ACCESS
LOS ANGELES

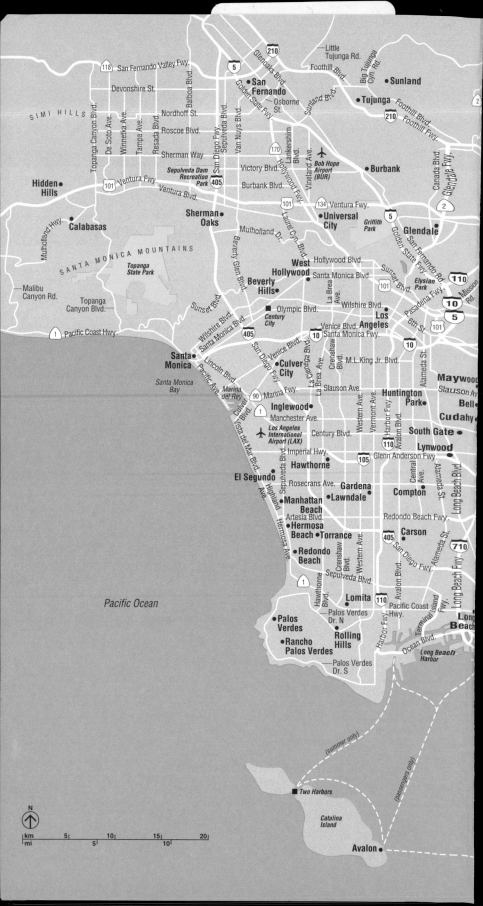

Welcome to LA!

Los Angeles is a peerless puzzle. Unique, often maligned by New Yorkers who think of it as one big backyard barbecue area, it is a mythical city where big breaks happen every day. It's a fairy-tale metropolis of dreams, schemes, and fortunes, where hordes of wannabe stars flock by plane, train, and bus hoping to someday see their names in the proverbial "lights." Fueled by pie-in-the-sky optimism, they act out their life stories like ideas for screenplays scribbled by aspiring writers on cocktail napkins. But of course, not everybody who comes to LA wants to be in pictures; some are just chasing their own versions of the American Dream.

Why? Because Los Angeles is a city where anything can happen—and almost everything does, from the sublime to the ridiculous and the tragic. In this picture-postcard setting, snow dusts the mountaintops while sandy-haired, suntanned surfers battle the waves just a few miles away. It is here youngsters can take a fantasy trip through one of the grandest amusement parks of them all, **Disneyland Resort** (in neighboring **Anaheim**). It's where TV game-show contestants spin wheels for fortunes, or try to become survivors (auditions are held at CBS Television Studios, 6121 Sunset Blvd., Hollywood, every spring; 323/460.3000—only the fittest need apply). This is a town where anything can happen, and has, from devastating earthquakes and riots to famous murders and mishaps. But it's also one that seems to weather all storms with flying colors and continues to enchant, entertain, and endure.

Part movie and entertainment capital, part social experiment, LA is a vast megalopolis where all types of lifestyles and cultures converge in a kaleidoscope of head-spinning contrasts. From cutting-edge architecture like the **Walt Disney Concert Hall** to fantastic food to warm sandy beaches, LA delivers. Unlike what is normally considered a "city," Los Angeles is actually composed of 9 distinct areas or neighborhoods—downtown LA, midtown LA, Hollywood, West Hollywood, Beverly Hills, West LA, Bel Air, Brentwood, and Santa Monica. To sample this City of Angels, cruise the storied boulevards—**Wilshire, Sunset, Santa Monica,** and **Olympic**—that snake like tributaries to the **Pacific Ocean** and its legendary beaches. Heading west on Olympic, stop for crab soup in **Koreatown,** and spy the Beverly Hills High School's oil rig as you approach the striking twin towers of **Century City.** On Sunset, pull over for a drink at the **Sky Bar** at Mondrian, the **Key Club,** or the Art Deco **Argyle** hotel, check out the scene at comedian Dan Aykroyd's **House of Blues** nightclub, pick up a movie-star map for a tour of the estates of the rich and famous, or turn off at **Will Rogers State Historic Park** to tour the Rogers home and hike the chaparral-covered hills. You can also ponder the beasts of millennia past at the **La Brea Tar Pits** along Wilshire, browse through the **Los Angeles County Museum of Art**'s gallery of German Expressionism, or inspect the latest in haute couture at the exclusive boutiques on **Rodeo Drive** in Beverly Hills. Head over to Santa Monica, where life's a beach by day and a playground by night. Pedal, rollerblade, or skate along the strand, but don't miss a stroll on the pier or to the **Third Street Promenade,** with its movie theaters, trendy restaurants, and bookstores.

In addition to all that, Los Angeles now boasts a thriving restaurant scene that has turned the area into a gastronomic delight as exciting new eateries blaze a culinary trail from downtown LA and beyond. For starters, there's a new **Patina** at the Walt Disney Concert Hall catering to the theater crowd. The young set flock to hot spots such as **A.O.C.,**

Bastide, Sona, Noe, Koi, Dolce, Table 8, Luna Park, Falcon, Grace, EM Bistro, Citrine, and Tantra—where most of the action is over trendy drinks at the bar. You'll find them all ranked and listed in this guide along with the usual popular suspects such as Spago, Water Grill, Le Dôme (which has been stunningly remodeled), Morton's, and The Palm Kate Mantilini. Dining out has never been this exhilarating in LA, and it's only just begun. More cosmopolitan than ever with the emergence of a pulsating after-hours club scene, Los Angeles has blossomed into a lean-and-mean metropolis. No one can ever kick sand in its face again. (And they know whom we're talking about.)

All this before you even tackle LA's notoriously congested freeway system with its unending on-ramps and 528 miles of clogged tarmac. But burning fuel personifies the Southern California experience, so when you're ready to venture beyond the city limits, fill up your tank, grab a road map, and buckle up for a fascinating tour of the most motorized region in the world. Drive north up the coastal highway and sink your feet into the gilt-edged sands of Malibu, home of the rich and beautiful. Or, for a complete contrast to such a privileged lifestyle, head back south to Venice Beach with its New Age hippies, bikini-

How To Read This Guide

ACCESS® LOS ANGELES is arranged so you can see at a glance where you are and what is around you. The numbers next to the entries in the following chapters correspond to the numbers on the maps.

The text is color-coded according to the kind of place described:

Restaurants/Clubs: Red

Hotels: Purple | Shops: Orange

 Parks/Outdoors: Green | Sights/Culture: Blue

WHEELCHAIR ACCESSIBILITY

An establishment (except a restaurant) is considered wheelchair accessible when a person in a wheelchair can easily enter a building (i.e., no steps, a ramp, a wide-enough door) without assistance. Restaurants are deemed wheelchair accessible only if the above applies, and if the rest rooms are on the same floor as the dining area and their entrances and stalls are wide enough to accommodate a wheelchair.

RATING THE RESTAURANTS AND HOTELS

The restaurant star ratings take into account the quality, service, atmosphere, and uniqueness of the restaurant. An expensive restaurant doesn't necessarily ensure an enjoyable evening; a small, relatively unknown spot could have good food, professional service, and a lovely atmosphere. Therefore, on a purely subjective basis, stars are used to judge the overall dining value (see the star ratings at right). Keep in mind that chefs and owners often change, which sometimes drastically affects the quality of a restaurant, and menus often change at the tip of a chef's toque. Our ratings are based on information available at press time.

The price ratings, as categorized below, apply to restaurants and hotels. These figures describe general price-range relationships among other restaurants and hotels in the area. The restaurant price ratings are based on the average cost of dinner for one person, excluding tax and tip. Hotel price ratings reflect the base price of a standard room for two people for one night during the peak season.

RESTAURANTS

★	Good
★★	Very Good
★★★	Excellent
★★★★	An Extraordinary Experience
$	The Price Is Right (less than $35)
$$	Reasonable ($35–$50)
$$$	Expensive ($50–$80)
$$$$	Big Bucks ($80 and up)

HOTELS

$	The Price Is Right (less than $125)
$$	Reasonable ($125–$175)
$$$	Expensive ($175–$325)
$$$$	Big Bucks ($325 and up)

MAP KEY

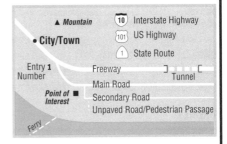

▲ Mountain	⑩ Interstate Highway
• City/Town	🛡 US Highway
	① State Route
Entry 1 Number	Freeway ⎯ ⎯ Tunnel
Point of Interest ■	Main Road
	Secondary Road
	Unpaved Road/Pedestrian Passage
Ferry	

clad roller skaters, well-oiled bodybuilders, and chain-saw jugglers who spend their days by the sea. Wherever you go, you'll enjoy ideal weather (it's practically perfect year-round) and a few surprises along the way. Just remember that almost anything can happen here.

Getting to Los Angeles

Airports

Los Angeles International Airport (LAX)

The principal hub of the Western Pacific Rim, the world's third-busiest airport hosts more than 100 air carriers in 10 terminals, each equipped with hotel/motel information boards, cafeterias, snack bars, cocktail lounges, newsstands, rest rooms, gift shops, and lockers. LAX also greets more than 65 million travelers a year. The central complex houses eight terminals (including the five-level, million-square-foot **Tom Bradley International Terminal**) around the perimeter of a two-level loop, which encircles parking, a restaurant, heliport, and control tower. Airlines frequently change terminals; call 310/646.5252 for up-to-date information.

The **Imperial Terminal,** just south of the central complex, handles charter flights and supplemental carriers. A free bus connects with the main terminal every half-hour until 12:30AM. Catch the bus from the center island at each baggage-claim area.

In each terminal, departures, ticketing, and check-in are on the upper level, and arrivals, baggage claim, car-rental booths, hotel information desks, and ground transportation are on the lower level. Blue, green, and white **Airline Connections** shuttles link each terminal at both levels, and buses take passengers to satellite parking lots.

Handicapped Connections is a free minibus with extra-wide doors and a ramp for wheelchairs. For additional airport information, pick up the yellow courtesy telephones inside the terminal to contact the **Airport Information Aides.**

AIRPORT SERVICES

Airport Police 310/646.6253

Business Service Centers are in all terminals.

Currency Exchange 310/417.0366

Customs and Immigration 310/215.2414

First Aid Station 310/215.6000

Ground Transportation 310/646.5252

Information..310/646.5252

Interpreters................................See information desk at ....Tom Bradley International Terminal.

Lost and Found.....................................310/417.0440

Parking.......................310/646.2911, 310/646.5252

Traveler's Aid 310/646.2270

Wheelchair/Disabled Services 310/646.5252

AIRLINES

Air New Zealand....................................800/237.6639, ...www.airnewzealand.co.nz

Alaska ....800/426.0333, www.alaskaair.com

Aloha Airlines ....800/367.5250, www.alohaairlines.com

American ....800/433.7300, www.aa.com

Continental ....800/525.0280, www.continental.com

Delta ....800/221.1212, www.delta-air.com

Hawaiian Air ....800/367.5320, www.hawaiianair.com

Jet Blue ....800/538.2583, www.jetblue.com

Mexicana Airlines ....800/531.7921, ...www.mexicana.com

Northwest ....800/447.4747, www.nwa.com

Singapore Airlines.................................800/741.3333, ...www.singaporeair.com

Southwest ....800/241.6522, www.flyswa.com

United ....800/241.6522, www.ual.com

USAirways..............800/428.4322, www.usairways.com

Getting to and from LAX

BY BUS

To help travelers avoid the hassle of driving and parking, door-to-door shuttles offer 24-hour service from the airports to most Los Angeles area destinations. A bewildering array of buses and vans circle the airport loop, stopping at the center island outside each baggage-claim area. Be sure to stand at the correct pick-up site. One of the most popular services is **Super Shuttle,** whose bright-blue vans offer door-to-door service from LAX to most destinations in Los Angeles and Orange Counties, including the other major airports. Prices vary, depending on your destination. For pickup at the airport, go outside your terminal to the designated stop or call 310/222.5500 after you have collected your baggage; for service from your home or hotel, call 800/554.3146 24 hours in advance. For more information, check out www.supershuttle.com. Other shuttle services include **Xpress Shuttle** (800/427.7483, www. expressshuttle.com), **All-American Shuttle** (310/641.4090), **Best Shuttle** (310/670.7080), and **Prime Time** (800/733.8267).

In addition, regular public bus service links many parts of town with the bus terminal at **Lot C.** A free connector bus stops at each of the airline terminals every 10 to 20 minutes, 24 hours a day.

BY CAR

The easiest way to reach downtown Los Angeles from the airport is to take **Century Boulevard** east to the **Harbor Freeway (I-110)** north. To get to LAX from downtown Los Angeles, take the **Santa Monica Freeway (I-10)** west to the **San Diego Freeway (I-405)** south and exit at either **La Tijera** or Century Boulevard. Alternatively, take the Harbor Freeway (I-110) south to the **Glenn M. Anderson Freeway (I-105)** west, which will funnel drivers into LAX,

SIGHTS FOR SORE EYES

On a clear day in LA (granted, that's a rarity in this smog-ridden city), you may not be able to see *forever,* but you can get some great views from these vantage points:

The **Los Angeles basin** from Griffith Park Observatory

Century City from the San Diego Freeway (I-405) transition southbound to the Santa Monica Freeway (I-10) eastbound

Santa Monica Bay from Toppers restaurant in the Radisson Huntley Hotel in Santa Monica

Whales, dolphin schools, and San Nicolas Island from the cliffs of Malibu Airplanes landing and taking off from the Observation Deck of the Theme Building at **Los Angeles International Airport**

Downtown Los Angeles from Windows Restaurant in the Transamerica Center

The **Los Angeles basin** and the **Hollywood Bowl** from Mulholland Drive between Outpost Drive and Cahuenga Boulevard

The **Westside, Century City, and the San Gabriel Mountains** from the rooftop parking garage of Westside Pavilion shopping mall

The **San Fernando Valley** from Fryman Canyon Overlook on Mulholland Drive

connecting the 605, 710, 110, and 405 Freeways between Norwalk to the east and the airport. In light traffic, the trip from LAX to downtown can be made in about 20 minutes, but always allow at least an hour.

RENTAL CARS

More than 30 national and local car-rental agencies are located at and around LAX, and all major hotels have car-rental counters. Options run the gamut— everything from your basic Ford to a Rolls-Royce, Ferrari, or a classic two-seater T-Bird. Weekly (a minimum of five days) or three-day weekend rates are usually the best deals, but you should always shop around. Contact the following major companies for their current rates:

Alamo ....800/327.9633, www.alamo.com

Avis ....800/331.1212, www.avis.com

Budget........................800/527.0700, 800/221.1203, ...www.drivebudget.com

Dollar ....800/800.0044, www.dollar.com

Enterprise ....800/RENT-a-CAR, www.enterprise.com

Hertz............................800/654.3131, www.hertz.com

National ....800/CAR-RENT, www.nationalcar.com

Thrifty ....310/645.1880, www.thrifty.com

Or, for the extremely budget-conscious:

Bob Leech's Auto Rental–LAX ....800/635.1240, ...www.bnm.com

Rent-a-Wreck ....800/535.1391, ...www.rent-a-wreck.com

And, for the extremely status-conscious:

Beverly Hills Rent a Car ....310/337.1400, ...800/479.5996, www.bhrentacar.com

Budget Rent A Car Beverly Hills ....310/821.1700, ...800/729.7350, www.budgetbeverlyhills.com

AIRPORT PARKING

Short-term parking options include the seven **Central Terminal** lots and the **West Imperial Terminal** lot (a total of 8,309 spaces). Rates are reasonable, but these lots are often full on holidays and during peak periods. Metered parking is available throughout the airport (for a two-hour maximum). Long-term and short-term parking is available at two major satellite lots (16,400 spaces): **Lot C** (at Sepulveda Boulevard and 96th Street) and **Lot B** (at La Cienega Boulevard and 111th Street). Both of these lots have 24-hour bus service running every 10 to 20 minutes to each of the eight terminals. For greater convenience (but higher cost), leave your car at one of the privately owned lots scattered around the airport such as **The Parking Spot**, a one-of-a-kind facility that caters to commuters with covered parking, courteous shuttle drivers who load and unload your bags, valet or self-parking, and even throw in a bottle of water, a newspaper, and emergency battery service when needed. Probably the best bang for your buck, at two convenient locations: 5701 W Century Blvd (between Bellanca and Airport Blvds), 800/745.2276; 9101 Sepulveda Blvd (at 92nd St), 866/826.2509. www.TheParkingSpot.com. For more information about airport parking, call 310/646.2911 or 310/646.5252. Email: infoline@airports.ci.la.ca.us.

BY LIMOUSINE

A luxurious transportation alternative, limo service between LAX and downtown can cost $65 and up (not including tip), depending on the size of the car. Limousine companies include the **A-List Limousine Service** (800/886.6644), **Dynasty Limousine** (800/670.6005), **DAV EL** (800/922.0343, www.davel.com), **elimos** (310/559.5164, www.elimos.com), and **Mercedes Limousine** (310/271.8559, www.mlslimo.com).

BY TAXI

Taxis wait for passengers at the authorized ranks located outside each terminal; the fare to downtown averages about $26-$35 (plus tip).

For other ground-transportation services, check with the ticket/information booths on the sidewalk outside each baggage-claim area.

Other Airports Serving Southern California

Bob Hope Airport ....818/840.8847, ...www.burbankairport.com

John Wayne Airport................................949/252.5171, ...www.ocair.com

Long Beach Municipal Airport ....562/570.2640, ...800/U-FLY-LGB

Ontario International Airport ....909/988.2700, ...www.lawa.org

Santa Monica Municipal Airport (small aircraft only) 310/390.7606

Getting Around Los Angeles

BICYCLES

Los Angeles County has more than 200 miles of bicycle trails. The most popular is the **South Bay Bicycle Trail**, which runs along 18 miles of shoreline from Santa Monica to Torrance Beach. Long Beach's three-mile **Oceanside Bike Path** offers a picturesque ride from Shoreline Village to Belmont Shore. The **San Gabriel River Trail** follows a 37-mile course from Santa Fe Dam in Azusa to Shoreline Village. And the eight-mile **Griffith Park Trail** takes in the Los Angeles Zoo, Travel Town, and the Autry Western Heritage Museum.

BOATS

You can charter a boat for **whale watching**, cruising to **Catalina Island**, or **fishing** for barracuda; boats depart from **Long Beach** and **San Pedro Harbors.**

There are a variety of **brunch and dinner tours of Los Angeles Harbor** from Seaport Village in Long Beach (for information, call **Spirit Cruises** at 562/495.5884). **Fishing charters** usually leave at 7AM, but check with the tour operator for specific departure time. A nonstop trip to Catalina takes about an hour, and a more leisurely trip lasts twice as long.

For more information, contact the following companies:

Belmont Pier Sportfishing 310/434.6781

Catalina Express....................................800/429.4601, ...www.catalinaexpress.com

Fantasea Yachts ....310/827.2220, ...www.fantaseayachts.com

The Gondola Getaway 310/433.9595

Hornblower Dining Yachts 800/950.1920

Spirit Cruises and Yacht Parties 562/495.5884

BUSES

Even some locals don't know this, but public transportation *does* exist in Los Angeles. More than 1.3 million people commute on public buses and subway lines daily. The **Metro** operates 208 bus routes in the greater metropolitan area. The fare is $1.35 and each transfer is 25 cents; weekly passes are $11. From **Spring Street** downtown, bus No. 27 takes you nonstop into **Century City**, and bus No. 439 will take you direct to **LAX**, as well as to **Manhattan, Hermosa,** and **Redondo Beaches.** For trips to and from the beaches along **Santa Monica's coast,** take bus No. 20 on Wilshire Boulevard or bus No. 4 on Santa Monica Boulevard. Both buses provide 24-hour service (213/626.4455). To obtain a copy of the Metro's *Self-Guided Tours* publication, write to Metro, 1 Gateway Plaza, Los Angeles, CA 90012. Municipal bus information is available through each city's chamber of commerce.

DASH

The Downtown Area Short Hop (DASH) operates 50 clean-fuel minibuses that shuttle between various spots in the Los Angeles area, including **downtown, Crenshaw, Pacific Palisades, Watts, Fairfax, Hollywood, southeast LA, Van Nuys/Studio City,** and **Warner Center**. There are three special DASH weekend routes: **Shoppers Paradise, Expo Direct,** and **Downtown Discovery**. Buses run every 15 minutes from 10AM to 5PM; call 800/COMMUTE or 213/580.5444. The fare's a mere 25 cents.

DRIVING

If you haven't heard already, you'll quickly learn that the traffic in LA is *always* unpredictable. **So always allow plenty of time to get anywhere in LA.** Tune in to local radio stations in the morning and late afternoon for minute-by-minute traffic reports. The state transportation department often publishes schedules of upcoming road construction in local newspapers, or you can call 213/628.7623 for information on highway conditions. Driving in downtown LA is a particular headache, thanks to the confusing one-way street system and expensive parking. Opt for walking or taking the DASH shuttle.

Distances

From downtown Los Angeles to:

Anaheim (Disneyland) ....26 miles

Beverly Hills ....10 miles

Big Bear Lake...100 miles

Bob Hope Airport ....13 miles

Griffith Park ....6 miles

Hollywood ....6 miles

Los Angeles International Airport ....17 miles

Pasadena..9 miles

Santa Clarita (Six Flags Magic Mountain) ....30 miles

Santa Monica..15 miles

Universal City (Universal Studios) ....9 miles

Venice Beach ....16 miles

Travel time varies widely depending on traffic.

Freeways

#	Name(s)
2	Glendale Freeway
5	Santa Ana Freeway/Golden State Freeway
10	Santa Monica Freeway/San Bernardino Freeway
22	Garden Grove Freeway
55	Costa Mesa Freeway
57	Orange Freeway
60	Pomona Freeway
90	Marina Freeway
91	Artesia Freeway/Riverside Freeway
101	Ventura Freeway/Hollywood Freeway
105	Glenn M. Anderson Freeway
110	Pasadena Freeway/Harbor Freeway
118	Simi Valley–San Fernando Valley Freeway
210	Foothill Freeway
405	San Diego Freeway
605	San Gabriel River Freeway
710	Long Beach Freeway

Metro Rail

The **Metro Rail system** (213/626.4455; 800/COMMUTE, www.mta.net) includes a light rail line, commuter trains, and even a subway. The **Red Line,** the city's only underground rail, runs from Union Station in downtown LA to Wilshire Boulevard and Vermont, Hollywood and Western, Highland, Universal City, and North Hollywood. The **Blue Line** travels between downtown and Long Beach, and the **Green Line** runs from Norwalk to Redondo Beach, connecting to the Blue Line at the Rosa Parks (Imperial/Wilmington) Station. The Blue Line also connects to the Red Line at the Seventh Street/Metro Center Station in downtown Los Angeles. The **Gold Line** links Pasadena to downtown Los Angeles. The 13.7-mile train ride starts in Sierra Madre with stops at Old Pasadena, the Southwest Museum, and Chinatown. www.la.pasblueline.org.

Taxis

Hailing a cab in LA is virtually unheard of, but you can find taxis in front of hotels and at **LAX, Union Station,** and other major ports of entry. In addition, downtown LA offers an inexpensive option of getting around with its **One Fare Zone,** which reaches to the 110 Freeway to the west, Main Street to the east, the Convention Center to the south, and the Hollywood Freeway to the north. Wait at the One Fare Zone taxi stand. At press time, the flat fare was $4. You also can call one of these major companies for a ride: **Independent Taxi Company** (323/666.0040, 800/521.8294), **LA Taxi** (310/715.1968), **United Independent Taxi Drivers, Inc.** (323/462.1088), and **Yellow Cab Company** (888/793.5569).

Trains

Thousands of passengers arrive daily in Los Angeles via the historic **Union Station** depot (800 N Alameda St, between the Santa Ana Fwy and E Macy St), an elegant hybrid of Art Deco and Spanish Mission architectural traditions, located downtown. **Amtrak** provides frequent service from LA to San Diego on its Pacific Surfliner—eight sleek double-decker trains fitted with special business-class compartments, stopping in several cities along the way. Great **day-trips by rail** are the coastal routes to Santa Barbara, San Luis Obispo, San Francisco, **San Juan Capistrano,** and the **Del Mar Racetrack.** The best way to ride is in Pacific Business class, where reclinable seats are equipped with laptop outlets, footrests, and audio/video devices. You get a free newspaper, soft drinks, wine (at special times), and snacks. There's also service to **Disneyland** in Anaheim. For information and reservations, call 800/872.7245, 800/USA-RAIL, or go online at www.amtrak.com.

FYI

Accommodations

It is not uncommon to check into an LA hotel and discover that the person checking in alongside you is a movie, television, or rock star. Celeb-style hotels will cost you dearly, however—and you'll need to make your reservations well in advance. But don't despair: If you're just looking for someplace to shower and sleep, sans megastars, you'll do well at one of the smaller hotels or motels throughout the area, and you probably won't need an advance reservation unless there's a convention in town. Generally speaking, accommodations are less expensive in the **San Fernando** and **San Gabriel Valleys** than in Hollywood, Beverly Hills, West LA, or downtown. For assistance in getting a room, call the **Los Angeles Convention and Visitors Bureau** hotel hotline (800/CATCH.LA).

Climate

Raincoats are rarely needed in LA: Rain falls an average of only 35 days a year, usually between the months of November and April. Typically, the sun shines 186 days a year in the city and 137 days at the beach. The average temperature is 74 degrees, with summer highs typically in the mid-80s and winter lows in the low 60s. In the desert, winter temperatures hover in the 70s, and summer highs range between 103 and 110 degrees.

Months	Average Temperature (°F)
January–March	69-48
April–June	77-59
July–September	83-63
October–December	77-49

Hours

Opening and closing times for shops and attractions in this book are listed by day(s) only, as long as they open between 8 and 11AM and close between 4 and 7PM. In all other cases, specific hours are given (e.g., 6AM-2PM, daily 24 hours, noon-5PM, and so forth).

Money

Most banks are open Monday through Friday from 9AM to 3 or 6PM and Saturday mornings. If you need to

FESTIVALS AND EVENTS

Los Angeles, always abuzz with activity, hosts a wide variety of special events and festivals throughout the year. The following is just a sampler of the many seasonal treats available in and around the city. For up-to-the-minute information, call the **Greater Los Angeles Convention and Visitors Bureau** multilingual events hot line (213/689.8822) or visit the website at www.LACVB.com.

January

What would **New Year's Day** be without the pomp and pageantry of the **Tournament of Roses Parade**? The promenade of floats down Colorado Boulevard in Pasadena starts at 8AM, but to get a good view, spectators start arriving in the wee hours of the morning. For a close-up look at the petal-bedecked floats, stop by Victory Park after the parade. Pasadena's New Year's Day celebration continues at the Rose Bowl with the **Annual Rose Bowl Game,** a showpiece of collegiate football. Rose Bowl, 626/419.ROSE. www.Tournamentofroses.com

Also on January 1 is the annual swim of **Cabrillo Beach Polar Bears**—hale and hearty souls who dive into the cold Pacific Ocean. Spectators may watch or join in the frigid fun. Free.

During the first week of the month, the **Greater LA Auto Show** takes place at the LA Convention Center, with more than 1,000 hot model cars, trucks, vans, SUVs, and futuristic vehicles on exhibit. Admission. 213/741.1151.

Memorabilia collectors will enjoy the **Vintage Poster Fair** at Santa Monica Civic Auditorium, where over 10,000 vintage posters from around the world are offered for sale. Admission. 415/546.9608.

February

Downtown merchants mark the beginning of Lent each year on the day before Ash Wednesday with an exuberant, Mexican-style **Mardi Gras** in historic El Pueblo de Los Angeles Plaza. Visitors are encouraged to wear costumes to enjoy the music, fun, and costume parade down Olvera Street.

The Annual **LA Bach Festival** is still going strong after more than 60 years. The tribute to Johann Sebastian Bach, held at the First Congregational Church (540 S Commonwealth Ave, at W Sixth St), not only features the music of its venerable namesake but also that of Corelli, Vivaldi, and Handel.

LA's Chinatown celebrates its own **Chinese New Year** anywhere from late January to February. The festivities include the colorful Golden Dragon Parade, a carnival, and a firecracker run. 213/617.0396. www.LAChinesechamber.org

March

Running mania reaches a fever pitch on the first Sunday in March with the **City of Los Angeles Marathon and Bike Tour.** The event, which attracts top-flight competitors from around the world, starts at Figueroa and Sixth and ends in front of the library on Fifth Street. Free. 310/444.5544.

The Oscars, Hollywood's biggest gala of the year, takes place on cue on the last Monday of the month, attracting tourists and lookie loos who camp out just for the chance to spot their favorite stars. But alas, no more bleachers at the new Kodak Theater in the heart of Hollywood.

April

People gather at El Pueblo de Los Angeles Historic Park on Holy Saturday, the day before Easter, for the **Blessing of the Animals.** The faithful dress up their pets—dogs, cats, birds, even pigs and chickens. Free. 213/896.1700.

Go back in time at the **Renaissance Pleasure Faire,** where foods of ye olde England, battling knights on horseback, medieval games, theater, and country dancing are celebrated at Glen Helen Regional Park near San Bernardino. 800/52.FAIRE. www.renfaire.com

May

The city's Mexican-American population commemorates **Cinco de Mayo** with colorful festivities featuring mariachi music, shows, folkloric dancing, and many other activities. The gala begins on the last Sunday in April with **LA Fiesta Broadway,** a big street party featuring ethnic food stands and international stars of Latin music.

exchange money, check with the major banks. Most banks have Automatic Teller Machines (ATMs), from which you can withdraw cash instantly.

PARKING

Fines for parking illegally can be high, so read all parking signs carefully before you enter into an agreement with the curb. Be particularly cautious in **West Hollywood,** where parking signs are among the most confusing in the country, listing all sorts of regulations and restrictions. Most meters in high-traffic commercial areas have a one-hour limit. For periods longer than 60 minutes, a parking garage is less painful on the pocketbook than a parking ticket. A **red curb** means no parking, a **green curb** permits parking for 20 minutes, and a **white curb** means loading and unloading only.

June

For two days, the Hollywood Bowl hosts some of the biggest names in jazz, big band, fusion, and blues for the annual **Playboy Jazz Festival.**

Gay and Lesbian Pride Celebration is a gala West Hollywood event that attracts thousands of onlookers, marchers, and participants. There's fun, food, dancing, and more. 323/658.8700.

July

Stock up on breath mints and don't miss the **Garlic Festival** on the grounds of the Federal Building. Dozens of LA's best chefs apply their talents to the aromatic root and create garlic-laced dishes ranging from appetizers to, yes, even desserts.

August

Downtown LA's Little Tokyo pulls out all the stops for its **Nisei Week Japanese Festival.** The celebration of Japanese culture features folk dancing, music, exhibits, carnivals, art shows, and parades.

September

Celebrate the 1781 founding of LA at **Los Angeles's Birthday Party** in El Pueblo de Los Angeles Plaza. Festivities feature live entertainment, games, and a huge birthday cake.

The huge **LA County Fair,** held at the County Fair Grounds in Pomona, features exhibits of some of the most luscious produce in America, plus carnival rides and entertainment ranging from rodeos to big-name concerts.

October

The **International Festival of the Masks** is among the city's more unusual events. The "mask-e-raid" is held in Hancock Park and features more than 40 booths exhibiting (and sometimes selling) beautiful-to-bizarre masks from around the world.

This is also when the gay community of West Hollywood rocks with their **Halloween Carnival** along Santa Monica Blvd. Open to the public regardless of persuasion, the event's a hoot, with booths, comedians, live music, and, as one might imagine, outrageous costumes. More than 400,000 revelers attend this event, and we mean 400,000. Free. 323/848.6547.

November

Día de los Muertos (Day of the Dead), held in El Pueblo de Los Angeles Plaza at the beginning of the month, is a festival unique to Latino culture. It begins with the celebration of life procession, which leads to ornately decorated altars. 213/485.9777. Free.

The **Doo Dah Parade** is Old Pasadena's parody of the Tournament of Roses parade, with more than 1,200 participants marching and stomping their way through the streets. It's a satirical riot with political pundits, midget gospel singers, dogs in drag, a flying toilet dirigible, the Doo Dah Lama, and more. Free. 626/440.7379.

Blockbuster Hollywood Spectacular (formerly Hollywood Christmas Parade) features celebrity guests, floats, and of course, Santa Claus. 323/469.2337. www.hollywood.christmas.com

December

As Christmas nears, the city goes up in lights and decorations (including plenty of artificial snow) and parades liven up the streets and waterways in and around LA. **Las Posadas,** held in El Pueblo de Los Angeles Plaza, is a weeklong celebration with a reenactment of Mary and Joseph's journey to Bethlehem as its centerpiece. From 16 December until Christmas Eve, nightly entertainment begins at 7PM; the procession starts at 8PM.

Colorful **nautical celebrations** of the holiday are held in Marina del Rey, Long Beach, San Pedro, and Redondo Beach.

New Year's Eve celebrations also overtake the town with events such as an annual **Shipwalk Party,** held on the *Queen Mary* in Long Beach, with music, entertainment, food, and fireworks. Admission. 562/435.3511. Similar action takes place at **Two Harbors,** 310/510.2800; **Gladstone's** at the beach, 310/GLA4-FISH; and on **Catalina Island** in the Casino ballroom. All admission. 310/510.1520.

PERSONAL SAFETY

It is generally safe to walk around downtown LA, Beverly Hills, Hollywood, West Hollywood, Brentwood, and Westwood Village during the day. At night, however, parts of the city are more dangerous, particularly **downtown, Hollywood,** and **South Central.** As with any large city, visitors to Los Angeles should exercise some commonsense precautions: Do not carry large amounts of cash or flash expensive jewelry. Know where your handbag and wallet are at all times. Try to blend in with your surroundings so it's not obvious you're a tourist. If you see trouble coming, get out of its way.

PUBLICATIONS

The *Los Angeles Times*, the only major metropolitan daily in the area, offers in-depth coverage of international and business news, along with suburban zone editions for

Phone Book

EMERGENCIES

AAA Motor Club (road service) 800/222.4357

AIDS Hot Line 800/367.2437

Ambulance/Fire/Police 911

Earthquake Emergency Services 510/893.0818, 818/304.8383

Missing Children 800/826.4743, 800/843.5200

Poison Control Center 800/876.4766

USC Medical Center and Women's Hospital ....
....800/872.2273

VISITORS' INFORMATION

Amtrak 800/872.7245

Beach Information 310/305.3547

Better Business Bureau..........................213/251.9696

Disabled Riders Hot Line.......................800/626.4455

Greyhound 800/231.2222, 213/629.8401

LA INC. (Convention and Visitors Bureau) ....
....213/689.8822

LA Convention and Visitors Bureau Hotel Hotline ....
....800/CATCH.LA

Surf Report 213/976.7873

Weather 805/988.6610

Time 213/853.1212

Transit Authority 818/888.7549

Women's Health Information 888/232.3299

---

local news. The Sunday "Calendar" section provides extensive entertainment listings. The *Daily News of Los Angeles* is a suburban daily based in the San Fernando Valley and offering local coverage; its "Weekend" section on Fridays has entertainment information. *Los Angeles Magazine* is published monthly and covers everything from politics to places to go, the best and worst of LA, and, of course, celebrities and fashion. For the most thorough arts and entertainment information, pick up the free *LA Weekly*, distributed on Thursday at restaurants and book, record, and convenience stores. Los Angeles's daily *La Opinión* is the largest Spanish-language newspaper in the country. And if you're looking for bargains, from used cars to computers, pick up the *Recycler* at liquor stores and corner markets.

RADIO STATIONS

Nowhere does radio boast a more captive audience than in LA, where the average commuter is trapped in his or her car for an hour a day. Morning talk shows range from racy "Mark and Brian" on **KLOS 95.5 FM** and shock radio with the infamous morning personality Howard Stern and testosterone-pumping, afternoon drive-time shock-jock host Tom Leykis on **KLSX 97.1 FM** to venerable DJ **Rick Dees**, who keeps LA morning freeway commuters entertained on **KIIS-FM**. The major LA stations include the following:

AM:

98 ....KFWB 24 Hours of News

570 ....KLAC Big Band Music

690 ....XTRA Talk

790 ....KABC Talk Radio

1260..KJAZ Jazz

1540...KMPC Sports

FM:

88.9.........................KXLU Electronic Synthesized Music

89.9 ....KCRW Public Radio

94.7 ....KTWV New Age

97.1 ....KLSX Talk

101.1 ....KRTH Oldies

102.7 ....KIIS Top 40

103.1 ....KACD Spanish

103.5 ....KOST Light Rock/Pop

104.3 ....KBIG Urban Contemporary

105.1 ....KMZT Classical

RESTAURANTS

Make your reservations weeks in advance whenever possible to avoid being forced to eat dinner at 6PM or 10PM. Except at funky little spots or fast-food joints, don't expect to just walk in and sit down without a reservation. At the trendiest and most expensive restaurants, reservations are essential, and sometimes even if you have one—say, at Spago or the Ivy—still expect a "wait at the bar." In LA even the most stylish establishments (like L'Orangerie) don't require ties for the gentlemen, but they do expect diners to show some dress decorum, and sports jackets are always welcome at the fine dining spots.

SHOPPING

For young, hip, cutting-edge designs, browse the boutiques along **La Brea Avenue** in midtown LA, **Old Pasadena, Melrose Avenue,** Santa Monica's chic **Third Street Promenade,** hip **Montana Avenue,** or groovy **Main Street.**

If you prefer shopping centers, your choices are plentiful, and include the behemoth 350-store **Del Amo Fashion Center** in Torrance; the stylish open-air **Westfield ShoppingTown Century City**; the indoor **Beverly Center** in midtown LA; the 200-store **South Coast Plaza** in Costa Mesa; and the upscale **Fashion Island** shopping complex in Newport Beach.

Wholesale shopping outlets can be found in the **Garment District** south of Seventh and Los Angeles Streets in downtown or at the **Citadel** complex in **City of Commerce.** For haute couture, head for **Rodeo Drive** in Beverly Hills.

Smoking

California won the war against smoking with a strictly enforced statewide ban on smoking in all indoor public places. (The feud is so fierce that anti-smokers have been known to turn in those who insist on lighting up anyway.) Unhappy with faltering business caused by the legislation, bar owners keep trying to get the law repealed.

Taxes

There is a sales tax of 8.25 percent. Hotel-room transient occupancy room tax is 14 percent for the city of Los Angeles; for other areas of the county, the levy varies from 11.5 to 14 percent.

Telephones

Los Angeles and its surroundings have a head-spinning number of area codes—more than any other comparable region in the US. Numbers in downtown LA have the **213** code; Hollywood and Griffith Park have the **323** code; Beverly Hills, Santa Monica, the Westside, and LAX have the **310** code (until a much opposed **412** area code is imposed to serve areas north of LAX); **714** is for most of northern Orange County, while **949** covers most of the southern portion. The **951** code is for Riverside, **909** for San Bernardino Counties and much of the San Gabriel Valley; **818** is for the San Fernando Valley from Agoura Hills to Glendale. **Los Angeles County** numbers have the 213, 310, 323, 626, 818, or 909 codes. Most of **Long Beach** is now **562,** while most of the **Desert Areas** (e.g., Palm Springs) are **760.** Area codes precede all phone numbers in this book.

Public phone booths are scarce in LA. And user beware: Independent public phone companies can charge as much as they want, and often do, so be careful or a local call could wind up setting you back several dollars instead of a few cents. For **directory assistance,** dial 411.

Tickets

Besides at the individual box offices, you can get tickets to cultural and sporting events through **Ticketmaster** (213/480.3232, www.ticketmaster.com) and **VIP Tickets** (818/907.1548, www.viptickets.com).

Time Zone

Los Angeles is in the Pacific Time zone, three hours earlier than New York City.

Tipping

While tipping is always at your discretion, it's a good idea to grease the palms of the people who assist you if you want to be treated well. Airport baggage handlers and hotel bellhops (at luxury hotels) get $1 to $2 per bag. Leave the hotel maid $1 per day (more at luxury properties). Valet parking attendants expect at least $1 or $2, paid upon return of the car. Leave a 15- to 20-percent gratuity in restaurants. Taxi drivers prefer a 15- to 20-percent tip, but 10 percent usually is adequate.

Visitors' Information

In LA's downtown financial district, **LA INC. The Convention and Visitors Bureau** (M-Sa; 685 S Figueroa St, at W Seventh St, 213/689.8822) provides maps, information on lodging, and discount tickets to amusement parks and cultural attractions. The bureau also offers a 24-hour multilingual **events hotline** (reached via the general number) that provides information in Spanish, French, Japanese, German, and English. Contact the following visitor information centers for more information:

Beverly Hills ....310/248.101 or 310/271.8174, www.itinet.com/beverlyhillscc

Long Beach ....562/436.3645, www.golongbeach.org

Palm Springs (hotel reservations)..........760/346.8800, 760/770.9000, 800/41.RELAX

Pasadena ....626/795.9311, email: cvb@pasadenacal.com

Santa Monica ....310/393.7593, 800/771.2322, email: smcvb@santamonica.com

West Hollywood ....310/289.2525, email: WHCVB@visitwesthollywood.com; www.visitwesthollywood.com

Chambers of commerce in these surrounding communities also provide free information:

Catalina Island (in Avalon)....................310/510.1520, email: chamber@Catalina.net

Century City ....310/553.2222, email: mkcccc@worldnet.att.net

Hermosa Beach ....310/376.0951, email: donsouzxa@gte.net; www.hbchamber.net

Hollywood ....323/469.8311, www.hollywoodchamber.net

Marina del Rey ....310/305.9546, email:bgbruin@aol.com

Santa Barbara ....805/966.9222, email:sbcvb@silcom.com; www.santabarbaraca.com

Torrance 310/792.2341

Venice ....310/827.2366, www.venice.net/chamber

At press time The Convention and Visitors Bureau, now called LA INC. The Convention and Visitors Bureau, was operating out of temporary headquarters at 6801 Hollywood Boulevard, in the Hollywood and Highland Complex. 213/689.8822. www.visitlanow.com.

Los Angeles's official flower is the Bird of Paradise; its tree is the coral tree.

More than 2.2 million anglers purchase some type of California fishing license each year. California Sport fishing licenses are valid 1 January through 31 December.

Well, it's not exactly what you might expect, but it's Angelenos' kind of downtown . . .

Yes, Virginia, there is a downtown of this behemoth, rambling region, flavored by assorted ethnic influences and an absorbing history. And, most of it can be explored by foot. For easier access we've divided downtown LA into the following three regions (see A, B, and C on the map at left):

A. Downtown/Historic Core, including **El Pueblo de Los Angeles** (site of the first settlement), **City Hall, Chinatown,** and **Little Tokyo;**

B. Downtown/Business and Financial, a corridor of high-rise offices to the east of the **Harbor Freeway** (see page 24); and

C. Downtown/Commercial and Exposition Park, an area that encompasses LA's classic commercial buildings, movie palaces, and markets, extending south to the **University of Southern California** (see page 32).

While the downtown district swells with commuters during the day (more than 210,000 people commute here daily), few Angelenos venture here at night, except perhaps for dinner and a show at the **Music Center**—though slowly increasing, the resident population is only about 20,000, and most downtown stores close right around the time commuters head home. However, with the opening of the **Walt Disney Concert Hall** in 2003 came an influx of visitors and second-nighters to downtown by night.

A. DOWNTOWN/ HISTORIC CORE

This is where Los Angeles began. Ever since 1781, when a handful of Spanish settlers founded the city, the central core has remained close to its origins throughout **El Pueblo de Los Angeles.** Los Angeles became part of Mexico in 1822, after winning independence from Spain. Twenty-five years later, the Stars and Stripes was raised, and local boosters roamed the nation singing the praises of a promised land. Yankee immigrants slowly began streaming in, sleeping in tents and bathtubs, but in 1887, when two competing railroads briefly dropped the fare to a dollar, the trickle turned into a flood.

The land boom quickly went bust, however, leaving downtown LA with twice as many permanent residents as before. The more affluent relocated to the west of downtown, leaving the center and east of the city to new arrivals. Over the years the influx took its toll, and the area around **City Hall** became a civic embarrassment.

Urban renewal began in the 1930s, with the institution of **Olvera Street** as a symbol of the original Spanish pueblo. In the late 1940s, the city created the Community Redevelopment Agency (CRA), which acquired properties for renovation and renewal, notably in **Little Tokyo, Chinatown,** and El Pueblo de Los Angeles.

Today, ethnic traditions flourish stronger than ever, and you can enjoy the culture and cuisine of almost every country of Latin America and the Pacific Rim here and in surrounding neighborhoods. Los Angeles's Hispanic population now accounts for an estimated 27% of the entire populace, making it one of the largest Spanish-speaking cities in the United States. There are two centers of Latino activity downtown: Olvera Street for tourists, and **Broadway** (in the "Downtown/Commercial and Exposition Park" section of this chapter) for locals.

1 EMPRESS PAVILION

★$$ Cantonese and Szechuan specialties are served in this spacious second-story restaurant in the **Bamboo Plaza.** Take-out food is available. ♦ Chinese ♦ Daily, breakfast, lunch, and dinner. 988 N Hill St (at Bernard St). 213/617.9898

2 PLUM TREE INN

★$$ Peking duck and kung pao chicken are specialties at this stylish restaurant. ♦ Chinese ♦ Daily, lunch and dinner. Reservations recommended. 937 N Hill St (between W College St and Chung King Ct). 213/613.1819 ♿

3 PHOENIX BAKERY

Locals line up, sometimes for hours, to purchase delicious sweets from this popular bakery. The strawberry cake is legendary. ♦ Daily. 969 N Broadway (at Bamboo La). 213/628.4642

4 SAN ANTONIO WINERY

LA's best-kept secret, this historic winery in the heart of downtown Los Angeles houses tasting rooms, aging cellars, a legendary restaurant, and a wine shop stocked with private-label wines and imported and domestic varieties. Founded in 1917 by Italian winemaker Santo Cambianica, who named it after his patron saint, Anthony, San Antonio is the only working winery in the city. Now operated by the Riboli family, who grow grapes in vineyards estates in Monterey, Santa Barbara, and Napa, the winery has garnered more than 1,000 awards for it private labels. Located just five minutes north of the Music Center, it is well worth a visit. Reservations are necessary for tours. Plaza San Antonio, 737 Lamar Street (at N Main St). 323/223.1401. www.sanantoniowinery.com

Within the San Antonio Winery:

MADDALENA RESTAURANT

★★$$ Named after a family member, this restaurant reflects the charm and graciousness of its owners. As you enter the large room you are greeted by tables of the day's signature dishes—the real thing, not plastic—from which to make your pick. The chicken Caesar salad is tangy, crispy, and one of the best in town; fish and chips is the fresh catch of the day, served with perfectly fried spuds. There's also a variety of Italian dishes, yummy chocolate biscotti, and a fantastic flan made from Mama Riboli's personal recipe. Of course, great wines are available to accompany it all. ♦ Daily, 11AM-7PM. 323/223.1401

5 HOP LI

★$$ A savvy seafood spot, Hop Li is one of many founded by renegade chefs from **Mon Kee** (see page 18). The food is similar but less expensive. ♦ Chinese/Seafood ♦ Daily, lunch and dinner. Reservations recommended

for six or more. 526 Alpine St (between N Hill and Yale Sts). 213/680.3939 ♿

6 DRAGON GATE INN

$ This Best Western–affiliated lodge (with 50 rooms) is strategically located in the heart of Chinatown. ♦ 818 N Hill St (between Alpine and W College Sts). 213/617.3077, 800/528.1234 ♿

7 YANG CHOW

★$$ Don't be turned off by the tacky décor. The Szechuan dishes that draw crowds here more than make up for the lack of ambience. Special kudos go to pan-fried dumplings, kung pao chicken, spicy Szechuan beef, and slippery shrimp. ♦ Szechuan ♦ Daily, lunch and dinner. Reservations recommended. 819 N Broadway (between Alpine and W College Sts). 818/625.0811 ♿

8 SAIGON PLAZA

This marketplace offers a good selection of merchandise, from color-splashed T-shirts to gold jewelry. ♦ Daily. 828 N Broadway (between Alpine and W College Sts). 213/972.1914

9 CHINATOWN

As early as 1852, a Chinese settlement was recorded near the site of today's Union Station. The community resettled a few streets over in 1938 with the dedication of Central Plaza, becoming the first modern American Chinatown, owned and planned from the ground up by Chinese. Today the area has turned into a thriving center for an avant-garde westside crowd that comes for the contemporary galleries, boutiques, and restaurants. The best way to explore Chinatown is to start with a visit to Central Plaza (947 N Broadway), where you will be enchanted by wind chimes and aromatic incense as you stroll through the quaint walkways and tiny shops. The sound of clicking mahjong tiles can be heard through upstairs windows from the halls where many of Chinatown's family associations hold their social meetings. **Central Plaza** is a popular place for filming, with its distinctive "Gate of Filial Piety," and also boasts a statue of Dr. Sun Yat Sen (founder of the Republic of China), a wishing well dating to 1939, and a five-tiered pagoda. A step outside and to the left of Central Plaza brings you to the doorstep of **Phoenix Bakery** (969 N Broadway; 213/628.4642), the oldest and largest bakery in Chinatown, with a citywide reputation for its strawberry whipped-cream cakes. Turn back and walk south along N Broadway. As you pass the curio shops and jewelry stores, stop to take in the beautiful tile murals on the wall at 913 N

DOWNTOWN/
HISTORIC CORE

Hollywood Fwy.
101
Beaudry Ave.
Sunset Blvd.
Figueroa Terr.
Stadium Way
Lilac Terr.
Lookout Dr.
N Broadway

NORTH CENTRAL

Pasadena Fwy.
110
Chung King Rd.
Bernard St.
Bamboo La.
N Spring St.
Elmyra St.

Adobe St.
W College St.

New Depot St.
Bunker Hill Ave.
Alpine St.

Grand Ave.
Hill Pl.
Yale St.
Ord St.
N Hill St.
N Broadway

CHINATOWN

Boston St.
Sunset Blvd.
New High St.
N Spring St.
Vignes St.

E Macy St.

Olvera St.

Harbor Fwy.
110
N Figueroa St.
W 1st St.
N Hope St.
N Grand Ave.
W Temple St.
N Hill St.
N Broadway
N Spring St.
W Aliso St.
Arcadia St.

Union Station

CIVIC CENTER

Olive St.
N Main St.
N Los Angeles St.

Federal Building

Commercial St.
Garey St.
E Temple St.
Vignes St.
Center St.
Lyon St.
Ramirez St.

101

E 1st St.
Onizuka St.
N Alameda St.
E 1st St.

LITTLE TOKYO

Boyd St.
E 2nd St.
Omar Ave.
E 3rd St.
S Central Ave.
E 2nd St.
E 3rd St.

E 4th St.
E 4th Pl.
E 4th St.

Los Angeles River

E 4th St.
E 5th St.
E 6th St.
E 7th St.
E 8th St.
Wall St.
S San Pedro St.
Towne Ave.
Gladys Ave.
S Alameda St.
Mateo St.
S Santa Fe Ave.
S Santa Fe Ave.

N

km
mi
1/8
1/4
1/4
1/2

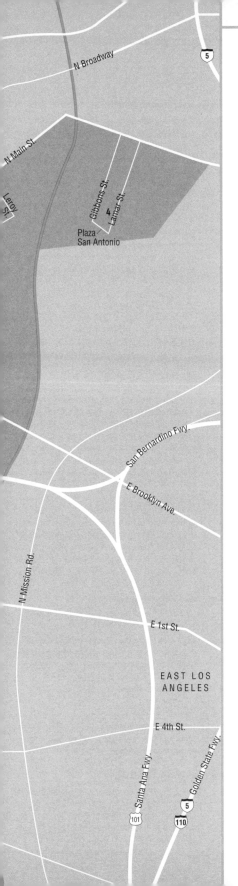

Broadway. Across the street, note **Little Joe's Restaurant,** a reminder of the large Italian population that also once lived here. The restaurant has recently been purchased, and development and restoration plans are underway. Continue south and you'll come to **Saigon Plaza, Chinatown Plaza,** and **Dynasty Center** (800 block of N Broadway). Chinatown's newest immigrants, from Laos, Vietnam, and Cambodia, own most of the shops and stalls in these bazaars, where you can find bargains on clothing, toys, and assorted knicknacks. As you walk on the west side of the street, your eyes will be caught by a number of jewelry stores sparkling with 18K and 22K gold and exquisite jade creations. On the corner of Alpine and Broadway is **Cathay Bank** (777 N Broadway), the first Chinese-American-owned bank in Chinatown. Also in this block is **Far East Plaza,** considered the first modern ethnic shopping mall in America. Originally constructed as a food center featuring 25 different dining establishments, Far East Plaza still houses the original Mandarin Deli, Sam Woo BBQ, Sam Woo Seafood, Pho 79, and Kim Chuy Restaurant, serving styles of regional cuisine that can be found here and nowhere else in Chinatown. The plaza is also home to **Wing Hop Fung Ginseng and China Products Center** (727 N Broadway; 213/626.7200; www.winghopfung.com), the largest store of its kind in the United States, fragrant with herbs and tea, and overflowing with chinaware, garments, and arts and crafts. A pharmacy and acupuncturist are located within. A little detour will take you into another world: an ornately decorated, incense-filled Taoist temple (750 Yale Street, open daily) that serves as a focal point of the immigrant community and is one of the most beautiful of its kind. As within any religious institution, please be respectful of worshippers and staff on the premises.

North along Hill Street you'll find the **Chinese United Methodist Church** (825 N Hill Street), which exemplifies a unique blending of Chinese and American architecture dating to the 1940s. The **Pacific Alliance Medical Center** at the corner of Hill and College Streets is one of the first hospitals in Los Angeles, built in 1868 to serve the city's French population and boasting a statue of Joan of Arc on its front lawn. Today, the hospital is run by enterprising Chinese doctors and serves the local Chinatown community. A little farther down is **West Plaza,** built in the late 1940s and mentioned in Lisa See's novel *On Gold Mountain.* The **F. See On** shop at the corner of the courtyard is actually run by See family members. West Plaza houses businesses on the ground floor and residences upstairs, and is also home to a burgeoning new art community whose avant-garde galleries and clothing boutique are interspersed among the curio shops. At the end of N Hill Street, a right turn onto Bernard

Street takes you to the headquarters of the **Chinese Historical Society of Southern California,** housed in two historic homes at 411 and 415 Bernard Street. French immigrants built both houses in the late 1880s. The visitor center showcases artifacts and historical photos recounting the history of the Chinese in Southern California. The center is open Sundays from noon to 4PM. Call 323/222.1918 for additional information.

For more details, call the **Chinese Chamber of Commerce** (777 N Broadway; 213/617.0396) or check out these web sites: www.camla.org (The Chinese American Museum), www.chssc.com (the Chinese Historical Society of Southern California), and www.chinatown.com (The Chinatown Business Improvement District).

10 OK SEAFOOD

★$$ Unusually cheerful waiters serve delicious, original renditions of standard and exotic Cantonese dishes (don't miss the crab in garlicky black bean sauce) in a spare room decorated with fish tanks. ◆ Cantonese/Seafood ◆ Daily, lunch and dinner until 1AM. 750 N Hill St (between Ord and Alpine Sts). 213/680.0640 &

11 WON KOK

★$ This busy, boisterous Cantonese restaurant stays open until the wee hours. Particularly satisfying after a night of carousing are their noodle dishes or a bowl of *jook*, a bland but wonderfully soothing thick rice porridge. ◆ Cantonese ◆ Daily, lunch and dinner until 3:30AM. 210 Alpine St (between N Spring and New High Sts). 213/613.0700

12 MANDARIN DELI

★$ Welcome to dumpling heaven: painless on the pocket but murder on the waistline. Everything is fresh. ◆ Chinese ◆ Daily, lunch and dinner. 727 N Broadway (between Ord and Alpine Sts), 213/623.6054. Also at 701 W Garvey Ave (at N Chandler Ave), Monterey Park, 818/570.9795; 9305 Reseda Blvd (at Prairie St), 818/993.0122

13 THANH-VI

★★$ Some of the best Vietnamese food in LA comes out of this raffish noodle bar, which might have been imported from Saigon. ◆ Vietnamese ◆ Daily, breakfast, lunch, and dinner. 422 Ord St (at N Hill St). 213/687.3522

14 ABC SEAFOOD

★★$$ Cantonese seafood is served in a bustling dining room. Lunch offers a wide assortment of dim sum, but dinner brings the best choices: fresh crab, calamari, or your favorite fish in season. ◆ Cantonese/Seafood

◆ Daily, breakfast, lunch, and dinner. 205 Ord St (between N Spring and New High Sts). 213/680.2887

15 CBS SEAFOOD

★$ Prawns with lobster sauce and wok-charred oysters are favorites in this popular restaurant. ◆ Chinese/Seafood ◆ Daily, breakfast, lunch, and dinner. 700 N Spring St (at Ord St). 213/617.2323 &

16 MON KEE

★★$$$ Chaotic and packed with people, Mon Kee is renowned for its fresh seafood, superbly prepared. Specialties include crab with garlic sauce and shrimp in spicy salt—both well worth the wait. ◆ Chinese/Seafood ◆ Daily, lunch and dinner. Reservations recommended for five or more. 679 N Spring St (between Sunset Blvd and Ord St). 213/628.6717 &

17 PHILLIPE'S ORIGINAL SANDWICH SHOP

★$ Legend has it that the French dip sandwich was invented here in 1908. Since then, loyal patrons have been coming here for the simple, honest food and the 10¢ coffee. The crowd is a cross section of LA society, from ballplayers to stockbrokers, and the décor consists of linoleum-topped tables on a sawdust floor. Be sure to have your sandwich double-dipped. ◆ American ◆ Daily, breakfast, lunch, and dinner. 1001 N Alameda St (at Ord St). 213/628.3781

18 PELANCONI HOUSE

Constructed in 1855, this was one of the first brick buildings in Los Angeles. The two-story balconied structure was named for its second owner, Antonio Pelanconi; the second floor is still a private residence. ◆ W-17 Olvera St (southwest of E Macy St)

Within the Pelanconi House:

CASA LA GOLONDRINA

★$$ Mariachis and dancers entertain while you enjoy Mexican food. ◆ Mexican ◆ Daily, breakfast, lunch, and dinner. Reservations recommended for four or more. 213/628.4349

18 CASA DE SOUSA

This shop carries Mexican and Central American folk art. ◆ Daily. W-19 Olvera St (southwest of E Macy St). 213/626.7076

19 ZANJA MADRE

A fragment of the city's original irrigation ditch, it was built in 1781 to carry water from the Los Angeles River near **Elysian Park** into the city. ◆ Olvera St (just southwest of E Macy St)

20 BAZAAR DE MEXICO

Brighten your wardrobe with Taxco silver jewelry and Mexican clothing and costumes. ♦ Daily. W-7 Olvera St (southwest of E Macy St). 213/620.9782

20 SEPULVEDA HOUSE

This redbrick building, a former boardinghouse built in 1887 by Eliosa Martinez de Sepulveda, houses a **Visitor Information Center.** An 18-minute film (available on request) chronicles the history of El Pueblo, and a walking-tour pamphlet is available in a variety of languages. ♦ M-Sa, 10AM-3PM. W-12 Olvera St (southwest of E Macy St). For a walking tour of Olvera Street, call 213/628.1274

21 AVILA ADOBE

LA's oldest adobe was built in 1818 by Don Francisco Avila, one-time mayor of the pueblo. Parts of the original two-foot-thick walls survive. The simple one-story structure is characteristic of Mexican design, with a garden patio in the rear. ♦ Free. Tu-Sa. 10 Olvera St (southwest of E Macy St). 213/680.2525

22 PLAZA CHURCH (CHURCH OF OUR LADY THE QUEEN OF THE ANGELS)

The oldest religious structure in Los Angeles, this church was originally a simple adobe, built between 1818 and 1822 by Franciscan padres and local Indians. ♦ 535 N Main St (between Arcadia and W Macy Sts). 213/629.3101

23 EL PUEBLO DE LOS ANGELES HISTORIC MONUMENT AND OLVERA STREET

The founding site of the city of Los Angeles encompasses **El Pueblo de Los Angeles Plaza,** Olvera Street, a park, and 27 historic or architecturally significant buildings. The entire area has undergone major urban renewal over the years. Olvera Street, named for a Los Angeles County judge and supervisor, was rebuilt in 1930 in the style of a Mexican marketplace. The brick-paved block is lined with shops and stalls selling Mexican handicrafts and confections. A number of stands and cafés along the street offer food, but for dessert go to the plaza, where peeled mangoes, papayas, and other tropical fruit is available. The confectioners at the center of Olvera Street tempt passersby with Mexican sweets such as candied squash or brown sugar cones, while delicious *churros*

(doughnuts) can be found at the bakery near the center of the north side of the street. There are free docent-led tours Tuesday through Saturday (call 213/628.1274 for group reservations). ♦ Bounded by N Alameda and N Spring Sts, and Arcadia and Macy Sts

23 LA LUZ DEL DIA

At this shop, you can watch women skilled in the fast-disappearing art of making tortillas by hand. ♦ Tu-Su. W-1 Olvera St (southwest of E Macy St). 213/628.7495

24 EL PUEBLO DE LOS ANGELES PLAZA (OLD PLAZA)

The center of **El Pueblo Historic Monument** and the hub of community life through the 1870s, the plaza now serves as the setting for public festivals that bring back the spirit of the Mexican era. Most notable are Cinco de Mayo (5 May), a Mexican Independence holiday; Día de los Muertos (Day of the Dead; early November), a religious festival in which the souls of the dead return to visit their living relatives; and Las Posadas (the nine consecutive days before Christmas), a parade that commemorates the birth of Christ with different nativity scenes. At the center of the plaza is the **Kiosko,** a hexagonal bandstand with filigree ironwork. ♦ Olvera St (southwest of E Macy St)

25 PICO HOUSE

This Italian palazzo was built by **Ezra F. Kysor** in 1870 for **Pio Pico,** the last Mexican governor of California. During its later heyday, the building was the finest hotel in California south of San Francisco. ♦ Closed to the public. 430 N Main St (between Arcadia and E Macy Sts)

26 MERCED THEATRE

Ezra F. Kysor also designed this three-story 1870 Italianate masonry building with a theater that's no longer in use today. At press time, the interior was being restored. ♦ 420 N Main St (between Arcadia and E Macy Sts)

26 MASONIC HALL

Designed in 1858, this was the city's first lodge, a two-story Italian Renaissance structure with a cast-iron balcony and three arched openings on each floor. ♦ 416 N Main St (between Arcadia and E Macy Sts). No tours or phone number at this time

27 OLD PLAZA FIREHOUSE

A castellated brick structure, this 1884 firehouse is now a museum containing firefighting equipment and photographs of

---

Restaurants/Clubs: Red | Hotels: Purple | Shops: Orange | Outdoors/Parks: Green | Sights/Culture: Blue

19th-century fire stations. Guided tours available. ♦ Free. Tu-Sa. 501 N Los Angeles St (between Arcadia and N Alameda Sts). 213/625.3741

28 GARNIER BLOCK

Philippe Garnier built this block in 1890 as commercial stores and apartments for the city's Chinese business population. It is constructed of buff brick with sandstone trim and has an unusual cornice of Victorian Romanesque design. ♦ 415 N Los Angeles St (between Arcadia and N Alameda Sts)

29 UNION STATION

One of LA's greatest—yet least appreciated—architectural treasures, and one of the last of the country's grand railroad passenger terminals, Union Station was designed by **John** and **Donald Parkinson** in 1939 and built jointly by the **Southern Pacific, Union Pacific, and Santa Fe railroad companies.** It is a free interpretation of Spanish Mission architecture, combining enormous scale with Moderne and Moorish details. The wood-beamed ceiling of the waiting room stands 52 feet high, the floors are made of marble, and deep scalloped archways lead to two patios. A food court offers Mexican food, bagels, and hot dogs. **Amtrak** (800/USA-RAIL, www.amtrak. com) offers comfortable daily service to just about anywhere in the country. Many local commuters forgo freeways to ride the rails to Santa Barbara and the Pacific Northwest and south to San Diego. And for you statisticians, nearly a million passengers go through the depot annually. ♦ 800 N Alameda St

(between the Santa Ana Fwy and E Macy St). General information 213/683.6875, schedule and ticket information 800/872.7245

Within Union Station:

TRAXX

★★$$ What could be more fitting than an Art Deco dining room in an Art Deco train station? This narrow little (100-seat) eatery has tables outside near the concourse and on the north patio, and a separate bar in the depot's old telephone room. An open kitchen, headed by chef Tara Thomas, produces such menu items as Manila clams in a Thai red curry sauce, crab cakes, lamb and pork chops, and an irresistible pecan pie. ♦ California ♦ M-F, lunch and dinner; Sa, dinner. 213/625.1999. www.traxxrestaurant.com

30 CITY ARCHIVES

Few people other than city officials know about these archives, but anyone can make an appointment to dig through the treasury of maps, papers, photos, and council records, which document LA since 1827. ♦ M-F. 555 Ramirez St (between Center and Lyon Sts), No. 320. 213/485.3512

31 LOS ANGELES COUNTY COURTHOUSE

Scene of the O.J. Simpson trial, this is where Marcia Clark and the "Dream Team" battled it out while TV crews and T-shirt vendors lined the street. Today it's business as usual—until the next big trial. ♦ W Temple St (between N Spring St and N Broadway)

Union Station

32 CIVIC CENTER

LA has the second-largest governmental center in the US outside of Washington, DC. Look for a sign that reads, "Abandon hope all ye who enter here." ♦ Bounded by N San Pedro St and N Grand Ave, and First and Aliso Sts

32 UNITED STATES FEDERAL COURTHOUSE BUILDING

The United States District Court occupies this handsome WPA-style structure designed by **Louis Simon & Gilbert Stanley Underwood.** ♦ M-F. 312 N Spring St (between W Temple and W Aliso Sts). 213/894.3650

33 LOS ANGELES CHILDREN'S MUSEUM

Children and adults alike enjoy this touch-and-play experience, where a kids' television station and changing exhibitions covering the city's streets and African-American roots encourage participation. Classes and workshops are scheduled regularly; call for current availability. Labels in Spanish and English explain the exhibitions. Weekday parking is available in the Los Angeles Mall garage. ♦ Admission; children under two free. Tu-Su. 310 N Main St (between E Temple and E Aliso Sts). General information 213/687.8801; recording 213/687.8800

34 CITY HALL

Designed by **John C. Austin, John Parkinson,** and **Albert C. Martin** in 1928, this classic monument underwent a much-needed restoration in 2001 thanks to Project Restore, a nonprofit that raised funds through corporations, individuals, and such organizations as the National Endowment for the Arts, the State Office of Historic Preservation, the City of Los Angeles, the Ahmanson Foundation, and the Community Redevelopment Agency. The restoration, which was guided by the architectural firm of Hardy Holzman Pfeiffer Associates, included the Main Street lobby and garage entrance, Spring Street forecourt, rotunda, third-floor lobbies, City Council chambers, Board of Public Works session room, main and secondary corridors, and the bridge to City Hall East. The project cleverly maintained the original design. Until 1957, City Hall with its pyramid-crowned tower was the only exception to the city's 150-foot building height limit. One of the most photographed buildings in LA, it has been featured in countless movies and television shows—most memorably as the *Daily Planet* building in the popular 1950s television series *Superman*. Inside, luxurious marble columns and an inlaid-tile dome give the public areas the feel of a cathedral. On a clear day, you can see forever from the 27th-floor observation deck. ♦ M-F. 200 N Spring St (between W First and W Temple Sts). 213/485.2121; www.cityofla.org

35 LOS ANGELES TIMES

Gordon Kaufman designed this stodgy Moderne block in 1935; the 1973 steel-and-glass addition is by **William Pereira Associates**. A free tour takes you through the making of the newspaper, from newsroom to printing. Children must be 10 or older. Meet the guide at the First Street entrance. Also available (by reservation) is a tour of the **Olympic Plant,** the paper's production facility. ♦ Free. M-F. 202 W First St (at S Spring St). 213/237.5757

36 PARKER CENTER

Named after a former chief of police, this is the headquarters of the Los Angeles Police Department. ♦ 150 N Los Angeles St (between E First and E Temple Sts). Tours are available by appointment only: 213/485.3205

37 VIBIANA PLACE/ST. VIBIANA'S CATHEDRAL

This Baroque-style cathedral was recently restored by Gilmore Associates of Los Angeles into a magnificent nonprofit performing arts center for Cal State Los Angeles. Originally designed in 1876 by **Ezra F. Kysor,** St. Vibiana is distinguished by a façade of pilasters and volutes crowned with a tower and cupola. Inside, relics of the early Christian martyr St. Vibiana are preserved in a marble sarcophagus. The site also contains 300 loft apartments, two Cal State L.A. performing arts and continuing higher education centers, a Little Tokyo Branch library, a restaurant, a small boutique hotel, and a rectory. ♦ 114 E Second St (at S Main St). 213/624.3941

LITTLE TOKYO

Bounded by **South Alameda, South Main, East Third,** and **East First Streets,** the heart of Southern California's Japanese-American community is home to more than 200,000 people. First settled more than 100 years ago, Little Tokyo began to flourish after World War I but was devastated by the forced evacuation of Japanese-Americans from the Pacific Coast during World War II. It has emerged in the past decade as an active and cohesive area, a mix of late–19th-century commercial buildings and modern structures. **Nisei Week,** held in August, is a major event, with a parade, street dancing, festival food, and demonstrations of flower arranging, *sumi* brush painting, the traditional tea ceremony, and other Japanese arts. If you're a bit skittish about dining here, many of the restaurants display their food in the

---

Restaurants/Clubs: Red | Hotels: Purple | Shops: Orange | Outdoors/Parks: Green | Sights/Culture: Blue

windows so you can see what you're getting. Those in the know, however, keep local woks sizzling. After dark, karaoke bars abound. Walking tours of Little Tokyo are available from the **Business Association** (213/620.0570); reservations are required.

38 NEW OTANI HOTEL

$$$ Far from the maddening crowd, this hotel offers a garden-like setting with its 434 rooms (including 20 suites) that boast either Japanese or American appointments. The pricey "Japanese Experience" package for two features a welcome from a kimono-clad attendant, and one night in a garden suite complete with futon, hot tub, and a sitting room with shoji screens. Also included in the package are a sauna, massage, and dinner at **A Thousand Cranes/Sen Bazuru** (see below). Worth a stop is the 24-hour **Rendezvous Lounge** in the main lobby. Nearby is a three-level shopping courtyard. Don't miss the fourth-story Japanese garden, a haven of tranquillity. On the same level, the **Genji Bar** is a lovely place to watch twilight deepen. ♦120 S Los Angeles St (between E Second and E First Sts). 213/629.1200, 800/273.2294 in California, 800/421.8795 in the US and Canada; fax 213/622.0980; www.newotani.com &

Within the New Otani Hotel:

A THOUSAND CRANES/ SEN BAZURU

★★$$$ This stylish restaurant overlooking the roof garden has separate rooms for sushi, tempura, and the *teppan* grill. The service is excellent. The Sunday buffet brunch is a spectacular offering of Asian and American food accompanied by Champagne and/or tea. ♦ Japanese ♦ Daily, lunch and dinner; Su, brunch. Reservations required. 213/629.1200

39 ASTRONAUT ELLISON S. ONIZUKA STREET

Formerly **Weller Court** but renamed to commemorate an astronaut who died in the *Challenger* explosion, this is a handsome pedestrian precinct. The major tenant is **Matsuzakaya,** a branch of Japan's oldest department store. ♦ Between E Second and E First Sts

40 GEFFEN CONTEMPORARY AT THE MUSEUM OF CONTEMPORARY ART (MOCA)

The transformation of two city-owned warehouses by architect **Frank Gehry** in 1983 was intended as a stopgap while a new

building was being readied a few blocks away (see page 26), but the 55,000-square-foot loft became a permanent facility. Exhibitions have included "Blueprints for Modern Living," "The Automobile and Culture," and "Tokyo: Form and Spirit." But the building would be worth seeing without the art: Gehry has preserved the raw character of the interior, adding a steel-and-chain-link canopy to create an outdoor lobby. A Barbara Kruger mural enlivens the south front. There's low-cost parking and easy access from the DASH shuttle. ♦ Admission (covers the MOCA and the Geffen Center); free for members, children under 12, and Th 5-8PM. Tu-W, F-Su; Th until 8PM. 152 N Central Ave (just north of E First St). 213/626.6222

41 JAPANESE AMERICAN NATIONAL MUSEUM

Housed in the historic **Nishi Hongwanji Buddhist Temple,** this private museum was designed in 1925 by **Edgar Cline** in a mix of styles, including Japanese and Middle Eastern. Exhibits preserve the Japanese experience as part of US history. A new $22 million pavilion by architect **Gyo Obata** increased the space by 300 percent. ♦ Admission. Tu-Su; F until 8PM. 369 E First St (at N Central Ave). 213/625.0414

42 JAPANESE VILLAGE PLAZA MALL

White stucco with exposed wood framing, blue tile roofs, and a traditional lookout tower distinguish this Japanese mini-mall, where you can pick up anything from a kimono to herbs and elixirs. Park on Central Avenue. ♦ 385 E Second St (between S Central Ave and S San Pedro St). 213/620.8861

43 RAFU BUSSAN

An unusually large selection of lacquerware and ceramics is sold here. ♦ Daily. 326 E Second St (between S Central Ave and S San Pedro St). 213/614.1181

44 JAPANESE AMERICAN CULTURAL AND COMMUNITY CENTER

The center houses many cultural groups and activities and is a major resource for the entire city. Special events and displays are organized in conjunction with annual community festivals, including Hanamatsuri (birth of the Buddha) in April, Children's Day in May, Obon (Festival of the Dead) in June and July, Nisei Week in August, and Oshogatsu (New Year's festivities). The Center's shop sells posters and distinctive crafts. ♦ 244 S San Pedro St (between E Third and E Second Sts). 213/628.2725

Within the Japanese American Cultural and Community Center:

GEORGE J. DOIZAKI GALLERY

This gallery features regular exhibitions of historical treasures and new art and graphics. ♦ Tu-Su. 213/628.2725

FRANKLIN D. MURPHY LIBRARY

Japanese magazines and books on Japan and Japanese-Americans are available here; an appointment is necessary to visit. ♦ Open Sa only. 213/628.2725

JAPAN AMERICA THEATER

The best in traditional and contemporary performing arts from Japan, including the Grand Kabuki, Bugaku, and Noh dramas, are presented here, along with Bunraku puppet theater and Western dance and chamber music. ♦ Box office: daily, noon-5PM. 213/680.3700

JACCC PLAZA

Designed by **Isamu Noguchi,** the monumental rock sculpture in the plaza is dedicated to the Issei (first generation of Japanese immigrants).

🌸 JAMES IRVINE GARDEN

A fusion of Eastern and Western cultures, this garden is a sunken oasis for strolling and meditation. It is also known as **Seiryu-en,** or "Garden of the Clear Stream." ♦ Call ahead for hours. 213/628.2725

45 YORO-NO-TAKI

★$ The name means waterfalls in Japanese. And the place is awash with businesspeople who crowd this wood-paneled room and down large quantities of sake and beer as they nibble on grilled fish, pickled vegetables, and oden, a fish-cake stew. ♦ Japanese ♦ M-Sa, dinner until 1AM. 432 E Second St (between S Alameda St and S Central Ave). 213/626.6055

46 HIGASHI HONGWANGJI BUDDHIST TEMPLE

This traditional structure by **Kajima Associates** was designed in 1976 for the Jodo Shinshu sect. A broad flight of stairs leads to the entrance; the blue tile roof is protected by two golden dragons. ♦ 505 E Third St (at S Central Ave). 213/626.4200

47 HANA ICHIMONME

★$ If you saw the movie *Tampopo,* you know how seriously the Japanese take ramen. Here the noodles are fresh, the broth rich and delicately spiced. ♦ Japanese ♦ Daily, lunch and dinner. Little Tokyo Square, 333 S Alameda St (between E Fourth and E Third Sts). 213/626.3514 &

THE RAW DEAL

If you already rave about raw fish, **Little Tokyo**—birthplace of the California sushi craze—will be your idea of *hamachi* heaven. But novices who feel intimidated by such exotic dishes may want to prep a little before dinner. Try walking around the neighborhood and looking at the sushi displays—most of the Japanese restaurants set up plastic models of their meals. If these tingle your tastebuds, but the names leave you tongue-tied, you can always bring your waiter outside and point. To make ordering easier, here's a glossary of some of the most common sushi terms:

Aji Spanish mackerel

Akagai Ark shell (red clam)

Amaebi Sweet shrimp

Aoyagi Round clam

Awabi Abalone

California roll Avocado and crab

Hamachi Yellowtail

Hashira Scallop

Hirame Halibut

Ika Squid

Ikura Salmon roe

Kaki Oyster

Kani King crab

Kappa maki Cucumber roll

Kazunoko Herring roe

Kohada Gizzard shad

Maguro Tuna

Masago Smelt roe

Mirugai Geoduck (jumbo clam)

Saba Mackerel

Sake Salmon

Shako Squilla

Tai Red snapper

Tako Octopus

Tekka maki Tuna roll

Toro Fatty tuna (or tuna belly)

Umeshiso maki Plum roll

Uni Sea urchin

Restaurants/Clubs: Red | Hotels: Purple | Shops: Orange | Outdoors/Parks: Green | Sights/Culture: Blue

B. Downtown/Business and Financial District

Wall Street it's not, but it's still well worth investing your time . . .

High-rise banks and corporate offices dominate a now-flattened **Bunker Hill** and a narrow corridor flanking the **Harbor Freeway**. Unlike the business and financial centers of many major US cities, the architecture in this part of downtown is generally undistinguished, and little has been done to make the pedestrian feel welcome. The whole area is a monument to local boosters who confuse growth with greatness. Massive urban redevelopment has obliterated neighborhoods and landmarks. The process began in the 1960s, and one of the latest installments, **California Plaza**, is only marginally better than what surrounds it.

At the turn of the century, **Bunker Hill** was the most desirable residential neighborhood in the city, with Victorian gingerbread mansions looking down on what was even then the city's business district. Over the years, the neighborhood fell into disrepair. In 1959, the Community Redevelopment Agency (CRA) decided that the dilapidated Victorian structures, many of which had been converted into seedy boardinghouses, should be demolished and the top of the hill be leveled (no thought of rehabilitation or adaptive reuse back then!).

Flower Street is the main avenue of this burgeoning financial district, which has boomed due to the widespread popularity of branch banking in Southern California and the emergence of Los Angeles as the American capital of the Pacific Rim. Of the six largest banks in California, four have built high-rise headquarters in LA, while the other two maintain their Southern California headquarters here. Overseas companies have invested heavily in downtown, too, since real estate in this area is a fraction of the cost of similar districts in Tokyo and Hong Kong.

1 Department of Water and Power Building

West of the Music Center (see below) is the headquarters of the largest utility company in the US. The glass-and-steel building, designed by **AC Martin Partners** in 1964, is an elegant stack of horizontal planes that looks its best when lit up at night. ♦ 111 N Hope St (between W First and W Temple Sts)

2 Bunker Hill Towers

These three high-rise blocks, designed by **Robert Alexander** in 1968, were the first residential structures on redeveloped Bunker Hill. ♦ 800 W First St (between S Hope and S Figueroa Sts)

3 Music Center

The addition of the Walt Disney Concert Hall, home of the LA Philharmonic—possibly the most spectacular auditorium ever conceived—ushered in a phenomenal new era for the city's major performing arts venue and quickly became the shining star of the four-theater facility. To welcome its new member, the grounds of this urban park/festival space were recently spiffed up with a new, more appealing entrance, a redesign of the seven-acre plaza by **Mark Rio Architects**, lavish landscaping, and a children's education pavilion. 111 South Grand Ave (at the intersection of First St and Grand Ave in Bunker Hill).

Within the Music Center:

Walt Disney Concert Hall

No structure ever built has received the accolades, oohs, aahs, and other distinguishable sounds than this mega-masterpiece. Fifteen years in the making with a cast of dream-team architects, designers, and acoustical designers led by **Frank Gehry**, this eagerly anticipated $274 million architectural wonder elevated Los Angeles to new cultural heights when it opened in October 2003. Wrapped in 9,000 panes of stainless steel sheathing, the extraordinary structure sits on a 3.6-acre site across from the Music Center. The phenomenal acoustical design provides a spectacular showcase home of the LA Philharmonic with a 360-degree wraparound stage offering fantastic viewing from any of its 2,265 seats. One of the most revered structures ever built in the city, it is almost sacrilege to criticize the Hall. Nevertheless, edgy us, we'll risk the wrath. While it's true this is one of the wonders of the world, what were they thinking when they made seats with leg room for Lilliputians? Unless you're stage front, your knees touch the seats in front of you. But the acoustics, setting, and incredible baton ballet by Philharmonic music director Esa-Pekka Salonen as he leads his orchestra more than make up for it.

The much bally-hooed project began in 1987 with a $50 million endowment by Lillian Disney to construct a world-class performing arts venue. Other members of the famed family later donated additional funds. In 1988, Frank Gehry was chosen to head the design team, with construction commencing in 1992. The result is a study in stainless steel—a metallic sculpture, almost, that curves and flaps around 293,000 square feet. The obvious centerpiece is the auditorium designed by Nagata Acoustics and Gehry Partners with its vineyard shape and curved wood ceiling, staggered seating, and unique intimacy. Even the entrance waxes grand, with an **Atrium Reception Hall** enclosed by glass windows that fold up, providing an indoor/outdoor venue. There's also the **BP Hall**, a pre-concert foyer set on travertine

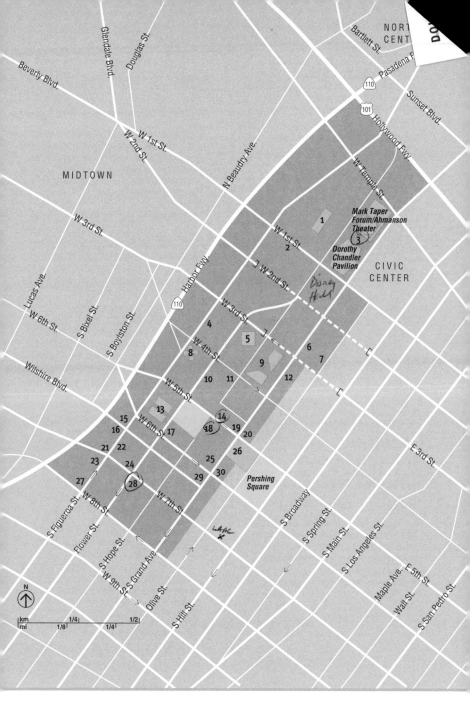

floors, where lectures and programs are staged. The **Founders Room**, anchoring the northernmost side, offers special amenities for the Center's major donors and guests, while the **W.M. Keck Foundation Children's Amphitheater** sits farthest south. There are two restaurants run by the Patina Group:

Patina, which was moved from its original Melrose Avenue location (which now houses Patina Prive, a catering and events venue), and **Patina Café**, a moderately priced self-serve snack bar. In keeping with the late Lillian Disney's wishes, a lavish garden, landscaped by Melinda Taylor, provides a

Restaurants/Clubs: Red | Hotels: Purple | Shops: Orange | Outdoors/Parks: Green | Sights/Culture: Blue

pleasant place to relax before or after concerts. Even if you don't go for a concert, you should at least head downtown for a glimpse and/or a tour of this magical/majestic music venue. 213/972.7211. www.LAPhil.com

Within the Walt Disney Concert Hall:

PATINA

★★★★$$$$ Joachim and Christine Splichal's decision to relocate this Patina Group flagship restaurant from its Melrose Avenue location to the Concert Hall in October 2003 shocked the city. More for the Music Center theater crowd now than leisure diners, the restaurant occupies a major corner space of the magnificent Hall, designed by **Hagy Belzberg**, a Santa Monica firm, to fuse with the Hall's dramatic décor. Not the Patina LA foodies came to know and love, the room is less intimate, with a wide-open setting and livelier ambience. And it's a long drive from the Westside, where most Patina patrons dwell. The menu reflects some of Splichal's signature dishes combined with new ideas. Still, it's too out-of-the-way for most of us, and we miss the Melrose location. ◆ French/California ◆ Daily, lunch and dinner. Reservations advised. 213/972.3331

THE CAFÉ AT WALT DISNEY CONCERT HALL

At this casual café, you hand-pick dishes from a marketplace menu of sandwiches, salads and soups, and daily entrée specials.

DOROTHY CHANDLER PAVILION

This big barnlike structure can be an exciting place to attend the opera or a play. The former home of the the Academy Awards (which moved to the new Kodak Theater in Hollywood), it also lost another distinction with the relocation of the LA Philharmonic to the Walt Disney Concert Hall in 2003. ◆ Box office: M-Sa, 213/972.7300; LA Opera, 213/972.7219; LA Master Chorale, 213/972.7282

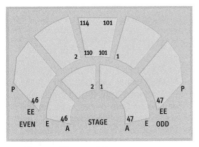

MARK TAPER FORUM

For more than 20 years, Gordon Davidson has made this one of the country's most

adventurous theaters (see seating chart above), beginning with a production of *The Devils,* which provoked a walkout by then-governor Ronald Reagan. The theater has offered more than 600 productions, including *Zoot Suit* and *Children of a Lesser God.* Readings and a literary cabaret are presented at the **Itchey Foot** restaurant down the street; experimental productions take place at the **Taper, Too** in the John Anson Ford Theater in Hollywood. ◆ M-Sa. 213/972.0700; www.taperahmanson.com

AHMANSON THEATER

This 2,140-seat theater underwent a $17.1 million renovation in 1997 that improved the acoustics, seating arrangements, and décor. The theater opened with *Miss Saigon.* ◆ M-Sa. 213/972.0700; www.taperahmanson.com

PRECONCERT DINING

Within the Dorothy Chandler Pavilion is **Kendall's Brasserie** (213/972.7322), a casual street-level room offering a seafood-bar menu of brasserie-style food.

The **Impresario Ristorante E Bar** on the fifth floor (213/972.7333) offers elegant dining Tuesday through Sunday and brunch on Saturday and Sunday. Other choices for pre-theater dining include the **Taipan** (213/626.6688) and the **California Pizza Kitchen** (213/626.2616), in the Wells Fargo Center (see page 28); and **Cicada** (213/655.5559) in the Oviatt Building (see page 35).

4 WORLD TRADE CENTER

This dull building, home to a number of import/export companies and law offices, is linked by bridges to the Bonaventure Hotel, Bunker Hill Towers, and the Sheraton Grande Hotel. A passport office and currency exchange are located in its shopping arcade. ◆ 350 S Figueroa St (between W Fourth and W Third Sts). 213/489.3337

5 BANK OF AMERICA

The well-detailed 55-story tower was designed in 1974 by **AC Martin Partners**. It is set at an angle to the street and anchored by a red Alexander Calder stabile outside the main entrance. ◆ 345 S Hope St (between W Fourth and Flower Sts)

6 MUSEUM OF CONTEMPORARY ART (MOCA)

The 1986 building is a dazzling fusion of Western geometry and Eastern tradition. The first major US building by Japan's leading architect, **Arata Isozaki,** it is also one of the city's finest. A sequence of luminous galleries with exposed vaults open off a sunken courtyard. Isozaki has even indulged his fascination with Marilyn Monroe in the sensuous curve of the parapet overlooking the courtyard. Highlights in this widely acclaimed facility include works from Franz Kline, Claes Oldenburg, Louise Nevelson, and Mark Rothko. Throughout the year, artists, critics, and curators give informative tours of current exhibitions. In the courtyard is what may be the best museum gift shop in LA. Below the galleries is a steep 162-seat auditorium used for film, video, and performing arts. Every Thursday night the museum stays open late; there is a bar, free hors d'oeuvres, and in summer, live performances in the courtyard. Parking is available at First and Grand (Lot 167) and at the Music Center; rates in garages below the museum are very high. The museum's second facility, the **Geffen Contemporary,** is a few blocks away in Little Tokyo at 152 North Central Avenue (see page 22). Parking close to the Geffen is much more reasonable and the DASH shuttle will get you to MOCA. ♦ Admission; free Th 5-8PM. Tu-Su; Th until 8PM. 250 S Grand Ave (between W Fourth and W First Sts). General information 213/621.2766; recording 213/626.6222. www.moca-la.org &

Within the Museum of Contemporary Art (MOCA):

PATINETTE

★★$ Probably the best restaurant to ever find its way into a museum, this one comes thanks to the creative efforts of Joachim Splichal, chef/owner of Patina, Cafe Pinot, Pinot Bistro, and Pinot Hollywood. Offering a Mediterranean menu with a rotating selection of appetizers, soups, sandwiches, salads, and yummy desserts in a casual setting, it provides an inexpensive way to sample this super-chef's coveted cuisine.
♦ Continental ♦ Tu-Su, lunch and dinner. 213/626.1178

OMNI ❀ LOS ANGELES HOTEL

7 OMNI LOS ANGELES HOTEL AT CALIFORNIA PLAZA

$$$ This 439-room luxury property, perched atop Bunker Hill, is perfect for business travelers who want to be close to downtown's business and financial district. It's a good-looking hotel with an interesting stylized lobby where Asia meets the West with a dramatic welded steel *Yellow Fin* by David Stomeyer sitting in a glass-walled atrium; a painted silk kimono done by California artist Marie-Laurie Ilie, housed in a Japanese frame; and black Chinese chairs by David Hockney. The rooms

are equally arty, done in neoclassic style with an Asian flair yet plugged in for the techno-needy, with work desks, dataports, three phones, video games for the kids, plus the usual creature comforts (robes, minibars, televisions). For nourishment there's the pretty, magnolia tree–framed **Grand Café** (★★$$) serving breakfast, lunch, and dinner as well as Sunday brunch. The eclectic international cuisine, created by executive chef Peter Dean, leans on the healthy, low-cholesterol side. For your tippling pleasure, there's the fireside **Angel's Flight Lounge** serving wines and champagnes by the glass, as well as the usual bar drinks and an interesting appetizer menu. And to keep you in shape, the fitness center has all the right stuff. Additional services include a full business center, complimentary town car transportation within a three-mile area, and the Omni Kids program, which keeps the little tykes amused. ♦ 251 S Olive St (between Olive and Fourth at California Plaza). 213/617.3300, 800-THE-OMNI; fax: 213/617.3399. www.omnilosangeles.com &

Within the Omni Los Angeles Hotel:

NOE

★★★$$$ Followers of chef Robert Gadsby will be happy to know that he's back in the kitchen at this elegant eatery. Accentuated by warm colors, international artwork, wood and glass, and recessed pin ceiling lights, the handsome setting, created by famed Hollywood production designer Curtis Schnell, provides an apt showcase for Gadsby's progressive American cuisine. Each artistically presented dish is outstanding, especially his gingered butternut squash cappuccino with almond cloud and toasted hazelnut veil, the filet of beef and braised short ribs, seared yellowfin tuna, and baked halibut. For a great Gadsby finale, opt for the banana tempura with boysenberries, banana walnut ice cream, and butterscotch sauce. If you have any culinary questions or just feel like chatting with the chef, chances are you'll have the opportunity. English-born Gadsby likes to stop by his tables and greet his guests personally. Then, if puffings your penchant, have a cigar and a cognac on the pleasant outdoor patio. ♦ American/Japanese fusion ♦ Daily, dinner. Reservations essential. 213/356.4100

8 WESTIN BONAVENTURE HOTEL

$$$ "Buck Rogers beside the Freeway" best describes this 1976 **John Portman** design of five mirror-glass silos with glass-bubble elevators and a huge, fanciful atrium. The hotel's 1,354 rooms are comfortable and

presentable. The bustling hotel is a popular venue for conventioneers, business travelers, and lookie-loos who wander about trying to make sense of the confusing eight levels of shops, fast-food places, and restaurants. Among these, the revolving **LA Prime,** a New York-style steakhouse, is notable for its prime cuts of beef served with a sweeping 360° view of the city and surrounding mountaintops. On a clear day you can even see the Pacific Ocean. Fitness/health amenities include a circular indoor running track with a multi-station weight training course and a 9,000-square-foot Asian-themed spa. There's also a half-acre garden deck and pool area for sun worshippers. For business travelers, there's a full-service center. Valet parking is available too. ♦ 404 S Figueroa St (at W Fourth St). 213/624.1000; fax 213/612.4800 ♿

9 WELLS FARGO CENTER

The twin knife-edge towers clad in polished brown granite and tinted glass were designed by **Skidmore, Owings & Merrill** in 1983 and developed by Maguire Thomas Partners. Between the towers is **The Court,** an exciting glass-walled garden designed by Lawrence Halprin, with sculpture by Jean Dubuffet, Joan Miró, Louise Nevelson, and Robert Graham. ♦ 350 S Hope St (between W Fourth and W Third Sts)

Within Wells Fargo Center:

WELLS FARGO HISTORY MUSEUM

From the company that helped civilize the West comes this museum, with a stagecoach, a two-pound gold nugget, and photos and videos recalling 130 years of history. ♦ Free. M-F. 213/253.7166

STARBUCKS

★$ Downtown's working populace flocks to this branch of Seattle's finest. ♦ M-F, until 5PM. 213/621.4191. Also at numerous other locations throughout the city

TAIPAN

★$$ The modern Mandarin cuisine includes orange-flavored beef and spicy Szechuan shredded pork. There's a full bar, too. ♦

Chinese ♦ M-F, lunch and dinner. Reservations recommended. 213/626.6688

CALIFORNIA PIZZA KITCHEN

★$$ The friendly staff at this branch of the restaurant chain serves acclaimed designer pizza (topped with barbecued chicken or roasted garlic shrimp, for example) as well as your basic cheese-and-tomato pie. There's pasta, salad, and wine, too. ♦ California ♦ Daily, lunch and dinner. 213/626.2616. Also at other branches all over LA

MCDONALD'S

$ LAPD veteran Don Bailey has turned his franchise into a classy joint for the budget-conscious. There's no anguish here over who gets the power table, just telephone connections to every seat, fresh flowers, and, at lunch on Thursday and Friday, a harpist or flutist to soothe executive stress. Weight-watchers can enjoy a chicken salad instead of the Big Mac and fries. Special events can be arranged. ♦ Fast food ♦ Daily, lunch and dinner. 213/626.0709

10 444 FLOWER BUILDING

This undistinguished corporate tower replaced the 1935 Sunkist Building, with its hanging gardens and statuary. Known by many as the *LA Law* building, it was seen weekly in the opening credits for the TV series. Steps and escalators lead up from a palm-shaded plaza to an upper garden on Hope Street; along the way is a distinguished collection of modern artworks by Mark di Suvero, Michael Heizer, Frank Stella, Bruce Nauman, and Robert Rauschenberg. A pedestrian bridge over Flower Street connects the building with the Bonaventure Hotel. ♦ 444 Flower St (between W Fifth and W Fourth Sts)

Within 444 South Flower:

THE TURKEY BASKET

★$ We're talking turkey here: Everything from burgers to pies (made from turkey) is on the menu at this popular self-service eatery. ♦ American ♦ M-F. 213/892.9500

11 STUART M. KETCHUM DOWNTOWN YMCA

This sleek coed facility features the latest equipment for sports enthusiasts: an indoor lap pool, a running track, and squash, racquetball, and tennis courts. ♦ Nonmembers pay a daily-use fee. 401 S Hope St (at W Fourth St). 213/624.2348

Within Stuart M. Ketchum Downtown YMCA:

CALIFORNIA CRISP

★★$ This small restaurant serves soup, salads, sandwiches, and pasta cafeteria style.

The fresh spicy chicken salad is a favorite. ◆ California ◆ Daily. 213/622.6749

12 CALIFORNIA PLAZA

This 11.5-acre site being developed by Bunker Hill Associates following **Arthur Erikson Architects'** master plan is highlighted by two slick-skinned office towers with curving glass walls anchored by granite. There's a residential tower, a spiral amphitheater, a museum, and a 1.5-acre outdoor performance space and garden. A restored version of the historic **Angel's Flight Railway** (the world's shortest railway) runs between Hill and Olive Streets. Outdoor concerts—featuring popular music, classical tunes, and such one-of-a-kind entertainment as El Vez, a Latino Elvis impersonator—are some of the popular events held here. ◆ S Grand Ave (between W Fourth and W First Sts). 213/687.2000

13 ATLANTIC RICHFIELD PLAZA

To replace the 1929 Richfield Building, a flamboyant black-and-gold Art Deco tower, the Atlantic Richfield Co. (ARCO) commissioned **AC Martin Partners** in 1972 to design twin 52-story charcoal-gray shafts— the architectural equivalent of a sober business suit—to house its own expanded offices and those of the Bank of America. Two 20-foot-high bronze doors from the old building are displayed in the lobby of the south tower. On the plaza is *Double Ascension*, a striking red helical sculpture by Herbert Bayer, who also designed the executive floors from the carpets on up. The escalators on Flower Street lead down to seven acres of subterranean shopping and eating, plus a church, fitness center, and post office. Yet another refurbishing began in 2003 when Los Angeles developer James A. Thomas announced plans for a $125 million face-lift that includes lots of freestanding illuminated glass signs, several fountains, a European-style central public plaza, a restaurant in each plaza, and a major upgrade of the underground shopping complex. The design by architects **A.C. Martin Partners**, according to Thomas, intends to entice you inside. ◆ M-Sa. Flower St (between W Sixth and W Fifth Sts). 213/625.2132

14 FIRST INTERSTATE WORLD CENTER

It's been called the tallest building in the West: a 1,017-foot, 73-story tower designed in 1990 by **Pei Cobb Freed & Partners Architects/Harold Fredenburg** and developed by Maguire Thomas Partners. The architects achieved an interplay between orthogonal and circular geometries, which are revealed in the setbacks that lead up to a circular crown. A number of attorneys and other professionals have their offices in this prestigious building. ◆ 633 W Fifth St (between S Grand Ave and Flower St)

At First Interstate World Center:

BUNKER HILL STEPS

Test your endurance by climbing this monumental stairway, designed in 1990 by Lawrence Halprin. The wide steps wrap up and around the base of the First Interstate tower, linking Bunker Hill to Hope Street (the two halves of the business district) and forming part of a sequence of landscaped pedestrian areas that Halprin calls "choreography for the urban dance." To come are his West Lawn for the library and Hope Street Promenade leading down to Grand Hope Park.

15 SANWA BANK PLAZA

Constructed in 1991 by **AC Martin Partners,** the granite, glass, and bronze tower has the dull and dated look of a chunky block—but don't let that stop you from seeing where all the design effort went. At its base, a 45-degree setback creates outdoor spaces that link the tower to the street. Interior screens stripe two dramatic 80-foot-high lobbies with light, accenting granite and marble floors and walls. ◆ 601 S Figueroa St (at W Sixth St)

Within Sanwa Bank Plaza:

PACIFIC GRILL

★★$$ American/Pacific Rim cuisine (try ahi tuna with risotto) is dished out at this charming indoor/outdoor restaurant. ◆ California ◆ M-F, lunch; Tu-Sa, dinner. 213/485.0927 ♿

16 WILSHIRE GRAND HOTEL

$$ This large, 903-room hotel boasts four restaurants, and is as popular with diners as with business travelers who bed down here. Amenities include a fitness center and an outdoor pool. ◆ 930 Wilshire Blvd (between S Figueroa and Francisco Sts). 213/688.7777, 800/773.2888

Within the Wilshire Grand:

KYOTO

★★$$ Designer sushi is served in a dramatic setting whose centerpiece is a 600-gallon aquarium filled with colorful

---

Restaurants/Clubs: Red | Hotels: Purple | Shops: Orange | Outdoors/Parks: Green | Sights/Culture: Blue

coral and saltwater fish. Chef Horii Hitoshi's lovely offerings include sashimi, crab legs, red snapper, and a delightful tempura bar. ♦ Japanese/Seafood ♦ M-F, lunch and dinner. Valet parking available. 213/896.3812

SEOUL JUNG

★★★$$ Chef Seek Soo Kim creates an exotic Korean menu centering on pork, beef, fish, and chicken. All are skillfully prepared on your marble-tabletop barbecue, in the style of the chef's homeland. ♦ Korean ♦ Daily, lunch and dinner. 213/629.4321

CITY GRILL

★$$$ City Grill's tasty Cobb salad helps business execs stick to their diets. ♦ California ♦ M-F, lunch and dinner. 213/623.5971

CARDINI

★★$$$$ New York architects **Voorzanger and Mills** designed the stunning postmodern interior of this restaurant in crisp tones of gray and blue. The space is beautifully lit and divided into enclosures by arches, columns, and open grilles. Chef Robert Segura creates such standout dishes as thin slices of veal with an herb-laden sauce; black ravioli filled with shrimp, cream, and chives; and risotto with seafood and porcini mushrooms. ♦ Italian ♦ M-F, lunch. Reservations recommended. 213/227.3464

17 CALIFORNIA CLUB

For years LA was in effect run by members of this private club. The Renaissance-style brick building, designed in 1930 by **Robert Farquhar,** is still a staid and elegant bastion of power and old money. Accept an invitation if you get so lucky; the food is surprisingly good. ♦ 538 S Flower St (between W Sixth and W Fifth Sts). 213/622.1391 &

18 LOS ANGELES CENTRAL LIBRARY

Designed in 1930 by **Bertram Goodhue and Carleton Winslow Sr.,** this LA landmark combines Beaux Arts monumentality with touches of Byzantine, Egyptian, and Roman styles in the surface ornament and incised lettering. There's even a hint of Art Deco. The building underwent a $214 million restoration in 1986, and a 1997 renovation by **Hardy Holzman Pfeiffer** added a lovely, bench-lined strolling garden and the Tom Bradley Wing, featuring an eight-story glass atrium and a children's reading room. Of special interest is Dean Cornwell's four-panel mural, which covers 48 square feet and is illustrated with 300 heroic-size figures that depict the history of California. As you enter at street level, notice the vaulted ceiling painted by Petropoulos. ♦ The hours change from time to time, so call ahead. 630 W Fifth St (between S Grand Ave and Flower St). 213/228.7000 &

18 CAFE PINOT

★★★$$ Right outside the Central Library, this lively spot is super-chef Joachim Splichal's gourmet version of a casual brasserie. Top items on the menu include a delightfully cheesy French onion soup; polenta with rock shrimp, pancetta, and asparagus; and escargot in wine sauce served on a brioche. Lighter spa cuisine is offered as well. Be sure to sample the homemade ice cream. There's also outdoor seating in a glorious patio filled with olive trees. ♦ California/French ♦ M-F, lunch and dinner; Sa, dinner. 700 W Fifth St (between S Grand Ave and Flower St). 213/239.6500 &

19 ONE BUNKER HILL

The former Southern California Edison building, built in 1931 by **Allison & Allison,** is a handsome Art Deco corner block with a lobby mural by Hugo Ballin. The building has been elegantly restored. ♦ S Grand Ave and W Fifth St

20 THE GAS COMPANY

Based on the plans of **Skidmore, Owings & Merrill/R. Keating** and developed by Maguire Thomas Partners, this elegant 62-story high-rise of polished granite and tinted glass steps and tapers around a core of boat-shaped elliptical blue glass. The shape of the 1991 building intentionally resembles the blue gas flame that is now the official symbol of The Gas Company. The lobby, reached by an escalator, faces a water garden and a 300-foot-high Frank Stella mural painted on the adjacent Pacific Bell/AT&T Building. The colorful, abstract *Dusk* is part of Stella's Moby-Dick series, which explores motion and travel themes. ♦ 555 W Fifth St (at S Grand Ave)

21 LA INC. THE CONVENTION & VISITORS BUREAU

Maps, fliers, and advice on Southern California's attractions are available from a helpful staff that can converse in English, Spanish, Japanese, French, German, and Italian. Tickets to TV tapings and discount coupons are sometimes offered. A multilingual events hotline is also available. ♦ M-Sa. 685 S Figueroa St (at W Seventh St). 213/689.8822, 800/228.2452. www.lacvb.com

22 ENGINE COMPANY NO. 28

★★$$$ This 1912 landmark firehouse has been reborn as a stylish bar and grill. It's just the place to unwind with a cocktail and comfort food: grilled fish, garlic chicken, and spicy french fries. The wine list is excellent. ♦ American ♦ M-F, lunch and dinner; Sa, Su, dinner 5-9. Reservations recommended. 644 S Figueroa St (between W Seventh St and Wilshire Blvd). 213/624.6996 &

" Z+FI6 " *Ernst + Young Tower*

23 SEVENTH MARKET PLACE

This urbane complex is found at the foot of Citicorp Plaza, three 42-story towers designed by **Skidmore, Owings & Merrill**. The sunken, palm-shaded patio is covered by a 144-foot canopy and ringed with three levels of specialty stores, as well as a Robinsons-May department store. Other tenants include Ann Taylor, Doubleday Books, and Johnston and Murphy. Choose between the cafés and restaurants or brown-bag it on a bench in the leafy, street-level plaza. The **Jerde Partnership** created this people-friendly space in a restrained neo-Victorian style. There's validated parking with a minimum purchase. ♦ M-Sa. 735 S Figueroa St (between W Eighth and W Seventh Sts). 213/955.7150

24 FINE ARTS BUILDING

Designed by **Walker & Eisen** in 1925, this splendidly eclectic landmark was first built as a complex of artists' studios enclosing an exhibition hall, and was later converted to office space. Brenda Levin & Associates restored the Romanesque façade and the high-ceiling tiled lobby with its gargoyles, fountain, and fanciful murals, and remodeled the interiors. ♦ 811 W Seventh St (between Flower and S Figueroa Sts)

25 HILTON CHECKERS HOTEL

$$$$ This small luxury hotel was created within the shell of the Mayflower, itself a posh establishment when it opened in 1927. The Mayflower has undergone several ownership changes, the Hilton group being its most recent. The 188 guest rooms and suites are furnished in a traditional style, with muted colors; niceties include writing desks and marble baths. Every room has three telephones, and the hotel offers a full range of electronic equipment, including personal fax machines, as well as 24-hour room service. There are also meeting rooms, limousine service, a multilingual staff, and a rooftop spa with a pool. ♦ 535 S Grand Ave (between W Sixth and W Fifth Sts). 213/624.0000, 800/757.HILTON; fax 213/626.9906. www.hilton.com &

Within the Hilton Checkers Hotel:

CHECKERS RESTAURANT

★★★$$$$ The dining room is an oasis of elegance and charm, with polished service and exceptional cuisine. Standout dishes include Pacific sashimi with daikon and ginger salad, wasabi rice-wine vinaigrette and caviar, grilled beef tenderloin with jam and pecan cake, medaillons of veal with spinach, forest mushroom ragout, and potato gnocchi. Best dessert choices are the Key lime pie, lemon meringue tart, and warm chocolate mousse cake. ♦ California ♦ Daily, breakfast, lunch, and dinner. Reservations recommended. 213/624.0000

26 THE MILLENNIUM BILTMORE HOTEL

$$$ This Italianate Beaux Arts structure was originally constructed in 1923 by **Schultze & Weaver** and was long considered a social hub. In 1927, at a lavish banquet here, Douglas Fairbanks Sr. announced that the newly incorporated Academy of Motion Picture Arts and Sciences would begin giving out awards to recognize distinctive achievement in the movies. The palatial décor of the public rooms has been refurbished and regilded several times over the years, as part of an ongoing renovation by Millennium Hotels and Resorts, owners of the 683-room hotel. Upgrades include new draperies, original artwork, and chairs upholstered in imported peacock-design tapestry. Bathrooms boast creamy beige fixtures and accents of marble and gold. The Premier Level rooms (floors 10 and 11) are ideal for business travelers, with fully stocked desks, voice mail, and data port capabilities. A private Premier Level Club Lounge offers concierge service, complimentary continental breakfast, and evening hors d'oeuvres. The Presidential Suite has a private elevator, the Music Suite a grand piano. The well-equipped health club offers exercise rooms and sumptuous Roman baths. There's also a full-service business center with all the latest techno gadgets, plus childcare and banquet rooms.

> During a trip to Los Angeles, Noël Coward once observed, "There is something so delightfully real about what is phony about what is real here."

Restaurants/Clubs: Red | Hotels: Purple | Shops: Orange | Outdoors/Parks: Green | Sights/Culture: Blue

The **LA Conservancy** (213/623.2489) offers tours of the hotel. ♦ 506 S Grand Ave (at W Fifth St). 213/624.1011, 866/866.8086 in CA; fax 213/612.1545. www.millennium-hotels.com &

Within the Millennium Biltmore Hotel:

SAI SAI

★★$$$ A split-level Japanese restaurant with a sushi bar and five private dining rooms that is open for lunch Monday to Friday and dinner Saturday. 213/624.1100

SMERALDI'S RISTORANTE

★$$$ Italian marble tables and plum-velvet Mies van der Rohe chairs, plus exotic plants and works of art that are changed seasonally, form an elegant setting for a delectable meal and for vintage wines served by the glass. The selection of fresh pastas and California Cuisine is superb. ♦ California ♦ M-Su, breakfast, lunch, and dinner. 213/612.1562

27 777 TOWER

Part of the Citicorp Plaza and home to a number of law firms and other professionals, this 53-story skyline standout, designed by **Cesar Pelli & Associates** in 1991, has a crisp profile of off-white metal that's luminous in sunlight. Indented corners with flared accents emphasize its vertical height, curving form, and solidity. The three-story lobby is glass-walled on the east and south, while a double-height colonnade faces the busy **Seventh Market Place** next door. ♦ 777 S Figueroa St (at W Eighth St)

28 MACY'S PLAZA

This shopping haven houses Macy's department store plus more than 30 other shops arranged around a skylit atrium. ♦ Daily. 750 W Seventh St (at Flower St). Mall information: 213/624.2891

Within Macy's Plaza:

HYATT REGENCY *Sheraton (2005)*

$$$ One of Hyatt's upscale chain members, this attractive, 485-room facility has two restaurants and a fitness center. Ask for accommodations on the Regency Floor—it's worth paying more for the concierge service and complimentary continental breakfast. ♦

The first issue of the *Los Angeles Times*, published in 1881, was delivered by horse-drawn wagons and carriages.

More women own businesses in the Los Angeles–Long Beach area than in any other metropolitan area in the country.

213/683.1234, 800/223.1234; fax 213/629.3230. www.hyatt.com

29 CASEY'S BAR

$$ This is a popular after-work meeting place for office workers. Simple fare is served in a setting of white-tile floors, dark paneling, and tin ceilings. ♦ American ♦ M-F, lunch and dinner. Reservations recommended. 613 S Grand Ave (between Wilshire Blvd and W Sixth St). 213/629.2353

30 WATER GRILL

★★$$ If seafood's your thing, this is the place. Begin your meal with mouthwatering oysters, then plow through a menu of exquisitely prepared seasonal fresh fish. Located on the ground floor of the Pacific Mutual Building, the softly lit dining room is done in leather and mohair. ♦ Seafood ♦ M-F, lunch and dinner; Sa, Su, dinner. Reservations recommended. 544 S Grand Ave (between W Sixth and W Fifth Sts). 213/891.0900 &

30 CARAVAN BOOK STORE

This fine antiquarian bookseller specializes in California history and memorabilia. ♦ M-Sa, and by appointment. 550 S Grand Ave (at W Sixth St). 213/626.9944

C. DOWNTOWN/COMMERCIAL AND EXPOSITION PARK

A unique mix of interesting things to do and see . . .

This area conveys an intriguing complexity, with several shops and hotels to the north; commercial, wholesale, manufacturing, and distribution sites to the east; and **Exposition Park** and the **University of Southern California (USC)** to the south. **Pershing Square,** the hub of the downtown business area, is active during regular business hours but almost deserted at night. Near the **Coliseum** and the **Shrine Auditorium** (the site of such events as the Grammy Awards and the American Music Awards), nighttime traffic jams occur when football and concert fans collide. The streets of the wholesale distribution centers are quiet until after midnight, when hundreds of trucks fill the roadways. And in the early dawn hours, movie crews may be filming on the deserted streets.

1 KAWADA HOTEL

$ Hidden on an undesirable stretch, this 116-room hotel built in the shell of a once-dilapidated 1920s brick building has retained its quaint exterior character with the original fire escapes and flower boxes. The interior is contemporary economy, with incredibly reasonable rates for downtown LA. ♦ 200 S Hill St (at W Second St). 213/621.4455, 800/752.9232; fax 213/687.4455

Within the Kawada Hotel:

EPICENTRE

★★$$ This fun, slightly bizarre bistro was designed by Janise Cooper & Associates to look like the aftermath of an earthquake, with faux fissures painted on the walls and artificial rubble strewn about. Some Angelenos are not amused. The tasty albeit gimmicky menu offers everything from seafood quesadillas to steak. ♦ California ♦ M-F, lunch and dinner. Reservations required for lunch. 213/625.0000

2 BROADWAY

Considered the main shopping street for Los Angeles's Latino community, Broadway's crowded sidewalks and exotic sounds and smells give it an intensely urban quality—much like upper Broadway in New York or even Mexico City. But changing tastes, neglect, and speculative greed threaten the architectural legacy of the prewar years, when Broadway was LA's "Great White Way." The once beautiful façades have been covered in plastic signs, the terrazzo sidewalk ornament is cracked and filthy, and, worst of all, the upper stories of several buildings have been lopped off in order to reduce tax assessments. Local restoration groups are working to protect the remaining structures.

2 HISTORIC THEATER DISTRICT

The first district of its kind to be listed on the National Register of Historic Places, this strip of theaters stretches from Third Street to Olympic Boulevard. Noteworthy sights include the **Million Dollar Theater** (307 S Broadway, at W Third St), a stunning building with a Churrigueresque exterior and a lavish Baroque interior; the **United Artists** (933 S Broadway, between W Olympic Blvd and W Ninth St), a **Walker & Eisen**-designed Spanish Gothic tower housing a cathedral-like theater that was financed by Mary Pickford, Douglas Fairbanks, and Charlie Chaplin; and the **Los**

Angeles Theater (615 S Broadway, at W Sixth St), a Baroque structure designed by **S. Charles Lee** that is thought by many to be the finest theater in the city (parts of the movie *Batman Forever* were shot here). The **LA Conservancy** (213/623.2489) offers guided tours of the district. ♦ S Broadway (between W Olympic Blvd and W Third St)

2 GRAND CENTRAL PUBLIC MARKET

Don't miss this indoor bazaar, which extends from Broadway to Hill Street. Ira Yellin, a developer with the vision to see Broadway's potential, commissioned Brenda Levin to undertake a major restoration. The stalls sell a wide range of food, from fish tacos to soups. Plastic wrap is unknown here—butchers use waxed paper and fruit and vegetable vendors select your produce from beautiful piles (don't help yourself) and brown-bag it. If you're thirsty, stop at **Tropical Zone Juice Bar.** ♦ Daily. 317 S Broadway (between W Fourth and W Third Sts). 213/624.2378

3 BRADBURY BUILDING

LA's most extraordinary interior is a Victorian treasure that was, in its time, futuristic. This office building was designed in 1893 by architectural draftsman **George Wyman,** who was inspired by a message from his dead brother, received via a Ouija board. Behind the plain brick façade is a skylit interior court that is a marvel of dark foliate grillwork, tiled stairs, polished wood, marble, and open-cage elevators. It was used to memorable effect in the movie *Blade Runner,* itself a vision of the future. Only the lobby level is open to the public. ♦ M-Sa. 304 S Broadway (at W Third St). 213/626.1893

4 SPRING STREET

What was once called the "Wall Street of the West" is slowly recovering from a long period of neglect. This National Register Historical District showcases a treasury of buildings from the first three decades of the century. Many have been imaginatively recycled, and new structures, including the huge **Ronald Reagan State Office Building** between Third and Fourth Streets, are being added. The **LA Conservancy** (213/623.2489) offers a useful flier to guide you through the area's architecture.

4 BANCO POPULAR

A German immigrant commissioned this Beaux Arts tower in 1903. Notice the fine ornamentation and the marble lobby with its stained-glass dome. ♦ 354 S Spring St (between W Fourth and W Third Sts)

Restaurants/Clubs: Red | Hotels: Purple | Shops: Orange | Outdoors/Parks: Green | Sights/Culture: Blue

5 TITLE GUARANTEE & TRUST BUILDING

John and Donald Parkinson's romanticized 1930 skyscraper has a Gothic crown and zigzag details on the façade. The lobby is designated as a future entry for **Metro Rail**. ♦ 401 W Fifth St (at S Hill St)

6 PERSHING SQUARE

SITE Projects, the New York architects best known for their surreal Best Co. stores, won a 1986 competition with a proposal to transform this site into an undulating landscape, but their plan was rejected by neighboring property owners who said it lacked accessibility. Working with developer Maguire Thomas Partners and the Community Redevelopment Agency, the property owners instead hired Mexico City architect **Ricardo Legorreta** to design a $14 million renovation plan with landscape architect **Hanna Olin.** The new layout includes an amphitheater for public performances, an eye-catching 120-

foot purple campanile (Legorreta's signature), and large shade trees. A crack in the ground was placed there to suggest earthquake damage. ♦ Bounded by S Hill and Olive Sts, and W Sixth and W Fifth Sts

7 ZUCCA

★★★$$ Another Patina Group/Joachim Splichal winner, this popular indoor/outdoor downtown eatery is big with the theater crowd and Splichal groupies who will follow him anywhere. The clubby room is done in rich

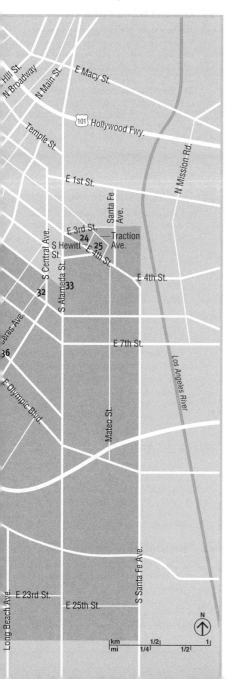

woods, Venetian crystal chandeliers, and treasures imported from Italy. The bar is always hopping and the tables are pretty much filled nightly. The menu takes an Italian twist and everything tastes great, from the antipasto to specialties such as *bistecca alla fiorentina*, roasted lamb sirloin with purple artichokes, and roasted striped sea bass. ♦ Italian. ♦ M-F, lunch and dinner; daily, dinner. Reservations necessary. 801 S Figueroa St (at W Eighth St). 213/614.7800; email: zucca@patinagroup.com www.patinagroup.com

8 OVIATT BUILDING

Designed in 1928 by **Walker & Eisen,** this was formerly an exclusive men's store, built for haberdasher James Oviatt, who had fallen in love with Art Deco during his many buying trips to Paris. Oviatt commissioned the decorative glass from **René Lalique,** imported the furnishings from France, and lived in a marvelous zigzag penthouse above the shop. In 1976, the building was bought by developer Wayne Ratkovich, who hired architect Brenda Levin to restore its original glories and leased the upper floors as offices. You can rent the thirteenth-floor penthouse for catered parties of up to 50 and dance under the stars on the 1,500-square-foot rooftop. ♦ 617 Olive St (between W Seventh and W Sixth Sts). 213/622.6096

Within the Oviatt Building:

CICADA

★★★$$$ This Nicolas Pasquale Valled–designed restaurant is simply stunning, with intimate cloverleafing leather banquettes, Italian landscape murals, beige chenille sofas, and leather club chairs. The superb Northern Italian menu teases the palate with such delicate appetizers as torchon of foie gras with chestnut honey and roasted apple, warm shallot flan with sautéed wild mushrooms carpaccio, smoked duck ravioli with shiitake mushrooms, oven-roasted John Dory with seafood cassoulet (for two), grilled veal chop with a vegetable tart in a port wine sauce, and a whole dover sole with sautéed spinach and roasted potatoes. For dessert, the Meyer lemon cheesecake and the poached pear wih almond mascarpone mousse and toasted hazelnuts, served martini-style, are a must. ♦ Northern Italian ♦ M-F, lunch; M-Sa, dinner. Reservations required. Valet parking available. 213/488.9488. www.cicadarestaurant.com

9 JEWELRY MART

Though this papery building does nothing for Pershing Square, the 1982 interactive neon artwork that runs the length of its façade—*Generators of the Cylinder* by Canadian Michael Hayden—is worth a look. If you're more interested in flashing diamonds than in flashing lights, the old jewelry district, offering highly competitive prices, extends a block south on Hill Street between Sixth and Seventh Streets. ◆ 550 S Hill St (at W Sixth St)

10 ALEXANDRIA HOTEL

$$ A fine hotel when it opened in 1906, the 400-room Alexandria once welcomed Theodore Roosevelt, Enrico Caruso, Sarah Bernhardt, and the first generation of moviemakers. Today it is a residence hotel only. ◆ 501 S Spring St (at W Fifth St). 213/626.7484

11 CONTINENTAL BUILDING

At 175 feet in height, this was LA's first skyscraper, an ornate pile designed in 1904 by **John Parkinson,** the architect of 17 other surviving buildings on the street. ◆ 408 S Spring St (at W Fourth St)

12 THE ORIGINAL PANTRY

★★$ This 1924 restaurant is the best place in town for hearty breakfast food served in generous portions. Later in the day, steaks, chops, meatloaf, and more are featured, as well as great cole slaw, sourdough bread, and hash browns. Owned by LA mayor Richard Riordan (who also is a frequent patron), the place never closes. Next door is the **Pantry's Bake & Sandwich Shoppe,** which offers just what the name promises (open daily, 6AM-3PM). ◆ American ◆ Daily, 24 hours. 877 S Figueroa St (at W Ninth St). 213/972.9279 ⑤

13 BROADWAY SPRING ARCADE

An Australian company turned this enormous skylit space linking Broadway and Spring Street into a three-level shopping arcade. The 1923 Spanish Renaissance office block is being renovated. ◆ 542 S Broadway (between W Sixth and W Fifth Sts)

14 LOS ANGELES CENTER STUDIOS

Originally a bank designed in 1916 by **John Parkinson,** this building was dramatically remodeled and expanded by John Sergio Fisher and Associates into a complex of four small, steeply raked theaters leading out of the original banking hall. Failing to garner broader public support, the center has become a major player in film and television productions, to which it leases state-of-the-art, high-tech soundstages, 72 furnished dressing rooms, a commissary, and screening rooms. ◆ 1201 W Fifth Street (at Spring St). 213/534.3000; fax 213/534.3001. www.lacenterstudios.com

15 FIGUEROA HOTEL

$$ This 280-room hotel has a superb location near the **Los Angeles Convention Center.**

Amenities include an enormous swimming pool and **The Clay Pit** restaurant. ◆ 939 S Figueroa St (between W Olympic Blvd and W Ninth St). 213/627.8971, 800/421.9092; fax 213/689.0305

16 STORY BUILDING & GARAGE

Morgan, Walls & Clements designed the 1916 Beaux Arts tower, faced with white terracotta and with superb zigzag garage gates. The garage was designed by **Clement Stiles** in 1934. ◆ S Broadway and W Sixth St

17 GRAND HOPE PARK

ⓟ This two-acre park, designed by **Lawrence Halprin,** comprises a series of outdoor rooms created by trellises, a fountain, a clock tower, and trees, all enhanced by the work of leading local artists. It will be the hub of the planned **South Park development,** a residential/commercial/office neighborhood bounded by Main and Eighth Streets and the Harbor and Santa Monica Freeways. Also in the works is a landscaped promenade along South Hope Street that will link the park with **Bunker Hill Steps** and the renovated library. ◆ W Ninth and S Hope Sts

18 GILL'S CUISINE OF INDIA

★$ The luncheon buffet includes hot curries and tandoori specialties. For dinner, don't miss the ground lamb sausage kabobs and the spicy cauliflower. Kulfi (homemade ice cream) is a great choice for dessert. ◆ Indian ◆ M-Sa, lunch and dinner. 838 S Grand Ave (between W Ninth and W Eighth Sts). 213/623.1050 ⑤

19 CLIFTON'S BROOKDALE CAFETERIA

$ You'll find a redwood forest interior with a waterfall and stuffed moose at this cafeteria. On the sidewalk are early-1930s terrazzo roundels depicting city landmarks. ◆ American ◆ Daily, breakfast, lunch, and dinner. 648 S Broadway (between W Seventh and W Sixth Sts). 213/627.1673 ⑤

20 COLE'S BUFFET

$ A bargain favorite of LA's workforce for years, this local hangout serves corned beef, roast beef, pastrami, and French dip sandwiches. ◆ American ◆ Daily, breakfast, lunch, and dinner until midnight. 118 E Sixth St (between S Los Angeles and S Main Sts). 213/622.4090

21 HOLIDAY INN CITY CENTER

$$ This 195-room hotel is convenient to the commercial center of downtown, and popular with business travelers. ◆ 1020 S Figueroa St (between W 11th St and W Olympic Blvd). 213/748.1291, 800/628.5240. www.holidayinnLA.com

LA STORY

Much has been written about the City of Angels—everything from fiction by such literary greats as F. Scott Fitzgerald to telltale historical accounts of Hollywood's rich and famous. If you'd like to brush up on the area before your trip, pick up any of these compelling and informative works:

Nonfiction

Architecture in Los Angeles by David Gebhard and Robert Winter (Peregrine Smith Books, 1985). Future editions of this architectural guide will cover all of Southern California.

California Crazy: Roadside Vernacular Architecture by Jim Heimann and Rip George (Chronicle, 1980). An amazing collection of architectural follies, nearly all of which have been demolished.

California Festivals by Carl and Katie Landau with Kathy Kincade (Landau Communications, 1989).

California People by Carol Dunlap (Peregrine Smith Books, 1982). Short biographies of men and women who made LA and the rest of the state what it is, from Earl C. Anthony to Frank Zappa.

The City Observed: Los Angeles, A Guide to its Architecture and Landscapes by Charles Moore, Peter Becker, and Regula Campbell (Vintage Books, 1984).

City of Quartz by Mike Davis (Vintage Books, 1990). A social history of LA, creatively researched and written with wit and irony.

East Los Angeles by Ricardo Romo (Texas, 1983). A history of the *barrio* from 1900 to 1930.

Ethnic LA by Zena Pearlstone (Hillcrest Press, 1990). Short histories of many of the city's ethnic groups, with statistical data from the 1980 census.

Golf in Hollywood: Where the Stars Come Out to Play by Robert Chew and Dave Pavoni (Angel City Press, 1998).

Inventing the Dream: California through the Progressive Era by Kevin Starr (Oxford University Press, 1985). Chapters on the growth of Southern California, Pasadena, and the movie industry, plus a thorough bibliography.

LA Freeway: An Appreciative Essay by David Brodsky (University of California, 1981).

LA Lost and Found by Sam Hall Kaplan (Crown, 1987). Photographs by Julius Schulman accompany an architectural history of the city.

Los Angeles: The Architecture of Four Ecologies by Reyner Banham (Penguin Books, 1971). An approving look at LA, years before it became fashionable, by a maverick English architectural historian.

Los Angeles: Biography of a City edited by John and LaRess Caughey (University of California, 1977). Brilliant anthology of writings on LA.

Raymond Chandler's Los Angeles by Elizabeth Ward and Alain Silver (Overlook, 1988). Quotations from LA's acerbic scribe juxtaposed with photos of real locations.

Southern California: An Island on the Land by Carey McWilliams (Peregrine Smith Books, 1973). An impassioned exposé of the dark side of the dream.

Fiction

Writers and journalists flocked to Hollywood with the coming of the talkies, and then bit the hand that fed them. Nathanael West's *Day of the Locust* (1939) is the classic put-down.

Budd Schulberg's *What Makes Sammy Run?* (1941) is a devastating portrait of greed and chicanery by a movie-industry insider.

F. Scott Fitzgerald's *The Last Tycoon* (published posthumously in 1941) is a romanticized portrait of Irving Thalberg, MGM's boy wonder.

Evelyn Waugh was invited by MGM to discuss a movie version of *Brideshead Revisited;* the visit yielded the funniest-ever poison-pen letter to LA, *The Loved One.*

John Fante created memorable portraits of Depression-era LA in *Dreams from Bunker Hill.*

F. Scott Fitzgerald, Henry Miller, and Raymond Chandler are just a few of several famed writers featured in John Miller's *Los Angeles Stories.*

Periodicals

Los Angeles Magazine is a hip, monthly city magazine that's heavy on celebrity, trends, and fashion, and is a good source for restaurants.

LA Style carries some of the city's sharpest restaurant reviews, as well as stories on cutting-edge music, fashion, architecture, and design.

LA Weekly seems torn between compulsive consumerism and outspoken radicalism, but is valuable for its comprehensive listings of movies, concerts, and theater.

Restaurants/Clubs: Red | Hotels: Purple | Shops: Orange | Outdoors/Parks: Green | Sights/Culture: Blue

22 Fashion Institute of Design and Merchandising

The **Jerde Partnership**'s characteristically eclectic 1990 design comprises a four-story arcade and terrace overlooking **Grand Hope Park**. The complex houses a fashion museum and gallery, shops, video production facilities, classrooms, and offices. ◆ 919 S Grand Ave (between W Olympic Blvd and W Ninth St). 213/624.1200

23 Spring Street Towers

Schultze & Weaver's handsome 1924 Beaux Arts bank has been recycled as an office building, though the exterior has changed little. ◆ 117 W Seventh St (between S Los Angeles and S Spring Sts)

24 Al's Bar

This crowded, smoky, and raw-edged bohemian hangout specializes in underground music, performance art, and theater. ◆ Daily, until 2AM. 305 S Hewitt St (between E Fourth Pl and Traction Ave). 213/625.9703

25 Avery Kitchen Supplies

Equip a restaurant or buy a single chef's pan at this discount emporium. ◆ M-Sa. 836 Traction Ave (between Merrick and S Hewitt Sts). 213/624.7832, 800/877.0905

26 849 Building

Formerly the Eastern Columbia, constructed in 1929 by **Claude Beelman,** this is downtown's finest Art Deco building since the Richfield Tower was razed. The 13-story tower, faced in turquoise terra-cotta with dark-blue and gold trim and ornamented with oddly twisted zigzag moldings, is now a wholesale apparel center. The **International Food Court** is open weekdays for breakfast and lunch. ◆ 849 S Broadway (between W Ninth and W Eighth Sts)

27 Los Angeles Convention Center

This municipal facility has been tripled in size, to 810,000 square feet, to lure major conventions, trade shows, and public events such as the Auto Show in January and the Travel Show in the spring. Twin 155-foot-high glass-and-steel lobby pavilions mark the $287 million project, designed by **Gruen Associates/Pei Cobb Freed & Partners Architects** on a 63-acre site. One of the most striking features is a massive curve of light-refracting blue-green glass just north of the intersection of the Santa Monica and Harbor Freeways. A four-acre open plaza named for late city councilman Gilbert W. Lindsay fronts Figueroa Street. As part of the Art-in-Architecture program, more than 60,000 feet of artist Alexis Smith's terrazzo

designs pave the floors, including a world map design featuring medallions derived from early Pacific Rim cultures. Future plans include tours of the convention center that focus on the lovely artwork. ◆ 1201 S Figueroa St (between Venice Blvd and W 11th St). 213/741.1151

Adjacent to the Convention Center:

Staples Center

This behemoth sports arena/entertainment center is the ultimate sports/entertainment venue and home to the LA Lakers and LA Clippers basketball teams, LA Kings hockey team, and LA Avengers arena football team. The complex is also used for concerts, ice shows (such as the 2002 Figure Skating Championship), and events (this is where the 2000 Democratic convention assembled). An ideal venue for any event, the center has 23 refreshments stands, 1,200 television monitors, 55 restrooms, over a dozen meeting rooms, 2,500 premier seats (roughly 20,000 total seating occupancy), and 160 high-priced ($900 to $7,000 a night) luxury suites (where Jack Nicholson, Tom Hanks, and other well-heeled sorts view events in style while being catered to by waiters and cocktail waitpersons). The suites, which can accommodate 20 to 140 people, are sold by event or season. Those who can't afford this kind of luxury have their pick of thousands of less expensive options. ◆ 1111 South Figueroa St. 213/742.7100; fax: 213/742.7269. www.staplescenter.com ♿

28 Sam's Deli Foods

$ Sam's Greek salad and walnut cake will revive your flagging energy. ◆ Deli ◆ M-F, breakfast and lunch. 121 E Ninth St (between S Los Angeles and S Main Sts). 213/622.2008

29 Mayan

An upscale nightclub now occupies what was once the **Mayan Theater,** built in 1927 by **Morgan, Walls & Clements**. The auditorium, which opened with a Gershwin revue and then was long relegated to porn, now contains a two-level dance floor and bar, popular among movie stars and top models. Warrior priests glare from the façade; inside is looming statuary and a riot of ornament inspired by an excavated Maya tomb (much as King Tut's launched a fad for ancient Egypt in the early 1920s). Next door is the **Belasco**, another theater by the same architects, and now

THE BEST

Susan Goldberg Kent

Director, Los Angeles Public Library

One of the greatest pleasures I have is working in the "new" **Central Library,** a building that is a blend of the old (Bertram Goodhue's original 1926 architecture, beautifully restored) and the new (the Tom Bradley Wing, designed by Hardy Holzman Pfeiffer). Situated in the **Maguire Gardens,** the Central Library offers residents and visitors to LA a place to read, to think, to use new technology, and to enjoy splendid public art as well as **cultural programs** sponsored by the Los Angeles Public Library.

It's hard to find a bad meal in LA. Joachim Splichal's **Patina** is the place for the most inventive and exciting cuisine, and its more casual sister **Cafe Pinot,** right outside the Central Library, features excellent risottos, salads, and rotisserie dishes. Make sure to visit **Monterey Park** for an almost endless selection of Hong Kong–style Chinese restaurants.

Bookstores abound in LA, including many excellent specialty bookstores like **The Cook's Library** on West Third Street, which features a vast array of cookbooks and wine guides. Its next-door neighbor, **The Traveler's Bookcase,** has something for everyone who is planning or dreaming of a trip.

available for rental. Across the street is **Tony's Burger,** a 1932 log cabin, while presiding over the parking lot is Kent Twitchell's 70-foot mural of Ed Ruscha—just one of LA's surreal juxtapositions. ♦ F-Sa. 1038 S Hill St (between W 11th St and W Olympic Blvd). 213/746.4287

30 GARMENT DISTRICT

Los Angeles has been a major center for high-quality garments at bargain prices since the 1930s, well before the advent of the outlet mall. First gaining fame for women's sportswear were Cole of California, Catalina, and Rose Marie Reid, three companies that transformed the nation's beaches. Today, jobbers and discount stores offering low prices on everything from children's wear to leather coats to knockoff T-shirts line Los Angeles Street from Seventh Street down to Washington Boulevard. A concentration of retail womenswear bargains can be found in the **Cooper Building** (860 S Los Angeles St, at E Ninth St; 213/622.1139). Across the street is **Academy Award Clothes** (811 S Los Angeles St; 213/622.9125), with a huge selection of quality men's suits and formalwear, and courteous service. ♦ Bounded by S San Pedro St and S Broadway, and Washington Blvd and Seventh St

30 CALIFORNIA MART

Apparel designers' manufacturer showrooms and independent representatives are housed here. Although normally open only to the trade, one weekend every month the public is welcome. ♦ Call ahead for the schedule. 110 E Ninth St (at S Main St). 213/620.0260

31 LOS ANGELES FLOWER MARKET

As at the **Wholesale Produce Market** (see page 40), the action here begins in the wee hours of the morning. The **American Floral Exchange** and the **Growers' Wholesale**

Terminal are huge halls of flowers reflecting the seasons that Southern California doesn't have. Wholesalers are willing to sell a box to anyone, and Wall Street is lined with stalls where smaller merchants offer potted plants to the public at substantial discounts. The best bargains are to be had after 9AM, and on Saturday mornings when the traders clear out their stocks for the weekend. ♦ M, W, 8AM-12PM; Tu, Th-Sa, 6AM-11PM. 754 Wall St (between W Eighth and W Seventh Sts). 213/622.1966

32 AMERICAN FISH & SEAFOOD COMPANY

Chefs shop at this market, which also sells to the public at wholesale prices. ♦ M-Sa. 550 Ceres Ave (between E Sixth St and S Central Ave). 213/612.0350

32 THE FISHERMAN'S OUTLET

★$ You can either buy fish to take home at this retail and wholesale establishment or eat at outdoor tables. There are a dozen varieties to choose from—broiled, deep-fried, or Cajun style—in large portions at rock-bottom prices. ♦ Seafood ♦ M-Sa 10AM-2:30PM, lunch. 529 S Central Ave (between E Sixth St and Ceres Ave). 213/627.7231 &

33 CIRRUS GALLERY

Contemporary paintings and fine art prints by Southern Californian artists are showcased here. ♦ Tu-Sa. 542 S Alameda St (between E Sixth and E Fifth Sts). 213/680.3473

34 HERALD EXAMINER BUILDING

Julia Morgan, the first woman trained at the Ecole des Beaux Arts in Paris and the designer of William Randolph Hearst's San Simeon castle, created this Spanish Mission Revival design in 1912, inspired by the California Building from the 1893 Chicago World's Fair. The newspaper is now defunct, but the building

---

Restaurants/Clubs: Red | Hotels: Purple | Shops: Orange | Outdoors/Parks: Green | Sights/Culture: Blue

itself is occasionally used as a filming site by major studios. Like so many of the city's historic landmarks, this too faces an uncertain future. ♦ 1111 S Broadway (at W 11th St)

35 TRANSAMERICA CENTER

This 32-story commercial structure has an observation deck with an outstanding view of downtown LA's high-rises. ♦ Free. M-F. 1150 Olive St (at W 12th St). 213/742.2111

Within the Transamerica Center:

WINDOWS

★$$$$ If you're looking for a high-powered martini lunch or steak dinner, this place offers expense-account dining with good service and a stunning view. ♦ California ♦ M, lunch only; Tu-F, lunch and dinner; Sa, dinner. Reservations recommended. 213/746.1554

36 WHOLESALE PRODUCE MARKET

A cornucopia of produce, sold by the lug or the bushel only, is available every weekday from 3AM to noon. The market is divided into two main sections: **Produce Court,** off Ninth Street just west of Central Avenue; and **Merchant Street,** off Eighth Street just west of Central Avenue. ♦ No phone

37 NORTH UNIVERSITY PARK

Feisty local preservation groups have protected a concentration of handsome late-Victorian houses that were laid out after the 1880s population explosion linked this prosperous residential neighborhood to downtown by streetcar. The residents have restored several of the finest examples, including the **Bassett House** (2653 S Hoover St) and the **Miller and Herriott House** (1163 W 27th St), all of which are private residences. ♦ Bounded by S Hoover St and Orchard Ave, and W 27th St and W Adams Blvd

38 THE INN AT 657

$ Here is a small, charming hotel with a friendly personality and an ideal downtown location. The 11 suites, which used to be separate apartments, are individually decorated with a mixture of contemporary furnishings and antiques; all have private baths and face either the garden or the patio. The amiable innkeeper, Patsy Carter, cooks up a lavish breakfast each morning (included in the rate) that may feature an egg dish, potato pancakes or hash browns, steak, fresh fruit, and croissants. ♦ 657 W 23rd St (between Harbor Fwy and Estrella Ave). 213/741.2200, 800/347.7512. www.patsysinn657.com &

39 DOHENY MANSION AND CHESTER PLACE

Thirteen grand and expensive houses were built here at the turn of the century on one block of a 15-acre residential park. The mansion, considered to be the finest structure on the block, was designed in 1900 by Theodore Eisen and Sumner P. Hunt for Oliver Posey. Shortly after its construction, oilman Edward Doheny bought the home. Few alterations have been made to the French Gothic château exterior. The house and park are now owned by **Mount St. Mary's College**. ♦ 8 Chester Pl (between W Adams Blvd and W 23rd St). 213/746.0450

40 STIMSON HOUSE

Originally designed in 1891 for prominent lumberman Douglas Stimson, this Queen Anne–style house has a tower and details reminiscent of a medieval fortress. The building is now occupied by the **Convent of the Infant of Prague** and is closed to the public. ♦ 2421 S Figueroa St (between W Adams Blvd and Harbor Fwy)

41 ST. VINCENT DE PAUL ROMAN CATHOLIC CHURCH

Oilman Edward Doheny donated the funds for this church, designed by **Albert C. Martin** in 1925 in the ornate Spanish style known as Churrigueresque, patterned after Baroque scrolled silverwork. The interior is decorated in brightly colored tiles and contains ceiling decorations painted by Giovanni Smeraldi. ♦ 621 W Adams Blvd (at S Figueroa St)

42 AUTOMOBILE CLUB OF SOUTHERN CALIFORNIA

This handsome Mission Revival building was completed in 1923. Services offered to members include insurance, towing, travel planning, and maps. Wall maps can be purchased by nonmembers. Check out the early road signs displayed in the courtyard. ♦ M-F. 2601 S Figueroa St (at W Adams Blvd). 213/741.3111

43 COCA-COLA BUILDING

In 1937, **Robert Derrah** took five plain industrial buildings and redesigned them so they would resemble an ocean liner. The streamlined forms, hatch covers, portholes, and flying bridge bring the semblance of a little salt air to the land of asphalt. Inset at the corners are two enormous replicas of Coke bottles, a reminder that the soft-drink giant used to be housed here. ♦ 1334 S Central Ave (between E 14th and E 12th Sts)

44 HEBREW UNION COLLEGE/ JEWISH INSTITUTE OF RELIGION

This institute of Jewish higher learning opened in 1954. The **Frances-Henry Library of Judaica** contains a special collection of material on the American Jewish experience.

Changing temporary exhibitions are also offered. ♦ Free. Hebrew Union College, M-F. S Hoover St (between W 32nd and W 30th Sts). 213/749.3424

45 STREET CLOCK

This vintage freestanding clock is the centerpiece of a delightful row of Art Deco storefronts in a section that has retained its original flavor. ♦ 2423 S Broadway (between W 25th and W 24th Sts)

46 SHRINE AUDITORIUM

This movie-set mosque, designed for and still used by the Shriners, was built in 1926. Neglected for years after the construction of the **Music Center** (see page 24), the cavernous auditorium gained worldwide recognition as the site of the annual Grammy Awards and the Academy Award ceremonies, now staged in the Kodak Theater in Hollywood. Concerts are also held here. ♦ 665 W Jefferson Blvd (at Royal St). 213/749.5123, concert information 213/748.4141

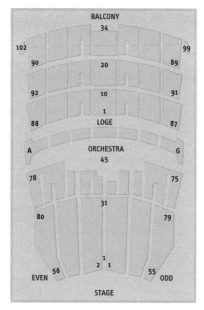

47 UNIVERSITY OF SOUTHERN CALIFORNIA (USC)

Founded in 1880, USC is the oldest major independent coeducational nonsectarian university on the West Coast, with a student body that's grown from 53 at its founding to 31,000. Among the professional schools are architecture, law, medicine, dentistry, social work, education, public administration, engineering, gerontology, cinema, performing

arts, pharmacology, and international relations. The campus has 191 buildings on 152 acres, and is open daily year-round; free hour-long **walking tours** of the campus are available. ♦ M-F. Bounded by S Figueroa St and Vermont Ave, and Exposition and W Jefferson Blvds. General information 213/740.2311

Within the University of Southern California (the letters preceding the entries refer to the map below):

A MCDONALD'S OLYMPIC SWIM STADIUM

This is where USC hosts its swimming and diving events. Closed to the public. ♦ Off McClintock St and W 34th St. 213/740.5127

B DAVID X. MARKS TENNIS STADIUM

USC tennis matches are held here. Closed to the public. ♦ 213/740.5127

C ARNOLD SCHOENBERG INSTITUTE

This complex, angular structure, designed in 1978 by **Adrian Wilson & Associates,** houses the archive of the great twentieth-century composer and a re-creation of the Brentwood studio in which he worked as an exile for the last 17 years of his life. Concerts of contemporary music are given in a small auditorium. ♦ Free. M-F. 3443 Watt Way. 213/740.4049

D BING THEATRE

In 1995, a version of the opera *The Ruffians* debuted at this little theater. ♦ Box office: M-F. 213/740.1249

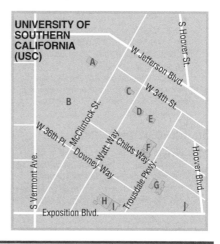

E NORRIS CINEMA THEATRE

Film programs in this luxurious theater are open to the public most evenings. ♦ Free. 213/740.1946

F BOVARD ADMINISTRATION BUILDING

John and Donald Parkinson's 1921 Romanesque brick block contains the 1,600-seat **Norris Auditorium,** which is used for a variety of cultural events.

G HANCOCK MEMORIAL MUSEUM

Original furnishings from a now-demolished mansion are incorporated into historical rooms. ♦ Free. M-F, by appointment. 213/740.5144

H FISHER GALLERY

Offers three rotating paintings and photography exhibits featuring different artists, eras, and styles. ♦ Free. Tu-Sa, Aug-May. 823 Exposition Blvd. 213/740.4561

I MUDD HALL

Since its opening in 1930, this has been an important philosophy library. The building was modeled on a medieval Tuscan monastery. ♦ M-F. 213/740.7434

J WIDNEY ALUMNI HOUSE

Built in 1880, this two-story clapboard house is furnished in period style.

48 SECOND BAPTIST CHURCH

Paul Williams's 1925 Lombardesque-Romanesque church serves as a center for African-American community activities. ♦ Daily. 2412 Griffith Ave (at E 24th St). 213/748.0318

49 RADISSON CROWNE PLAZA

$$ Formerly the University Hilton, this comfortable 240-room hotel is located across the street from USC's **Davidson Conference Center.** Facilities include a spa, swimming pool, restaurant, and complimentary transportation to area attractions. ♦ 3540 S Figueroa St (between Exposition and W Jefferson Blvds). 213/748.4141, 800/333.3333; fax 213/746.3255. www.radisson.com

50 EXPOSITION PARK

🅿 This is the location of the **Memorial Coliseum, Sports Arena,** the **Museums of Science and Industry, Space,** and **Natural History,** a community clubhouse, and several landscaped areas, including a rose garden. The park began as a casual open-air market, and in 1872 was formally deeded as an agricultural park for farmers to exhibit their products. Fairs and carnivals on the grounds were organized by the Southern California Agricultural Society, including occasional horse races (and sometimes camel races) on the lot to the rear of the park. In the early twentieth century, it was home to bicycle and automobile competitions. During the park's decline in the early 1890s, it became a hangout for society's lower elements and home to three saloons. The transformation of the rowdy park into a major state, county, and city museum center was accomplished by Judge William Miller Bowen after the park's seductive attractions had made truants of the students in Sunday school classes he taught nearby. One Sunday he followed his class to discover their secret destination (a saloon), then spearheaded a drive to create a landmark of worthwhile cultural significance on the site of the infamous watering hole. By 1910, work on the **County Museum of Natural History** had begun. ♦ Bounded by S Figueroa St and Menlo Ave, and South Park Dr and Exposition Blvd

Within Exposition Park:

NATURAL HISTORY MUSEUM OF LOS ANGELES COUNTY

This handsome Spanish Renaissance building was restored in 1988 for the museum's seventy-fifth anniversary. Some of the finest traveling exhibitions in LA are presented here, on topics as varied as Hollywood, nomads, volcanoes, and Indonesian court art. But the image of the museum is indelibly set by its celebrated collections of reptile and mammal fossils (including several dinosaurs), its innovative **Schreiber Hall of Birds,** and its minerals and pre-Columbian artifacts. The **Hall of American History** shows machinery and memorabilia. Native American and folk art festivals are presented every year, and the annual **Dinosaur Ball** is a major social event. Children and adults will enjoy the **Discovery Center,** where they learn by handling and working with artifacts. The **Insect Zoo** features over 25 live insect exhibits, including giant beetles and hissing cockroaches. The museum also has a bookstore, a gift shop, and a cafeteria serving low-priced meals. ♦ Admission; free on the first Tu of every month. M-Su; daily in summer. 900 Exposition Blvd (at Menlo Ave). General information 213/763.3515. www.nhm.org

CALIFORNIA AFRO-AMERICAN MUSEUM

This museum is dedicated to African-American achievements in politics, education, athletics, and the arts. The front part of the museum is a 13,000-square-foot sculpture court with a sloping space-frame ceiling covered with tinted glass. Inside are a research library, theater, and gift shop. ♦ Free. Tu-Su. 600 State Dr (between S Figueroa St and N Coliseum Dr). 213/744.7432

THE BEST

Paul R. Ellis

Wine Broker, Fourcade & Hecht

Saturday morning at the **Farmers' Market** in Calabasas, shopping for great vegetables and fruit—especially the exotic selection of chilies!

Driving down **Malibu Canyon** to the ocean for a romantic meal at **Granita,** where my wife Yun-Hwa and I had our first dinner date.

Because of my job, I do plenty of driving: **Sunset Boulevard** defines LA if you take it from downtown (after lunch at the **Water Grill**) and follow it all the way to the beach and then drive over to **Venice.**

There is great hotel dining in LA, with the superb setting and food at the **Hotel Bel-Air**; the other great spot is the wonderful **Peninsula Beverly Hills**, which also puts out some of the best food and wines in town. When we want to go out for the kind of food that we would not generally make at home (Yun and I cook a lot), we love to go to **Koutoubia**, on Westwood Boulevard, for great Moroccan cuisine.

It only takes us just over an hour (but what a world away) to drive to **Santa Barbara** to walk the streets and head "over the hill" to some of the finest wine country in America.

Back at home in **Agoura**, we hike through the hills and make lunch; or we listen to the coyotes at night and have friends over for dinner—we love LA!

CALIFORNIA MUSEUM OF SCIENCE AND INDUSTRY AEROSPACE HALL

A black-walled hangar, with echoes of radomes and space-assembly buildings, and an F-104 Starfighter pinned to the façade, seemingly frozen in flight, catch your eye when you first see this museum, designed by **Frank Gehry** in 1984. Inside, open walkways give you close-ups of suspended planes: a 1920 Wright glider, a 1927 Mono Coupe, a T-38 Air Force Trainer, and a Gemini 11 space capsule. ◆ Free. Daily. 700 State Dr (between S Figueroa St and N Coliseum Dr). 213/744.7400

Next to California Museum of Science and Industry Aerospace Hall:

MITSUBISHI IMAX THEATER

Frank Gehry's octagonal theater shows IMAX films on a five-story-high, 70-foot-wide screen. ◆ Admission. Call for schedule. 213/744.2014

CALIFORNIA MUSEUM OF SCIENCE AND INDUSTRY

A great place for kids of all ages, this museum gets more visitors each year than any other LA museum. Its exciting displays include the **Mark Taper Hall of Economics and Finance, Charles Eames**'s **Mathematica,** talking computers, and the **Kinsey Hall of Health.** Innovative exhibitions allow you to check your health, understand electricity and earthquakes, and explore DC-3 and DC-8 aircraft. There's a gift shop and a **McDonald's** cafeteria, too. ◆ Free. Daily. 213/744.7400

EXPOSITION PARK ROSE GARDEN

This sunken garden contains more than 19,000 rose bushes representing 190-plus varieties. At the center are latticework gazebos. When the roses are in bloom, this is the most fragrant spot in town. ◆ Reservations required for weddings. 701 State Dr (between S Figueroa St and N Coliseum Dr). 213/748.4772

LOS ANGELES MEMORIAL COLISEUM & SPORTS ARENA

Built in 1923, the coliseum was the major venue for the **1984 Olympics,** as it was for the **1932 Games.** It has also been the site of two Super Bowls (in 1967 and 1974) and a papal visit (in 1987). The stadium was damaged during by the 1994 Northridge earthquake and was later remodeled, though since the Raiders returned to Oakland the space is often empty, aside from hosting **USC football games,** other sporting events, and the occasional concert. ◆ 3911 S Figueroa St (between South Park and State Drs). 213/748.6136

In front of Los Angeles Memorial Coliseum:

OLYMPIC ARCH

Robert Graham's massive sculpture in front of the Coliseum is a permanent memento of the **1984 Summer Olympics.** It is topped by two headless bronze nudes; water polo player Terry Schroeder was the model for the male figure.

SPORTS ARENA

Built in 1958, this sister facility to the Coliseum is used as a multipurpose indoor sports and entertainment facility. The main auditorium is home to the **LA Clippers,** the **USC basketball team,** and the **Ice Dogs** (LA's member of the International Hockey League). In addition, the stadium hosts ice shows, track meets, car shows, concerts, rodeos, wrestling, and conventions. ◆ 3939 S Figueroa St (at South Park Dr). 213/748.6131

Restaurants/Clubs: Red | Hotels: Purple | Shops: Orange | Outdoors/Parks: Green | Sights/Culture: Blue

MIDTOWN

We're talking an eclectic, ethnic infusion here . . .

Los Angeles embraces several diverse neighborhoods, with the largest concentration clustered in Midtown, which stretches from downtown to the edge of Beverly Hills and the Westside. The easternmost section, from the **Harbor Freeway** to **Lafayette Park**, is home to thousands of immigrants from Central America, Mexico, Southeast Asia, and Korea. West to **La Brea Avenue** is a transitional area, with landmark commercial buildings that date back to the 1920s. In the 1930s, **Wilshire Boulevard** from La Brea to Fairfax Avenue was developed into a prestigious business and shopping district that was dubbed Miracle Mile; following a long decline, this strip has been extensively rebuilt. The final section, west to **La Cienega** and **Robertson Boulevards**, is a fashionable residential district, studded with design showrooms and art galleries.

Wilshire Boulevard, now the backbone of this corpulent entity, was originally a trail followed by the Yang-Na Indians from their Elysian Hills settlement to the tar pits of

Hancock Park, where they obtained pitch to waterproof their homes. The bustling boulevard, which runs 16 miles west to the ocean, was named after **H. Gaylord Wilshire** (1861-1927), a puckish entrepreneur from Ohio who made and lost fortunes in orange and walnut farming, gold mining, therapeutic electric belts, and real estate development. The thoroughfare didn't reach its current renown until oil fever captured the city and Edward Doheny struck a small pool after digging with a shovel 16 feet into a hillside near First Street and Glendale Boulevard. By 1905 the area was dotted with oil wells, and fortunes were made—among them the Hancock family's, whose farm included the tar pits near Wilshire Boulevard and Fairfax Avenue. This field was soon exhausted, leaving only the tar pits and a few camouflaged wells as reminders of the boom years. Today the famous **La Brea Tar Pits** showcase fossils from over one million years ago.

1 TRASHY LINGERIE

Diaphanous, lacy, and racy only begins to describe the ultra-sexy array of intimate apparel sold here. The enticing window displays stop traffic. However, a membership fee is charged to discourage voyeurs from lingering in the store. ♦ M-Sa. 402 N La Cienega Blvd (at Oakwood Ave). 310/652.4543

2 CANTER'S FAIRFAX RESTAURANT DELICATESSEN AND BAKERY

★$ A legend in its own time, this is the largest, liveliest deli on Fairfax, and is a popular breakfast spot with the lox-and-bagel crowd and morning people who like to wake up with big, hearty plates of food. The interior never changes. In fact, it's remained virtually untouched since Doris Day was a girl. The corned beef hash and eggs are a must, any sandwich will satisfy, and the pastrami is top grade. The neon sign on the façade is a classic. ♦ Deli ♦ Daily, 24 hours. 419 N Fairfax Ave (between Oakwood and Rosewood Aves). 323/651.2030

3 RAPPORT CO.

This is the place to shop for really top-quality home furnishings and accessories. You're bound to find some really cool pieces to decorate your home or apartment, and the sales staff is friendly and helpful. ♦ Tu-Sa. 435 N La Brea Ave (between Oakwood and Rosewood Aves). 323/930.1500

4 LA BREA AVENUE

La Brea bustles with art galleries, design-oriented stores, and restaurants, especially around the junction with Melrose Avenue and south to Wilshire Boulevard, where the long-neglected Art Deco and Spanish 1930s buildings are being renovated. Leading galleries include **Couturier Gallery** (166 N La Brea Ave; 323/933.5557), **Iturralde Gallery** (154 N La Brea Ave; 323/937.4267), **Fahey/Klein Photography** (148 N La Brea Ave; 323/934.2250), **Jan Baum** (170 S La Brea Ave; 323/932.0170), and **Ovsey** (170 S La Brea Ave; 323/935.1883).

4 LINDERDESIGN

Reproductions of classic early-modern lamps and furnishings by designers Desny, Josef Hoffmann, and Otto Wagner are showcased here. ♦ Daily. 440 N La Brea Ave (between Oakwood and Rosewood Aves). 323/939.4020

5 CADILLAC CAFE

★★$ A short walk from the Beverly Center, this fun little café on the boulevard is a good spot to refuel for a shopping spree. Good offerings include deviled eggs with chives and black caviar, walnut/spinach pâté with honey-raspberry aioli, Chinese chicken salad, and frittatas. ♦ American ♦ M-F, lunch and dinner; Sa, Su, breakfast, lunch, and dinner. 359 N La Cienega Blvd (between Beverly Blvd and Melrose Ave). 310/657.6591

6 HOTEL SOFITEL

$$$ The exterior of this French chain hotel is rather klutzy looking, but the recently renovated interiors more than make up for this lapse in architectural judgment. Guest rooms have been refreshed with lighter hues and colorful blue-and-yellow Pierre Deux fabrics; bathrooms now boast prestigious Nina Ricci amenities. Half of the 311 rooms provide views of the Hollywood Hills. Executive rooms sport country French furnishings, a good working desk, and fax/printer/data port hookups available on request. Amenities include a pool, an expanded health club with a sauna and personal trainers, and **Gigi,** a simple brasserie. Weekend rates are lower. ♦ 8555 Beverly Blvd (between N La Cienega Blvd and Beverly Pl). 310/278.5444, 800/521.7772 (direct to hotel), 800/763.4835 (Sofitel reservations); fax 310/657.2816. www.sofitel.com

7 ÉLAN

$$ If you like your hotels small, cozy, and uncluttered, this one's for you. Situated just a stroll from **Beverly Center,** boutiques, shops, and restaurants, the 50-room, ultra-techno-styled charmer offers royal deluxe, 200-thread-count bedding, down comforters and pillows, 25-inch TVs, high-speed Internet, two phones, voice mail, mini fridge, coffeemaker, and robes in every tidy room. There's no restaurant, but food can be ordered in from a restaurant (Jan's) across the street, and a free continental breakfast is served in the cyber-lounge daily. There is a small fitness center and accessibility to a nearby health club. ♦ 8435 Beverly Blvd (at Croft St), 323/658.6663, 888/611.0398. www.elanhotel.com

7 FUN FURNITURE

Treat the kids to whimsical architect-designed pieces such as a skyscraper dresser, a taxi toy box, or a fire-engine bed at this unique children's furnishings shop. ♦ Daily. 8451 Beverly Blvd (between N Croft Ave and N Alfred St). 323/655.2711

7 CORONET THEATER

Set back in an almost hidden courtyard, this intimate playhouse features children's theater productions by the Serendipity Theater Company. ♦ 366 N La Cienega Blvd (between Beverly Blvd and Oakwood Ave). 310/657.7377

7 CORONET PUB

This cute little neighborhood watering hole is popular with actors, writers, and musicians. ♦ M-Sa, until 2AM. 370 N La Cienega Blvd (between Beverly Blvd and Oakwood Ave). 310/659.4583

8 KINGS ROAD CAFE

★$ Folks congregate outside while waiting for tables at this happening café. The clientele is an eclectic mix of writers, artists, and industry execs who go there to sip rich espresso, cappuccino, or *caffè lattes* and munch on gourmet sandwiches prepared with fresh-baked sourdough bread and fillings such as herb-roasted chicken, Black Forest ham, fontina cheese, onions, and roasted eggplant. The croissants and pastries are good, too. ♦ Coffeehouse ♦ Daily, until midnight. 8361 Beverly Blvd (at N Kings Rd). 323/655.9044

9 MIMOSA

★★★$$ This charming French bistro showcases the culinary flair of Jean-Pierre Bosc, one of LA's finest chefs. The bistro-style menu is a throwback to Bosc's French background with such dishes as French onion soup, leeks vinaigrette, macaroni and cheese gratin, roasted chicken, and filet of sole. Desserts are equally yummy, from the fresh fruit "minestrone" and sherbet to the sinfully rich crème brûlée. All are served in a soothing room with plank floors and pale yellow walls adorned with photographs of friends, family, and customers, or on a patio that's heated on cool days. ♦ French/Italian ♦ M-F, lunch and dinner; Sa, dinner. Reservations recommended. 8009 Beverly Blvd (at N Edinburgh Ave). 323/655.8895

9 EM BISTRO

★★$$ A popular date night/couples spot, this casual bistro offers simple food served in a sophisticated two-level setting. The homemade potato chips with a crème fraiche dip are addictive. Everything on the menu is nicely presented and tasty, from the heirloom tomato bean soup to the short ribs and polenta. A blackberry tart or strawberry shortcake rounds out the meal nicely. ♦ American ♦ Tu-Sa, dinner; Su, brunch. Reservations suggested. 8256 Beverly Blvd (between N Harper and N Sweetzer Ave). 323/658.6004

10 AL'S NEWS

A profusion of newspapers and magazines line the racks here. ♦ Daily. 370 N Fairfax Ave (at Oakwood Ave). 323/935.8525

11 AUTHENTIC CAFE

★★$ Be prepared to stand in line most of the time at this tiny, terminally trendy spot. Rest assured, the tasty, generous portions, always served with a smile, are worth the wait. Tortilla-crusted chicken breast, Jamaican jerk chicken, Asian noodle salad, marinated and wood-grilled Yucatecan chicken, and skirt steaks are among the best choices. ♦ International ♦ Daily, breakfast, lunch, and dinner. No reservations. 7605 Beverly Blvd (between N Curson and N Stanley Aves). 323/939.4626

11 SONRISA FURNITURE

Here's the place to pick up some unique pieces for home or office made from vintage American steel, much of it recycled from medical facilities. There are great industrial-looking bookshelves, desks, and cabinets. ♦ M-Sa. 7609 Beverly Blvd (between N Curson and N Stanley Aves). 323/935.8438

12 A. J. HEINSBERGEN COMPANY

This tiny medieval brick castle, with drawbridge and moat, is still occupied by the design company that built it in 1925. ♦ 7415 Beverly Blvd (between N Martel Ave and N Vista St). 323/934.1134

13 SKANK WORLD

It looks like a Goodwill store with punk overtones, but this is the place to find classic 1950s furniture at affordable prices, including Eames plywood chairs and the rare example of Alvar Aalto. ♦ Opens at 2:15PM Tu-Sa or by appointment (323/965.1757). 7205 Beverly Blvd (between N Formosa Ave and N Alta Vista Blvd). 323/939.7858 &

14 EAST INDIA GRILL

★$$ Enjoy original dishes such as basil-coconut curries, tandoori ribs, and savory soups at this friendly bistro. ♦ Indian ♦ Daily, lunch and dinner. 345 N La Brea Ave (between Beverly Blvd and Oakwood Ave). 323/936.8844. Also at 318 Santa Monica Blvd (between Third St Promenade and Fourth St), Santa Monica. 310/917.6644

15 CHAN DARA

★$$ The slightly sleeker, fancier spin-off of the Thai favorite in Hollywood is a winner with the Hancock Park crowd. Specialties include

---

Restaurants/Clubs: **Red** | Hotels: **Purple** | Shops: **Orange** | Outdoors/Parks: **Green** | Sights/Culture: **Blue**

sausage with ginger and lime, stuffed chicken wings, barbecued beef, and flamed banana fritters with coconut and sesame seed. ◆ Thai ◆ M-F, lunch and dinner; Sa, Su, dinner. Reservations recommended. 310 N Larchmont Blvd (at Beverly Blvd). 323/467.1052

16 KENTUCKY FRIED CHICKEN

The architecture is the attraction here, not the food. **Grinstein/Daniels** created this superb piece of innovative 1990 design, with a curving façade and floating geometric masses. ◆ 340 N Western Ave (at Oakwood Ave)

17 CASA CARNITAS

★$ Kitsch décor, Latino crowds, and Mexican music create an appropriate context for searingly soulful food. Rich Yucatecan specialties include excellent fish and shellfish, pork-and-black-bean stew, and fried plantains. ◆ Mexican ◆ Daily, lunch and dinner. 4067 Beverly Blvd (between N Kenmore and N Alexandria Aves). 323/667.9953

18 THE IVY–LA DESSERTS

★★★$$$ Perennially hip, it's so in to lunch at the Ivy but not that easy to get a reservation. Dinner's a tough ticket, too, and there's always a long wait unless you're somebody. But the setting is pretty, the food good, and, well, it's just the place to go. The décor reflects a Southwestern feeling, with adobe walls, open hearths, antiques, and an ivy-strewn terrace. Simple dishes are best: Try the corn chowder and mesquite-grilled shrimp. But save room for the desserts that made this restaurant's reputation, especially the lemon cake topped with white chocolate mousse. And carry some home from LA Desserts, which shares space with the restaurant. ◆ American ◆ M-Sa, lunch and dinner; Su, brunch, lunch, and dinner. Reservations required. 113 N Robertson Blvd (between Alden Dr and Beverly Blvd). 310/274.8303 ⓖ

19 AGNÈS B.

Shop here for classic French-style women's linen suits, cotton sweaters, and snap sweatshirts. ◆ Daily. 100 N Robertson Blvd (at Alden Dr). 310/271.9643

19 PACIFIC THEATER BUILDING

This mall/office complex of white stucco across the street from The Ivy–LA Desserts houses shops, restaurants, retail outlets, and

> Los Angelenos are the largest consumers of seafood in the United States, eating some $1.5 billion worth annually.

a movie theater. The layout features a charming, well-landscaped courtyard. ◆ 120 N Robertson Blvd (between Alden Dr and Beverly Blvd)

Within the Pacific Theater Building:

STORYOPOLIS

The best in children's book illustrations are displayed in this 6,000-square-foot showroom that is part shop, part gallery. Both the illustrations and the books themselves can be bought here. Operated by the eponymous production company that also makes films based on children's books, it presents craft and story hours the first Saturday of every month. ◆ Days of operation vary, so call ahead. 116 N Robertson Blvd. 310/358.2500

NEWSROOM

★★$ Healthy food is the specialty at this eatery. The menu features generous portions of Caesar salad (in several low-fat variations using just egg whites), turkey burgers, and reduced- and low-fat chicken and vegetarian dishes. True vegans will delight in the "Moroccan mixed-up wild grains" (grilled chopped vegetables tossed with couscous, four kinds of rice, and Moroccan spices). Breakfast is served all day. The large dining room is sparsely decorated, with simple wooden furnishings; there's also a bar and a take-out counter. The service is friendly and efficient. ◆ Health food ◆ Daily, lunch and dinner. 310/652.4444 ⓖ

19 CHAYA BRASSERIE

★★★$$ The marvelous interior by Elyse Grinstein and Jeff Daniels combines a Japanese esthetic (skylit, pine-framed bamboo grove and upturned parasol lampshades) with the friendly informality of a Parisian brasserie. Chefs Goto Shingi and Shigefumi Tachibe pull off the same East-meets-West magic in such innovative dishes as tuna tartare and seaweed salad, plus Japanese-accented French and Italian fare. There's a hot bar scene, too. ♦ Japanese/French/Italian ♦ M-F, lunch and dinner; Sa, Su, dinner. Reservations recommended. 8741 Alden Dr (at N Robertson Blvd). 310/859.8833. Also at Venice Renaissance Building, 110 Navy St (at Main St), Venice. 310/396.1179 &

20 CEDARS SINAI MEDICAL CENTER

Though it's inspirational for the philanthropy that made it possible (and fashionable because of the celebrities and other bigwigs who come for the medical services), this hospital's unimaginative gigantism makes it a fit companion for the Beverly Center. A bright spark, architecturally, is the outwardly inconspicuous cancer clinic, designed by Morphosis in 1988. ♦ 8700 Beverly Blvd (between N San Vicente and N Robertson Blvds). 310/855.5000

21 BEVERLY CENTER

A much-needed multimillion-dollar face-lift transformed this windowless eight-story bastion of consumerism into a more stylish, upbeat, contemporary spot to spend cash. It's still windowless but now with brighter, more upbeat colors schemes, modern lighting, and comfortable places to sit in between spending sprees. A 32-by-46-foot shoji screen showcases the Grand Court displaying a pixilated California landscape on 252 panels. The Café L.A. food court on level 8 received the most attention, with an outdoor rooftop patio and Terrace restaurant providing great views of the areas below. Level 6 now sports **The Wave** restaurant ($★★) and lounge, an unusual dining venue for a mall that actually serves great food. And even deserves two stars. Open from 11AM until the last shop closes, The Wave offers an inviting bar or several tables on which to sample the eclectic California/Asian cuisine. The service is unusually competent; the prices are moderate, and it's well worth a stop even if you just go for tapas (prawn rolls, salmon asparagus, melted brie with candied walnuts and garlic). There are also great soups, salads, and sandwiches. Anchored by Bloomingdale's and Macy's, Beverly Center proffers all the essentials for major consumerism in more than 160 outlets such as Club Monaco, BOSS, Laundry by Shelli Segal, ISSI, Up Against the Wall, Williams-Sonoma Grande Cuisine, Traffic, Lucky Brand Dungarees, and DKNY. In addition to the food court, several full-service restaurants provide fuel for shoppers, including PF Chang's China Bistro, Hard Rock Café, California Pizza Kitchen, and others. Late movies are offered on the 13 screens on level 8. Beverly Center attracts its share of tinsel-town types. So, keep your eyes wide open. You just might spot Ben Affleck, Matthew Perry, Drew Barrymore, Jackie Chan, Jennifer Lopez, and even Tom Cruise—or so the p.r. folks for Beverly Center claim, anyway. You'll also find ample parking on four open decks. ♦ 8500 Beverly Blvd. (bounded by La Cienega and San Vicente Blvds, and W Third St and Beverly Blvd). 310/854.0070. www.beverlycenter.com

22 LAPALOMA DESIGNS

A trove of sturdy Southwestern furniture and bric-a-brac fills this shop. ♦ Tu-Sa. 8408 Beverly Blvd (between N Orlando and N Croft Aves). 323/655.2195

23 I. MARTIN IMPORTS

This place is a haven for anyone in training for the Tour de France, or who wants to race up the side of Mount Wilson riding the best bike money can buy. ♦ Daily. 8330 Beverly Blvd (at N Flores St). 323/653.6900

23 OPERA SHOP OF LOS ANGELES

Everything under the sun for opera, dance, and music can be purchased in this small shop. In addition to memorabilia relating to the works of Mozart, Verdi, Puccini, and other great masters, the store is well stocked with *Phantom of the Opera* merchandise. ♦ T-Sa. 8384 Beverly Blvd (between N Kings Rd and N Orlando Ave). 323/658.5811

23 MANDARETTE

★★$$ The food is outstanding and portions intentionally small so you can sample all the wonderful choices. Ask your waiter to help you choose from the eclectic selection of regional Chinese dishes. The room is smart and simple, with white walls and accents of sky blue and a most calming shade of celadon. ♦ Chinese ♦ Daily, lunch and dinner. 8386 Beverly Blvd (at N Orlando Ave). 323/655.6115 &

24 PASTIS

★★★$$ This special little find dishes out great food, from a delightful tuna tartare and asparagus salad to spicy Chilean sea bass on a bed of wild mushrooms, lovely lamb as only the French can fix, and fabulous salads, with friendly service and moderate prices. The place is always packed, so call ahead. ♦ French ♦ M-Sa, dinner. Reservations recommended. 8114 Beverly Blvd (between N Crescent Heights Blvd and N Kilkea Dr). 323/655.8822 &

Restaurants/Clubs: Red | Hotels: Purple | Shops: Orange | Outdoors/Parks: Green | Sights/Culture: Blue

25 FAIRFAX AVENUE

Since World War II, this has been Main Street for the Jewish community of Los Angeles. Although the majority of Los Angeles Jews currently reside on the Westside and in the San Fernando Valley, the Eastern European Jewish tradition continues as a strong influence in this area.

26 CBS TELEVISION CITY

This massive complex of television studios and offices was built in 1952 by **Pereira & Luckman** and renovated in 1976 by Gin Wong Associates. Free tickets to shows can be picked up at the information window; age restrictions vary. For groups of 20 or more, call 323/852.2455. ♦ Daily. 7800 Beverly Blvd (between N Genesee and N Fairfax Aves). 323/852.2624

27 GRACE

★★$$$ Cutting-edge hip with waiters donned in safari chic, this is one of the top spots for LA's young and restless. The over-the-top design features a frivolous but tasty menu that begins with a soup tasting and moves along to John Dory accompanied by potato gnocchi or salmon with Catalan-style peppers stuffed with brandade, braised short ribs with langoustines, or a bacon-wrapped saddle of rabbit. Vegans can enjoy tofu stuffed into peppers alongside basmati rice and butternut squash. Dress outrageously hip and you'll fit right in. ♦ French ♦ Dinner, Tu-Su. Reservations a must. 7630 Beverly Blvd (between N Fuller and N Martel Aves). 323/934. 4400; fax: 323/934.0485. www.gracerestaurant.net

28 STEVE TURNER GALLERY

This gallery features American modernist paintings from the 1930s and 1940s, and international poster design from 1910 to 1950. ♦ W-Su. 7220 Beverly Blvd (between N Formosa Ave and N Alta Vista Blvd). 323/931.1185

28 INSOMNIA

★★$ This stylish literary coffeehouse, operated by UCLA graduates' and frequented by aspiring screenwriters, is set in a converted Art Deco building. Fresh breads, pastries, and light fare sustain those who are reading, playing chess, or listening to the Wednesday and Sunday night readings of poetry and fiction. ♦ Coffeehouse ♦ Daily. 7286 Beverly Blvd (between N Alta Vista Blvd and N Poinsettia Pl). 323/931.4943

28 TYLER TRAFFICANTE

On sale here are tailored suits and coats for men and women, all with a winning blend of old-world elegance and very contemporary theatrics, all designed by Australian expatriate Richard Tyler. The fashions are housed in a dramatic Art Deco corner building. ♦ M-Sa. 7290 Beverly Blvd (at N Poinsettia Pl). 323/931.9678

29 FARFALLA

★★$$ This larger version of the North Central LA trattoria on Hillhurst Avenue serves delicious pizza, pasta, and desserts to a smartly dressed film industry crowd. Any dish with eggplant is worth a try. ♦ Italian ♦ M-F, lunch and dinner; Sa, dinner. Reservations recommended. 143 N La Brea Ave (between W First St and Beverly Blvd). 323/938.2504

29 PATINA

Choose from custom-made hats in felt and straw, trimmed with vintage lace, ribbons, and flowers, in period and contemporary styles. ♦ W-Sa; M-Tu by appointment. 119 N La Brea Ave (between W First St and Beverly Blvd). 323/931.6931

30 HANCOCK PARK

Captain G. Allan Hancock—son of Henry Hancock, who bought Rancho La Brea in 1860—began this exclusive residential section in the 1910s. The palatial mansions were once owned by such notable California families as the Dohenys, Huntingtons, Van Nuyses, Jansses, Bannings, Crockers, and others. ♦ Bounded by S Lucerne, Larchmont, and Wilshire Blvds and Highland and Melrose Aves

31 LARCHMONT VILLAGE

Don't miss this shopping street of small-town charm and urban sophistication. Nearby is the Wilton Historic District, a modest area of California bungalows dating from 1907 to 1925. ♦ N Larchmont Blvd (between W First St and Beverly Blvd)

At Larchmont Village:

PRADO

★$$ The setting—pale-blue walls, painted angels floating above the chandeliers—enhances the cuisine prepared by chef Javier Prado. The dishes, while exotic, are often overspiced, and the tiny room is sometimes overwhelmed with diners. ♦ Caribbean ♦ M-Sa, lunch and dinner; Su, dinner. Reservations recommended. 244 N Larchmont Blvd. 323/467.3871

32 BEVERLY CONNECTION

This annex to **Beverly Center** (see page 49) has undistinguished industrial-chic designs but is much more pedestrian-friendly than its giant neighbor. Among the tenants are a consumer electronics store, a market, and specialty shops including **Greenpeace,** an environmentalist's paradise for politically correct knickknacks; **Bookstar,** an upscale discount bookseller; **Sports Chalet,** an athlete's wonderland; and **Strouds,** for fine linens and bath supplies at discount prices. Among the small restaurants are a branch of the **Daily Grill** (310/659.3100) for meat loaf, pasta, or a Cobb salad. And of course, there's the omnipresent Starbucks. ♦ Daily. 100 N La Cienega Blvd (between W Third St and Beverly Blvd).

33 THIRD STREET

This booming half-mile corridor hosts a collection of worthwhile little restaurants, antiques shops, and lots of hair salons. Hip without the hype, Third Street is more off the beaten path than offbeat. The street's denizens, mainly apartment dwellers who reside north and south of Sunset Strip, can stroll around the corner and grab a sandwich at **Who's on Third,** walk in for a restyled coif at **Object Hair Salon,** purchase new threads at **Atlas Clothing Co.,** and wash those threads at the **Washing Machine** self-serve laundry. ♦ Between S Sweetzer Ave and S La Cienega Blvd

34 THE TRAVELER'S BOOKCASE

Browse through an extensive collection of books for armchair globe-trotters and serious adventurers at this delightful shop. ♦ Daily. 8375 W Third St (between S Kings Rd and S Orlando Ave). 323/655.0575

34 THE COOK'S LIBRARY

Owner Ellen Rose turned her hobby into an occupation when she opened the only LA store that concentrates entirely on cookbooks—new, old, and out-of-print. ♦ M-Sa. 8373 W Third St (between S Kings Rd and S Orlando Ave). 323/655.3141

35 FOUR SEASONS HOTEL

$$$$ This is about as good as a hotel gets, with outstanding service and style. Each of the 179 rooms and 106 suites is outrageously comfortable and luxurious. But then, this is what one comes to expect of this prestigious hotel chain. The public areas are exquisite, with fine furnishings, marble floors, fine art (including a Picasso in the lobby), and fresh floral arrangements everywhere. The hotel spa is one of the prettiest in town, with aromatic scented treatment rooms, top-notch therapists, and a fitness-friendly, outdoor/tented workout area. There's also a charming garden, a terrace pool with a café, and complimentary limo service to Rodeo Drive in Beverly Hills. ♦ 300 S Doheny Dr (at W Third St). 310/273.2222, 800/332.3442; fax 310/859.3874. www.fourseasons.com ♿

Within the Four Seasons:

GARDEN'S

★★★$$$ This elegant dining room offers excellent service and consistently good fare: Try the braleed artichoke salad, Norwegian smoked salmon with whitefish gravlax on a potato pancake, or duck breast with figs and pears in a honey and green peppercorn sauce. A divine finale is the chocolate truffle cake with banana rum ice cream. Every month Garden's highlights a region of the world with special five-course tasting menus that include regional wine pairings for a mere $75 a person. A recent Spanish sampling was superb. ♦ California ♦ Daily, breakfast, lunch, and dinner. 310/273.2222, ext 2171

36 MICHEL RICHARD

★$$ There are tables for petit déjeuner, salad-and-quiche lunches, and steak-and-shrimp dinners. Each dessert is a work of art. ♦ French ♦ Daily, breakfast, lunch, and dinner. 310 S Robertson Blvd (between Burton Way and W Third St). 310/275.5707

37 KATSU 3RD

★★$$ The cool minimalist room has hand-painted furniture and an atmosphere that might be described as hip Zen. Sushi and tempura are the name of the game here. But there's also a short, innovative menu that fuses East and West with creative fish dishes done with scallops, halibut, and eel, or beef fillet stuffed with monkfish mousse. ♦ California/Japanese ♦ M-F, lunch and dinner; Sa, dinner. 8636 W Third St (between Willaman Dr and Hamel Rd). 310/273.3605 ♿

37 LOCANDA VENETA

★★★$$ Owner Jean Louis de Mori and chef Massimo Ormani head up this terrific trattoria that continues to lure foodies with such winners as handmade mozzarella, duck, chicken dumplings with onion confit, organic free-range chicken grilled with sage and lemon zest in a spicy garlic sauce, and any of the pastas or risottos—not to mention the vanilla ice cream with chocolate sauce. ♦ Italian ♦ M-F, lunch and dinner; Sa, dinner only. 8638 W Third St (between Willaman Dr and Hamel Rd). 310/274.1893 ♿

37 ORSO

★★$$ Joe Allen's, the legendary showbiz hangout, has been transformed into a great-looking trattoria with the most seductive patio in town. The bread is fabulous, the hand-painted plates gorgeous,

---

Restaurants/Clubs: Red | Hotels: Purple | Shops: Orange | Outdoors/Parks: Green | Sights/Culture: Blue

the service friendly (if casual and a bit hands-off), and the cosmopolitan clientele star-studded. The ambitious menu changes daily, but you can always get such delicacies as pan-fried calf's liver or a margarita pizza, and if you're there at the right time, veal kidney, tripe, dandelion greens, and Italian cheeses, along with pastas and grilled fish. However, some dishes are overpriced. ♦ Italian ♦ Daily, lunch and dinner. Reservations recommended. 8706 W Third St (at Hamel Rd). 310/274.7144 &

37 BAREFOOT

★★$$ Light and dark wood, aged copper, stone, and floral prints are blended to great effect in this restaurant, with its cozy bar and airy rooftop terrace. The creative menu features sautéed whitefish, stuffed chicken breast with goat cheese, and seafood risotto. Don't miss the crème brûlée-it's gotten raves all over town. Because it stays open until midnight, this is a perfect place for late-night dining. ♦ California/Italian ♦ M-F, lunch and dinner; Sa, Su, brunch, lunch, and dinner. 8722 W Third St (between Hamel Rd and Arnaz Dr). 310/276.6223 &

38 BEVERLY PLAZA HOTEL

$$ This attractive 98-room hotel is recommended for those who want to shop 'til they drop at nearby **Beverly Center** (see page 49). The rooms are charming and come with terry robes, coffeemaker, natural soaps and shampoos, daily newspaper, fresh fruit, and yummy chocolates at turndown. There's a pool, fitness center, spa, and free transportation within a five-miles radius of the hotel. ♦ 8384 W Third St (at S Orlando Ave). 323/658.6600, 800/624.6835; fax 323/653.3464 &

38 BUTTON STORE

Amiable shopkeeper Omid Hashemi stocks nothing but buttons, from contemporary designer styles to vintage, centuries-old pieces. It's the only store of its kind in the city. ♦ M-Sa. 8344 W Third St (between S Sweetzer and S Orlando Aves). 323/658.5473

39 FARMERS' MARKET

A favorite with locals and tourists, this market was established in 1934 as a cooperative where local farmers could sell their produce. Today, more than 160 vendors set up shop every day, including dozens of stalls offering hot and cold dishes from around the world. Go to **Johnny Rockets** (Stall 706) for the best burgers and hot fudge sundaes; **Sushi A Go Go** (No. 618) for yummy sushi, or **Du-pars** (No. 210) for yummy pancake breakfasts. Browse around the retailers, munch on a nosh here, an entrée there, but save room for pastry at **Thee's Continental Bakery** (Stall 361) or **Thee's Pie Shop** (Stall 530), and find a seat beneath the umbrellas and awnings. **Mr. Marcel Gourmet Grocery** (Stall 150) sells all sorts of gourmet treats; try **Farm Fresh Produce** (Stall 816) for exotic fruits. Several of the fruit and nut stalls will create and ship gift boxes, as will some of the confectioneries, where you can watch candy being made. Complete your outing with flowers from **Black Orchid Boutique** (Stalls 230, 234) or a place called simply **Florist** (Stall 328). ♦ Daily. 6333 W Third St (corner of S Fairfax Ave and Third). Three hours free parking. 323/933.9211; www.farmersmarketla.com

Within the Farmers' Market:

KOKOMO

★$ The New Age counter here offers great granola, gumbo, and BLTs. ♦ American ♦ Daily, breakfast, lunch, and dinner. 323/933.0773

GUMBO POT

★$ Spicy gumbo, fresh oysters, blackened fish, and meat loaf are the specialties, and the weekend brunches are hearty. ♦ Cajun/Creole ♦ M-F, breakfast, lunch, and dinner; Sa, Su, breakfast, brunch, lunch, and dinner. 323/933.0358

39 THE GROVE AT FARMERS' MARKET

A major departure from the over-the-top-consumerism of Beverly Center, this picture-postcard pretty, European-village-like mall, which attracts shoppers, moviegoers, and even busloads of tour groups to the droves, is one of the most successful commercial centers in the city. The stunning 640,000-square-foot annex to Farmers' Market provides a study in architectural styles ranging from Italian Renaissance to Art Deco. An assortment of retail outlets, anchored by Nordstrom, offers consumers opportunities to buy just about anything under one multimillion-dollar roof. You have Abercrombie & Fitch, All American Sausage Co., Amadeus Spa, Apple Computers, Banana Republic, Barnes and Noble, Lucky Brand Dungarees, Gap, Victoria's Secret, several restaurants, and an acoustically advanced multiplex movie theater. 888/315.8883, 323/900.8000. www.TheGroveLA.com. 189 The Grove Drive (between W 3rd St and Beverly Blvd).

40 AMERICAN RAG COMPANY

This is where to pick up hip and trendy recycled duds at designer prices. You'll find racks and racks of blue jeans, cool jackets, and more. Next door is a home-furnishing store and the **Maison et Cafe** (No. 148) for a quick lunch or espresso. Steps away: **American Rag Cie Shoes** (No. 144). ♦ Daily. 150 S La Brea Ave (between W Second and W First Sts). 323/935.3154

SONORA CAFÉ

40 SONORA CAFÉ

★★$$ This gourmet cousin of LA's beloved Mexican eatery **El Cholo** serves deliciously sophisticated Mexican-influenced Southwestern dishes such as Texas barbecue pork chop with sweet potato tamale and mango-papaya salsa, chicken enchiladas, southwestern mixed grill with Texas antelope, Sonoma quail, venison sausage, and roasted poblano-tomatillo salsa. Desserts take on a continental twist, with offerings like flourless chocolate cake, lime tart, eggnog cheesecake, and a to-die-for trio of crème brûlée (vanilla, coffee, and chocolate). The margaritas are really robust. The dining room has a warm Southwestern feel, with wood floors, large chandeliers, and antique rugs, and a lovely patio encourages outdoor dining. ♦ Southwestern/Mexican ♦ M-Sa, lunch and dinner; Su, dinner. Reservations advised. 180 S La Brea Ave (at W Second St). 323/857.1800 &

41 LOWENBRAU KELLER

★$$ Huge helpings of German food—sausages, sauerbraten, and a good choice of local wine and beer—are enhanced by the Bavarian setting. ♦ German ♦ M-F, lunch and dinner; Sa, dinner. Reservations recommended for five or more. 3211 Beverly Blvd (between N Dillon and Robinson Sts). 213/382.5723

42 SHIBUCHO

★★$$ Sushi and sashimi of high quality are served in a traditional, woodsy interior with pebble floors ♦ Japanese ♦ M-Sa, dinner until 3AM. 3114 Beverly Blvd (between S Vendome and S Dillon Sts). 213/387.8498

43 ARNIE MORTON'S THE STEAK HOUSE

★★★$$$ This carnivore's paradise serves the biggest, juiciest steaks you've ever eaten—and possibly the most expensive, too. Grilled to taste, beef just doesn't get any better than the melt-in-your-mouth filet mignon, New York, porterhouse, and rib-eye steaks accompanied by à la carte piles of mashed or fried potatoes, asparagus, or fresh spinach sautéed with mushrooms. The New York cheesecake, chocolate velvet cake, and Key Lime pie wage a conspiracy against your diet resolutions. ♦ American ♦ Daily, dinner. Reservations recommended. 435 S La Cienega Blvd (at Colgate Ave). 310/246.1501 www.mortons.com

44 THE LITTLE DOOR

★★★$$$ Organic, Mediterranean-style cuisine attracts health-minded gourmets to this trendy bistro. A favorite of models and celebrities, the handsome St. Barth's–style eatery features wide curtained windows, rich wood furnishings, and soft lighting. Chef Nicolas Peter's seasonally changing menu is downright spectacular, with spinach ricotta and potato gnocchi primavera, veal shank osso bucco, foie gras with poached figs, goat cheese and pistachio tart, and celery root–crusted sea bass. The primo tables are out front or in the back room. ♦ French/Mediterranean ♦ Daily, dinner; Sunday, lunch, 11AM-3PM. 8164 W Third St (between S Crescent Heights Blvd and S La Jolla Ave). 323/951.1210

45 SOFI RESTAURANT

★$$ This lively, family-run restaurant serves excellent moussaka and other Greek specialties. ♦ Greek ♦ M-Sa, lunch and dinner; Su, dinner. 8030 W Third St (between S Edinburgh Ave and S Crescent Heights Blvd). 323/651.0346

46 TAHITI

★★★$$ Chef/owner Tony Di Lembo opened this Polynesian-style eatery in 1997, attracting a loyal coterie of foodies with such signature dishes as Chilean sea bass baked in banana leaves, chicken and spinach pot stickers, papaya salad, and chicken in red curry-coconut sauce. Less exotic (but equally tasty) dishes include pizzas, pastas, and grilled fish—the creation of which can be viewed through the glassed-in kitchen. The setting is breezy South Seas, with palm trees, an open-air shuttered patio, and a graceful fountain. ♦ Polynesian ♦ Tu-F, lunch and dinner; Sa, dinner. Reservations recommended. Visa and Mastercard only. 7910 W Third St (at S Fairfax Ave). 323/651.1213 &

46 AOC

★★$$ This chic neighborhood-style restaurant run by partners Suzanne Groin and Caroline Styne, of Lucques fame, is one of the hottest tickets in town. The scene's a hoot, with a mix of the young and restless, Cosmopolitan-swirling set and foodies just there for the great eats. The name stands for Appellation d'Origine Controlée, an official French classification for wines and cheeses. Designed more like a tapas "tasting menu," portions are small. Waiters suggest sharing, and so do we. Choose from dishes of braised pork cheeks; skewers of lamb, skirt steak, and arroz Negro with squid, roasted date,

---

Restaurants/Clubs: Red | Hotels: Purple | Shops: Orange | Outdoors/Parks: Green | Sights/Culture: Blue

parmesan, and bacon; duck fat potatoes; and brioche with prosciutto, Gruyère, and egg. The wine list is sensational, with 50 choices by the glass. ♦ French with a California flair ♦ Daily, dinner. Reservations required. 8022 W Third St (between Fairfax Ave and Crescent Heights Blvd). 323/653.6359

47 FORMER SELIG STORE

This streamlined gem designed in black-and-gold glazed terra-cotta and glass brick dates back to 1931. ♦ S Western Ave and W Third St

48 TOMMY'S

$ More than a million people have enjoyed a burger or two at this legendary hamburger joint (circa 1946). Best known for its world-class chili burgers and chili cheese burgers, now available at more than two dozen locations throughout the Southland, Tommy's is the place to go when you want quality beef ground into the best burger you've ever eaten. It's just a funky, little stand and there is always a line. But believe us, it's worth the wait. Extra portions of tomato, chili, onions, or pickles are on the house. ♦ Burgers ♦ Daily. 2575 W Beverly Blvd (at Rampart Blvd). 213/389.9060. www.originaltommys.com

49 BROOKLYN BAGEL BAKERY

The bagels here will bring tears to the eyes of New York expatriates—the crisp, shiny crusts garnished with onion are great. ♦ Daily. 2217 Beverly Blvd (between N Lake St and Roselake Ave). 213/413.4114

50 PARK LA BREA HOUSING AND TOWERS

Built in the 1940s, the large Regency Moderne complex of low- and high-rise garden apartments is surrounded by a 176-acre park. ♦ Bounded by Cochran and S Fairfax Aves, and W Sixth and W Third Sts

51 IL LITERATURE

An eclectic mix of books, frames, candles, cards, and unique gifts is stocked here. ♦ Daily. 456 S La Brea Ave (between W Sixth and W Fourth Sts). 323/937.3505

52 ARUNEE

★★$ A family-run restaurant with modest décor. The crab with cellophane noodles and the spicy seafood stew rate high among the best Thai dishes in LA. ♦ Thai ♦ Daily, lunch and dinner. 401 S Vermont Ave (at W Fourth St). 213/385.6653

53 WILSHIRE CREST

$$ This 34-room hotel has great rates, with a daily continental breakfast thrown in. ♦ 6301 Orange St (at S Crescent Heights Blvd). 323/936.5131; fax 323/936.2013

54 MUSEUM OF CONTEMPORARY ART (MOCA)

Housed in the original May Co. Department Store—an immense gilded cylinder set into the southwest corner of this rectangular block, designed in 1940 by **Albert C. Martin** and **S.A. Marx**—the facility is an extension of the Los Angeles County Museum of Art (LACMA; see below), and offers exhibits throughout the year. ♦ 6067 Wilshire Blvd (at S Fairfax Ave). 323/857.6000 රු

55 LA BREA TAR PITS

The tar (*brea* in Spanish) that seeps from these pits was used by Native Americans and early settlers to seal boats and roofs. In 1906, geologists discovered the pits had entrapped 200 varieties of mammals, plants, birds, reptiles, and insects from the Pleistocene Era and preserved them as fossils. Disneyesque sculptures of doomed mammals add a surreal touch. ♦ Hancock Park, Wilshire Blvd (between S Curson Ave and S Ogden Dr)

At the La Brea Tar Pits:

GEORGE C. PAGE MUSEUM OF LA BREA DISCOVERIES

Established in 1977 within grassy berms topped by a steel-frame canopy, the museum offers exhibitions, films, and demonstrations describing the evolution of the pits. Children will revel in the holographic displays (which give flesh to the bones of a tiger and a woman that were excavated here) and in a hands-on demonstration of how sticky tar is. Summer visitors can watch paleontologists at work in Pit 91. There's a gift shop, and free parking is available in back. ♦ Admission. Tu-Su. 5801 Wilshire Blvd. 323/936.2230

55 LOS ANGELES COUNTY MUSEUM OF ART (LACMA)

A pastiche of architectural styles, this is one of the finest, most varied art museums in the US. The permanent collections of Western art include works by Degas, Monet, and Gauguin. In addition, huge holdings of Asian and Near Eastern art, costumes, and textiles are on display. The **Rifkin Collection of German Expressionism** is justly famous. The **Japanese Pavilion**, overlooking the tar pits, was conceived by the late Bruce Goff in 1988, and realized by his protégé, Bart Prince. Some find this gallery reminiscent of Eero Saarinen's TWA Terminal at New York's Kennedy Airport, while others discover echoes of 1950s Googie-style coffeehouses. To avoid internal divisions, the building is suspended from a frame of concrete posts and beams and is lit from fiberglass wall panels that evoke shoji screens. Visitors take an elevator to the third floor and walk down a winding ramp through the east wing, past a series of wall niches that frame a constantly changing selection of 30 artworks. The west wing contains netsuke and other highlights from the museum's rich collections, along with a book/gift store. The **Robert O. Anderson Building,** designed by **Hardy Holzman Pfeiffer** and completed in 1986, comprises a vast wedge of limestone, glass brick, and green terra-cotta that pays homage to the Coulter's Store (a former Streamline Moderne highlight of Miracle Mile). An entry portal of Babylonian proportions frames the steps leading up to the original pavilions and the courtyard, which is now roofed over. The sculpture garden has been restored and a Japanese garden added. Some of LA's best film series and concerts of contemporary music are regularly presented in the 500-seat auditorium of the **Bing Center,** where there is also an outstanding museum store. Jazz concerts are presented in the Plaza on Sunday afternoons, and with cocktails and hors d'oeuvres on Friday evenings. Members may rent selected artworks, and, if they decide to keep them, apply the charges to the purchase price. The Plaza Cafe offers food of a quality far above most museum cafeterias, and is a favorite meeting place for young (art) lovers. You may notice construction on your next visit as an ambitious redesign develops. Created by world-renowned architect **Rem Koolhaas**, plans call for a three-level building that will replace existing structures. ♦ Admission; free on the second Tuesday of each month. Tu-Su; F until 9PM. Hancock Park, Wilshire Blvd (between S Curson Ave and S Ogden Dr). Recording 323/857.6000; fax 323/857.6214. www.lacma.org

56 EL REY

This streamlined movie house, designed by W. Clifford Balch in 1936, has led a checkered life, going from thriving Wall Street nightclub and restaurant to lively theater and, finally, to a flophouse for the homeless. Recently reborn, the Art Deco theater is now alive with the sounds of music, movie wrap parties, fund-raisers, and other special events. ♦ 5519 Wilshire Blvd (between Dunsmuir and Burnside Aves)

57 CAMPANILE

★★★$$$ Architect **Josh Schweitzer** placed a glass roof over a street-front courtyard of a 1928 Spanish-style building (once owned by Charlie Chaplin) to create a two-story atrium. The pretty tile fountain and signature tower

that serves as the entrance to one of the most romantic dining spots in LA were kept intact. The menu is a rustic blend of Italian and California, with signature dishes such as prosciutto and melon, squash blossom and ricotta ravioli, risotto cakes with Portobello mushrooms, cedar-smoked king salmon, and a big, juicy porterhouse steak. Sweet treats include macadamia nut tart, panna cotta, and chocolate sorbet, along with a selection of dessert and port wines. Late breakfast lovers should go for the Saturday and Sunday brunch (which starts at 9:30). The big, thick slices of French toast and the buttery scrambled eggs with creamed spinach are worth waiting for. ♦ M-F, lunch and dinner; Sa, breakfast and dinner; Su, breakfast. Reservations required. 624 S La Brea Ave (between Wilshire Blvd and W Sixth St). 323/938.1447

58 MIRACLE MILE

In 1920, visionary A.W. Ross bought 18 acres of empty land along Wilshire Boulevard, which he then developed as a prestigious business and shopping district. A friend dubbed it "Miracle Mile." Ross closely supervised the designs of individual buildings, and a few relics survive ongoing redevelopment.

58 LUNA PARK

★★$$ Hot, hot, hot. This San Francisco import has hosted an SRO crowd since opening its smart and casual bar/restaurant in 2003. Bar noshing is big here, but tables also get their fill of diners. The eclectic menu is interesting, with the emphasis on French and Italian and hints of Asian. Sample fare includes warm goat cheese fondue with grilled bread and sliced apples, which didn't cut it for us, but some folks seem to eat it up. Other interesting items to consider are the fontina-stuffed raviolis with mushrooms, spinach, and truffle oil; a great grilled yellowtail with wild mushroom ragout; hunter's pie with venison, port, spinach, and mashed potatoes; or the tender lamb shank with cranberry beans and brown butter polenta. We said it was a diverse menu. Desserts aren't worth the extra calories, except for a plate of tasty cookies. Plan time to sip a trendy mojito at the bar. There's a nice wine list but a limited selection by the glass. ♦ French/Italian/Asian ♦ M-F, lunch and dinner; daily, dinner. Reservations suggested. 672 S La Brea Ave (at Wilshire Blvd). 323/934.2110. www.lunaparkla.com

59 GETTY HOUSE

This half-timbered English-style house, built in 1921, was donated to the city by the Getty Oil Company and was once used as the mayor's official home. It is now a private residence. ♦ 605 S Irving Blvd (at W Sixth St)

Restaurants/Clubs: Red | Hotels: Purple | Shops: Orange | Outdoors/Parks: Green | Sights/Culture: Blue

60 St. Basil's Catholic Church

The massive, modernist reinforced-concrete church was designed by **AC Martin Partners** in 1974. ♦ 3611 Wilshire Blvd (between S Kingsley Dr and S Harvard Blvd). 213/381.6191

61 Radisson Wilshire Plaza Hotel and Garden

$$ This 391-room hotel has a pool and small fitness room, along with two restaurants. ♦ 3515 Wilshire Blvd (at S Normandie Ave). 213/381.7411, 800/382.7411; fax 213/386.7379

62 Chapman Shopping Center

Originally designed in 1929 by **Morgan, Walls & Clements,** this vintage shopping center was rehabilitated by the indispensable Los Angeles urban developer Wayne Ratkovich. It boasts a motor court and Churrigueresque façade, a quality market, florist, retail shops, and restaurants. ♦ 3451 W Sixth St (at S Kenmore Ave). 213/487.6155

63 Cassell's Patio Hamburgers

★$ Homemade hamburgers, out-of-sight turkey burgers, potato salad, and fresh-squeezed lemonade are served at this landmark, no-frills joint. ♦ American ♦ Daily, lunch until 4PM. 3266 W Sixth St (at S Berendo St). 213/480.8668

64 CNA Building

The mirrored slab of this 1972 building reflects the sky and the 1932 English Gothic First Congregational Church across the street. ♦ W Sixth St and S Commonwealth Ave

65 Lafayette Park

This park includes a recreation and senior citizens' center, tennis courts, a picnic area, and a scent garden with numerous fragrant flowers. ♦ 625' S Lafayette Park Pl (between Wilshire Blvd and W Sixth St). 213/387.9426

66 Caffe Latte

★$ An interesting crowd frequents this friendly place, known for its innovative fare and artistic modern décor. Home-baked breads and roasted-on-the-premises coffee beans can also be purchased. ♦ American ♦ M-Sa, breakfast, lunch, and dinner. 6254 Wilshire Blvd (at McCarthy Vista). 323/936.5323

67 Los Angeles Museum of the Holocaust

This archival storehouse honors the survivors and six million Jewish victims of Nazi persecution and internment. The gallery displays photomurals, documents, artifacts, and memorabilia recounting this tragic period

in history. Names of the victims are inscribed on the walls of the **Martyrs Memorial,** designed to resemble the cattle-car transports that carried millions to their deaths. In a wing dedicated to the children of the Holocaust is a scaled model of Terezin, a concentration camp that imprisoned 15,000 youth between 1942 and 1944. Also here is the **Jewish Community Library,** which contains literature on Jewish history and culture. ♦ Free. Gallery: M-F, Su. Library: M-F. 6006 Wilshire Blvd (at S Ogden Dr). 323/761.8176

67 Petersen Automotive Museum

This 340,000-square-foot exhibition space showcases the largest automotive collection in the country. There's also a restaurant. ♦ Admission. Tu-Su. 6060 Wilshire Blvd (at S Fairfax Ave). 323/930.CARS. www.petersen.org

68 Wilshire Courtyard

Clad in brown marble and handsomely landscaped, **McLarand & Vasquez**'s sleek stepped-back commercial development is a welcome relief from the bland towers and fake-classical boxes that dominate LA's most prestigious artery. The development was completed in 1988. ♦ 5750 Wilshire Blvd (between Masselin and S Curson Aves)

69 Commercial Building

Frank M. Tyler's 1927 twin turrets look like towering Japanese origami. ♦ 5464 Wilshire Blvd (between Cochran and Dunsmuir Aves)

69 Desmond's

Note the rounded corners on the low wings of **Gilbert Stanley Underwood**'s handsome eight-story tower, which was completed in 1928. Housed in this building is the **Ace Gallery** (Tu-Sa; 323/935.4411), showcasing such artists as Roger Herman, Bob Zoeli, and Pauline Stella Sanchez. ♦ 5514 Wilshire Blvd (between Dunsmuir and Burnside Aves)

70 The Dark Room

The façade of Marcus P. Miller's 1935 building is that of a period camera in black vitrolite. ♦ 5370 Wilshire Blvd (between S Detroit St and Cloverdale Ave)

70 Dominguez-Wilshire Building

In 1997, Los Angeles's Art Deco Society joined forces with the owners of this 1930 **Morgan, Walls & Clements** structure to completely restore the finely detailed tower and two-story retail base to its former glory. ♦ 5410 Wilshire Blvd (at Cloverdale Ave)

71 WILSHIRE EBELL THEATER AND CLUB

Because of its Renaissance-style façade, this 1924 building is popular with movie and television companies. The theater is noted for its cultural and educational programs as well as for stage plays. ♦ 4401 W Eighth St (at S Lucerne Blvd). 323/939.1128

72 WILTERN CENTER

Another Art Deco masterpiece, this tower was designed by **Morgan, Walls & Clements** in 1931. Wayne Ratkovich rescued the building from an insurance company that wanted to clear the site. The corner tower and side wings are clad in green terra-cotta; closely spaced, lively moldings make the tower seem far more imposing than its 12 stories. Architect Brenda Levin restored them for lease as offices, stores, and the **Upstage Cafe** (213/739.9913). ♦ Wilshire Blvd and S Western Ave

Within the Wiltern Center:

WILTERN THEATRE

This grand theater has an imposing marquee and a patterned terrazzo forecourt. Built in 1931 by **G. Albert Lansburgh,** the venue has been restored by Brenda Levin and Anthony Heinsbergen Jr., son of the original interior designer, for use as a performing arts center. It is a fairyland of Art Deco ornament embellished in pink and green hues with gold trim. A masterly sequence of spaces guides the audience into an auditorium whose proscenium is crowned with a sunburst of low-relief skyscrapers. ♦ Box office: noon-6PM on the first day tickets are released and three hours before the event on show day. 3790 Wilshire Blvd. 213/380.5005

73 I. MAGNIN WILSHIRE

The grandest Art Deco monument in LA was completed in 1928. Designed by **John & Donald Parkinson,** it was the city's most handsome store, from its stepped profile to its soaring green-crowned tower. The store closed in 1993 because of poor sales, but the exterior is still a sight to see. ♦ 3050 Wilshire Blvd (at S Westmoreland Ave)

74 GRANADA BUILDING

Spanish Colonial architecture is combined with Mission-style arches and arcades in this 1927 building. ♦ 672 S Lafayette Park Pl (between S Hoover St and Wilshire Blvd)

75 PARK PLAZA HOTEL

$ Open only for special events during a massive renovation, this landmark hotel occupies the 1925 Elks Building, a close relation of the Central Library, with its grand arches, massive parapet sculptures, and interiors decorated by Anthony B. Heinsbergen. In addition to 140 rooms and 10 suites, the hotel features three ballrooms, a gym with an Olympic-size pool, and free parking. However, there's no on-site restaurant. ♦ 607 S Park View St (between Wilshire Blvd and W Sixth St). 213/384.5281; fax 213/480.1928

75 OTIS SCHOOL OF ART AND DESIGN

LA's oldest college of art and design, established in 1918, offers undergraduate and master's degrees in fine and applied arts, plus public evening classes and varied community outreach programs. Kent Twitchell painted one of his best murals, a Holy Trinity of soap opera stars, on a wall overlooking Carondelet Street. The **Otis/Parsons Art Gallery** presents notable exhibitions. ♦ Free. Tu-Sa. 2401 Wilshire Blvd (at S Park View St). 213/251.0500

75 LA FONDA

★$$ **Los Camperos,** one of the finest mariachi groups anywhere, entertains in this popular spot. The margaritas are especially good and the atmosphere is one of the most festive in town. ♦ Mexican ♦ Tu-F, lunch and dinner; Sa, Su, dinner. Reservations recommended. 2501 Wilshire Blvd (at S Carondelet St). 213/380.5055

76 BOB BAKER MARIONETTE THEATER

Since 1963, this has been one of LA's most delightful experiences for children of all ages. Ticket prices include refreshments and a backstage tour. ♦ Performances: Tu-Su. Reservations required. 1345 W First St (at Glendale Blvd). 323/250.9995

77 CARTHAY CIRCLE

Don't miss this charming, leafy neighborhood of 1930s stucco cottages that mix Spanish and Art Deco themes. Consistent in style and scale, this historic district is now threatened by predatory developers. ♦ Bounded by S Fairfax Ave and Schumacher Dr, and W Olympic and Wilshire Blvds

78 KOREATOWN

Rambling, repainted old bungalows, storefronts provisioned with Korean foodstuffs, and distinctive angular calligraphy identify this dynamic ethnic neighborhood, bounded roughly by Vermont and Western Avenues, Pico Boulevard, and Eighth Street. It is the

---

Restaurants/Clubs: Red | Hotels: Purple | Shops: Orange | Outdoors/Parks: Green | Sights/Culture: Blue

hub for Korean cultural, social, and business life, but only a third of LA's 160,000 Koreans (the largest Korean population in the US) actually live here. It is now home to twice as many Latino immigrants, many from Central America.

78 DONG II JANG

★$$ Natural wood and subdued lighting are featured at this restaurant. Your order of beef or chicken is cooked on a grill hidden under the removable tabletop. ♦ Korean ♦ Daily, lunch and dinner. 3455 W Eighth St (at S Hobart Blvd). 213/383.5757

79 TAYLOR'S PRIME STEAKS

★$$ This place is everything a steak house should be: a clubby, wood-paneled space with the finest meat, generous portions, and very reasonable prices. The menu offers seafood and chops as well as steak. ♦ American ♦ M-F, lunch and dinner; Sa, Su, dinner. 3361 W Eighth St (between S Normandie Ave and Irolo St). 213/382.8449

80 MACARTHUR PARK

One of LA's first public gardens, this was originally worthless swampland. In the 1880s, Mayor William H. Workman arranged to have topsoil brought in and planted trees and shrubbery. A lake was created by filling a low ravine with water, which inspired the name Westlake Park because of its geographical location in town. Later the park was renamed as a tribute to General Douglas MacArthur. Today it provides badly needed recreation space for local immigrant communities. It contains more than 80 species of rare plants and trees, a lake with paddleboats for rent, a small bandshell for summer entertainment, snack bars, and children's play areas. More than 11 site-specific artworks have been installed in the park, including Judy Simonian's *Pyramids* (two tiled ziggurats linked by a speaking tube), Eric Orr's *Water Spout* (which rises up to 500 feet from the lake), and George Herm's *Clock Tower* (constructed from discarded materials in the spirit of Watts Towers). The neon signs around the park and along Wilshire Boulevard have been relit to evoke the 1930s; especially notable is the marquee of the **Westlake Theatre,** a handsome 1926 movie palace overlooking the park. The area is currently threatened by drug-related violence, so be careful. ♦ Wilshire Blvd (between S Alvarado and S Park View Sts)

81 MARY ANDREWS CLARK MEMORIAL RESIDENCE OF THE YWCA

Arthur Benton designed this enormous French château in 1913. ♦ 306 Loma Dr (at W Third St).

82 PACIFIC STOCK EXCHANGE

The exchange relocated to this bland, modern structure from its landmark building on Spring Street. ♦ Free. Viewing gallery: M-F, 8AM-1PM. 233 S Beaudry Ave (between W Third and W Second Sts). 323/977.4500

83 THAI KATSERINE

★★$ The menu lists some of the best northern regional Thai dishes in LA, including meat-and-vegetable chili, *kaeng hung lae* (pork curry), and *ap pla* (catfish with basil steamed in banana leaves). ♦ Thai ♦ Daily, lunch and dinner. 2810 W Ninth St (between S Westmoreland and S Vermont Aves). 213/384.7049

83 LA PLANCHA

★$$ If you're looking for a gastronomic adventure, you've come to the right place. Specialties include meats and fish marinated in orange and lime, ripe plantain stuffed with cotija cheese, and nactamales (giant tamales). Beer, wine, and refreshing *cacao* (a chocolate drink) are also available. ♦ Nicaraguan ♦ Daily, breakfast, lunch, and dinner. Reservations recommended. 2818 W Ninth St (between S Westmoreland and S Vermont Aves). 213/383.1449

83 YONGSUSAN

★$$ You can be your own barbecue chef at this lively restaurant, but come prepared for spicy food and clouds of smoke. ♦ Korean ♦ M-F, lunch and dinner; Sa, Su, dinner. 950 S Vermont Ave (between W Olympic Blvd and San Marino St). 213/388.3042

84 LANGER'S DELICATESSEN

★$ One of the few pastrami places that a New Yorker would applaud; other delectables include braised lamb shank and grilled liver and onions. ♦ Deli ♦ M-Sa, breakfast and lunch until 4PM. 704 S Alvarado St (at W Seventh St). 213/483.8050

85 PACIFIC DINING CAR

★★★★$$$$ This LA institution, opened in 1921, resembles a luxurious dining car of yesteryear—in fact, the front dining room *was* once a railroad car. The food and service are excellent. The prime beef (aged on the premises) and spinach salad are great choices, and there's also a great selection of desserts and a remarkable wine cellar. The place fills up in the morning with power breakfast meetings and with local folks and office workers who want to start their day with a hearty meal and good, strong coffee. ♦ American ♦ Daily, 6AM-2AM. Reservations recommended. 1310 W Sixth St (at Witmer St). 323/483.6000. Also at 2700 Wilshire Blvd (at Princeton St), Santa Monica. 310/453.4000

86 BEST WESTERN MAYFAIR HOTEL

$$ Not for the luxury-seeker, but just fine if you're on a budget, this vintage 295-room hostelry has a restaurant and lounge and provides a free shuttle to downtown. ♦ 1256 W Seventh St (at Witmer St). 323/484.9614, 800/821.8682 in CA; fax 323/484.2769

87 HARBOR FREEWAY OVERPASS

Between Figueroa Street and Beaudry Avenue, Wilshire Boulevard passes over the Harbor Freeway. A few blocks north is the stack interchange where the Hollywood, Harbor, and Pasadena Freeways form the hub of the freeway system. Driving north gives you the closest view you will want of two unusually inept buildings: pseudoclassical towers for Coast Savings and Home Savings.

88 VERSAILLES

★★$ Built to accommodate loyal patrons from the Midtown area, this larger version of the original restaurant (see page 123) serves the same gutsy garlic chicken, pork with black beans, oxtail, and strong coffee. ♦ Cuban ♦ M-F, lunch and dinner; Sa, Su, dinner. 1415 S La Cienega Blvd (between Alcott St and W Pico Blvd). 310/289.0392. Also at 10319 Venice Blvd (at Vinton Ave). 310/558.3168

89 MAURICE'S SNACK 'N' CHAT

★$$ This popular soul food restaurant serves large platters of meat loaf, short ribs, and liver and onions, accompanied by yams, beets, or black-eyed peas. ♦ Soul Food ♦ M-F, breakfast, lunch, and dinner; Sa, Su, breakfast and dinner. 5549 W Pico Blvd (at S Sierra Bonita Ave). 323/931.3877

90 SOUTH BONNIE BRAE STREET

Westlake (now MacArthur Park) was one of LA's first suburbs. Most of it has been rebuilt, but this street survives as a treasury of houses built in the 1890s. Among the standouts are **No. 818**, a regal Queen Anne with an immense veranda, elaborate woodwork, and several types of columns and piers; **No. 824**, the Charles B. Boothe and Carriage House, with its Islamic domed tower; and many on the **1000 block**. ♦ Between W 11th and W 8th Sts

91 LOYOLA LAW SCHOOL

An idiosyncratic version of Thomas Jefferson's "Academical Village" has given new spirit to what was formerly a drab commuter school. Completed in 1987, **Frank Gehry**'s stylized versions of a classical temple and a Romanesque chapel are deployed on a tight-knit campus. Outside stairs create a forced-perspective centerpiece on the administration building and encourage social intercourse. The school has established a fine art collection that includes Claes Oldenburg's *Toppling Ladder*, a whimsical construction. ♦ 1441 W Olympic Blvd (at Valencia St). 323/736.1000

92 ALVARADO TERRACE

Laid out in the first decade of the century, this gently curving street is a fashionable suburb at the western boundary of the original pueblo of Los Angeles. It's a smorgasbord of architectural styles, including Queen Anne, Mission Revival, Shingle, and English Tudor. It's named after Juan Bautista Alvarado, the Mexican governor of California from 1836 to 1842. ♦ Between W Pico Blvd and S Hoover St

93 L'ADELITA

★$ This Mexican and Central American emporium offers baked goods, fresh tortillas, tamales, *pupusas* (Salvadoran cornmeal turnovers), sandwiches, and hot entrées. ♦ Mexican/Central American ♦ Daily, breakfast, lunch, and dinner. 1287 S Union Ave (at W Pico Blvd). 213/487.0176. Also at 5812 Santa Monica Blvd (at N Van Ness Ave). 323/465.6526

94 PAPER SOURCE

Owner Rose Marie Dawes adores paper, and stocks her shop accordingly with the finest materials for artists, designers, and archivists, who shop here for handmade, marbleized, and gold-leaf sheets. ♦ M-F. 1506 W 12th St (at Valencia St). 323/387.5820

95 ST. ELMO'S VILLAGE

Artist Roderick Sykes organized friends and neighbors to transform this derelict courtyard into a painted quilt of faces, figures, and inspirational messages whose verve would have delighted Picasso. ♦ Su, noon-6PM. 4830 St. Elmo Dr (between Rimpau Blvd and Longwood Ave). 323/936.3595

96 FRED'S BAKERY

Only in LA would bagels aspire to elegance, but these are good enough for movie stars. Other tempting treats includes cakes, cookies, and fresh-baked breads. ♦ Daily. 2831 S Robertson Blvd (between Olin and Hargis Sts). 310/838.1204

Restaurants/Clubs: **Red** | Hotels: **Purple** | Shops: **Orange** | Outdoors/Parks: **Green** | Sights/Culture: **Blue**

Tinseltown meets urbanity in a tale of two cities . . .

A bit of a letdown at first sight, Hollywood has a seamy, underbelly sensibility, a little like New York's old 42nd Street. First-time visitors expect to see movie stars on every corner; instead they find hand- and footprints on the sidewalks or stars embedded in a Walk of Fame where celebrities rarely tread (save to immortalize their extremities in cement or dedicate their stars). On the other side of the coin, recently titivated West

Hollywood exudes a tidy sophistication combined with a literally and figuratively gay attitude.

Back to Hollywood. We hate to be the ones to break the news, but contrary to popular belief, the American film industry wasn't born there. Actually, the fledgling business of the "flickers" emerged from the borough of Queens in New York City, and didn't move west until the second decade of the 20th century, when the first movie moguls realized that their product could be made more conveniently year-round in sunny California. At first, they settled in an area of Los Angeles called Edendale (which today is **Silverlake**,

Echo Park, and Los Feliz), but soon afterward they moved west to Hollywood, where the land was cheaper. Here, a legend was born: As a mecca for established and aspiring actors, directors, producers, and other film people, Hollywood came to symbolize glamour and excitement around the world. And it still does, even though most of the major studios have relocated (only **Paramount Pictures** remains).

Hollywood is divided economically and geographically into two communities: the flatlands and the hills. Older houses, elegant remnants of Hollywood's Golden Age, hide in the low hills to the north, secluded because of the confusing, narrow roads snaking into them. Small, often decrepit bungalows from the 1910s and 1920s, battered, faceless apartment buildings, and the characterless offices of small entertainment-industry service companies make up most of the rest of the "flats."

The hills, on the other hand, exhibit the rustic charms of **Nichols Canyon** and the raffish counterculture of **Laurel Canyon.** They feature a bizarre mixture of castles and cottages, Spanish haciendas and Moorish temples, and winding streets and wild areas of chaparral. Prosperous and settled, the hills appeal to literary and artistic types (some of the folks who live or have lived there include Jane Seymour, Jay Leno, Frank Zappa, Arsenio Hall, Kevin Costner, David Hockney, Marlon Brando, and Judy Collins). Recent immigrants, especially from Southeast Asia, Latin America, the Middle East, and the former Soviet Union, make up much of the lower flatlands population. Sadly, the part of Hollywood that the average tourist knows best is also one of the seediest sections of LA. World-famous stretches along **Hollywood Boulevard, Sunset Boulevard,** and **Vine Street** are often overcrowded, honky-tonk, or just run down. A major revitalization effort by the Community Redevelopment Agency has made the area more eye pleasing, but if you're planning to stroll along the **Walk of Fame** to check out any of the 2,160 stars immortalized in concrete or their concrete foot- and handprints in front of **Mann's Chinese Theatre,** do so during daylight. Non-celebrity issues include the addition of an ambitious retail/residential/entertainment complex between Highland, Hollywood Boulevard, and Vine, which has greatly enhanced the area's appeal.

In contrast to Hollywood, West Hollywood—a pistol-shaped area in the flatlands west of Hollywood and east of Beverly Hills—provides a vibrant, relatively carefree environment. An independent city since 1984, its problem is not decay but excessive growth and trendiness. But just when many thought the city planners had wisely applied the brakes, along came a mega-million-dollar project to widen, beautify, and showcase **Santa Monica Boulevard.** The task, which closed the boulevard to parking and traffic and/or caused major delays, took three years and many retail casualties to complete. On the plus side, it groomed the area into a tropical SoHo with bustling sidewalk cafés, beautifully landscaped plazas, and pretty foliage. Designer showrooms, fashionable shops, restaurants, and hotels abound. The predominantly gay and lesbian community, with a small bohemian population, is generally more affluent than the rest of LA.

West Hollywood's core is Santa Monica Boulevard from **La Brea Avenue** west to **Doheny Drive.** But its boundaries—from **Beverly Boulevard** to the **Sunset Strip** in the west, narrowing to a few blocks in the east—are so ragged that it's more practical to describe the area's attractions along with those of Hollywood. WeHo's (that's the nickname for West Hollywood) hub is a stretch of Santa Monica Boulevard from **La Cienega** to **Robertson Boulevard,** which sees most of the action. Transformed into a mini Greenwich Village or SoHo, the area throbs with bars, restaurants, and boutiques. The greatest change runs along a small district on Robertson Boulevard between Santa Monica Boulevard and **Melrose Avenue.** Wedged in among a sprinkling of attractive office buildings and an inviting day spa are trendy bars and eateries that run packed day and night.

Historically, Hollywood was a winter campground for the Cahuenga Indians and later, because of its proximity to the **Cahuenga Pass,** it became a way station on the Camino Real and a major stop on the Butterfield Stage route. When Harvey Wilcox registered the subdivision of Hollywood in 1887, it had few residents, and only 165 citizens participated in the 1903 vote to incorporate as a city. Wilcox's wife, Deaida, named the area after the Chicago summer home of a woman she met on the train, and she was its greatest supporter, giving land for churches and schools, keeping demon drink at bay, and welcoming French artist Paul de Longpre, whose garden became Hollywood's first tourist attraction. Hollywood surrendered its independence in 1910 to guarantee its access to city water, but it remained a staid farming community of citrus orchards and sheep, with unpaved streets lined with pepper trees and a scattering of houses.

Then moviemakers arrived from the East like the Goths invading Rome, taking over a saloon on Sunset as the first Hollywood film studio, hiring cowboys who rode over front lawns in the excitement of the chase, and greasing intersections to film motorists' skids. Today, although the big studios have moved on, their lots and stages have been taken over by small independents—many of which are producing the more interesting work to come out of Hollywood these days—and TV production facilities and recording studios still flourish here. However seedy, the reality and the myth still endures.

1 HOLLYWOOD SIGN

The 50-foot-high letters that sit near the summit of Mount Lee were first erected in 1923 to advertise **Hollywoodland,** a residential development. In 1949, the deteriorating sign and its acreage were deeded to the Hollywood Chamber of Commerce, which took down the "land" to create a civic advertisement. A new sign was erected in 1978. The sign has been a favorite target of stealthy typographers: from the one who blanked out the "H" to create "Ollywood" (for Iran-contra messenger Colonel Oliver North) to those who draped the sign in a gigantic yellow ribbon to honor the US troops in Desert Storm. Nowadays, there's a high-tech security system to keep visitors at a safe distance. ♦ Mount Lee Dr (north of Mulholland Hwy)

2 LAKE HOLLYWOOD

This reservoir up in the hills offers a splendid view of the Hollywood sign, a rustic jogging trail, and a sense of what this place must have looked like a hundred years ago. ♦ Daily. Lake Hollywood Dr (east of Barham Blvd)

3 VILLAGE COFFEE SHOP

★$ The good food and warm atmosphere make the tables worth waiting for in this homey rendezvous for the area's actors, writers, and singers—the aspirants who live below the **Hollywoodland** gates and the more established who live in the hills above. ♦ American ♦ M-Sa, breakfast, lunch, and dinner. 2695 N Beachwood Dr (at Belden Dr). 323/467.5398

4 HOLLYWOOD BOWL

This natural amphitheater was developed in the 1920s with the construction of a concert shell and seating, and now hosts the summer season of the **Los Angeles Philharmonic,** visiting musicians, and jazz and pop concerts. Popular perennials include the Easter sunrise service, the Fourth of July, and closing-night concerts with fireworks. The acoustics have greatly improved over the years, but the hard seats haven't, so bring a soft cushion for comfort. The **Deck** restaurant serves supper alfresco (reservations required a week in advance); there's also **The Deli** (serving fast food, wine, and beer), as well as several refreshment stands. But to have a really fun night of it, pack a picnic and arrive early—the Bowl fills up quickly. Many local restaurants and even some hotels (**Pinot Bistro** and **Hotel Bel-Air,** to name a couple) sell great picnic baskets designed for the Bowl. Parking at the Bowl on Highland Avenue is quite expensive and chaotic; a cheaper choice is the park-and-ride lots that provide free bus service from different parts of LA. For the Deck

---

Restaurants/Clubs: Red | Hotels: Purple | Shops: Orange | Outdoors/Parks: Green | Sights/Culture: Blue

NAUGHTY NIGHTS ON SUNSET AND BEYOND

Casinos, pretty call girls, and flashy nightclubs lined the Sunset Strip from Crescent Heights to Doheny in the 1930s and 1940s, when Hollywood stars used to relax at famous clubs such as **Ciro's** and **Mocambo** on their way home from the studios to Beverly Hills. This stretch of boulevard (part of the city of West Hollywood since 1984) was governed by LA County, and was free of city restrictions on alcohol, gambling, and prostitution. A steady stream of limousines dropped off glamorous carousers for dining, drinking, and dancing. Some stars kept apartments at the **Château Marmont** or the Art Deco tower that is now **The Argyle** hotel.

In the 1960s, the strip was a haven for hipsters and flower children. Today it's lined with record shops, rock clubs, bookstores, sidewalk cafés, restaurants, and cool boutiques. The hottest spots on the Strip are **The Sky Bar** (at Mondrian), **House of Blues,** the **Key Club,** and the super sizzlers: **Star Shoes** on Hollywood Boulevard, **White Lotus** on Cahuenga, and **Here Lounge** on Robertson Boulevard. This stretch of the Strip is famous for its eye-catching, over-the-top, custom-made billboards, referred to in the industry as "vanity boards." Or head over to the **Beauty Bar** on North Cahuenga; **Ruby** on Hollywood Boulevard; **Blue** on Las Palmas, or **El Cid** on West Sunset Boulevard for Flaming Flamenco plus.

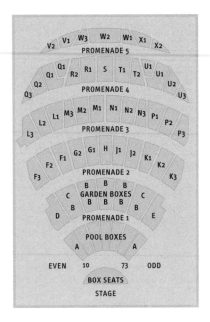

restaurant and picnic baskets (order the previous day), call 323/851.3588. ♦ Grounds daily until dusk, July-September. 2301 N Highland Ave (at Cahuenga Blvd W). 323/850.2000; www.hollywoodbowl.org

At the Hollywood Bowl:

HOLLYWOOD BOWL MUSEUM

Exhibitions on the history of the Bowl include original drawings of concert shell prototypes by **Lloyd Wright** (son of Frank). Visitors may listen to tapes of Bowl performances in small booths. ♦ Tu-Sa. 323/850.2058. www.hollywoodbowl.org/museum

5 SAMUELS-NAVARRO HOUSE

Designed by architect **Lloyd Wright** in 1928, this house stretches horizontally along a natural ridge ending with a swimming pool (now enclosed) at one end and a garden at the other. Josh Schweitzer remodeled the private residence. ♦ 5609 Valley Oak Dr (off Verde Oak Dr)

6 LOFT TOWERS

With a nod to nearby **High Tower** (see below), Australian architects **Koning & Eizenberg** created a pair of suburban lofts, each of which comprises three 20-square-foot rooms for working and living. The 1987 residences are private. ♦ 6949 Camrose Dr (between Glencoe Way and N Sycamore Ave)

7 HIGH TOWER

This 1920 campanile is an elevator shaft that rises to the villas on either side. Stepped streets reinforce the impression of San Gimignano in the Hollywood Hills. ♦ High Tower Dr (south of Camrose Dr)

8 HOLLYWOOD HERITAGE MUSEUM

Cecil B. DeMille rented this horse barn in 1913 and used it as a set, offices, and changing rooms for *The Squaw Man,* the first feature-length movie shot in Hollywood. It originally stood at Selma Avenue and Vine Street, and was moved to its present site in 1985, where it was restored by **Hollywood Heritage** and furnished with exhibitions. ♦ Only open to the public when volunteers are on duty, so your best bet is to call before going. 2100 N Highland Ave (at Milner Ave). 323/874.2276

9 YAMASHIRO'S RESTAURANT

$$ The oldest building in LA is a 600-year-old pagoda, imported by Adolphe and Eugene Bernheimer as an ornament for the Japanese palace and gardens they built in 1913. The food here is borderline, but the sunset view is worth the climb and the price of a drink. ♦ Japanese ♦ Daily, cocktails and dinner. 1999 N Sycamore Ave (at Fitch Dr). 323/466.5125

10 FREEMAN HOUSE

The **Frank Lloyd Wright**–designed, Maya-influenced 1924 residence was completely restored by USC. ♦ 1962 Glencoe Way (between Hillcrest Rd and Camrose Dr). No public phone number

11 WHITLEY HEIGHTS

Developed in the 1920s and 1930s by Hobart J. Whitley, these old Italian villa-style houses are built into the hillside. Marion Davies, Gloria Swanson, and Ethel Barrymore are among those who once lived here. ♦ North of Franklin Ave (between Cahuenga Blvd and N Highland Ave)

12 AMERICAN FILM INSTITUTE (AFI)

Offices of the AFI and its **Center for Advanced Film Studies** now occupy what was once the campus of Immaculate Heart College. The **Louis B. Mayer Library,** open to serious film scholars, has the most extensive collection of movie scripts in the country. The AFI and its **Sony Video Center** presents regular screenings and classes, plus annual film and video festivals. ♦ 2021 N Western Ave (between Franklin Ave and Los Feliz Blvd). 323/856.7600

13 LA POUBELLE

★★$$ How to resist a brasserie that calls itself "The Garbage Pail"? French waiters shout orders to the kitchen, Edith Piaf recordings play, and owner Jacqueline Koster guides you through the menu. Crepes, omelets, and coq au vin are staples. ♦ French/Italian ♦ Daily, dinner. 5907 Franklin Ave (at N Bronson Ave). 323/465.0807

14 SOWDEN HOUSE

This private residence was designed by Frank Lloyd Wright's son, **Lloyd Wright.** Built in 1926, its décor is a fusion of Maya and Deco themes. The house is built around a courtyard with a unique entrance through a cave framed with decorative concrete blocks. ♦ 5121 Franklin Ave (between N Normandie Ave and Laughlin Park Dr)

15 WATTLES MANSION & GARDENS

Hollywood Heritage restored this 1905 house and the formal gardens, which were a top tourist attraction in Hollywood's early years. Just beyond is a wilderness area that links up to **Runyon Canyon Park.** The staff is all volunteer workers, and because of this you never know when someone will be on duty to show you around. When someone is there, he or she will be happy to give you the five-minute tour. ♦ 1824 N Curson Ave (north of Hollywood Blvd). 323/874.4005 (or check at the Hollywood Studio Museum). 323/874.2276

16 CASE STUDY APARTMENTS

Adele Naude Santos's design for a villagelike cluster of low-income apartments was chosen by the Museum of Contemporary Art to be built as homage to the Case Study House Program that *Arts+Architecture* magazine ran from 1945 to 1966. ♦ Franklin and N La Brea Aves

17 IVAR AVENUE

This block above Yucca Street still has many 1920s and 1930s apartment buildings. The **Parva Sed** is where Nathanael West lived when he originally conceived the plan for *Day of the Locust.* Farther up the block is **El Nido,** the fictional home of the luckless screenwriter played by William Holden in the movie *Sunset Boulevard.* ♦ Between Yucca St and Hollywood Fwy

18 5390 FRANKLIN AVENUE

This flamboyant apartment building, formerly the **Château Elysée,** is now owned by the Church of Scientology. ♦ Between N Harvard Blvd and N Western Ave

19 MANN'S CHINESE THEATRE

Master showman Sid Grauman commissioned **Meyer & Holler** to create this fanciful Chinese temple in 1927 so that he would have a new stage for his prologues—extravagant spectacles keyed to the movies they accompanied. Legend has it that Norma Talmadge accidentally stepped into the wet cement of the forecourt, inspiring Sid to round up Mary Pickford and Douglas Fairbanks to repeat the trick with their hands and feet, thus inaugurating the world's largest autograph album. He also created the first gala premiere, lining Hollywood Boulevard with klieg lights as the limousines arrived for the opening night of DeMille's *King of Kings* on 18 May 1927.

> Charlie Chaplin built an eclectic group of cottages for workers at his La Brea Avenue studio, including the Hampton Towers in West Hollywood.

Restaurants/Clubs: Red | Hotels: Purple | Shops: Orange | Outdoors/Parks: Green | Sights/Culture: Blue

♦ 6925 Hollywood Blvd (between Orchid Ave and N Orange Dr). 323/464.8111

At Mann's Chinese Theatre:

GRAVE LINE TOURS

This ghoulish tour—in a classic Cadillac hearse—is a treat for lovers of gallows humor. The two-hour treks of the homes where stars met their maker are an improvement on the conventional trips around the houses from which stars have long since moved. Tours depart Tuesday through Sunday from the east side of the theater. ♦ Reservations 323/469.4149, information 323/469.3127

20 HOLLYWOOD ENTERTAINMENT MUSEUM

A state-of-the-art homage to Hollywood provided through interactive exhibits and video presentations where you can take a tour of the original *Star Trek: The Next Generation* and *Cheers* sets. ♦ Admission. Th-Tu, 11AM-6PM; Tu-Su, 10AM-6PM; closed Mondays and holidays. 7021 Hollywood Blvd (between Sycamore Ave and Orange Dr). 323/465.7900. www.hollywoodmuseum.com &

20 GALAXY CONCERT THEATRE

You get it all at this popular concert hall: Eric Burdon, SR-71, Nazareth, the Bellamy Brothers, Ultimate Pro Wrestling, and more under one galactic roof. Open depending on attractions, so call the concert hotline (714/957.0600) or check it out online at www.galaxytheatre.com. ♦ 7021 Hollywood Blvd (between Sycamore Ave and Orange Dr). 213/480.3232

20 THE KNITTING FACTORY

This happening nightspot features big-name entertainers on one stage and lesser knowns in the intimate AlterKnit lounge. There are also "web booths" for surfing for music on the information highway, interactive video links with the club's original New York City branch, and a restaurant serving eclectic cuisine. ♦ Cover. Daily, lunch and dinner. Showtime's usually 8 or 9PM, bar's open until 2AM. Reservations needed. 7021 Hollywood Blvd (beneath the Galaxy Theatre)

21 LAS PALMAS

One of the hottest spots in town, this place rocks with stars, stargazers, and Y-Gens over 21. The beat is hip-hop with a jungle theme, the vibes are sexy, and the mood is rad. Keep an eye open for Britney—you never know what she might be wearing (or not). There are two bars and a patio on which to chill out. ♦ Hours vary, so call ahead. Reservations strongly suggested. To ensure entry, dress the part (trendy, chic). 1714 N Las Palmas Ave

(at Hollywood Blvd, two blocks from Highland Ave). 323/464.0171

22 MUSSO AND FRANK GRILL

★★★$$ Opened in 1919, Hollywood's oldest restaurant has hosted plenty of celebrities over the years. Gossip columnists Hedda Hopper and Louella Parsons held court here, and Dashiell Hammett, Papa Hemingway, F. Scott Fitzgerald, William Faulkner, and Aldous Huxley dined regularly at what was called the "Algonquin Round Table West." The place remains reassuring, with its paneled permanence, great martinis, and comfortable counter for solitary diners. The short ribs or macaroni and cheese (made with cheddar, Parmesan, and breadcrumbs) are sure winners. Waiters can be brusque unless they know you, however. ♦ American ♦ Tu-Sa, breakfast, lunch, and dinner. Reservations recommended for lunch and dinner. 6667 Hollywood Blvd (between Cherokee and N Las Palmas Aves). 323/467.7788 &

22 BOOK CITY

A huge selection of new and used books on all topics is stocked here. ♦ Daily. 6627 Hollywood Blvd (between Whitley and Cherokee Aves). 323/466.2525. Also at 308 N San Fernando Blvd (between E Palm Ave and E Magnolia Blvd), Burbank. 818/848.4417

23 JANES HOUSE

Constructed in 1903, this last survivor of the Victorian mansions that lined the boulevard until the 1920s was the home of a family-run school whose famous students included the children of Douglas Fairbanks, Cecil B. DeMille, Thomas Ince, and Charlie Chaplin. It is currently an official **Visitors Information Center.** ♦ M-Sa. 6600 Hollywood Blvd (between N Hudson and Whitley Aves). 323/461.9520

24 JOSEPH'S CAFE

★$ This long-established favorite serves fabulous gyros, lentil soup, and rice pudding. ♦ Greek/Mediterranean ♦ M-Sa, breakfast, lunch, and dinner. 1775 Ivar Ave (at Yucca St). 323/462.8697

25 HOLLYWOOD PALACE

This 1920s Art Deco landmark looks great after a million-dollar face-lift. The 1,200-seat, bi-level dance club boasts a state-of-the-art light-and-sound system and performances by groups like Green Day, Sterolab, and Nine Inch Nails (if you haven't heard of 'em, it's probably not your scene). There's a strict dress code: Be cool, but not in bad taste. ♦ Performances F and Sa nights, other events scheduled during week; call for program. Vine St (between Hollywood Blvd and Yucca St). 323/467.4571, recorded hot line 323/462.3000. www.hollywoodpalace.com

26 PANTAGES THEATER

Once a movie palace, the Pantages is now a showcase for Broadway musicals such as the Tony award–winning production of *The Lion King*. It's a dazzling example of adaptive reuse. Originally designed by **B. Marcus Priteca** in 1929, the theater rivals the **Wiltern** (see page 57) as an anthology of zigzag Moderne, from the vaulted lobby to the fretted ceiling of the auditorium, designed by Anthony B. Heinsbergen. ◆ 6233 Hollywood Blvd (between Argyle Ave and Vine St). 323/468.1770. www.nederlander.com

26 EXINCENDO

★★$$ This two-floor restaurant is enclosed by crimson walls illuminated by soft red lights, providing a distinctive mood to savor the interesting take on American food. The seared sea scallops accompanied by wild mushrooms with a truffle vinaigrette and the roasted rack of lamb with butternut squash and chestnut honey are wise choices. So is the chocolate ooze cake. There's a fun bar filled with a Gen-X crowd and lots of attitude. ◆ American with a twist ◆ M-F, lunch; Tu-Sa, dinner. Reservations suggested. 6282 Hollywood Blvd (across the street from the Pantages between Argyle Ave and Vine St). 323/465.3257 &

26 COLLECTOR'S BOOK STORE

For film fans and collectors, this shop is a treasure trove of movie books, stills, and memorabilia. ◆ Tu-Sa. 6225 Hollywood Blvd (between Argyle Ave and Vine St). 323/467.3296

26 CAPITOL RECORDS TOWER

An example of programmatic architecture on an epic scale, this 1954 tower by **Welton Becket & Associates** looks like a stack of records topped by a stylus. A rooftop beacon flashes the word "Hollywood" in Morse code at night. In December, it's lit to create Hollywood's tallest Christmas tree. ◆ 1750 Vine St (at Yucca St). www.hollywoodandvine.com

27 HOLLYWOOD BOULEVARD

Originally laid out as Prospect Avenue and lined with ornate mansions, this stretch of road was rebuilt in the 1920s and 1930s as the movie colony's Main Street. For a decade or so, it boasted fashionable stores, hotels, and restaurants, though the movie stars came out only at night—for gala premieres at **Mann's Chinese Theatre** (see page 65) and other movie palaces. Nearly 50 years of decline have given the boulevard a seedy reputation, but the architecture has remained almost intact. Hollywood Heritage, a lively preservation organization, secured official recognition for the heart of the boulevard as a National Historic District—though this may not protect it from massive redevelopment. Look up to enjoy such treasures as the Gothic Moderne tower of the **Security Pacific Bank** at Highland Avenue, the lively zigzag façades flanking **Frederick's of Hollywood**'s purple tower, the streamlined drugstore on the corner of Cahuenga Boulevard, and the 1933 marquee of the **Hollywood Theatre** (which now houses the **Guinness World of Records Museum**). Look down for the 2,200-plus terrazzo stars of the **Walk of Fame,** commemorating celebrities from every branch of entertainment.

27 HOLLYWOOD ROOSEVELT HOTEL

$$ This restored 1927 landmark was the site of the first Academy Awards ceremony and the former social hub of the movie colony. Errol Flynn invented his recipe for gin in a back room of the barber's shop; Scott Fitzgerald, Ernest Hemingway, and Salvador Dalí patronized the **Cinegrill** upstairs; and Bill "Bojangles" Robinson taught Shirley Temple to tap dance up the lobby staircase—or so the legends go. The two-story Spanish Colonial lobby with its painted ceiling is worth stopping in to see, and **Theodore's** restaurant off the lobby and the Cinegrill (which offers live entertainment nightly) are both sleekly retro in feeling. All of the 335 rooms are soundproofed to drown out the street noises, and come with coffeemakers, minibars, hair dryers, and other amenities. David Hockney painted the Olympic-size pool. ◆ 7000 Hollywood Blvd (at N Orange Dr). 323/466.7000, 800/950.7667 in CA, 800/858.2244 in the US; fax 323/462.8056. www.hollywoodroosevelt.com &

27 LA FILM PERMIT OFFICE

Free daily listings of location filming are available here. ◆ M-F. 6922 Hollywood Blvd (between N Highland Ave and N Orange Dr), Suite 602. 323/485.5324

28 PACIFIC EL CAPITAN THEATER

Fields & Devereaux Architects artfully restored this 1926 single-screen movie palace, a magnificent blend of Baroque, Moorish, East Indian, and Churrigueresque ornamentation created by architects **Morgan, Walls & Clements** and theater designer G. Albert Lansburgh. A team of conservators re-created the stenciled ceiling coves, cornice moldings, and balcony boxes. Thanks to Disney's Buena Vista Pictures and Pacific Theaters, the preservation saved the elaborate interior from being partitioned into soulless multiscreen boxes. Today, perhaps in gratitude to its

---

Restaurants/Clubs: Red | Hotels: Purple | Shops: Orange | Outdoors/Parks: Green | Sights/Culture: Blue

rescuer, the theater shows mostly Disney movies. Call for showings. ◆ 6838 Hollywood Blvd (between N Highland Ave and N Orange Dr). 323/467.7674

28 HOLLYWOOD & HIGHLAND

This $567 million retail and entertainment complex at Hollywood Boulevard and Highland Avenue was spearheaded by TrizecHahn. The 1.3-million-square-foot facility features a pair of elephants replicated from the 1916 D. W. Griffith movie *Intolerance* looming over the central courtyard. The massive production also includes the **Renaissance Hollywood Hotel** (see below), four movie theaters, nightclubs, a broadcast studio, and major shopping outlets such as Duty Free Stores, Aveda, Tommy Hilfiger, Louis Vuitton, Origins, Gap, Banana Republic, Benetton, Swatch, Café Med, Celine, a trendy bowling club, and others. But the main attraction is the spiffy 3,300-seat **Kodak Academy Awards Theatre,** the new home of the Oscars. Located on the northwest corner of Hollywood Boulevard and Highland Avenue, the facility was designed specifically for the annual event, with a dramatic entrance, cable tunnels, a red terrazzo floor, and a Governors Ballroom with views of Hollywood Boulevard and the Hollywood Hills. During the other 364 days of the year the theater hosts concerts and stage performances. Guided tours are offered daily, every half hour, and worth it just for a look at the 26 four-foot-wide by five-foot-high images of such Oscar winners as Grace Kelly, Jack Nicholson, Tom Hanks, and Marlon Brando. 323/308.6300, 323/308.6363. www.kodaktheatre.com. ◆ 6834 Hollywood Blvd (between N Highland and N La Brea Aves). Information 323/460.2626. www.hollywoodandhighland.com

Within the Hollywood & Highland Complex:

LUCKY STRIKE LANES

It's a bowling alley, it's a restaurant, it's hip, it's happening, and it's a lot of fun. Created by entrepreneurs Steven and Gillian Foster, this 12-lane upscale bowling alley/lounge attracts a high-visibility celebrity crowd and young trendoids who go as much to be seen as to throw strikes. Comforts include a custom lounge, billiards tables, outdoor smoking patio, private VIP room, and a bustling bar/restaurant (which is more like a food service than a sit-down facility). The food, which is served at the lanes or at the bar, is what you'd expect and a little more—burgers, hot dogs, and pizzas, skewered rock shrimp, baked clams, tomato cheese s'mores, Buffalo wings with a blue cheese dip—you get the picture. There are plenty of dessert options to fuel you for action. ◆ Daily, 11AM-2AM. 323/467.7776. www.bowlluckystrike.com

28 THE RENAISSANCE HOLLYWOOD HOTEL

$$$ This 640-room Marriott International hotel, which was under construction at press time, is the cornerstone of Hollywood's revitalization efforts. The 22-story building was designed in a midcentury/modern style with all the creature comforts a traveler would want: fitness center, swimming pool, restaurant, lounge, 50,000 square feet of multifunctional meeting space, a 30,000-square-foot Grand Ballroom with food catered by Wolfgang Puck, and a few over-the-top features, such as a pool deck that rises 50 feet in the air and a 3,000-square-foot Presidential suite with floor-to-ceiling glass windows. ◆ 6834 Hollywood Blvd, northwest corner of Hollywood Blvd and Orange, adjacent to Mann's Chinese Theatre. Pre-opening offices: 310/856.1205, 800-HOTELS-1. www.renaissancehotels.com

29 GUINNESS WORLD OF RECORDS MUSEUM

Oddities and world-record displays are featured in the refurbished **Hollywood Theatre,** Hollywood's first movie house. The most popular exhibit is the $30,000 tribute to singer Michael Jackson's *Thriller* album, which set a record when it sold 48 million copies. ◆ Admission. M-Th, Su, until midnight; F, Sa, until 2AM. 6764 Hollywood Blvd (between N McCadden Pl and N Highland Ave). 323/463.6433. www.guinessrecords.com

29 THE HOLLYWOOD WAX MUSEUM

Only in LA can you find more than 200 wax replicas of such famous figures as *Playboy*'s Hugh Hefner, who took his enshrined spot alongside a bevy of wax beauties. A bit spacey, you bet, but hey, this is Tinseltown. So go on over and take a look at the eerie likenesses of Marilyn Monroe, Pamela Anderson, Bob Hope, various sports figures, and even Hannibal the Cannibal Lecter, aptly ensconced in the Chamber of Horrors. ◆ Admission. Daily, 10AM to midnight, until 2AM on weekends. 6767 Hollywood Blvd (just east of N Highland Ave). 323/462.8860

29 HOLLYWOOD HISTORY MUSEUM

Housed in the recently restored Art Deco–style Max Factor Building, the museum's exhibits take you on a tour of Hollywood past and present. There's a restaurant, gift shop, and lounge. ◆ Admission. Daily. 1666 N Highland Ave (north of Hollywood Blvd). 323/464.7776, www.hollywoodhistorymuseum.com

30 EGYPTIAN THEATER

Sid Grauman's first Off-Broadway movie palace, designed by **Meyer & Holler,** was inspired by the 1922 discovery of King Tut's tomb, complete with sphinxes, hieroglyphics, and winged cobras adorning the walls. Facing competition from multiplex movie houses, owner United Artists shut down the theater in 1992, but thanks to local preservationists, this national institution is making a comeback under **American Cinematheque.** Plans include restoring the theater to its original splendor, with period signs, a marquee, and an organ. Films on the history of Hollywood, independent and foreign flicks, documentaries, and classic film festivals will fill the schedule. ♦ 6712 Hollywood Blvd (between N Las Palmas Ave and N McCadden Pl)

30 Pig 'n Whistle

★★$$ This historic 1927 landmark was recently restored to its original glory, and now looks as it did when movie stars and moguls flooded the place after attending premieres at the Egyptian Theater. Designed by noted architects **Morgan, Walls & Clements**, the restaurant relives the glamour that was Hollywood with a refurbished marquee sporting a dancing-pig-and-fife motif, hand-painted tiles, and hand-carved wood. The food is Hollywood bistro, with Scottish salmon, peppered filet, shepherd's pie, seafood salads, and an original selection of Pig 'n Whistle soda fountain drinks. After 10PM the neon sign changes from Pig 'n Whistle to **NuBar** when the restaurant turns into a nightclub/martini bar. ♦ Hollywood Bistro ♦ Su-Th, 11AM-midnight; F, Sa, 11AM-2AM. 6714 Hollywood Blvd (between N Las Palmas and N Highland Aves, on the west side of the Egyptian Theater). 323/463.0000

30 Universal News Agency

This newsstand is one of the best sources of hometown (whether Bangor or Bangkok) newspapers and international magazines. ♦ Daily. 1655 N Las Palmas Ave (at Hollywood Blvd). 323/467.3850

31 Les Deux Café

★★★$$$$ Ooh la la! It doesn't get more French than this. We're talking waiters with an attitude and food that makes you want to sing praises to the chef. The entrance is in a dark parking lot, but don't let the location fool you: Eating here is an experience you won't want to miss if you really care about good food. The crowd is beautiful, with lots of models and showbiz types, all dressed in trendy black outfits, who arrive late and hang around the patio bar before dining. The menu, which changes frequently according to what's fresh and available, is French bistro with hearty soups, rigatoni with white bean

ragout, and great desserts. ♦ French. ♦ Reservations *mai oui*! 1638 N Las Palmas (between Sunset and Hollywood Blvds). 323/465.0509

32 Larry Edmunds

A mecca for lovers of film and theater, this place has a wide selection of books, posters, and stills, but it's not all it used to be. ♦ M-Sa. 6644 Hollywood Blvd (between N Hudson and Cherokee Aves). 323/463.3273

32 Frederick's of Hollywood

The 1935 purple-and-pink Art Deco tower designed by **Frank Falgien** and **Bruce Marteney** is an appropriate symbol for the company's flamboyantly sexy apparel. During the 1992 riots, thieves made off with, among other items, Madonna's studded brassiere from the **Celebrity Lingerie Hall of Fame.** A few days later, a guilt-plagued young man handed a priest a bag containing Ava Gardner's pantaloons and a bra belonging to actress Katey Sagal, saying he was too afraid to return them himself. It took a few years longer for the Madonna bustier to find its way back. ♦ Daily; F until 9PM. 6608 Hollywood Blvd (between N Hudson and Cherokee Aves). 323/466.8506, 24-hour mail orders 800/323.9525

32 Hollywood Toys and Costumes

LA's largest and best place for compulsive exhibitionists rents Halloween costumes year-round, along with masks, wigs, and all kinds of makeup. ♦ Daily. 6562 Hollywood Blvd (between N Hudson and Cherokee Aves). 323/465.3119

33 Los Angeles Contemporary Exhibitions (LACE)

This nonprofit interdisciplinary arts organization offers diverse gallery and community art programs. Since 1977, the group has presented significant audio/video performances, sculpture, drawings, paintings, and installation pieces by both emerging and well-known artists. There's also an art periodical bookstore. ♦ W-Su. 6522 Hollywood Blvd (between Wilcox and N Hudson Aves). 323/957.1777

34 Frances Goldwyn Regional Branch Library

To replace the Hollywood Library, which was destroyed by arson, **Frank Gehry** created this cluster of luminous boxes (the illumination comes from light bouncing off water in shallow reflecting pools) in 1986. So outdoorsy is the overall feel that you hardly

---

Restaurants/Clubs: Red | Hotels: Purple | Shops: Orange | Outdoors/Parks: Green | Sights/Culture: Blue

notice how well the building is protected—
"tighter security than the American Embassy
designed for Damascus," says the architect. ♦
M-Sa; M, W until 8PM. 1623 N Ivar Ave
(between Vine St and Hollywood Blvd).
323/467.1821

35 JAMES DOOLITTLE THEATER

This spot is one of the best places in LA to
enjoy one-person shows and quality drama. ♦
1615 Vine St (between Selma Ave and
Hollywood Blvd). 323/462.6666

36 DADDY'S

This sexy little late lounge, with its 28-foot-
long curvaceous bar, curving interior, and lack
of attitude, provides a cool hangout for legal-
age Y'ers (21 or over) and industry types who
sit for hours in double-sized moveable
ottomans, banquettes, or booths, sipping
drinks and playing the jukebox. ♦ M-Sa, 8PM-
2AM; Su, 9PM-2AM. 1610 Vine St (between
Selma Ave and Hollywood Blvd).
323/463.7777

37 HENRY FONDA THEATER

The conversion of the former **Music Box** is a
brave attempt to bring quality drama to a
depressed neighborhood. ♦ 6126 Hollywood
Blvd (between Gower St and El Centro Ave).
323/468.1700

38 BARNSDALL PARK

Located at the top of a hill and ringed by olive
trees, this oasis and cultural center is in the
flatlands of eastern Hollywood. ♦ 4800
Hollywood Blvd (between N Vermont Ave and
Edgemont St)

Within Barnsdall Park:

HOLLYHOCK HOUSE

Oil heiress Aline Barnsdall commissioned this
house—architect **Frank Lloyd Wright's** first in
LA, completed in 1920—as part of a complex
of cultural and residential structures. It has
been restored and includes many of the
original Wright furnishings. The guided tour is
interesting. ♦ Admission. Tours, Tu-Su.
323/913.4157

MUNICIPAL ART GALLERY

This exhibition space is a visual forum for
cutting-edge Southern California art. The
theater presents a lively and varied bill of
films and concerts. ♦ Admission. Tu-Su.
323/485.4581

JUNIOR ARTS CENTER

The center offers an extensive program of
sophisticated and innovative studio art
classes for children and young people ages 3
to 18. Designed for a young audience, the
gallery's changing shows emphasize

participation and activity. ♦ M-F. Gallery,
Tu-Su. 323/485.4474

39 HOLLYWOOD HIGH SCHOOL

Decorative reliefs and uplifting inscriptions
embellish the surface of these 1935
Streamline Moderne buildings. Farmers called
the $67,000 three-story Roman temple-style
school a "ridiculous piece of extravagance"
when it was being built over a century ago.
The "piece of extravagance" schooled famous
folk such as Judy Garland, Mickey Rooney,
Sally Kellerman, James Garner, and Nobelist
William Shockley—to name a few.♦ Sunset
Blvd and N Highland Ave

40 CAFE DES ARTISTES

★★$$ Picture
yourself on a
back street in
Cannes while
dining at Silvio
de Mori's idyllic
neighborhood
French bistro
with its leafy patio,
cool dining room,

and friendly service. Some of the most
delicious *plats du jour* include macaroni and
cheese, mussels, or steak with *pommes frites*.
The trendy spot attracts a young, hip, late
crowd. The Sunday brunch is very good, too.
♦ French ♦ Tu-F, lunch and dinner; Sa,
dinner; Su, brunch, lunch, and dinner.
Reservations recommended. 1534 N
McCadden Pl (between Sunset Blvd and
Selma Ave). 323/469.7300

40 STAGES TRILINGUAL THEATER

Paul Verdier produces some of LA's most
innovative theater here, including plays by
Ionesco, Marguerite Duras, and René-Daniel
DuBois, in English, French, and Spanish.
Seating is limited, so book well in advance ♦
1540 N McCadden Pl (between Sunset Blvd
and Selma Ave). General information
323/463.5356, box office 323/465.1010

41 CHATEAU MARMONT HOTEL

$$$ This 1927 Norman castle, where Greta
Garbo stayed and John Belushi died, once
guarded the approach to the Sunset Strip. The
interior of the hotel is handsome and intimate
enough to continue attracting movie and
music celebrities. The 63 accommodations
include 30 luxury suites with balconies and
views, and cottages around the pool. The
dining room is open 24 hours, as is room
service. If you're into vintage wheels and
power cars, take a peek into the parking
garage: It will blow you away. ♦ 8221
Sunset Blvd (at Marmont La), West
Hollywood. 323/656.1010, 800/242.8328;
fax 323/655.5311; email: chateau@aol.com

42 COCONUT TEASZER

This funky, Generation Y–powered rock 'n' roll joint is a disco-dancing madhouse on weekends, with beer and food included in the cover charge. ♦ Cover. M-Th, Su, until 2AM; F, Sa, until 4AM. 8117 Sunset Blvd (at Laurel Canyon Blvd). 323/654.4773

43 GREENBLATT'S DELICATESSEN

★$ This haven for expatriate New Yorkers serves typical deli fare (pastrami, cheesecake, cold cuts, sides, etc.) to eat in, take home, or bring to the Hollywood Bowl in the summer. There's a full bar, a nifty wine cellar, and a friendly staff. ♦ Deli ♦ Daily until 2AM. 8017 Sunset Blvd (between N Laurel Ave and Laurel Canyon Blvd). 323/656.0606

44 SAMUEL FRENCH

Plays from Shakespeare to Stoppard as well as books on the theater are stocked in this bookstore. ♦ M-Sa. 7623 Sunset Blvd (at N Stanley Ave). 323/876.0570. Also at 11963 Ventura Blvd (between Colfax and Radford Aves), San Fernando Valley. 818/762.0535. www.samuelfrench.com

44 DAR MAGHREB

★$$$ The Arabian Nights décor and good renditions of the standard dishes (couscous, lamb, and quail) are popular with tour groups. ♦ Moroccan♦ Daily, dinner. 7651 Sunset Blvd (at N Stanley Ave). 323/876.7651

45 FALCON

★★★$$$ This lofty lair, named for Falcon Lair, the luxurious sanctuary of silent-film star Rudolph Valentino, throbs with young sophisticates decked out in designer black. The minimalist décor, outdoor patio, and perceptive wait staff add to the charm. The food doesn't hurt either. Get in the mood with an exotic martini—chocolate espresso, keylime, or Topaz. Then savor starters such as pan-seared diver scallops, beef carpaccio, or ahi tuna and keep the juices flowing with wild mushroom, grilled chicken, and goat cheese pizza, lobster chopped salad, herb-crusted pork tenderloin, or red-wine-braised bee short ribs, then finish with a succulent savory. ♦ Su-W, 7PM to midnight; Th-Sa, to 1 AM. California ♦ Reservations required. Valet parking. 7113 Sunset Blvd (at Poinsettia). 323/850.5350. www.falconslair.com.

46 CROSSROADS OF THE WORLD

Designed in 1936 by **Robert Derrah,** this is a paradigm of fantasy architecture in pristine condition: a liner (center building) sailing into a foreign port (surrounding English, French, Spanish, and Moorish shops). ♦ 6671 Sunset Blvd (at N Las Palmas Ave)

47 CHAN DARA

★$ This pioneering Thai restaurant has a large and loyal clientele, so you may have to wait to eat. Best bets from the long menu include *mee krob* (sweet fried noodles), satay, squid with mint and chili, and wonderfully spicy soups. ♦ Thai ♦ M-F, Su, lunch and dinner; Sa, dinner. Reservations recommended for five or more. 1511 Cahuenga Blvd (between Sunset Blvd and Selma Ave). 323/464.8585

47 BEAUTY BAR

Only in LA or Hollywood (or New York, where it originated) could you find a bar where you can get a pedicure or manicure with your martini. Well, actually, just order a froufrou drink like a Shampoo, Prell, or Platinum and the preening's on the house. No joke! It's a no-brainer that the '60s-styled place, with its hair dryers, retro bar stools, and vintage fixtures, attracts a young crowd, mostly single women (so if you're looking . . .). ♦ Doors open at 6PM and close 2AM most nights. 1638 Cahuenga Blvd (between Selma Ave and Hollywood Blvd). 323/464.7676

47 SPACE 6507 HOLLYWOOD

This is the spot for some late-night fun and lots of action. The no-nonsense minimalist interior has a full bar and spacious dance floor, and live music is performed every night. An imaginative booking policy features rap, punk, R&B, and jazz, as well as local DJ celebrities and a midnight drag show. Admission charge varies, and you must be at least 21. ♦ Cover. M-Sa until 2AM. 6507 Sunset Blvd (at Wilcox Ave). 323/466.8557

48 SUNSET & VINE

Urban renewal hits Hollywood big time with this ambitious $3\frac{1}{2}$ acre development project by The Sagan Group and Bond Capital, which will transform a large chunk of Sunset Boulevard and Vine Street into a major retail/residential/entertainment center that includes 300 residential units and 900,000 square feet of retail space with such shops as Borders Books and Bed, Bath & Beyond. 310/395.4250

48 360 (DEGREES)

Picture a penthouse way up in the sky where you can dine and dance in a glamorous setting. That's exactly what you get at this late-night club, which highlights a different musical theme each night—Wednesday it's R&B, Thursday it's hip-hop and R&B, Friday and Saturday it's jazz. ♦ Supper Club

---

Restaurants/Clubs: Red | Hotels: Purple | Shops: Orange | Outdoors/Parks: Green | Sights/Culture: Blue

♦ Tu-Su. Reservations essential. 6290 Sunset Blvd (at Vine St). 323/871.2995

49 HOLLYWOOD PALLADIUM

Famous since 1940, the Palladium has swung to the sounds of the Dorsey Brothers, Glenn Miller, Stan Kenton, and Lawrence Welk. Current attractions vary from dancing to conventions, but big names still make frequent appearances. A full bar and à la carte dinners are offered. ♦ Cover. Call for show times. 6215 Sunset Blvd (at El Centro Ave). 323/962.7600

50 HOLLYWOOD HOUNDS

This one's for dog lovers. If you're traveling with Fido or just want to treat him to a "pawdicure," this canine day spa is the place to go. You can board your pups, throw them a birthday party or barkmitvah, or even walk them down the aisle in holy muttramony at this wild and wonderful one-of-a-kind facility. There's even pick-up and delivery from your home or hotel. ♦ 8218 Sunset Blvd (just west of Crescent Hts and across the street from the Chateau Marmont). 332/650.5551

50 THE FALLS

★★$$$ Tucked away in a house once occupied by Charlie Chaplin sits an ornate retro-Hollywood supper club embellished with Italian marble, chenille, and hand-carved wood. A private VIP room offers a view of a wild outdoor dining area and a cascading candlelit waterfall. More than just a place to eat, it's a hip nightspot, dance club, cigar club (in the special Crystal Lounge), and a mecca for a young, ultra-hip/Hollywood crowd who swarm around its four bars. The menu created by former L'Orangerie chef Seth Meo features lamb in a puff pastry, Sonoma duck, Kansas City strip steak with sautéed spinach, and macaroni and cheese with horseradish sauce along with the usual fish and meats with extraordinary touches. Weekends rock, but be sure to don your hippest outfit and be cool. ♦ Continental ♦ Tu-Sa, dinner. Reservations required. Valet parking available. 8210 Sunset Blvd (on the south side of the boulevard, one block west of Crescent Heights). 323/822.2082

51 GAUCHO GRILL

★$ Good, solid Argentinean-style steaks and chicken are smothered in garlic and served with French fries (or rice and salad). The décor encourages quick meals. Wear earplugs; it's loud. ♦ Argentinean ♦ Daily, lunch and dinner. 7980 Sunset Blvd (at N Laurel Ave), 323/656.4152. Also at 11754 San Vicente Blvd (at Gorham Ave) 310/447.7898; 11838 Ventura Blvd (between Blue Canyon Dr and Carpenter Ave), San Fernando Valley. 323/508.1030

51 8000 SUNSET BOULEVARD

This complex of shops and restaurants looks like a modern take on Art Deco. Its biggest tenant is the **Virgin Megastore** (323/650.8666), the first US link in the international chain of music shops. Other noteworthy establishments include **Buzz** (323/650.7742), serving dynamite espressos and pastries in an outdoor setting; a **Wolfgang Puck Cafe** (323/650.7300), offering designer pizzas, pastas, and salads; **Los Angeles Sporting Club** (323/650.1166), purveyors of hip clothing for the "lifestyle-conscious" (such as workout wear, jeans, active wear, and accessories); **Sam Ash** (323/654.4922), a musical instrument megastore and more; and **Crunch** (323/654.4550), a branch of the New York health club. Those preoccupied with pampering can indulge themselves at **Burke Williams Day Spa** (323/822.9007). ♦ Daily. At N Laurel Ave

52 DIRECTORS GUILD OF AMERICA

This overpowering curvilinear bronze-glass tower is a textbook example of how not to build on Sunset. Constructed in 1989, it is out of scale and character with everything around it. It does have three excellent auditoriums, though, which are currently being used by the **American Cinematheque** (323/461.9622) for public programs. ♦ 7920 Sunset Blvd (between N Fairfax and N Hayworth Aves). 310/289.2000

Sunset Room

53 SUNSET ROOM

★★★$$$ The Cuban-style room sizzles to a salsa beat and is frequented by the body-pierced, skintight-clad, and tightly wound, who are there to see and be ogled. It's a club, it's a restaurant, and it's a fun spot to go if you can get by the surly doormen. Just be or look young and dress cool. The fine food is worth the effort and so are the people-watching ops. Menu winners include the carrot and ginger soup, glazed Chilean sea bass marinated in soy sauce and sake, and the warm apple tart. ♦ French with a California cuisine twist ♦ Reservations a must. Tu-Sa, dinner; dancing in the lounge on weekends. 1430 N Cahuenga Blvd (one-half block south of Sunset Blvd). 323/463.0004 ₺

54 ARCLIGHT HOLLYWOOD & CINERAMA DOME

This amazing theater complex is showcased by the Conerama Dome. Fourteen other screens show the latest films on techno-advanced equipment using the latest in acoustics and sight lines. There's free parking and popcorn. 630 Sunset Blvd (at Ivar Ave). 323/464.4226. www.arclightcinemas.com

55 OFF VINE

★$$ A shark juts through the roof of this frame house, heralding such dishes as tender filet mignon, super lamb chops, pork chops, and turkey burgers with three sauces. The chocolate soufflé is a must, as is the chocolate pecan caramel pie ♦ California ♦ M-F, lunch and dinner; Sa, dinner; Su, brunch and dinner. Reservations recommended. 6263 Leland Way (between El Centro Ave and Vine St). 323/962.1900

56 PINOT HOLLYWOOD AND THE MARTINI BAR

★★★$$ Immensely successful LA chef Joachim Splichal—the guiding force behind Patina, Pinot Bistro, Cafe Pinot, and Pinot Bistro Hollywood—created this charming bistro, decorated in rich woods, velvet drapes, and deep-pile carpeting. Consistently excellent, the hearty French menu includes such tasty items as butter brioche with chanterelle mushrooms, roasted onion, and parsley sauce; New Zealand snapper; escargots; orange-infused seafood risotto; grilled veal chops; and garlic-soaked prawns. You're more apt to spy celebrities at lunch, when they are working at or visiting the studios. ♦ French Bistro ♦ M-F, lunch and dinner; Sa, dinner. Reservations recommended. 1448 Gower St (at Sunset Blvd). 323/461.8800 &

57 STARSTEPS

A 40,000-pound steel sculpture by artist John David Mooney has been perched atop the **Metromedia TV** studio since 1981. Brightly illuminated at night, it seems to float above the freeway. ♦ Sunset Blvd (between N Wilton Pl and Hollywood Fwy)

58 PARU'S

★$ Standouts on Paru's vegetarian menu include the *masala dosa* (a foot-long lentil flour crepe filled with potato curry), *samosas* (turnovers), and *idli* (rice pancakes with lentil gravy). ♦ Indian Vegetarian ♦ Daily, lunch and dinner. 5140 Sunset Blvd (between N Normandie Ave and N Kingsley Dr). 323/661.7600

The Standard

59 THE STANDARD HOTEL

$ This place is so hip and trendy the name is actually written upside down on the marquee. Carved out of a '60s motel, this youth-driven, 138-room hotel caters to its clientele in a big way. Generation X'ers love it for the wild and free ambience and the cool rooms, all with CD players and VCRs, cordless phones, and platform beds with condoms on the pillows. Although the price is right, the "kids" who stay here are hardly needy. The lobby rules with its pair of bubble-like glass swings, constant R&R or rap music, and a cozy corner with oversized, cushy seats and arcing lamps. There's a wacky 24-hour coffee shop and bar serving everything from sandwiches and pizza to sushi and ahi tuna. It attracts a wild-and-crazy crowd all through the night. There's also a smoking room, barbershop, gift shop, pink pool on a wide-open deck, and day passes to nearby Crunch, the hottest health club in town. And get this: the housekeepers don't rev up their vacuums until noon. ♦ 8300 Sunset Blvd, West Hollywood (between N Sweetzer Ave and Olive Dr). 323/650.9090; fax 323/650.2820; www.standardhotel.com. A second Standard Hotel is located in downtown LA. This 200-room branch of Andre Balazs's hotel empire provides some rooms specially designed for the NBA, with 1,000 square feet of space, nine-foot beds, and huge bathrooms with eight-foot-long tubs. Other accommodations cater to a young, hip, corporate clientele. There's also a Bond Street restaurant straight out of the Big Apple, a spa, a gym, and a pool. And it's hot, hot, hot!

60 VILLA D'ESTE APARTMENTS

This 1928 structure is one of several lushly planted courtyard apartments in Los Angeles that evoke romantic Mediterranean villas. Other cherished examples are located within walking distance at **1400** and **1475 Havenhurst Drive, 8225 Fountain Avenue,** and **1338 North Harper Avenue.** All are private residences. ♦ 1355 Laurel Ave (between Fountain Ave and Sunset Blvd), West Hollywood

61 HAMPTON'S

★$ Sink your teeth into world-class hamburgers made from freshly ground beef, half-pound turkey burgers, and an outstanding salad bar offering everything from avocados to peanut butter. ♦ American ♦ Daily, lunch and dinner. 1342 N Highland Ave

---

Restaurants/Clubs: Red | Hotels: Purple | Shops: Orange | Outdoors/Parks: Green | Sights/Culture: Blue

(between Fountain and De Longpre Aves). 323/469.1090

61 AMMO

★★★$$ One of the city's most popular catering concerns runs this neighborhood restaurant with élan. The décor is funky, with hanging paper lanterns, exposed pipes, and metal chairs. And the food's downright delicious. Go for breakfast and feast on 10-grain flapjacks, have a turkey burger for lunch, and enjoy anything from tuna tartare and beef carpaccio to grilled chicken, a double-cut pork chop, or pan-seared halibut for dinner. Or just drop by for a piece of chocolate mousse layer cake with mocha icing when you get a craving for sweets that just won't quit. ◆ American ◆ M-F, breakfast and lunch; daily, dinner; Sa, Su, brunch. Reservations suggested for dinner. 1155 N Highland Ave (between Fountain Ave and Sunset Blvd). 310/323.2666; www.ammocafe.com

62 MILLENNIUM ON SUNSET

This expansive 110,000-square-foot contemporary commercial complex stretches east from La Cienega Blvd to Sunset Plaza. An assortment of upscale shops and boutiques are housed in three separate buildings—including Madison for fine Italian shoes, O Boutique featuring French fashions, L'Occitane for cosmetics and beauty products, and Vertigo for women's clothes. There's also a Japanese restaurant called **Rika** and straight from Florida, a **Norman's** (★★★$$$) restaurant showcasing the Latin American culinary talents of famed chef, restaurateur, and celebrated cookbook author Norman Van Aken. There's also a mega-modern health club and two 300-room luxury hotels—one on the corner of Sunset and La Cienega Blvds and the other, smack in the middle of the compound—that are scheduled to open in 2005. 8560-8590 Sunset Blvd, West Hollywood

Within the Millennium:

EQUINOX

Spread out on 32,000 square feet of stunningly appointed space, this state-of-the-art exercise/health emporium burst onto the LA fitness scene when it opened in 2003. The stiff yearly fee doesn't faze its wanna-be buff membership—probably because of the dynamite design coupled with ultramodern equipment. There are panoramic views of the area from wide windows, treadmills facing big-screen TVs, a congenial staff, private trainers, and a charming, full-service spa. Not to mention a Pilates studio staffed with a Windsor Pilates team, a kids' spa, and a head-spinning variety of fitness classes from Ashtanga Yoga to Aerobagogo (an aerobic dance workout done to rock music). Guests of the Sunset Marquis Hotel receive reciprocal privileges at the health club. 310/289.1900. Also in Pasadena at 260 E Colorado Blvd, 626/685.4800, and throughout New York City. www.equinoxfitness.com

63 THE COMEDY STORE

This place is perennially packed by folks who just want to laugh and comedians who go to practice their craft before a critical audience. It is probably the most important showcase for comedians trying to break into show business. The **Main Room** presents established comics; the **Original Room** offers continuous shows of rising new comedians; and the **Belly Room** presents female talent. ◆ Two-drink minimum. Call for hours. 8433 Sunset Blvd (between N Kings and Queens Rds), West Hollywood. 323/656.6225

64 THE ARGYLE

$$$$ Originally the **Sunset Tower,** built in 1929, this landmark 16-story Art Deco architectural gem is timeless. Listed on the National Register of Historic Places, the hotel is rich in Hollywood lore (John Wayne was one former tenant of the twelfth-floor penthouse—where he reportedly kept a cow on the balcony). The hotel was restored to its original splendor in 1995 under the direction of designer David Becker, who added steel window frames and a multi-spandrelled glass exterior. The 64 guest rooms include two townhouse suites, two penthouse suites, 41 one-bedroom suites, and 19 deluxe rooms, each tastefully appointed in Art Deco style, with striking pieces imported from Italy. In-room amenities include fax/copy machines, computer modem hookups, two-line phones, robes, TV, VCR, and large marble bathrooms stocked with Aveda products. The small rooftop pool is a popular gathering place for Hollywood celebs, and there's also a health club, meeting facilities, a concierge, a bar/lounge, and a restaurant. ◆ 8358 Sunset Blvd (between N Sweetzer Ave and Olive Dr), West Hollywood. 323/654.7100, 800/225.2637; fax 323/654.9287. www.argylehotel.com

Within The Argyle:

FENIX AT THE ARGYLE

★★★$$$$ Sweeping views of Hollywood make this dining spot one of the best in town. Celebrities, film executives, and captains of industry come here to dine on such signature dishes as Tuna 3 Ways (that's yummy any style); Arctic Char in a scallion pesto sauce;

F. Scott Fitzgerald wrote *The Last Tycoon*, his great unfinished novel about Irving Thalberg and the Golden Age of Hollywood, in his Laurel Avenue apartment in West Hollywood.

Red snapper baked in banana leaves; an amazing crispy whole catfish and more. Like its parent hotel, the room is decorated in elegant Art Deco style, with black lacquer furniture, white napery, and a purple carpet; the space overlooks a patio for outdoor dining and a pool lined by a row of concrete palm trees. ♦ French ♦ M-Sa, breakfast, lunch, and dinner; Su, breakfast and brunch. Reservations required. 323/848.6677 &

65 HOUSE OF BLUES

$$ The brainchild of Isaac Tigrett and "Blues Brother" Dan Aykroyd, this is one of a chain of eatery/nightclubs that pays homage to blues music and Southern cooking. There are nightly performances of blues and blues-inspired music. Food is served in **The Porch** (★★$$), which is separated from the showroom by soundproof glass to afford peaceful enjoyment of the Southwestern comfort cuisine. Wending your way through the menu can be fun, with everything from crispy Caesar salads and blackened chicken sandwiches to cedar plank–roasted salmon with Dijon glaze, voodoo shrimp with Dixie beer, rosemary cornbread, and pan-seared crab cakes. Yummy desserts include warm chocolate-chip pie with cookie-dough ice cream and peppermint sauce, white chocolate banana bread pudding with crème Anglaise and whipped cream, and a to-die-for chocolate pecan terrine. ♦ Southern ♦ Cover varies. Restaurant: M-Sa, lunch; daily, dinner (until midnight Su-Th, 1AM on F-Sa); Su, gospel brunch and dinner. Club: daily until 2AM. 8430 Sunset Blvd (at Olive Dr), West Hollywood. 323/848.5100. www.houseofblues.com or simply www.hob.com

65 MONDRIAN

$$$ Hip hotelier Ian Shrager (owner of boutique properties such as the Paramount, Royalton, and Morgans in New York and the Delano in Miami) turned this 188-suite hotel into one of the hottest properties in town. French designer Philippe Starck was responsible for restoring this landmark building to its original splendor, dressing it up in an all-white, contemporary California look. The place rules as the too-hip spot for movie and recording industry stars, moguls, and wannabes who jam the popular **Sky Bar** or bring their drinks down to the starlit pool (drinks are served in plastic for that purpose). Reservations are not easily gotten at this outrageously expensive restaurant, although hotel guests have a better shot than non-guests. If sake's your preference, you'll find the largest selection in LA at the **Seabar**. ♦ 8440 Sunset Blvd (at Olive Dr), West Hollywood. 323/650.8999, 800/525.8029; fax 323/650.5215. www.mondrianhotel.com

Within the Mondrian:

ASIA DE CUBA

★★★$$$$ Ian Schrager picked a winner when he opened this quirky Asian/Cuban fusion restaurant. The trendoids who frequent the Sky Bar love the long, narrow dining room with its stark white walls and black-and-white lithographs. The creative menu includes duck tacos, mahi-mahi, oxtail spring rolls, black bean soup, satays, and some of the best pan-seared salmon ever made. Dieters beware. Desserts are served in huge portions, like a skyscraper of coconut and butter cream cake topped with chocolate sauce, or a banana split that serves two. ♦ Reservations vital, and earlier is better as the regulars dine fashionably late. 323/848.6000

65 THE GRAFTON

$$-$$$ According to the desk clerk, the price varies depending on occupancy of the hotel. No kidding. It could range from $119 to $300-plus a day, so call ahead. The place is about as cool as its next-door neighbor, with trendy minimalist designs and a young clientele. There are 108 rooms (including five lavish suites), all simply but nicely appointed according to feng shui. Facilities include a bistro, a stunning Venetian-influenced pool and garden with a graceful waterfall, a bar, and a fitness center. To help you get around town, there's complimentary transportation in the hotel's PT Cruiser. ♦ 8462 Sunset Blvd, West Hollywood (next door to Mondrian, near Olive Dr). 323/654.4600; fax 323/654.5918. www.graftonsunset.com

Within the Grafton:

BALBOA RESTAURANT & LOUNGE

★★$$ Over-the-top trendy with an innovative design, this is where the steaks are prime and the clientele ripe, especially at night. At least twice there have been sightings of former president Bill Clinton eating here. We've been assured it wasn't a Hollywood double. Best menu choices are the New York steak or sirloin burger. All drinks are big and potent. The lounge rocks in the evening; so if you don't go for dinner, hop over for a drink and a great scene. Be sure to dress in your coolest duds. ♦ Daily, lunch and dinner. Reservations suggested. 323/650.8383

66 ARTURO'S FLOWERS

This shop has a goofy genius for oddball promotion, and though the selection of flora is limited, the hours make this place a lifesaver

Restaurants/Clubs: **Red** | Hotels: **Purple** | Shops: **Orange** | Outdoors/Parks: **Green** | Sights/Culture: **Blue**

75

for any occasion. ◆ Daily, until 9PM. 1261 N La Brea Ave (at Fountain Ave), West Hollywood. 323/876.6482

67 MEL'S DRIVE-IN

★★$ This fun spot serves the usual diner fare—hamburgers, shakes, fries—as well as vegetarian dishes. All the action takes place indoors (sorry, no car service), with booths, counter service, and a jukebox. ◆ Daily, 24 hours. 8585 Sunset Blvd (between Londonderry Pl and Sunset Plaza Dr), West Hollywood. 310/854.7200

67 SUNSET PLAZA

A strip mall may not have been what architect **Charles Selkirk** had in mind back in the 1930s, but **Honnold and Russell** have revamped his design and created a genteel centerpiece of a cluster of exclusive stores and restaurants. Many of them have been restored to their original Colonial Revival, Neoclassical, and Regency styles. Among the style-setting establishments to shop in are **Nicole Miller** (No. 8635; 310/652.1629) for the designer's colorful clothing and accessories; **Oliver Peoples** (No. 8642; 310/657.2553) for optical-wear; **Origins** (No. 8645; 310/659.2797) for aromatherapy items and cosmetics; **Plaza Kids** (No. 8646; 310/652.1675) for the young jet set; A/X Armani Exchange (No. 8700, 310/659.0171); Hugo Boss Shop (No. 8625, 310/360.6931); Dolce & Gabbana (No. 8641, 310/360.7272); Club Monaco (cool clothes for men and women) (No. 8569, 310/659.3821). ◆ 8589-8720 Sunset Blvd (at Sunset Plaza Dr), West Hollywood. 310/652.7137

At Sunset Plaza:

CAFE MED

★★$ **Bice** restaurant's Roberto Riggeri also owns this fun indoor-outdoor café for the budget conscious. Daily specials might include rack of lamb, risotto with seafood, and Dover sole. ◆ Mediterranean ◆ Daily, lunch and dinner. Reservations recommended for large parties. No. 8615. 310/652.0445 ♿

WATHNE

Formerly Madeleine Gallay, this sartorial accessory and leather goods outlet is great for upscale gifts. ◆ M-Sa. No. 8710. 310/358.9500

LE DÔME

★★★★$$$$ This legendary power drinking/dining establishment, where recording industry bigwigs and celebrity hotshots hang, looks better than ever after a $2 million makeover by noted restaurant designer Dodd Mitchell. The dramatic, 600-year-old Tuscan villa–like décor, while over the top, somehow manages to maintain Le Dôme's inimitable classic style. Mitchell remodeled the popular circular bar using an up-lit Italian marble top with a firebox that glows from below and surrounding it with 200-year-old European stone columns. He also removed the restaurant's signature rotunda, exposing the original wood rafter ceilings. The front patio now spans the entire length of the building. The entrance has been dramatized with tall archways made of carved stone and concrete. The lower level of the restaurant now resembles a Champagne cave from France. A new penlight-illuminated rooftop lounge allows smokers a pretty place to puff. Mitchell's interior design divides the restaurant into five intimate rooms bathed in brick and cobblestone. Executive chef Sam Marvin completes the leitmotif with his creative California/French menu. Best bets begin with goat cheese gnocchi or vertical of caviar, a beluga lentil dish with warm fingerling potatoes, pickled red onion, and endive prosciutto, followed by a main course of dry aged New York steak, a buttery veal chop, or steamed turbot. For dessert, the soufflés are supreme. ◆ California/French ◆ M-Sa, lunch and dinner. Reservations a must. 310/659.6919

OLEHENRIKSEN

This peaceful Japanese-style day spa provides the perfect panacea after a busy day shopping or sightseeing. Spend a whole or half day of salubrious pleasures that begin with a leisurely soak in a scented hydrotherapy tub surrounded by lighted candles (there are actually two tubs, so bring a close friend). Then have a superb hot rock massage, sports rub, incredible facial, or any of a number of top-notch treatments personally created by Danish dynamo Ole Henriksen, skin care guru to the stars. We do mean big-name celebs, so keep your eyes open if you're into stargazing. ◆ 8622A West Sunset Blvd, (in Sunset Plaza on the south side of Sunset Blvd, West Hollywood). 310/854.7700. ww.olehenriksen.com. OleHenriksen treatments are also available at Shutters at the Beach in Santa Monica in a sparkling new facility designed by Michael Smith. 1 Pico Blvd (at Appian Way). 310/458.0030. A word of advice: If you go to one of his day spas be sure to pick up supplies of OleHenriksen's botanically based product line Face/Body—perhaps some of the best beauty products available. And when you need more, just call 800/327.0331.

68 SUNSET MARQUIS

$$$$ This oasis hidden in the midst of Hollywood is *the* place for show and music biz types. Billy Joel, U2, Bruce Springsteen, and

the like come for such perks as 24-hour security and room service, multiline phones, and a workout room with two trainers. There are 106 suites and 12 palatial one- and two-bedroom villas that sit on parklike grounds along with two pools, a fishpond, and exotic birds in cages. The restaurants are for guests and friends of guests only. A stretch limousine provides complimentary service within seven miles of the hotel. An especially attractive lure for visiting recording stars and producers is the acoustically engineered 1,200-square-foot recording studio, set in an underground garage. ♦ 1200 Alta Loma Rd (between Holloway Dr and Sunset Blvd), West Hollywood. 310/657.1333, 800/858.9758; fax 310/652.5300. www.sunsetmarquis.com

Within the Sunset Marquis:

WHISKEY

This late-night bar pulsates with a hip Hollywood crowd after 11PM, making it a prime stargazing spot. The dimly lit room with comfortable upholstered sofas is also perfect for a romantic rendezvous. ♦ Cover. Daily, until 2AM. 310/657.1333

69 ROXY

This Art Deco dance club is jammed every night with a mix of hip young trendies, older fans of rock 'n' roll, and recording industry bigwigs. Rock and jazz performers, already famous or on the right path, are the headliners here. The club is frequently booked by the local music industry to showcase hot new talent. ♦ Cover. Show times vary, so call ahead for the schedule. 9009 Sunset Blvd (between Hilldale Ave and N Wetherly Dr), West Hollywood. 310/276.2222. www.theroxyonsunsetn.com

69 KEY CLUB

This cool, three-story nightspot with its red and blue metal trim is the place to go to see big-name performers (Ricky Martin, Dennis Quaid, the Sharks, and Living Color are a few past headliners). There's dancing on weekends, when the name changes to **Elysium** (on Fridays) and **God's Kitchen** (on Saturdays). There's also a pleasant horseshoe-shaped restaurant on the second floor serving decent California cuisine, along with great views of the action and a plush VIP lounge. Hours vary depending on who's on stage, but it's always open 'til at least 2AM. ♦ 9039 Sunset Blvd (between N Wetherly and N Doheny Drs), West Hollywood. 310/274.5800. www.thekeyclub.com

69 TALESAI

★★$$ Some of LA's most distinctive food is served in this chic, upscale Thai restaurant. Specialties include *hor mok* (shrimp and squid with lemongrass, basil, and coconut), squid with chili, and *masman* lamb (with chili-coconut sauce, curry style). ♦ Thai ♦ M-F, lunch and dinner; Sa, dinner. Reservations recommended. 9043 Sunset Blvd (between N Wetherly and N Doheny Drs), West Hollywood. 310/275.9724

70 WHISKY A GO GO

Live rock music is the attraction at this thriving nightspot. There's dancing on the floor up front by the stage. ♦ Cover. Call for hours. 8901 Sunset Blvd (at Clark St), West Hollywood. 310/652.4202

70 DUKES

★$ This popular West Hollywood coffee shop has a fast pace, good food, and a friendly feel. They seat you wherever they can, which is usually with strangers—but they won't be strangers for long. Expect a long wait for brunch on Sunday. ♦ Coffee shop ♦ Daily, breakfast, lunch, and dinner. No credit cards. 8909 Sunset Blvd (between Clark St and Hilldale Ave), West Hollywood. 310/652.9411

70 HUSTLER HOLLYWOOD

What can we say: It's a sex shop, filled with all the paraphernalia one would expect and more (like pierced babes who hang out at the entrance). There's also a café and newsstand serving light fare daily from 8AM. The shop is open daily, 10AM-2AM. ♦ 8920 Sunset Blvd (between N San Vicente Blvd and Hilldale Ave, across the boulevard from Dukes), West Hollywood. 310/860-9009; fax 310/860.9029; email sexstore@pacbell.net

71 TOWER RECORDS

Tower bills itself as the largest record store in the world. Across Sunset is an annex selling classical recordings (310/657.3910) and videos (310/657.3344). ♦ Daily, until midnight. 8801 Sunset Blvd (at Horn Ave), West Hollywood. 310/657.7300

72 HUGO'S

★★★$$ Such head-turning stars as Julia Roberts, Bette Midler, and Geena Davis, as well as funnyman Jerry Seinfeld, have been spotted breakfasting at this hip spot. Many a million-dollar deal has been made over pumpkin pancakes, pasta alla Mamma (linguine, eggs, garlic, and Hugo's secret seasoning), and smoked salmon omelets with tomato and sour cream. Go early; primo window tables fill up fast. ♦ Italian ♦ Daily, breakfast, lunch, and dinner. 8401 Santa Monica Blvd (between N Kings Rd and Olive Dr), West Hollywood. 323/654.3993 ♿

72 GLOBE PLAYHOUSE

The charming replica of Shakespeare's wooden O-shaped theater is host to the Bard's plays and dramatic readings of his sonnets. ♦ 1107 N Kings Rd (between Santa Monica Blvd and Fountain Ave), West Hollywood. 323/654.5623

73 MARIX TEX-MEX

★$$ Huge margaritas help pass the time while you're waiting for your table in this boisterous cantina. Fajitas and blue-corn tortillas are the specialties. ♦ Tex-Mex ♦ M-F, lunch and dinner; Sa, Su, brunch and dinner. 1108 N Flores St (between Santa Monica Blvd and Fountain Ave), West Hollywood. 323/656.8800 ♿

73 O-BAR

★★★$$ You feel good the minute you walk into this dynamite-looking restaurant. The hosts and wait staff are cheerful and efficient. The décor is a knockout, with large chunks of raw, recycled glass, bamboo floors, pebble-crusted columns, and replica busts of classical sculpture set under a high ceiling. Extraordinary-looking white powder–coated iron reeds hang in synthesis over the two-sided bar. Adding to the look, created by SCHOOS Incorporated (a design firm that also owns the restaurant), is a glassed-in meditation garden. Located in the center of activity in WeHo, the restaurant attracts a large gay crowd, but thanks to amiable and above-average-looking waiters and waitresses, everybody feels at home here. The food is innovative and good if you stick to less complicated offerings. Signature dishes include lobster macaroni and cheese, pot roast, short ribs, and butternut squash ravioli. Desserts here are sinfully rich, especially the best banana split you'll ever eat, made with tons of chocolate, ice cream, cookies, and plenty of calories. ♦ Fusion Asian/California ♦ Daily, dinner. Reservations suggested. 8279 Santa Monica Blvd (at N Sweetzer Ave). 323/822.3300

74 BELLY

While we're usually cynical about new clubs, when this lively lounge opened in 2001 it

More than 2,000 residents of West Hollywood are members of the Screen Actors Guild.

Hollywood High School alumni include Linda Evans, Carol Burnett, Ricky Nelson, and Warren Christopher.

seemed destined to survive—as it has! Billed as a tapas lounge (the little snacks are served nightly along with a full bar menu), the stylish room attracts a happening singles crowd. The room feels like the tummy of a whale, with cushions everywhere and a no-attitude wait staff. There's a live DJ spinning discs, and a tiny dance floor. There are no velvet ropes, no cover, and no guest list—everybody age 21 and over is welcome here, even smokers: There are two outdoor sections for puffers. ♦ Club/lounge ♦ Doors open at 6PM and close at 2AM. 7929 Santa Monica Blvd (a half-block west of N Fairfax Ave), West Hollywood. 323/692.1068 ♿

75 THE PLEASURE CHEST

The catalog of naughtiness here is as prosaically displayed as produce in a supermarket. ♦ Daily, until 1AM. 7733 Santa Monica Blvd (at N Genesee Ave), West Hollywood. 323/650.1022

76 PLUMMER PARK

Part of a ranch that operated as a farm and dairy from 1877 to 1943, this three-acre park now contains recreational facilities and the original **Plummer home** (323/848.6530). A **farmers' market** is held here every Monday from 10AM to 2PM. ♦ 7377 Santa Monica Blvd (between N Fuller Ave and N Vista St), West Hollywood

77 JONES HOLLYWOOD CAFE

★★★$$ This hip, clublike restaurant attracts young trendies in designer jeans who go for the good food and fun ambience. The menu offers a blend of California and continental fare, including calamari, grilled ahi tuna, grilled Portobello mushrooms with polenta, and a large selection of salads. The setting is casual, with tables draped in red-and-white checkered oilcloths, a large banquette adorned with a bandana-like print, and Jack Daniels bottles standing behind chicken wire on a shelf. An eclectic mix of recorded music plays in the background. ♦ California/Continental ♦ M-F, lunch and dinner; Sa, Su, dinner. Reservations required for dinner. 7205 Santa Monica Blvd (at N Formosa Ave), West Hollywood. 323/850.1726

78 MAROUCH

★★★$ This little sleeper gained recognition in Zagat as one of the best of its kind in the city. It's plain and simple, with a storefront façade, but the food's delicious. Middle Eastern appetizers such as tabouleh, falafel, and dishes like *kibbeh* (veal mixed with crushed wheat stuffed with ground beef and pine nuts), *shawarma* (beef topped with sesame sauce), *shawarma* chicken, *lekkos ramly* (fresh sea bass), and assorted baklavas for dessert make for a perfect meal. There's a tiny patio for smokers who can't resist, and a belly dancer who entertains on weekends. What more can you ask for? ♦ Lebanese ♦ Tu-Su, lunch and dinner. Reservations recommended for four or more. 4905 Santa Monica Blvd (at N Edgemont St). 323/662.9325

79 BEZJIAN'S GROCERY

Exotic spices and ingredients for Middle Eastern cooking, such as chutneys, basmati rice, imported feta and olives, hummus, and flat breads, are sold here at very low prices. ♦ Daily. 4725 Santa Monica Blvd (between N Vermont and N New Hampshire Aves). 323/663.1503

80 JOSS

★★$$ East meets West in this stunning, clean-lined restaurant with a select, reasonably priced wine list. Owner Cecile Tang offers innovative but often overpriced and modest-size dishes from her home territory of Hong Kong. Best bets include sweet-and-sour soup, Mongolian lamb, and Peking duck. There's a counter for late suppers, and a terrace for dim sum lunch. Service can be erratic. ♦ Chinese ♦ M-F, lunch and dinner; Sa, Su, dinner. Reservations recommended. 9255 Sunset Blvd (at Phyllis St), West Hollywood. 310/276.1886

81 THE VIPER ROOM

Hot groups like Pearl Jam and REM drop by regularly for a few impromptu sets at this cool music club. On a somewhat creepier note, this is also the place where actor River Phoenix died in 1994 after a particularly wild night. The clientele's dress code runs from miniskirts with work boots to tight jeans and tank tops. ♦ Cover. M-Sa, until 2AM. 8852 Sunset Blvd (at Larrabee St), West Hollywood. 310/358.1880

81 WYNDHAM LE BEL AGE

$$$$ After being purchased by the Wyndham hotel group in 1994, this 188-room property underwent a complete refurbishment. The building looks plain and undistinguished on the outside, but the interior décor is opulent and refined. Amenities include **Ten 20,** a lounge, piano bar, and restaurant with open mics on Thursday and Friday nights, and a rooftop sports club complete with sauna, pool, steam bath, and a knockout view. ♦ 1020 N San Vicente Blvd (between Cynthia St and Sunset Blvd), West Hollywood. 310/854.1111, reservations only 800/424.4443; fax 310/854.0926. www.wyndham.com &

Within Wyndham Le Bel Age:

DIAGHILEV

★★$$$$ Caviar served with flavored vodkas, *koulibaca* (puff pastry filled with salmon, rice, and herbs), and quail stuffed with foie gras are among the specialties of this hotel restaurant of czarist splendor. ♦ Russian ♦ Tu-Sa, dinner. Reservations recommended. 310/854.1111, ext 480

81 SAN VICENTE INN/RESORT

$$ The city's only true gay hostelry, this tiny 40-room B&B has a variety of accommodations, including rooms with private or shared baths, suites, and cottages. All have phones, televisions, microwaves, coffeemakers, refrigerators, and VCRs, and come with continental breakfast. Outside there are pretty gardens, a pool, a clothing-optional sundeck, a hot tub, and a fitness center. ♦ 845 N San Vicente Blvd (200 yards from Santa Monica Blvd, two blocks from Sunset Blvd). 310/854.6915; fax 310/289.5929. www.gayresort.com

82 BOOK SOUP

This marvelous store specializes in current and classic literature, books on the arts, and a remarkable choice of American and foreign magazines. ♦ Daily, until midnight. 8818 Sunset Blvd (between Holloway Dr and Larrabee St), West Hollywood. 310/659.3110

83 SUMMERFIELD SUITES HOTEL

$$ Any of the 103 nicely appointed suites provides a perfect setting for a quiet getaway. Amenities include a workout room and a rooftop pool and Jacuzzi. There's no restaurant, but several are within walking distance. ♦ 1000 Westmount Dr (at West Knoll Dr), West Hollywood. 310/657.7400, 800/253.7997; fax 310/854.6744. www.sshhollywood@attmail.com

84 ROSAMUND FELSEN GALLERY

New and established LA artists, including Mike Kelley, Chris Burden, and Roy Dowell, are showcased here. ♦ Tu-Sa. 8525 Santa Monica Blvd (at West Knoll Dr), West Hollywood. 310/652.9172

85 CAFE LA BOHÈME

★★★$$ The epitome of dining as theater, designer Margaret O'Brien's setting combines a castle's great hall with the atmosphere of a subterranean abode fit for the Phantom of the Opera. Gauzed illumination and a reflecting pool help to offset the vastness of the two-

---

Restaurants/Clubs: Red | **Hotels: Purple** | Shops: Orange | Outdoors/Parks: Green | Sights/Culture: Blue

level dining area. Impeccably attired and attentive waiters serve filet mignon, free-range chicken cooked in cilantro and peppers, and deliciously prepared fish. ◆ International ◆ Daily, dinner; Sa, Su, brunch and dinner. Reservations required for dinner. 8400 Santa Monica Blvd (at N Orlando Ave), West Hollywood. 323/848.2360 ઼

86 LE MONTROSE

$$$ Located one block from Beverly Hills and just south of the Sunset Strip in a quiet residential area, this recently renovated hotel boasts a lobby with Art Nouveau furniture and 133 tastefully decorated suites (including 45 executive suites). Many feature kitchenettes, sunken living rooms, balconies, and VCRs, and such luxuries as fax machines, fireplaces, irons and ironing boards, and terry-cloth robes. A fruit basket and mineral water are in each executive suite upon guests' arrival, and homemade cookies and milk are served upon their departure. There's a fitness center with a sauna, a rooftop heated pool with private cabanas, and Jacuzzi, and a lighted tennis court. The **Library** restaurant is open to hotel guests and their friends only. Visiting rock bands and performers make this their Los Angeles home. ◆ 900 Hammond St (at Cynthia St), West Hollywood. 310/855.1115, 800/776.0666; fax 310/657.9192. www.lemontrose.com ઼

87 RAMADA PLAZA WEST HOLLYWOOD

An Art Deco/Miami–South Beach façade, added in 2003, featuring bright pastels and colorful accents, seems a little out of place on this stretch of Santa Monica Boulevard, but you get used to it. The colorful metal flower sculptures by Peter Shire were left intact. Accommodations include 175 rooms, of which 20 are two-bedroom corporate and apartments and eight are studio units. Newly added is a Panini Café serving breakfast, lunch, and dinner, a fully equipped fitness center, and a branch of Wells Fargo Bank. There are several sidewalk cafés (Starbucks, Jamba Juice) just a stroll from the entrance along the boulevard. ◆ 8585 Santa Monica Blvd (between West Knoll and Westmount Drs), West Hollywood. 310/652.6400, 800/845.8585; fax 310/652.4207. www.ramada-wh.com

88 BENVENUTO

★★★$$ Oozing with ambience, this tiny trattoria dishes out great Italian food in an inviting café that once served as a recording studio for Jim Morrison and The Doors. It's now a popular late-night rendezvous for celebrities, who linger over espresso and cappuccino after meals of focaccia and olive oil, pizza, fresh fish, and divine desserts. ◆ Italian ◆ Tu-F, lunch and dinner; Sa, Su,

dinner. 8512 Santa Monica Blvd (at N La Cienega Blvd), West Hollywood. 310/659.8635 ઼

89 858 NORTH DOHENY DRIVE

Frank Lloyd Wright designed this concrete-block house with a dramatic two-story living room in 1928. A private residence, it's located on a tiny corner lot. ◆ At Vista Grande St, West Hollywood

90 REVOLVER

This video/discotheque extravaganza pulsates with a young gay crowd who come to dance the night away. There's a small espresso bar upstairs. ◆ Cover. Daily, until 2AM. 8851 Santa Monica Blvd (at Larrabee St), West Hollywood. 310/659.8851

90 VALADON

$$ This intimate 80-room hotel features split-level suites and a rooftop heated pool and spa. Room service is available. ◆ 8822 Cynthia St (at Larrabee St), West Hollywood. 310/854.1114; fax 310/657.2623

91 L'ORANGERIE

★★★★$$$$ Still the grandest and most formal French restaurant in LA—and perhaps in the country—L'Orangerie has been lavishly redesigned by architect **Valerian S. Rybar**. With an immense bouquet of seasonal flowers, Versailles-like landscape murals, arched doorways, and exquisite Louis XVI furnishings, the high-ceilinged dining room resembles the orangerie of an eighteenth-century château. Alas, chefs have been playing musical tables at this normally unwavering restaurant. At last look, the sous chef was running the show with a menu of new offerings along with some favorite signature dishes. The very popular (and expensive, at about $110) signature appetizer of Tsar Osetra caviar with blini and crème fraiche is still available, as are the house smoked salmon and roasted John Dory. The desserts here are outstanding—especially the apple tart, chocolate soufflé, and the three crème brûlées served with crunchy pralines. Plan to spend an evening, beginning with a drink at the handsome bar/lounge and ending with a rich espresso or after-dinner libation. Many local foodies consider this the best French restaurant in Los Angeles. After years of savoring the exceptional cuisine and service, we have to agree, no matter who's in the kitchen. ◆ French ◆ Tu-F, lunch and dinner; Sa, Su, dinner. Reservations necessary. 903 N La Cienega Blvd (between Sherwood Dr and Santa Monica Blvd), West Hollywood. 310/652.9770 ઼

92 LOLA'S

★★$$ Owner Lola Dunsworth left **House of Blues** to dish out comfort food at this charming little cottage. The vaulted ceiling shelters a décor of wrought-iron chairs upholstered in cheetah-patterned velveteen, a cozy alcove with leopard-skin sofas, and an antique billiards table. Some of the fish dishes are heavenly, and the chicken potpie is just like somebody's mother used to make. Martini lovers are drawn to the 45 varieties served, from banana to cranberry. ◆ American ◆ Daily, dinner. Reservations recommended. Valet parking available. 945 N Fairfax Ave (between Willoughby Ave and Romaine St), West Hollywood. 323/736.5652 &

93 BURNETT MILLER

Minimalist and conceptual American and European artworks and installations by Charles Ray and Wolfgang Laib are featured. ◆ Tu-Sa. 964 N La Brea Ave (between Willoughby Ave and Romaine St). No phone

94 HOLLYWOOD MEMORIAL CEMETERY

Ⓟ A galaxy of top stars found refuge from their fans in this 65-acre oasis. Douglas Fairbanks has the most elaborate memorial, and Valentino is in wall crypt No. 1205, though the lady in black who used to bring flowers on the anniversary of his death comes no more. Here, too, are Cecil B. DeMille, Tyrone Power, and Peter Lorre. Close by is the **Beth Olam Cemetery,** where rests mobster Bugsy Siegel. ◆ Daily. 6000 Santa Monica Blvd (between N Van Ness Ave and Gower St). 323/469.1181

95 MAC CENTER FOR ART AND ARCHITECTURE/ L.A. SCHINDLER HOUSE

LA's most innovative house has been lovingly restored. **Rudolph Schindler** came from Vienna to work with Frank Lloyd Wright, and built this studio/residence in 1921. He lived and worked here until his death in 1953. Inspired by a desert camp, the architect combined tilt-up concrete slab walls, canvas canopies, and open-air sleeping lofts—techniques and spatial treatments that were novel at the time. Richard Neutra lived here in the late 1920s, and the house was a meeting place for the avant-garde. ◆ Admission. Free on F, 4-6PM. W-Su, 11AM-6PM and by appointment. 835 N Kings Rd (between Waring and Willoughby Aves), West Hollywood. 323/651.1510 www.maccenter.com

96 CHIANTI CUCINA

★★$$ Splendid pasta and the best breadsticks anywhere (from the same kitchen as the restaurant's parent, **Ristorante Chianti**; see below) are served in the noisy, informal, white-tiled room at this place, which is filled to capacity with a young, attractive crowd. Try it for a late-evening dessert and a cup of espresso. ◆ Italian ◆ M-Sa, lunch and dinner; Su, dinner. Reservations recommended. 7383 Melrose Ave (at N Martel Ave). 323/653.8333

96 RISTORANTE CHIANTI

★★$$$ At this grande dame of Italian cuisine, with etched glass and dark wood booths, the dishes are as tasty as they are beautiful. Favorites include shrimp, lobster, and pasta with porcini mushrooms. ◆ Italian ◆ Daily, dinner. Reservations recommended. 7383 Melrose Ave (at N Martel Ave). 323/653.8333 &

97 PROPAGANDA FILMS

Franklin Israel's brilliant 1988 adaptation of an old warehouse features sculptural enclosures in a cavernous space. ◆ 940 N Mansfield Ave (between Willoughby Ave and Romaine St)

98 MARGO LEAVIN GALLERY

Claes Oldenburg, John Baldessari, and Alexis Smith strike again, with a blade slicing through the stucco façade like a knife through pastry. It's just the thing to enliven a side street and win attention for serious contemporary art. ◆ Tu-Sa. 817 Hilldale Ave (between Santa Monica Blvd and Keith Ave), West Hollywood. 310/273.0603. Also at 812 N Robertson Blvd (between Santa Monica Blvd and Keith Ave), West Hollywood

99 THE ABBEY

★$ Perhaps the best lemon squares in any LA coffee shop can be had here, but don't shortchange the other delicious pies, cakes, and shortbreads. Patio dining is available. ◆ Coffee shop ◆ M-Th, 7AM-2AM; F, 7AM-3AM; Sa, 8AM-3AM; Su, 8AM-2AM. 692 N Robertson Blvd (between Melrose Ave and Santa Monica Blvd), West Hollywood. 310/289.8410

100 KOONTZ

Russell Wilson offers one of the best selections of craft tools and housewares in the city. Notable items are lighting fixtures and German-made miniature toy trains. ◆

Restaurants/Clubs: Red | Hotels: Purple | Shops: Orange | Outdoors/Parks: Green | Sights/Culture: Blue

Daily. 8914 Santa Monica Blvd (between N San Vicente and N Robertson Blvds), West Hollywood. 310/652.0123

100 LE PARC

$$$ This pretty, 150-room, all-suite hotel has an inviting marble lobby and pretty accommodations that come with CD players and terry robes. There are also tennis courts, a rooftop swimming pool, a fitness facility, and a garden. **Cafe Le Parc** serves everything from spring rolls to quesadillas. ♦ 733 West Knoll Dr (between Melrose Ave and Sherwood Dr), West Hollywood. 310/855.8888, 800/578.4837; fax 310/659.7812. www.leparcsuites.com

101 KOI

★★★$$$ Have a yen for creative Japanese food? This stylish, feng shui–correct restaurant is the place to go. The indoor and outdoor dining areas are equally inviting with Buddhas and bamboo, ornately carved wooden doors, and a popular bar and lounge. Koi's Zen-like interior actually sparkles, and so does the food. The crispy salmon skin salad, with just the right amount of zest, and tangy tuna tartare with avocado in a crisp won ton are superb; the spicy seared albacore with crispy onion is another winner, as is the Kobe–style filet mignon Toban-Yaki, black cod bronzed with miso, and any tempura on the menu. The bar bustles with the young and hip, who sip drinks before and after dinner. It's a scene, and worth showing up for. ♦ Japanese-inspired with California accents ♦ M-F, lunch and dinner; daily, dinner. Reservations recommended, especially for dinner. Valet parking available. 730 N La Cienega Blvd (near Melrose Pl). 310/659.9449

101 BASTIDE

★★★★$$$$ Chef Alain Giraud, formerly of Citrus and Lavande, created an exceptional menu for this chic spot, designed by Andre Putman. Plan to make a night of it, as the five-course prix-fixe meal is a leisurely affair. Considering the price, you might as well sit back and enjoy yourself. There are three intimate dining rooms, the most popular of which sits at the entrance in a romantic, candlelit courtyard garden. Tables are superbly set. The well-trained wait staff ranks among the best. Expect to pay a premium for wines and drinks; an $18 glass of California chardonnay was a shocker. However, the meal was so good we easily forgot about it. A sample menu might include a tender, succulent lobster salad, sautéed foie gras with fig Banyuls sauce, rack of lamb with black olive sauce, or veal daube with carrots and olives. For dessert a tray of perfectly ripened cheeses, lavender ice cream, or dark chocolate tart provide a fitting finale. ♦ French ♦ M-Sa, lunch and dinner.

Reservations a must. Dress chic. 8475 Melrose Place (between Orlando Ave and La Cienega Blvd). 323/651.5950

102 GEMINI G.E.L.

Fine art prints by David Hockney, Jasper Johns, Robert Rauschenberg, and Ellsworth Kelly are spotlighted in this workshop/gallery designed by **Frank Gehry.** ♦ M-F. 8365 Melrose Ave (between N Kings Rd and N Orlando Ave). 323/651.0513

103 AGENT PROVOCATEUR

This London-based lingerie boutique was put together by Joseph Corre (son of the fashion world's Vivienne Westwood and former Sex Pistols manager Malcolm McLaren) and his wife, Serina Reese. The sensuous shop was a big hit with Tinseltown's A-list crowd: Naomi Campbell, Kate Moss, Madonna, Courtney Love, and Oscar winners Gwyneth Paltrow and Julia Roberts. If you're looking for a sexy gift, or something naughty for yourself, you're bound to find it among the fabulous international collection of mink collars, slave chains, bustiers, corsets, panties, and nighties. There's a private little dressing room for the timid. ♦ M-Sa, 11AM-7PM. 7921 Melrose Ave (between N Fairfax Ave and Crescent Heights Blvd). 323/653.0229

103 CARLITOS GARDEL

★★$$$ Terrific Argentinean food is served in this contemporary, bustling restaurant. Specialties can change nightly: On Thursdays, there's a wonderful garlic-laced *linguine alle puttanesca*, a tasty paella, and superb gnocchi (Argentina was heavily settled by Italians). There's a good selection of Argentinean wines, too. ♦ Argentinean ♦ M-F, lunch and dinner; Sa, Su, dinner. Reservations recommended. 7963 Melrose Ave (between N Hayworth and N Edinburgh Aves). 323/655.0891

104 GENGHIS COHEN

★$$ Catering to a neighborhood crowd and a smattering of show-biz types, this upscale Szechuan restaurant serves black-bean crab, crackerjack shrimp, and *kung pau* chicken (in a sauce of red chilies, peanuts, soy, and scallions). The décor has a stylish New York feel. ♦ Chinese ♦ Daily, lunch and dinner. 740 N Fairfax Ave (between Melrose and Waring Aves). 323/653.0640 ౽

105 MATRIX THEATRE COMPANY

As good as any Off-Broadway theater, this adventurous, Equity-waiver playhouse received the LA Drama Critics' Circle Award for its productions of *The Tavern* and *The Seagull* in 1994. Other shows have included Samuel Beckett's *Endgame*, Harold Pinter's *Betrayal* and *The Homecoming*, Lyle Kessler's *Orphans*,

and Simon Gray's *The Common Pursuit*. ◆
7657 Melrose Ave (between N Stanley and N
Spaulding Aves). 323/852.1445.
www.tix.com

105 TABLE 8

★★$$ Smack in the middle of quirky Melrose
and perched aptly enough under a body-
piercing salon, this replacement for Bouchon
fast became an in spot when it opened in
2003. The restaurant features a minimalist
1960s New York–style décor with lots of
banquettes and comfy chairs. Co-owner Chef
Govind Armstrong offers an inventive seasonal
menu that plays on fresh vegetables. The
wood-roasted chicken or the 30-ounce porter-
house steak for two is worth ordering.
Desserts are spectacular here, especially the
peach crisp. There's a lounge menu for light
fare like grilled cheese sandwiches or
asparagus and morel omelets and a jiggy bar.
◆ French Bistro ◆ Daily, dinner. Reservations
suggested. 7661 Melrose Ave (between N
Stanley and N Spaulding Aves).
323/782.8558

106 LA EYEWORKS

Eyeglasses are treated as art in this shop,
which has a stark setting and inventive
displays to rival the best galleries. Both
classic and outrageous frames of high quality
are sold at high prices. ◆ Daily. 7407 Melrose
Ave (between N Martel Ave and N Vista St).
323/653.8255

107 GROUNDLINGS THEATRE

This resident company does sleight-of-mouth
improvisation using suggestions from the
audience. ◆ 7307 Melrose Ave (at N
Poinsettia Pl). 323/934.9700.
www.groundlings.com

107 TOMMY TANG'S

★$ Popular with a young, hip clientele, this
restaurant calls its food "modern Thai."
Specialties include Thai toast, barbecued
chicken, and Malaysian clams. Eat in the
large, attractive dining room or at a table on
the pretty tiled patio. There's also a sushi bar.
◆ Thai ◆ M-Sa, lunch; M-Su, dinner. 7313
Melrose Ave (between N Poinsettia Pl and N
Fuller Ave). 323/937.5733 ♿. Also at 24 W
Colorado Blvd (between S Fair Oaks and S De
Lacey Aves), Pasadena. 818/792.9700

108 PINK'S FAMOUS CHILI DOGS

★$ Serving what are arguably the city's best
hot dogs, hamburgers, and tamales since
1939, this funky little place is an LA
institution. The chili dogs are what make this
place world famous. ◆ American/Take-Out

◆ M-Th, until midnight; F-Sa, until 3AM; Su,
until 2AM. 709 N La Brea Ave (between
Melrose and Waring Aves). 323/931.4223

109 DANZIGER STUDIO

It was this minimalist house/studio built for
designer Lou Danziger in 1965 that launched
Frank Gehry's career. Three blank stucco
boxes, adroitly positioned, transform LA's
industrial vernacular into high art. It's a
private residence. ◆ 7001 Melrose Ave (at N
Sycamore Ave)

110 ALEX

★★★★$$$$ Expect to be dazzled by the
gorgeous room and even more so by chef Alex
Scrimgeour's eloquent menu. The open
kitchen provides a nice view of the Paris
Cordon Bleu chef at work while the room, with
its mahogany beams, canvas ceiling, and
subtle colors, presents a fitting showcase for
his talents. Order drinks or a bottle of wine to
sip while scanning the all prix-fixe menu;
you'll need time to make your selection.
Sample choices might include a
complimentary *amuse-bouche* such as a
crepe stuffed with wild mushrooms; Maryland
blue crab cakes or grilled radicchio with
Roquefort, blood oranges and pine nuts; goat
cheese soufflé with roasted pear, Applewood
bacon, and frisée; Maine lobster done three
ways; grilled venison tenderloin, or John Dory
cooked to perfection and served with polenta.
There is always a spectacular finale, like the
triple chocolate marquise with hazelnut
crunch and warm ganache. ◆ Modern British
◆ Dinner, M-Su. Reservations a must. 6703
Melrose Ave (at Citrus Ave). 323/933.5233.
www.Alexrestaurant.com

111 HIGHLAND GROUNDS

★$ LA bohemians engage in esoteric
discussions here over generous bowls of latte.
There's a fun Tex-Mex menu, wine and beer,
and nightly entertainment. Breakfast and
lunch menus are available. ◆
Coffeehouse/Tex-Mex ◆ Tu-Su, until 1AM; M,
until 7PM. 742 N Highland Ave (between
Melrose and Waring Aves). 323/466.1507

112 PATINA

This flagship of the Patina Group relocated to
the **Walt Disney Concert Hall** in downtown LA
in October 2003. In its place is an exclusive
private venue for events and entertaining also
known as "Patina." Please see Walt Disney
Concert Hall for more information.
Reservations recommended. 5955 Melrose
Ave (between Cole and Wilcox Aves).
323/467.1108 ♿

Restaurants/Clubs: Red | Hotels: Purple | Shops: Orange | Outdoors/Parks: Green | Sights/Culture: Blue

113 A-1 RECORD FINDERS

The best place to find a disc nobody else has. If they don't have it, they'll send out a posse. ◆ M-Sa. 5639 Melrose Ave (between Gower St and El Centro Ave). 323/732.6737

114 PARAMOUNT STUDIOS

The last of the major studios in Hollywood. The original entrance gate, through which Gloria Swanson was driven by Erich von Stroheim in *Sunset Boulevard*, is tucked away at the end of Bronson Avenue, its purpose supplanted by a new double gate on Melrose. The stages along Gower Street were formerly part of **RKO Studios,** and the trademark globe can be seen at the corner. The studio is closed to the public, but the site is full of atmosphere. ◆ 5555 Melrose Ave (between Bronson Ave and Gower St)

115 PALM RESTAURANT

★★★$$$ The best steak and lobster in town—and also the most expensive—are served here along with super side orders of onion rings, mashed potatoes, creamed spinach, and fries. Portions are big, but if you have room left, go for the New York cheesecake. The dining room is always jammed, but the waiters are speedy. ◆ American ◆ M-F, lunch and dinner; Sa, Su, dinner. Reservations recommended. 9001 Santa Monica Blvd (between N Robertson Blvd and N Doheny Dr), West Hollywood. 310/550.8811. Also in downtown LA at 1100 S Flower St. 213/763.4600 ♿

116 DOUG WESTON'S TROUBADOR

This long-established rock 'n' roll shrine now specializes in heavy-metal bands. ◆ Cover. Call for schedule. 9081 Santa Monica Blvd (at N Doheny Dr), West Hollywood. 310/276.6168

116 LA MASIA

★$$ Celebrate a special occasion at this versatile restaurant, which has a tapas bar upstairs and Latin jazz and salsa music downstairs from 9PM. Paella and other standard Spanish fare is served. ◆ Spanish ◆ M-F, dinner; Sa, brunch and dinner. Reservations recommended. 9077 Santa Monica Blvd (between Nemo St and N Doheny Dr), West Hollywood. 310/273.7066

117 JAN TURNER GALLERY

Tony Delap, John Alexander, Guy Dill, and the late Carlos Almarez are among the artists shown here, where innovative landscapes are a specialty. The gallery shares its space with **Turner/Krull** (310/271.1536), which shows nineteenth- and twentieth-century photography. ◆ M-Sa. 9006 Melrose Ave (at N Almont Dr), West Hollywood. 310/271.4453

117 MAXFIELD

Shop here for avant-garde couture at drop-dead prices in a spare concrete shell designed by Larry Totah. The window display is often worth a detour. ◆ M-Sa. 8825 Melrose Ave (between N Robertson Blvd and N La Peer Dr), West Hollywood. 310/274.8800

118 FAT FISH

★★$$ Locals love this little spot at night (probably because there is no valet parking at lunchtime and it's difficult finding a place to park your car). The dining area is roomy and minimally decorated. The service is sometimes slow. There's a pleasant patio for alfresco dining or drinks and a little bar hidden off in the back. The menu centers around fresh fish with an Asian twist, such as grilled salmon with long beans, and seared bass carefully marinated in sake and miso with candied ginger, baby choy sum, lemongrass, and basil mousse. There's also duck breast, sushi, and other choices. ◆ Asian Bistro ◆ M-F, lunch; dinner. Reservations suggested. 616 N Robertson Blvd (between Melrose Ave and Santa Monica Blvd), West Hollywood. 310/659.3882. www.fatfishla.com

118 HEDLEY'S

★★$ Forget fancy-schmansy spots; this simple little joint dishes out great food at low prices in a fun, family-style atmosphere. Go for lunch or dinner and enjoy home-style cooking such as pork loin with grilled yams, roasted turkey with stuffing, tofu steak seasoned with ginger, veggie burgers, or even a New York steak for half the price you'd pay anywhere else. The ambience combined with the price attracts a big crowd day and night that jams into the tiny dining room or outside patio. There's a small selection of wines and beers and luscious desserts such as peach and blueberry cobbler with oat strudel, key lime pie, or warm chocolate bread pudding. There are napkins on the tables and smiles on the wait staff's faces. ◆ American ◆ Tu-F, lunch and dinner; Tu-Su, dinner; Sa, Su, brunch. Reservations not required except for large parties. 640 N Robertson Blvd (between Melrose Ave and Santa Monica Blvd). 310/659.2009

118 KINARA

This charming, transcendental day spa owned, operated, and conceived by Olga Lorencin and Christine Splichal, wife of LA super-chef Joachim Splichal, is designed to calm and relax through exotic treatments designed by Lorencin. You feel the bliss the minute you walk through its glassed front portals. The mood is friendly and honest, and the treatments are divine. Products are natural, herbal concoctions that are beneficial to your skin. A pleasant plus is a yummy restaurant where you can dine inside or out, all day until 7PM, on a charming patio. The menu relies on organic, healthy fare created by Joachim Splichal. ◆ Tu-Su. 656 N Robertson Blvd (a block south of Santa Monica Blvd). 310/657.9188. www.kinaraspa.com

119 PACIFIC DESIGN CENTER

These mammoth, glass-clad geometric structures by **Cesar Pelli** and **Gruen Associates** house around 130 interior furnishings and accessories showrooms. The public may visit **Center Blue** or **Center Green;** most showrooms allow you to browse on your own, but purchasing requires the services of an interior-design professional. Visitors can learn more about the designers and their work by taking a free one-hour tour. On the plaza that separates the center from San Vicente Boulevard is the **MOCA Gallery,** which presents high-quality art and design exhibitions (213/626.6222). Throughout the year, public exhibitions are held. ◆ M-F. Tours: M-F, 10AM. Reservations required for large groups. 8687 Melrose Ave (at N San Vicente Blvd), West Hollywood. 310/657.0800. www.pdclacworldnet.att.net

Within the Pacific Design Center:

ASTRA WEST

★★$$ Famed chef/restaurateur Charlie Palmer oversees the menu at this knock-down gorgeous luncheon/catering spot. Huge bouquets of fresh flowers accentuate the linear, modular, minimalist design of the glamorous room. The simple menu offers sandwiches, salads, grilled beef and fish, desserts, and a full bar. ◆ Creative California ◆ M-F, lunch. Astra doubles as an event site and is one of the most popular in town. 310/652.3003; e-mail: astrawest@charliepalmer.com. www.charliepalmer.com

CHRIS MICHAELS

★★$$ A pleasant place to get a quick bite while browsing around the Center, offering morning coffee and pastries and lunchtime salads, sandwiches, soup, and turkey chili. ◆ American ◆ M-F, breakfast and lunch. Reservations not required. 310/289.8877

119 THREAD

Designers Beth Blake and Sophie Simmons create stylish bridesmaid's dresses and other special-occasion frocks that are sold at this charming shop. ◆ Tu-Sa; hours vary, so call ahead. 8575 Melrose Ave (across from Pacific Design Center), West Hollywood. 310/360.5943

120 BODHI TREE

Books on philosophy, health, women's issues, astrology, and religion stock the shelves, along with herbs, soaps, and tarot cards. ◆ Daily, until 11PM. 8585 Melrose Ave (between Westmount and Westbourne Drs), West Hollywood. 310/659.1733

120 LE PAIN QUOTIDIEN

★★$$ This charming white-shingled café would deserve three stars if only they used cloth napkins; paper doesn't hack it for us. Still, the food and service are great and the prices are affordable. There's outdoor seating on a long, inviting porch, where most folks sit. Belgian-born chef/owner Alain Coumont's cuisine is a healthy mix of organic and fresh produce, simply prepared but quite tasty. Coumont's cooking is homey, creative country French. We loved the Portabello mushrooms stuffed with curried chicken and the braised boneless short ribs. A great choice for vegetarians is the lasagna stuffed with tofu and cheese. There are also gourmet sandwiches like brie with pecans and seafood choices. *Le pain quotidien* means "daily bread," which is the LPQ's specialty and truly about as good as it gets (loaves are available for purchase at the little retail outlet by the entrance). You'll want to take a few loaves home while you're it, a muffin or dessert or two. Speaking of sweets, desserts are luscious, especially the fruit tarts. ◆ California with some French twists ◆ Daily, 7AM-10:30 PM. Reservations suggested for dinner. 8607 Melrose Ave (corner of Westbourne, 2 blocks west of La Cienega Blvd). 310/854.3700. Also at 9730 Little Santa Monica Blvd (between Bedford and Camden). 310/859.1100; and 11702 Barrington Court (corner of Barrington and Sunset Blvd). 310/476.0969. Both open 7AM-7:30PM. www.painquotidien.com

LUCQUES

121 LUCQUES

★★★$$$ French for "olive," Lucques (pronounced Luke, no "s") is a foodie's paradise where the in crowd goes to savor chef Suzanne Goin's fabulous French fare. Dress casual chic, preferably in something

---

Restaurants/Clubs: Red | Hotels: Purple | Shops: Orange | Outdoors/Parks: Green | Sights/Culture: Blue

black. Sip some wine, then feast on some jumbo asparagus, Tuscan bean soup, saddle of rabbit, grilled club steak for two, or the fish du jour. Finish with vanilla pot de crème or some other delightful dessert. ◆ French ◆ Reservations a must (request a table in the garden, among the cool crowd). 8474 Melrose Ave (one-half block east of N La Cienega Blvd), West Hollywood. 323/655.6277 ♿

121 AGO

★★★$$$ Named for noted chef Agostino Sciandri, this uptown trattoria, with its wood-burning pizza oven, tempts with such artfully prepared dishes such as *costata di manzo* (18-ounce rib eye), *fritto misto di mare* (battered seafood), Tuscan-style chicken cooked in wine and herbs, grilled polenta with salt cod in a spicy tomato sauce, and Agostino's signature steak Florentine. The charming room, set under corrugated roofing and halogen spotlights, is a throwback to the Tuscan countryside, with a villa courtyard shaded by six 30-foot-high Italian cypress trees and four olive trees on a terra-cotta floor. The wait staff is delightful, and the crowd comes in late. ◆ Italian ◆ M-F, lunch and dinner; Sa, dinner. Reservations recommended. 8478 Melrose Ave (at Clinton St), West Hollywood. 323/655.6333

122 KIYO HIGASHI

The work of Larry Bell, Penelope Krebs, Guy Williams, and Lies Kraal is shown in this austerely handsome space. ◆ Tu-Sa. 8332 Melrose Ave (at N Flores St). 323/655.2482

123 DECADES, INC.

This Art Deco building showcases a vintage collection of 1960s and 1970s designs by Cardin, Halston, Pucci, and others, plus outfits from the estates of such Hollywood types as Ginger Rogers and Audrey Meadows. Accessories range from jewelry to girdles. ◆

> "People here still believe. The sun comes out every day and smacks them in the face and they march off gamely to face insurmountable odds. Los Angeles may be the most renewable city in the world."—Tom Shales, *Washington Post* television critic

M-Sa. 8214 Melrose Ave (between N La Jolla and N Harper Aves). 323/655.0223

123 DAILEY RARE BOOKS & FINE PRINTS

This shop carries art and illustrated books and literary first editions. ◆ Tu-Sa. 8216 Melrose Ave (between N La Jolla and N Harper Aves). 323/658.8515

123 DOLCE

★★★$$ Little Italy meets LA at this modish hot spot filled with lovely, lean women baring pierced bodies and taut bare bellies who mostly hang at the bar and make lots of noise. Designed by Douglas Dodd (who created interiors for Falcon, Avenue, and Katana), the clubby room is swathed in black leather and so is much of the young clientele. The food's good, from the antipasto to the assorted pasta, meat, and fish dishes (go for the halibut or sea bass). The Caesar salad is one of the best in town. The crepes stuffed with ricotta, the prime rib, and the risottos are not to be missed. ◆ Italian ◆ Daily, dinner. Reservations essential. 8284 Melrose Ave (at N Sweetzer Ave). 323/852.7174

124 FRED SEGAL

It's *so* overpriced. But the "I want to be hip" set that shops here doesn't care. Racks and display tables are filled with everything trendy, from T-shirts to shoes. Sales clerks have attitude. The parking lot's filled with Mercedes, Porsches, Z-3s, and other cool wheels. And, for the less privileged style-seekers, there is a sale every September that's so popular, parking spots are filled for six blocks around—which only goes to show you there's no shame in bargain hunting. ◆ Daily. 8100 Melrose Ave (at N Crescent Heights Blvd). 323/651.4129

124 IMPROVISATION

The bar here is two or three deep on weekends, but you can catch the best (and worst) of stand-up comedy every night. Top names sometimes stop in to watch a show or try out new material. ◆ Cover. Daily; call for performance times. 6182 Melrose Ave (between N Kilkea Dr and N La Jolla Ave). 323/651.2583

125 FANTASIES COME TRUE

Disney animation cels and character figurines from the great movie cartoon families are showcased here. ◆ Tu-Sa, noon-4PM. 8012 Melrose Ave (between N Edinburgh and N Laurel Aves). 323/655.2636

126 LA LUZ DE JESUS GALLERY

With its array of colorful *Día de los Muertos* figurines, Mexican ceremonial masks, and other Indo-Hispanic folk art, this upstairs gallery/bookstore is a manifestation of *Rod Serling's Night Gallery*. The entrance is on Martel Avenue. ◆ Daily; F-Sa, until midnight. 7400 Melrose Ave (at N Martel Ave). 323/666.7667

127 WOUND AND WOUND

Toy fanatics get all wound up about this place. ◆ Daily. 7374 Melrose Ave (between N Fuller and N Martel Aves). 323/653.6703

128 MELROSE AVENUE

Until the 1980s, this was just another sleepy little LA street. But then it began to find its identity as the "funky" part of town. The drab buildings were replaced with adventurous restaurants, fast-food places, galleries and design stores, and shops selling radical, vintage, and used clothing. On weekends, sidewalks are thronged and parking is difficult. Wear comfortable shoes; it's a three-mile stroll from Highland west to Doheny. Don't miss the Italian food at **Luce** (No. 7371; 323/658.6340). For racy adult gifts and videos, browse around **Drake's** (No. 7566; 323/651.5600). Stop for a jolt of joe and dessert at **Caffe Luna** (No. 7463; 323/655.8647) or some of the best Mexican food north of the border at **Antonio's** (No. 7470; 323/655.0480), where mariachis serenade while you dine. Pick up some really outrageous vintage outfits at **Aardvark's** (No. 7579; 323/655.6769) or begin a great gallery hop at **Tasende** (No. 8808; 310/276.8686), then continue on to **Chac-Mool** (No. 8920; 310/550.6872) and **William A. Karges Fine Art** (No. 9001; 310/276.8551). For your reading pleasure, **A Different Light** (No. 8853; 310/854.6601) provides a mix of lesbian and gay and conventional literature. For a real sense of LA fashion style, stop in at **James Perse** (No. 8914; 310/276.7277), where Perse's picks include clothes for men and women, togs for tots, and home accessories. ◆ Between N Highland Ave and N Doheny Dr

129 ZUMAYA

★★$ The fish tacos, special enchiladas, and chicken in spicy sauce are among the standouts in this cozy, upscale, family-run restaurant, with pleasant service. ◆ Latin ◆ M-F, lunch and dinner; Sa, Su, dinner. 5722 Melrose Ave (between N Lucerne and N Arden Blvds). 323/464.0624

129 SEAFOOD VILLAGE

★$ Fresh seafood from the fish market next door is served in this popular neighborhood establishment. ◆ Seafood ◆ Daily, lunch and dinner. 5732 Melrose Ave (between N Lucerne and N Arden Blvds). 323/463.8090

130 RINCON CHILENO

★$ Chile is a long coastal country, hence the emphasis on seafood at this warm, homey spot. Try the *paila de mariscos* (seafood stew), eel, or *pastel de choclo* (an unusual corn casserole), plus a bottle of strong Chilean wine. The place can be crowded on weekends, and speaking a bit of Spanish doesn't hurt. ◆ Chilean ◆ Tu-Su, lunch and dinner. 4354 Melrose Ave (at Heliotrope Dr). 323/666.6075

131 CHA CHA CHA

★★$ The crowds just keep on coming to this little out-of-the-way hot spot, which has an infectiously friendly spirit, spicy food, and wonderful daily specials. The corn tamale with golden caviar, the giant shrimp in black pepper sauce, and the chicken *poblano* (in a sauce with chocolate and almonds) are not to be missed. ◆ Latin/Caribbean ◆ Daily, lunch and dinner. Reservations recommended. 656 N Virgil Ave (at Melrose Ave). 323/664.7723 ಓ. Also at 762 Pacific Ave (at W Eighth St), Long Beach. 310/436.3900

132 SANTO COYOTE

★★$$ No ordinary Mexican restaurant, this one pulsates with plasma-screen TVs, Latin music, and tequila-swigging hipsters who go more to see and be seen than for the food. Celebs (Matthew Perry, Carmen Electra) and just plain folk fill up this place nightly. The inviting décor mingles calfskin chairs, ceramic pottery, and brass lanterns, with wooden ceiling beams. Named after a famous Guadalajara restaurant, Santo Coyote dishes out authentic fare. The heady margaritas are mixed with top-of-the-line tequilas. Do be careful with the tequila you select; some run as high as $35 a shot. The food is good, but sometimes spotty. The high-testosterone scene, coupled with lots of eye candy, revs up the mojo, should you require a jolt. ◆ M-F, lunch; daily, dinner. Reservations a must for dinner. 9010 Melrose Ave (between Doheny and Almont Drs), West Hollywood. 310/860.9333. www.santocoyotela.com

133 JAY WOLF

Designer Waldo Fernandez adds his signature decorative touches to this sophisticated imported menswear store. ◆ M-Sa. 517 N Robertson Blvd (between Rangely and Melrose Aves), West Hollywood. 310/273.9893

Restaurants/Clubs: Red | Hotels: Purple | Shops: Orange | Outdoors/Parks: Green | Sights/Culture: Blue

134 MORTON'S

★★★$$$ Still on the best-seller list after dozens of years, this power-lunch and dinner spot caters to celebrities who go to see, be seen, and work the room, especially on Friday nights. If you pass on people-watching and arrive early, you'll have less of a wait, but you'll miss the point of this restaurant, which is so in that it doesn't need a sign. The Caesar salad is top-notch and so is the sesame-crusted ahi tuna with shiitake mushrooms, basmati rice, baby bok choy, and ponzu sauce; the New York steak; *cote de boeuf* (a thinly sliced, grilled rib eye); Morton's lime grilled chicken; and the lamb loin. Killer desserts include warm chocolate espresso truffle cake with coffee ice cream, banana walnut beignets with vanilla ice cream and caramel sauce, and apple tart with caramel sauce and ice cream. ◆ California/Continental ◆ M-F, lunch and dinner; Sa, dinner only. Reservations required. 8764 Melrose Ave (between N San Vicente and N Robertson Blvds), West Hollywood. 310/276.5205

135 SOOLIP MARIE PAPIER

If you're looking for unique paper products, stationery, gifts, or albums, you're sure to find them and more at this adorable designer paper shop. ◆ M-Sa. 8574 Melrose Ave (across from **Pacific Design Center**—see page 85), West Hollywood. 310/360.0581

135 ROBERT KUO LTD & KUO DESIGN

Right across from the **Pacific Design Center** (see page 85), this marvelous shop offers very impressive limited-edition and one-of-a-kind repoussé and cloisonné pieces created by Chinese artist Robert Kuo. You'll also find the most unusual pieces of jewelry created by Alice Kuo, Robert's wife. ◆ Shop: M-F; Sa, noon-4PM. Kuo Design open by appointment only. 8686 Melrose Ave (at N San Vicente Blvd), West Hollywood. 310/855.1555

135 DU VIN WINE & SPIRITS

Ask owner René Averseng for current bargains in French wines, and while you're here, pick up some cheese and sandwiches. ◆ M-Sa. 540 N San Vicente Blvd (between Rosewood and Melrose Aves), West Hollywood. 310/855.1161. www.duvin.net

135 NISHIMURA

★★★$$$ Keep your eyes open, as it's easy to miss the tiny building that houses this upscale sushi joint. The gracious entrance sits off to the side next to a pretty garden. An inviting portal, adorned with a bright blue basin filled with water and a bamboo ladle, opens to a modern, white-walled, high-ceilinged room decorated with brilliant ceramic pieces by Mineo Mizuno. Once inside, you'll find some of the best sushi this side of the Orient presented on hand-painted ceramic plates. Owned and operated by master sushi chef Hiro Nishimura, who made his mark at Katsu in Los Feliz, the place is perfect for digging into Nishimura's tantalizing concoctions. The lightly grilled *unagi* (eel) threaded on a bamboo skewer, dabbed with miso and green peppers, is fantastic. So are the steamed razor clams, oysters, scallops or octopus sushi and sashimi. For tipplers, there's a large selection of Japanese beers and sakes. ◆ Sushi Bar ◆ M-F, lunch, M-Sa, dinner. Reservations advised. 8684 Melrose Ave (across the street from the Pacific Design Center). 310/659.4770

136 ELIXIR

This shop proffers healthy remedies, from herbs and teas to natural tonics. Browse among Chinese antiques and natural body-care products, or sit down at the outdoor "tonic bar" amid beautiful botanical gardens. ◆ M-Sa; Su, noon-5PM. 8612 Melrose Ave (between Westbourne and Huntley Drs), West Hollywood. 310/657.9311

137 HOMEBODY

At this sugar-and-spice boutique, customers create their very own bath and body fragrance from 160 varieties of natural and essential oils. ◆ Daily. 8500 Melrose Ave (at N La Cienega Blvd), West Hollywood. 310/659.2917

137 HERITAGE BOOK SHOP

Early manuscripts, seventeenth- to twentieth-century first editions, fine bindings, and autographs are some of the treasures in this shop. ◆ Tu-Sa; M, by appointment only. 8540 Melrose Ave (between West Knoll and Westmount Drs), West Hollywood. 310/659.3674

137 ELLIOTT KATT BOOKSELLER

This is possibly the best bookshop in Los Angeles for old and new publications on film, radio, television, and theater. ◆ M-Sa. 8568 Melrose Ave (at Westmount Dr), West Hollywood. 310/652.5178

138 CITRINE

★★$$$ Alas, several restaurants have come and gone at this location, so let's hope this one makes it. Indications are it should. The room, created by LA interior designer Michael Berman, unfolds through a massive front door modeled after Judy Garland's home. An Asian theme continues with oversized lampshades on backlit sconces set on a wall of iron leaves. The imaginative menu, created by David Slatkin (former chef at Mojo at the W

Hotel in LA, and the Fenix at the Argyle, West Hollywood), fuses Asian, Caribbean, and Cuban dishes from sashimi to grouper wrapped in banana leaves, foie gras with corn arepa, and a whole lot more. ♦ Asian/Cuban/California ♦ Daily, dinner. Reservations suggested. 8360 Melrose Ave (at N Kings Rd). 323/655.1690

139 DETAILS

Redecorating your home? Stop by this boutique for upscale architectural accessories by contemporary American and European designers. ♦ M-F. 503 N La Cienega Blvd (between Rosewood and Melrose Aves). 310/659.1550

140 IL PICCOLINO

★★$$ Owner Marco Tencanera is proud of his attractive trattoria and his excellent menu selections: baby artichoke salad with shaved parmesan and walnuts, spaghetti Bolognese, pizza *alla agniola* (fresh vegetables on a thin crust), freshly prepared pastas, fish, veal dishes, and steaks. Desserts are well worth the caloric splurge, especially the world-class tiramisù, flourless chocolate cake, Napoleon, or lemon champagne sorbet. There's a nice, affordable wine list. ♦ Italian ♦ M-Sa, lunch and dinner. 350 N Robertson Blvd, West Hollywood. 310/659.2220

141 DIVA

Offbeat contemporary lighting and furniture pack this showroom. ♦ M-Sa. 8801 Beverly Blvd (at N Robertson Blvd), West Hollywood. 310/278.3191

141 MADEO

★★$$$ The chic dining experience here is worth the price. Superb veal chops, extraordinary risotto, and delicious desserts are just some of the specialties. It helps if you know Italian, as the staff doesn't speak much English. ♦ Italian ♦ M-F, lunch; daily, dinner. Reservations recommended. 8897 Beverly Blvd (between N Robertson Blvd and N Almont Dr), West Hollywood. 310/859.0242 &

142 SONA

★★★$$$ Hot, hot, hot from the day it opened in 2003, this throwback to fine dining is the brainchild of co-chef/owners David and Michelle Meyers, who have a self-professed passion for food, which is a good thing for chefs and diners alike. With the help of Parisian architect Anthony Eckelberry, they created a minimalist room done in white, gray, and black, highlighted by a wine-decanting table carved from a six-ton granite boulder by Japanese sculptor Yoshikawa. The cuisine is an outrageously creative combination of Asian, French, and California. The menu offers small portions of items such as a foie gras with blood plum blaze, tuna and tartare with pickled watermelon rind, red and yellow tomato soup with vodka crème fraiche, miso-marinated prime beef, and fried lotus chips. You can order off the menu or just take a seat and ask the chef to surprise you—which he will with multiple mouthwatering courses paired with appropriate wines and served on Izabel Lam china along with Reidel stemware. ♦ Modern French ♦ Tu-Sa, dinner. Reservations essential. 401 N La Cienega Blvd (between Beverly Blvd and Melrose Ave). 310/659.7708. www.sonarestaurant.com

143 TAIL-O'-THE-PUP

$ This hot dog stand, built in 1946, is the most celebrated of LA's few remaining programmatic structures. Hot dogs are sold from a 17-foot-long wiener in a bun. Don't miss it. ♦ Daily. 329 N San Vicente Blvd (between Beverly Blvd and Ashcroft Ave), West Hollywood. 310/652.4517

LINQ

144 LINQ

★★★$$$ The stunning black-and-white décor complements the clientele, who tend to dress in trendy all-black and crowd knee-deep around the sleek, inviting bar, or snuggle up in a booth in the charming candlelit lounge before dinner. The service is leisurely, but then you don't want to hurry this culinary event. Start with sweet white corn soup, smoked salmon quesadilla, or crab cakes, and move right along to the sweet sake-glazed Chilean seabass with wasabi mashed potatoes, whole sizzling catfish (it will make you purr), mushroom risotto, Moroccan seared chicken with a mango-ginger chutney and couscous, or tender filet mignon with porcini mushroom–cabernet sauce. Desserts are just as enticing, especially the chocolate-and-vanilla-layered crème brûlée, banana walnut torte, brownie and brioche bread pudding with Frangelico sauce, and, for lighter tastes, the "Jewel Box" of lemon, mango, and raspberry sorbets. ♦ Asian/French Fusion ♦ Reservations a must. 8338 W Third St (east of La Cienega Blvd between N Sweetzer Ave and N Kings Rd). 323/655.4555 &

Restaurants/Clubs: Red | Hotels: Purple | Shops: Orange | Outdoors/Parks: Green | Sights/Culture: Blue

BEVERLY HILLS/ CENTURY CITY

Money, moguls, and movie stars, and mo' money . . .

Beverly Hills moves to the beat of a different drummer, where it's difficult to differentiate fantasy from reality. The home of rich, famous, and buff-bodied beauties, where plastic surgery and liposuction are household words and limousines, Mercedeses, Rolls-Royces, and vintage wheels are the preferred mode of transportation, Beverly Hills is all about looks and appearances. Neat and clean, chockablock with expensive adult toy stores and lined with Old World buildings, Beverly Hills is a gilded paradise of tree-shaded streets, low crime, and narcissistic opulence. Stately mansions with swimming pools, impeccably manicured lawns, and tennis courts typify the residential areas north and south of **Sunset Boulevard**, but a few simple cottages and modest apartments can be found high up in the hills and south of **Wilshire Boulevard**. The area's been a haven for Hollywood moguls, mavens, and movie stars since the 1920s, when one of its most famous couples, Mary Pickford and Douglas Fairbanks, first set up house here at what is now known as Pickfair. Beverly Hills flaunts its wealth in a manner that has gone out of style elsewhere, but hey, that's because it can.

Until the 1880s, what is now Beverly Hills was just a bunch of lima bean farms. According to local legend, founder **Burton Green** picked the original name, Beverly Farms, from a place in Massachusetts where President William Howard Taft vacationed. In 1907, Wilbur Cook designed the present city for the Rodeo Land and Water Company, laying out the triangular grid of business streets at a 45-degree angle to Wilshire and the curving residential streets north to Sunset. The Olmsted brothers

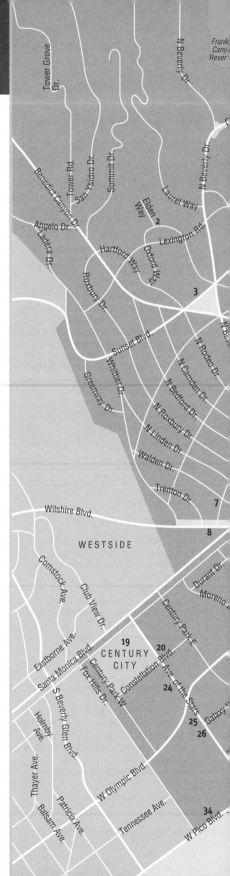

created the picturesque streets that wind through the hills above Sunset Boulevard as though in a landscaped park. One of the first buildings was the **Beverly Hills Hotel**, which was completed around 1912, but much of the surrounding area remained undeveloped until long after. As late as 1946, agent Leland Hayward was offered a snake-infested tract of hilly land in a prime location at a bargain price; that miserable property is today's affluent **Trousdale Estates**. The residential streets are lushly planted with stately and well-trimmed shrubbery and flowers. In spring, gorgeous jacarandas bloom along **Palm** and **Whittier Drives**. The houses, when not obscured by perfectly preened hedges or high walls, exhibit every known architectural style and many hybrids.

Tourists flock here to shop (unless you have a big budget, prepare for a major price shock), stargaze (especially along **Rodeo Drive**, where celebrity-toting limousines line up in front of the chic shops and boutiques), and generally to ogle the good life. The main retail area—bounded by **North Cañon Drive**, Wilshire Boulevard, and **Little Santa Monica Boulevard**—is known as the **Golden Triangle**. Rodeo Drive, which slices north and south through this gilded gateway, is LA's answer to London's Bond Street, Rome's Via Condotti, and Paris's Rue du Faubourg-St-Honoré. From Armani to Versace, Cartier to Tiffany, Chanel to Hermès, every top fashion name is represented in this high-rent retail district and along the blocks of Wilshire Boulevard. In 2003 The Golden Triangle received a major $18 million face-lift, spearheaded by the Pasadena architectural firm of **Moule & Polyzoides**, that included new palms, flowering trees, hip streetlights, and wider sidewalks. **Century City** sits strategically between Beverly Hills and the booming Westside. Once Twentieth Century-Fox's backlot, it was sold in the late 1950s and developed by the Alcoa Corporation. Lacking the glitz of its neighbors, the sterile commercial center offers no street life and little redeeming architecture. It does, however, boast the deluxe **Century Plaza Hotel**, the **St. Regis**, the **Park Hyatt**, and **Westfield Shoppingtown Century City**, a consumer haven of boutiques and outlets sprawled over 18 acres.

1 GREYSTONE PARK

Oil millionaire Edward L. Doheny built this 55-room English Tudor mansion for his son in 1928. Long abandoned, it was used as a set for *The Loved One* and later leased by the American Film Institute. City authorities seem unable to decide what to do with the house, which is closed to the public. But the 16-acre garden, with its balustraded terraces and grassy slopes, is one of LA's loveliest public parks. ♦ Daily. 905 Loma Vista Dr (at Doheny Rd). Concert and event information 310/550.4654

2 VIRGINIA ROBINSON GARDENS

Forget touring the homes of the stars; by calling a week in advance, you can enjoy the oldest residence in Beverly Hills, plus six acres of lush gardens, groves of palms, azaleas, and camellias in spring. It's a treasury of rarities and specimen trees, including the largest monkey hand tree in California. ♦ Admission. Tu-F, 10-11:30AM, 1-2:30PM. 1008 Elden Way (just north of N Crescent Dr). 310/276.5367

The Beverly Hills Hotel
and Bungalows

3 BEVERLY HILLS HOTEL

$$$$ This doyenne of LA is nicknamed "the Pink Palace." A sprawling Mission Revival hotel that is seen as the unofficial symbol of the city and its hedonistic lifestyle, the graceful building was constructed in 1912, enhanced in the 1940s, and restored, remodeled, and renovated several times since. The 12 acres of lush tropical gardens are cleverly landscaped to prevent intrusion from traffic noise and prying eyes. The 194 rooms (including the 21 luxurious bungalows where such luminaries as Chaplin, Garbo, Gable, and Lombard stayed) are large, modern, and lavishly decorated. A fitness center, two tennis courts, five meeting spaces, an inviting pool with cabanas, and a LaPrairie full-service spa are added amenities. ♦ 9641 Sunset Blvd (between N Crescent Dr and Hartford Way).

310/276.2251, 800/283.8885; fax
310/887.2887. www.thebeverlyhillshotel.com

Within the Beverly Hills Hotel:

POLO LOUNGE

★★★$$$ The bar is jammed during the
cocktail hour even though some of the usual
suspects have found greener pastures in the
lounges of the Peninsula Hotel, Raffles'
L'Ermitage, or the Four Seasons. Chef Katsuo
"Suki" Sugiura's food can be top-notch,
especially the sautéed tenderloin of beef,
penne pasta with oolong tea, smoked free-
range chicken and crispy Asian vegetables,
and the perfectly prepared Chilean sea bass.
End with a chocolate soufflé or chocolate
sensation. ◆ California ◆ Daily, breakfast,
lunch, and dinner. Reservations necessary.
310/276.2251

THE FOUNTAIN COFFEE SHOP

★★★$ Whether for the 1950s-style
countertop dining or for the floats and malts,
some of the most recognizable people in the
world come here for breakfast. ◆ Coffee Shop
◆ Daily, breakfast, lunch, and light dinner.
310/276.2251

4 MAPLE DRIVE

★★★$$$ This large, bustling, and *très*
fashionable restaurant features an attractive
interior with a handsome, inviting bar. After
14 years in business, Maple Drive underwent
a major menu change in 2003 spearheaded
by chef Eric Klein and his partner Douglas
Wickard. Together the duo created what they
call an "upper echelon of dining events." The
seasonally changing cuisine, now called
"Eric's Food," features old standbys (meat
loaf, Caesar salad) along with some daily
surprises (foie gras spring rolls, crispy
calamari, braised veal cheeks, and a mighty
fine pear upside-down cake). Don't miss the
Sunday jazz brunch—a scrumptious
assortment of specialties that includes
homemade granola, barbecued salmon, eggs
Benedict and Florentine, and other yummy
delights. A jazz combo provides background
music Wednesday through Saturday nights.
This is also a great spot for celebrity sightings.
California ◆ M-Su, dinner; M-F, lunch and
dinner. 345 N Maple Dr (between W Third St
and Alden Dr). 310/274.9800 &

5 IL CIELO

★★$$ Forks down, this is one of the most
romantic restaurants. Choose from creative
raviolis stuffed with ricotta, veal, and truffles,
cheese and nut pasta, salmon with peppers
and grilled baby eggplant, or chicken stuffed
with peanuts, ricotta, and shallots. Dine

alfresco in either of two charming courtyards,
or in the white-walled room with a trompe l'oeil
sky. ◆ Italian ◆ M-F, lunch and dinner; Sa,
dinner. 9018 Burton Way (between N Almont
and N Wetherly Drs). 310/276.9990 &

5 PRATESI

Hand-embroidered silk sheets, cashmere
blankets, and huge fluffy towels for
millionaires can be found here. ◆ M-Sa. 9024
Burton Way (between N Almont and N
Wetherly Drs). 310/274.7661

6 LE MERIDIEN HOTEL

$$$ This French-style 304-room hotel sits just
off busy La Cienega Boulevard's restaurant
row. Awash in high-tech electronics, all rooms
have fax machines, computer hookups, and
sophisticated remote-control gadgetry, as well
as deep soaking tubs. Other amenities
include Le Festival, a French/Mediterranean
restaurant; a health club; and an outdoor
pool. ◆ 465 S La Cienega Blvd (at Clifton
Way). 310/247.0400; fax 310/247.0315.
www.lemeridienbeverlyhills.com &

7 SPADENA HOUSE

Hansel and Gretel would have lived here if
they'd made it big with their screenplay. The
thatch-roof house was designed by **Henry
Oliver** in 1921 as a combined movie set and
office. It's a private residence. ◆ Walden Dr
and Carmelita Ave

8 MERV GRIFFIN'S BEVERLY HILTON HOTEL

$$$ Balconied rooms surround the large pool,
giving this 582-room luxury hotel the feel of a
resort. Guest rooms are comfortable and
subtly decorated in light, soft colors. There are
two restaurants, a business center, and a
well-equipped fitness center. ◆ 9876 Wilshire
Blvd (just west of Santa Monica Blvd).
310/274.7777, 800/HILTONS; fax
310/285.1313. www.merv.com &

9 KATE MANTILINI

★★$$ When owner Marilyn Lewis requested a
roadside café, the architects at Morphosis
gave her one of the most exciting interiors in
LA, spread out in layered space, indirectly lit,
with a jagged steel sundial extending from the
floor through the ceiling. Enclosed booths line
the 100-foot-long outer wall. The restaurant is
named for a boxing promoter of the 1940s,
and the menu pays homage to Hollywood's
famous Musso and Frank Grill, offering hearty
meat loaf with crisp kale, roast chicken with
mashed potatoes, and a delectable calf's
brain omelet. ◆ American ◆ M-F, breakfast,
lunch, and dinner; Sa, Su, brunch and dinner.

Restaurants/Clubs: Red | Hotels: Purple | Shops: Orange | Outdoors/Parks: Green | Sights/Culture: Blue

9101 Wilshire Blvd (at N Doheny Dr).
310/278.3699 &

10 ACADEMY OF MOTION PICTURE ARTS & SCIENCES

LA's finest thousand-seat theater houses Oscars and lobby exhibitions, plus occasional public screenings. ♦ 8949 Wilshire Blvd (between N La Peer and N Almont Drs). 310/247.3000

11 REIGN

★★$$$$ This is the place to go when you're in the mood for fine soul food. After all, the menu was created from original recipes by owner, epicure, and Dallas Cowboys wide receiver Keyshawn Johnson's mother and aunt. Portions are big and choices are many, like crunchy fried chicken, smothered pork chops, beef short ribs, baby back ribs, gumbo, and catfish, accompanied by options such as mashed potatoes, collard greens, macaroni and cheese, and candied yams. And if you have a football player's appetite, finish with peach cobbler or sweet potato pie. Between bites, check out the scene at the bar, where smartly clad cosmopolitan swillers congregate. ♦ Soul Food ♦ Dinner, nightly. Reservations recommended. 180 N Robertson Blvd (at Wilshire Blvd). 310/273.4463 & (The physically challenged should request a table on the lower level.)

11 WILSHIRE-ROBERTSON PLAZA

Designed by the provocative firm **Arquitectonica** in 1990, this commercial block stands out from the tedious succession of savings and loan offices. ♦ 8750 Wilshire Blvd (at S Robertson Blvd)

12 MATSUHISA

★★★$$$ Behind this storefront restaurant and innovative sushi bar is a sushi master with more than 20 years of experience. ♦ Japanese ♦ M-F, lunch and dinner; Sa, Su, dinner. 129 N La Cienega Blvd (one block north of Wilshire Blvd). 310/659.9639

12 DELMONICO'S LOBSTER HOUSE

★★$$ Lobster lovers rejoice, as you can feast on your favorite crustacean prepared 17 different ways at this tiny seafood house. Have a stuffed two-pounder or a crispy Maine lobster roll, lobster cocktail, lobster cobbler, lobster linguini, cutlet, or risotto. Chef Tony De la Cruz also grills a mean prime aged steak, veal, poultry, and a variety of fresh fish dishes. The dining room is inviting, with vanilla-toned marbles, Mediterranean-style fabrics, and attractive artwork. ♦ Daily, dinner. Reservations suggested. 133 N La Cienega Blvd (one block north of Wilshire

Blvd). 310/854.9077. Also in Encino at 16358 Ventura Blvd (at Havenhurst). 818/986.0777

13 LAWRY'S PRIME RIB

★★$$ Prime rib is always the *plat du jour* at this carnivore's emporium set in retro 1940s décor. It seems silly to go here unless you're into beef, but for those who aren't, there are other choices on the menu. There's always a fairly long wait for a table. ♦ American ♦ Daily, dinner. 100 N La Cienega Blvd (between Wilshire Blvd and Clifton Way). 310/652.2827 &

14 GAYLORD INDIA

★★$$ The name has changed, but everything else is still the same at this understated and beautiful local outpost of the upscale chain, which began in New Delhi in 1941. The food is consistently first-rate. ♦ North Indian ♦ Daily, lunch and dinner. 50 N La Cienega Blvd (between Wilshire Blvd and Clifton Way). 310/652.3838

15 WILSHIRE THEATRE

The stylish zigzag movie house, designed by **S. Charles Lee** for Fox in 1929, has been restored as a stage for musicals and dramas. ♦ 8440 Wilshire Blvd (at S Hamilton Dr). 323/468.1700

16 RUTH'S CHRIS STEAK HOUSE

★★$$$ Some say this acclaimed restaurant serves the best steaks in town. Order your favorite cut from their traditional menu. ♦ American ♦ Daily, dinner. 224 S Beverly Dr (between Gregory Way and Charleville Blvd). 310/859.8744

17 ROSEBUD CAKES

Head here for a selection of Memphis-inspired white-chocolate cakes and other delectable confections. ♦ Tu-Sa; Su, 10AM-noon (pickups only). 311 S Robertson Blvd (between Olympic Blvd and Gregory Way). 310/657.6207

18 CENTER FOR MOTION PICTURE STUDY

Fran Offenhauser and Michael J. Mekeel did the imaginative conversion of this 1928 landmark building. The project represented a triumph for local preservationists, offsetting the loss of the zigzag Beverly Theater on North Beverly Drive. The **Margaret Herrick Library,** with one of the country's finest collections of film books, magazines, and archival treasures, is open without charge to serious students of cinema. ♦ Free. M-F. Tours on first day of the month at 10AM by reservation only. 333 S La Cienega Blvd (between W Olympic Blvd and Gregory Way). 310/247.3000

19 WESTFIELD SHOPPINGTOWN CENTURY CITY

This is one of LA's first malls. It's easy to maneuver in, lively, houses more than 100 stores, and has ample free parking. Major attractions include the Marketplace, AMC Theaters (in which the quality of sound, projection, and sightlines is far above average), and Gelson's, one of LA's top markets. Macy's and Bloomingdale's anchor the rest of the mall, which includes such shops as Brentano's (an exemplary general bookstore), Crabtree & Evelyn, Abercrombie & Fitch, Gap, Banana Republic, Rand McNally, Tiffany's, Crate & Barrel, Godiva Chocolatier, and Aveda. New York's Metropolitan Museum of Art also has an extensive gift shop here. ♦ Daily. Free parking with validation. 10250 Little Santa Monica Blvd (between Avenue of the Stars and Century Park W). 310/277.3898. www.westfieldshoppingtowncenturycity.com

20 CENTURY CLUB

★★$$$ This gargantuan space (25,000 square feet) is a combination café/nightclub, with three dance floors and patio and indoor dining areas. There is a mix of entertainment styles: For example, on Mondays they play the blues; on Fridays, the score heats up with Latin salsa; on Sundays, rap and hip-hop is highlighted. The menu at the **Banana Cafe** offers such dishes as pasta primavera, grilled Norwegian salmon, and filet mignon. ♦ Continental ♦ Cover charge, plus a minimum food purchase. M, W-Su lunch and dinner. Reservations required; jacket required. 10131 Constellation Blvd (at Avenue of the Stars). 310/553.6000 と

21 AVALON HOTEL

$$ This is one of LA's best-kept secrets, and the TV, film, recording, and other entertainment types who stay here like it that way. If you prefer small, out-of-the way hotels, this legendary triplex hide-away on the southern tip of Beverly Hills is for you. Carved from a 1950s relic that once hosted Marilyn Monroe and served as a location for the *I Love Lucy* show, the hotel's interior was reinvented by Kelly Wearstler of KWID Designs, with a hip and cozy décor defined by sharp curves and clean lines. Each of the homey 88 rooms features Charles Eames–inspired chairs, George Nelson bubble

lamps, and Isamu Noguchi tables highlighted by bright colors and equipped with the usual TV, CD, Internet access, fax, and room service (which is the dining option of choice for its Tinseltown clientele). In-room manicures, pedicures, facials, massages, and even acupuncture are available. There's also an outdoor pool. **Blue on Blue Restaurant** (★★$$) is a fun, cheery three-meals-a-day eatery with good food and signature drinks like "A Walk in Space" with Pearl vodka, watermelon liqueur, and Tang, or the "Librarian's Martini"—Southern Comfort, amaretto, and fresh limes and cranberries. ♦ California ♦ Daily from 7AM. ♦ 9400 W Olympic Blvd (corner of Beverly Dr). 310/277.4928, 800/535.4715; www.avalon-hotel.com

22 CHRISTOPHER HANSEN

In 1990, **Kirkpatrick Associates** designed this museum-like setting for custom audio installations and home-entertainment centers. ♦ M-Sa. 8822 Olympic Blvd (between S Robertson Blvd and S Clark Dr). 310/858.8112

23 WOSK APARTMENT

Frank Gehry and **Miriam Wosk**'s surreal 1983 penthouse—with its gold ziggurat, blue dome, black marble arch, and turquoise-tile walls clustered atop a pink apartment building—juices up an otherwise bland street. It's a private residence. ♦ 440 S Roxbury Dr (between S Bedford Dr and Olympic Blvd)

24 CENTURY PLAZA HOTEL & SPA

$$$$ You don't have to be rich *and* famous to stay at this opulent landmark—just rich. The original hotel, an elliptical block designed by **Minoru Yamasaki,** opened in 1966. All spiffed up after a multimillion-dollar renovation (completed in 2001), the hotel sports a showcase lobby and world-class, 30,000-square-foot, Asian-themed day spa. There are 727 rooms (all with balconies) attractively designed with cherry wood paneling, unique glass vanities, porcelain flooring, polished chrome, and lavish bathrooms. In-room extras include Internet access, 27-inch televisions, robes, deluxe bath products, safes, three phones, and private bars. As always, the Plaza's focus is banquet and convention groups, and there's plenty of space dedicated to both in the new design. There's also a 10-acre garden with an oversized pool. ♦ Valet and self-parking. 2025 Avenue of the Stars (between W Olympic and Constellation Blvds). 310/277.2000, 800/WESTIN1; fax 310/551.3355. www.centuryplazala.com

Restaurants/Clubs: Red | Hotels: Purple | Shops: Orange | Outdoors/Parks: Green | Sights/Culture: Blue

Within the Century Plaza Hotel:

BREEZE

★★★$$$ Indoor/outdoor dining is offered at this bright and airy restaurant, with its muted gold-and-white-striped motif and lively atmosphere. Talented chef John Hart creates tasty dishes from fresh seasonal produce and herbs and truffles picked from his garden, including an awesome yellowfin tuna tartare with avocado; fresh calamari from Point Judith, Maine; Artic char artichoke mascarpone ravioli, and assorted fresh fish dishes.

The veal chop with cipollini onions and chanterelles is divine. There's also a seafood bar where you can snack on house-cured smoked fish, oysters, shellfish, and even a selection of gazpachos. Dessert winners are the chocolate sensation, a flourless cake with chocolate mousse, and the pineapple cream cheese beignet with mango salsa and caramelized bananas. The pretty room is done with glass walls, terrazzo flooring, laminated glass ceiling with a rice-paper and bamboo motif, and grassy plants that sway from the breeze of special air diffusers. There's a fun ellipse-shaped bar and a patio highlighted by a giant California coral tree. ♦ Daily, breakfast, lunch, and dinner. 310/551.3334

24 ST. REGIS LOS ANGELES

$$$$ Adjacent to the Century Plaza Hotel and carved out of the landmark building that once housed the Plaza's Tower section, this super-swank member of the prestigious St. Regis hotel chain features 297 luxuriously appointed rooms. You can feel just how swank this place is the moment you walk through the spiffy new entrance into the luscious lobby. Each room is wired up with technologically advanced electronic equipment and doodads. There are CD and DVD players with surround sound, high-speed Internet access, a laptop safe with battery recharging capability, fax/copier/printer, and, for a touch of class, 24-hour butler service. Hotel facilities include a full-service spa and fitness room overlooking the large pool area, where on a clear day you can see the ocean. Joining the bandwagon of the burgeoning in-room pampering phenomena, the hotel now offers a variety of treatments from the "Morning Call"—a half-hour Swedish massage with a newspaper, fruit smoothies, and

Los Angeles is a multiethnic mosaic of people and cultures. The 9.6 million residents of Los Angeles County include people from about 140 countries. This population includes the largest group of Asian/Pacific people in the US outside of Honolulu; the second-largest populations of Armenians, Koreans, Filipinos, Salvadorans, and Guatemalans in the world; and the largest Hispanic population in the US.

mineral water thrown in—to a "Late Night Bubbles" for two that includes a 50-minute rub, a bottle of Dom Perignon, chocolate-dipped strawberries, and a candlelit bubble bath. Ah, the good life. 2055 Ave of the Stars (between W Olympic and Constellation Blvds) ♦ 310/277.6111, 800/325.3589; fax 310/277.6311. www.luxurycollection.com &

Within the St. Regis:

ENCORE

★★$$$ Chef Bruno Davaillon, a talented import from Michelin-rated restaurants in France and Great Britain, oversees the creative menu for this branch of the New York restaurant of the same name. Choice options include Dungeness crab and potato, mille-feuille with a beurre blanc emulsion, pan-seared duck foie gras; roast dry-aged New York steak with stewed shallots, pommes Anna, horseradish, and oxtail in a black olive sauce; roasted Alaskan halibut with fingerling potatoes, haricots vert, fried shallots, and truffled chicken jus; and desserts like caramel and chocolate mousse, almond shortbread, and black sesame Napoleon with Granny Smith apples, raisins, calvados, and vanilla ice milk. Be sure to have a drink at the stylish King Cole Bar before or after dinner. ♦ M-Sa, breakfast, lunch, and dinner; Su, brunch and dinner. 310/277.6111

25 FOX PLAZA

Johnson, Fain & Pereira Associates' 1987 design represents the most dramatic addition to Century City since the original twin towers. This handsome 34-story office tower is faceted like a crystal, banded in salmon granite and gray-tinted glass, and positioned to dominate the sweep of Olympic Boulevard and the Midtown skyline. ♦ 2121 Avenue of the Stars (between W Pico and W Olympic Blvds). 310/282.0047

26 PARK HYATT LOS ANGELES AT CENTURY CITY

$$$$ The 367-room, 181-suite property features an exterior peach pyramid design with a softly tinted interior décor. Guests are pampered with such special services as packing and unpacking of luggage on request, limousine service, and a 24-hour mending and pressing service. Each comfortable, recently refurbished room comes with a terry-cloth robe, fine toiletries, multiple phones, and a balcony. In addition to the Park Grill restaurant, there's a new spa and fitness-center pool and sundeck with an inviting Jacuzzi and extensive business services. ♦ 2151 Avenue of the Stars (between W Pico and W Olympic Blvds). 310/277.2777, 800/233.1234; fax 310/785.9240. www.parkhyattlosangeles.com &

27 LOEWS BEVERLY HILLS HOTEL

$$$ A hotel of many incarnations, now owned and operated by Loews, this 136-room hillside inn sits a bit off the beaten track, just outside of Beverly Hills proper. Every room and suite is nicely appointed. Most feature Tempur-Pedic beds—simply divine mattresses that conform to your shape and size—a coffeemaker, high-speed Internet access, and the usual upscale amenities from hair dryers to robes. A major plus is Loews' company-wide Star Service, which provides in-room exercise gadgets (Pilates balls, stair stepper, ankle weights, tummy roll, barbells, and more) at the touch of the star on your in-room phone. Another asset is the private balconies that offer sweeping views of Century City, Beverly Hills, and Hollywood Hills. The **Lot 1224 Restaurant** (**$$) (pronounced "twelve twenty-four," as in the hotel's address) offers an inviting venue for breakfast, lunch, and dinner along with a friendly, bustling bar/lounge. In addition to full-course meals, the eclectic menu offers a variety of "small bites" lounge food. You'll love breakfast here, where choices range from "Toad in a Hole" (sourdough toast stuffed with eggs over easy) to French toast. Dinners are designed so you can have fun with your food and mix and match courses with such choices as Asian-style halibut, Tuscan bread salad, and glazed eggplant or Mediterranean mussels. An entertainment room sits adjacent to the dining area, where you can relax and watch television on a flat-screen. There's also a special executive club floor that comes with privileges such as continental breakfast and nightly hors d'oeuvres in an exclusive lounge. Other amenities include a large swimming pool with private cabanas and a fitness facility. ◆ 1224 S Beverwil Dr (at W Pico Blvd), Beverly Hills. 310/277.2800, 1/800/23.LOEWS. www.loewshotels.com

28 OSTERIA ROMANA ORSINI

★★$$ Perhaps it's the lunching execs from nearby Twentieth Century-Fox who give this place such a clubby feel. The kitchen serves and the bountiful lunchtime antipasto buffet is memorable. Nevertheless, the nightclub upstairs persists in such amusingly antediluvian behavior as charging women less for admission than they charge men. ◆ Italian ◆ Restaurant: M-F, lunch and dinner; Sa, dinner. Club: Th-Sa, until 2AM. 9575 W Pico Blvd (between Smithwood and Edris Drs). 310/277.6050

29 DELMONICO'S

★★$$ This large, airy seafood restaurant, with ceiling fans and tables crowded in the center of the room, is reminiscent of an old Parisian brasserie and filled with the same fearsome din; to avoid the racket, try for one of the wooden booths that hug the walls. The long, lively bar serves fresh oysters and great Bloody Marys. ◆ Seafood ◆ M-F, lunch and dinner; Sa, Su, dinner. 9320 W Pico Blvd (between Glenville and S Rexford Drs). 310/550.7737 &

30 HYMIE'S FISH MARKET

★$$ Top showbiz types come to this no-nonsense place for the lobster bouillabaisse, clams, oysters, and so on. It also has a fresh fish market. ◆ Seafood ◆ Restaurant: M-F, lunch and dinner; Sa, Su, dinner. Fish market: M-F, until 10PM; Sa, Su, 3-10:30PM. 9228 W Pico Blvd (between Cardiff Ave and Glenville Dr). 310/550.0377

31 BEVERLYWOOD BAKERY

Some of the best pumpernickel and rye this side of Central Europe is baked on these premises. ◆ Bakery ◆ Daily. 9128 W Pico Blvd (at Oakhurst Dr). 310/550.9842

32 RAJA

★$$ Kashmiri specialties, tandoori, and vegetable dishes are served here at reasonable prices. An all-you-can-eat lunch buffet is available, too. ◆ Indian ◆ Daily, lunch and dinner. 8875 W Pico Blvd (between S Clark and S Swall Drs). 310/550.9176

33 MUSEUM OF TOLERANCE

This high-tech multimedia center was created to raise everyone's consciousness of bigotry and racism, with a focus on the Nazi Holocaust and prejudice in American history. The new **Point of View Diner** (which serves no food) encourages visitors, through video monitors, to consider the moral responsibility of such social issues as First Amendment rights and drunk driving. ◆ Admission. M-F, Su. 9786 W Pico Blvd (at S Roxbury Dr). 310/553.8403. www.weisenthal.com

34 TWENTIETH CENTURY-FOX FILM CORP

This film company has survived more predators than a maiden in a melodrama. There are no tours offered here, but you can drive up to the gate and get a glimpse at the *Hello, Dolly!* street, a re-creation of turn-of-the-century New York. This was Hollywood's first studio planned for sound, created by pioneer William Fox, who then lost control of the company he had established. Darryl Zanuck ruled here over such eminent subjects as Shirley Temple, Carmen Miranda, and director John Ford. It was also home to

---

Restaurants/Clubs: Red | Hotels: Purple | Shops: Orange | Outdoors/Parks: Green | Sights/Culture: Blue

Marilyn Monroe, *Cleopatra*, and *M.A.S.H.* ♦ 10201 W Pico Blvd (between Ave of the Stars and Fox Hills Dr). 310/277.2211

35 BEVERLY HILLS CITY HALL

The unique scroll ornament and colorful aquatie dome of **William Gage**'s splendid 1932 Baroque pile were scrubbed clean in a recent restoration. ♦ 455 N Rexford Dr (at Santa Monica Blvd)

35 BEVERLY HILLS CIVIC CENTER

Architect **Charles Moore** won a competition with his romantic/historical design for a diagonal sequence of three landscaped courtyards that link the library, fire and police stations, offices, and parking to the remodeled City Hall. The grand vista toward the hills works well, but the buildings have the insubstantial quality of a movie set—you wonder if they will still be there next week. Repetitive rusticated arches and tile inserts along the courtyard compete with the frilly decoration of old City Hall. ♦ N Rexford Dr (between Little Santa Monica and Santa Monica Blvds)

36 US POST OFFICE

Ralph Flewelling created this noble 1933 structure in the Italian Renaissance style, with terra-cotta, brick, and classically framed windows and doors. This may be the only post office in the country (or even the world) that offers valet parking. It could also end up being the only mail center with a museum-quality retail store, café, theater, and visitors information center, if the Beverly Hills Cultural Center Foundation raises enough funds for the project. ♦ 9300 Santa Monica Blvd (at N Crescent Dr)

37 UNION 76 GAS STATION

The swooping cantilevered 1950s concrete canopy is extraordinarily daring for this area. ♦ N Rexford Dr and Little Santa Monica Blvd

38 RAFFLES L'ERMITAGE HOTEL

$$$$ Hidden in a residential section on the fringes of Beverly Hills, this stylish hotel attracts a big record company/entertainment industry crowd who appreciate its off-the-beaten-track location and luxurious digs. The décor is minimalist/Asian modern accented by maple, marble, and interesting works of art. The 124 suites are spacious and sumptuous, with plush carpeting, silk-covered queen-sized beds, and English sycamore furnishings. Lovely latticework separates the bedroom from a well-stocked bar (with free soft drinks) and walk-in closet, and the lavish marble-and-tile bath offers an array of Aveda amenities. Other enticing touches include 40-inch televisions, CD/DVD players, free local calls, fax machines, and cell phones. There's a cozy library bar with a fireplace, attractive

rooftop gardens, a pool, a nicely equipped fitness center, and a spa, along with a very accommodating staff. While room service is the most popular mode of dining among the celebrity in-house guests (many rarely leave their suite), the restaurant (see below) is definitely worth trying. ♦ 9291 Burton Way (at Foothill Rd). 310/278.3433; fax 310/278.8247. www.lermitagehotel.com

Within Raffles L'Ermitage Hotel:

JAAN RESTAURANT AT RAFFLES

***$$$ Talented chef Bruno Lopez created a seasonally changing, light, and lively menu that excites the palate. You can order à la carte or by six-course tasting menu (we recommend the latter), but be sure to ask for the fresh halibut served on potato gnocchi or foie gras pâté. The gorgeous dining area sits under a dome ceiling. Dancing fountains, lit up at night, visible through a floor-to-ceiling window add to the romance of the room. A striking Oriental flower arrangement provides a regal centerpiece for the dining area. The adjacent lounge overflows with before- and after-dinner drinkers, while an outdoor patio attracts those who still smoke. ♦ Daily, lunch and dinner. Reservations advised. 310/278.3344

RAFFLES AMRITA SPA

This pretty little pamper spot, named after a mystic nectar of the gods, offers an array of salubrious services from facials to pedicures. Conveniently located on the eighth floor, just below the rooftop pool and adjacent to the fitness center, the spa features Zen-like treatment rooms, changing rooms for men and women with steam baths, showers, and lockers, and a superb staff. A recent massage ranked as one of the top 10 ever experienced by a self-admitted spa snob. ♦ Daily, 6AM–10PM.

39 O'NEILL HOUSE

Antonio Gaudí is alive and well in Beverly Hills! The architect would be proud of the writhing stucco on **Don Ramos**'s 1989 Art Nouveau house, and of the more whimsical guest house behind. It's a private residence. ♦ 507 N Rodeo Dr (between Santa Monica Blvd and Carmelita Ave)

40 MUSEUM OF TELEVISION & RADIO

Architect **Richard Meier** redesigned this former bank building to house the 23,000-square-foot museum. Visitors can choose from more than 60,000 television and radio programs and commercials to watch at private consoles. Special exhibits are shown in a 150-seat theater as well. ♦ Admission. W-Su. 465 N Beverly Dr (at Little Santa Monica Blvd). 310/786.1000

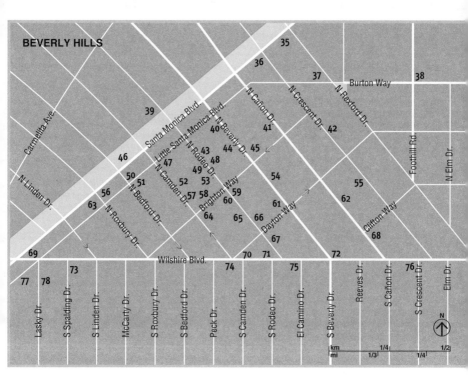

41 CARROLL & CO.

Proffering menswear for the old guard—including such odd bedfellows as Ronald Reagan, George McGovern, and Gregory Peck—this popular, upscale shop moved here in 1997. ♦ M-Sa. 425 N Cañon Dr (between Brighton Way and Little Santa Monica Blvd). 310/273.9060

42 WESTERN ATLAS

Paul Williams's 1940 American Federal Revival office building has a grand portico. ♦ 360 N Crescent Dr (between Dayton Way and Little Santa Monica Blvd)

43 POLO/RALPH LAUREN

No, you haven't wandered into an English country house; it's just the latest of Lauren's emporia for visiting squires and Anglophiles. ♦ M-Sa. 444 N Rodeo Dr (between Brighton Way and Little Santa Monica Blvd). 310/281.7200

Above Polo/Ralph Lauren:

FRÉDÉRIC FEKKAI

This chic salon, named for the New York wunderkind stylist, is just too hip. His top-to-toe beauty treatments are the hottest ticket (and among the priciest) in Beverly Hills, and his clientele is the prettiest and richest. ♦ M-Sa. 310/777.8700

44 THE FARM OF BEVERLY HILLS

★★$$ Formerly known as Jacksons Farm, this friendly eatery offers generous portions of comforting home-style fare. At times inconsistent, the food is generally very good, and the place is packed night and day. Favorites include halibut with warm red and yellow tomatoes, grilled marinated steak with shoestring potatoes and three-grain mustard sauce, and rotisserie chicken. The deli offers food to go—perfect for a picnic at the beach or the Hollywood Bowl. ♦ American ♦ M-F, breakfast, lunch, and dinner; Sa, Su, brunch and dinner. 439 N Beverly Dr (between Brighton Way and Little Santa Monica Blvd). 310/273.5578 ♿

45 NATE 'N' AL

★$$ Big-name stars often frequent this celebrated deli on weekends to read their Sunday newspapers and visit with friends. ♦ Deli ♦ Daily, breakfast, lunch, and dinner. 414 N Beverly Dr (between Brighton Way and Little Santa Monica Blvd). 310/274.0101

46 CACTUS GARDEN

Cacti and succulents from around the world occupy one section of the most handsome

---

Restaurants/Clubs: Red | Hotels: Purple | Shops: Orange | Outdoors/Parks: Green | Sights/Culture: Blue

landscaping to be found on any city boulevard. ◆ Santa Monica Blvd (between N Camden and N Bedford Drs)

47 EXOTICAR MODEL GALLERY

Sly Stallone, Bill Clinton, Jerry Seinfeld, and Tim Allen are just a few of the better-known customers of this museumlike miniature car shop. If you're into vintage or luxury wheels, you can pick up a one-eighteenth-scale replica of anything from a 1950 Chevrolet Cameo Pickup to a 1997 Mercedes CLK-GTR-11-D2. ◆ Daily. 9532 Little Santa Monica Blvd (between N Rodeo and N Camden Drs). 310/276.5035

48 GIORGIO ARMANI

The largest and glitziest of Italian designer Giorgio Armani's ultra-stylish clothing stores attracts Steven Spielberg, Sir Elton John, and other big-name regular customers. ◆ M-Sa. 436 N Rodeo Dr (between Brighton Way and Little Santa Monica Blvd). 310/271.5555

48 HERMÈS

Designed by Rena Dumas, this behemoth haute couture emporium, with towering archways, lush greenery, and slender furnishings, is designed to provide an appropriately elegant backdrop for Hermès signature scarves, high fashion, and leather goods. ◆ M-Sa. 434 N Rodeo Dr (between Brighton Way and Little Santa Monica Blvd). 310/278.6440

49 FRETTE

Exquisite Italian lingerie and table, bath, and bed linens are sold here. ◆ M-Sa. 449 N Rodeo Dr (between Brighton Way and Little Santa Monica Blvd). 310/273.8540

50 AIRSTREAM DINER

*$ This whimsical 24-hour breakfast, lunch, and dinner diner, set in a vintage Aluminum Airstream trailer with retro Formica, linoleum, and Snow White statues for stools, is one big loopy restaurant. Even so, it works for locals who go for the Billion Dollar Babies silver-dollar-size pancakes, fresh lemonade, Cuban sandwiches, burgers, and homemade berry pop tarts. ◆ American ◆ Daily, 24 hours. 9601 S Santa Monica Blvd (at Bedford Dr). 310/440.8883

51 CRUSTACEAN

★★★$$$ Like its San Francisco namesake, this dynamite Eurasian eatery features food as attractive as the place itself. An awesome aquarium, built into the floor, winds from the entrance to the dining room. Chef/owner Helene An's busy open kitchen creates such scrumptious tapas as prawn-filled rice-paper rolls and lemongrass-sesame beef satay.

Artfully prepared entrées include Chilean sea bass pan-seared with ginger-citrus reduction and rack of lamb flambéed in Chardonnay. ◆ Eurasian ◆ M-Sa, lunch and dinner. Reservations required. Valet parking available. 9646 Little Santa Monica Blvd (at N Bedford Dr). 310/205.8990

52 MANDARIN

★★$$$ Peking duck, braised lamb, and Beggar's Chicken highlight the Mandarin menu at this fun eatery. ◆ Chinese ◆ M-F, lunch and dinner; Sa, Su, dinner. Reservations recommended. 430 N Camden Dr (between Brighton Way and Little Santa Monica Blvd). 310/859.0638, 323/272.0267

53 RODEO COLLECTION

Within this pink marble shopping mall are upscale designer boutiques such as La Perla, Sumer Collection, Sonia Rykiel, Stuart Witzman shoes, and Fila. ◆ Daily. 433 N Rodeo Dr (between Brighton Way and Little Santa Monica Blvd)

DE MORI

***$$ The debonair host with the most, Silvio De Mori (Mimosa and Café des Artistes) originally opened this characteristically charming, casual café. Alas the charming De Mori sold the place in 2004, but his signature remains and so does the fine Italian cuisine. A gracious outdoor patio provides an inviting setting for alfresco dining, especially on warm summer nights. The food puts the icing on the cake: luscious linguini, spaghetti Bolognese, mouthwatering veal chops, or grilled eggplant polished off with a great wine. Desserts are just as good. The new owners have livened up the scene with a violinist and a guitarist to entertain nightly and Cuban dance nights a few times a month. ◆ Italian with a California twist. ◆ Tu-Su, lunch and dinner. Reservations suggested. Downstairs at the Rodeo Collection. 310/274.1500; email: sdemori@msn.com

54 TASCHEN BOOKSTORE

This highbrow bookstore, operated by the German-based Taschen Company, specializes in scholarly and pop coffee-table books of various genres from photography to sex. Designed by Philippe Starck, the stunning 3,000-square-foot literary emporium looks more like an art gallery than a bookstore. Careful cerebral touches include a private glassed-in reading room on the mezzanine and a relaxing terrace area. To keep you on your intellectual toes, there are regularly scheduled events and lectures as well as special weeks highlighting celebrity curators. ◆ Daily. 354 N Beverly Dr (between Dayton and Brighton Ways). 310/274.4300. www.taschen.com

55 WHOLE FOODS MARKET

This bustling yuppie haven is the place to stock up on fresh organic produce, meat raised humanely and without hormones, healthy breads, yummy natural desserts, and other politically correct goodies. ♦ Daily. 239 N Crescent Dr (between Clifton and Dayton Ways). 310/274.3360. Also at 3476 Centinela Ave (at Palms Blvd), Westside. 310/391.5209

56 THE NOSH OF BEVERLY HILLS

★★$ Stop for a quick, delicious bite at this New York–style "haimish" deli serving everything from lox and bagels to chicken soup and cheesecake. ♦ Jewish Deli ♦ Daily. 9689 Little Santa Monica Blvd (at N Roxbury Dr). 310/271.3730

57 LA SCALA

★★★$$$ An institution once known for its celebrity clientele, snooty service, and steep prices, this spot has a new attitude. It is now a kinder, gentler neighborhood restaurant, serving good food with a smile, including ever-changing pasta dishes, osso buco, and fresh fish. The wine list is excellent. ♦ Italian ♦ M-Sa, lunch and dinner. Reservations recommended. 410 N Camden Dr (between Brighton Way and Little Santa Monica Blvd). 310/275.0579 ♿ Also at 3821 Riverside Dr (between Hollywood Way and Kenwood St), Burbank. 818/846.6800 ♿; 11740 San Vicente Blvd (at Gorham Ave), Brentwood. 310/826.6100

58 EMPORIO ARMANI

You can really bust your budget at this posh Italian designer-wear emporium, but hey, his stuff's worth it. ♦ 9533 Brighton Way (between N Rodeo and N Camden Drs). 310/271.7790

59 LUXE HOTEL RODEO DRIVE

$$$ A special little find in the heart of Beverly Hills, this minimalist 86-room hotel, designed by Vicente Wolf, blends classic and contemporary styles through the use of copper, marble, and glass. Each adorable room comes with upscale features such as Frette linens, signature robes, Rene Furterer toiletries, and CD players. Other in-room amenities include speedy Internet access, 27-inch televisions, and 24-hour room service. There are two Valentino boutiques (one for him, the other for her) at the entrance of the hotel, where big-budget shoppers can find exquisite designer duds. Even if you can't afford the price tags, just browsing through these chic shops is a trip. And, who knows, you just might spot a favorite celebrity or two. Since there is no pool or tennis courts, the hotel provides free shuttle service to its sister property, the **Summit Belair,** which provides those facilities. ♦ 360 N Rodeo Dr (between Dayton and Brighton Ways). 310/273.0300, 800.HOTEL.411; fax 310/859.8730. www.luxehotels.com ♿

60 BANG & OLUFSEN

The selection of high-concept electronic systems at this massive, museum-like shop will delight the senses of any audiophile. The Danish company's showroom houses wide-screen and interactive digital televisions, sound systems, computers, and other high-end play toys and gadgets. If you're into high design and equipment that looks like an artistic piece of furniture, this is the place. ♦ Daily except Christmas, Columbus Day, and Easter. 369 N Rodeo Dr (between Dayton and Brighton Ways). 310/247.7785. www.bangandolufsen.com

61 IL FORNAIO

★★$ One of the few bargains in an otherwise pricey town, this bright and cheerful café serves great food—from hearty soups and salads to pizzas, pastas, and fish. The bakery turns out designer breads (whole wheat and olive, walnut, rosemary, potato) and yummy desserts. ♦ Italian Bakery/Café ♦ Bakery: daily. Café: daily, breakfast, lunch, and dinner. 301 N Beverly Dr (at Dayton Way). 310/550.8330 ♿. Also at 1800 Rosecrans Ave (at Manhattan Village Mall, corner of Sepulveda Blvd), Manhattan Beach. 310/725.9555

61 GRAFFEO COFFEE ROASTING COMPANY

This shop offers just three coffee blends—light, dark, and decaf—but it may yield the best cup you've ever savored. ♦ M-Sa. 315 N Beverly Dr (between Dayton and Brighton Ways). 310/273.4232

62 MASTRO'S STEAKHOUSE

★★★$$$ This stylish steak house appeals to meat eaters with big, juicy prime rib beef and great service. The 18-ounce Kansas City strip of 40-ounce porterhouse is recommended. Be sure to order the baked potato or fried onion rings on the side. There's a great bar and drinks are large, like everything else served here. ♦ Steak House ♦ M-F, lunch; daily, dinner. Reservations necessary. 246 N Cañon Dr (between Clifton and Dayton Ways). 310/888.8782

63 THE WINE MERCHANT

Dennis Overstreet offers classes, tastings, and rental vaults as well as an outstanding

Rodeo Drive Shopping

SANTA MONICA BOULEVARD

womenswear **Boulmiche Boutique**

LITTLE SANTA MONICA BOULEVARD

young casuals **BB1**

handbags and accessories **Bottega Veneta**
womenswear **Theodore**
menswear **Theodore Man**
linens **Frette**
sportswear **Lacoste**

RODEO DRIVE

Celine *Parisian womenswear*
Zaiko Muraoka *womenswear*
Mila Schlön *Milanese womenswear*

Polo/Ralph Lauren *classic mens-, womens-, and childrenswear*
Frederic Fekkai *beauty salon*
Holland & Holland *menswear*
Giorgio Armani *mens- and womenswear*

Rodeo Collection
Gianni Versace, Sonia Rykiel, Kenneth Jay Lane, and other boutiques
beauty salon **Vidal Sassoon**
womenswear **La Perla**
jewelry **Fred Joaillier**

Hermes *womenswear*
Galerie Michael *masterworks*
Bijan *menswear*
Hugo Boss *menswear*

Chanel *womenswear*

BRIGHTON WAY

jewelry **Harry Winston**
Bang and Olufsen
audio equipment and accessories
men's and women's shoes **A. Testoni**
women's shoes **Ferragamo**
Gucci
men's and women's fashions/accessories **Hermes**
women's fashions/accessories **Hermes**
art **Dyansen Gallery**
European menswear **Bardelli**
leather goods **Gold Pfeil**
menswear **Ted Lapidus**
art **Hanson Gallery**
womenswear **BCBG**
womenswear **Ungaro**
womenswear **Alaia Chez Gallay**
womenswear **Dior**
menswear **Ermenegildo Zegna**
leather goods/luggage **Louis Vuitton**
womenswear **Chanel Boutique**

Cartier *jewelry*
Benetton *womenswear*

Bernini I *menswear*
Luxe Hotel
Valentino Boutiques *mens- and womenswear*
Bernini II *European menswear*
Bally of Switzerland *men's shoes and accessories*

David Orgell *jewelry/silver*
Bowles-Sorokko Galleries *contemporary art*
Georgette Klinger *beauty salon*
Frances Klein Estate Jewels *rare antiques*
Sotheby's *auction house*
Battaglia *menswear/men's shoes*
Van Cleef & Arpels *jewelry*

DAYTON WAY

1 Rodeo Drive
Denmark Jewelers, Dunhill, Isis Unlimited, and other boutiques

2 Rodeo Drive *Cartier, Charles Jourdan, Christian Dior, Valentino, Cole Haan, Tiffany & Co., and other boutiques*

WILSHIRE BOULEVARD

Regent Beverly Wilshire Hotel
jewelry **Buccellati**

---

selection of rare vintages; there's also a cigar-smoking room in the cellar. ♦ M-Sa. 9701 Little Santa Monica Blvd (at N Roxbury Dr). 310/278.7322

64 PREGO

★★$$ Tantalizing pizzas are prepared in wood-burning ovens, but the pies hardly upstage the carpaccio, gnocchi, pasta, and grilled entrées. This is an attractive, bustling restaurant with a lively (separate) bar scene and service that is tremendously congenial, if a bit harried. ♦ Italian ♦ M-Sa, lunch and dinner; Su, dinner. 362 N Camden Dr (between Wilshire Blvd and Brighton Way). 310/277.7346 ₺

65 GIORGIO BEVERLY HILLS

This tiny boutique offers a great selection of signature scents, body products, and pricey designer casual wear and jewelry, and shares space with BCBG Max Azria, which carries cutting-edge women's clothing. ♦ Daily. 327 N Rodeo Dr (between Dayton and Brighton Ways). 310/274.0200

66 DAVID ORGELL

The sparkle of superb jewelry and antique English silver will catch your eye at this smart boutique. ♦ M-Sa. 320 N Rodeo Dr (between Dayton and Brighton Ways). 310/273.6660

67 2 RODEO

Across the street from 1 Rodeo resides the crowning jewel of the boulevard. Perched atop Spanish-style steps is an ersatz European village with a cobblestone street designed by Kaplan/McLaughlin/Diaz in 1990. The corner of Rodeo and Wilshire houses the largest **Tiffany & Co.** store outside of New York. Other tony tenants include José Eber, Cartier, Pierre Deux, Sulka, and Judith Ripka. Perhaps the most striking occupant, though, is **Gianni Versace**—in a Greco-Roman acropolis featuring fluted Corinthian columns, mosaic tile floors, and a dramatic glass oculus, and offering high-fashion men's and women's clothing (310/205.3921). ♦ N Rodeo Dr (between Wilshire Blvd and Dayton Way)

Within 2 Rodeo:

PIAZZA RODEO

$ The quaint terrace restaurant mimics a Parisian sidewalk café and evokes some of the same charm. The food is very casual gourmet, with open-face sandwiches, pasta, and fish. ♦ International. ♦ Daily, lunch and dinner. Reservations recommended. 208 Via Rodeo. 310/275.2428

GINZA SUSHI-KO

★★★★$$$$ This branch of a Tokyo-based sushi bar is famous for its perfect cuisine. Chef Masa Takayama prepares multicourse feasts that are unforgettable both for the culinary experience and the tab—at least $150 per person for lunch and twice that for dinner. Even at these prices, it's packed every night. ♦ Japanese ♦ M-Sa, lunch and dinner.

Reservations recommended. 218 Via Rodeo. 310/247.8939

68 SPAGO BEVERLY HILLS

★★★★$$$$ Call right now for a reservation at this shining star of super-chef Wolfgang Puck's culinary empire. Reservations are still tough to get at prime time, unless you're "somebody." Puck's former wife, Barbara Lazaroff, and architect Stephen Jones are responsible for the inviting design, which wraps the dining area around a garden patio where tall, willowy pepper trees and two-century-old olive trees shade a fountain. Some favorites from the menu include sweet corn soup spiced with lobster nuggets; rare beef on the bone, thickly sliced with potato and garlic purée whipped with Cantal cheese; and simply prepared fresh fish such as whole dorado or turbot. The desserts are to die for: crepes with berries and cheese dumplings stuffed with apricots or plums. The place hops nightly with major industry players and celebrities who get top priority for primo tables. ♦ California ♦ M-Sa, lunch and dinner; Su, dinner. Reservations essential; be sure to call weeks in advance to assure a table at the usual dinner time (7:30 PM and on). Valet parking available. 176 N Cañon Dr (at Clifton Way). 310/385.0880 ₺

69 CREATIVE ARTISTS AGENCY (CAA)

Former CAA president Michael Ovitz commissioned **Pei Cobb Freed & Partners Architects** to design this sleek but understated palace in 1989. Its curved marble, steel, and glass façade, circular glass lantern, and very precise detailing give an awkward intersection a big lift. ♦ Santa Monica and Wilshire Blvds

70 THE GRILL ON THE ALLEY

★★★$$$ Chef John Sola has won applause for his assurance with corned beef hash, braised short ribs, and Cobb salad, along with oak-charcoal-grilled fish and meats. One of the most popular restaurants in the city, this is a place with a warm, woodsy setting, professional waiters, and huge helpings at fair prices. ♦ American ♦ M-Sa, lunch and dinner. Reservations required. 9560 Dayton Way (at Wilshire Blvd). 310/276.0615 ₺

71 1 RODEO

This building, fronted by a whimsical pastiche of Palladio-style façades by Johannes Van Tilburg, houses such swank boutiques as Bulgari and Denmark Jeweler. ♦ 201 N Rodeo Dr (at Wilshire Blvd)

Restaurants/Clubs: Red | Hotels: Purple | Shops: Orange | Outdoors/Parks: Green | Sights/Culture: Blue

72 STERLING PLAZA

The stunning Art Deco office tower built by Louis B. Mayer in 1929 as the MGM Building has been beautifully refurbished. Ironically, the movie company has moved a block away behind a bland white-marble-and-black-glass façade. Mayer would not have approved. ♦ Wilshire Blvd and Beverly Dr

73 MOSAIC HOTEL

$$ Devotees of boutique hotels will enjoy this 57-room charmer with its stylish interior and warm ambience. Amenities include a fitness room outfitted with a treadmill, Elliptical machine, weights, and exercise videos, and free laptops set up in the lobby to check your e-mail or surf the net. Each attractive room comes with upscale toiletries as well as Frette sheets, towels, and robes. There is a full-service restaurant with an active bar where you can nosh on tapas, and 24-hour room service. ♦ 125 S Spalding (just south of Wilshire Blvd). 310/278.0303, 800/463.4466. www.mosaic.com

74 WILSHIRE BOULEVARD

Some of the city's best department and specialty stores line this stylish stretch of LA's Main Street. Handsome old buildings and contemporary slick glass high-rises reflect a mix of architectural styles, and the boulevard, shaded by lofty palm trees, boasts a lively pedestrian scene. Shopping highlights include **Niketown; Burberry** (No. 9560; 310/246.0896); **Neiman Marcus** (No. 9700; 310/550.5900), which also houses a full-service **Estée Lauder day spa** (310/550.2056); and **Saks Fifth Avenue** (No. 9600; 310/275.4211): There's also **Calibar** (No. 9667½; 310/777.0065), a late-night tapas lounge imported from London and New York that swings from 4 in the afternoon until 2 in the morning. It's hot and trendy yet laid back, with dim lighting, interesting art, and an eclectic clientele. ♦ Between Crescent and Roxbury Drs

74 BARNEYS

The LA branch of the New York department store is a five-level, 108,000-square-foot shopping emporium of cutting-edge fashions (at inflated prices), along with a Chelsea Passage Gift Department offering collectibles from all over the world. ♦ 9570 Wilshire Blvd (between S Camden and Peck Drs). 310/276.4400

74 SPORTS CLUB LA/BEVERLY HILLS

This swank $25 million offspring of the fast-growing chain of elite health clubs takes fitness to new heights. Pass through the Zen-like lobby, adorned with bamboo gardens and waterfalls, and you enter a 10,000-square-foot gym, a Cardiovascular Center with 100 pieces of select equipment, each with a personal TV. There's also a Flexibility Center, Functional Training Performance Center, and four exercise studios. Members stay in shape through REV group cycling, Pilates, yoga, aerobics, and specially designed classes. *Après*-workout amenities include Splash, a destination day spa, a boutique, and Linq Café, operated by famed restaurateur Mario Oliver and open for breakfast, lunch, and dinner. Sports Club LA has branches in Washington DC, Boston, San Francisco, Miami, and Irvine. ♦ 9560 Wilshire Blvd (at Camden Dr). 310/888.8100. www.thesportsclubla.com

75 REGENT BEVERLY WILSHIRE HOTEL

$$$$ The doyenne of luxury hotels, thanks in part to the fine management by Four Seasons Hotel and Resort, this stellar property was originally designed by **Walker & Eisen** in 1928. Today the completely renovated 402-room (of which 123 are suites) hotel boasts a brighter yet still luxurious look that unites marble with mahogany, plush carpeting, and outstanding works of art. Each room is sumptuously appointed with every creature comfort imaginable. A dramatic 5,000-square-foot, three-bedroom penthouse suite, added in 2000, is worth all of the $7,500 a day it commands from the rich and famous who stay there regularly. Besides spectacular views from a wraparound balcony, the suite has a Jacuzzi tub in an over-the-top marble bathroom, an entertainment center, a formal dining room, a butler's pantry, and special privileges. The service throughout the hotel is *par excellence*, from the 24-hour concierges to the fastidious room stewards on every floor. On the ground floor is a handsome, clubby bar where well-heeled guests might enjoy an after-dinner cognac or cigar. The exquisite Lobby Lounge serves breakfast, lunch, and dinner along with an elegant afternoon tea, snacks, and cocktails. Other amenities include a full-service spa, a well-equipped fitness center (with amenities like TV monitors, towels, ice water, coffee, fruit and nuts, and attendants on hand), and an outdoor swimming pool. And to keep you well coiffed, the **Sylvain Melloul Salon**, manned by the famous Paris, France/Washington DC stylist, offers the gamut of hair care services along with manicures, pedicures, and makeup applications. For an appointment, call 310/385.7007. ♦ 9500 Wilshire Blvd (at El Camino Dr). 310/275.5200, 800/545.4000; fax 310/274.2851. www.regenthotels.com &

Within the Regent Beverly Wilshire Hotel:

REGENT BEVERLY WILSHIRE DINING ROOM

At press time, plans were underway to replace the Dining Room with an as-yet unnamed restaurant.

76 RADISSON BEVERLY PAVILION HOTEL

$$$ Decorated with a handsome rusticated stone façade and stylish interior, this 110-room European-style hotel offers complimentary limousine service, valet parking, a rooftop pool, and a spectacular view of the city. It's small, but sophisticated. ♦ 9360 Wilshire Blvd (at S Crescent Dr). 310/273.1400, 800/441.5050; fax 310/859.8551. www.radisson.com ♿

Within the Radisson Beverly Pavilion Hotel:

EARTH

★★$$$ Only in health-conscious Beverly Hills would you find a quintessential restaurant that uses only organic ingredients free from hormones, pesticides, and other harmful additives, and that still tastes great. Menu bests include fried calamari, popcorn shrimp, bruschetta, chicken quesadilla, salads, pastas, pizzas, steak, salmon, and garlic chicken—all good for you. Perhaps not quite as healthy are mouthwatering desserts such as apple tart, lemon tart, strawberry puff pastry, and tiramisù. ♦ Healthy American ♦ Daily, breakfast, lunch, and dinner. 310/273.1400

77 PENINSULA BEVERLY HILLS

$$$$ This bustling French Renaissance–style hotel offers 196 well-appointed rooms (including 32 suites and 5 two-story villas) and outstanding service, making it a favorite of well-heeled celebrities and business travelers. Along with spectacular landscaped grounds, the low-rise hotel boasts fine antiques, European marbles, polished woods, and tapestries. It offers courtesy chauffeured Rolls-Royce service in Beverly Hills and Century City. Other amenities include a rooftop pool; a full-service spa offering world-class facials, massages, and body treatments in a serene atmosphere; a well-equipped fitness center; terrace dining; and a business center. During the Oscars, Tinseltown takes over the property. Although the rich and famous are regulars here, this is one hotel that truly does treat all guests equally—maybe you won't be upgraded to a suite, but you will get the same service as everybody else. ♦ 9882 Little Santa Monica Blvd (between Lasky Dr and Charleville Blvd). 310/551.2888, 800/462.7899; fax 310/788.2319. www.peninsula.com ♿

Within the Peninsula Beverly Hills:

THE BELVEDERE

★★★★$$ This is one pleasant hotel dining room for any meal. Classic and exquisitely designed, with big windows and a comfortable ambience, it's worth a trip even if you're not staying at the hotel. The award-winning restaurant provides a fitting showcase for the outstanding menu created by executive chef Bill Bracken. Some of his best creations include smoked salmon on a scallion pancake with crème fraiche and caviar; lightly spiced corn chowder with house-smoked shrimp; truffle-roasted chateaubriand of veal; a pan-charred 18-ounce prime beef T-bone to die for; pistachio-crusted roasted John Dory you wouldn't believe, and potato-crusted Chilean sea bass that melts in your mouth. Desserts are also divine, particularly the Valrhona Manjari chocolate obsessions with caramel ice cream, chocolate soufflé tart with melted bananas and banana ice cream, burnt lemon mousse with blackberry sorbet and caramelized fruit, and warm apple tart with cinnamon ice cream and caramel sauce. If you have trouble deciding, you can order a sampler plate that includes a bite-size portion of each one. Sunday brunch at the Belvedere is a special-occasion event with fabulous food and endless glasses of French champagne. ♦ Continental ♦ M-Sa, breakfast, lunch, and dinner; Su, brunch and dinner. Reservations recommended; jacket required. 310/788.2306

78 MAISON 140

$$ If you prefer your hotels adorable and sweet, you'll love it here. Located in a residential area on the periphery of the shopping district, this 45-room boutique hotel oozes charm. A touch eighteenth-century France, a tad modern, the Kelly Wearstler-designed hotel has interesting touches such as dormers with potted topiaries, a white-lacquered floor-to-ceiling screen of suspended classical ceiling medallions resting on the foyer's black hardwood floor, crystal French chandeliers, Lucite bar stools, and gobs of hand-selected antiques. Each colorfully charming (and little) room contains vintage pieces and custom-designed appointments like overstuffed French Bergère chairs and Rothko-inspired oil paintings, along with contemporary must-haves: cordless phone, high-speed Internet access, data ports, minibars, and safes. They also throw in a generous complimentary continental breakfast, which makes the moderate price even more attractive. ♦ 140 Lasky Dr (between Charleville and Little Santa Monica Blvds). 310/281.4000, 800/432.5444; fax 310/281.4001. www.maison140.com

---

Restaurants/Clubs: Red | Hotels: Purple | Shops: Orange | Outdoors/Parks: Green | Sights/Culture: Blue

WESTSIDE

Yuppie heaven . . .
    Ever so chic and trendy, with a zip code fast becoming nearly as prestigious as Beverly Hills 90210, the Westside hosts a growing community of movie and record industry tycoons and rich young couples. Space, greenery, picturesque hills, clean air, and proximity to the ocean are the palpable attractions of this region, located just west of Interstate 405. With cool ocean breezes, air conditioning is rarely needed, even during

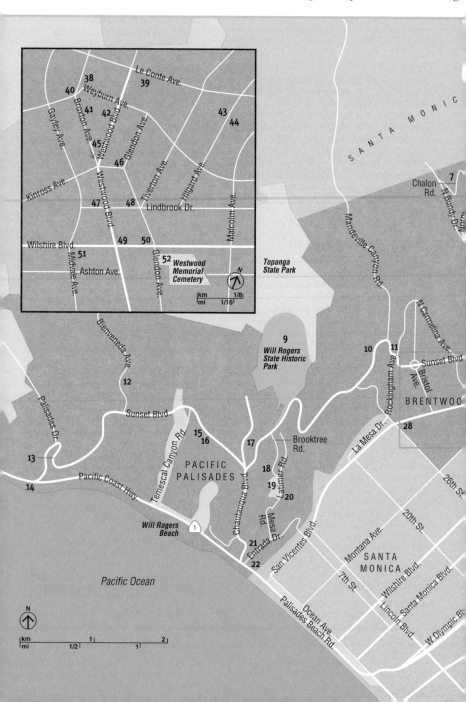

the height of summer. The area is primarily residential, with a sharp contrast between the modest houses and apartments that predominate south of Wilshire Boulevard and the lushly planted estates of **Bel Air, Brentwood,** and **Pacific Palisades** to the north of that axis.

Private tennis courts, swimming pools, Porsches, Mercedeses, BMW Z3s, Range Rovers, and high-end SUVs are commonplace in this affluent area, which also happens to sport five major country clubs. But unlike Beverly Hills, which flaunts its wealth, the golden ghettoes of the Westside are noticeably restrained.

Just east of I-405 but often included as part of the Westside is **Westwood Village,** an upscale residential area that also houses the **University of California at Los Angeles** (UCLA). Originally part of the 1843 land grant of Rancho San Jose de Buenos Ayres, Westwood became the John Wolfskill Ranch after 1884. In 1919, Arthur Letts, founder of the Broadway and Bullock's department stores, bought the farmland and then sold it to the Janss Company. In 1926, Westwood was annexed to Los Angeles in a civic enlargement that included a large portion of the Santa Monica Mountains, the Pacific Palisades, and Brentwood. In 1929, when UCLA opened its Westwood campus, the Janss Company had already built 2,000 houses and a shopping district called Westwood Village.

Bustling with college kids and young professionals from neighboring offices, Westwood Village boasts numerous restaurants, shops, and movie theaters. Its intersection of Wilshire and Westwood Boulevards is one of the city's busiest. The **Village Center Westwood** at Weyburn and Tiverton Avenues has 13 movie screens, 26,000 square feet of restaurant space, and a five-story retail/residential building. And although high rents drove out several quality stores in previous years, a major gentrification and civic push is now drawing many back, luring fine dining establishments and slowly filling up some of the empty retail spaces. Because parking is difficult, many merchants offer one hour free with a minimum purchase at their shops.

In recent years Westwood lost some of its luster, and with it its older weekend audience (who replaced it with the revitalized Third Street Promenade in Santa Monica), but it's still popular with nearby UCLA students, who like to gather at local cafés, go to movies, shop, and jam the sidewalks on weekends. Fast noshing remains the dominant activity today, with a croissant shop or cookie store on virtually every block, a score of pizza places and ice cream and frozen yogurt parlors, plus hamburger and falafel joints. You'll also find clothing shops (from preppy to pop, but mostly athletic), video outlets, Tower Records, and several bookstores, including B. Dalton and Crown.

BEL AIR

This posh hillside community, developed by Alphonzo E. Bell in the early 1920s, rapidly became a preferred location for stars and other celebrities who valued the privacy and the views. There's not much for the outsider to see along the winding roads with their Mediterranean names, since the best houses are hidden from sight.

FOUR OAKS
RESTAURANT

1 FOUR OAKS RESTAURANT

★★$$$ This charming rural restaurant, hidden in a quaint canyon in the Hollywood Hills, thrives under the talented hands of chef Peter Roelant, who creates memorable, magical meals. This is the type of place you want to linger over a special dinner, warmed by a glowing fireplace (it gets cool at night in the hills). Begin with a salad of arugula with glazed walnuts, winter pear, and crumbled blue cheese topped with balsamic vinegar, and an appetizer of lobster spring rolls with passion fruit, mint dip, and wasabi mustard. Then move right along to a Great Lakes whitefish in a wild mushroom crust with shaved asparagus and lemon vodka sauce, or lamb culotte with creamy potatoes gratin, grilled artichoke, basil, and Provençal tomato. Then finish with frozen almond crumble nougat with orange/cranberry syrup or raspberry mousse with a crispy meringue and chocolate shavings. Yum. ♦ California ♦ M, dinner; Tu-Sa, lunch and dinner; Su, brunch and dinner. Reservations recommended. 2181 N Beverly Glen Blvd (at Scenario La). 310/470.2265; fax 310/475.5492

1 MULHOLLAND GRILL

★★$$ Barbara Lazaroff originally helped transform this tiny storefront into the colorful, cavelike southwestern restaurant Shane. It was so adorable that when the new Italian owners took it over, they retained the décor and simply added tablecloths. The ambience is lively, the food superbly prepared, especially the seafood risotto with shrimp, scallops, and Manila clams sautéed with garlic, white wine, parsley, and tomato sauce; the *salada bella* (baby arugula with goat cheese and sun-dried tomatoes); *tonno di sicilia* (seared center-cut crusted ahi tuna with Italian peppers and sesame seeds over julienned mixed vegetables and crispy carrots in an orange ponzu sauce); and *osso buco agnello* (lamb shank with vegetables in Tuscan-style red wine sauce served with polenta). For dessert there's a flourless chocolate cake à la mode, chocolate truffle oozing with dark chocolate, and caramelized banana tart. ♦ Italian ♦ M-F, lunch and dinner; Sa, Su, dinner. Reservations recommended. 2932 Beverly Glen Cir (north of N Beverly Glen Blvd). 310/470.6223 &

2 BEL AIR BAR & GRILL

★★★$$ After touring the **Getty Center** (see page 110), drive a mile down the road for a bite to eat at this handsome neighborhood restaurant/bar carved out of a 60-year-old ranch house. The retro '50s supper-club décor is replete with French mahogany-framed countryside doors, cushy booths, banquettes, and a real brick-wall fireplace set under a high vaulted ceiling. The night scene is filled with well-heeled locals and foodies who drive from other parts of town to sample the simple but tasty selection of items like grilled swordfish with tomatoes, capers, and anchovies served with garlic rapini; New York steak grilled to your gusto; and braised veal shank that melts in your mouth (no kidding). There are also creative sandwiches such as a house-cured salmon with dill mayo, tomatoes, and capers, and the Bel-Air Club, which is stacked with grilled chicken, Canadian bacon, and avocado served on panini bread, as well as pastas and more. For your sweet tooth, the caramelized banana split, chocolate soufflé, and apple tart à la mode do the trick. ♦ American Bar and Grill ♦ Daily, lunch and dinner, bar open 'til 2AM. Reservations required. 662 N Sepulveda Blvd (just north of Sunset Blvd at Moraga Drive, about a mile from the Getty). 310/440.5544, fax 310/475.5492. www.belairbarandgrill.com &

3 HOTEL BEL-AIR

$$$$ This ultra-exclusive hideaway, perched high above the city in a wooded canyon, offers a dynamite romantic setting surrounded by 11 pastoral acres of gardens highlighted by a beautiful lake filled with graceful white swans. Even the entrance waxes poetic. You stroll across a bucolic bridge past towering sycamores, over a tranquil lake, into the gracious European-style lobby where you are greeted like an old friend. Spiffier than ever after an extensive renovation under the able guidance of managing director Carlos Lopes, this exclusive hideaway redefines luxury with a seamless style. Special touches make all the difference. Like an elegant tea service delivered to your room a few minutes after you check in, bottled water and fruit provided poolside throughout the day, and attentive guest service personnel. For an extraordinary, albeit budget-busting, treat, book the Grace Kelly, Swan Lake, or Spa suite. Each provides the ultimate in luxurious living. While plans are underway to add a day spa, until that time you can enjoy "virtual spa" in the privacy of your own room. Any treatment—facial, makeup, hairstyling, manicure, pedicure, body wrap, scrub, massage, and more—is possible. All it takes is a call to the concierge staff and a therapist is dispatched to your room within a couple of hours. This definitely qualifies as the ultimate in pampered living. If you have unruly tots in tote who need some etiquette training, you might want to consider enrolling them in the hotel's unique Petite Protocol workshop. The half-day session, headed by an internationally recognized instructor, teaches basic manners and decorum from writing thank-you notes to serving food and beverages. Sessions with Ms. Manners cost $250 a tiny head and include a child's size multi-course lunch with the chef. Classes are held three or four times a year. For information or reservations, call 310/207.5175. You can't help but love any of the 92 uniquely designed Mediterranean-style rooms and suites, neatly tucked within rambling Mission-style buildings. Each exudes a distinctive charm provided by needlepoint rugs, canopy beds, wood-burning fireplaces, natural stone or marble, and always-lovely floral arrangements. One of the most exceptional is the Chanock Suite, a

freestanding bungalow (named after a former guest who resided in the hotel for more than 40 years) that boasts terra-cotta paver floors, a limestone fireplace from France, and French doors that open to a walled back garden lush with azaleas, camellias, philodendrons, and a large silk-floss tree. The very pricey hotel caters to a very high-end clientele comprised mostly of movie stars and music industry mavens. Attention to privacy and discretion make you feel like the only guest in residence. During the day, the rich, famous, handsome, and beautiful-bodied congregate at the pool for sunning, reading, lunching, and drinking. A nice touch is the pitchers of ice water, tons of towels, and bowls of fresh fruit set out on the deck for all to enjoy. There's also a nicely equipped fitness center with a legend: It was carved out of Marilyn Monroe's favorite bungalow. The inviting center features high-quality state-of-the-art equipment and apparatus. It's free and open 24 hours. ◆ 701 Stone Canyon Rd (at Chalon Rd). 310/472.1211, 800/648.4097; fax 310/476.5890. www.hotelbelair.com

Within the Hotel Bel-Air:

THE RESTAURANT

★★★★$$$$ Warmed by a roaring fireplace, the courtly dining room provides a romantic setting for the fine continental cuisine. Chef Douglas Dodd, formerly of the Phoenician in Scottsdale, Arizona, arrived in 2003 and revamped the menu, bringing back the fine cuisine Hotel Bel-Air expected. The food is now as good as it gets. Wisely maintaining favorites such as the tortilla soup and white bisque with truffle flan, Dodd lightened up the fare while still giving the illusion of rich gourmet (save for the fois gras). When white asparagus, not on the menu, were requested, the chef sent out an exquisite plate of tender spears touched perfectly with truffle oil. In keeping with Hotel Bel-Air tradition, he does such things. For main courses you can't go wrong with his seared Petrale sole, wildflower honey-lacquered duck, roast rack of lamb, and mustard-crusted salmon. Scrumptious desserts include fresh donut Parisienne with fondue and a knockout Grand Marnier soufflé. Take a few foodie friends out for a night at "Table One"—specially prepared chef's dinners for eight people served in a charming room adjacent to the kitchen, where diners can watch the action through a glass window; make reservations at least two weeks in advance. The more casual terrace overlooking the swan-filled lake offers a tranquil spot to enjoy a hearty breakfast. ◆ California/French ◆ Daily, breakfast, lunch, and dinner. 310/472.1211. www.hotelbelair.com

4 UCLA HANNAH CARTER JAPANESE GARDEN

The enchanted garden, designed by Nagao Sakurai in 1961, is a tranquil retreat amid private estates, with rocks, wooden structures, trees, and plants imported from Japan. Behind the teahouse is a Hawaiian garden. ◆ Free. Tu-W. Reservations required. 10619 Bellagio Rd (between Stone Canyon Rd and Siena Way). UCLA Visitor's Center: 310/825.4574

5 THE GETTY CENTER

Richard Meier designed this billion-dollar paean to fine art that opened in December 1997 with much worldwide brouhaha and press. Perched dramatically on 110 hilltop acres in the Santa Monica Mountains, seven stunning, low-scale geometric-shaped pavilions—each devoted to a period in art history—are linked by bridges and lush formal gardens. Half the project sits underground, where all the buildings are connected. The amazing, crisply detailed complex, with rough travertine marble cladding alternated with metallic-finished porcelain steel panels, offers changing exhibits along with the extensive Getty art collection. The center unites several programs of the J. Paul Getty Trust: a study center for comparative archeology and culture, the Getty Conservation Institute, and the Getty Center for History of Art and Humanities. Orientation talks and gallery lectures are given daily, concerts are held Friday afternoons and evenings, and educational programs are offered regularly. A pleasant restaurant/café has outdoor seating on balconies and terraces with awesome views of the Pacific. ◆ Fee for parking only. Tu-Su. Note: Parking reservations are no longer required, but spaces are limited. Visitors may take the MTA bus no. 561 or the Santa Monica Big Blue bus no. 4; request a museum pass from the driver. 1200 Getty Center Dr (west of San Diego Fwy). 310/440.7300, 310/440.7722. www.getty.edu &

6 LUXE SUMMIT HOTEL BEL-AIR

$$$ Few people know about this little gem hidden away on seven acres just below the Getty Center. It's a little off the beaten track but perfect for a peaceful hideaway. There are 162 rooms equipped with the usual business tech tools as well as the usual hair dryers, robes, and amenities. Recreational facilities include a pool, spa, fitness center, and tennis courts. The Café Bel-Air (★★$$) is a perfect place to enjoy breakfast, lunch, or dinner indoors or out on the patio, though the dinner menu's rather humdrum; recommended dishes inlcude tasty lamb chops, filet mignon, chicken, and pastas. ◆ Daily. 11461 Sunset Blvd (between Church La and N Gunston Dr). 310/476.6571, 800/HOTEL411; fax 310/471.6310. www.luxehotels.com

PACIFIC PALISADES

Now one of the most affluent communities in and around Los Angeles, with real estate values that have skyrocketed to supersonic levels, Pacific Palisades was founded in 1922 as a new Chautauqua by the Southern Conference of the Methodist Episcopal Church. Highlighted by a western border of oceanfront bluffs that frequently crumble down onto the Pacific Coast Highway, particularly after bad rainfalls, the Palisades boasts the highest median income of any area in the city of Los Angeles—we're talking big bucks here, folks. Film and television stars, moguls, mavens, and even some wannabes make up the majority of the residents, who pay a premium for the prestigious address and lifestyle. You would think that streets would be named after some of the famous Hollywood folk who live or lived here, but instead, many bear the names of Methodist Church bishops.

7 MOUNT SAINT MARY'S COLLEGE

The small, private liberal arts college sits atop a hill with one of the most beautiful views in the city. ♦ 12001 Chalon Rd (between Norman Pl and N Bundy Dr). 310/476.2237

Within Mount St. Mary's College:

CHAMBER MUSIC IN HISTORIC SITES

Among the annual attractions that make Los Angeles a mecca for music lovers is this series of concerts organized by Dr. Mary Ann Bonino for the Da Camera Society of Mount St. Mary's College. Many of the performances, by top groups and soloists, are held under the Tiffany glass dome of the **Doheny Mansion,** the society's home. But that's just for starters. The Bartok String Quartet has performed in Frank Lloyd Wright's Ennis-Brown House; Prague's Music da Camera in the Grand Salon of the *Queen Mary;* the New World Basset Horn Trio in a former Masonic lodge. ♦ 310/440.1351

8 MARIA'S CUCINA

★$ Standout pizza with a variety of toppings is the highlight of this mostly take-out place. ♦ Pizza/Take-out ♦ Daily. 11723 Barrington Ct (just south of S Barrington Ave). 310/476.6112

9 WILL ROGERS STATE HISTORIC PARK

🅟 This 187-acre park was the home of cowboy/ humorist/writer/performer Will Rogers between 1924 and 1935. Inside the house is memorabilia from his busy career. A nearby visitor's center sells "Rogersiana" and shows a 10-minute film on his life, narrated by friends and family. Rogers was an avid polo player, and his 900-by-300-foot polo field is the site of matches on the weekend year-round, weather permitting. The extensive grounds and the chaparral-covered hills invite hiking and picnicking. No barbecues are allowed. ♦ Free. Daily. 14253 Sunset Blvd (between Amalfi Dr and Rivas Canyon Rd). 310/454.8212

10 CLIFF MAY OFFICE

Cliff May, renowned master of the California ranch-style house, designed this wood-paneled studio in 1952. It is tucked into a corner lot on Sunset Boulevard near his residences on Riviera Ranch and Old Oak Roads. Immediately recognizable with their broad shingle roofs and stucco walls, most of the homes are partially visible through the foliage, with the exception of May's former residence, Mandalay, which is gated and hidden by plantings. ♦ 13151 Sunset Blvd (at Riviera Ranch Rd)

11 TEMPLE HOUSE

As a child, actress Shirley Temple lived with her parents in this delightful small-scale European farmhouse designed by **John Byers** and **Edla Muir** in 1936. It's a private residence. ♦ 231 N Rockingham Ave (between Sunset Blvd and Oakmont Dr)

12 ST. MATTHEW'S EPISCOPAL CHURCH

Charles Moore of Moore Ruble Yudell worked closely with the parishioners when designing this replacement for a church destroyed by fire. The result is indisputably modern, but the subtle use of historic design elements, from Renaissance to California Craftsman, grounds the building in tradition. ♦ 1030 Bienveneda Ave (between Las Pulgas Rd and El Hito Cir). 310/454.1358

13 SELF-REALIZATION FELLOWSHIP LAKE SHRINE

Once a movie set, the open-air temple was founded in 1950 by followers of Paramahansa Yogananda. Ponds, lakes, waterfalls, windmills, and gazebos make this a pleasant place for walking or meditation. ♦ Tu-Su. 17190 Sunset Blvd (between Pacific Coast Hwy and Marquez Pl). 310/454.4114

14 GLADSTONE'S MALIBU

★★$ One of the best beachfront restaurants for a casual meal, this funky fish house offers alfresco picnic-style dining. Fish is the dish here, served with a huge salad. ♦ Seafood ♦ Daily breakfast, lunch, and dinner.

Restaurants/Clubs: Red | Hotels: Purple | Shops: Orange | Outdoors/Parks: Green | Sights/Culture: Blue

Reservations recommended. 17300 Pacific Coast Hwy (at Sunset Blvd). 310/454.3474; www.gladstones.com

15 GELSON'S MARKET

A cornucopia of fresh produce, specialty meat cuts, and exotica fills the shelves. ♦ Daily, until 10PM. 15424 Sunset Blvd (at Via de la Paz). 310/459.4483

15 TIVOLI CAFE

★$$ An upscale spot, this place offers designer pizzas, sandwiches, and tiramisù, along with daily specials. ♦ Italian ♦ Daily, lunch and dinner. 15306 Sunset Blvd (at Swarthmore Ave). 310/459.7685

16 MODO MIO CUCINA RUSTICA

★★$$ A little taste of Italy, tucked away on a side street, oozing with charm, reeking of garlic, and serving some of the best risotto, gnocchi, and cioppino this side of owner Rino Brigliadori's native country. ♦ Italian ♦ M-F, lunch and dinner; Sa, Su, dinner. Reservations recommended. 15200 Sunset Blvd (at La Cruz Dr). 310/459.0979

17 BRIDGES HOUSE

In 1989, **Robert Bridges** designed and engineered this woodsy three-level house/office atop concrete piers. It rises from a precipitous site 70 feet above the traffic on Sunset Boulevard. It's a private residence. ♦ 820 Chautauqua Blvd (between Sunset Blvd and Gallaudet Pl)

18 KAPPE HOUSE

The founder of the Southern California Institute of Architecture, **Raymond Kappe**, built this expansively scaled concrete-and-wood home for himself. It's a private residence. ♦ 715 Brooktree Rd (between Hightree Rd and Ranch La)

19 RUSTIC CANYON RECREATION CENTER

The quiet sylvan glade is perfect for picnics and barbecues. ♦ 601 Latimer Rd (between Hilltree and Brooktree Rds). Groups of more than 20 should call ahead: 310/454.5734

20 UPLIFTERS CLUB CABINS

In the early 1920s, an offshoot group of the Los Angeles Athletic Club (L. Frank Baum, author of the *Wizard of Oz* books, was one member of this splinter group) built cottages in the hills of the Pacific Palisades. Many of the residences were log cabins, but some were intended as stage sets. They are now private residences. ♦ Nos. 1, 3, 18 Latimer Rd (just north of Upper Mesa Rd); nos. 31, 32, 34, 38 Haldeman Rd (between Latimer and Brooktree Rds)

21 CHANNEL ROAD INN

$ A bit off the beaten track (but not too far, and worth the trip), this small, luxurious inn oozes charm, and the price is right. Designed in 1910 by **Frank Kegley** as the home of oil magnate Thomas McCall and his family, the Colonial Revival–style structure still features many of its original characteristics, including stately fireplaces, birch wood floors, and cream-colored walls. The public areas are plush and comfortable, with furniture upholstered in pastel silks and lavender-accented Oriental carpeting, and each of the 14 rooms (two with Jacuzzis) and suites is attractively decorated with antique four-poster beds and lace bedspreads or Amish quilts. All rooms have private baths; two suites feature fireplaces. The rate includes a continental breakfast and afternoon refreshments such as wine and cheese. ♦ 219 W Channel Rd (between E Rustic Rd and Chautauqua Blvd). 310/459.1920. www.channelroadinn.com &

22 MARIX TEX MEX PLAYA

★$$ This branch of the rambunctious West Hollywood restaurant offers the usual southwestern/Mexican-style fare, from nachos and tostadas to chili rellenos and *mas*, all easily washed down with some of the best margaritas mixed north of the border. ♦ Tex-Mex ♦ Daily, lunch and dinner. 118 Entrada Dr (between Ocean Way and Pacific Coast Hwy). 310/459.8596

BRENTWOOD

Nestled due west of Belair, this ritzy residential area still suffers the worldwide notoriety it gained in 1995 during the "Trial of the Century," as O. J. Simpson stood accused of the murders of his ex-wife, Nicole Brown Simpson, and her friend Ronald Goldman. Lookie-loos from all over the world flocked to Bundy Drive, where the brutal murders took place, and Rockingham Avenue, the location of O.J.'s estate. Both areas have quieted down somewhat—especially since Simpson was forced to sell his house—but they still attract attention and visitors. Chic, casual, and countrified, this section of town is populated with stucco and clapboard cottages and huge, sprawling mansions. In spite of the notoriety (or perhaps because of it), real estate values and rents here just keep on climbing.

San Vicente Boulevard is Brentwood's main drag. The attractive, coral tree–shaded street is popular with joggers, walkers, and cyclists. The roads that wind up into the hills have an even more rustic feel. Most of the activity centers around the sleek, multi-story **Brentwood Gardens** complex with its high-end fashion boutiques and patio dining at the **California Pizza Kitchen** (310/826.3573). Across the street is an outdoor mall, **Brentwood Town & Country**, home to **Flowers with Love** (310/207.3075), a petite but colorful floral stand, and **Salutations, Ltd.** (310/820.6127), where you'll find home adornments that can transform your residence into the cover story for *Metropolitan Home.*

23 DUTTON'S BOOKSTORE

Music and the humanities are the strong suits here, but there's a good choice of new and used books in every major field, plus CDs and tapes, readings, and book signings. The service is expert and friendly. ◆ Daily; M-F, until 9PM. 11975 San Vicente Blvd (at S Saltair Ave). 310/476.6263. Also at: 5146 Laurel Canyon Blvd (between Hartsook St and Magnolia Blvd), San Fernando Valley. 818/769.3866; 3806 W Magnolia Blvd (at Screenland Dr), Burbank, 818/840.8003

24 EL DORADO

★★★$$$ A tequila lover's paradise, this swinging restaurant sports more than 100 varieties of the potent liquor. Olé! You can do a tequila tasting or even tequila pairing with the menu. Be sure to have a designated driver available. The food's amazing, too. The chicanitas tacos, infused with onions, cilantro, and salsa roja, are exceptional, and quesadillas, tostaditos, and ceviche are so authentic you'll think you're south of the border. The whole boneless red snapper staged with roasted peppers, epazote, onions, and tomatoes is delicious. You can't go wrong with any of the Mexican delicacies on the menu, and we mean that. Even desserts sing. Go for the chocolate-chip bread pudding dripping with caramel, or warm apple empanada with cinnamon topped with vanilla ice cream and spiced cider syrup. ◆ Mexican ◆ M-F, lunch; daily, dinner. Reservations for dinner a must. 1177 San Vicente Blvd (between S Barrington and Montana Aves). 310/207.0150

25 DAILY GRILL

★★$$ Sibling of **The Grill** in Beverly Hills (see page 103), this place is located upstairs in an upmarket mall. The mood is fun and the food dependable. Chicken potpie, Cobb salad, great onion rings, french fries, and rice-pudding pie are favorite choices. ◆ American ◆ Daily, lunch and dinner. 11677 San Vicente Blvd (between Darlington and S Barrington Aves). 310/442.0044

26 TOSCANA

★★★$$ Splendid rustic food is served in a bright, modern restaurant that hums with a crowd of satisfied diners at lunch and dinner. Standouts from chef Pietro Topputo's menu include pizzas and perfect risottos, a variety of grilled meats including an

TOSCANA

authentic *battuta al rosmarino* (pounded tenderloin with rosemary and garlic), and *salmone alla rugola* (poached salmon with arugula, lemon, and extra-virgin olive oil). In season, fresh porcini mushrooms are served with the grilled items. There's a marvelous list of wines by the glass or bottle to enhance the meal. For dessert, the tiramisù is unbeatable. ◆ Italian ◆ M-Sa, lunch and dinner; Su, dinner. Reservations recommended. 11633 San Vicente Blvd (at Darlington Ave). 310/820.2448

27 SAWTELLE VETERANS' CHAPEL

This picturesque white gingerbread chapel was designed by **J. Lee Burton** at the turn of the century. It's part of the Sawtelle Veterans' Hospital complex, one of the first veterans' facilities opened in the US after the Civil War. ◆ Wilshire Blvd and Bonsall Ave

27 WADSWORTH THEATER

Located near the Veterans' Chapel, the auditorium is used by UCLA for chamber music, plays, and special film screenings. Free jazz concerts are offered on the first Sunday of the month; call for details. ◆ Eisenhower Ave (between Bonsall and Brigham Aves). 310/825.2101

28 BRENTWOOD COUNTRY MART

This red barn houses a post office and more than 26 shops, including an espresso bar and a fresh juice bar. Standouts include the **Brentwood Camera Shop** (310/394.0256), **Hansel 'n Gretel,** for really adorable clothing and stuff for kids (310/394.2619), **Loupilou** for adult clothing (310/394.4118), and **Shokos,** where you can pick up gorgeous floral arrangements or flowers (310/394.1856). This is a favorite shopping spot for local celebrity residents. ◆ 26th St and San Vicente Blvd. 310/395.6714

29 VINCENTI RISTORANTE

★★★$$ Chef Gino Angelini creates show-stopping dishes such as *strozzaprette* (handmade pasta spirals) in a spicy lobster sauce, blackened red snapper, and tripe simmered in tomato with Parmesan flan. The ambience is contemporary yet Old World, with a sleek marble bar, burnished aubergine walls, and rounded booths. ◆ Italian ◆ Tu-Th, Sa, Su, dinner; F, lunch and dinner. Reservations recommended. 11930 San Vicente Blvd (between Montana Ave and S Bundy Dr). 310/207.0127 ♿

30 GAUCHO GRILL

★$ This meat-eaters' haven in waistline-conscious Brentwood is similar to its

---

Restaurants/Clubs: Red | Hotels: Purple | Shops: Orange | Outdoors/Parks: Green | Sights/Culture: Blue

Hollywood sister. The great take-out menu features Argentinean-style ribs designed for 2 or 10. ♦ Argentinean ♦ Daily, lunch and dinner. 11754 San Vicente Blvd (at Gorham Ave). 310/447.7898

31 BERTY'S

★$$ Try the blue-crab ravioli and a grilled veal chop before moving on to a tempting dessert. This restaurant is casual, with a cool, tranquil environment. ♦ California ♦ M-F, lunch and dinner; Sa, dinner. Reservations recommended on weekends. 11712 San Vicente Blvd (at S Barrington Ave). 310/207.6169

31 CHIN CHIN

★★$ Brent Saville designed this offshoot of the popular café on Sunset Strip. Dim sum and other light Chinese dishes are served in a bright tiled room and on a handsome roof terrace with large white umbrellas. ♦ Chinese ♦ Daily, lunch and dinner. 11740 San Vicente Blvd (at Gorham Ave). 310/826.2525. Also at several southland locations, including 8618 Sunset Blvd (between Alta Loma Rd and Palm Ave), West Hollywood. 310/652.1818; 12215 Ventura Blvd (between Laurel Canyon Blvd and Laurelgrove Ave), San Fernando Valley. 818/985.9090; 13455 Maxella Ave (at Del Rey Ave), Marina del Rey. 310/823.9999

32 NEW YORK BAGEL COMPANY

★$ To the delight of his friends and bagel aficionados, ex–New Yorker Dave Rosen has brought his bagel business to the sunnier pastures of Los Angeles. Slap everything from cream cheese and lox to fruit jams on 11 varieties of the ringed rolls, including cinnamon raisin, pumpernickel, garlic, and sesame. Rosen's old friend, master architect **Frank Gehry**, created a design for this deli/diner (located in the Brentwood Town & Country outdoor mall) that reminds patrons the best bagels come from the Big Apple: A 33-foot-long replica of the Chrysler Building floats over the high-ceilinged structure like an armored zeppelin. ♦ Deli ♦ Daily, breakfast and lunch. 11640 San Vicente Blvd (at Darlington Ave). 310/820.1050

32 ZAX

★★★$$ This is truly the quintessential neighborhood restaurant. The stylized room is welcoming, with exposed brick walls, an open kitchen behind a wood bar, and friendly, happy vibrations. The food is as good as the setting: great salads like roasted fig and beets with hazelnuts in a goat cheese vinaigrette, perfect pastas such as pea ravioli, and a slow-roasted halibut with orange tomato sauce that melts in your mouth. Nothing is over the top, but everything is tasty. Don't

miss the lemon tart or the coffee and doughnuts for a special ending to a great meal. ♦ California Bistro ♦ Tu-F, lunch and dinner; Sa-Su, dinner. Reservations a must. 11604 San Vicente Blvd (between S Barrington Ave and Wilshire Blvd). 310/571.3800

33 INDIA'S OVEN

★★$$ Great tandoori chicken and curries are served in a posh second-floor restaurant. ♦ Indian ♦ Daily, lunch and dinner. 11645 Wilshire Blvd (between Barry and S Barrington Aves). 310/207.5522

WESTWOOD AREA

34 TISCHLER HOUSE

This geometrically sculptured house was designed by **Rudolph Schindler** in 1949; the private residence was one of the architect's last and most successful works. ♦ 175 Greenfield Ave (between Cashmere St and Sunset Blvd)

35 UNIVERSITY OF CALIFORNIA AT LOS ANGELES (UCLA)

This world-renowned university has grown to be a city within the city. It was established in 1919 as the University of California's "Southern Branch," a small two-year college. The fledgling institution grew rapidly, and in 1929 moved to Westwood. Today, UCLA has the largest enrollment (37,600 students) of the nine University of California campuses. The first four buildings—Italian Romanesque brick palazzos laid out around a grassy quadrangle known as the **Royal Quad**—remain the best. The 419-acre campus is beautifully landscaped, with plenty of paths for walking, jogging, or quiet reverie. Many of the departments and professional schools have exceptional reputations, including chemistry, earth and space sciences, philosophy, linguistics, history, medicine, law, the John E. Anderson Graduate School of Management, and theater, film, and television. Library holdings total more than 6.1 million volumes—among the world's largest.

The best way to get to the campus is by bicycle or shuttle bus; cars are restricted to a few ring roads. Local authorities have covered the area with meters and created ordinances that restrict parking, often by permit only. RTD, Santa Monica, and Culver City bus lines have direct routes to UCLA.

Free **Campus Express buses** circulate from Westwood Village through the campus every five minutes on weekdays. Limited parking is available in campus structures; access tokens are sold at the information kiosks on

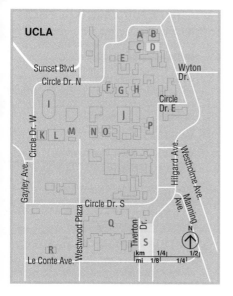

Westwood and Sunset Boulevards and Hilgard Avenue. ◆ 405 Hilgard Ave (between Le Conte Ave and Sunset Blvd). 310/825.4321. www.UCLA.edu/resources.html

Within the University of California at Los Angeles (the letters preceding the following entries refer to the map above):

A UCLA WIGHT ART GALLERY

A vital, innovative force within the Southern California art community, the gallery is located within the **Dickson Art Center.** It encompasses exhibition galleries as well as the **Grunwald Center for the Graphic Arts** and the **Franklin Murphy Sculpture Garden.** Exhibitions are complemented by a wide range of programs, including lectures, tours, educational workshops, and publications. The museum shop sells books, posters, jewelry, and crafts. ◆ Free. Grunwald Center: Open by appointment. Wight Art Gallery: Tu-Su. Docent tours: Sa, Su, 1:30PM or by appointment. 310/825.3281

B UCLA FILM AND TELEVISION ARCHIVE

Screenings of more than 500 films a year are a major activity in the former Melnitz Hall, dedicated to the preservation, study, and exhibition of the moving image. In addition, the archive presents major retrospectives, festivals, tributes, and documentaries. The **Archive Research and Study Center** (310/206.5388), located in Powell Library, makes available to the UCLA community and general public on-site viewing of archival material for research purposes. ◆ Information about public screenings: 310/206.8013

C UNIVERSITY RESEARCH LIBRARY

Designed by **A. Quincy Jones** in 1964, this library houses a superb reference collection. It's open to the public for reading; loans are available to the university community and library card purchasers. Exhibitions of literary material from the Department of Special Collections are displayed on the first floor. ◆ For hours, call 310/825.8301. Reference desk 310/825.1323

D FRANKLIN MURPHY SCULPTURE GARDEN

This idyllic five-acre greensward looks its best when the jacaranda trees bloom in April. Major works by Jean Arp, Henri Matisse, Joan Miró, Henry Moore, Auguste Rodin, David Smith, Francisco Zuniga, and others are here.

E NORTH CAMPUS STUDENT CENTER

This popular campus dining spot offers the same low prices as all UCLA restaurant facilities. ◆ M-Sa. 310/206.0720

F FOWLER MUSEUM OF CULTURAL HISTORY

The three-story museum houses one of the nation's leading collections of African, Oceanic, and American Indian art and cultural artifacts, with more than 750,000 pieces in all. There are also four exhibition galleries, an amphitheater, a museum store, and a library. ◆ Free. W-Su. 310/825.4361

G ROYCE HALL

Designed by **Allison & Allison** in 1919, this is part of the original quadrangle, with classrooms, offices, and an auditorium that is a year-round venue for big-name artists and professional music, dance, and theatrical presentations. ◆ UCLA Central Ticket Office 310/825.2101

H HAINES HALL

This 1928 building, also one of the original buildings on the quadrangle, houses classrooms.

I DRAKE STADIUM

The track-and-field stadium seats 11,000. ◆ Event information 310/825.4546

J POWELL LIBRARY

Located here is the college library, which houses the undergraduate collection. The rotunda and grand staircase of the 1928 building are notable. ◆ Reference desk 310/825.1938

Restaurants/Clubs: Red | Hotels: Purple | Shops: Orange | Outdoors/Parks: Green | Sights/Culture: Blue

K LA TENNIS CENTER

Built for the 1984 Summer Olympics, the center is the current home of the annual Volvo Tennis/Los Angeles Men's Tournament. ♦ Event information 310/825.5995

L PAULEY PAVILION

Welton Becket & Associates designed this 1965 home of the UCLA Bruins women's and men's basketball teams. Concerts, cultural events, gymnastic meets, and volleyball games are also held. ♦ UCLA Central Ticket Office 310/825.2101, 310/825.4546

M UCLA ATHLETICS HALL OF FAME

A two-story display of trophies, photos, and memorabilia relating to the UCLA athletic tradition is located in the J.D. Morgan Intercollegiate Athletics Center. ♦ M-F. 310/825.8699

N ACKERMAN STUDENT UNION

A bustling center of campus activity, the union houses the **Student's Store** and the **Treehouse Restaurant**. Actually several restaurants in one, the eatery has fresh fruit and salads and a full meal section, all at very low prices. The store on the first floor carries a fine selection of academic books, with a full range of UCLA insignia merchandise in the "Bearwear" department. ♦ For hours, call 310/825.7711

O KERCKHOFF HALL

Student activity offices and a moderately priced coffeehouse are located here. ♦ Coffeehouse, daily. 310/206.0729

P SCHOENBERG HALL

The hall is named for the Austrian composer **Arnold Schoenberg,** who was a professor of music at UCLA from 1936 to 1951. The departments of music, musicology, ethnomusicology, and systematic musicology are located here, as well as the **Schoenberg Auditorium** (see seating chart below) and the **Jan Popper Theater**. ♦ UCLA Central Ticket Office 310/825.2101

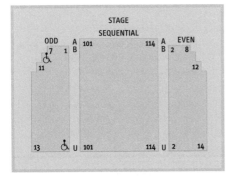

Q CENTER FOR HEALTH SCIENCES

The entire southern end of the campus is occupied by one of the largest medical complexes in the nation. The UCLA Hospital and Clinics, also in the center, operates a 24-hour emergency room, which is reached via an entrance at Tiverton Dr and Le Conte Ave. ♦ Emergency 310/825.2111, physicians referral: 800/825.2631

R VISITORS' CENTER

Walking tours depart from Room 1417 of the Ueberroth Building on weekdays at 10:30AM and 1:30PM. Free maps in English, Japanese, Spanish, and French are available there. ♦ M-F. 10945 Le Conte Ave (between Westwood Plaza and Gayley Ave). 310/825.4321, group tour information 310/825.8764

S MATHIAS BOTANICAL GARDENS

This eight-acre shaded canyon was planted to create a peaceful, woodsy retreat with mature specimens of unusual size. There are no restroom facilities. ♦ Free. Daily. Tiverton Dr (north of Le Conte Ave). 310/825.3620

36 STRATHMORE APARTMENTS

When **Richard Neutra**'s modern bungalow court rose from a then-empty hillside in 1937, its stark lines attracted such tenants as Orson Welles, Charles and Ray Eames, Clifford Odets, and Luise Rainer. A private residence, it remains one of the best preserved of several Neutra apartment buildings in and around the village. ♦ 11005 Strathmore Dr (at Glenrock Ave)

37 BEVERLY HILLS PLAZA HOTEL

$$$ This low-key, reliable hotel in a converted apartment building has a homey feeling that makes it popular with guests on extended visits. Each of the 116 suites has a living room, dining area, kitchen, and one or more bedrooms. After sightseeing, take a dip in the pool. The restaurant features steak, pastas, seafood, and salads. ♦ 10300 Wilshire Blvd (at Comstock Ave). 310/275.5575, 800/800.1234; fax 310/278.3325. www.placestostay.com &

38 MANN'S BRUIN THEATRE

Denoted by a sensuously curved and neon-lit marquee, this streamlined 1937 movie house carries the design signature of architect **S. Charles Lee**. ♦ 948 Broxton Ave (at Weyburn Ave). 310/208.8998

39 UCLA–WESTWOOD CENTER

Restored and refurbished in the 1960s by A. Quincy Jones, this pleasant compound houses a theater and a second-floor photographic exhibit chronicling the history of Westwood Village. ♦ Exhibit hours: Daily. 10886 Le Conte Ave (between Tiverton Ave and Westwood Blvd). 310/208.4108

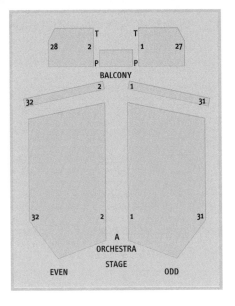

```
              T        T
   28    2          1      27
              P    P
           BALCONY
             2    1
  32                           31




  32         2    1           31
              A
          ORCHESTRA
            STAGE
   EVEN                  ODD
```

39 GEFFEN PLAYHOUSE

This little theater is undergoing a $17 million renovation and will be closed through 2005. In the meantime programming will continue at an alternative location. Call for details. 310/208.5454

40 MANN'S VILLAGE THEATRE

This marvelous 1931 Spanish Moderne tower still dominates the village. Architect **P.O. Lewis** designed the gleaming white-stucco moldings, porte cochere with freestanding box office, and golden flourishes within. Fox Studios built a chain of Spanish theaters before the Depression put them out of business; the Deco "FOX" sign that crowns the tower has been refurbished and relit, and today the theater shows first-run films. ◆ 961 Broxton Ave (at Weyburn Ave). 310/208.5576

41 MYSTERIOUS BOOK STORE

Formerly in West Hollywood, this intriguing bookshop attracts fans of spies, sleuths, gumshoes, and all sorts of unsavory sorts. ◆ Daily. 1036 C Broxton Ave (between Kinross and Weyburn Aves). 310/659.2959 www.mystery-bookstore.com. For orders: orders@mystery-bookstore.com &

42 BEL AIR CAMERA

This 45-year-old shop offers a wide range of photo, audio, and video equipment at competitive prices, with expert service. ◆ Daily. 10925 Kinross Ave (at Gayley Ave). 310/208.5150

43 HILGARD HOUSE HOTEL

$$ The elegant, 47-room hotel is located a few minutes from the village and UCLA. Complimentary continental breakfast is served. ◆ 927 Hilgard Ave (between Weyburn and Le Conte Aves). 310/208.3945, 800/826.3934; fax 310/208.1972

44 W LOS ANGELES– WESTWOOD HOTEL

$$$$ Over-the-top trendy, this branch of Starwood's Generation Y- and X-oriented hotels features 258 outstanding suites. Formerly the Westwood Marquis, the building underwent a multimillion-dollar renovation spearheaded by the Starwood Design Group with the help of Hollywood set designer Dayna Lee and architect Jon Brouse, and opened in February 2001. The dramatic finished product begins with a frosted glass entrance that leads to a fiber-optically illuminated waterfall in a dynamite, modernistic lobby of exposed cement, custom-designed furnishings, and cozy corners in which to sit and play W board games. Each suite has a W bed with a pillow-top mattress, 250 thread-count linens, goose down comforter, louvered window shutters, big desk, coffeemaker, snack and beverage bar, signature robes, Aveda bath products, and the gamut of techno tools for the cyber savvy (printer, copier, scanner, direct Ethernet modem connection—you name it), plus a state-of-the-art entertainment system. There are two restaurants, 24-hour room service, an inviting bar and lounge, a full-service spa/fitness facility (Westwood's AWAY Spa and Gym), two pools, meeting rooms, valet parking, and concierge service. ◆ 930 Hilgard Ave (between Weyburn and Le Conte Aves). 310/208.8765, 800/421.2317; fax 310/824.0355; 877-WHOTELS. www.whotels.com &

Within the W Hotel:

LUDO

Chef Ludovic, formerly of L'Orange, and a team of restaurateurs took over Mojo and renamed it Ludo (after the chef) in spring 2004. Although I was not able to personally sample or rate it, the big local buzz bets on a dynamite dining venue. The interior design paints a tropical Southeast Asian picture in which to enjoy Ludovic's cuisine, which he calls "contemporary French with a heavy emphasis on Asian ingredients." Days and hours of operation were unavailable at press time, but dinner definitely will be served nightly.

45 TANINO RISTORANTE BAR

★★★$$ From the Italianate Renaissance arches above the sidewalk café to the original

1920s interior design (modeled after the Pitti Palace in Florence), it doesn't get more Italian than this. A bustling bar sets the mood for a festive feast of chef/owner Tanino Drago's culinary delights. Begin with a fantastic antipasto and/or soup such as *pappa al pomodoro* (thick bread and tomato soup) and continue on with *pasta incaciata* (penne with beef ragu, peas, boiled eggs, and provolone cheese, baked in an eggplant dome), risotto with squid ink and calamari, roasted leg of veal with polenta, or lamb shank osso buco. Then, for a grand finale, a tiramisù, *torta al cioccolato* (flourless chocolate cake with raspberry sauce), or panna cotta—all equally delicious. ◆ Italian ◆ Daily, dinner; M-F, lunch. Reservations suggested. 1043 Westwood Blvd (between Kinross and Weyburn Aves). 310/208.0444; fax 310/208.2344. www.tanino.com ⌂

45 EUROCHOW

★★$$$ Michael Chow created a showplace out of this former Wherehouse Records shop, but his food is so ho-hum and so unlike his original **Mr. Chow's of Beverly Hills** that it isn't funny. His name alone attracts plenty of business and the room, in this historic domed building, is reason enough to visit the place, but we want more Chinese on the menu. Set under a 55-foot-high ceiling is a 25-foot-high marble obelisk that reflects prisms of light. There's a Venetian-style bridge that connects a balcony dining area and a 2,000-bottle wine cellar viewable from the glass dining room below. The long bar was designed to resemble the one in Stanley Kubrick's movie *The Shining*; the art is eye-opening (Andy Warhol's *Hamburger*, for one); and glass tables are illuminated from below while 600 lights of varying intensity shine on diners in a flattering way. The odd menu has offerings such as pizza, pasta, sandwiches, chicken, pork chops, lamb, and fish. ◆ Italian/Chinese ◆ Daily, lunch and dinner. Reservations recommended. 1099 Westwood Blvd (at Kinross Ave). 310/209.0066

46 WESTWOOD BREWING COMPANY

★★$ Stop in for a handcrafted brew served in 4.5-ounce testers and pints. Beyond the great pizzas, sandwiches, and burgers served at this wide-windowed brew pub, the menu also offers such tasty items as quesadillas, pot

stickers, Creole swordfish, and Louisiana catfish. ◆ American ◆ Daily, lunch and dinner. 1097 Glendon Ave (at Kinross Ave). 310/209.2739

47 CITY BEAN COFFEE

This tiny European-style indoor/outdoor micro-roaster serves some of the best coffee in the city, made from dozens of varieties of freshly roasted beans. Coffee lovers will go ballistic over the jump-starting espresso, cappuccino, and just plain joe poured here. You can also buy the beans by the bushel on site or through mail order (888/248.9232). ◆ M-Sa. 10911 Lindbrook Dr (between Westwood Blvd and Gayley Ave). 310/208.0108. Also at 2121 Avenue of the Stars (lower level of the Fox Plaza, at Olympic). 310/556.1721

48 GARDENS ON GLENDON

★★$$ This popular, savvy restaurant is set in a Spanish-style brick rotunda. The hamburgers, salmon tartare, pizzas, salads, and grills justify the high prices. ◆ California ◆ Daily, lunch and dinner. Reservations recommended. 1139 Glendon Ave (at Lindbrook Dr). 310/824.1818

48 NAPA VALLEY GRILLE

★★$$ Wine and food is what this relative newcomer is all about. Chef Frank Fronda takes seasonal products and pairs them with one of the 700 wines carefully chosen from the vast wine cellar. Fonda's signature dishes include oven-roasted monkfish with sweet-and-spicy chorizo and peppers; thyme-braised veal cheeks with spaghetti squash potato cake, forest mushrooms, and thyme jus; seasonal crusted Chilean sea bass; braised lamb shanks; and a variety of pasta dishes—the roasted beet and goat cheese ravioli is superb. Chef Verite Mazzola is no slouch in the dessert department, with offerings such as dark chocolate mousse torte, Meyer lemon parfait, espresso crème brûlée, and other sinfully rich choices. Designed by Bay area architect Mark Stevens, the sprawling restaurant is inviting in warm earth tones and rough-hewn materials accented by a life-size hand-painted mural of the Napa Valley in springtime. Two fireplaces keep the room warm on cool winter nights and an attractive garden is welcoming for warm-weather alfresco dining. ◆ California Cuisine ◆ Reservations recommended. M-F, lunch; daily, dinner. 1100 Glendon Ave (one block north of Wilshire Blvd at the corner of Tiverton). 310/824.3322; fax 310/824.3232

49 UCLA HAMMER MUSEUM AND CULTURAL CENTER

The late chairman of Occidental Petroleum broke a pledge to donate his art to the Los

Angeles County Museum of Art (LACMA) in order to build this monument, which squats beneath his corporate tower. Designed by **Edward Larrabee Barnes**, the museum opened in 1990, shortly after Hammer's death. The basic concept of this museum is to promote and interpret the works of underrepresented, up-and-coming artists. It is also a showcase for the **Armand Hammand Collection** of Old Master, Impressionist, and Post-Impressionist paintings, such as the works of Mary Cassatt, Claude Monet, Pissarro, Rembrandt, and Vincent van Gogh. The **Contemporaries Collection** highlights the painting, sculpture, and lithography of nineteenth-century French satirist Honoré Daumier and his peers. There's also the must-see **Franklin D. Murphy Sculpture Gardens**, an outdoor collection spread out on five acres of land at the northern end of UCLA's campus, showcasing such greats as Jean Arp, Isamu Noguchi, and Auguste Rodin. A recent $25 million enhancement added features such as an auditorium with TV and movie archives, a courtyard bookstore, a Great Hall lecture area for educational programs, a café/restaurant/coffee bar, and a new entrance on Lindbrook that provides better accessibility for the physically challenged. Thanks to a $5 million donation by Audrey L. Wilder, widow of famed director/writer Billy Wilder, the museum now sports a 288-seat theater named after her husband, who died in 2002 at the age of 95. ◆ Tu-Su. 10899 Wilshire Blvd (at Westwood Blvd). 310/443.7020; fax 310/443.7099. www.hammer.ucla.educ &

PALOMINO

50 PALOMINO

★★$$$ One of the slew of more upscale entries to Westwood's revitalized dining scene, this eclectic urban eatery was a hit the minute it opened. The mood is friendly and the décor a blend of rare African quartered Sapele veneers, sliced mahogany, and broken-stripe Makore veneer accented by Spanish Roo Alicante marble floors and countertops and Italian Vagli Calicatta Roas bar tabletops. Gorgeous hand-blown chandeliers and pendant lamps by artist Martin Blan and reproductions of expressionist wall art by northwest artists Kevin Koch and Shawn Hair complete the leitmotif. The food may seem almost a secondary consideration, but it isn't. Everything's quite tasty, especially signature

dishes like rotisserie chicken, applewood-grilled wild Alaskan halibut, and oven-roasted garlic prawns. The seafood sampler (salmon, scallops, and prawns with sun-dried tomato risotto and raspberry vinaigrette), paella, and rotisserie pork loin are also winners. ◆ American/Southern European Bistro ◆ Reservations suggested. M-F, lunch; daily, dinner. Valet parking. 10877 Wilshire Blvd (corner of Glendon Ave). 310/208.1960; fax 310/208.3366. www.palomino-euro-bistro.com &

51 THE TOWER

This striped marble concoction was designed in 1988 by the meister of slick, **Helmut Jahn.** Its pretentiousness is all the more obvious amid the mediocrity of Westwood's high-rises. ◆ 10940 Wilshire Blvd (at Midvale Ave)

52 WESTWOOD MEMORIAL CEMETERY

The graves of Marilyn Monroe, Natalie Wood, and Buddy Rich are tucked away behind the Avco Center movie houses. ◆ Daily. 1218 Glendon Ave (between Wellworth Ave and Wilshire Blvd). 310/474.1579

53 DEL CAPRI HOTEL

$$ Yet another great budget find, this one has 80 comfortable rooms with kitchens, and an outdoor pool. Rates include a daily continental breakfast. ◆ 10587 Wilshire Blvd (at Westholme Ave). 310/474.3511, 800/444.6835; fax 310/470.9999. www.hoteldelcapri.com &

54 CENTURY WILSHIRE HOTEL & SUITES

$$ This 99-room hotel is the perfect budget-saver with its pretty garden patio, outdoor pool, and free parking. Most units have fully equipped kitchen units. ◆ 10776 Wilshire Blvd (between Selby and Malcolm Aves). 310/474.4506, 800/421.7223; fax 310/474.2535. www.centurywilshirehotel.com

55 LUNARIA

★★★$$$ Bernard Jacoupy's restaurant is a treasure: a cool, spacious dining room, caring service, good acoustics, and reasonable prices. Standout dishes include smoked salmon tart, braised veal Provençale, braised Chilean sea bass, and mouthwatering desserts like hot chocolate soufflé tart, caramelized banana linzer torte, and to-die-for homemade espresso profiterole. And, to enhance the experience, there's live jazz nightly. ◆ French ◆ M-F, lunch; Tu-Sa, dinner. Reservations

Restaurants/Clubs: Red | Hotels: Purple | Shops: Orange | Outdoors/Parks: Green | Sights/Culture: Blue

recommended. 10351 Santa Monica Blvd (between Comstock Ave and S Beverly Glen Blvd). 310/282.8870

56 BEL AIR CAVIAR MERCHANT

This roe shop sells 15 varieties of caviar packaged to go or to ship anywhere in the country. ♦ W, Th, F only. 10421 Santa Monica Blvd (between S Beverly Glen Blvd and Pandora Ave). 310/474.9518

57 LA CACHETTE

★★$$$ This charming hideaway, set in a residential area, offers the superb bistro fare of chef/owner Jean François Meteigner (formerly of L'Orangerie) in a romantic setting. The dining room is reminiscent of a French country inn, with cedar paneling, wood beams, and Impressionist paintings on the walls. Meteigner changes the menu frequently, so it's hard to say what's cooking. However, some choice items we've enjoyed include warm Maine lobster with roasted red beets, baby artichoke, and French walnut oil; Napoleon of sautéed foie gras and foie gras terrine with rhubarb and strawberry chutney and black currant sauce; seared farm-raised squab with English peas, baby carrots, and prosciutto with roasted garlic and foie gras sauce; and Marseilles-style bouillabaisse. For dessert, the baked chocolate mousse and passionfruit lemon tart are hard to beat. ♦ French ♦ M-F, lunch and dinner; Sa, dinner. Reservations required. 10506 Little Santa Monica Blvd (between Thayer and Fairburn Aves). 310/470.4992; fax 310/470.7451. www.lacachetterestaurant.com &

58 MORMON TEMPLE

Designed by **Edward Anderson** in 1955, this is the largest temple of the Church of Jesus Christ of Latter Day Saints outside of Salt Lake City. The 257-foot tower crowned with a 15-foot gold-leaf statue of the angel Moroni is a familiar landmark on the LA skyline. It's open only to church members, but visitors may tour the grounds and the Visitor Information Center. ♦ Daily until 9PM. 10777 Santa Monica Blvd (between Manning and Selby Aves). 310/474.1549

59 LA BRUSCHETTA

★★★$$ The elegant service and décor here are as savory as the excellent Northern Italian cuisine. The portions are hearty, and there's a very enticing wine list. Recommended are the osso buco (veal shank), roasted squab, and any pasta dish. ♦ Italian ♦ M-F, lunch and dinner; Sa, dinner. 1621 Westwood Blvd (between Massachusetts and Ohio Aves). 310/477.1052 &

60 LA BOTTEGA

★★$ Stop for a bite at this deli/restaurant before or after an art film at the neighboring Nuart or Royal Theaters. The extensive menu features everything from great antipasti to homemade pasta and pizzas, sandwiches, and heartier fare. The risotto pescatore with calamari, shrimp, clams, and mussels in a red sauce is a winner. ♦ Italian ♦ Deli, M-Sa, lunch and dinner. Restaurant closed Sunday. 11363 Santa Monica Blvd (at Purdue Ave). 310/477.7777

60 THE ISLE OF CALIFORNIA

The much-faded classic mural, created in the late 1960s by the LA Fine Arts Squad, shows the rugged Arizona coastline after the "Big One" has sent California off into the Pacific. ♦ Santa Monica Blvd and Butler Ave

61 JAVAN

★$ This Persian restaurant has a crisp black-and-white interior and delicious offbeat dishes. Specials have included zereshk polo (chicken with rice pilaf flavored with dried barberries), gheymeh (lamb shank with split yellow peas), and steamed spinach with tart yogurt. Baklava is the dessert of choice. ♦ Persian ♦ Daily, lunch and dinner. 11628 Santa Monica Blvd (between Federal and Barry Aves). 310/207.5555

62 NUART THEATER

One of LA's last surviving movie repertory houses, this theater shows adventurous new work, theme series, classics, and camp favorites. Notice the fine streamline neon marquee. ♦ 11272 Santa Monica Blvd (at Sawtelle Blvd). 310/478.6379

62 LULU'S BLUEPLATE

★$ Around the corner from the arty movie house Nuart, this Westside coffeehouse offers a more relaxed atmosphere than many of its Midtown counterparts. In addition to espresso, they are famous for deep fried Twinkies. ♦ Coffeehouse ♦ Daily, breakfast, lunch, and dinner. 1640 Sawtelle Blvd (between Iowa Ave and Santa Monica Blvd). 310/479.6007 &

63 THE SPORTS CLUB LA

This acropolis of fitness is typically filled with an all-star cast of body-conscious celebrities such as Dyan Cannon, Linda Fiorentino, Marisa Tomei, Dennis Rodman, Diana Ross, plus many directors, screenwriters, and more. Famous and trendy, the lavish body-buffing emporium offers yoga and exercise classes, carpeted aerobics rooms, and locker rooms with steam baths, saunas, whirlpools, towels, toiletries, and lots of telephones. Personal trainers are available for a fee. Scripts are pored over, big movie deals are made, and singles meet at the bar or one of the two power restaurants. There's not only valet parking, but you can have your car washed, waxed, and/or detailed while you work out. Now a thriving chain, Sports Club LA is expanding faster than Rambo's biceps, with reciprocal memberships available in New York, Washington DC, San Francisco, and Boston. ◆ Daily. 1835 S Sepulveda Blvd (between Missouri and Nebraska Aves). 310/473.1447 Also in Beverly Hills at 9560 Wilshire Blvd (at Camden Dr). 310/888.8100

64 SHAMSHIRY

★$ The setting may be bare-bones, but this popular family restaurant serves huge portions of shish kebab, chicken faisanjan (braised in pomegranate sauce), and pilaf. ◆ Persian ◆ Daily, lunch and dinner. 1916 Westwood Blvd (between La Grange and Missouri Aves). 310/474.1410

65 SAWTELLE BOULEVARD

Named for a subdivision that didn't take, this area is now a Japanese/Mexican community of restaurants and small businesses, most related to the gardening trade. ◆ Between W Olympic and Santa Monica Blvds

65 HIDE SUSHI

★★$$ The counter chefs never get a moment's rest in this perpetually crowded café, but they seem to relish the attention and praise for the excellent sushi delicacies and finger appetizers. ◆ Japanese ◆ Tu-Su, lunch and dinner. 2040 Sawtelle Blvd (between Mississippi and La Grange Aves). 310/477.7242

66 ODYSSEY THEATRE

Artistic Director Ron Sossi heads this three-stage avant-garde theater. ◆ 2055 S Sepulveda Blvd (between Mississippi and La Grange Aves). 310/477.2055

67 WALLY'S LIQUOR AND GOURMET FOODS

Within this high-tech California redwood store is the best in food and wine, including boutique vineyard labels unavailable elsewhere, and a cheese department that includes buffalo mozzarella, California goat cheese, pizzas, and chili dogs. The ever-present owner, Steve Wallace, is an expert on California wines. ◆ Daily. 2107 Westwood Blvd (between W Olympic Blvd and Mississippi Ave). 310/475.0606

68 KOUTOUBIA

★★$$$ Named for a famous mosque in Marrakesh, this tent, with its hassocks and low brass tables, is a showcase of the cuisine of the Magreb. Chef/owner Michael Ohayon is a master of couscous and *tajines* (well-done lamb cooked with onion, parsley, cilantro, honey, and raisins), but will prepare special treats if you call ahead—fresh brains with coriander sauce, b'stilla (flaky pastry stuffed with chicken, cinnamon, and spices) with squab, and sea bass with red chilies. Delicious anise bread accompanies every entrée. For dessert there's a luscious mango tartin. ◆ Moroccan ◆ Tu-Su, dinner. 2116 Westwood Blvd (between W Olympic Blvd and Mississippi Ave). 310/475.0729 ♿

69 LAX LUGGAGE

One of a row of discount stores, this shop has good prices on name-brand bags. ◆ Daily. 2233 S Sepulveda Blvd (between Tennessee Ave and W Olympic Blvd). 310/478.2661

70 WINE HOUSE

Their huge and eclectic stock of wines, beers, and spirits is competitively priced. ◆ Daily. 2311 Cotner Ave (between W Pico Blvd and Tennessee Ave). 310/479.3731

71 MATTEO'S

★★★$$$$ This celebrity hangout caters to the older generation, especially on Sunday nights. A long bar near the entrance provides the perfect place to see and be seen; in the main dining room, try for a booth against the wall for better people-watching. In addition to antipasti and great pasta, the menu offers such signature dishes as chicken Beckerman (roasted with parsley, garlic, and roasted potatoes), veal Matteo with eggplant parmigiana, and baked ziti with ricotta and marinara sauce. The service is exceptional—it's

---

Restaurants/Clubs: Red | Hotels: Purple | Shops: Orange | Outdoors/Parks: Green | Sights/Culture: Blue

attentive without being fawning, friendly without being overly familiar. ◆ Italian ◆ Tu-Su, dinner. Reservations required. 2321 Westwood Blvd (between W Pico Blvd and Tennessee Ave). 310/475.4521

71 NIZAM

★★$ This is truly one of LA's nicest Indian restaurants. Exemplary renditions of standards and such unusual dishes as *dai papri* (lentil wafers with potatoes, onion, cilantro, and yogurt) are among the highlights. ◆ Indian ◆ M-F, lunch and dinner; Sa, Su, dinner. Reservations required on weekends. 10871 W Pico Blvd (between Westwood Blvd and Midvale Ave). 310/470.1441

72 COMPACT DISC-COUNT

This shop is filled wall-to-wall with new, vintage, and used CDs. You can review your choices on a CD player before putting your money down. ◆ Daily, until 10PM. 10741 W Pico Blvd (between Selby and Malcolm Aves). 310/475.4122

73 JOHN O'GROATS

★$ Great breakfasts (especially the pancakes and oatmeal) and lunches with tartan touches (biscuits, fish-and-chips, and shortbread) are the specialties here. ◆ Scottish ◆ Daily, breakfast and lunch. 10516 W Pico Blvd (between Patricia and Prosser Aves). 310/204.0692

74 WESTSIDE PAVILION

Architect **Jon Jerde** (of San Diego's Horton Plaza fame) makes retail whimsical in this 1985 indoor shopping mall, centered around an elongated glass-vaulted atrium and accented with trendy paste-on Postmodern design. **Nordstrom** and **Robinsons-May Co.** anchor three levels of retail establishments. The **Samuel Goldwyn Cinemas** (310/475.0202) often have exclusive runs of the better independent releases. A skybridge above Westwood Boulevard connects the mall to another complex that has the same details. Within, the 1950s-style merry-go-round (310/446.8811) and **Disney Store** (310/474.7022) are appropriate tenants, given the mall's theatricality. ◆ Daily. 10800 W Pico Blvd (between Westwood Blvd and Overland Ave). 310/474.6255. www.westsidepavilion.com

Within Westside Pavilion:

NORDSTROM

The stock and service are exemplary at this branch of the Seattle-based chain. Shoes and stylish American clothes are specialties. ◆ Daily. 310/470.6155

SISLEY

★$$ Dependable pizzas and homemade pastas energize exhausted shoppers. ◆ Italian ◆ Daily, lunch and dinner. 310/446.3030

75 JIMMY'S TAVERN

★★$$ Jimmy Murphy is back in business after a long sabbatical. And so are his Bentley-driving, vintage-car-owner customers. The host with the most, who closed his signature Beverly Hills restaurant a few years back, returned to the culinary scene with a bustling tavern where folks linger over drinks and dinner and have a good time doing so. The room is brightened by a huge skylight and kitsched up with carriage lights and porcelain pagodas, and bears little resemblance to a saloon, but it works. The menu recalls some of Jimmy's past, with a few added touches. Best plates include smoked Irish salmon, lamb stew, and corned beef and cabbage. ◆ Irish/American. ◆ M-F, lunch and dinner; Sa, dinner. Reservations suggested. 10543 W Pico Blvd. (between Patricia and Prosser Aves) 310/446.8808

76 BOMBAY CAFÉ

★★$ The combination of excellent tandoori-style food and low prices keeps this place hopping day and night. An open kitchen provides a first-hand view of the chef's specials along with fragrant, appetite-teasing aromas. Everything on the menu is worthy of praise, from the tandoori chicken to the samosas and beyond. There are fun, tasty samplers and great curries. ◆ Indian ◆ M-F, lunch and dinner; Sa, Su, dinner. 12113 W Pico Blvd (at S Bundy Dr). 310/473.3388

77 RENT-A-WRECK

Owner Dave Schwartz has successfully franchised his idea worldwide, but he still manages this original facility. Once just a place to "rent a wreck," it now has hundreds of cars of every make, model, and year. Vintage Mustang convertibles are a specialty here. The scruffy surfaces are deceptive; the old cars rarely let you down and will dramatize your disdain of conventional status symbols. In the land of Mercedes, a battered Chevy is king. However, you might feel even better in a late-model Rolls, Corvette, or Porsche. And while you're deciding, there are free bagels to nosh on and dozens of magazines to read. ◆ Daily. 12333 W Pico Blvd (at Centinela Ave). 310/826.7555. www.wrentawreck.com

78 CHAN DARA

★★$$ Don Carsten's neon-accented interior glows with rich lacquers, and the kitchen also sparkles with vegetable soup (crammed with goodies), huge and flavorful shrimp, pan-fried noodles with chicken, and beef *panang* (in a thick curry gravy). This is the third in a family that began in Hollywood and Larchmont Village. ♦ Thai ♦ M-F, lunch and dinner; Sa, Su, dinner. 11940 W Pico Blvd (between Granville Ave and S Bundy Dr). 310/479.4461

79 PETAL HOUSE

Architect **Eric Moss** has taken a modest suburban house and, using the simplest materials, opened it up like a flower. This is a private residence. ♦ 2828 Midvale Ave (between Coventry Pl and Brookhaven Ave)

80 TRADER JOE'S

Known as the "poor man's gourmet shop," this is the place to find really great deals on wine, champagne, liquor, cheese, coffee, chocolate, and nuts, plus exotica that are wittily described in the monthly catalog. There are branches all over town. ♦ Daily. 10850 National Blvd (at Westwood Blvd). 310/470.1917

81 CIRCUIT CITY

This store is part of a national chain that offers electronics and appliances at competitive prices, with efficient and helpful service. ♦ Daily. 3115 S Sepulveda Blvd (between Clover Ave and National Blvd). 310/391.3144

82 HU'S SZECHWAN RESTAURANT

★$ Bring your own beer and wine to this bare-bones joint, which is packed with locals digging their chopsticks into the spicy Szechuan specialties. ♦ Chinese ♦ M-Sa, lunch and dinner; Su, dinner only. 10450 National Blvd (at Rose Ave). 310/837.0252

83 VERSAILLES

★★$ The roast pork with black beans, chicken with garlic, and paella are all delicious in this modest restaurant. For dessert, stick with the flan. ♦ Cuban ♦ Daily, lunch and dinner. 10319 Venice Blvd (between Vinton and Motor Aves). 310/558.3168

Matthew S. Morrow

Santa Monica/Venice

SANTA MONICA/VENICE

Oh to ride a scooter or roller blade down by the seashore in a thong bikini . . .
Youth-oriented, high energy, and *testosterone-driven* are active terms that best describe this dynamic duo of adjacent seaside communities. Beach seekers were attracted to this area more than a century ago—so much so that they spent a half-day riding in a stagecoach just to get from downtown Los Angeles for overnight camping trips in **Santa Monica Canyon.** Today a similar trip could take nearly as long due to the heavy traffic that often throttles the city. But, all kidding aside, it really should take only about 20 to 40 minutes by freeway, and if you're lucky it sometimes does. On a typical hot summer Sunday, commuting sybarites sit in bumper-to-bumper for nearly 40 miles driving up and down the **Pacific Coast Highway,** especially around Santa Monica and Venice with their long, unbroken line of beaches—the most accessible to the city. Sun, surf, sand, cool ocean breezes, and smog-free air lure millions of visitors to the Los Angeles County coast, but don't expect the Pacific to be balmy: It's very rare for the water temperature to reach 70 degrees, even in midsummer.

SANTA MONICA

Santa Monica, and the original amusement area of **Ocean Park** to the south, started out as a seaside resort in the 1870s. Hotels and stores sprouted up soon after, attracting year-round residents. In 1887, Santa Monica was incorporated as an independent city, and in the 1930s led a dual existence as both a quiet residential suburb and bustling haven for offshore gambling ships. But the opening of the **Santa Monica Freeway** in 1966 permanently altered the sleepier tempo. Affluent, family-oriented residents mostly populate the northern sector of Santa Monica. The central and southern parts attract the upwardly mobile and young singles drawn to an upscale, casual lifestyle. This well-heeled populace once began their relocation by moving to rent-controlled apartments or leased condos until they'd saved enough for a down payment on a house, but the dot-com riches of the '90s afforded many the opportunity to buy right away, and they did. And once the deed was signed, a devoted remodeling began that would put Martha Stewart to shame. A recent $15 million face-lift of the six-block area between **Ocean Avenue** and **Seventh Street** further enhanced the city's oceanfront charm. Sidewalks were widened and embellished with mosaic tiles patterned after Japanese kimonos. To help visitors find their way around, 35 sandblasted granite map tiles were added. Streetlights, made in Barcelona, brighten the boulevards, while a dozen stainless-steel bronze and art-glass bus shelters make waiting for a bus more pleasurable. There are even electronic touch-screen kiosks offering visitor information at the touch of a finger. For a virtual tour of the town, go to www.Santamonica.com. To live in Santa Monica it's simply *de rigueur* to be, or at least look, hip.

1 LA MESA DRIVE
Huge Moreton Bay fig trees canopy this lovely street, which is lined with fine Spanish-Colonial 1920s houses by **John Byers.** Examples are at **nos. 1923, 2102,** and **2153.** They are all private residences. ◆ from about 19th St to 25th St

2 WILSHIRE BOOKS
A diverse collection of new and used books is found here. ◆ Daily. 3018 Wilshire Blvd (between Berkeley and Stanford Sts). 310/828.3115

3 SONNY MCLEANS FISH PUB AND RESTAURANT
This cozy place is a fun spot for a light meal and bit of ale, music, pool, and darts. ◆ Irish ◆ Daily; bar until 2AM. 2615 Wilshire Blvd (between Princeton and 26th Sts). 310/828.9839

4 GEHRY HOUSE
Renovated by master architect **Frank Gehry** himself, this is a mecca for students of architecture but an outrage to the neighbors. Gehry described the original Dutch-gabled cottage as "a dumb little house with charm." In 1978, he built a carapace of corrugated metal, plywood, chain link, and glass around the house, creating a design statement that might have been concocted by a Russian Constructivist of the early 1920s. It's a private residence. ◆ 22nd St and Washington Ave

5 Pacific Dining Car

★★$$ This Westside branch serves up the same high-quality steaks, prime ribs, and lobster as its flagship on W Sixth St in downtown LA (which has been around since 1921). It's a great spot for a power breakfast or lunch or a lively dinner. ♦ American ♦ Daily, breakfast, lunch, and dinner. 2500 Wilshire Blvd (at 27th St). 310/453.4000. www.pacificdiningcar.com

6 Drago

★★$$ Another bellissimo production of Celestino Drago and his brothers, this one features an old-world charm imparted by the late designer Brent Saville, who went for the understated with Italian tiled floors and a kitchen framed by artwork from local talent. The food is consistently Celestino *buono*, especially the *branzino* (striped bass) and grilled veal chop. The signature panna cotta with fresh berries completes a fine dining experience. ♦ Italian ♦ Daily, dinner; M-F, lunch. Reservations suggested. 2628 Wilshire Blvd (at 26th St). 310/828.1585

7 French Rags

Savvy designer Brenda French turned her cottage industry into a thriving fashion emporium with her unique knitwear for women. Her styles appeal to the likes of Hillary Rodham Clinton, Ann Richards, and Barbara Boxer (to drop a few fan names). You can have an entire wardrobe created by Brenda or one of her consultants while you sip some coffee, tea, or wine. Price tags are moderately high, but the quality and style is exceptional and long-lasting. There's also a sales rack to browse through for prêt-à-porter items. Call for an appointment or just drop by to browse through the showroom; you'll love it. ♦ 11599 Tennessee Ave (near Colby and Olympic Blvd), 310/479.5648, 800/347.5270. www.frenchrags.com

8 A.B.S. California

It's worth the trip to browse through the casual and career-womenswear and costume jewelry on sale here. ♦ Daily. 1533 Montana Ave (at 16th St). 310/393.8770

9 17th St. Cafe

★$ Known by locals as the "Pink Shoebox" because of its rectangular dining room in pink accents, this café serves great tortilla soup, cioppino, roasted lamb loin, and homemade desserts. The name's a little misleading, though; the restaurant is actually on Montana Avenue southwest of 17th Street. ♦ California ♦ Daily, breakfast, lunch, and dinner. 1610 Montana Ave (between 17th and 16th Sts). 310/453.2771 ♿

9 Montalvo on Montana

If you're hankering for a custom-made suit or shirt, you don't have to fly to London or Hong Kong; just drop in here and the expert tailors will dress you for success with dynamite, hand-stitched clothing for men and women. ♦ Tu-Sa. 1624 Montana Ave (between 17th and 16th Sts). 310/828.7748

10 Wolfgang Puck Cafe

★$$ Bustling and terribly popular, this is another link in the famous chef's chain of informal, affordable cafés. While Puck does not work the kitchen himself, the pizzas, pastas, salads, and other California/Italian dishes are prepared in his signature style. The décor is contemporary, with colorful tiles, a high, beamed ceiling (with a huge skylight), and modern pottery. True, this place isn't as good as **Spago** or **Chinois on Main**, but it's a lot cheaper and easier to get into. ♦ California/Italian ♦ Daily, lunch and dinner. 1323 Montana Ave (between 14th and 13th Sts). 310/393.0290 ♿ Also at 8000 Sunset Blvd (at N Laurel Ave), Hollywood. 213/650.7667; Woodland Hills Promenade, Topanga Canyon Blvd (between Oxnard and Erwin Sts), San Fernando Valley. 818/884.7090

10 Le Marmiton

For the most elegant of picnics, or when you would love to eat in a very fine French restaurant but can't afford it, this takeout is the answer. ♦ Tu-Su. 1327 Montana Ave (between 14th and 13th Sts). 310/393.7716

11 Federico

Native American and Mexican textiles, antiques, and jewelry are sold here. ♦ M-Sa. 1522 Montana Ave (between 16th and 15th Sts). 310/458.4134

11 Cafe Montana

★$ This local favorite is flooded with natural light and has a contemporary interior design by Eddie Silkaitis. The pleasing menu emphasizes soups, salads, and grilled fresh fish, plus excellent breakfasts and desserts. ♦ California ♦ Daily, breakfast, lunch, and dinner. Reservations recommended. 1534 Montana Ave (at 16th St). 310/829.3990

12 Weathervane

Sophisticated dressers love the women's sportswear by Matsuda and others. For the

---

Restaurants/Clubs: Red | Hotels: Purple | Shops: Orange | Outdoors/Parks: Green | Sights/Culture: Blue

guys, there's **Weathervane for Men** (1132 Montana Ave; 310/395.0397). ♦ Daily. 1209 Montana Ave (between Euclid and 12th Sts). 310/393.5344

12 BRENDA CAIN

Vintage textile furnishings, draperies, home accessories, yard art, and antique jewelry are available here. ♦ Daily. 1211 Montana Ave (between Euclid and 12th Sts). 310/395.1559

13 THE AMBROSE

$ Set in a residential part of town, next door to St. John's Hospital, this 77-room hideaway is the perfect place for chilling out, especially *après* surgery. The Gustav Stickley–inspired early California artisan design includes a fireplace library, inviting entry foyer/living room, and study. Rooms come with two-tone cherry wood–paneled vestibules, beds covered with pretty chenille spreads, terraces, and bathrooms touched with chrome, limestone countertops, and Gasgon blue floors. A complimentary breakfast buffet is served in the living room. Room service, provided by local restaurants, is available but not always 24 hours as the management claims. Amenities include a recreation room stocked with fitness videos, chilled towels, and lockers where frequent guests can store their workout gear. To sweeten your stay the hotel also offers free underground parking, free wireless high-speed Internet access in guest rooms and public areas, and complimentary transportation to downtown Santa Monica via the hotel's own London taxi. You can also stroll a block up to Wilshire Blvd and browse at the Gap, Borders Books, or a number of shops and boutiques that line the street. If you're up to it, walk the 17 blocks to the Third Street Promenade. For a good workout, trek the mile and a half to the beach. ♦ 1255 20th St (at Arizona Ave). 877/AMBROSE, 310/315.1555; fax 310/315.1556. www.ambrosehotel.com

14 LA FARM

★★★$$ A wooden gate with a steer's head leads to this noisy, hip, and citified version of the rural and rustic, with a lovely patio surprisingly situated in an office building. Jean-Pierre Peiny, former chef of the genteel **La Serre,** offers corned beef and cabbage, but the menu is primarily cosmopolitan and worldly. Try fresh salmon marinated in aquavit or zucchini tempura. ♦ International ♦ M-F, Su, lunch and dinner; Sa, dinner. 3000 Olympic Blvd (between Centinela Ave and Stewart St). 310/449.4000

15 IMAGINE

Imported toys and gifts for children inhabit this shop. ♦ Daily. 927 Montana Ave (between 10th and 9th Sts). 310/395.9553

16 BABALU

★$ Many come here for the tropical décor, folk art on the walls, and tasty light dishes such as crab cakes and shrimp quesadillas. ♦ Caribbean/Mexican ♦ Daily, lunch and dinner; Sa, Su breakfast. 1002 Montana Ave (at 10th St). 310/395.2500

16 LOUISE'S TRATTORIA

$ This chain member is a favorite with the young crowd, which gathers for the pizzas, calzone, focaccia with roasted garlic, and homemade pastas. ♦ Italian ♦ Daily, lunch and dinner. 1008 Montana Ave (between 11th and 10th Sts). 310/394.8888 &

16 MY FATHER'S OFFICE

This friendly tavern is a really cool place to hang out and sample some 35 different brewskies while nibbling on bar food such as tapas or big juicy burgers and fries. Food is ordered at the bar and delivered to big tables designed to help customers mingle easily. ♦ Daily. 1018 Montana Ave (between 11th and 10th Sts). 310/393.2337

16 PALMETTO

The skin, hair, and bath products are natural, homeopathic, and therapeutic at this upscale store. The handsomely packaged soaps and scents have attracted such celebrity customers as Demi Moore, Annette Bening, Lauren Bacall, and Angela Lansbury. ♦ Daily. 1034 Montana Ave (at 11th St). 310/395.6687

17 MONTANA AVENUE

Slicing through the ritzy residential areas of Santa Monica and Brentwood, this perky street offers 11 blocks of shopping options, from funky furnishings and vintage clothing to cutting-edge fashions and string bikinis. At last count there were more than two dozen women's clothing stores, 21 hair and beauty shops, 9 laundries and dry cleaners, 20-plus restaurants and gourmet takeouts, 19 gift boutiques, and a half dozen specialty stores, plus offices of 12 doctors and 10 dentists. This is a fun place to window-shop and celebrity-watch—stars are best spotted in the more upscale stores, although they also can be seen browsing in the funkier establishments. ♦ Between 17th and Seventh Sts

17 MARMALADE

The fancy take-out food in this cozy and bustling European-style deli includes pastries, cheeses, and smoked salmon, as well as such home-style treats as cookies and chicken potpie. There's limited café seating. ♦ Deli ♦ Daily. 710 Montana Ave (between Lincoln Blvd and Seventh St). 310/395.9196

17 VINCENZO

★★$$ Yes, there is a Vincenzo and he's very proud of his homemade pastas, pastries, and breads. The rest of the menu's pretty typical, with seafood, veal chops, and rack of lamb. Vincenzo recommends the tiramisù, cannoli, or fresh fruit pie for dessert, and you should listen to him. ♦ Italian. ♦ Tu-Su, dinner. Reservations recommended. 714 Montana Ave (between Lincoln Blvd and Seventh St). 310/395.6619

18 SANTA MONICA BEST WESTERN GATEWAY HOTEL

$$ This 125-room, four-story hotel, centrally located at a busy intersection, is a modern version of the familiar Best Westerns. Suites are available. There's no restaurant on-site, but there is an **International House of Pancakes** next door. ♦ 1920 Santa Monica Blvd (at 20th St). 310/829.9100, 800/528.1234; fax 310/829.9211

19 BERGAMOT STATION

Art lovers will feel like kids in a candy store at this five-acre art center, housed in a former trolley car station designed by architect **Frederick Fisher.** Some of the city's most prestigious galleries are housed here, including the **Robert Berman Gallery** (310/315.9506), **Patricia Correla Gallery** (310/264.1760), **Frumkin/Duval Gallery** (310/453.1850), **Rosamund Felsen Gallery** (310/453.6463), **Frank Lloyd Gallery** (310/264.3866), **Gallery of Functional Art** (310/829.6990), and **Shoshana Wayne Gallery** (310/451.3773). ♦ 2525 Michigan Ave (northeast of Cloverfield Blvd). General Information 310/829.5854

Adjacent to Bergamot Station:

THE SANTA MONICA MUSEUM OF ART

This new contemporary art museum has changing exhibits featuring performers as well as works by local and European artists and photographers. ♦ Admission. W-Th, Sa, Su; F until 10PM. 310/586.6488

20 McCABE'S GUITAR SHOP

On weekends there are live performances by well-known musicians. Call for show times. ♦ Daily. 3101 Pico Blvd (between Urban and Dorchester Aves). 310/828.4497, recording 310/828.4403

VALENTINO

20 VALENTINO

★★★★$$$$ Sicilian-born owner Piero Selvaggio and his talented chefs make culinary magic at this popular Italian restaurant. Among the mouthwatering signature dishes are the smoked mozzarella-stuffed black cod with roasted tomato sauce; bucatini with ricotta and zucchini; beef carpaccio with capers and radicchio; mushroom timbale with saffron; marinated shiitake mushrooms, French beans and sliced mozzarella; Maine lobster salad with couscous, olives, and orange-infused oil or potato-and-spinach gnocchi in a Gorgonzola sauce; perfect pastas; and risotto. There's also a great grilled squab in honey-fig and red wine sauce, osso bucco braised in veal stock with mushrooms and Marsala, super shrimp and scallop dishes, Dover sole, and leg of lamb. Desserts are to die for. To truly sample the chef's culinary talents, go for the tasting menu that might include lobster salad with tomatoes, Gulf shrimp and garlic sauce, veal cheeks done in red wine sauce, and Italian savories such as *lamponi con zabaglione al moscato gratinato e gelato. Buon appetito.* All the desserts are *magnifico,* but the pear tart and trio of gelatos are sure winners. The captain will happily help you create a special menu for the evening and suggest the proper wine pairings from the 115-page list—one of the best in the country. Expect an enjoyable evening with friendly service in a gorgeous room that combines elegance, comfort, and striking contemporary style. FYI: Should you book a cruise on Crystal Cruises' *Crystal Symphony* or *Harmony* you'll find Piero's food served in the alternative Prego restaurant on board. ♦ Italian ♦ M-Sa, dinner; F, lunch and dinner. Reservations recommended. 3115 Pico Blvd (between Urban and Dorchester Aves). 310/829.4313 ♿

21 CALIFORNIA MAP & TRAVEL CENTER

Owner Sheldon Mars has LA's best stock of maps, both local and of other areas of the country and the world. ♦ Daily. 3312 Pico Blvd (between 34th and 33rd Sts). 310/396.6277

22 EL CHOLO

★★$ Formerly **Tampico Tilly's,** this clone of Ron Salisbury's popular Mexican eatery recreates the ambience of his original

---

Restaurants/Clubs: Red | Hotels: Purple | Shops: Orange | Outdoors/Parks: Green | Sights/Culture: Blue

Midtown location. The romantic entry leads to a gracious patio with a flower-filled Guadalajara-style fountain and hand-painted walls by local artist Sally Lamb. Everything is authentic Mexican, from the tasty margaritas and nachos to the enchiladas, tostadas, green corn tamales, and fajitas. ♦ Mexican ♦ Daily, lunch and dinner. Valet parking available. 1025 Wilshire Blvd (between 11th and 10th Sts). 310/899.1106. Also at 1121 S Western Ave (between Country Club Dr and W 11th St), Midtown. 321/734.2773; 958 S Fair Oaks Ave (between California and E Del Mar), Pasadena. 626/441.4353

23 THE ADDRESS
Make a splash without going broke at this boutique, which sells slightly worn designer wear. ♦ Daily. 1116 Wilshire Blvd (between 12th and 11th Sts). 310/394.1406

23 MELISSE
★★★$$$ This popular spot offers fine French cuisine served à la carte or by a tasting menu. The fare tends to be a little heavy for some tastes, but if you love foie gras and the likes, you'll find happiness here. ♦ French/ California. ♦ Daily, dinner; W-F, lunch. Reservations a must. 1104 Wilshire Blvd (at southeast corner of 11th St), Santa Monica. 310/395.0881

24 ANASTASIA'S ASYLUM
$ This dark, bohemian space offers entertainment of an alternative nature. Specially priced coffee and espresso are served to early-morning risers and during happy hour. ♦ Coffeehouse ♦ Daily, breakfast, lunch, and dinner. 1028 Wilshire Blvd (at 11th St). 310/394.7113

25 SANTA MONICA SEAFOOD
Shop here for the largest, freshest selection of fish outside of downtown. ♦ M-Sa. 1205 Colorado Ave (at 12th St). 310/393.5244

26 BUFFALO CLUB
★★★$$$$ This star-filled club, owned by TV producer Anthony Yerkovitch (best known for *Miami Vice*), does not enjoy the best location: It's off the beaten track, in a somewhat seedy neighborhood. But the ambience of the elegant, mahogany-accented dining room and the hearty American fare offer a memorable dining experience—that is, *if* you can get in: The place is about as snobby as it gets. If you can name-drop your way through the door, you'll soon be rubbing elbows with such LA luminaries as Robert De Niro, Quentin Tarantino, Arnold Schwarzenegger, and Maria Shriver. Signature dishes include hush puppies with lamb chops, onion rings made with chili, pork roast, oyster shooters, Buffalo

wings, shrimp and lobster dumplings, and great pork chops. For a dessert sensation, try the pecan pie crumble sundae with bittersweet chocolate sauce. ♦ American ♦ M-Sa, dinner; M-F, lunch. Reservations required (and very hard to get). 1520 Olympic Blvd (between 16th and 15th Sts). 310/450.8600 &

27 JOSIE
★★★$$$ Chef Josie LeBlach (formerly with Remi and Saddle Peak Lodge) and spouse Frank Delzio took over the former 2424 Pico Restaurant and transformed it into an elegant eatery with banquettes upholstered in light green, pretty framed prints, and soft lighting. The extensive menu has something for every taste, from sautéed sardines fried with celery leaves and ravioli stuffed with oxtail to Texas wild boar, vegetarian barley prepared like risotto, and campfire trout. ♦ American, with French and Italian influences ♦ Dinner, M-Sa. Reservations recommended. 2424 Pico Blvd (between 25th and 24th Sts). 310/581.9888 &

28 SUN TECH TOWN HOUSES
Urban Forms designed this striking high-tech terrace of condominiums in 1981. A similarly scaled group, with a false classical façade, is located at **2332 28th Street.** These are private residences. ♦ 2433 Pearl St (at 25th St)

29 IL FORNO
★$$ Exceptional pizza and pasta are served in a noisy, crowded room. ♦ Italian ♦ M-F, lunch and dinner; Sa, dinner. 2901 Ocean Park Blvd (at 29th St). 310/450.1241

30 BAY CITIES IMPORTING
Mediterranean foods, a deli counter, sandwiches, pastas, cheeses, wines, and extra-virgin olive oils make this a one-stop shop for creating your favorite meal. ♦ Daily. 1517 Lincoln Blvd (between Colorado Ave and Broadway). 310/395.8279

31 TYPHOON
★$$ The dramatic two-level space in the **Santa Monica Municipal Airport** terminal was designed in 1991 by Grinstein/Daniels. An eclectic menu mixes dim sum and curry with an offering of, believe it or not, fried crickets (we're not kidding; it's an old Asian recipe), all served in a cherry-paneled

JOLTIN' JOE (AND WE DON'T MEAN DIMAGGIO!)

Coffeehouses have arrived on the LA scene with a jolt. Just about every street now boasts its share of java joints. There's **Starbucks**—although not yet on every corner, they're getting there—and plenty of other brands offered up in a variety of shops. But for those seeking a little ambience with their eye-opener, here are a few choice places to go.

The Abbey Savor a cup of espresso, cappuccino, or just plain gourmet coffee in a lovely setting with statuary gardens and indoor and outdoor fountains. There's also a selection of 50 desserts to enhance the experience. Each month, works by a different artist decorate the walls. ♦ M-Th, 7AM-2AM; F, 7AM-3AM; Sa, 8AM-3AM; Su, 8AM-2AM. 692 N Robertson Blvd (between Melrose Ave and Santa Monica Blvd), West Hollywood. 310/289.8410

Anastasia's Asylum Popular with vegetarians and coffee-lovers who like their joe powerful and their vegetables cooked properly, this bi-level, antiques-furnished hangout is warm and comfortable, just right for a cozy cup or two. ♦ M-F, 7AM-2AM; Sa, Su 8AM-2AM. 1028 Wilshire Blvd (at 11th Street), Santa Monica. 310/394.7113

Buzz This relaxed coffeehouse attracts an eclectic crowd of writers, actors, playwrights, artists, and other creative types, who linger over coffee. ♦ M-Th, Su, 7AM-midnight; F-Sa, 7AM-1:30AM. 8200 Santa Monica Blvd (at Havenhurst Dr), West Hollywood. 323/650.7742

City Bean Coffee This funky, no-frills café, with indoor and outdoor seating, micro-roasts specially selected estate coffees from around the world. (Micro-roasting means that the beans are roasted in small batches for optimum freshness.) The coffee's so good it's impossible to walk away without buying a pound or two. ♦ M-F, 6AM-8PM; Sa, Su, 7AM-4PM. 10911 Lindbrook Dr (between Westwood Blvd and Gayley Ave). 310/208.0108. Also at 8457 Santa Monica Blvd (between Olive Dr and N La Cienega Blvd), West Hollywood. 323/848.8500

Coffee Junction This is the place to kick-start a weekend night on the town. On Friday and Saturday, this fun joint accompanies its good, strong coffee with entertainment by blues bands, country rockers, and aspiring singers. ♦ M-Th, 7AM-7PM; F, 7AM-11PM; Sa, 8AM-11PM; Su, 9AM-5PM. 19221 Ventura Blvd (between Vanalden and Tampa Aves). 818/342.3405

The Kindness of Strangers Comforting as its name suggests, this cozy, living-room-like café has bookcase-lined walls, great coffee, and free entertainment nightly to boot. ♦ Tu-F, 5-11PM; Sa, Su, 9AM-11PM. 4378 Lankershim Blvd (between Bloomfield and Moorpark Sts). 818/752.9566

The Coffee Bean & Tea Leaf Stop off at any one of this trio of casual java joints for a yummy iced mocha or cup of joe or tea and then pick out some coffee beans from 30 varieties. ♦ M-F, 6:30AM-midnight; Sa, Su, 7AM-midnight. 8591 Sunset Blvd, 310/659.1890; 8793 Beverly Blvd, 310/659.4592; and 8735 Santa Monica Blvd, West Hollywood, 310/659.8207

dining room with a mirror-glass map of the world, or on an observation terrace shaded by pierced metal silhouettes of vintage airplanes. ♦ Asian ♦ M-F, Su, lunch and dinner; Sa, dinner. 3221 Donald Douglas Loop S (off 28th St). 310/390.6565

31 THE HUMP

★★★$$$ Just one floor up in the building that houses Typhoon, this outstanding Japanese restaurant offers a creative menu in a unique setting. Your entry into this Asian delight, designed by architect Stephen Jones, begins when you walk through intricate steel doors onto pebble stone floors. Propeller-shaped fans hang from a ceiling made of mahogany, bamboo, and seagrass. Seating is in teak/leather chairs from Indonesia, and food is served in Asiatic ceramic or pieces of bamboo. There's also an observation deck with a telescope where you can watch the planes taking off or landing. Chef Hiro Nishimura's cuisine matches the view. Begin with a cup of sake and feast on miso soup, assorted tempuras, grilled salmon skin and crabmeat salad, tuna sashimi (with cilantro, ginger, and garlic), broiled or steamed black cod, soft-shelled crabs, y-ma-dai (steamed whitefish with shiitake mushrooms), and other delights. There's also a sushi bar to die for. ♦ Japanese ♦ M-F, lunch; daily, dinner. Reservations a must. At Santa Monica Airport, 3221 Donald Douglas Loop South (off 28th St and upstairs from Typhoon). 310/313.0977

32 RADISSON HUNTLEY HOTEL

$$$ This 18-story hotel has great ocean views from the 213 guest rooms, decorated

---

Restaurants/Clubs: Red | Hotels: Purple | Shops: Orange | Outdoors/Parks: Green | Sights/Culture: Blue

in an elegant blend of European cosmopolitan and Art Deco. ♦ 1111 Second St (between Wilshire Blvd and California Ave). 310/394.5454, 800/333.3333; fax 310/458.9776

Within the Radisson Huntley Hotel:

TOPPERS

★$ Located atop the hotel, this Mexican restaurant and bar has a lively happy-hour crowd and a wide array of hors d'oeuvres. There's nightly musical entertainment in the bar. ♦ Mexican ♦ Daily, lunch, dinner, and late-night snacks. Reservations recommended. 310/393.8080

33 THE FAIRMONT MIRAMAR HOTEL (FORMERLY THE SHERATON MIRAMAR)

$$ Situated on the bluffs above Santa Monica, this legendary 302-room luxury hotel has the ambience of a private seaside residence. A $14 million refurbishment by Fairmont Hotels under the direction of LA-based designer Virginia Ball of VB Designs Inc. brought a new, modern design to this century-old property. In addition to hotel rooms there are 32 super-special bungalows with private patios hidden among tropical flowers and palm trees. We suggest staying in one of the completely renovated bi-level units, which feature an upstairs living room and balcony, a sauna, and a whirlpool bath (where Greta Garbo, Humphrey Bogart, Betty Grable, Marilyn Monroe, and other box-office biggies bedded down in decades past). Other accommodations include 176 ocean-view rooms and suites and a "historic" wing with oversized rooms. Special amenities include in-room coffeemakers, robes, two-line phones, data ports, Nintendo games, minibars, and daily newspaper. Facilities include a bi-level spa and fitness complex where you can look out at the ocean while you pump, flex, and sweat it out on the latest machines. There's also a steam room, sauna, and whirlpool, a gamut of salubrious treatments, and an outdoor pool. There are two place to eat: **The Grille** for California cuisine served indoors or alfresco on the patio, and **The Café,** where local luminaries like to go for casual fare. The enormous Moreton Bay fig tree in the center courtyard was planted in the 19th century. ♦ 101 Wilshire Blvd (at Ocean Ave). 310/576.7777,

800/866.5577; fax 310/458.7912. www.fairmont.com/santamonica.htm

33 HENNESSEY & INGALLS

This is LA's best resource for books and magazines on art, architecture, and design, with a spiky Constructivist façade designed by Morphosis. ♦ Daily. 214 Wilshire Blvd at Second St. 310/458.9074

MICHAEL'S

34 MICHAEL'S

★★★★$$$ Any meal at this Michael McCarty white-on-white restaurant is a magical experience. The cutting-edge restaurateur pioneered the new California cuisine, and also has a talent for breaking imported chefs into the LA scene. His most recent prize is chef de cuisine Olivier Rousselle, a Parision who earned his toque abroad in a busy Paris bistro, Boodle's gentlemen's club in London, where under chef Keith Podmore he cooked for London luminaries and members of the royal family. After a stint in South Africa's wine country at La Couronne Hotel, he returned to the London, where he cooked at several trendy eateries. Then, *voilà*, Michael discovered him. Like those of his predecessors, Rousselle's menu is both sensational and seasonal. If it's summer, you might find items such as oysters on the half shell, chilled avocado soup, hazelnut-crusted goat cheese, ahi tuna tartare, roasted sardines, seared California squab and foie gras, or grilled Mediterranean *loup de mer*. The best dessert is the lemon crème brûlée. And from zee pastry cart, your very own apple crumble pie with caramel ice cream, hot Valrhona chocolate fudge cake, or the cookie and confection plate are sure to please the sweet tooth. Adding to the culinary enjoyment is the flower-filled patio with its big white umbrellas and the works of David Hockney and Jasper Johns that adorn the dining room walls, not to mention the beautiful people who frequent this popular spot. Do dress up for the occasion in fashionably casual attire. ♦ California ♦ M-Sa, dinner; M-F, lunch and dinner. Reservations required. 1147 Third St (between Wilshire Blvd and California Ave). 310/451.0843. www.michaelssantamonica.com

35 THIRD STREET PROMENADE

This three-block pedestrian street with its faded stucco façade has been landscaped (with topiary dinosaur fountains) and given a major face-lift, revealing such architectural gems as the **Keller Building** (at Broadway), restored by Frank Dimsterr, and the **W.T. Grant**

Building (1300 block). Architect **Johannes Van Tilburg** designed the block at Arizona Avenue in the style of the Viennese Werkstatte. The area is home to the best specialty bookstores west of New York's SoHo, including **Arcana Books on the Arts** (no. 1229; 310/458.1499), as well as a rare book dealer, **Kenneth Karmiole** (two blocks away at 509 Wilshire Blvd; 310/451.4342). A bustling nightlife thrives throughout the outdoor mall, thanks to several movie theaters and a good selection of restaurants and bars, many with sidewalk patios. The shops are a mixed bag of everything from optical boutiques and New Age crystal shops to clothing outlets such as Old Navy (no. 1234), Lucky Brand Jeans and casual wear (no. 1215), and Johnny Rockets (no. 1322). Most of the shops stay open late. On Wednesday, California farmers market their produce on Arizona Avenue between Fourth and Second Streets. ♦ Between Broadway and Wilshire Blvd

35 LOCANDA DEL LAGO

★★★$$ A spunky Italian trattoria, it has oversize windows that face the bustling promenade. Bring a big appetite and dig into chef Enrico Gladuo's wonderful Northern Italian menu: *mossarella ala Sorrentina* (fresh mozzarella and tomato with oregano and basil), *carpaccio di bue all'Albese* (thin slices of raw beef tenderloin brushed with lemon-truffle dressing and shaved Parmesan and celery), filet of trout coated in a porcini mushroom breading, *fritto misto* (calamari, white shrimp, and lightly fried freshwater smelts), and the best risottos you've ever tasted. ♦ Italian ♦ Daily, lunch and dinner. Reservations recommended. 231 Arizona Ave (at Third St Promenade). 310/451.3525

36 SHANGRI-LA HOTEL

$$$ Like the monastery in the classic 1937 movie *Lost Horizon*, this is a Streamline Moderne gem, and—with its view over **Palisades Park** and the ocean—it's almost as idyllic. There's no lounge or restaurant, just a quiet, unassuming lobby. The 55 rooms and suites have been remodeled with a clean-edged 1930s look, including Deco posters, grays and pinks, and frosted glass. Most have ocean views; many have sundecks. It's within walking distance of shops and the beach. ♦ 1301 Ocean Ave (at Arizona Ave). 310/394.2791, 800/345.STAY. www.shangrila-hotel.com

37 BRAVO CUCINA

★$$ This is a charming sidewalk café to stop for a bite while strolling the Promenade. Pasta's the specialty here and it's *molto*

bene. ♦ Italian ♦ Daily, lunch and dinner. 1319 Third St Promenade (between Santa Monica Blvd and Arizona Ave). 310/394.0374

38 PINK ICE

This is where to find outrageously hip, tattoo/pierced-friendly fashions. ♦ Daily. 1340 Third St Promenade (between Santa Monica Blvd and Arizona Ave). 310/393.5877

39 HOOTERS

$$ It all depends on how you feel about scantily clad waitresses in tight T-shirts serving you chicken wings, hot dogs, hamburgers, and other greasy food in a noisy, high-octane environment. If the idea appeals, this two-hundred-and-thirtieth member of the quirky chain serves food as spicy as its women. ♦ Daily. 321 Santa Monica Blvd (between Fourth and Third Streets). 310/458.7555

40 OCEAN AVENUE SEAFOOD

★★$$ Superlative fresh fish, raw oysters, and genuine New England clam chowder are served in a yuppified Las Vegas setting. Patio dining overlooks **Palisades Park.** ♦ Seafood ♦ Daily, lunch and dinner. Reservations recommended. 1401 Ocean Ave (at Santa Monica Blvd). 310/394.5669

41 YE OLDE KING'S HEAD

$ Members of the local British colony tend to congregate for dart games and a sustenance of fish-and-chips and warm beer at this traditional English pub. ♦ English ♦ Daily, lunch and dinner; bar until 2AM. 116 Santa Monica Blvd (between Second St and Ocean Ave). 310/451.1402

41 YE OLDE KING'S HEAD SHOPPE

Homesick Brits know to come here for English candies, bangers (sausages), marmalades, and biscuits; teapot collectors will find a fabulous selection. British men's toiletries, dart supplies, and, of course, teas can be found in this quaint corner shop. ♦ Daily. 132 Santa Monica Blvd (at Second St). 310/394.8765

42 JIRAFFE

★★★$$$ Chef/owners Josiah Citrin and Raphael Lunetta (formerly of **Jackson's**) continue to please diners with great food and a comfortable setting. The two-story dining room features big, arched windows, dark-wood library chairs, and attractive ironwork sconces. Tables are set with retro-French silverware, white tablecloths, and baskets

---

Restaurants/Clubs: Red | Hotels: Purple | Shops: Orange | Outdoors/Parks: Green | Sights/Culture: Blue

filled with thick, buttery brioches. The creative menu includes such heavenly choices as truffled artichoke hearts, wild mushroom salad, fresh fig and arugula salad, ahi tuna tartare, seafood, lamb, and rabbit. ◆ American ◆ Tu-F, lunch and dinner; Sa, Su, dinner. Reservations required. 502 Santa Monica Blvd (at Fifth St). 310/917.6671

42 Union Restaurant and Bar

★★$$ Manhattan meets Santa Monica at this city-like spot with its sleek gentlemen's club–like décor of rich woods and unfinished steel. An upper deck features an aquatic theme with Robert Orr–designed waterfalls and an aquarium behind the bar. A brick-walled outdoor dining area boasts big booths and lots of alfresco ambience. The menu goes from light to heavy. Even appetizers run the gamut, from tuna tartare to buttermilk pancakes layered with Maine lobster, scrambled eggs, and honeycomb. Then come entrées like John Dory with homemade white truffle angel-hair pasta, Maine lobster flavored with vanilla bean, crispy duck confit, lamb osso buco, and filet mignon. Flavors are subtle, but servings are not. ◆ New American. ◆ Reservations suggested. M-F, lunch; daily, dinner. 1413 Fifth St (at Santa Monica Blvd). 310/656.9688

43 Voda

★★★$$$ The name translates to "water" in several languages, but vodka drinks are really the big draw here, with lots of different brands and types served with caviar. Stone walls accentuated by brown carpets and candles set the scene for the hip young crowd that frequents this lively spot. The eclectic menu ranges from designer pizzas to hearty steaks. ◆ Italian ◆ Tu-Sa, dinner. Reservations a must. 1449 Second St (near Santa Monica Blvd). 310/394.9774

43 Midnight Special Bookstore

The specialties here are politics, sociology, and literature. Call for a schedule of readings. ◆ Daily. 1450 Second St. 310/393.2923

44 Urban Outfitters

Steel girders frame 10 huge panels of floor-to-ceiling windows on the façade of this converted meatpacking plant, which now houses a funky sportswear shop for hip young metropolitanites. The raw, cavernous interior,

Thanks to California's stringent air-quality standards, Los Angeles has the most-improved air of any major city in the world over the past 20 years. The city is also a leading center for the development of environmental technology.

with its open beamed ceiling and cement floor, showcases trendy labels such as Bull Dog, Wheat, Free People, and Anthropology. ◆ Daily. 1440 Third St Promenade (between Broadway and Santa Monica Blvd). 310/394.1404

45 Gotham Hall/Sessions

Bon vivants and just plain night owls will enjoy this two-story European-style club, spread out in a mammoth six-room facility. The scene is young and hip, and often outlandish (there's a TV screen running replays of Jerry Springer's "Transsexual Tales," and performers in diamond-studded black-leather bikinis), with DJs from local radio stations spinning the latest hits. ◆ Cover. Must be 21 or older. F, Sa, 10PM-2AM. 1431 Third St Promenade (between Broadway and Santa Monica Blvd). 310/394.8865

46 Border Grill

★★$$ Half Mexican cantina, half punk nightclub (designed by Josh Schweitzer), this place literally vibrates with sound and color. Chefs Mary Sue Miliken and Susan Fenniger are known for their inventive cuisine, everything from green corn tamales and shrimp ceviche to bread soup, braised duck, and lamb tacos. Communal tables are provided for single diners and those without reservations. ◆ Mexican ◆ Tu-Su, lunch; daily, dinner. Reservations recommended. 1445 Fourth St (between Broadway and Santa Monica Blvd). 310/451.1655. www.bordergrill.com

47 Palisades Park

This park is one of the oldest and best maintained in the city, and the steep, crumbly cliffs along the edge of the ocean are a traditional spot for Angelenos to watch the sunset fade over the ocean. Towering palms and semitropical trees form beautiful bowers for strolling or jogging, as well as a haven for the elderly, who gather here to gossip and play chess, and for the homeless. Steps lead down to the beach. ◆ Ocean Ave (between Colorado Ave and Adelaide Dr)

Within Palisades Park:

Camera Obscura

In the **Senior Recreation Center** is an upstairs room where startling projections of the outside world appear on a circular white surface. ◆ Free. Daily. 1450 Ocean Ave (at Broadway). 310/394.1227

Visitors' Information Stand

Pick up free sightseeing maps and bus and tour information here. ◆ Daily. Ocean Ave and Santa Monica Blvd. 310/393.7593

PALISADES PARK GATES

The Craftsman-style fieldstone gates were made in 1912 and decorated with tiles by Ernest Batchelder of Pasadena.

48 CARMEL BY THE SEA

$ This well-kept economy hotel with 102 rooms and eight suites is close to **Santa Monica Place.** There's a convenient coffee shop just outside the building. ♦ 201 Broadway (at Second St). 310/451.2469

49 LONE WOLF

Celebrities James Belushi and Chuck Norris opened this bustling cigar shop, where smokers can relax in oversize leather chairs and puff to their heart's content on private-label brands and selections from around the world. Humidors keep the stogies fresh. ♦ M-F, 10AM-10PM; Sa, 10AM-11PM; Su, 10AM-8PM. 223B Broadway (between Third St Promenade and Second St). 310/458.5441

50 BROADWAY DELI

$ Steven Erlich designed this stripped Deco interior with stylish simplicity. They serve sandwiches, salads, grills, and deli basics, plus a good choice of beers and wines by the glass. ♦ Deli ♦ Daily. 1457 Third St Promenade (at Broadway). 310/451.0616

51 BURKE WILLIAMS DAY SPA AND MASSAGE CENTER

When this fortress of salubrious indulgence opened in Santa Monica more than a decade ago, it was the only act in town of its kind. Pamper seekers flocked here for the ultimate massage. It was truly one of the best. You can still enjoy a top-notch rub if you get the right therapist. Unfortunately, some regulars have experienced more misses than hits. But it still packs them in, somewhat to the consternation of regulars who feel it's become too factory-like. Still, it's convenient for locals, and the facility itself is quite pleasant and attractively put together. There are steam rooms, hot tubs, bubbling baths, relaxation rooms, showers, lockers, and a wide range of services from hair care, facials, and manicures to reflexology and pedicures. Body scrubs, sea salts, and massages are best bets. Facials can be very spotty. ♦ Daily. 1460 Fourth St (at Broadway). 310/587.3366. Also at 8000 Sunset Blvd (at Laurel Ave), Hollywood. 310/833.9007; 39 Mills Place, Pasadena. 626/440.1222; 27741 Crown Valley Pkwy, Mission Viejo. 949/367.9717; 20 City Blvd, West Bldg, Orange. 714/769.1360; and

15301 Ventura Blvd, Sherman Oaks. 818/789.3339. www.burkewilliamsspa.com

52 I CUGINI

★$ Owned by the same successful restaurateurs who opened **Water Grill** downtown and **Ocean Avenue Seafood** down the street, this restaurant has a split personality: noisy at night inside; quiet and candlelit on the outdoor patio, where diners enjoy views of **Palisades Park** and the Pacific Ocean. The veal chops, sea bass, and spaghetti with seafood are popular entrées. The décor is turn-of-the-century Northern Italian, with mahogany wainscoting, marble accents, and cove ceilings. A lobby bakery sells fresh rosemary bread sticks, spinach bread, and an olive purée that's great for spreading on bread. ♦ Italian ♦ Daily, lunch and dinner. 1501 Ocean Ave (at Broadway). 310/451.4595

53 FRED SEGAL FOR A BETTER ECOLOGY

The burgers are turkey; the bed sheets, clothing, face products, and paints are bleach- and chemical-free; and ecology and energy information is displayed alongside products. But don't confuse this complex with earthier, more bohemian stores: It has upscale fare for environmentalists who drive Range Rovers. ♦ Daily. 420 Broadway (between Fifth and Fourth Sts). 310/394.6448

54 FRED SEGAL

A spin-off of its Melrose sister, this cluster of specialty stores is like a tiny village under one roof, with gourmet takeout and an espresso bar; youthful, hip, and classy upscale goods; and a DJ spinning oldies and Top 40 hits. Hats, jewelry, clothing, and scents for women, a pricey kids' shop with handmade quilts, men's clothing and gifts, and the latest eyewear are all available. The latest addition is a sleek, contemporary day spa proffering the gamut of head-to-toe services from professional hair-color consultations to a grooming parlor for men. The quirky décor includes doohickeys such as a graffiti pole, an oversized black-and-white cowhide-covered bench in the waiting room, Takara Belmont wall-mounted shampoo bowls, and stylists and manicure stations on wheels for faster service. And for those really in the fast lane, a concierge who makes dinner reservations, arranges alterations and dry cleaning, walks and/or grooms your dog, has your car washed or detailed, gets theater tickets, and more. What more can you ask for? 310/451.5155 ♦ Daily. 500 Broadway (at Fifth St). 310/393.2322

Restaurants/Clubs: Red | Hotels: Purple | Shops: Orange | Outdoors/Parks: Green | Sights/Culture: Blue

55 IVY AT THE SHORE

★★$$$ This informal oceanfront version of the more stylish Ivy in Midtown is spacious and airy, with big rattan chairs and an outdoor terrace. The menu includes crab cakes, grilled fresh fish, steaks, pasta, and salads. It's a good place to bring out-of-town visitors looking for the elusive "LA lifestyle." ◆ California ◆ Daily, lunch and dinner. Reservations recommended. 1541 Ocean Ave (between Colorado Ave and Broadway). 310/393.3113

56 SANTA MONICA PLACE

Architect **Frank Gehry**'s 1979-81 design of this huge white skylit galleria features three levels of shops. The cutaway façade with its balcony views of the ocean, the mesh screen on the parking garage, and the asymmetrical plan show that an architectural intelligence rather than a cookie-cutter mind was involved. **Robinsons-May** and **Macy's** anchor the complex, which includes **Eddie Bauer, Compagnie BX** (Michael Glasser's boutique), **Natural Wonders, Cotton Kids,** more than a dozen specialty carts selling everything from candles to jewelry, and 150 other stores as well as the **Santa Monica Visitor's Center** (at no. 203). If you need help navigating the area, drop into this state-of-the-art help center where a multilingual staff can assist with hotel reservations or tickets to attractions and give advice on restaurants. There are also interactive computer displays. 310/393.7593. The **USC School of Fine Arts** shows innovative Southern California artists in its **Atelier.** ◆ Daily. Bounded by Fourth and Second Sts, and Colorado Ave and Broadway. 310/394.1049. www.santamonicaplace.com

57 SANTA MONICA PIER

The aroma of popcorn, cotton candy, and corn dogs, the soft resonance of the boardwalk underfoot, the calliope of the merry-go-round, and the metallic din of the penny arcade characterize this pier, which really began as two piers. Built side by side between 1909 and 1921, the piers were threatened with demolition in 1973 and badly damaged by storms 10 years later. Citizens rallied to save them, and the city backed a Pier Restoration Corporation development plan that resulted in such additions as the **UCLA Ocean Discovery Center** (310/393.6149), a hands-on aquarium/learning center focusing on the study of underwater sea life. Open to the public daily 11AM to 5PM, the facility offers computer links to scientific sources around the world, tanks filled with many kinds of sea creatures, and a small auditorium for lectures. **Pacific Park** (310/260.8744), a two-acre "fun zone" at the southwest corner of the pier, features 12 rides, including a roller coaster and a giant Ferris wheel that soars 100 feet above the ocean. Other additions include a food court, arcade games, strolling performers, shops, and boutiques. www.pacpark.com.

The **Looff Hippodrome** is popular with children, who enjoy riding on its **Philadelphia Toboggan carousel.** Brought to the pier in 1947 and restored in 1981, the carousel played a supporting role in the movie The Sting. Free concerts with dancing under the stars are presented on the pier on Thursday nights in summer. At night, the long strand of white lights along the pier's edge creates a poetic landmark for those coming down the coast highway from the north. Nearby, the architectural firm **Moore, Ruble, and Yudell** created **Carousel Park** (Colorado and Ocean Aves) as a stepped gateway to the pier, an open theater for beach sports, and a children's park with a dragon made of river-washed granite boulders. To the south, the same architects have landscaped a section of **Ocean Park Beach,** and the entire three-mile stretch of beach has been turned into the **Natural Elements Sculpture Park.** Already installed in this park is Douglas Hollis's Wind Harp (singing beach chairs). Carl Cheng's Santa Monica Art Tool is a concrete roller towed by a tractor to imprint a miniature metropolis on the sand. ◆ Fee for Pacific Park rides and carousel. Pacific Park and Looff Hippodrome: daily. Carousel Park: Tu-Su in summer; Sa, Su in winter. Shuttle buses run from the parking structure at 2030 Barnard Way. Colorado Ave (just southwest of Ocean Ave). General information 310/260.8747

At the Santa Monica Pier:

SOUTH BAY BICYCLE TRAIL

This beachside trail runs from the pier 18 miles south to the city of Torrance.

58 SANTA MONICA FREEWAY

Known as the "Christopher Columbus Transcontinental Highway," it sweeps through a curved tunnel to Route 1, setting you on a new course filled with dramatic scenery.

59 ANGELS ATTIC MUSEUM

Miniatures, toys, and dolls are displayed in this restored Victorian-style house, while tea and cookies are served on the porch from 12:30 to 3:30PM. ◆ Admission. Th-Su. 516 Colorado Ave (between Sixth and Fifth Sts). 310/394.8331

60 DOUBLETREE SUITES

$$$ Sweeping views, a terrace restaurant, business center, outdoor pool, and fitness facilities are only some of the amenities

provided at this all-suite hotel (formerly **Guest Quarters**). It's a great buy for families, as the 253 suites here each sleep four. ♦ 1707 Fourth St (at Santa Monica Fwy). 310/395.3332, 800/222.8733 (weekends only); fax 310/458.6493. www.doubletreeSantaMonica.com

61 SANTA MONICA CIVIC CENTER

The complex includes the **Santa Monica Civic Auditorium** (310/393.9961), which presents big-name rock and jazz concerts, exhibitions, and trade shows. ♦ Bounded by Fourth and Main Sts, and Pico Blvd and Santa Monica Fwy

62 LOEWS SANTA MONICA BEACH HOTEL

$$$$ This attractive luxury hotel just above the beach provides sweeping views of the sea. Just a short walk from the **Santa Monica Pier**, it offers 350 recently renovated rooms and suites flanking a lofty glass-roofed atrium, out of which flow the restaurants and a half-covered pool. The spa and fitness center, operated by trainer-to-the-stars Jackson Sousa, is one of the best of the hotel variety. The **Lavande** (★★★$$$) features creative California cuisine with a Mediterranean twist by chef Jeffrey Nimer. Bouillabaisse with saffron shellfish, grilled New Zealand snapper with blood sausage and beluga lentils in a veal reduction, and lobster salad with haricots vert and teardrop tomatoes in an herb vinaigrette are dishes to enjoy while savoring the spectacular ocean view. There's also the **Papillon Lobby** bar and fireside lounge for drinks and tapas. An array of business facilities and meeting spaces is available. ♦ California/Mediterranean ♦ Reservations suggested. Daily, dinner. 310.576.3180. 1700 Ocean Ave (between Seaview and Seaside Terrs). 310/458.6700, 800/223.0888; fax 310/458.0020. www.loewshotels.com &

62 IL FORNAIO

★★$$ You can make the short two-block stroll over here from the Loews Hotel and enjoy a fabulous feast of Sicilian delights like thick-crust pizzas, rotisserie meats and poultry, imported pastas, grilled local fish, and great breads and desserts. ♦ Italian ♦ Reservations suggested. Daily, lunch and dinner; Sa, Su, brunch. 1551 Ocean Ave (between Pico Blvd and Colorado Ave). Also at 301 N Beverly Dr (at Dayton Way), Beverly Hills. 310/550.8330 &

LE MERIGOT

62 LE MERIGOT

$$$ Although there are 175 rooms, Le Merigot (a JW Marriott beach hotel and spa) has the feel of a smaller, more intimate hotel thanks to a friendly staff and relaxed atmosphere. Even the lobby is serene with its large, open spaces and comfy chairs and sofas. All the rooms are spacious and nicely appointed, with an understated elegance. The linens are Frette and the toiletries are from Bare Escentuals. There are feather beds, robes, slippers, 24-hour mending and pressing of clothing, free shoe shine, newspaper, fax, cellular phone, and even the option of having someone pack and unpack your bags. (For a real treat, book room no. 449, which comes with a big balcony and great views of the sea.) Dining choices include **Cézanne's** (★★$$$), a good, serviceable three-meal-a-day restaurant, and room service. There's also **Le Troquet**, a lobby bar where drinks, hors d'oeuvres, and cigars are proffered. A well-equipped fitness room and nice-sized pool help keep guests in shape, while a full-service spa provides the ultimate in pampering treatments—massages here are not to be missed. The newest kid on the beachfront block, Le Merigot opened on New Year's Day Y2K. The hotel is literally steps from the sea and Santa Monica's shopping areas. ♦ 1740 Ocean Avenue (between Pico Blvd and Colorado Ave). 310/395.9700, 888/539.7899; fax 310/395.9200. www.lemerigothotel.com or www.marriott.com

63 VIDIOTS

This is the place to rent or buy unique independent, foreign, and cult movies. ♦ Daily. 302 Pico Blvd (at Third St). 310/392.8508

64 MARLOW'S BOOKS

And here's where to pick up new and used books of all kinds, along with sheet music and magazines. ♦ Daily. 2314 Lincoln Blvd (between Kensington Rd and Strand St). 310/392.9161

65 VICEROY

$$$ Interior designer Kelly Wearstler performed miracles on the aging landmark Pacific Shore Hotel when hired by the Kor Hotel Group, who took over the place in 2002, to do the remodel. The result is an over-the-top stunning design with lots of white, splashes of yellow, charcoal, and

---

Restaurants/Clubs: Red | Hotels: Purple | Shops: Orange | Outdoors/Parks: Green | Sights/Culture: Blue

minimalism mixed with Colonial—cane and wicker furnishings combine with chandeliers, oversized chairs, and chaises done in white faux leather. It's hip and happening, with 170 sleek rooms done in blinding white with yellowish trim. Nice touches include 300-thread-count Frette sheets, surround-sound CD/DVD players, and attractive tile baths with lavish amenities. The two pools double as a guest facility, providing a meeting place for after-work locals who flop on oversized chaises and sip martinis and other libations. There's also a fitness center and a popular restaurant called **Whist** (see below). ♦ 1819 Ocean Ave (at Pico Blvd). 800/622.8711, 310/451.8711; fax 310/394.6657. www.viceroysantamonica.com

Within the Viceroy:

WHIST

★★★$$$ A crowd scene on almost any night of the week, this quirky-looking restaurant combines metallic wallpaper with pentagonal, Escher-esque glass chandeliers, limed wood floor, wingback chaises, smoky mirrors, and a green-mirrored wall filled with 250 pieces of English china. The noise level (mostly from high-testosterone tipplers) makes conversation difficult. The food is so good you'll want to concentrate on what you're eating anyway. Signature dishes include hot smoked king salmon, braised prime short ribs with polenta, and hand-rolled gnocchi. Everything's done to perfection most of the time. Desserts are divine. ♦ California ♦ Daily, breakfast, lunch, and dinner. Reservations a must for dinner. 310/451.8711

66 SHUTTERS ON THE BEACH

$$$$ Antebellum unites with modern-day luxury at this 198-room plantation-style beachfront budget-buster. The showstopping guest rooms are done in dark walnut on blue-and-white carpeting, with Laura Ashley–like prints, tufted lounge chairs, and, of course, shuttered windows. Other creature comforts include pretty terry robes, in-room and outdoor Jacuzzis, a health club, a pool, two restaurants, and a plucky waterfront saloon called **Handles**. One of the best amenities is the **OleHenriksen** day spa. A branch of the West Hollywood facility, the transcendental pamper spot offers hand-picked, trained therapists who provide head-to-toe treatments. Facials are about as good as it gets. Call the concierge for appointments at 310/458.0030. (OleHenriksen is also located at 8622A W Sunset Blvd, in Sunset Plaza on the south side of Sunset Blvd, West Hollywood. 310/854.7700.) www.olehenriksen.com ♦ 1 Pico Blvd (at Appian Way). 310/458.0030, 800/336.3000; fax 310/458.4859 ♿

Within Shutters on the Beach:

ONE PICO

★★$$$ Plate-glass windows at this charming restaurant provide ringside views of Santa Monica's beach people—joggers, volleyball players, and sun worshipers. The food is great, especially the fresh seafood and pasta dishes and the divine strawberry shortcake. ♦ California ♦ Daily, lunch and dinner. Reservations required. 310/587.1717

66 CASA DEL MAR

$$$$ This 129-room sister of Shutters Hotel sits just across the street from its sibling yet is worlds apart. Originally built as a beach club/hotel more nearly 75 years ago, the historic landmark underwent a $60 million face-lift before reopening in 1999. The lobby lounge caught on quickly with locals (who jam the place nightly), and the charming hotel rooms have lured lots of business. There's a decent restaurant, a nice-size pool, a fitness center, and all the usual upscale amenities. ♦ 1910 Ocean Front Walk (across the street from Shutters at Pico Blvd). 310/581.5533

67 MAIN STREET

Slightly south of Santa Monica proper is Ocean Park, once a seaside resort with thousands of tiny beach cottages and a large Coney Island–style amusement park. The neighborhood now includes an active shopping and trendy dining area covering several blocks of this street. It's a pleasant place for walking and window-shopping. There is a high concentration of restaurants, many with rear patios or sidewalk seating.

67 AMICI MARE (FORMERLY GILLILAND'S)

★★$$ As the name implies, much of the fare is from the sea (*mare* in Italian). The tomato-based fish soup is a great starter or meal in itself. The place is fun and the food is good. ♦ Italian ♦ Reservations are a good idea. M-F, lunch; daily, dinner. 2424 Main St (between Ocean Park Blvd and Hollister Ave). 310/314.2119

68 HORATIO WEST COURT

These impressively modern two-story apartments, designed by **Irving Gill** in 1919, were far ahead of their time. They are private residences. ♦ 140 Hollister Ave (between Neilson Way and Ocean Ave)

69 HIGHLIGHTS

Owners Ron Rezek and Lori Thomsen have displayed their choice of the "50 best lights in the world," and can order up many more if you still can't find just the right lamp. Call ahead if you plan to drop by at lunchtime. ♦

M-Sa. 2427 Main St (between Ocean Park Blvd and Hollister Ave). 310/450.5886

69 EDGEMAR

Developer Abby Sher commissioned **Frank Gehry** to design this urban village in 1989. The mixed-use development points to the numbing mediocrity of the mini-malls elsewhere in the city. Instead of the typical façade with a car park in front, Gehry has created a cluster of unique sculptural forms (high-tech, streamline, and minimalist) that relate well to neighboring buildings and define a series of pedestrian spaces. An eclectic mix of businesses occupies the development, including an art museum, an upscale restaurant, and retail stores offering functional art, pricey retro children's clothing, business services, records, and **Ben & Jerry's** ice cream. ♦ 2435 Main St (between Ocean Park Blvd and Hollister Ave)

Within Edgemar:

RÖCKENWAGNER RESTAURANT & BRASSERIE

★★★$$$ Hans and Mary Röckenwagner are personally involved in the cooking at their restaurant, and it shows. Hans Röckenwagner redesigned the restaurant into a casual, moderate-priced brasserie but kept an area with a few tables dedicated to a prix-fixe menu of his original dishes. The brasserie fare features lamb cassoulet, grilled flank steak, oysters, roasted half chicken, and veal goulash. A take-out deli offers breads by a German master baker and excellent plum strudel. ♦ California ♦ Daily, lunch and dinner; Sa, Su, brunch. Reservations recommended. 310/399.6504 ⅃

70 CALIFORNIA HERITAGE MUSEUM

Period rooms, local archives, and photographs are preserved in this restored 19th-century house designed by **Sumner P. Hunt** for Roy Jones, a son of one of the city's founders. ♦ Admission. W-Su. 2612 Main St (at Ocean Park Blvd). 310/392.8537

71 JADIS

Even if you're not a set designer, you might get a kick out of Parke Meek's place of movie props. Meek makes scientific and industrial props that have appeared in such films as *Batman*, *Casper*, *Mystery Men*, and *Waterworld*, as well as TV's *The X Files*. His kitschy window displays are reason enough to visit the shop—and Meek always welcomes visitors. ♦ 2701 Main St (right next door to Paris 1900 at Hill St). Call ahead to be sure someone's there, if you want to go inside. 323/396.3477

PARIS 1900

71 PARIS 1900

Martha Stewart meets Laura Ashley at this adorable boutique, which carries a wonderful assortment of white vintage lace gowns, bridal accessories, antique table linens, bedding, and museum-quality antique clothing and accessories. ♦ M-Sa by appointment, or take a chance and stop by; if someone's there they'll let you in. 2703 Main St (at Hill St). 310/396.0405

71 CHINOIS ON MAIN

★★★★$$$$ **Wolfgang Puck**'s noisy, crowded, and expensive restaurant is not to be missed by anyone who loves indulging in inventive cuisine in the most stylish of settings. Puck's creations fuse East and West: Try the warm curried oysters, Cantonese duck, barbecued salmon, or ginger-stuffed whole sizzling catfish with sweet pepper sauce. Desserts are special here, the standout being an assortment of three petites crèmes brûlées. Barbara Lazaroff (Puck's former wife) did the wonderful décor, which incorporates a fine screen by Miriam Wosk. Ask for a table away from the open kitchen. ♦ French/Chinese ♦ Daily, dinner; W-F, lunch and dinner. Reservations required. 2709 Main St (between Ashland Ave and Hill St). 310/392.9025

72 MAX STUDIO

Trendy Generation Y'ers shop here for Leon Max's casuals, suits, and special dresses. ♦ Daily. 2712 Main St (between Ashland Ave and Hill St). 310/396.3963

73 HOMEWORKS

You will certainly find unusual items at this novelty gift shop, which prides itself on its oddball eclectic inventory. ♦ Daily. 2923 Main St (between Pier and Ashland Aves). 310/396.0101

74 ENTERPRISE FISH COMPANY

★★$$ This fish-eater's haven captures the seafaring ambience of the Chesapeake Bay

---

Restaurants/Clubs: **Red** | Hotels: **Purple** | Shops: **Orange** | Outdoors/Parks: **Green** | Sights/Culture: **Blue**

and the Pacific Northwest. Steamed mussels, chunky clam chowder, and fried calamari are great openers for swordfish, mahi mahi, orange roughy, and fresh Pacific salmon broiled on an open mesquite grill. Japanese tourists come here by the busload. ♦ Seafood ♦ Daily, lunch and dinner. Reservations recommended. 174 Kinney St (at Main St). 310/392.8366

75 SCHATZI ON MAIN

★\$\$ Arnold Schwarzenegger and Maria Shriver's restaurant/bar is casual, comfortable, and cheery, with colorfully upholstered banquettes, brick cove ceilings, and a garden patio. The menu features lots of homey food, and veers from his contributions (bratwurst on a pretzel roll) to hers (chicken potpie) to theirs (crab blintzes with tomato salsa). The quality of the food doesn't match the celebrity draw, but try the excellent homemade corned-beef hash for breakfast or the linguine with shrimp, mussels, and calamari for dinner. ♦ California ♦ Daily, lunch and dinner; closed first M of each month for invitation-only cigar dinner. Reservations recommended. 3110 Main St (between Navy and Marine Sts). 310/399.4800

VENICE

At the turn of the century, tobacco magnate Abbot Kinney tried to create a model community fashioned after Venice, Italy, that would spur Americans to achieve their own cultural renaissance. A network of canals drained the marshy land and fed into the **Grand Lagoon,** and a three-day opening celebration, beginning on 4 July 1905, featured gondola and camel rides. The community was briefly self-governing, but in 1925, residents voted for annexation by the city of LA, which soon paved over all but three of the original 16 miles of canals and closed the speakeasies and gambling houses that thrived during Prohibition. The arcades along **Windward Avenue** and a few surviving waterways to the south (which are slowly being refurbished) are all that survive of Kinney's grand design.

But Venice and neighboring **Ocean Park** continued to flourish as "Coney Island West," defying the bluenoses and devastation by storm and fire. Flanking the boardwalks and several piers were Arabian bathhouses and Egyptian bazaars, roller coasters, and freak shows. As the area became more raffish and run-down, it lured those who couldn't afford to live—or didn't feel at home—elsewhere. Beats gave way to hippies and Hell's Angels to drug gangs, with the elderly, the artistic, and the adventurous finally settling here in a crazy quilt of humanity. The diversity is on display in the weekend circus on **Ocean Front Walk,** where jocks, executives, panhandlers, hipsters, families, bikini-clad women, and cops in shorts promenade or roll along the famed **Venice Beach Boardwalk** on every imaginable wheeled device. It has become a compulsory stop for tourists

from Tokyo to Topeka. You can rent skates or bikes and join the scene. For a map of **Venice Beach,** contact the **Venice Chamber of Commerce** (310/396.7016, www.venice.net/chamber) and ask for the *Venice Visitors Map,* a valuable guide to the area's rich selection of public art, historic sites, and more.

A ferment of cultural activity away from this colorful craziness are the studios and galleries of leading artists, many of which can be explored on the annual **Art Walk** (for more information, call 310/392.8630). Some of LA's most adventurous new architecture and restaurants are slotted in amid the peeling stucco and clapboard cottages. The greatest threats today are from crime and gentrification, not physical deterioration. When there's no room at the beach parking lots, you can leave your car in the city lot at Abbot Kinney and Venice Boulevards and ride to the beach on the DASH shuttle, which runs every 15 minutes on Saturday and Sunday.

76 VENICE RENAISSANCE BUILDING

Johannes Van Tilburg's design for this 1990 building was lauded for its mixed-use concept. The 34-foot-high ballerina clown sculpture mounted at its southeast prow has become a landmark; the bizarre kinetic work unites the contrasting images of a classical performer and a lowbrow comedian. Artist Jonathan Borofsky designed the vulgar, kitschy image to echo Venice and to contrast the upscale site. ♦ Rose Ave and Main St

Within the Venice Renaissance Building:

CHAYA≈VENICE
CHAYA VENICE

★★\$\$ This stunning restaurant was designed by Grinstein/Daniels, who created the interior for **Chaya Brasserie** in West Hollywood and **El Chaya** in Hollywood. Bronze and copper, natural woods and stone, and a Japanese ceiling mural achieve a pleasing harmony. And the food is equally enjoyable, especially the miso or spicy white bean soup, shrimp and pork pot stickers, and paella. For dessert, the brownie sundae and the "Banana, Banana, Banana" tart coated in chocolate are musts. ♦ International ♦ M-F, lunch and dinner; Sa, dinner; Su, brunch, lunch, and dinner. Reservations recommended. 110 Navy St (at Main St). 310/396.1179

77 340 MAIN BUILDING

Designed by **Frank Gehry,** this unique building has two sections flanking the entry—a boat-shaped white office wing on the north and an innovative abstract tree form made of copper-clad steel on the south—were already designed when former tenant Jay Chiat pushed for an entry solution. Gehry grabbed a nearby Claes Oldenburg maquette of a pair of binoculars and placed it on the model as an example. Chiat liked it. The result is an unusual building (completed in 1991) designed to create a three-part streetscape in scale with the neighborhood. The structure still appears massive because it reaches the edge of the site (to compensate for coastal height limits). The treelike form creates a sunscreen for the west-facing building, and the binoculars contain two small meeting rooms. ♦ 340 Main St (at Rose Ave)

77 ROSE CAFÉ AND MARKET

★$$ Eclectic modern dishes are served in the dining area; lighter fare, including breakfasts and great pastries, can be ordered at the counter, to go or to eat on the patio. ♦ International ♦ M-Sa, breakfast, lunch, and dinner; Su, breakfast and lunch. 220 Rose Ave (between Hampton Dr and Main St). 310/399.0711

77 GOLD'S GYM

This is the original home of the unbelievably well-oiled buff bodies and rippling abs. There's a "we will pump you up" mentality, no frills, and lots of equipment to get the job done. There are several individually owned branches throughout Southern California. ♦ Daily. 360 Hampton Dr (between Sunset and Rose Aves). 310/392.6004. Also at numerous locations throughout the area

78 VENICE BISTRO

★$$ Mexican-American dishes, including pasta and a variety of salads, are served at this popular patio restaurant. There's live music Wednesday through Sunday evenings. ♦ Mexican/American ♦ Daily, lunch and dinner. 323 Ocean Front Walk (between Dudley and Rose Aves). 310/392.3997

79 FIG TREE

$$ Grilled fish and flavorful vegetarian dishes are served both indoors and on a peaceful patio just off the boardwalk. ♦ California ♦ Daily, breakfast, lunch, and dinner. 429 Ocean Front Walk (between Paloma and Dudley Aves). 310/392.4937

80 AMUSE CAFÉ

★★$$ This little charmer set in a two-story historic railroad bunkhouse was conceived by two young LA super-chefs, Brooke Williamson and Nick Roberts, who set out "to create an approachable space for our neighbors." Which they did and more, attracting folks from far and near. The food's great and the ambience enhanced by oversized china plates and cobalt blue glassware set on white tablecloths, dark oak wood chairs, polished hardwood floors, wide windows, and friendly service. The menu

changes daily and includes something for everybody. The fish (especially the halibut in season) and tender grilled flatiron steak are good choices. For dessert, a banana split, chocolate fondue, or vanilla-bean panna cotta does the trick. ♦ Daily (except Tu), breakfast, lunch, and dinner. Reservations recommended for lunch and dinner. 796 Main St, Venice (between Abbot Kinney Blvd and Brooks Ave). 310/450.1956; email: chefs@amusecafe.com www.amusecafe.com. (Physically challenged should request lower-level seating, as there are stairs to climb.)

81 JOE'S RESTAURANT

★★★$$ Yes, there really is a Joe: chef Joe Miller, who staffs the kitchen and creates good, honest California food at modest prices. The room has a New York/San Francisco flair, a laid-back elegance that makes you want to dress for lunch or dinner. Attractive artwork is hung on the walls. There's a welcoming outdoor patio (heated in winter). The service is consistently efficient. ♦ California ♦ Tu-Su, lunch and dinner. Reservations suggested. 1023 Abbot Kinney Blvd (near Broadway). 310/399.5811. www.JoesRestaurant.com

81 LILLY'S FRENCH CAFÉ & BAR

$$ Chef Francis Bey treats diners to delicious French fare in a California-casual bi-level patio setting. The roasted chicken breast; goat cheese, wild mushroom, and leek tart; and juicy sirloin steak are ooh la la, and the baba au rhum is a nice finishing touch. ♦ French ♦ Daily, lunch and dinner. Reservations suggested for dinner. 1301 Abbot Kinney Blvd (between Westminster Ave and Broadway). 310/314.0004

81 AXE

★★$$$ This eclectic little café dishes out some dandy eats, from the grilled flatbread smothered with hummus, eggplant, and caramelized onions to the poached halibut or duck leg laced with plum, orange, and cilantro. And for dessert, a chocolate brownie pudding will satisfy your sweet tooth. ♦ Eclectic ♦ Reservations suggested. Tu-F, lunch; Tu-Su, dinner. 1009 Abbot Kinney Blvd (between Brooks Ave and Broadway). 310/664.9787

82 CAPLIN HOUSE

This quirky house by **Frederick Fisher** was built in 1979 for the editor of *Wet* magazine;

The city of Santa Monica collects more than $5 million in parking fees yearly.

Restaurants/Clubs: Red | Hotels: Purple | Shops: Orange | Outdoors/Parks: Green | Sights/Culture: Blue

the design was a stylistic statement for both the architect and the client. It's a private residence. ◆ 229 San Juan Ave (between Riviera Ave and Main St)

83 HAL'S BAR & GRILL

★$$ A favorite with local artists, this place has a casual interior and offers salads, pasta, and other basic fare. ◆ California ◆ M, Tu, dinner; W-F, lunch and dinner; Sa, Su, brunch and dinner. Reservations recommended. 1349 Abbot Kinney Blvd (between California and Santa Clara Aves). 310/396.3105

84 BEYOND BAROQUE LITERARY/ARTS CENTER

Don't miss the adventurous readings, lectures, and performances that sustain the bohemian tradition of Venice. Abbot Kinney would have approved. Call ahead for program information. ◆ 681 Venice Blvd (between Oakwood and Shell Aves). 310/822.3006

85 SPILLER HOUSE

In 1980, **Frank Gehry** designed this pair of houses, each with two parking spaces and a garden, shoehorned onto a very tiny plot. They combine a corrugated-steel exterior with a woodsy interior, thus creating an archetypal low-cost Venice landmark. This is a private residence. ◆ 39 Horizon Ave (between Pacific Ave and Speedway)

86 SIDEWALK CAFE

$ Skateboarders and young "dig me" types go here to enjoy salads, pizzas, and burgers. ◆ American ◆ Daily, breakfast, lunch, and dinner. 1401 Ocean Front Walk (at Horizon Ave). 310/399.5547

87 GLOBE VENICE BEACH

★★$$$ Joseph Manzare, former chef at Granita and owner of the Globe in San Francisco and Mucca in Sonoma, took over the former **72 Market** restaurant and remodeled it into a sister of his San Francisco eatery. The menu is typical Manzare: grilled meats, fish, and homemade pastas. ◆ American ◆ M-F, lunch and dinner; Sa, Su, brunch, lunch, and dinner.

Not surprisingly, you can see lots of LA locales at your neighborhood movie theater. Just a few examples: In *Lethal Weapon*, Mel Gibson took a dramatic leap from the roof of the Emser Building in West Hollywood; in *Annie Hall*, Diane Keaton defended LA culture to Woody Allen at The Source restaurant on Sunset Strip; and Tim Robbins held his famous poolside meeting in *The Player* at the St. James's Club (now The Argyle).

Reservations required. 72 Market St (between Pacific Ave and Speedway). 310/392.8720

88 WINDWARD CIRCLE

From 1905 to 1929 it was known as the "Grand Lagoon." Architect **Steven Erlich** has tried to awaken its ghosts with three complementary buildings that use concrete-filled culvert pipes to suggest Venetian porticoes. The giant **Race Through the Clouds roller coaster** finds an echo in the neon loop of a retail block; metal frames flank a food market, recalling the steam-driven dredgers that excavated the canals. A residential block occupies the site of the **Antlers Hotel**, which was demolished in 1960. To the south is a post office containing Edward Biberman's mural of the history of Venice. ◆ Main St and Windward Ave

At Windward Circle:

HAMA SUSHI

★$$$ This well-lit eatery decorated with blond wood furnishings is a favorite neighborhood sushi bar. If perchance you're not in the mood for sushi, try the lobster dynamite (lobster sautéed in soy sauce with mushrooms). ◆ Japanese ◆ M-F, lunch and dinner; Sa, Su, dinner. 213 Windward Ave. 310/396.8783

89 CAPRI

★★$$ Owner Alana Hamilton Cooke offers superb food in a minimalist setting. Chef John Beriker, formerly of Spago, conjures up some excellent pasta, poultry (don't miss the quail), and seafood creations. Cooke boasts an impressive but reasonably priced Italian wine list, and she has introduced some wonderful desserts, from tiramisù to flourless chocolate cake. ◆ Italian ◆ Tu-Su, dinner. Reservations recommended on weekends. 1616 Abbot Kinney Blvd (between S Venice Blvd and Rialto Ave). 310/392.8777

90 VENICE MURAL

Terry Schoonhoven's large, much-faded mural shows a mirror image of the city on a very clear day, with the distant mountains in view. Venice is full of murals—one of the best, Jon Werhle's *The Fall of Icarus*, is a block north—and in fact French filmmaker Agnes Varda, a local resident, did a poetic documentary about them called *Murs Murs*. A local agency, SPARC, is commissioning more murals to be created with city funds. ◆ Windward Ave and Speedway

91 L.A. LOUVER GALLERY

Works by important LA artists, including David Hockney, Ed Moses, Tony Berlant, and Michael McMillen, are showcased here. ◆ Tu-Sa. 55 S Venice Blvd (at Pacific Ave).

THE BEST

Larry Lipson

Restaurant Critic, **Daily News,** LA/Restaurant Reporter and Reviewer, K-NEWS (KNNS-AM 1260; KNN2-AM 540)

Taking the **Metrolink** train downtown to **Union Station,** ambling across the road to **Olvera Street,** nibbling on seviche while sipping a chilled margarita at **Casa La Golondrina** while the mariachis play, and taking the train back.

Capping an evening out to dinner with an assorted dessert plate and a glass of house champagne at **Spago,** or a late cognac at the **Polo Lounge,** where maitre d' Nino Osti fills me in on all the celebrities that are in the room, or those who have been in lately.

Celebrating a special occasion with a romantic dinner overlooking the beach and the Pacific at **Monroe's** in Malibu.

Eating any meal, anytime, at any one of Joachim Splichal's restaurants (**Patina, Pinot Bistro, Cafe Pinot, Pinot Hollywood**) or ditto at any one of Piero Selvaggio's restaurants (**Valentino, Posto, Primi**).

Caffè latte at **Puccino's** in CityWalk, Universal City, after a movie at the **Odeon Cineplex,** and sometimes oysters and cheap Sauvignon Blanc at the oyster bar at **Gladstone's Universal** before the flick.

A premium cigar after a long (three- to four-hour) **Westwood Wine and Food Society dinner** at one of LA's top restaurants.

310/822.4955. Also at 77 Market St (at Pacific Ave). 310/822.4955

92 JAMES BEACH

★★★$$ Partners James Evans and Daniel Samakow did a complete makeover of this cheerful café (formerly **West Beach Cafe**). Designed by Billy Al Bengston, the place now sports spare white walls, classic "potato chip" chairs created by Charles Eames, and cozy booths by the back wall. The food continues to garner rave reviews from critics and patrons, especially the "Towering Shrimp Louis" (a mound of plump pink shrimp on crisp iceberg lettuce), tuna tartare, grilled Portobello mushrooms with spinach and mashed potatoes, hearty chicken potpie, turkey burgers, and sandwiches. ◆ American ◆ Daily, dinner; W-F, lunch. Reservations recommended. Valet parking available. 60 S Venice Blvd (at Pacific Ave). 310/823.5396

93 VENICE CANALS

A frail remnant of Abbot Kinney's vision can be found along this succession of side canals and Venetian bridges. The city would like to fill the canals in, so catch them while you can. ◆ Southeast of S Venice Blvd and Strongs Dr

94 NORTON HOUSE

Frank Gehry created this 1984 house for a Japanese-American artist (notice the log *torii* over the gate, two upright beams supporting a concave crosspiece that are typical of a Shinto temple gatewFay) and her screenwriter husband, who works at a lifeguard shelter overlooking the beach. Gehry's design provides privacy and complexity on a minuscule site. This is a private residence. ◆ 2509 Ocean Front Walk (between 26th and 25th Aves)

95 THE VENICE BEACH HOUSE

$$ Just off the oceanfront, this charming bed-and-breakfast is located in a quiet part of Venice. Each of the nine rooms is individually decorated. ◆ 15 30th Ave (between Pacific Ave and Speedway). 310/823.1966

96 SIAMESE GARDEN

★★$$ The specialties served in this delightful little place include barbecued chicken, grilled shrimp, steamed crab claws, and fine pad thai noodles. The courtyard is delightful, too. ◆ Thai ◆ M-F, lunch; daily, dinner. Reservations recommended. 301 Washington St (at Strongs Dr). 310/821.0098

Restaurants/Clubs: Red | Hotels: Purple | Shops: Orange | Outdoors/Parks: Green | Sights/Culture: Blue

Where the rich and famous play in the sun and surf . . .

Sun, surf, movie stars, and million-dollar beachfront homes hidden behind gilded gates epitomize the mystique of celebrity-packed Malibu, a high-rent district where the mountains meet the sea and reality and illusion sometimes clash discordantly. Just about everything you've heard about its laid-back hedonism is true. Bikini-clad

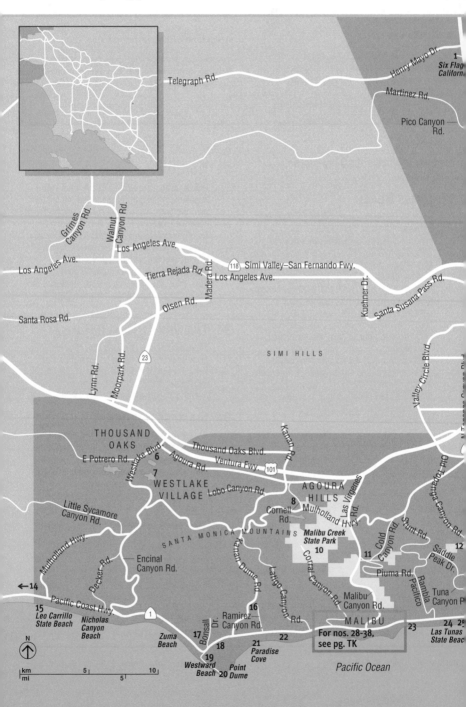

Telegraph Rd.

Henry Mayo Dr.

1
Six Flags
California

Martinez Rd.

Pico Canyon Rd.

Grimes Canyon Rd.

Walnut Canyon Rd.

Los Angeles Ave.

Los Angeles Ave.

Tierra Rejada Rd.

Madera Rd.

118 Simi Valley–San Fernando Fwy.

Los Angeles Ave.

Olsen Rd.

Kuehner Dr.

Santa Susana Pass Rd.

Santa Rosa Rd.

Lynn Rd.

Moorpark Rd.

23

SIMI HILLS

Valley Circle Blvd.

THOUSAND OAKS

E Potrero Rd.

Westlake Blvd.

Thousand Oaks Blvd.

Agoura Rd.

6

Ventura Fwy.

101

Kanan Rd.

7

WESTLAKE VILLAGE

Lobo Canyon Rd.

AGOURA HILLS

8

Cornell Rd.

Mulholland Hwy.

Las Virgenes Rd.

Old Topanga Canyon Rd.

Little Sycamore Canyon Rd.

SANTA MONICA MOUNTAINS

Malibu Creek State Park

10

Cold Canyon Rd.

Stunt Rd.

Mulholland Hwy.

Decker Rd.

Encinal Canyon Rd.

Kanan Dume Rd.

Latigo Canyon Rd.

Corral Canyon Rd.

11

Piuma Rd.

Saddle Peak Dr.

12

Rambla Pacifico

← 14

Pacific Coast Hwy.

Malibu Canyon Rd.

Tuna Canyon Rd.

15
Leo Carrillo State Beach

Nicholas Canyon Beach

1

Zuma Beach

17

Bonsall Dr.

Ramirez Canyon Rd.

16

MALIBU

For nos. 28-38, see pg. TK

23

24 25
Las Tunas State Beach

N

18

21
Paradise Cove

22

19
Westward Beach 20
Point Dume

Pacific Ocean

km
mi 5 10
5

sunbathers, die-hard surfers, and star-struck tourists eager for a glimpse of a famous resident all succumb to the allure. Rural, hilly, and isolated from the city, Malibu is about the same size as the rancho it replaced, and tends to hide its riches: Million-dollar estates along the **Pacific Coast Highway** reveal only their usually scruffy backsides or hide behind anonymous gates, and Malibu's scattershot commercial strip is as ordinary and undistinguished as most beach towns, making one wonder just where Malibu actually is. After nearly two decades in the planning, Malibu is about to get its first luxury resort.

The **Rancho Malibu Hotel,** built by Adamson Hotels, offers 146 villa and bungalow suites wrapped around a garden courtyard, a 10,000-square-foot spa, pools, tennis courts, a restaurant, and a cultural center featuring Chumash Indian relics discovered in Malibu.

The Chumash Indians were the area's earliest settlers; in 1887, wealthy easterner Frederick Rindge bought the Topanga-Malibu-Sequit rancho, an expanse that included more than 22 miles of pristine Pacific oceanfront. Rindge built a private railroad and pier, planted alfalfa, and spent the rest of his life trying to shut out newcomers, even taking his argument to the Supreme Court. The government eventually prevailed, however, and in 1929 the Pacific Coast Highway (then the **Roosevelt Highway**) officially opened, paving the way for more development. The first film star to settle in **Malibu Beach** was Anna Q. Nilsson, who built a house on a deserted beach just west of **Malibu Creek** in 1928. Clara Bow, Gloria Swanson, Ronald Colman, and Frank Capra soon followed, and by 1930 the area had been dubbed the "Malibu Motion Picture Colony." Now simply "The Colony," Malibu Beach is still home to Larry Hagman, Johnny Carson, Shirley MacLaine, Tom Hanks, Bruce Willis, Tom Arnold, and Barbra Streisand, and other celebrities own houses and estates along the beaches or in the canyons.

Hikers find respite here in the chaparral-covered **Santa Monica Mountains,** which separate the Los Angeles basin from the **San Fernando Valley.** Affluent homeowners, who have carved a place of their own in the hills and canyons, enjoy some of the best views anywhere. For a 360-degree panorama of ocean, mountains, and the San Fernando Valley, drive up into the hills to the end of Corral Canyon Road, beyond **Malibu Canyon,** and climb to the boulders on the crest of the hill. While the canyon-marked hills trap the smog in the flatlands of the city they define, they also give urban dwellers a rim of rural wilderness.

Paradise is not without its problems, however. Mudslides, caused by infrequent but heavy rains in an otherwise arid area, have been known to reduce palatial homes to tumbles of plywood, and the ever-present threat of brushfires keeps residents' hoses at the ready. But for every blow Mother Nature deals them, Malibu dwellers just shrug philosophically—and rebuild. Once you see this magical place, you'll understand why.

SANTA CLARITA VALLEY

One of the fastest-growing areas in Southern California, this picturesque valley surrounded by majestic mountains is blessed with clean air, a low crime rate, and some of the friendliest people in Los Angeles County. Credit **Six Flags Magic Mountain** for putting the area on the map and a major development company for attracting businesses and residents.

1 SIX FLAGS CALIFORNIA

For more than 30 years, **Six Flags Magic Mountain** has offered thrill rides and grand spectacles to delight both kids and adults. A recent expansion has transformed the site from a theme park to an "Xtreme" park, with three new daredevil rides. It is also in the *Guinness Book of Records* for having the most roller coasters (15) of any attraction. ♦ Magic Mountain Pkwy (west of Golden State Fwy). 818/367.5965

At Six Flags California:

SIX FLAGS MAGIC MOUNTAIN: THE XTREME PARK!

This gigantic theme park gets its name from the fast and scary thrill rides offered. Spread out on 260 beautifully landscaped acres atop the rolling hills west of Santa Clarita, this is the kick-ass amusement park of all times, with 15 roller coasters to test your mettle. For true white-knuckle thrills, there's **Déjà Vu,** a super-boomerang roller coaster that plummets 196 feet and flies at a speed of 65 mph over the outside of a vertical loop and a giant 110-foot-tall boomerang turn. If that's not scary enough, climb onboard **X,** where you race in prototype vehicles that spin 360

degrees forward or backward and let you fall (albeit safely) 299 feet to the ground, head first, face down, and race at 76 mph spinning head-over-heels through a huge 3,600-foot twisting steel maze—we're feeling dizzy just writing about it. The two make **Colossus** seem tame even though it's billed as the largest, fastest, highest, and steepest wooden roller coaster ever built. After you've ridden 9,200 feet at speeds of up to 65 mph, you won't want to argue the point. **Zonga**, a loopy, 112-foot-tall roller-coaster ride featuring wild blue, purple, red, yellow and green towering metal twists—four full-circle, full-tilt loops and two big back-to-back circuits—marks the sixth and wildest roller coaster added to the Park's 35 rides in the last six years. Then there's **Scream!** And you surely will after riding this Guinness Book world record winner, with its flying chairs hurtling at mega-speeds through the air and no track above your head or coach around the seats. Now that's Xtreme. The **Revolution** offers a 360-degree vertical loop at 60 mph; the **Shock Wave** gives thrill-seekers the opportunity to loop the loop while standing up; the **Gold Rusher** is a theme roller coaster on which you become a passenger aboard a runaway mine train; and **Flashback** is the world's only hairpin-drop roller coaster, with six spiral dives. If you enjoy getting drenched, try the **Tidal Wave,** which takes you by boat over a 50-foot waterfall; the **Jet Stream,** which whisks you across the water in speedboats; and the **Roaring Rapids,** a whitewater rafting trip straight out of *The River Wild.* For extreme adventure of the bungee-jumping kind, **Dive Devil** dares participants, who are strapped in a harness and suspended from steel cables, to dive from towers more than 150 feet tall. "Fliers" plunge in a 50-foot freefall, reaching 60 mph, and swing only six feet from the ground before arching back up.

For those who would prefer to watch someone else perform fantastic feats, the **Lazer Dome** presents a live show featuring enough acrobatics, in-line skating, and stunts to satisfy any kid's craving for spectacle. For views of the surrounding territory, take the **Eagle's Flight Tramway,** a 40-degree inclined funicular, to the top of the mountain, or the **Sky Tower,** a ride to the observation deck of a 384-foot space-needle structure.

Nor is the past forgotten here. The **Grand Carousel** is an exquisitely restored 1912 merry-go-round. At **Spillikin Handcrafters Junction,** traditional American crafts such as glassblowing and blacksmithing are demonstrated, and the goods are sold in quaint shops.

Nighttime attractions for teenagers include **Back Street,** a high-energy city block, and **After Hours,** a high-tech dance club. The **Magic Moments Theater** presents *California Dreamin*; and there's plenty of rocking at the **Contempo Pavilion.** Divers and dolphins star at the **Aqua Theater.** A fireworks extravaganza explodes over **Mystic Lake** nightly through summer.

Bugs Bunny, Daffy Duck, Wile E. Coyote, and other Warner Brothers cartoon characters welcome youngsters to the six-acre **Bugs Bunny World** with its 15 pint-size rides, and kids can enjoy a magic show through the summer in the **Valencia Falls Pavilion.** And be sure to check out the petting zoo.

Food is plentiful in the park, although it's recommended that you wait a half-hour after meals before hitting the larger rides. The **Four Winds** offers a delicious salad buffet at lunchtime and hot meals in the evening. The **Timbermill** serves hearty American-style food. **Food Etc.** is a fast-food restaurant with a surprisingly sophisticated décor by Shari Canepa. ◆ Admission (one fee covers all rides and attractions, except Dive Devil). Daily, Memorial Day through Labor Day; Sa, Su, and school holidays the rest of the year. There are height and weight restrictions on some rides. 661/255.4111, 661/255.4100. www.sixflags.com

SIX FLAGS HURRICANE HARBOR WATER PARK

Adjacent to Six Flags Magic Mountain, this water park has a tropical jungle setting with lagoons, rafting adventures, replicas of ancient ruins, and playful sea creatures, and provides fun for the whole family. Children love **Castaway Cove,** a pirate-themed water play area; **Shipwreck Shores,** a play area with swings and slides; and **Lizard Lagoon,** a 3.2-acre tropical paradise with a 7,000-square-foot, 3½-foot-deep pool with basketball hoops, a lizard slide, volleyball, and more. There are also fun rides for all ages, like open-flume body slides, high-speed flume rides, and a wave pool. ◆ Admission (a combination ticket can be bought for both Six Flags Magic Mountain and Six Flags Hurricane Harbor). Daily, Memorial Day through Labor Day. 661/255.4111, 661/255.4100. www.sixflags.com

2 HYATT VALENCIA

$$$ Situated in a self-contained community that resembles a movie set of a turn-of-the-century New York or European city—with its varied architecture that combines stark stone, wrought-iron balconies, and tile roofs—this 244-room hotel oozes with charm. The staff is friendly. Rooms are pleasantly appointed, many with terraces that look out onto the nearby golf course or mountains. An inviting courtyard hosts a heated pool nestled by a two-sided fireplace. The **Vines Restaurant and Bar** (**$$) is a pleasant spot for breakfast, lunch, and dinner, with indoor and outdoor seating. A scrumptious buffet brunch is served on Sunday. Dinner menus have seasonal twists with French, Asian, Caribbean, and California influences. Winemakers' weekends are sponsored throughout the year. Just a short stroll from the hotel entrance awaits the centerpiece of the community, **Valencia Town Center** (661/287.9050), a major mall housing dozens of shops, cafés, restaurants, movie theaters, an IMAX 3-D theater, and a major sports club. Hyatt guests have the benefit of privileges at the TPC at Valencia, a 27-hole golf course designed by PGA Tour Design Services and Mike O'Meara. Six Flags Magic Mountain, the area's main attraction, is just a short drive down the road (see above). ◆ 24500 Town Center Dr (between Magic Mountain Dr and McBean Pkwy), Valencia. 661/799.1234; 800/233.1234. www.hyatt.valencia.com

3 CALIFORNIA INSTITUTE OF THE ARTS

Founded with an endowment from Walt Disney in 1970, Cal-Arts is an elite, cutting-edge college with schools of film, dance, theater, art, and music. Graduates here (including David Salle and Eric Fischl) have invigorated the fine arts world on both coasts. ◆ 24700 McBean Pkwy (just east of Golden State Fwy), Santa Clarita. 805/255.1050

4 WILLIAM S. HART PARK

◐ "While I was making pictures, the people gave me their nickels, dimes, and quarters. When I am gone, I want them to have my home." With this testament, silent-film cowboy star William S. Hart bequeathed his 253-acre ranch for use as a public park. Some 110

Restaurants/Clubs: **Red** | Hotels: **Purple** | Shops: **Orange** | Outdoors/Parks: **Green** | Sights/Culture: **Blue**

147

acres have been preserved as a wilderness area. The developed portion of the property includes an animal compound, picnic sites, and Hart's ranch-style home, **La Loma de los Vientos,** which contains paintings and sculpture by Charles M. Russell. ♦ Free. Park: daily. Museum: W-Su. 24151 San Fernando Rd (at Newhall Ave), Santa Clarita. 805/254.4584

5 PLACERITA CANYON PARK

This 314-acre native chaparral park is located in a canyon amid stands of California live oak. The **Nature Center** and self-guided tour are designed to illustrate the relationships of the plants and animals in the area. ♦ Free. Daily. 19152 Placerita Canyon Rd (east of Antelope Valley Fwy). 805/259.7721

SANTA MONICA MOUNTAINS

A national recreation area administered by the National Park Service, the Santa Monicas are part of a mountain chain that rises from the floor of the Pacific, forming the **Channel Islands,** the beach plateau, and a series of peaks that extend into the city center at heights averaging 1,000 to 2,000 feet. These mountains offer breathtaking views of the Los Angeles basin and the San Fernando Valley from their summits, while retaining a wild environment within their ridges and valleys. The slopes are covered with a collection of evergreen shrubs and scrubby trees known as chaparral. Other plant life includes chamise and sage on the lower, drier hills and a denser cover of scrub oak, sumac, wild lilac, and manzanita along the streambeds. The wild plants you see on these mountains were introduced only 200 years ago by the Franciscan padres. Fire is a major hazard in this region, as the plant life is bone-dry in the summer, and the smallest spark or flame can ignite a raging brushfire—you may remember watching the Santa Monicas burn on television in October 1993 in a firestorm that ultimately destroyed more than 175,000 acres, leveled 750 houses, and caused approximately $500 million in damage.

For a quick look at the wilderness and the housing that imperils it, cruise the length of **Mulholland Drive** and **Mulholland Highway,** which snake 50 miles along the crest of the Santa Monicas from the **Hollywood Freeway** to **Leo Carrillo State Beach.** The narrow country roads were named for the self-taught Irish engineer who developed the first major aqueduct in the city, thus spurring its rapid growth.

Malibu's Point Dume, like several other landmarks along the coast, was named by English explorer Captain George Vancouver. It was given the name on 24 November 1782 in honor of Padre Francisco Dumetz of the Ventura Mission.

6 TUSCANY

★★$$ Come here for serious eating in a remote location. Try the herb-flavored veal chops, cheese-stuffed chicken breast, and inventive antipasti. Tommaso Barletta runs a tight ship. ♦ Italian ♦ M-F, lunch and dinner; Sa, Su, dinner. 968 Westlake Blvd (at Townsgate Rd), No. 4. Thousand Oaks. 818/880.5642

7 BOCCACCIO'S

★★$$$ Despite its location in the midst of a housing development, this dependable standby offers a degree of sophisticated service, a formal, elegant atmosphere, and a truly marvelous oak-tree and lakeside view. Salmon in potato crust, pasta with sausage in a light tomato and cream sauce, and tiramisù are standouts. ♦ Italian/French ♦ M-F, lunch and dinner; Sa, Su, dinner. Reservations recommended. 32123 Lindero Canyon Rd (at Lakeview Canyon Rd), Westlake Village. 818/889.8300

8 PARAMOUNT RANCH

Since the early 1920s, westerns have been shot on the standing set of what was formerly a 4,000-acre expanse of hills. Ranger-guided hikes over the ranch and movie set are offered once a month, and 436 acres of wooded countryside are open daily for riding, walking, and picnicking. Silent films are shown under the stars in July and August. ♦ Free. Daily, dawn to dusk. 2813 Cornell Rd (north of Mulholland Hwy). 818/735.0876

9 WILL GEER'S THEATRICUM BOTANICUM

This outdoor theater, established by the late Will Geer (grandpa on the TV show *The Waltons*), stages Shakespeare and new and classic modern plays from June through September. ♦ 1419 N Topanga Canyon Blvd (between Oakwood and Cheney Drs). 310/455.3723

10 MALIBU CREEK STATE PARK

Four thousand acres of park, including Malibu Creek, two-acre Century Lake, and ageless oaks, chapparal, and volcanic rock, are found here. There is excellent day hiking on almost 15 miles of trails, and camping is allowed. ♦ Parking fee. 28754 Mulholland Hwy (between Las Virgenes Rd and Lake Vista Dr). 818/880.0367

11 SADDLE PEAK LODGE

★★★$$$$ The hearty game food menu—exotic antelope, kangaroo, venison, and quail—is so befitting of the lodge-like atmosphere here, where a roaring fire, dimly lit hurricane lamps, cushy armchairs, and a high-beam ceiling hung with assorted stag's heads enhance the rustically elegant setting. If game isn't your thing, there are other superb choices such as vodka-cured salmon, lobster and black truffle ravioli, and a carpetbagger steak. It's well worth the long drive. Lots of folks have discovered this hideaway, so be sure to make a reservation. ♦ American ♦ W-F, dinner; Sa, brunch and dinner; Su, brunch. Reservations required. 419 Cold Canyon Rd (between Piuma Rd and Mulholland Hwy). 310/456.7325. 818/222.3888. www.saddlepeaklodge.com

12 TOPANGA CANYON

A quaint, artistic community shaded by bamboo and sycamore trees and covered with heavy brush and flowers, Topanga Canyon (whose name means "Mountains That Run into the Sea," as the long, curving canyon road really does) once boasted Jim Morrison, Charlie Chaplin, Peter Lorre, and Humphrey Bogart as residents. The quiet, bucolic setting still attracts celebrities, as well as screenwriters, producers, architects, teachers, and assorted hippies (though even before hand-painted VW buses, when only Mexicans wore huaraches, this was an alternative community). An eclectic group of homes (some looking pretty shabby, but surprisingly expensive) sit sheltered under groves of sycamores or scattered along the creek that flows through the base of the canyon. It's believed that Native American settlements date back at least 5,000 years. And because of its rich history and fecund land, The American Land Conservancy of San Francisco wants to purchase 1,659 acres along what is called Lower Topanga and sell it to the state for use as a park. While this may sound like a good thing, the problem is the devastating effect on the number of residents (it affects about 56 houses and 10 businesses) who would have to relocate should the deal go through—and it appeared at press time that it very well might. We told you anything can and does happen in LA. Some of the denizens have inhabited the Canyon for decades, and do so because they prefer its rural charm. Should all appeals to abort the project go to deaf ears, by the time you visit the area you will find a major park spreading from Pacific Coast Highway up Topanga Canyon and virtually connecting the mountains to the sea—just like the name Topanga implies. www.topangaonline.com

12 INN OF THE SEVENTH RAY

★★$$ This charming, ephemeral eatery sits snugly perched off a funky canyon road about four miles from the Coast Highway. Although it has always catered to vegetarians, there's now something for everybody on the New Age menu. And you can't beat the bucolic setting, where tables nestle outside beside a gently flowing stream, accompanied by Baroque and New Age melodies. Somehow dining here always calls for a bottle of crisp Chardonnay to accompany a meal of, say, vegetarian lasagna, mango-papaya duck, lobster, or swordfish, and really outstanding freshly baked breads. ♦ California ♦ Daily, dinner; M-Sa, lunch; Su, brunch. Reservations recommended for brunch and dinner. 128 Old Topanga Canyon Rd (just west of N Topanga Canyon Blvd). 310/455.1311. www.innoftheseventhray.com

13 TOPANGA STATE PARK

ⓟ With 9,000 untouched acres to explore and enjoy, this park offers a soothing respite from civilization. The high peaks beckon, with superb views of the ocean and the San Fernando Valley, while the grassy meadows and woodlands are perfect for picnics and long walks. A self-guided trail explains the ecology. Water and sanitary facilities are available in the park. You can camp in the backcountry for $1 a person. Note: There are no park signs, so keep a sharp lookout for the turnoff from Topanga Canyon Boulevard. ♦ Daily. Parking is only $2. 20825 Entrada Rd (off Topanga Canyon Blvd). 310/455.2465

14 POINT MUGU STATE PARK

ⓟ The secluded and idyllic park, with 70 miles of trails, a tall-grass prairie preserve, beautiful sycamores, and lovely canyons, is excellent for day hikes and picnics. Advance camping reservations are required. ♦ Admission. 9000 Pacific Coast Hwy (between Pacific View and Las Posas Rds). 818/880.0350

15 LEO CARRILLO STATE BEACH

ⓟ This beach was named for the Los Angeles–born actor, who died in 1961. A descendant of one of California's oldest families and son of the first mayor of Santa Monica, Carrillo became famous as Pancho, the sidekick on TV's *The Cisco Kid.* Surfers should head for the western end of the beach. ♦ Pacific Coast and Mulholland Hwys

16 STREISAND CENTER

Barbra Streisand donated her lavish 22.5-acre, four-house estate to the Santa Monica Mountains Conservancy in 1993. The property houses the **Streisand Center for Conservancy Studies,** an environmental think tank. The $30 entrance fee includes a guided tour of three homes and the grounds (which encompass lush botanical gardens, landscaped meadows, and orchards) as well

---

Restaurants/Clubs: Red | **Hotels: Purple** | Shops: Orange | **Outdoors/Parks: Green** | Sights/Culture: Blue

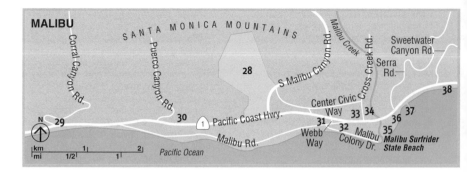

as afternoon tea. ◆ Admission. Tours: W, 1-4PM; Tu, Th, by appointment. 5750 Ramirez Canyon Rd (north of Pacific Coast Hwy). 310/589.2850

17 ZUMA CANYON ORCHIDS

Prizewinning plants bred here are sent all over the world. ◆ M-Sa. 5949 Bonsall Dr (north of Pacific Coast Hwy). 310/457.9771

18 ZOOMA SUSHI

★$ College students and casual celebrities such as Emilio Estevez and Nick Nolte frequent this 25-seat sushi bar and restaurant located in architect **Ed Niles**'s woodsy office building. The most popular is the Vegas Roll—five kinds of fish rolled in seaweed, deep fried, and wrapped in spicy crab—but more traditional fare is also available. ◆ Japanese ◆ Daily, dinner. 29350 Pacific Coast Hwy (between Heathercliff and Westward Beach Rds). 310/457.4131

19 GRAY WHALE

★★$$$ Isn't it romantic to sit in a cozy room just across from sensational Zuma Beach, dining on fine California /Mediterranean-style food and maybe even spotting a whale or two in season? You bet it is at this precious dining

---

Malibu was founded on 28 March 1891. The median household income is $80,198 for a population of 14,233 people. The median age is 37.9.

Coyote, mule deer, rabbits, rattlesnakes, skunks, and foxes all live in the Santa Monica Mountains. The largely undeveloped range bisects the city of LA.

---

spot. ◆ California/Mediterranean ◆ 6800 Westward Beach Rd (south of Pacific Coast Hwy). 310/457.5521

20 POINT DUME

This residential area with a hard-to-get-to beach was named in 1782 by George Vancouver, the English explorer, for Father Dumetz, a Jesuit at the **Ventura Mission.** Until the 20th century, Point Dume was high and peaked, but the top was shaved off to build a housing development. ◆ Westward Beach Rd (south of Pacific Coast Hwy)

21 PARADISE COVE

This private beach is full of nooks and crannies for walking and exploring. **The Sandcastle** (310/457.2503), a staid, inexplicably popular restaurant, overlooks the ocean. ◆ Admission. Paradise Cove Rd (south of Pacific Coast Hwy)

22 GEOFFREY'S

★★★★$$$$ Go for the fabulous cliff-edge terrace with its sweeping 180-degree ocean view; the handsome **Richard Neutra** interior; and the eclectic menu that includes nori-wrapped ahi tempura with red pepper coulis and wasabi, grilled fish, salads, and Geoffrey's Egg Fabergé, seared rare Hawaiian ahi, sautéed monkfish. There's live piano music nightly. ◆ Cal-Asian/New American ◆ Daily, lunch and dinner; Su, brunch. 27400 Pacific Coast Hwy (at Escondido Beach Rd). 310/457.1519. www.geoffreysmalibu.com

23 ACKERBURG RESIDENCE

Designed by **Richard Meier & Partners,** this 1991 beachfront house translates Meier's white rational design into Southern California courtyard living. On the same strip of beach are the contrasting styles of two other renowned architects. **John Lautner**'s 1979 **Segal Residence,** a heavily landscaped curving wood and concrete house, is located at no. 22426, and a **Gwathmey, Siegel & Associates** wood-and-glass house is located at no. 22350. All three are private residences. ♦ 22466 Pacific Coast Hwy (between Carbon Canyon and Sweetwater Canyon Rds)

24 MOONSHADOWS

★$$$ Bountiful salads, steaks, the piped-in sounds of the surf, and the view of the breakers are the attractions here. ♦ American ♦ M-Sa, dinner; Su, brunch and dinner. Reservations recommended. 20356 Pacific Coast Hwy (between Big Rock Dr and Las Flores Canyon Rd). 310/456.3010. www.moonshadowsmalibu.com

24 DUKES

★★$$ Aloha comes to town with big, welcoming mai tais and great food at this West Coast version of Hawaii's popular restaurant. Try the sugar cane shrimp with Thai chili beurre blanc and tropical salsa, or any fresh fish or seafood dish. ♦ Seafood ♦ Tu-Sa, lunch; daily, dinner. Reservations suggested. 21150 Pacific Coast Hwy (between Big Rock Dr and Las Flores Canyon Rd). 310/317.0777

25 LAS TUNAS STATE BEACH

The name does not refer to canned fish; it's Spanish for the fruit of the prickly pear cactus. ♦ Pacific Coast Hwy (between Tuna Canyon Rd and Big Rock Dr)

26 REEL INN RESTAURANT AND FRESH FISH MARKET

★$ Fresh fish is prepared in the kitchen daily, grilled or pan-blackened Cajun style, and served alongside hearty home-fried potatoes, Cajun rice, and coleslaw. The setting is rustic boathouse, with long wooden picnic tables and a patio. Celebrities like to slip in here unnoticed. However, should the American Land Conservancy have its way and turn the area on which it sits into a state park, the restaurant will become one of its victims. ♦ Seafood ♦ Daily, lunch and dinner. 18661 Pacific Coast Hwy (between S Topanga Canyon Blvd and Topanga Canyon La). 310/456.8221. Also at 1220 Third St Promenade (between Arizona Ave and Wilshire Blvd), Santa Monica. 310/395.5538; 2533 Pacific Coast Hwy (at Crenshaw Blvd), Torrance. 310/530.40470

27 THE GETTY VILLA

The former **J. Paul Getty Museum** closed its doors when the Getty Center opened in Brentwood and at press time still hadn't reopened. It was last slated to be back in business in late 2005 following a $275 million renovation. Exhibits focus on Greek, Etruscan, and Roman antiquities. ♦ 17985 Pacific Coast Hwy (at Coastline Dr). 310/458.2003, hearing impaired 310/394.7448 ঙ

The Getty Villa

PEPPERDINE
UNIVERSITY

28 PEPPERDINE UNIVERSITY

Popularly known as "Surfers U" for its oceanfront site, Pepperdine is actually a respected institution that offers bachelor's and master's degrees in 50 major subject areas. It has a law school, four satellite centers in Southern California, and a year-in-Europe program at Heidelberg University. Also on campus is the **Frederick R. Weisman Museum of Art,** which displays pieces from the industrialist's personal collection of modern art, as well as changing exhibits on such themes as British photography, turn-of-the-century arts and crafts in America, and modern glass sculpture. ♦ Free. Tu-Su. 24255 Pacific Coast Hwy (at S Malibu Canyon Rd). General information 310/456.4000, museum 310/456.4851

29 BEAU RIVAGE

★$$$ This warm and cozy roadhouse with a piano indoors and a patio out back has a rich, steeply priced international menu of fish, pasta, and game dishes with a touch of France, Italy, Morocco, and Spain. The food has drawn mixed reviews, but locals still throng in. ♦ Mediterranean ♦ M-Sa, dinner; Su, brunch and dinner. 26025 Pacific Coast Hwy (between Puerco Canyon and Corral Canyon Rds). 310/456.5733

30 24955 PACIFIC COAST HIGHWAY

This crisp low-rise development designed by **Goldman Firth Architects** in 1989 lifts the spirits of motorists speeding by. ♦ Between John Tyler Dr and Puerco Canyon Rd

31 GRANITA

★★★$$$ Wolfgang Puck and Barbara Lazaroff, owners of **Spago** bistros, **Chinois on Main,** and assorted **Wolfgang Puck Cafes** around the city, also run this great restaurant in the **Malibu Colony Plaza.** Full of artisan-crafted details and curves, the oceanic interior with seafoam ceramic glazes and hand-blown glass is an original design. Signature dishes include the Mediterranean fish soup with half a lobster and couscous, and fritto misto with shrimp. There's also the usual list of designer pizzas; superior takes on John Dory, monkfish, and salmon; and a yummy Chinese-style duck. ♦ California/Mediterranean ♦ Daily, dinner; W-F, lunch; Sa, Su, brunch. Reservations recommended. 23725 Malibu Rd (at Webb Way). 310/456.0488

31 THEE FOXES' TROT

Another tenant of the **Malibu Colony Plaza,** this general store offers arty furnishings and personal accessories. ♦ Daily. 23733 Malibu Rd (at Webb Way). 310/456.1776

31 CAMPBELL-TOLSTAD STATIONERS

A survivor of a more gracious age, this shop in the **Malibu Colony Plaza** sells fine pens and writing papers alongside more prosaic items. ♦ M-Sa. 23823 Malibu Rd (at Webb Way). 310/456.9838

32 MALIBU BEACH COLONY

"The Colony," as insiders call it, has been an exclusive and very private beach community for the famous and wealthy since 1926. Many of the beach cottages have bedrooms sufficient to sleep the cast of *Melrose Place* and hot tubs big enough to soak the Olympic swim team. The drives and beach here are private, but the dramatic **Stevens House** by **John Lautner** can be seen from the Pacific Coast Highway as a double-height, concrete quarter-circle rising into the sky. ♦ Malibu Colony Dr (south of Malibu Rd)

33 NOBU MALIBU

★★★$$$ The Malibu cousin of Matsuhisa in LA and the sister of Nobu New York, this one is a little more affordable, but still has much the same great Japanese fusion menu. Order the *tiradito* plate, a pretty-as-a-picture flower-shaped dish of thinly sliced whitefish. Any sushi is superb, as are the whole grilled sizzling fish, chicken, lobster, and steak dishes. A fun dessert is the bento box filled with green-tea ice cream and chocolate soufflé. The broiled plums with a meringue puff and ginger ice cream with a cookie taste pretty good, too. ♦ Japanese ♦ Daily, dinner. Reservations suggested. Country Mart, 3835 Cross Creek Rd (between Pacific Coast Hwy and Civic Center Way). 310/317.9140

33 MALIBU BOOKS

This bookstore is an invaluable resource for resident writers and compulsive readers. The stock is rich and varied. ♦ Daily. 23410 Civic Center Way (at Cross Creek Rd). 310/456.1375

33 TOPS MALIBU

Eclectic and whimsical handmade American furniture, jewelry, and accessories are all sold here. ♦ Daily. 23410 Civic Center Way (at Cross Creek Rd). 310/456.6002

34 GUIDO'S

★$$ The flower-filled patio at this restaurant overlooking Malibu Creek is a lovely place for lunch; for dinner guests, there's a cozy interior. Smoked salmon, pasta with eggplant, risotto, and herbed roast chicken all come recommended. ♦ Italian ♦ Daily, lunch and dinner. Reservations recommended. 3874 Cross Creek Rd (north of Pacific Coast Hwy). 310/456.1979

35 SURFRIDER STATE BEACH

Ⓟ Affectionately known as "The Bu" by surfers, this beach has a world-famous right reef point break. The surfing here is best in August and September, when south swells are at their peak. ♦ Pacific Coast Hwy (between Sweetwater Canyon Rd and Malibu Colony Dr)

36 ADAMSON HOUSE

This romantic Spanish Colonial house, designed by **Stiles Clements** in 1929, is preserved just as its owner, Rhoda Rindge Adamson, left it at her death in 1962. It is a showcase of colorful Malibu tiles and a reminder of the imperious family that once owned 17,000 acres in and around Malibu. The house and adjoining **Malibu Lagoon Museum** are accessible only on guided tours, which take about 45 minutes. ♦ Admission. Tours: W-Sa, 11AM-3PM. 23200 Pacific Coast Hwy (at Serra Rd). 310/456.8432

37 MALIBU PIER

Frequently filmed for movie backdrops, the landmark structure was built in 1906 as a landing point for ranch supplies and for Frederick Rindge's private railroad. A 4.8 million restoration rescued the structure from rot and disrepair and restored it to its original

glory. ♦ 23000 Pacific Coast Hwy (between Sweetwater Canyon and Serra Rds)

38 CASA MALIBU INN ON THE BEACH

$$ This charming historic hideaway, draped in bougainvillea and copa de oro, dates back to 1949, when it was a popular place for celebs to flee to for weekends. The 21 rooms and suites boast a contemporary style; each has a king-size or double bed, coffeemaker, and refrigerator; some also have private decks, fireplaces, and fully equipped kitchens. The **Catalina Suite**, once a favorite of Lana Turner's, features a cozy sitting room with a fireplace, bookshelves that reach the ceiling, a TV set, and a sofa bed. There's another fireplace in the bedroom, which also boasts a king-size four-poster bed and grand ocean views. Though the hotel does not have a restaurant, there are several in the neighborhood. ♦ 22752 Pacific Coast Hwy (just east of Sweetwater Canyon Rd). 310/456.2219, 800/831.0858; email: casamalibu@earthlink.net &

38 LA SALSA

★$ A huge rooftop figure of a man in a sombrero marks this popular take-out place overlooking the ocean. The fresh vegetables, grilled chicken, fish, and meat tacos have won acclaim. ♦ Mexican/Take-out ♦ Daily, lunch and dinner. 22800 Pacific Coast Hwy (just east of Sweetwater Canyon Rd). 310/317.9476. www.lasalsa.com

38 MALIBU BEACH INN

$$$ This Spanish-style beachfront hotel offers romantic vistas of the Pacific sunset from each of its 47 pleasingly appointed, recently renovated rooms. Decked out in deep, rich colors like forest green and maroon, each has its own fireplace and oceanfront balcony; all ground-floor rooms feature a private Jacuzzi where you can watch the sea while you soak. There is no restaurant, but a very satisfying complimentary continental breakfast buffet is served daily. There are plenty of places for other meals nearby. ♦ 22878 Pacific Coast Hwy (at Sweetwater Canyon Rd). 310/456.6444, 800/462.5428; fax 310/456.1499. www.malibubeachinn.com

---

Restaurants/Clubs: Red | Hotels: Purple | Shops: Orange | Outdoors/Parks: Green | Sights/Culture: Blue

SAN FERNANDO VALLEY

Like, we're talking the other side of the mountain . . .
Made famous by the the teens who shop till they drop at the local malls and speak
a "Valley girl" language few adults can decipher, the sprawling San Fernando just keeps
on growing. To really get a handle on its scope, take an evening drive along **Mulholland
Drive** to the top of the LA basin and gaze straight down from the crest of the hills. On a
clear night, it looks like Christmas, with countless twinkling lights illuminating the basin.
Go during the day to catch a bird's-eye view of the awesome **Santa Monica Mountains**,
which separate the valley from the rest of the city. Although somewhat connected to Los

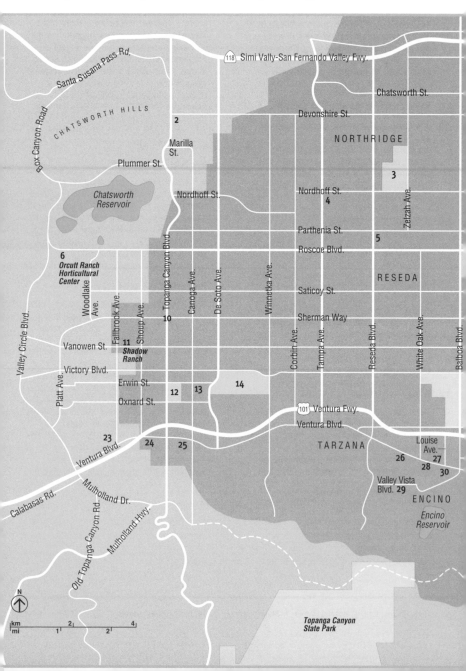

Angeles, the Valley does have a distinctive personality: lots of space (most of it flat), high temperatures (the Valley is usually 10 to 20 degrees warmer than the LA basin), trauma (it was the epicenter of the 1994 Northridge earthquake), and traffic (an extended grid of seemingly endless boulevards and streets crossing its length and breadth, reinforcing its dominant car culture). For visitors from eastern American or European cities, the sprawl of the Valley could prove difficult to grasp: When the City of Los Angeles originally annexed the San Fernando Valley on 22 May 1915, it effected a land grab that added 177 square miles to its existing 108 square miles.

Until the early 1900s, land use in the Valley was limited to ranching and nonirrigated agriculture. Then speculators, anticipating the arrival of the **Owens River Aqueduct** in

1913, began to buy up thousands of acres of Valley property. To share in the water brought by the aqueduct, ranchers voted to join the municipality of Los Angeles. Property values soared, and people savvy enough to invest in real estate profited handsomely. Boom succeeded boom, and hundreds of thousands moved into the Valley, encouraged by jobs in the nearby aviation, electronics, and entertainment industries. Several decades of accelerated development made the area famous for rapid-start tract-house neighborhoods and instant shopping centers. The vast spaces quickly filled up due to a low-density development pattern: only 7.2 people per acre here compared to the Wilshire district's 38.9 persons per acre. Today, the Valley is predominantly residential, with an increasingly diverse population: Whites still make up a slight majority (around 60%) and Hispanics represent the second-largest segment (around 30%). The west and south sides are more affluent than the east, and heavy industry is almost exclusively concentrated in the northern area around **San Fernando, Sylmar,** and **Pacoima.** With these few exceptions, the Valley is basically all of one fabric, very middle class, and extremely mobile. Single-family ranch-style houses outnumber multiple dwellings nearly two to one, leaving this a place where it's still possible to maintain a semblance of the American dream: to own a home with a spacious yard and a two-car garage.

1 MISSION SAN FERNANDO REY DE ESPAÑA

Until the dissolution of the missions in the mid-1830s, San Fernando was an essential part of the economic life of Los Angeles, supplying a great portion of the foodstuffs for the fledgling community. Founded in 1797 by Friar Fermin Lasuen, the mission was completed in 1806 but was subsequently destroyed by an earthquake and replaced in 1818. History repeated itself in the 1971 Sylmar/San Fernando earthquake, when the church again sustained damage so grave that it had to be reconstructed. The adobe construction of the early period had a simple yet monumental quality that achieved richness through the repetition of structural elements. This quality is best observed in the 243-foot-long *convento,* where 19 semicircular arches supported by massive square pillars form a loggia over time-hollowed tiles. Tours of the mission include working, sleeping, and reception areas, giving visitors a sense of day-to-day life during the early days. ♦ Admission. Daily. 15151 San Fernando Mission Blvd (between Sharp Ave and Sepulveda Blvd). 818/361.0186

2 LES SISTERS SOUTHERN KITCHEN

★$ Authentic down-home fare is served in this restaurant, including shrimp jambalaya, potent gumbo, fried chicken, and hushpuppies. There is no bar, and no alcohol is served. ♦ Southern ♦ Tu-F, lunch; Tu-Su, dinner. Reservations recommended for five or more. 21818 Devonshire St (between Jordan and Vassar Aves), Chatsworth. 818/998.0755

3 CALIFORNIA STATE UNIVERSITY AT NORTHRIDGE (CSUN)

One of the most popular branches of the **California State University** system, CSUN offers undergraduate and graduate courses in liberal arts and science disciplines. Recent government cutbacks have forced the university to curtail programs and classes, making the traditional four-year baccalaureate pursuit more difficult. **Richard Neutra** designed the 1961 **Fine Arts Building.**
♦ 18111 Nordhoff St (between Zelzah and Darby Aves). 818/885.1200

4 ALEXIS GREEK RESTAURANT

★★$ This fun spot combines Greek and Portuguese food and ambience. The unusual menu has it all: roast leg of lamb, filet mignon strip steak, white bass baked in wine with mushrooms and feta cheese, spicy chicken pirii, six different Greek salads, and all sorts of wonderful sausages. It also boasts a lavish dessert menu that includes an outstanding tiramisù; light and delicious almond cookies made with egg whites, almonds, and sugar, and a different chocolate cake every night. Beer and wine are the only alcoholic beverages served. ♦ M-Sa lunch; daily, dinner. 9034 Tampa Ave (at Nordhoff St). 818/349.9689

5 THAI BARBEQUE

★$ The great northern Thai/Laotian food at this restaurant is absolutely the spiciest in town, so unless you want smoke pouring out of your ears, don't ask them to make it hot. Not for everyone, but certainly interesting, is a jackfruit ice cream made with garbanzo beans. ♦ Thai ♦ M-F, lunch and dinner; Sa, Su, dinner. 8650 Reseda Blvd (at Parthenia St). 818/701.5712

6 ORCUTT RANCH HORTICULTURAL CENTER

Originally part of a 200-acre estate belonging to William and Mary Orcutt, the extensive gardens, lush landscaping, and venerable trees accented by statuary are relaxing and lovely. Picnic spots, hiking trails, and horticultural demonstrations count among the attractions. Tours of the 1920 house designed by **C. G. Knipe** are given the last Sunday of each month from 2 to 5PM from September through June. ♦ Free. Ranch: daily. 23600 Roscoe Blvd (between Jason and March Aves). 818/346.7449

7 94TH AERO SQUADRON HEADQUARTERS RESTAURANT

★$$ Located near the Van Nuys Airport, this 1973 version of a French farmhouse comes complete with bales of hay in the front yard. American standards—burgers, prime rib, fried chicken—make up the menu. It's a fun place to take the kids. ♦ American ♦ Daily, lunch and dinner. Reservations recommended. 16320 Raymer St (west of Woodley Ave). 818/994.7437

8 DR. HOGLY-WOGLY'S TYLER TEXAS BBQ

★★$ This is the real thing, tangy enough to bring tears to the eyes of a Lone Star exile. People line up to eat down-home ribs, links, chicken, and beans, despite the lack of amenities. ♦ Barbecue ♦ Daily, lunch and dinner. 8136 Sepulveda Blvd (between Sepulveda Pl and Roscoe Blvd). 818/780.6701

9 WESTERN BAGEL

Jalapeño and blueberry are among the 18 varieties of freshly baked bagels sold here. ♦ Daily, 24 hours. 7814 Sepulveda Blvd (between Stagg and Raymer Sts). 818/786.5847. Also at 11628 Santa Monica Blvd (between Federal and Barry Aves). 310/826.0570

10 ANTIQUE ROW

More than 28 shops specialize in Americana, ranging from memorabilia to publications. ♦ Daily. Sherman Way and Topanga Canyon Blvd

11 SHADOW RANCH

This restored 1870 ranch house built by LA pioneer Albert Workman is located on nine acres that were once part of a 60,000-acre wheat ranch. The eucalyptus trees on the property were planted in the late 19th century by Workman, who brought them from Australia; they are purported to be the parent stand of the trees that are now one of the most prominent features of Southern California botany. The ranch is presently used as a community center. ♦ Free. Daily; Tu-Th until 9PM. 22633 Vanowen St (between Sale and Ponce Aves). 818/883.3637

12 WESTFIELD SHOPPINGTOWN WOODLAND HILLS

This is one of the poshest of the indoor malls, with **Macy's** and **Macy's Men's Store** anchoring some 80 other upscale shops and boutiques, such as **818 Freight Dakota Blues** for jeans and sportswear. Also lining the tiled corridors are a state-of-the-art movie theater with stadium-like seating and a food court that has a branch of the **Wolfgang Puck Cafe.** Lighting, fountains, and indoor landscaping add to the cool elegance of the place. ♦ Daily; M-F until 9PM. 6100 Topanga Canyon Blvd (between Oxnard and Erwin Sts). 818/884.7090. www.westfield.com

13 PYRAMID PALMS

This striking building is the headquarters for the cosmetics conglomerate Wella Sebastian International, and has a simulated rain forest inside (see below). ♦ 6109 De Soto Ave (at Erwin St). 800/829.7322

Within Pyramid Palms:

SEBASTIAN'S RAINFOREST

On display in a large room within Pyramid Palms is a replica of the Brazilian rain forest that was built by John Sebastian, the ecology-minded founder and former CEO of Sebastian, as an educational tool for both children and adults. There is also a large manmade pond. ♦ By appointment only. 800/829.7322, 818/829.4422

14 LOS ANGELES PIERCE COLLEGE

This branch of the **Los Angeles Community College** system specializes in agriculture, horticulture, landscape architecture, and animal husbandry. ♦ 6201 Winnetka Ave (between Oxnard St and Victory Blvd). 818/347.0551

Restaurants/Clubs: Red | Hotels: Purple | Shops: Orange | Outdoors/Parks: Green | Sights/Culture: Blue

Magical Mulholland Drive

Mulholland Drive, LA's mountain roadway, twists along a ridge high above the **Los Angeles Basin** to the south and sprawling **San Fernando Valley** to the north. Here celebrities seclude themselves in hilltop mansions or gated estates far from the street; lovers drive up at night for the romantic setting enhanced by the twinkling lights of the city below; and Sunday drivers cruise to escape the week's pressures.

Named for William Mulholland, who engineered the aqueduct connecting LA and the San Fernando Valley, the two-lane road with numerous switchbacks opened in 1924. Apart from celebrity residents such as Marlon Brando, Kevin Costner, and Arsenio Hall, it hasn't changed much since. Riding the ridge of the **Santa Monica Mountains** (an east-west spur of the Coastal Range referred to as the Hollywood Hills), Mulholland Drive rises 1,400 feet above sea level—just high enough to afford spectacular views.

The 22-mile-long portion of the road between Hollywood and the San Diego Freeway at Bel-Air is the neighborhood known as **The Hills,** where well-heeled businesspeople, writers, entertainers, rock stars, and artsy-crafty sorts live the cantilevered life. Mule deer, bobcats, coyotes, great horned owls, red-tailed hawks, and even the odd mountain lion roam and roost along the canyon-riven roadway. There are few curbs here, lots of rural mailboxes, and plenty of native chaparral. The only commerce is a country store and the popular **Four Oaks Restaurant** in Beverly Glen Canyon. Yet just short drives away are all the important business addresses, restaurants, and nightspots of LA. The locals relish the relative isolation and have fought—somewhat successfully—to keep it.

15 Sepulveda Basin Recreation Area

The 2,000-acre basin is leased by the City of Los Angeles from the US Army Corps of Engineers. Within the park are three 18-hole golf courses, a 20-acre picnic area, a cricket field, a model airplane field, an archery range, and plenty of bicycle and roller-skating paths. ◆ Daily, sunrise to sunset. 17017 Burbank Blvd (between Balboa Blvd and Aldea Ave). General information 818/756.8189, golf reservations 213/485.5515

16 Louise Bianco Skin Care

In a town sated with day spas, it's always a bonus when you find a talent like Louise Bianco. She's been called a "miracle worker," "facialist to the stars," and the "tops in town"—and rightly so. Relocated from her Beverly Hills salon, Bianco performs her magic in the comforts of her own home. If you need wrinkles ironed out or a facial pep-up, make an appointment with this wonder woman. Just one treatment lifts, rejuvenates, and even firms the skin. Try it; you'll thank us for it. While you're there, be sure to stock up on her signature cosmetics. ◆ 13655 Chandler Blvd (between Woodman and Buffalo Aves), Sherman Oaks. 310/278.2164; to order products, call 818/786.2700 in LA or nationwide: 800/782.3067. www.louisebianco.com

17 Great Wall of Los Angeles

The world's longest mural (a half-mile and still unfinished) occupies the west wall of a concrete flood control channel and tells the history of California from the age of the dinosaurs to the present. Anger brings history to life, as in the revolutionary murals of Mexico City, and though this collaborative effort by more than 215 of the city's young people is no artistic masterpiece, it's a provocative learning experience for participants and visitors. Judy Baca has directed the project over the past dozen or so years for SPARC, a nonprofit Venice arts group. ◆ Coldwater Canyon Ave (between Burbank Blvd and Oxnard St)

18 Norah's Place

★$ Quinoa, the sacred grain of the Inca, is a key ingredient in the distinctive cuisine of Bolivia. So are a few of that country's 100-plus kinds of potatoes. Other dishes served here are more familiar—such as empanadas and *lomo saltado* (sirloin tips). Enjoy live folk music and dancing on weekends. ◆ Bolivian ◆ W-Su, dinner. 5667 Lankershim Blvd (between Burbank Blvd and Collins St). 818/980.6900

19 Salomi

★$$ The curries here are exceedingly hot. For the faint of heart, there are also tamer tandoori and kabob dishes. ◆ Indian ◆ M-F, lunch and dinner; Sa, Su, dinner. 5225 Lankershim Blvd (between Magnolia Blvd and Weddington St). 818/506.0130

20 Arte de Mexico

Create your own hacienda from the items in seven warehouses crammed with crafts from Mexico and the Southwest. ◆ Daily. 5356

Riverton Ave (north of Magnolia Blvd). 818/769.5090

21 DUTTON'S BOOKSTORE

A well-stocked branch of the Brentwood store. ♦ Daily. 5146 Laurel Canyon Blvd (between Hartsook St and Magnolia Blvd). 818/769.3866. Also at 11975 San Vicente Blvd (at S Saltair Ave), 310/476.6263; 3806 W Magnolia Blvd (at Screenland Dr), Burbank. 818/840.8003

22 CHAING SHAN

★$$ Tasty Thai cooking is served in a nondescript setting. The beef curry and the special seafood dish, which includes shrimp, squid, and clams in a delicious spicy sauce, are highly recommended. ♦ Thai ♦ Daily, lunch and dinner. 5145 Colfax Ave (between Hartsook St and Magnolia Blvd). 818/760.1283

23 ADAGIO

★★$$ Pastas, fish, and meat dishes all excel, and the *penne all'amatriciana* and fried calamari have won applause. ♦ Italian ♦ Tu-F, lunch and dinner; Sa, Su, dinner. 22841 Ventura Blvd (between Fallbrook and Royer Aves). 818/225.0533

24 VILLA PIACERE

★$$ Pasta and seafood are the specialties of this stylish Italian restaurant. ♦ Northern Italian ♦ Daily, lunch and dinner. 22160 Ventura Blvd (at San Feliciano Dr). 818/704.1185

25 THREE 6 NINE

Tammy Kranzo decided to rename her C.E.N.T.E.R. salon "Three 6 Nine" for her favorite lucky numbers. Men and women flock from near and far (all the way from Palm Springs) to have their tresses stylishly trimmed, permed, and colored at this adorable, no-attitude salon with its Old European/Mediterranean décor. Big, colorful starfish hang from the exposed pipe ceiling, muted yellow tones cover the walls and floors, and plates of cookies, fruit, and assorted beverages are proffered freely. Many go for a makeover by super-stylist Kranzo, the owner/operator and former head colorist for Sebastian International. If Tammy's not available, you'll be in good hands with any of her skilled staff. Besides being just about the best in the business, their prices are more affordable than those puff-puff shops over the mountain in Beverly Hills. And when you have your hair washed you get a dreamy, tension-reducing scalp massage. Not to mention how

the organic shampoos and conditioners leave your hair feeling soft and silky. ♦ M-Sa. 21132 Costanso (one block off Ventura Blvd, between Canoga Ave and Topanga Canyon Blvd). 818/347.1900

25 BROTHER'S SUSHI

★★$$ The sushi is wonderful, but don't miss the ultra-fresh oysters or the crackly salmon skin. ♦ Japanese ♦ M-Sa, dinner. 21418 Ventura Blvd (at Canoga Ave). 818/992.1284

26 MON GRENIER

★$$$ The French name of this place means "my attic," and the dining room certainly resembles one. It's almost always crowded in the evenings. Favorite Franco-Gallic specialties include salmon *en croûte* and pheasant with wild mushrooms. The service is sometimes surly, but just smile and pretend you're in Paris. ♦ French ♦ M-Sa, dinner. Reservations required. 18040 Ventura Blvd (between Newcastle and Lindley Aves). 818/344.8060

SKIN SPA

A LUXURIOUS EUROPEAN DAY SPA

27 SKIN SPA

The south of France meets Encino at this delightful spa spread out atop the charming **Courtyard Center.** Owner Jonathan Baker provides a salubrious setting and high-quality service unmatched in the Valley. The tranquil facility has a terraced spa deck, a "Niagara" waterfall that massages your entire body with 20 jets, couples' suites for a massage *à deux,* a private therapy bath soak, and special full-body regimens that include massage with exotic oils, antioxidant skin treatments, and mud baths. If you're the "no pain, no gain" type, head for a **CHI sports massage,** 55 minutes focusing on every sore or overused muscle in the body. There's also a **SuperStrech**—85 blissful minutes of Pilates-style body movements combined with a super massage. You can also arrange an entire day of pampering, which includes spa treatments, catered lunch on the patio, leisurely soaks in the hot tubs, and even (for an extra charge) limousine service to and from your hotel. ♦ Tu-Su. 17401 Ventura Blvd (between Louise and Encino Aves).

Restaurants/Clubs: Red | Hotels: Purple | Shops: Orange | Outdoors/Parks: Green | Sights/Culture: Blue

818/995.3888, 877-SKIN SPA. www.
skinspa.com

27 CHA CHA CHA

★★$$ Chicken, pastas, and pizzas are given
a spicy, tropical treatment here. Notables are
the sizzling corn chowder and the ferocious
camarones negros—shrimp in a dark and
challenging chili sauce. High-back chairs in
aqua, green, and orange juxtaposed to animal
objects give a playroom-like sensitivity to the
expansive whitewashed dining room. Though
originally part of Mario Tamayo's chain of Cha
Cha Cha outlets, the restaurant now runs solo.
♦ Latin/Caribbean ♦ Daily, lunch and dinner;
Sa, Su, brunch. Reservations recommended,
especially on F and Sa. 17499 Ventura Blvd
(at Encino Ave). 818/789.3600

28 DOMINGO'S

Pick up imported cheeses, salami, olive oil,
pastas, and great sandwiches and other food
to go at this family-run Italian grocery/deli. ♦
Tu-Su; 17548 Ventura Blvd (between Encino
and Texhoma Aves). 818/981.4466

29 JUEL PARK

Edwina Skaff creates lingerie for
perfectionists, continuing the tradition of her
mother, Sue Drake, who joined the firm a year
after its founding in 1929 and created
form-fitting, bias-cut silk gowns for Jean
Harlow, Carole Lombard, and Norma Shearer.
Custom-made negligees and teddies come in
satin, lace, and organdy. ♦ By appointment
only. 17940 Rancho St (between Zelzah and
Lindley Aves). 818/609.7342

30 ENCINO TOWN CENTER

This little mini-mall has a couple of shops,
one specializing in home furnishings, the
other in bargain books. Its most distinguishing

A contest to rename the San Fernando Valley was
staged by the *Los Angeles Times* after surrounding
neighborhoods began adopting fancy nicknames to
improve their image.
    The winning name in the tongue-in-cheek
competition: Twenty-Nine Malls. Some runners-up:
Beige-Air, Minimalia, McValley, Valle de Nada, and
West Emphysema.

characteristic is an old oak tree estimated to
be more than a thousand years old. The
branches spread out 150 feet and the trunk
measures more than eight feet in diameter. ♦
Daily; M-F until 9PM. 17200 Ventura Blvd
(between Oak Park and Louise Aves).
818/788.6100

31 RANCHO DE LOS ENCINOS STATE HISTORICAL PARK

Leave the traffic behind and recall the stage-
coach era, when dusty travelers stopped off
here to refresh themselves. Among the five
acres of expansive lawns, duck ponds, and tall
eucalyptus are a nine-room adobe built in 1849
by Don Vicente de la Osa and a two-story
limestone French-style home designed in 1870
by Eugene Garnier. ♦ Admission. Grounds:
W-Su. Home tours: W-Su, 1-4PM. 16756
Moorpark St (at La Maida St). 818/784.4849

32 TEMPO

$ The taste of the Middle East served here will
be welcome for those unfamiliar with its
charm. Try the falafel, hummus, or shish
kebab. ♦ Middle Eastern ♦ Daily, lunch and
dinner. 16610 Ventura Blvd (at Rubio Ave).
818/905.5855

33 BENIHANA OF TOKYO

★$$$ The *teppan*-grill tradition of Japan is
raised to the level of theater by a chef trained
to handle a knife like a samurai. ♦ Japanese
♦ Daily, lunch and dinner. Reservations
required. 16226 Ventura Blvd (between
Woodley and Libbit Aves). 818/788.7121

34 SHIHOYA

★★$$ This is another traditional sushi bar,
where you are rewarded with outstandingly
fresh and beautiful sashimi and sushi. ♦
Japanese ♦ M-F, lunch and dinner; Sa,
dinner. 15489 Ventura Blvd (between Orion
and Firmament Aves). 818/986.4461

35 INDIA PALACE

★$$ Chicken *tikka* (marinated in masala
sauce and baked in a clay oven) and lamb
vindaloo (with potatoes and curry) are
standouts at this Indian restaurant. ♦ Indian
♦ M-Sa, lunch and dinner; Su, dinner. 4523
Sepulveda Blvd (between Greenleaf and
Dickens Sts). 818/986.8555

36 LA FRITE

$$ Crepes, omelettes, and quiche are all
nicely prepared and served until late. ♦
French ♦ Daily, lunch and dinner.
Reservations recommended. 15013 Ventura
Blvd (between Lemona and Noble Aves).
818/990.1791. Also at 22616 Ventura Blvd
(between Sale and Ponce Aves).
818/225.1331

37 MILLENNIUM DENTAL SPA

Next time you need dental work, consider this unusual facility operated by Dr. Eddie Siman, which actually pampers patients with manicures, pedicures, foot reflexology, and leg and ankle massages while in the chair during any procedure that lasts an hour or more. While the dentist does his stuff, your face is covered in hot towels, a scented seed pillow is place over your eyes and you can put on headphones to listen to DVDs. There's even an attractive aromatherapy-scented, candlelit "relaxation room." Talk about taking the angst out of dentistry. Get this: You can even have your car washed and detailed while you're there. The best part is it's all included in Dr. Siman's fee. ♦ 14629 Ventura Blvd (between Kester Ave and Van Nuys Blvd), Sherman Oaks. 818/784.6666

38 PANZANELLA

$$ (unrated) At press time, Piero Selvaggio sold what was once **Posto** to the three Drago brothers, Tanino, Calogero, and Giacomino. The Dragos then opened a Tuscan-style eatery featuring assorted pastas, risottos, and such. ♦ Italian ♦ Tu-F, lunch; M-Sa, dinner. Reservations suggested. 14928 Ventura Blvd (between Kester and Noble Aves). 818/784.4400

39 FORBIDDEN PLANET

This is the place for contemporary pop culture—American and European adult comics, fantasy, and science fiction—and artworks and collectibles. ♦ Daily. 14513 Ventura Blvd (at Van Nuys Blvd). 818/995.0151

40 SUNKIST HEADQUARTERS BUILDING

This striking concrete crate was designed in 1969 by **AC Martin Partners**. ♦ 14130 Riverside Dr (at Hazeltine Ave)

41 WESTFIELD SHOPPINGTOWN FASHION SQUARE

Macy's and Bloomingdale's anchor one of the first large indoor shopping malls built in the area. Just about anything you want can be found at this two-story structure, from lingerie (Victoria's Secret) to sporting goods, household gadgets, jewelry (real and costume), shoes, and even vitamins (GNC). There's a fun food court where you can fuel up on pastries, pizza, frozen yogurt, ice cream, and assorted ethnic fare. ♦ Daily; M-F until 9PM, Sa until 7, Su until 6. 14006 Riverside Dr (at Hazeltine Ave). 818/783.0550

42 ROBBIE MAC'S

*$ For cheap eats, it's hard to beat this family-style fun designer pizza joint. Brick walls, a hardwood floor, and a friendly staff add to the comfortable neighborhood ambience. The freshly made pies and pastas are tasty. The draft beer runs good and cold. (Wine is served, but no booze.) Sports fans have three TVs (one flat-screen) for their viewing pleasure. The New York–style cheesecake and chocolate mousse are killer desserts. ♦ Pizzas and Pastas. ♦ Daily, 11AM to midnight. 14502 Ventura Blvd, Sherman Oaks (at Van Nuys Blvd). 818/906.3000

43 FAB'S ITALIAN KITCHEN

★$ This friendly restaurant and storehouse of imported specialties from the old country offers hearty pizzas and traditional pasta favorites. ♦ Italian ♦ M-Sa, lunch and dinner. Opens at 3PM on Su. Reservations recommended for five or more. 4336 Van Nuys Blvd (at Dickens St). 818/995.2933

44 CAFE BIZOU

★★★$$ Gourmets discovered this wonderful French bistro the minute it opened, and it's now so popular that you need to make your reservation at least a week in advance. Decorated in beige and white, the pleasant, casual dining room is the perfect showcase for chef/owner Neil Rogers's creative menu, which includes such scrumptious specialties as shrimp and scallops served on a bed of black tagliarini mixed with tomato and basil, and salmon coated with sesame seeds presented on a bed of potato pancakes. Among the list of simple desserts, the tarte tatin takes the cake. The very reasonable prices are another great attraction—you can even bring your own bottle of wine for an unheard-of low $2 corkage fee. ♦ Continental/French ♦ Daily, lunch and dinner; Sa, Su, brunch and dinner. Reservations required. 14016 Ventura Blvd (between Costello and Murietta Aves). 818/788.3536 ♿ Also at 91 N Raymond Ave (between Holly and Colorado Blvds), Pasadena. 626/792.9923; 2450 Colorado Ave (at Cloverfield Blvd), Santa Monica. 310/582.8203

THE BEST

Diana Rosen

Editor, *Tea Talk*

Great Stuff About LA:

Anything and everything you can imagine is available in Los Angeles. It is now a premier art city, theater city, and shopping mecca, and has the best restaurants where you don't need to break into a Brink's truck to enjoy yourself. It's hip, it's hep, it's what's happening.

The **Netsuke Room** at the Japanese Pavilion in the **Los Angeles County Museum of Art.** (LACMA) is a treasure of hundreds of intricately carved sculptures that tell reams of stories despite their small size. Exquisite! Also at LACMA, the **Betty Asher Collection** of whimsical teacups from the best contemporary artists in America.

The sunny California look and feel of the main lobby of the **Peninsula Beverly Hills,** and its perfect afternoon tea.

Before or after any venture downtown, I stop at the **Brooklyn Bagel Bakery** on Beverly; it's not the same since they put up barriers so you can't peer into the vats of boiling water, but they still make the best poppy-seed bagels anywhere, and the price is right!

Downtown's **Fountain Pen Shop**—a step back in time with the greatest technicians ever to fix that beloved Waterman or Sheaffer pen you got from a favorite relative.

Driving along **Sunset Boulevard,** beginning at the **Beverly Hills Hotel** and going west and fantasizing about which home I'll buy when I win the lottery.

The **Larchmont Family Fair,** the weekend before Halloween; small-town fun in LA's best residential neighborhood, where the girls are almost pretty, the boys are doing well, and the parents are all nicknamed Skip and Muffy.

The pure Americana of **Dodger Stadium,** with instant replay on giant screens, always off-key organ for the music, and a pig-out on hot dogs, popcorn, drippy nachos, and watery Coke (eschewing the yuppie stuff like sushi). Oh, do you go to see the game?

Anything at the **Mark Taper Forum,** my favorite theater of all time.

Walking along **La Brea** between Second Street and Willoughby and **Melrose Avenue** between San Vicente and Highland and practicing "Safe Shopping"—aka looky-looing. I don't drive (believe it or not), so I walk, bus, or cab it.

Riding the elevators of the **Central Library** and "reading" the walls—check it out and you'll see what I mean.

Climbing up to the top of **City Hall** and going out (without security seeing you) to the very top cupola to view the city—scary, height-wise, but fun.

Pasadena's gorgeous library; beauty everywhere you look.

45 SEÑOR FRED

★★★$ Andre Guerrero and Michael Lamb teamed up to open this sprightly eatery, named after Guerrero's son, on the heels of their successful MAX Restaurant about a mile down the boulevard. The design by interior architect Kristopher Keith echoes Mexico circa the turn of the 20th century, with two complementing areas. One offers oversized tooled-leather booths that seat 10, with dim lighting from hanging lamps covered by giant fabric-covered charcoal lampshades. The spacious dining room features freestanding tables and a stucco and tile-covered fireplace. A long, attractive walnut-stained bar, which takes up much of the place, is a popular gathering spot for local singles and couples. For non-barflies, there's a cozy lounge with an inviting couch. Tinted French doors lead to an outdoor patio, equipped with heat lamps for cool nights, where tables book up fast. It's a happy-go-lucky setting. Exceptional dishes include *Róbalo* (pan-roasted sea bass accented with mango and black bean salsa tostada and topped off with a tangy sauce) and Quesadilla de Huitlacoche (prepared with the mushroom-like corn truffle filled with asadero cheese, epazote, and pieces of poblano chile and served with guacamole and other south-of-the-border-style dishes). The best desserts are the chocolate *con leche y galletas* flavored with cinnamon, almonds, and vanilla, served with freshly baked cookies; and the flan *con lima*. ◆ Mexican ◆ Daily, lunch and dinner. Reservations recommended for dinner. 13730 Ventura Boulevard (at Mammoth Ave, just west of Woodman Ave), Sherman Oaks. 818/789.3200; fax: 818/789.3232. www.SenorFred.com

46 PREZZO

★$$ The food is quite tasty at this favorite meeting place of the Valley's *jeunesse dorée*. Scallops in red pepper sauce, pasta with smoked chicken, and grilled swordfish come highly recommended. ◆ Italian ◆ Daily, dinner. Reservations recommended. 13625 Ventura Blvd (between Ventura Canyon and Woodman Aves). 818/905.8400

47 MAX

★★$$ Chef Andre Guerrero tipped his toque to Linq, where he worked culinary magic for two years, and opened his own little neighborhood charmer. Named after his son, the storefront eatery is adorned with white damask walls, cozy banquettes, and soft lighting. There's a special niche, off to the side of the main dining room, set aside for celebrities who like to go unnoticed. The food is a fusion of California and Asian with offerings such as shrimp and pork spring rolls; Thai lemongrass coconut soup; crab ravioli; tea-smoked salmon cured in soy sauce mirin, and fresh ginger; roasted chicken; Applewood-smoked baby back ribs; New York pepper steak; and much more. The lemon mascarpone icebox cake, chocolate brownie, and brioche bread pudding should satisfy your sweet tooth. The service is good and the ambience inviting. ◆ California-Asian Fusion ◆ Daily, dinner; M-F, lunch. Reservations suggested for dinner. Valet parking available. 13355 Ventura Blvd (between Dixie Canyon and Fulton Ave), Sherman Oaks. 818/784.2915. www.maxrestaurant.com

48 THE GREAT GREEK

★\$\$ Greek food is served in an exuberant atmosphere here, but the appetizers are a better bet than the entrées. The 14-course banquet, intended to serve one, is enough for three people. There's music and dancing nightly. ◆ Greek ◆ Daily, lunch and dinner. Reservations recommended. 13362 Ventura Blvd (at Dixie Canyon Ave). 818/905.5250

48 MISTRAL

★\$\$\$ This French bistro offers a warm atmosphere and a touch of Provence in the generous use of herbs to flavor the baked mussels and grilled steak. ◆ French ◆ M-F, lunch and dinner; Sa, dinner. Reservations recommended. 13422 Ventura Blvd (between Dixie Canyon and Greenbush Aves). 818/981.6650

49 IROHA SUSHI

★★\$\$ Excellent sushi is prepared at this quiet, caring bar that's well hidden from the street. ◆ Japanese ◆ M-Sa, lunch and dinner; Su, dinner. 12953 Ventura Blvd (between Coldwater Canyon and Ethel Aves). 818/990.9559

49 PINOT

★★★\$\$ Master chef **Joachim Splichal** (of **Patina** fame) brings his culinary expertise to this busy bistro. As with his Melrose Avenue restaurant, Splichal enlisted the expertise of Cheryl Brantner, whose designs for the interior complement the flavors of French cooking with a simple but very

elegant country French setting. Whether you order fish, grilled veal chop, or some exotic specialty of the day, expect culinary ecstasy. ◆ French ◆ M-F, lunch and dinner; Sa, Su, dinner. 12969 Ventura Blvd (between Coldwater Canyon and Ethel Aves). 818/990.0500

49 MARRAKESH

★★\$\$ Couscous with lamb, chicken with olives, and *b'stilla* (chicken with spices, nuts, and fruit beneath a flaky pastry crust) are enjoyed amid authentic décor. ◆ Moroccan ◆ Daily, dinner. Reservations recommended. 13003 Ventura Blvd (between Coldwater Canyon and Ethel Aves). 818/788.6354

49 PINZ

The late, great James Dean bowled here years ago when it was called the Sports Center Bowl. Even under new management and a different name, it continues to attract young, attractive celebrities such as Jennifer Aniston, Brad Pitt, Cameron Diaz, Drew Barrymore, and that crowd. The appeal is the 32 state-of-the-art lanes, full game arcade, billiards, dancing, laser shows, and food and bar service from Jerry's Deli. Not to mention a private screening theater, comedy club, sushi bar, and a full schedule of theme nights held throughout the year. ◆ Daily. 12655 Ventura Blvd (across the street from La Knitterie Parisienne and next door to Jerry's Deli). 818/769.7600. www.pinzbowlingcenter.com

50 LA KNITTERIE PARISIENNE

If you want to learn how to knit, or already do but need some yarn, go see Edith Eig at her charming knitting emporium in Studio City. An amazing assortment of yarns (13,000 to be exact) include imported fibers such as silk, cotton, angora, linen, wool, mohair, corde, soutache, and hand-dyed and blended yarns. She also offers free knitting and crochet lessons. While you're there, browse through the collection of extraordinary sweaters and accessories. ◆ Daily. 12642 Ventura Blvd (between Whitsett and Coldwater Cyn), Studio City. 818/766.1515; e-mail: laknitpar@earthlink.net. www.laknitterieparisienne.com

50 BISTRO GARDEN

★★★\$\$\$ Although the Beverly Hills branch is long closed, the "ladies who lunch bunch" and well-heeled, mostly surgically enhanced Westsiders trek over the mountain to continue the tradition. The room is light and airy, with a traditional décor. The menu is extensive and includes signature dishes such as French

---

Restaurants/Clubs: Red | **Hotels: Purple** | Shops: Orange | **Outdoors/Parks: Green** | Sights/Culture: Blue

onion or sweet potato, corn, and jalapeño soup; tuna tartare with ginger soy vinaigrette, goat cheese and walnut cake; penne pasta with peppers, eggplant, zucchini, fresh mozzarella, and red bell pepper coulis; lemon pepper linguini with shiitake mushrooms, asparagus, sun-dried tomatoes, and extra-virgin olive oil; Parmesan risotto with beef tenderloin; broiled whitefish in lemon butter; braised Chilean sea bass in a Dijon mustard dill sauce; chicken curry; osso buco; grilled veal porterhouse; and on and on. Desserts worth the caloric splurge include a heavenly chocolate or pumpkin soufflé, crème brûlée, pineapple cheesecake, and chocolate mousse cake with vanilla sauce. ♦ French Continental ♦ M-F, lunch and dinner; Sa, Su, dinner. Reservations recommended. 12950 Ventura Blvd (between Coldwater Canyon and Van Noord Aves). Valet parking. 818/501.0202; fax 818/501.2244. www.bistrogarden.com

51 Oyster House Saloon and Restaurant

★$$ The oyster bar and the pasta with seafood are the main attractions at this popular watering hole. ♦ Seafood ♦ M-Sa, lunch and dinner; Su, light snacks and dinner. Reservations recommended. 12446 Moorpark St (at Whitsett Ave). 818/761.8686

52 Out Take Café

★★★$$ This funky little eatery proffers some of the best home-style cooking around. Few tables mean there's often a wait, but the food's well worth some patience. The eclectic menu includes wonton soup, Ukrainian borscht, Southwest turkey chili, spinach salad, Asian chicken satay, sandwiches, and pasta dishes. ♦ Café ♦ Daily, lunch and dinner. 12159 Ventura Blvd (between Laurel Canyon Blvd and Laurelgrove Ave). 818/760.1111 ♿

On any given day, an average of 25 productions are filming on the streets of Los Angeles.

52 Mexicali

★★$ A feisty little Mexican restaurant it gets all dressed up in scarecrows and pumpkins in October and Christmas trees and lights in December, and offers a tasty menu with everything from enchiladas to ahi tuna. The garlic-and-chipotle-roasted chicken and the tortilla soup are superb. Cozy booths and a friendly staff make this a very special place. ♦ Mexican ♦ Daily, lunch and dinner. 12161 Ventura Blvd (between Laurel Canyon Blvd and Laurelgrove Ave). 818/985.1744 ♿

52 Siesta Specialties

If pottery's your thing, you'll find a great selection in a variety of styles and colors at this adorable shop. ♦ Closed M. 12401 Ventura Blvd (between Vantage and Whitsett Aves). 818/752.7200

53 Wine Bistro

★$$ Enjoy a variety of wines with a wonderful bistro menu served in a cozy woodsy setting. Start with escargot or pâté de foie gras with crusty French bread and continue with bouillabaisse, roasted duckling, or whitefish with sweet caramelized red onion. Luscious endings include crème brûlée, chocolate mousse cake, and a traditional cheese plate. ♦ French ♦ M-F, lunch and dinner; Sa, dinner. 11915 Ventura Blvd (between Colfax and Radford Aves). 818/766.6233

54 Barsac Brasserie

★★$$ This charming little bistro caters to the nearby studio set, who dine here between scenes. The menu changes every three months, but you can usually count on items such as the quail salad, black and white linguine with bay scallops, ravioli stuffed with goat cheese, tournedos of salmon, or sautéed whitefish to satisfy your taste buds. ♦ French ♦ M-F, lunch and dinner; Sa, dinner. 4212 Lankershim Blvd (between Cahuenga Blvd and Valley Spring La). 818/760.7081

55 Dari

Melanie Shatner, daughter of William Shatner, *Star Trek*'s Captain Kirk, runs this earthly shop of trendy duds and accessories from designers such as Diane von Furstenberg, Laura Urbinati, and Isabella Fiore. ♦ Daily; Su until 5PM. 12184 Ventura Blvd (between Laurel Canyon Blvd and Whitsett Ave). 818/762.3274

55 Art's Deli

★$ This full-service deli is a favorite among Valley tennis players. Pastrami is a house specialty. ♦ Deli ♦ Daily. 12224 Ventura Blvd (between Vantage and Laurelgrove Aves). 818/762.1221

56 LA LOGGIA

★★$$ Movie moguls and power brokers keep this modern trattoria jumping. Its popularity hasn't waned since the day it opened—locals describe it as the Valley's answer to Spago. Pasta (linguini with seafood; angel hair with fresh tomatoes, garlic, and basil), risotto with saffron and asparagus, farm-raised roasted chicken au jus, and pork chop with caramelized Bartlett pears and Gorgonzola sauce are standouts. Forget calorie counting and finish with a scrumptious banana Napoleon, upside-down chocolate soufflé, or tiramisù. ♦ Northern Italian ♦ M-F, lunch and dinner; Sa, Su, dinner. 11814 Ventura Blvd (between Blue Canyon Dr and Carpenter Ave). email: laloggia@earthlink.net. www.calendarlive.com/LaLoggia/; 818/985.9222

56 TERU SUSHI

★$$ This hugely popular sushi bar launched what is now LA's favorite grazing fare. The theatrical presentation by the chefs adds flair to the other specialties as well. ♦ Japanese ♦ M-F, lunch and dinner; Sa, Su, dinner. 11940 Ventura Blvd (between Carpenter Ave and Laurel Canyon Blvd). 818/763.6201

56 FIREFLY

★★★$$$ Hidden in a vine-shrouded building—and we do mean concealed, with no signage—this is without doubt the hippest spot in the Valley. Fashion-plate, bare-bellied, tattooed, pierced, and trendy foodies flock from all over town to be part of this over-the-top scene. An open-air dining room, big bar lined with bookcases, velvet sofas, an outdoor fireplace, and dim lighting set the mood for the eclectic, seasonally changing menu. Order the pan-roasted scallops served on a bed of succotash with vanilla-bean vinaigrette or the calamari sprinkled with almond flour if you see them on the list. Any salad will please your palate, and so will the Tahitian vanilla-bean crème brûlée or banana walnut cake. Dress as hip as your wardrobe allows. Bring a few friends; people tend to travel in groups here. ♦ American Eclectic ♦ M-Sa, dinner. Reservations necessary. 11720 Ventura Blvd (between Blue Canyon Dr and Carpenter Ave), Studio City. 818/762.1833. (Look for the vine-covered building, as there's no name posted.)

57 HORTOBAGY

★$$ Since it's named for the plains region of Hungary, home of the fabled Hungarian horsemen, it's no surprise that the food here is solid, spicy, and unpretentious. There are stews, rich soups, grilled and breaded meats, and amazing homemade sausages, as well as a selection of Hungarian wines. Great dessert choices are the chocolate torte or plum dumpling. ♦ Hungarian ♦ M, dinner only; Tu-Su, lunch and dinner. Reservations recommended for four or more. 11138 Ventura Blvd (between Fruitland and Eureka Drs). 818/980.2273

57 SUSHI NOZAWA

★★$$ Victorian table manners are observed at this splendidly old-fashioned restaurant, but the stern warnings on what not to do or eat are worth it: Chef Nozawa offers some of the best sushi in town. ♦ Japanese ♦ M-F, Su, lunch and dinner; Sa, dinner. 11288 Ventura Blvd (at Eureka Dr), Unit C. 818/508.7017

58 THE BAKED POTATO

Guitar gods Lee Ritenour and Larry Carlton got their starts here at one of LA's best-established clubs for contemporary jazz. It's loud and yet intimate. Twenty-one varieties of stuffed potatoes are served (shrimp-and-cheese are one of the favored choices). ♦ Cover. Daily, 7PM until 2AM. 3787 Cahuenga Blvd (at Lankershim Blvd). 818/980.1615

Some of Southern California's shakiest quakes:

17 January 1994 in Northridge: 6.6 magnitude, 55 deaths, 1,000 injuries, $30 billion in damages

28 June 1992 in Landers and Big Bear Lake: 7.4 and 6.5 magnitude (respectively), one death, 350 injuries, $92 million in damages

28 February 1990 in Upland: 5.5 magnitude, no deaths, 38 injuries, $10.4 million in damages

1 October 1987 in Whittier Narrows: 5.9 magnitude, eight deaths, more than 200 injuries, $358 million in damages

8 July 1986 in North Palm Springs: 5.9 magnitude, no deaths or injuries, $5.3 million in damages

9 February 1971 in Sylmar/San Fernando Valley: 6.4 magnitude, 58 deaths, 2,000 injuries, $511 million in damages

21 July 1952 in Tehachapi: 7.7 magnitude, 12 deaths, 18 injuries, $50 million in damages

---

Restaurants/Clubs: Red | Hotels: Purple | Shops: Orange | Outdoors/Parks: Green | Sights/Culture: Blue

GRIFFITH PARK/NORTH CENTRAL

L A's hidden treasures . . .

These two stylish neighborhoods nestle in the foothills of the **Santa Monica Mountains,** just northeast of Hollywood. The 4,000-acre **Griffith Park,** one of the largest urban green spaces in America, was named for Colonel Griffith J. Griffith, who bought the land in 1882 and then donated it to the city in 1896.

Two distinctive communities, **Los Feliz** and **Silverlake,** sit south of the park. Built in

the 1920s before the advent of pad construction, many of the houses here conform to the picturesque undulations of the land. The winding roads and tiled roofs massed on the slopes around the **Silver Lake Reservoir** resemble a Mediterranean hill town. The pretty lake provides the perfect setting for jogging, bicycling, or strolling. The region also boasts LA's highest concentration of modern architectural masterpieces, notably by **Richard Neutra, Rudolph Schindler, Gregory Ain,** and **John Lautner.**

The first residents of North Central were the Yang-Na Indians, who camped in the **Elysian Park Hills** and hunted for small game with bows and arrows. Around 1910,

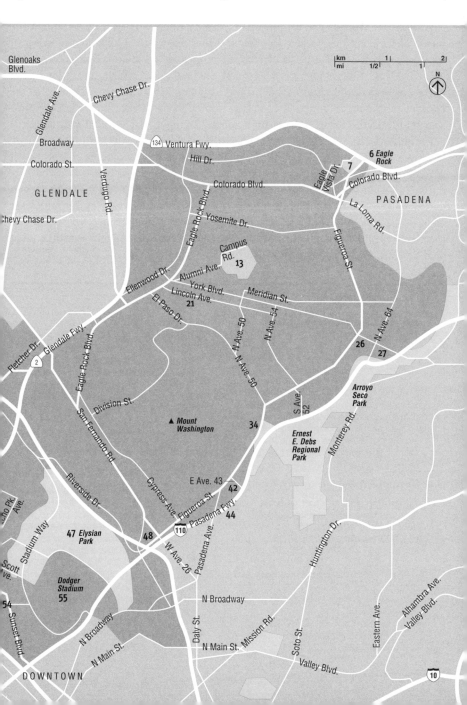

moviemakers came to the neighborhood, among them Mack Sennett, who built his first studio near **Glendale Boulevard.** Today, North Central is predominantly a blue-collar Hispanic-American district, tucked into two pockets of steep hills and bordered by freeways at the northern end of downtown LA. The small frame houses perched high on the tightly woven streets give the appearance of a rural setting, and huge stands of eucalyptus trees run across the hillsides and into the canyons. Trails form a network through the overgrown wilderness across slopes and ravines leading up to **Mount Washington.** A mix of romance and economy makes this residential area attractive to creative young people.

The park is divided into two main parts: the flatlands, with their lush golf courses, picnic areas, pony and train rides, tennis courts, merry-go-round, zoo, museum of transportation, observatory, and **Greek Theatre;** and the mountainous central and western areas, undeveloped save for numerous hiking and horse trails. Four main entrances lead to the park: **Ferndell Drive,** off Los Feliz Boulevard, leading to the **Ferndell; Vermont Avenue,** off Los Feliz, leading to the Greek Theatre and the **Bird Sanctuary; Crystal Springs Drive,** off Los Feliz, leading to the **Ranger Station,** merry-go-round, and golf courses; and the junction of the **Golden State** and **Ventura Freeways,** leading to the zoo and museum. Rangers lead a hike on the first Saturday of the month at 9AM from the merry-go-round parking lot. **Sierra Club tours** include evening outings during full moons. There are no specific bike paths, but regular paved roads are open to cyclists; bikes aren't permitted on the fire roads or horse trails. Some of the 18 picnic areas in the park have benches and tables; those in the Ferndell and Vermont Canyon have barbecues and water. **Park Center** and **Mineral Wells** have some areas with cooking facilities. Visitors may also picnic on the grass. The park is open daily until 10PM.

---

1 EQUESTRIAN CENTER AND CRICKET FIELDS

Two fields are located in the center of the equestrian track near Riverside Drive. The track functions as a practice area and leads to all trails. There are 43 miles of horse trails within the park. Several commercial stables on the outskirts of the park rent horses by the hour. All accept cash only and require a security deposit. ◆ Daily. Riverside Dr and Main St, Burbank. 818/840.8401

2 TRAVEL TOWN

The romance of the rails lives on at this open-air museum of transportation, which displays many antique railroad and trolley cars, locomotives, planes, and automobiles. An enclosed structure houses fire trucks and a circus animal wagon. Many exhibits allow children to climb on board, a treat they'll not forget. Members of a model train club work on an enormous train layout on Saturdays. ◆ Free. Daily. 5200 Zoo Dr (just north of Griffith Park Dr). 323/662.5874. www.ci.la.ca.us/rap/grifmet/ tt/information.htm

3 LIVE STEAMERS

The Los Angeles Live Steamers Club brings its tiny steam locomotives to an area just east of **Travel Town** each Sunday. The trains run on tracks only seven inches wide, but they're authentic in every detail and powerful enough to pull several fully loaded cars. Children get free rides and a chance to examine the miniatures. ◆ Su, 11AM-2:30PM. Zoo Dr (between Crystal Springs and Griffith Park Drs). 323/662.8030

4 AUTRY MUSEUM OF WESTERN HERITAGE

Gene Autry, the singing cowboy of movies, radio, and television, opened this wonderful tribute to the spirit of the West in 1988. Walt Disney Imagineering has brought the memorabilia, artwork, and movie clips to life so you can get a visceral sense of what it was like to be a settler, a cowboy, or a sheriff. Scholarship and showbiz are fruitfully combined, and the museum presents regular exhibitions along with the permanent collection. The architecture firm of **Widom Wein Cohen** designed the museum. ◆ Admission. Tu-Su. 4700 Western Heritage Way (at Zoo Dr). 323/667.2000. www.autry-museum.org

5 LOS ANGELES ZOO

The 75-acre zoo, which opened in 1966, has more than 2,000 animals grouped according to continent of origin. Many of the animals are in environments that simulate their natural habitats, with surrounding moats that allow you to see them without bars. The zoo preserves 78 endangered species. Explore the **Koala House** and the **Aviary,** ride a camel or an elephant, and take in a bird show. The **Animal Nursery** proudly displays the newest arrivals. The 4.5-acre **Pachyderm Forest** houses elephants, hippos, and other creatures in a setting of tropical hardwoods, lagoons, and an Asian topiary. **California Sea Lions Cliffs** is a saltwater exhibit affording underwater viewing. Baby stroller and wheelchair rentals are available along with picnic tables, a snack bar, and a tram tour. ◆ Admission. Daily. 5333 Zoo Dr (just west of Golden State Fwy). General information 323/644.6400. www.lazoo.org

Within Los Angeles Zoo:

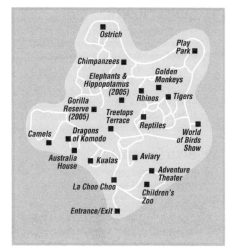

WINNICK FAMILY CHILDREN'S ZOO

Added in the summer of 2001, this petting zoo lets you touch the animals in various "safe zones." Fun for the whole family, the former Adventure Island area also offers storytelling, puppet shows, and close-up and personal looks at ferrets and chickens.

RED APE RAIN FOREST

A three-quarter-acre rain forest that replicates the natural Southeast Asian habitat for orangutans with 20-foot-high bamboo, fruit, and ficus trees. Bring the children to meet Eloise, Bruno, Rosie, and Kalim, a family of apes, ages 18 to 31.

6 EAGLE ROCK

The massive sandstone rock, 150 feet high, resembles an eagle in flight on its southwest side. Described by Dr. Carl Dentzel, late director of the Southwest Museum, as the most distinctive natural landmark in the city, it is visible from the Ventura Freeway traveling east from Glendale to Pasadena. ◆ N Figueroa St and Scholl Canyon Rd

7 EAGLE ROCK PLAYGROUND CLUBHOUSE

Richard Neutra designed this building in 1953. It boasts a magnificent view. ◆ Figueroa St (between Colorado Blvd and Ventura Fwy)

8 GOLF

Two 18-hole courses (**Harding** and **Wilson**) and two nine-hole courses (**Roosevelt** and **Los Feliz Pitch & Putt**) in the park are open to the public. City-registered golfers may make reservations. Others will be allowed on the green as space becomes available. ◆ Harding and Wilson: 4730 Crystal Springs Dr (between Los Feliz Blvd and Zoo Dr), 323/663.2555. Roosevelt: 2650 N Vermont Ave (at Commonwealth Canyon Dr), 323/665.2011. Los Feliz Pitch & Putt: 3207 Los Feliz Blvd (between Garden Ave and Golden State Fwy), 323/663.7758

9 MERRY-GO-ROUND

The well-preserved merry-go-round on the green was constructed in 1926 and moved to the park in 1936. ◆ Admission. Daily, mid-June to mid-Sept; Sa, Su, and LA public school holidays, mid-Sept to mid-June. Park Center Picnic Area (west of Griffith Park Dr). 323/665.3051

10 RANGER STATION

The **Griffith Park Visitors' Center** operates here. Stop in to pick up information and free road and hiking trail maps. ◆ Daily until 10PM. 4730 Crystal Springs Dr (between Los Feliz Blvd and Zoo Dr). 323/913.7390; fax 323/485.8775

10 BASEBALL

A baseball diamond in the **Crystal Springs Picnic Area** is used by city college teams for league games. Open by permit only. ◆ Crystal Springs Dr (between Los Feliz Blvd and Zoo Dr)

Restaurants/Clubs: Red | Hotels: Purple | Shops: Orange | Outdoors/Parks: Green | Sights/Culture: Blue

11 SUNSET RANCH

The Old West flourishes in the heart of the city at this ranch, with photogenic stables and moonlit rides to the top of the mountains, where you'll have stupendous views of LA. Night rides every Friday at 5PM are on a first-come, first-served basis; groups must make appointments on other nights. ♦ Daily. 3400 N Beachwood Dr (north of Franklin Ave). 323/469.5450

12 BIRD SANCTUARY

Rangers planted protective foliage to encourage birds to nest in this wooded canyon with ponds and a stream. Picnic while you keep an eye out for sparrows, hawks, and scrub jays, among others. ♦ Daily, dawn to dusk. Vermont Canyon Rd (between Commonwealth Canyon and Mount Hollywood Drs)

13 OCCIDENTAL COLLEGE

This small liberal arts college, founded in 1887, was formerly affiliated with the Presbyterian Church. The campus core was designed by **Myron Hunt** after the college's move to the Eagle Rock area in 1914. Occidental figures as Tarzana College in Aldous Huxley's *After Many a Summer Dies the Swan*. The inventively designed **Keck Theatre** (323/259.2737) presents a wide range of plays and dance performances throughout the year. ♦ 1600 Campus Rd (at Alumni Ave). 323/259.2500

14 GRIFFITH-VERMONT CANYON TENNIS COURTS

Free play is available at the 12 day-use-only courts before 4PM. No reservations are taken. ♦ Fee after 4PM. Daily. Commonwealth Canyon Dr (between Vista del Valle Dr and N Vermont Ave). 323/664.3521

15 WOODY'S BICYCLE WORLD

Griffith Park is full of bike trails, and this is the place to rent your wheels. ♦ Daily. 3157 Los Feliz Blvd (between Garden Ave and Golden State Fwy). 323/661.6665

16 TAM O'SHANTER INN

★★$$ **Lawry's** runs this haven for expatriate Scots. The prime rib is tops. But many folks go for the toad-in-the-hole and Scotch rarebit, mustard-encrusted pork, and the super salmon and swordfish. For true believers, haggis is served on Robert Burns's birthday. ♦ Scottish ♦ M-F, lunch and dinner; Sa, dinner; Su, brunch and dinner. Reservations recommended. 2980 Los Feliz Blvd (at Boyce Ave). 323/664.0228

17 OBSERVATORY AND PLANETARIUM THEATRE

Closed to the public during a $63 million renovation and expansion that began in January 2002, the Observatory is scheduled to reopen in late 2005. ♦ 2800 Observatory Rd (between Vermont Canyon and Western Canyon Rds). 323/664.1191

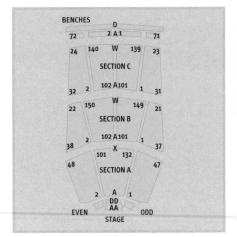

18 GREEK THEATRE

All spruced up after a multimillion-dollar major face-lift, this imposing amphitheater now boasts more plaza areas, upgraded concession stands, state-of-the-art sound and lighting systems, and a more inviting picnic lawn area. The renovation also included restoration of the 1930s façade. The redo was timed to coincide with the Greek Theatre's 75th anniversary. The amphitheater presents mostly popular music from June through the first week of October. Box suppers may be purchased from concessionaires inside. Beer and wine are available. Bring a sweater—nights get chilly in LA. ♦ Admission. 2700 N Vermont Ave (north of Los Feliz Blvd). Tickets and schedules 323/665.5857, subscription information 323/468.1767. www.nederlander.com/greek.html

19 PONY RIDES

This safe, small track offers pony rides for children. ♦ Tu-Su. Crystal Springs Dr (north of Los Feliz Blvd). 323/664.3266

19 TRAIN RIDE

Another tiny train, but this one is for adults as well as children. ♦ Fee. Daily. 4400 Crystal Springs Dr (north of Los Feliz Blvd). 323/664.6788

20 OSTERIA NONNI

★★$$ The high-tech setting here accentuates the sharply focused menu, inspired by the

Trattoria Angeli in West LA. Tiny clams in a white-wine-and-prosciutto sauce, designer pizza, lightly fried baby salmon, and breaded calamari are all choice entrées. ♦ Italian ♦ M, Sa, Su, dinner; Tu-F, lunch and dinner. Reservations recommended on Friday and Saturday. 3219 Glendale Blvd (between Edenhurst and Brunswick Aves). 323/666.7133

21 SPARKLETT DRINKING WATER

Corporate LA is full of Islamic pastiches, and this 1929 mosque is one of the finest. The minarets came down in the 1971 earthquake and were rebuilt. ♦ 4500 Lincoln Ave (at N Ave 45)

22 SWIMMING POOL

An Olympic-size pool is open during the summer at the **Griffith Recreation Center.** ♦ Free. Daily, mid-June to mid-Sept. Riverside Dr and Los Feliz Blvd. 323/665.4372

23 THE FERNDELL

This natural glade along a spring-fed stream is planted with native and exotic ferns. Paths and picnic tables make this an outstanding place to retreat from the world for an alfresco meal. ♦ Daily. Ferndell Dr (between Black Oak and Red Oak Drs)

24 ENNIS-BROWN HOUSE

Frank Lloyd Wright built this "Maya temple," the most impressive and best-sited of his concrete-block houses, on a hill overlooking the city in 1924. It is a private residence; however, tours are offered of the interior, which has been restored to its original appearance. ♦ Admission. Tours: Second Sa of each odd-numbered month from noon on. 2655 Glendower Ave (between Bryn Mawr Rd and N Catalina St). Tour reservations 323/660.0607

25 LOVELL HOUSE

Richard Neutra created LA's finest example of International-style architecture: a steel-framed, stucco-clad composition of stacked planes flowing out from a hillside. Completed in 1929, the design launched Neutra's 40-year career as the most productive and prestigious of LA's modern architects. This is a private residence. ♦ 4616 Dundee Dr (west of N Commonwealth Ave)

26 SAN ENCINO ABBEY

The hybrid of California Mission and European Gothic styles was created by **Clyde Brown** between 1909 and 1925. Brown imported parts of old European castles and monasteries to create his own medieval environment. It's a private residence. ♦ 6211 Arroyo Glen St (at Figueroa St)

27 JUDSON STUDIOS

This studio has been well known for its stained-glass work since 1897. The Moorish and Craftsman-style building is owned by a fourth-generation Judson descendant. ♦ Lobby, M-F. 200 S Ave 66 (between Marmion Way and York Blvd). 323/255.0131

28 SANSUI

★$ "Healthy food in a peaceful room" is the goal of owner/chef Shinichi Kishi, and he delivers on both promises. The Shojin dinner includes 10 small vegetarian courses, and the music that wafts through sounds like wind on a mountaintop. ♦ Japanese ♦ M-F, lunch and dinner; Sa, Su, dinner. Reservations recommended for parties of five or more. 2040 Hillhurst Ave (at Price St). 323/660.3868

29 TRATTORIA FARFALLA

★$ Delicious pizzas, pastas, fish, and, according to the owner, "everything else" are served in this hole-in-the-wall. Save room for the delectable desserts. ♦ Italian ♦ Daily, lunch and dinner. Reservations recommended for parties of six or more. 1978 Hillhurst Ave (between Clarissa and Finley Aves). 323/661.7365. Also at 143 N La Brea Ave (between W First St and Beverly Blvd). 323/938.2504

30 SAY CHEESE

This shop is a great neighborhood resource for fresh cheeses, teas, coffees, and imported delicacies. ♦ Daily. 2800 Hyperion Ave (between Griffith Park Blvd and Rowena Ave). 323/665.0545

31 FRED 62

★★$ This eccentric little coffee shop espouses the motto "Eat now, dine later." Perfect for families, the quirky menu offers kids such choices as MacDaddy and Cheese (macaroni and cheese) and Bearded Mr. Frenchy (French toast breaded with cornflakes). Adults might prefer the Thai Cobb salad, Seoul Caesar, or eggs and omelets. ♦ Coffee Shop ♦ Daily, 24 hours. 1850 N Vermont Ave (at Russell Ave). 323/667.0062 &

32 ELECTRIC LOTUS

★★$$ The long, narrow restaurant, named after a nightclub in Goa, is definitely wired with the hip and happening (and young celebs) who go to enjoy Northern Indian cuisine and stay up late listening to live Indian music. The food's tasty and interesting, with offerings like

---

Restaurants/Clubs: **Red** | Hotels: **Purple** | Shops: Orange | Outdoors/Parks: **Green** | Sights/Culture: **Blue**

chicken tikka masala, *palek paneer* (steamed spinach with tofu), tofu curry, and a choice of two desserts: rice pudding and yummy *gulab jamon* (pastry balls spiced with ginger and sweetened with honey). ♦ Indian ♦ Daily, lunch and dinner (open until 11PM weeknights, 1AM weekends). Reservations suggested. 4656 Franklin Ave (between Hillhurst and N Vermont Aves). 323/953.0040

32 AMOK BOOKSTORE

An eclectic range of literature, from the macabre to the philosophical. ♦ Tu-Su. 1764 N Vermont Ave (between Kingswell and Melbourne Aves). 213/239.0030

33 RED LION TAVERN

★$ Not a nook for nibbling, this unpretentious, inexpensive neighborhood restaurant is the real home-cooked German article, with delicious food and lots of it: schnitzel, bratwurst, smoked pork loin, veal loaf, sauerkraut, potato salad, etc. There's also weiss beer and Dortmunder Ritter on tap, and a fine selection of after-dinner liqueurs, such as kirschwasser, slivovitz, and apple schnapps. ♦ German ♦ Daily, lunch and dinner. Reservations recommended for parties of eight or more. 2366 Glendale Blvd (at Brier Ave). 323/662.5337

34 SOUTHWEST MUSEUM

One of the city's sleepers, this museum houses a magnificent collection of Native American art in a Mission-style building on Mount Washington overlooking the Pasadena Freeway. The permanent displays of art and artifacts from the Southwest, Great Plains, Northwest coast, and California have been dramatically improved over time. Notable among the holdings are the **Poole Collections** of American Indian basketry, Navajo blankets, pottery, and a full-size Blackfoot tepee. Loan exhibitions, lectures, and workshops for the entire family are held throughout the year. The **Festival of Native American Arts**, with food, music, and dance, is held every October. There is also a well-stocked gift and bookstore and the important **Braun Research Library** for scholarly reference. ♦ Admission. Tu-Su. 234 Museum Dr (just north of Marmion Way). Recorded information 323/221.2163, offices 323/221.2164

35 EL CHAVO

$ The menu features *riñones fritos* (sautéed kidneys with chopped vegetables); tongue in Spanish sauce and mole; a wonderful, tender poached chicken; and excellent grilled steaks. The soft lighting is pleasant and the music is, thankfully, unobtrusive. ♦ Mexican ♦ Daily, lunch and dinner. 4441 Sunset Blvd (between N Hoover St and Sunset Dr). 323/664.0871

36 CASITA DEL CAMPO

$ Go here for enjoyable eating on an outdoor patio. ♦ Mexican ♦ Daily, lunch and dinner. Reservations recommended. 1920 Hyperion Ave (between Landa St and Lyric Ave). 323/662.4255. www.casitadelcampo.com

37 OLIVE HOUSE

This wonderfully complex house was designed by **Rudolph Schindler,** Richard Neutra's compatriot and rival, who was more innovative and less successful in his LA career. This street has a uniquely rich concentration of classic modern houses, all of which are private residences. ♦ 2236 Micheltorena St (between Rock and Angus Sts)

38 NEUTRA HOUSE

Richard Neutra built this daringly experimental house for himself in his first decade of work in 1933. When it was destroyed by fire in 1963, he created a more romantic version, completed one year later. On Silverlake's **2200 block** there's a concentration of Neutra houses dating from 1948 to 1961: nos. **2250, 2242, 2240, 2238, 2226, 2218, 2210,** and **2200.** All are private residences. ♦ 2300 Silverlake Blvd (between Earl St and Edgewater Terr)

39 EL CID FLAMENCO SHOW RESTAURANT

$$ The food in this Spanish Colonial cabaret is only run-of-the-mill, but the flamenco guitar and flamenco dancing are remarkable. It's located on the site of D. W. Griffith's studio, where the 150-foot-high set of *The Grand Babylon Hotel* rose in 1916. ♦ Mexican/Spanish ♦ W-Su, dinner. Reservations recommended. 4212 Sunset Blvd (at Myra Ave). 323/668.0318

41 SOMPUN THAI

★$ Excellent noodles are served in this family-style restaurant. Dine on the charming patio. ♦ Thai ♦ M, W-Su, lunch and dinner. 4156 Santa Monica Blvd (between Manzanita St and Myra Ave). 323/669.9906

41 TANTRA

★★★$$ The scene is tantra-lizing with seductive Bhangra music and subtle, sexy colors, designs, and scents. You feel like you walked into an opium den or forbidden garden. Designed by Sat Garg, the whimsical, mystical décor of mottled deep yellow plaster walls, a giant statue of Lord Ganesha (God of Prosperity), and plasma-screen television showing old Hollywood movies teases the senses, while the food rouses gastric juices into a frenzied state of pure delight. Every menu morsel is fantastic, from the tandoori salmon kebob to the lamb biryani. The Tantra Platter is a winner, with salmon, green chicken tikka, and spinach tofu samosas served with masala cheese naan; as is the Jhinga Khichdi, an Indian-style risotto with red onion and coriander topped with a crispy prawn. The after-hours set fills the bar until early morning. ♦ Indian ♦ Dinner, T-Su. Reservations required. 3705 Sunset Blvd (between Edgecliff Dr and Lucille Ave). 323/663.8268; e-mail: tantrasunset@hotmail.com. www.tantrasunset.com

42 LUMMIS HOUSE

This unique owner-built residence was conceived and executed between 1898 and 1910 by Charles Fletcher Lummis, founder of the **Southwest Museum** (page 172) and the first city librarian. Constructed of granite boulders from the nearby arroyo, hand-hewn timbers, and telephone poles, the structure is a romantic combination of styles. Most of the original furniture is gone, but the home and gardens remain as a monument to a most extraordinary man. ♦ Free. F-Su, noon-4PM. 200 E Ave 43 (at Midland St). 323/222.0546

43 NETTY'S

$ Soups, pasta, grilled chicken, and dishes of the day, to go or to eat at a few teensy tables, are the mainstays of the menu here. ♦ American ♦ M-Sa, lunch and dinner. 1700 Silverlake Blvd (at Effie St). 323/662.8655

44 HERITAGE SQUARE MUSEUM

The president of the National Trust described this as an "architectural petting zoo," and certainly these vintage houses had a greater impact on the city when they occupied their original sites. But just as zoos preserve endangered species, so the LA Cultural Heritage Board has rescued these eight historic buildings, built between 1865 and 1920, from the insatiable greed of developers. They include the **Hale House,** the **Palms Railroad Depot,** and the **Lincoln Avenue Methodist Church.** Ask about tours and special events. There's also a gift shop. ♦ Admission. F-Su, noon-4PM. 3800 N Homer St (south of E Ave 43). 626/449.0193

45 LONGEST STAIRCASE

The earliest movie makers built studios in Silverlake and filmed on its streets. Laurel and Hardy tried to carry a grand piano up these steps in *The Music Box* (1932). ♦ 927 N Vendome St (between N Dillon St and Sunset Blvd)

46 CAFÉ TROPICAL BAKERY

Guava-cream-cheese pie and piping-hot coffee are specialties. ♦ Daily, until 10PM. 2900 Sunset Blvd (at Parkman Ave). 323/661.8391

47 ELYSIAN PARK

The second-largest park (more than 600 acres) in the Los Angeles area occupies several hills and valleys. The parkland was set aside for public use at the founding of the city in 1781. The main part of it has been left in its natural state, its slopes covered with the shrubs and low trees known as chaparral and crisscrossed with hiking trails. A scenic plaza with a small artificial lake is located a quarter-mile north of the Academy Road/Pasadena Freeway intersection. There's also a children's play area. A café at the Police Academy opens to the public weekdays from 6AM to 3PM, serving hearty, reasonably priced meals. ♦ Free. Daily, until 9PM. 1880 Academy Dr (north of Academy Rd). 323/222.9136

48 LAWRY'S CALIFORNIA CENTER

The restaurant and gift shop have closed, and the building is now home to Lawry's corporate offices. Note the distinctive Spanish-style architecture. ♦ 570 W Ave 26 (between N Figueroa St and San Fernando Rd)

49 OLIVE SUBSTATION

Restored by the Jerde Partnership, this 1907 structure was one of several Mission-style stations in the city taken over by the Pacific Electric Railway Company in 1911. It now houses a private office. ♦ 2798 Sunset Blvd (at N Occidental Blvd)

50 TAIX

★★★$$ The largest and oldest of LA's French restaurants, this dining spot offers fixed-price, full-course *très très* French meals. Favorites include signature roast chicken *fermière* (covered in a light Bordelaise sauce), a superior filet mignon served on Monday nights, a divine lamb shank on Wednesdays, about the best short ribs you'll ever eat on Fridays, and a duck à l'orange to make you drool on Saturdays. Although you get sherbet *après* your meal, the chocolate mousse or crème brûlée are well worth the splurge. Wines are the most reasonably priced around. ♦ French ♦ Daily, lunch and dinner. 1911 Sunset Blvd (at Reservoir St). 213/484.1265. www.taixfrench.com

51 BARRAGAN CAFE

★$$ This neighborhood favorite for Mexican food serves honestly prepared platters of the usual dishes (tacos, tostadas, enchiladas, rellenos) all dished out in combo plates with lots of chips and salsa. There's nightly entertainment in the bar. ♦ Mexican ♦ Daily, breakfast, lunch, and dinner. Reservations recommended. 1538 Sunset Blvd (between Laveta Terr and Echo Park Ave). 213/250.4256

Restaurants/Clubs: Red | **Hotels: Purple** | Shops: Orange | **Outdoors/Parks: Green** | Sights/Culture: Blue

TINSELTOWN—TAKE ONE

Early moviemakers shot their scenes primarily in the streets of LA, making everyday life a part of the action. The Keystone Kops comedies, Harold Lloyd's *Safety Last* (1923), and Laurel and Hardy's *Big Business* (1929) document the city as it was then. Some of the best films featuring the City of Angels include the following:

Annie Hall (1977) Arguably Woody Allen's finest film, this stinging social comedy won Academy Awards for Best Picture, Actress (Diane Keaton), Director (Allen), and Screenplay (Allen and Marshall Brickman). In one scene, Alvy Singer (Allen) sits with Annie (Keaton) in the restaurant **The Source** and delivers the line that LA's greatest cultural contribution was its law allowing a right turn at a red traffic light.

The Big Lebowski (1998) Joel and Ethan Coen's darkly hilarious tale about an LA slacker (potently brought to life by Jeff Bridges) caught in a web of kidnap and murder features some nifty skewering of LA stereotypes, all in the name of entertainment. The Busby Berkeley–esque musical sequence is a highlight.

Blade Runner (1982) Ridley Scott's fantasy of LA in the year 2019 as a megalopolis of 90 million people makes inspired use of the **Bradbury Building** and Frank Lloyd Wright's **Ennis-Brown House.**

Boogie Nights (1997) This loving ode to the late-'70s porn industry that grew out of California makes the best use of LA's sprawling suburbs to tell the story of the rise and fall of Dirk Diggler (Mark Wahlberg) and his eclectic family of porn stars. Funny and heartbreaking.

Boyz N the Hood (1991) The hood means "neighborhood" in this realistic drama about college-bound teenagers and gang members growing up in **South Central L.A.** It was written and directed by South Central native John Singleton, who was nominated for a Best Director Oscar.

Clueless (1995) Babe-of-that-moment Alicia Silverstone plays a way-cool **Beverly Hills** high-school student in this salute to teenage fun, fads, and LA jargon. Amy Heckerling's film, based on Jane Austen's *Emma,* is a consistently enjoyable flick that has held up well over the years.

Colors (1988) A violence-choked **East LA** is the setting for this police drama starring Robert Duvall and Sean Penn, but much of it was filmed in **Venice,** where director Dennis Hopper lives.

Day of the Locust (1975) Directed by John Schlesinger, the film takes a devastating look at moviemaking in the 1930s—the ultimate Hollywood horror story. It is in front of **Mann's Chinese Theatre** that Donald Sutherland incites the riot.

The Doors (1991) The Oliver Stone film biography stars Val Kilmer as legendary rock star Jim Morrison, following the UCLA film student/poet/musician from **Venice Beach** to **Sunset Boulevard** and the **Château Marmont.**

E.T. The Extra Terrestrial (1982) TV-perfect suburbia, as exemplified by the **San Fernando Valley,** is the setting for this Steven Spielberg movie, as well as many of his other films.

Falling Down (1993) Joel Schumacher's best film to date features a searing performance from Michael Douglas as "D-Fens," a man caught in LA's traffic hell who decides that he's had enough and sets out on a one-man vigilante rampage against all that's wrong with American society. Robert Duvall is especially affecting as the retiring cop who's chasing him down.

Grand Canyon (1991) Chance encounters change lives from **Brentwood** to **Inglewood** in Lawrence Kasdan's

52 ANGELUS TEMPLE

In the 1920s and 1930s, Aimee Semple McPherson preached her "Foursquare Gospel" within this circular structure. The large domed classical building was based on the design of the Mormon Tabernacle in Salt Lake City. ♦ M-F. Services: Su, 10:45AM, 6PM; W, 7:30PM. 1100 Glendale Blvd (between Park Ave and Sunset Blvd). 213/484.1100

53 ECHO PARK

🅟 During the 1870s, **Echo Park Lake** provided water for nearby farms. In 1891, the land was donated to the city for use as a public park. Joseph Henry Tomlinson designed the layout utilizing the plan of a garden in Derbyshire, England. This 26-acre park is attractively landscaped with semitropical plants and a handsome lotus pond. The lake has paddle boats available for hourly rental. Special events include an annual celebration by the local Samoan community. ♦ Daily, until 10:30PM. Bounded by Echo Park Ave and Glendale Blvd, and Bellevue and Park Aves

54 ANGELINO HEIGHTS

This was LA's first commuter suburb, begun in the land boom of 1886 to 1887, when it was linked by cable car along Temple Street to the stores and offices downtown, just over a mile away. The hilltop site offered views and a cool refuge from the noise and dust of Spring Street. Professionals moved

redemption film starring Danny Glover and Kevin Kline.

LA Confidential (1997) Early 1950s LA, from its fabulous mansions to sizzling nightclubs, is brought to life in this Oscar-nominated crime-solver directed by Curtis Hanson and featuring Kevin Spacey, Kim Basinger, and Danny DeVito.

L.A. Story (1991) Steve Martin's valentine to the city where he met his former wife, Victoria Tennant, stars both. Martin dates a Venice Beach valley girl and roller skates through the **Museum of Contemporary Art** in the comedy that embraces LA and satirizes its lifestyles.

Lethal Weapon (1987) In this action flick and its three sequels, Mel Gibson and Danny Glover pull pranks and catch bad guys all over LA.

Magnolia (1999) P. T. Anderson's ambitious story about fathers and their children features frogs raining down all over the city of angels, and some very brilliant performances from Tom Cruise, Julianne Moore, Melora Walters, and the rest of a stellar cast.

Mulholland Drive (2001) The latest mind-warp from David Lynch is an endlessly fascinating homage to himself. Mixing the naïve sleuths of *Blue Velvet,* the bizarre denizens of *Twin Peaks,* the reality/fantasy switcheroo of *Lost Highway,* and none of *Dune,* this is Lynch's most provocative film in a long time.

The Player (1992) Robert Altman's insider view of today's movie business stars Tim Robbins as a studio dealmaker who kills a screenwriter. More than a dozen stars make cameo appearances in this ironic, funny, and accurate portrait of the industry.

Pretty Woman (1990) Julia Roberts got her big break in this chic flick playing a woman for hire. Most of the interior scenes were staged at the **Wilshire Beverly Regent** hotel in Beverly Hills, where Roberts's character shacked up with Richard Gere.

Pulp Fiction (1994) Quentin Tarantino's much-imitated film about a day in the life of a bunch of criminals and other ancillary characters takes viewers all around town in the search for a "Royale with Cheese."

Rebel Without a Cause (1955) James Dean became a Hollywood sensation overnight thanks to his powerhouse performance in this film about a troubled teen who gets in over his head. The rumble that forms the centerpiece of the movie takes place at the **Griffith Park Observatory.**

Ruthless People (1986) Designer Lilly Kilvert exploits the surreal juxtapositions of LA architecture to comic effect in this viciously clever satire, starring Bette Midler and Danny DeVito.

Short Cuts (1993) A stark portrayal of virtually every layer of LA society, from the well-to-do to the poor, this intricate three-hour film by Robert Altman is based on a collection of Raymond Carver short stories. The large, all-star cast includes Jennifer Jason-Leigh, Tim Robbins, Madeleine Stowe, Jack Lemmon, Tom Waits, and Lily Tomlin.

Speed (1994) The ultimate proof that LA does indeed have public transportation—though you may not want to take it after watching this action thriller about a bomb-laden bus. Keanu Reeves plays the cop who has to defuse the situation, and Sandra Bullock got rave reviews as a plucky passenger. (A piece of future LA trivia: This is the first Hollywood movie to use the city's new subway system as a setting.)

The Sting (1973) Robert Redford tracks down a scruffy Paul Newman at the carousel on **Santa Monica Pier** in this classic romp about a pair of con men. Directed by George Roy Hill, it won seven Academy Awards, including Best Picture.

10 (1979) At the end of this slight but trend-setting Blake Edwards picture, Dudley Moore watches as Bo Derek, the woman he has been chasing throughout the film, gets married to another man in **All Saints Episcopal Church** in Beverly Hills.

---

into Queen Anne and Eastlake houses, but the boom soon fizzled. The 1300 block of Carroll Avenue is a time capsule of the period, lovingly restored by its residents, who organize an annual house tour in May to raise money for improvements, including the installation of period street lamps. It's a favorite location for film and television crews, but has kept an authentic neighborhood atmosphere, especially on the adjoining streets, where Craftsman bungalows are interspersed with Victorians. For tour information and other events, call the **Carroll Avenue Restoration Foundation** at 213/626.9968. The houses are private residences. ♦ Carroll Ave (between Edgeware Rd E and Edgeware Rd W)

55 DODGER STADIUM

The Dodgers baseball team fled Brooklyn for the sunny skies of LA in 1958, but it wasn't until 1962 that the stadium designed by **Emil Prager** was completed. The home of the "blue-and-white" is located at the heart of Chavez Ravine, and is surrounded by one of the world's largest parking lots. All levels of the stadium are well supplied with food stands selling the famous Dodger Dogs; you might ask for the unadvertised spicy dog—a Polish sausage on an onion roll. And this is one of the only fields in America that sells sushi. The ticket office is in the parking lot. ♦ Ticket office: M-Sa. 1000 Elysian Park Ave (at Stadium Way). 323/224.1400, 877/LAD-EVENTS. www.dodgers.com

---

Restaurants/Clubs: Red | Hotels: Purple | Shops: Orange | Outdoors/Parks: Green | Sights/Culture: Blue

BURBANK/GLENDALE

Beautiful downtown Burbank and environs . . .

Although the small, stubbornly independent Los Angeles County cities of Burbank and Glendale both started life at the turn of the century as quiet, middle-class bedroom communities for settlers from the Midwest, they couldn't be more different from each other today. While Glendale retains the aura of an unobtrusive, rather ordinary hometown, Burbank has boomed into such a thriving center for the entertainment industry that it might accurately be called "New Hollywood."

It is, therefore, difficult to remember that the cities share a common location and a similar history. Both are set at the eastern end of the **San Fernando Valley,** where the **Verdugo Mountains** to the north and the terminus of the **Santa Monica Mountains** at Griffith Park funnel into the Los Angeles Basin and the **San Gabriel Valley.** Both were originally part of **Mission San Fernando,** deeded in 1794 to José Maria Verdugo, the captain of the guards at the San Gabriel Mission. The 433-square-mile **Rancho San Rafael** remained in the Verdugo family until a financial crisis forced foreclosure in 1869. By 1883, 13 Americans had arrived and were farming a site they named Glendale (after the title of a painting one of them had seen), and in 1887

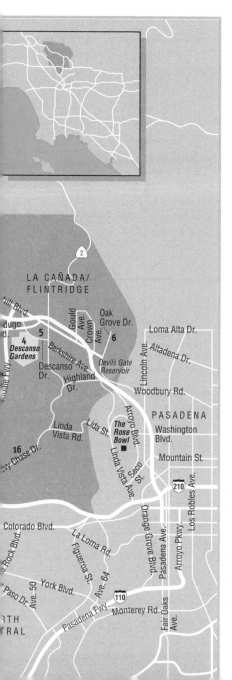

five speculators filed plans for the town. Within the year, real estate promoters founded another small town on the nearby site of the **Rancho La Providencia,** its name borrowed from physician/sheep rancher Dr. David Burbank, the former owner.

The two cities grew slowly until 1904, when the extension of the Pacific Electric Railway brought hundreds of new citizens. In 1906, Glendale became incorporated, and Burbank followed in 1911. **Tropico,** a competing city (and the site of photographer Edward Weston's first studio), sprang up south of Glendale that same year, its main economic activity being strawberry farming. Glendale annexed Tropico in 1918.

Many of Glendale's houses date from the 1920s, when it flourished as a suburban haven; more expensive subdivisions were later constructed on the steep mountain hillsides. Glendale still retains a Main Street USA image on some of its older downtown streets. Minutes from downtown Los Angeles, its southern portion is predominantly commercial, while the northern side has its original residential grid filled with modest stucco houses.

Burbank too has a good number of simple houses attesting to its residential past (although it also has pricey enclaves like **Toluca Lake,** where Bob Hope's has an opulent estate). But even though it's smaller than Glendale, it has a higher profile nationally for two reasons: aircraft construction and the motion picture and television industry. In 1914, Carl Laemmle was the first of the movie moguls to head "over the hill" from Hollywood when he turned a 230-acre chicken ranch adjacent to Burbank into his **Universal City** production facility. The Burbank studio that has been the home of **Warner Bros.** for decades opened in 1918, and **Walt Disney Studios** came in 1940. Meanwhile, Allan Loughead (he later changed the spelling to Lockheed) opened an aircraft manufacturing facility in 1928, an event that eventually spawned a huge aerospace and electronics industry employing tens of thousands. Lockheed's airport eventually became the **Burbank-Glendale-Pasadena Airport,** which was recently renamed **Bob Hope Airport.**

Even with all this, Burbank stayed relatively quiet until the mid-1980s, when a construction boom created the **Media District,** a cluster of studios and industry offices in the area surrounding Warner Bros. Whereas before there had been a three-floor height limit to buildings here, skyscrapers have now been erected. One of the major reasons for all the flurry of business activity is that Burbank imposes no gross receipts tax, as Los Angeles does. Even the long-overlooked downtown area at the base of the northern hills has begun a cleanup program as a result of the increased business presence here.

With this explosion of growth in Burbank's entertainment industry, it hardly seemed to matter when the Lockheed Corporation, formerly the town's largest single employer, left town in 1990. Burbank bounced back almost immediately, and now Lockheed's huge property next to the airport is being turned into more production space for the area's studios. Today, Burbank's fame and fortune rests almost totally in the hands of its major film and television studios—Walt Disney, Warner Bros., Universal, and **NBC.** (Not to be outdone, there are plans in the works for Glendale to become the site of **SKG Dreamworks'** new animation facility.) With the exception of the Disney lot, which is closed to visitors, guided studio tours are available to show "civilians" how all that incredibly lucrative fantasy is created.

1 McGroarty Cultural Arts Center

This historic house is the former home of John Steven McGroarty, a congressman, poet, and historian. It's now operated by the City of Los Angeles as a showcase for mementos and a community arts center. ♦ Free. M-Sa. 7570 McGroarty Terr (just south of McGroarty St). 818/352.5285

2 Theodore Payne Foundation

The preservation and propagation of native California flora are the goals of this organization, which is named for the pioneer California botanist. There's a well-kept nature trail up the hillside and a nursery where seeds and plants are sold at reasonable prices. The book room offers informative literature. ♦ Free. W-Sa. 10459 Tuxford St (between Ledge and Wheatland Aves). 818/768.1802

3 Montrose Bowl

If you like tenpins and want to play where the rich and famous bowl, check out this charming, old-fashioned alley, which opened in 1936. Celebrities often rent the establishment for private parties, among them Tony Danza, Roseanne, Janet Jackson, and David Cassidy—check out their photos on the wall. ♦ 2334 Honolulu Ave (between Ocean View Blvd and Wickham Way). 818/249.3895

4 Descanso Gardens

These 165-acre gardens are famous for their collection of camellias, with more than 600 varieties. The landscaping also includes azaleas, roses, and bulb flowers, all located in a mature California live-oak grove. The variety of plants ensures that there is almost always something blooming. (The camellias bloom from late December through early March.) Tea and cookies are served daily from 11AM to 4PM in a teahouse nestled in a Japanese-style garden featuring a stream that forms waterfalls and pools. If you're in town during the Christmas season, check out the special holiday garden and displays. ♦ Nominal admission. Daily. Tram tours on the hour: Tu-F, 1-3PM; Sa, Su, 11AM-3PM. 1418 Descanso Dr (between Encinas Dr and Verdugo Blvd), La Cañada-Flintridge. 818/952.4400. www.descanso.com

5 MIN'S KITCHEN

★★★$$ This casual Thai restaurant offers a good selection of authentically spicy fare, including seafood talay. The service is friendly, too. ◆ Thai ◆ Daily, lunch and dinner. 1040 Foothill Blvd (at Chevy Chase Dr), La Cañada-Flintridge. 818/790.6074

6 JET PROPULSION LABORATORY (JPL)

More than 50 years ago, a group of **Cal Tech** graduates performed what one described as rather odd experiments in rocketry. Today, the laboratory covers 175 acres of the San Gabriel foothills and has 200 buildings. From the 1958 *Explorer 1*, America's first satellite, to the *Voyager* missions that blazed a trail to the edge of the solar system, it has brought the sights and sounds of space to scientists and into living rooms all over the world. Two-hour guided tours, offered on weekdays, include a multimedia presentation about the facility and a visit to the **Space Craft Museum.** ◆ Fee for tours. Call ahead for tour schedule. 4800 Oak Grove Dr (north of Foothill Blvd), La Cañada-Flintridge. 818/354.2180

7 BOB HOPE AIRPORT

Burbank Airport commissioners recently voted to rename Burbank-Glendale-Pasadena Airport "Bob Hope Airport," marking the fifth time the name has been changed during the airport's 73-year history. Hope, a longtime resident of Toluca Lake, died July 27, 2003, at the age of 100. Apparently he was somewhat envious when Orange County Airport was renamed "John Wayne Airport," and once remarked that it would be nice to have a facility named after him. The powers to be felt it would be a fitting tribute to the entertainer. The airport code will remain "BUR," but new signage will use Hope's name and perhaps likeness.

Six airlines serve a variety of domestic destinations, making this a convenient alternative to LAX for those living on the north side of LA. The airport is located between the Hollywood, Ventura, and Golden State Freeways. Adjoining the terminal are expensive short- and long-term parking lots, which can be entered from Empire Avenue. A free shuttle runs to a 24-hour economy lot located north of the airport on Hollywood Way. Ground transportation to and from the airport is available through **SuperShuttle** (818/556.6600). ◆ 2627 Hollywood Way (between Empire Ave and N San Fernando Blvd). 818/840.8847

8 MEDIA CITY CENTER

You can shop 'til you drop or max out your plastic at more than 100 shops such as **Sears, Gap, Ikea, Idea, Mervyns,** and **Macy's.** There are also movie theaters and restaurants. The promenades between the stores make for interesting strolling. ◆ 201 E Magnolia Blvd (between N First and N Third Sts). 818/566.8617 ⑆

9 BURBANK CITY HALL

This 1941 WPA Moderne classic is distinguished by its tall fretted screen, fountain, and jazzy lobby. ◆ E Olive Ave and N Third St

10 BOULDER BUNGALOWS

These 1929 private bungalows are a good example of the use of boulders, which were popular building materials in the foothills in the 1920s. ◆ E Olive Ave and Ninth St

11 BRAND LIBRARY

Housed in an exotic "El Miradero" (meaning "view from a high place"), built in 1904 for Leslie C. Brand and inspired by the East Indian Pavilion at the 1893 Chicago World's Fair, this is a delightful place to do research or some quiet reading. Brand donated the white-domed Saracenic-style house and grounds to the city of Glendale with the stipulation that it be used as a public library and park. It is currently the art and music branch of the **Glendale Public Library,** housing a gallery for contemporary Southern California art, a lecture and concert auditorium, and an arts-and-crafts studio. The extensive, beautifully landscaped grounds are lovely for picnicking. The Queen Anne–style **Doctor's House,** furnished with period antiques, has been moved onto the grounds and restored. Tours of the Doctor's House can be arranged. ◆ Free. Tu-Th, 1-6PM; F, Sa, 1-5PM. 1601 W Mountain St (at Grandview Ave). 818/548.2051

12 CATALINA VERDUGO ADOBE

Part of the original **Rancho San Rafael,** this single-story adobe was built in 1875 for José Maria Verdugo's blind daughter, Doña Catalina. It is now a private residence. ◆ 2211 Bonita Dr (between Camulos Ave and Opechee Way)

13 GENIO'S

$$$ Genio's upbeat Italian menu changes constantly, but the quality is consistently good. ◆ Italian ◆ M-F, lunch and dinner; Sa, dinner. Reservations recommended for parties of five or more. 1420 W Olive Ave (at S Beachwood Dr). 818/848.0079 ⑆

Restaurants/Clubs: Red | Hotels: Purple | Shops: Orange | Outdoors/Parks: Green | Sights/Culture: Blue

14 Casa Adobe de San Rafael

Thomas A. Sanchez, onetime sheriff of Los Angeles County, lived on Rancho San Rafael. Huge eucalyptus trees planted by Phineas Banning, founder of the Los Angeles Harbor, surround this one-story hacienda. The historic house was restored in 1932 by the city of Glendale. ◆ Free. W, Su, 1-4PM. 1330 Dorothy Dr (between W Stocker and Spencer Sts). No phone

15 First Church of Christ, Scientist

Moore, Ruble, and Yudell designed this beautifully lit church in the Arts and Crafts tradition in 1989. ◆ 1320 N Brand Blvd (between E Randolph and E Mountain Sts)

16 Derby House

This 1926 house by **Lloyd Wright** (Frank's son) is a superb example of the architect's precast concrete-block houses, patterned after pre-Columbian designs. Also in the neighborhood are Lloyd Wright's **Calori House** (3021 E Chevy Chase Dr), a free interpretation of the Spanish Colonial Revival style, and his **Lewis House** (2948 Graceland Way, south of Golf Club Dr). All three are private residences. ◆ 2535 E Chevy Chase Dr (between St. Andrews and Kennington Drs)

17 Safari Inn/Anabelle

$ These surprisingly inexpensive side-by-side small hotels provide lots of comfort and extras in any of their combined 102 oversized rooms (47 at Anabelle, 55 at Safari), all with safes, voice mail, free local calls, iron and board, robes, and mini refrigerator. There's even free shuttle service to the local airport; a great bistro and lounge for breakfast, lunch, dinner, and/or drinks; a fitness room; a swimming pool; and a sun deck—and you can't beat the location: just a stone's throw from Burbank, Disney, NBC Studios, and Warner Bros. studios, seven miles from Universal Studios, and 10 miles from Hollywood. ◆ 1911 W Olive Ave (between N Parish Pl and N Lamer St). 818/845.8586, 800/782.4373, 800/426.0670; fax 818/845.0054. www.westcoasthotels.com/anabelle

18 Gennaro's

★$$$ Discreet décor, honest food (including clam soup, Caesar salad, and osso buco), and a solid wine list are the elements at work here. ◆ Italian ◆ M-F,lunch and dinner; Sa, dinner. Reservations recommended. 1109 N Brand Blvd (between W Dryden and W Stocker Sts). 818/243.6231 &

19 Bob's Big Boy

$ This is the nation's oldest in the acclaimed coffee shop chain, built in 1949 by owner Bob Wian and architect **Wayne McAllister**. Through preservation efforts, it is the only one of the original six not yet demolished. ◆ Coffee Shop ◆ Daily, 24 hours. 4211 Riverside Dr (at W Alameda Ave). 818/843.9334

20 Arnie Morton's the Steak House

★★★$$$$ This Valley version of the Chicago-based nationwide chain dishes otherworldly cuts of beef that almost melt in your mouth in a clubby-looking setting of mahogany paneling, leather banquettes, and walls festooned with celebrity photos and LeRoy Neiman serigraphs. The cooked-to-order double filet mignon or 24-to-48-ounce porterhouse will satisfy any carnivore and perhaps Fido, too (doggie bags are prevalent here). Should you be dining with non-beef lovers, they too can find contentment in the lemon oregano chicken, broiled Block Island swordfish, or Sicilian veal chop. Be sure to order a soufflé for two (chocolate, Grand Marnier, or lemon). The Key lime pie is also good, and the fresh raspberries or strawberries are a lighter choice if you ask them to omit the Sabayon sauce. ◆ Steak House ◆ M-F, lunch and dinner; Sa, Su, dinner. Reservations advised. 3400 W Olive (between Riverside Drive and Alameda), Burbank. 818/238.0424. Also at 435 S La Cienega Blvd (at Colgate Ave), Midtown. 310/246.1501. www.mortons.com

21 NBC Television Studios

Famous as the home of The Tonight Show, where Jay Leno rules as king of the late-night talk shows, this is the largest color facility in the US. Tickets to attend tapings of NBC shows are available, some on a standby basis. Out-of-state visitors should write to: Tickets, NBC Television, 3000 W Alameda Ave, Burbank, CA 91523. No tickets will be sent out of state, but a letter of priority will be returned, which gives you priority at the Burbank ticket line. Because of frequent changes in availability, it is recommended that anyone wishing to attend a taping call the studio for current information. Don't miss the 70-minute tour through a number of soundstages, The Tonight Show studio, the prop warehouse, and the wardrobe department. ◆ Admission; show tickets free. Taping times vary. Tour: M-F. 3000 W Alameda Ave (between Bob Hope Dr and W Olive Ave). General information 818/840.3538, recorded information 818/840.3537

THE BEST

Steve Harvey

"Only in LA" columnist for the Los Angeles Times

Some of my favorite things in Southern California:

Plunking a quarter into the tabletop jukeboxes for two tunes at **Johnnie's Pastrami** in Culver City.

Seeing the grin on my eight-year-old son Jamie's face when **Dodger Stadium** vendor Richard Aller unleashes his trademark cry, "Nuts!"

Dining upstairs at **Philippe's** near Chinatown and wondering if any of the patrons around me know that the many doorways indicate it was probably a brothel a century or so ago.

Playing the eighteenth hole on the **Rancho Park Golf Course** and knowing I'll probably fare better than Arnold Palmer did at the 1961 Los Angeles Open. Probably. (Palmer shot a 12 on that hole.)

Gazing at the statuary at **USC,** including the sculpture of a student in a football uniform gazing at a football atop Bridge Hall, the gargoyle who appears to be giving a one-fingered salute outside Mudd Hall, and the cement monkey thumbing his nose at former chancellor Rufus B. Von "KleinSmid" on the **Student Union Building**—reportedly an architect's sly revenge against the interfering Von KleinSmid.

Showing visitors the photo display of scary-looking characters inside the **Original Pantry Cafe** on Figueroa Street—ex-waiters whose grim visages reinforce the urban myth that the eatery used to hire ex-cons to wait tables.

Spelunking inside the dark caverns of **Acres of Books** in Long Beach, an ancient warehouse with 6.5 miles of shelves on which are balanced 750,000 second-hand tomes, give or take a few Micheners. I never forget my flashlight.

Checking out L.A.'s oldest homicide victim—a reconstructed skeleton of a 9,000-year-old female called **La Brea Woman** at the Page Museum on Wilshire Boulevard. Scientists believe she died from a blow to the head. The crime is unsolved.

22 CIRCLE 'K' STABLES

This equestrian center appeals to couples and families who go to spend the day horseback riding through the picturesque trails of **Griffith Park.** Group rides can be arranged in advance. ♦ Daily. 914 S Mariposa St (south of Riverside Dr). 818/843.9890

23 BAR 'S' STABLES

Another equestrian's delight, this one offers more than 45 horses to mount. It's popular with adults, and children over the age of seven can ride any of the more than 45 horses. Group rides with guides are available. Riding lessons are offered by appointment only. ♦ Daily. 1850 Riverside Dr (between Western Ave and Main St). 818/242.8443

24 HILTON HOTEL

$$$ Situated at the eastern door to the San Fernando Valley, this 18-story, 348-room glass-sheathed luxury hotel perfectly matches Glendale's contemporary skyline and affords panoramic views of the San Gabriel Mountains and downtown Los Angeles. Within is **100 West,** a gourmet restaurant offering a wide selection of continental cuisine, plus three bar/lounges and a three-meal-a-day restaurant. There are convention facilities, too. ♦ 100 W Glenoaks Blvd (at N Brand Blvd). 818/956.5466, 800-HILTONS; fax 818/956.5490. www.hilton.com

25 FALCON THEATRE

Noted producer/director Garry Marshall founded this 130-seat theater in order to "bridge the gap between Hollywood and legitimate theater." Workshops, children's summer acting classes, and assorted performances are offered throughout the year. There's plenty of parking, comfortable seats (bought from a synagogue), and cake by the slice at the concession stand. It's open whenever there's a show, so call ahead. ♦ 4252 Riverside Dr (at N Rose St). 818/955.8004

26 SMOKE HOUSE

★$$ This long-established steak house takes care with the thing that really matters: meat. They age their own and grill it over hickory. ♦ Steak House ♦ Daily, lunch and dinner. Reservations recommended. 4420 Lakeside Dr (at W Olive Ave). 818/845.3731

27 WARNER BROS. STUDIOS

Movie buffs will enjoy this unique museum, offering more than 75 years of cinema memorabilia, including a massive wardrobe section. Visitors can take guided tours through the studios, observing live productions and rehearsals. It's a good idea to wear comfortable walking shoes. In contrast to the **Universal Studios** tours (see page 183), these are an introduction to the actual

Restaurants/Clubs: Red | Hotels: Purple | Shops: Orange | Outdoors/Parks: Green | Sights/Culture: Blue

behind-the-scenes technical workings of the motion picture crafts. A limited amount of photography is permitted, and keep a sharp eye out—you never know who you're going to run into. ♦ Admission. Tours: M-F, 9AM-3PM. Reservations required. 4000 Warner Blvd (corner of Olive Ave and Hollywood Way). 818/954.1744. www.warnerbros.com

28 Kix Banquets

Once a cozy restaurant under the able toque of chef Michael Levin (previously with **La Serre**), Kix is now a full-fledged catering service and well worth considering for any affair. ♦ 343 N Central Ave (at W Lexington Dr). 818/956.7800

29 The Exchange

A unique collection of upscale shops and boutiques, plus fine restaurants and movie theaters. ♦ Bounded by N Louise St and N Brand Blvd, and E Broadway and E Wilson Ave

29 Panda Inn

★$ Very reliable Chinese food is the specialty of this spartan restaurant. ♦ Chinese ♦ Daily, lunch and dinner. 111 E Wilson Ave (between N Maryland Ave and N Brand Blvd). 818/502.1234

29 Far Niente

★$$ The rich menu draws crowds, though the cooking is uneven. Penne Far Niente or the veal chops are winners, though; and the chocolate soufflé is a good bet and should take care of your calorie intake for the week. ♦ Italian ♦ M-F, lunch and dinner; Sa, Su, dinner. Reservations recommended. 204½ N Brand Blvd (between E Wilson and E California Aves). 818/242.3835 ♿

29 The Alex Theatre

The fluted pylon of this dramatic 1939 Streamline Moderne movie house once dominated the cityscape along Glendale's Brand Boulevard. After becoming a victim of the rise of multiplex movie theaters nearby, the theater closed down for a time. Now completely restored, it's the perfect setting for shows, performances, concerts, and movies. ♦ 216 N Brand Blvd (between E Wilson and E California Aves). 818/243.2539

30 Glendale Galleria

This complex of more than 150 shops, boutiques, and restaurants is anchored by **Macy's, Nordstrom,** and **JC Penney.** There's

ample parking. ♦ Daily; M-F until 9PM. S Central Ave (between W Colorado St and W Broadway)

31 Scarantino

★$ Home-cooked minestrone, chicken rollatini, baked zucchini, and spaghetti Napoletana are the top choices here. Bring your best appetite—the portions are generous. ♦ Italian ♦ M-Su, dinner. 1524 E Colorado St (between Lincoln Ave and Lafayette St). 818/247.9777

32 Forest Lawn

Founder Hubert Eaton envisioned "the greenest, most enchanting park you ever saw in your life . . . vistas of sparkling lawns, with shaded arborways and garden retreats and beautiful, noble statuary." The cemetery contains reproductions of **The Church of the Recessional,** modeled after a 10th-century English church; **Wee Kirk o' the Heather,** a copy of a 14th-century church in Glencairn, Scotland; and the **English church** in Thomas Gray's poem "Elegy in a Country Churchyard." All three may be visited when they're not being used for services.

The **Memorial Court of Honor** in the **Great Mausoleum** contains a stained-glass interpretation of Leonardo da Vinci's *The Last Supper.* The world's largest religious painting (measuring 195 feet by 45 feet), *The Crucifixion* by Jan Stykam, is displayed every hour on the hour in the **Hall of Crucifixion-Resurrection.** A companion behemoth, *The Resurrection* by Robert Clark, is revealed every hour on the half-hour in the same hall. The **Court of Freedom** displays objects from American history as well as a 20-by-30-foot mosaic copy of *The Signing of the Declaration of Independence.* Additional attractions include the collection of originals of every coin mentioned in the Bible; the **Court of David,** containing a reproduction of Michelangelo's famous sculpture; and the chance to pay your respects to the earthly remains of Hollywood luminaries such as Clark Gable, W.C. Fields, Nat King Cole, and Jean Harlow. The exact whereabouts of graves are never disclosed by the staff. ♦ Free. Daily. 1712 S Glendale Ave (between San Fernando and Mission Rds). 818/241.4151

33 Campo de Cahuenga

The treaty ending the war between Mexico and the United States was signed here on 13 January 1847 by Lt. Col. John C. Frémont and General Andreas Pico in a historic meeting that opened the way for California's entry into the Union. The declaration was known as the Treaty of Cahuenga, after the building constructed by Thomas Feliz in 1845. The existing structure is a 1923 replica of the original, which was demolished in 1900.

Unfortunately, it's no longer open to the public. ♦ 3919 Lankershim Blvd (between Ventura Blvd and Bluffside Dr)

34 SHERATON UNIVERSAL HOTEL

$$ Casual California-style living and attractive weekend packages add to the appeal of this 436-room hotel. Located smack on the backlot of Universal Studios, the hotel caters to business travelers, groups (there are lots of meeting and banquet facilities), and folks who want to be close to the theme park. Facilities include a casual dining room (with rather mundane food), bar/lounge, outdoor pool, and health club. Rooms are typical Sheraton (save for some spiffier suites and special Club Floor accommodations), with the usual furnishings and amenities. ♦ 333 Universal Terrace Pkwy (east of Lankershim Blvd). 818/980.1212, 800/325.3535; fax 818/985.4980. www.sheraton.com

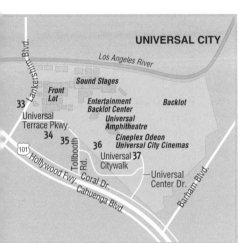

35 HILTON UNIVERSAL CITY AND TOWERS

$$ This attractive, 24-story steel-and-glass tower features 483 spacious, nicely appointed rooms that provide welcome amenities such as coffeemakers, daily newspaper delivery, three phones, iron and ironing board, fax machines, voice mail, writing desks, and safes. In addition to the lobby lounge, with a big-screen television and light menu, the pleasant restaurant serves California cuisine. Facilities include an outdoor pool, fitness center, and 17 meeting rooms. ♦ 555 Terrace Pkwy (east of Lankershim Blvd). 818/506.2500, 800/727.7110; fax 818/509.2058. www.hilton.com &

36 UNIVERSAL STUDIOS HOLLYWOOD

Anticipating the need for a huge backlot, movie mogul Carl Laemmle moved his studio from Hollywood to the undeveloped hills of Universal City in 1915. This visionary augmented his revenues with the first studio tour: For a mere quarter, visitors could watch films being shot. The tour was discontinued when it proved distracting to moviemakers, but in 1964 a tram ride was inaugurated. It has since drawn more than 80 million visitors, making it the most popular manmade attraction in the US after Disney's two theme parks.

Compulsively humorous guides accompany the 45-minute tram tour around the lot, bringing you face-to-face with a 30-foot-high **King Kong** (smell the bananas on his breath!) and the giant mechanical shark from *Jaws.* You will barely survive an avalanche, a collapsing bridge, an earthquake registering 8.3 on the Richter scale (although some Angelenos feel this is in poor taste following the real 1994 quake), and the parting of the Red Sea. Visitors are invited to participate in demonstrations on the **Cinemagic Stage** that reveal the astounding developments in movie magic, from the early years to today's creations by director Steven Spielberg. Experience 10,000 degrees of excitement in **Backdraft,** based on Ron Howard's film about firefighters.

From the tram you can glimpse more than 500 outdoor sets, ranging from the **Bates Mansion** from *Psycho* to the façades for *Back to the Future* and *Kojak.* Artificially aged streets are redressed for every new movie and TV series: here are the New England village; Six Points, Texas; and Old Mexico you've seen a hundred times in different guises on the screen. After the tour, wander at will in the **Entertainment Center,** with its exciting live shows, including the **Wild, Wild West Stunt Show** and **Animal Planet Live!** For more thrills, there's the exciting **Back to the Future** ride (housed in the world's tallest twin-domed **Omnimax Theater**—it's 13 stories high), where passengers sit in their own Delorean cars and take a simulated trip that goes back in time 4,000 years and 25 years into the future. Newer additions include **Nickelodeon Blast; Shrek 4-D,** starring voice-overs by Mike Myers, Eddie Murphy, Cameron Diaz, and John Lithgow; "Spiderman Rocks"—a musical performance portraying Marvel Comics' Peter Parker; "Revenge of the Mummy," a high-speed, breathtaking rollercoaster ride; and **Terminator 2:3D. Jurassic Park** still thrills all ages with its realistically re-created prehistoric dinosaurs. Star look-alikes (from Charlie Chaplin and Marilyn

Monroe to the Phantom of the Opera) will pose with you for photos, and special celebrations are held in the center throughout the year. A **Studio Center** facility features the futuristic **Universal Starway** people-mover plus **Lucy: A Tribute,** open-to-the-public video production stages, and the **Studio C Commissary.** Food stands and gift stores abound, and there are 50 acres of free parking.

For those who hate crowded buses, book the special **VIP Experience,** a personal tour in a comfortable private tram that whisks you hassle-free around the park. It's $129 well spent when you consider the extras: front-of-the-line privileges, reserved show seating, a commemorative photo, and lounge access. Several attractive, money-saving ticket options are also available, such as **Celebrity Annual Pass,** which gives you unlimited visits; **Hollywood CityPass,** which includes entry to Universal as well as other area attractions; **Front Line Pass,** which affords front-of-the-line privileges, reserved show seating, and a souvenir photo, and more, so check them out before you head to the park. Universal also offers free **shuttle service** from Anaheim-area hotels via colorfully decorated 50-passenger buses equipped with video monitors that show highlights of Southern California attractions. In order to get the free ride, tickets to Universal Studios must be pre-purchased at the AirportBus Terminal, 1415 Manchester Avenue (next to Disneyland). ◆ Admission. Call ahead for hours and tours. 100 Universal City Plaza. 818/508.9600 or 818/622.3036. www.universalstudioshollywood.com

37 UNIVERSAL CITYWALK

It's Rodeo Drive, Melrose Avenue, Venice Beach, and Hollywood Boulevard all rolled into one jazzy, neon-lighted retail complex designed by **Jon Jerde** of Jerde Partnership. The bustling open-air promenade houses several dozen individual façades, each dedicated to a different architectural style of Southern California, surrounded by signature animated graphics, towering palm trees, plants, flowers, fountains, Postmodern ornaments, and brightly colored awnings, trellises, and canopies. While some urban critics initially dismissed the structure as an artificial and contrived mishmash, visitors—most of whom are locals or tourists who stroll over from **Universal Studios Hollywood,** the cinema complex, or the **Universal Amphitheatre**—not only love it, many stay until the lights go out. ◆ Universal Center Dr (north of Hollywood Fwy)

Los Angeles is the only city in the United States to have hosted the Summer Olympics twice.

Within Universal CityWalk (there are currently more than 60 venues represented, here are just a few prime examples. Please note, all restaurants are open from 11AM to 10 or 11PM daily):

CAMACHO'S CANTINA

★$ This Mexican restaurant is decorated in the charming style of LA's historic Olvera Street. The atmosphere is everything; the food is ordinary. ◆ Mexican ◆ Daily, lunch and dinner; Su, brunch and dinner. 818/622.3333 ☐

GLADSTONE'S UNIVERSAL

★★$$ Fresh fish and pasta dishes are the specialties at this inland version of the popular Santa Monica establishment **Gladstone's 4 Fish.** Try the New England Maine lobster bake, a two-foot-long tray of lobster, clams, mussels, crab, and vegetables. ◆ Seafood ◆ Daily, lunch and dinner. 818/622.8680 ☐

WIZARDZ

★$$ This club/restaurant offers dinner theater for family audiences. While you eat, you'll be entertained by magicians who are often funny as well as mystifying. The show gets raves from all ages. ◆ American ◆ Daily, lunch and dinner. 818/506.0066 ☐

B. B. KING'S BLUES CLUB

★★$$ This is the second link in this chain of music and supper clubs owned by the blues legend. King reportedly opened this branch because his guitar, Lucille, wanted to go to Hollywood. Patrons can enjoy tasty Southern food like fried catfish and Mississippi mud pie as they listen to the blues music played live by top artists (including, sometimes, King himself). The place keeps late hours—until 1AM during the week and 2AM on weekends. ◆ Southern ◆ M-Sa, lunch and dinner; Su, brunch and dinner. 717/622.5480 ☐

Additional CityWalk restaurants worth sampling (most are walk-in, but reservations can't hurt at the finer establishments) include:

Benita's

F R I T E S

BENITA'S FRITES

★$ When you just feel like snacking on fried finger food, this cozy place, shaped like a gigantic french fry, is just the ticket. They serve some of the best *pommes frites* this side of France, spiced with a variety of sauces (mayo, jalapeño, remoulade, blue cheese, sun-dried tomatoes, peanut curry

CHILD'S PLAY

Seen enough of Disneyland, Knotts Berry Farm, Magic Mountain, and other amusement parks? There are plenty of other delightful, less time-consuming, and more affordable diversions for children visiting Los Angeles. Here are a few of the better ones.

Visit the **La Brea Tar Pits,** a rich deposit of Ice Age fossils. Okay, so they're not dinosaurs, but these mammals were larger than their modern counterparts. Nearby is the **Page Museum,** which displays fossils and models of the animals stuck in the ancient goo.

Soar 100 feet above the ocean on a Ferris wheel or ride an antique horse on the indoor carousel at the newly refurbished **Santa Monica Pier.** Touch sea stars at the **Cabrillo Marine Aquarium** in San Pedro.

Cruise the open Pacific on a **whale-watching tour.** Between December and April the big, beautiful mammals make their way along the LA coast in the company of dolphins, seals, and seabirds. Tours depart from Long Beach and San Pedro Harbors.

Learn about nature and model all kinds of wonderful costumes at the **Los Angeles County Museum of Natural History's Discovery Center.**

Laugh at a puppet show at the **Bob Baker Marionette Theater,** the oldest marionette theater in the US.

Climb aboard a vintage train, plane, or car at **Travel Town** in Griffith Park.

See the many endangered species at the **Los Angeles Zoo.**

Play with the fascinating, interactive nature exhibits at **Kidspace** in Pasadena.

Hear a story, read, and see some favorite illustrations from children's books at **Storyopolis.**

satay, and more). They also offer sugar waffles called *gauffre de liege* (which we warn can be addictive) and beignets topped with powdered sugar. ♦ Fast Food ♦ Daily, from 11ish. 818/505.8834

TU TU TANGO
★★$$ The chimerical vibe at this bohemian-style café makes you feel like dancing. The room is adorned with wall-to-wall artwork and enlivened by paintings in progress, spontaneous song and dance performances, and visits from psychics, tarot card readers, and body painters. The delicious tapas, chicken potpie, and steak with mashed potatoes are best bets. ♦ Spanish/Eclectic ♦ Daily, lunch and dinner. 818/769.2222

HARD ROCK CAFÉ HOLLYWOOD
★★$$ Okay, it's a chain, but you can still find exceptional burgers, shakes, salads, and fries at this zany spot, filled with such rock 'n' roll memorabilia as musical instruments and costumes once used by Jimi Hendrix, the Rolling Stones, the Beatles, Elvis, and Billy Idol, plus ZZ Tops' pumpkin-colored Cadillac convertible rotating from the ceiling. ♦ American. ♦ Daily, lunch and dinner. 818/622.7625

TONY ROMA'S
★★$$ Ribs, ribs, and more baby back ribs are the order of the day here, perfectly

cooked, succulent, and tangy. There are also sandwiches, hot wings, and other choices. ♦ Rib Joint ♦ Daily, lunch and dinner. 818/763.7662

VERSAILLES
★★$$ This is where to stop for a quick bite of delicious Cuban-style garlic-soaked chicken, fried plantains, and other ethnic specialties. The service is *muy rapido* and the food's good.♦ Cuban ♦ Daily, lunch and dinner. 818/505.0093

ALL STAR COLLECTIBLES
The sports memorabilia on sale here includes a football signed by Joe Montana, a hockey stick autographed by Wayne Gretzky, and Mickey Mantle's bat. ♦ M-F, 10AM-9PM; Sa, Su, 10AM-11PM. 818/622.2222

Adjacent to Universal CityWalk:

UNIVERSAL AMPHITHEATRE
The theater presents a full range of entertainment year-round. ♦ 818/980.9421, ticket charge line 213/480.3232

CINEPLEX ODEON UNIVERSAL CITY CINEMAS
One of the world's largest multiplexes has 18 theaters seating 5,600 people and a 1,400-car parking garage. ♦ 818/508.0588

Restaurants/Clubs: Red | Hotels: Purple | Shops: Orange | Outdoors/Parks: Green | Sights/Culture: Blue

PASADENA

Home of the Rose Bowl . . .

Pasadena's claim to fame rests on a single day's activities: the annual New Year's Day **Tournament of Roses Parade** and the post-parade **Rose Bowl** football game. Parade festivities have been held here yearly since 1890, when citizens first draped garlands of fresh blossoms over horse-and-buggy teams and carts in a celebration of the Southland's mild winter climate. The "Battle of the Flowers" originally climaxed with a gala Roman chariot race. The races were thought to be too dangerous, however, so a substitute event— the national football college championship game known as the Rose Bowl—has been held since 1916.

Those who feel overwhelmed by the epic scale and relentlessly wholesome quality of the Roses Parade may enjoy a rival venture, the November **Doo Dah Parade,** which has fast become an institution. The Doo Dah has no floats, no queens (except, perhaps, in drag), and, best of all, no television celebrities. Its stars are the precision briefcase drill team and assorted zanies with lawnmowers, supermarket carts, and odd musical instruments.

Pasadena had a false start in 1873, after Midwestern pioneers established a farming community here, giving it a name that means "Crown of the Valley" in the Chippewa Indian language. The tiny settlement exploded during the land boom of 1886, when Pasadena had 53 active real estate agencies for a population of less than 4,500 people. Promoters arranged five daily trains to Los Angeles and a special Theater Express to the downtown area three nights a week. Salespeople advertised the region's sunny, healthful climate, hotels were quickly erected, and get-rich-quick schemes proliferated. The city incorporated in 1886, but the boom collapsed, the population dwindled, and once-clamored-for town lots grew weeds. But soon the clear air, citrus blooms, and mountain views (now but a memory) began to draw a steady stream of affluent Easterners. The **Ritz-Carlton Huntington Hotel & Spa** and the **Hotel Green** (now converted to apartments) are reminders of an era when this was a fashionable winter resort. And the Craftsman bungalows, designed by architects Charles and Henry Greene, evidence that some travelers stayed on.

Pasadena's population increased through several small booms in the 1920s, until it became the most important suburb of Los Angeles. LA's first freeway—the 1942 **Arroyo Seco Parkway**—stimulated commuter traffic. Today, Pasadena has 140,000 residents, a mixture of old money to the south and low income to the north, along with opulent houses, lush gardens, and outstanding scientific and cultural resources.

1 SAN GABRIEL MOUNTAINS

True wilderness is found in the San Gabriel Mountains, which were inaccessible to anyone but a seasoned adventurer until 1935 when the **Angeles Crest Highway** (Route 2) opened. The highway begins in La Cañada-Flintridge and leads to the 691,000-acre **Angeles National Forest.** Some of the more remote sections of the region have colorful histories. The discovery of placer gold deposits triggered a small gold rush as early as 1843 near the east and west forks of the San Gabriel River. Gold fever revived during the Depression, when jobless Southern Californians improvised camps and panned for hardscrabble gold with kitchen utensils. During the boom of the 1880s, Angelenos made the horse trail up 5,710-foot Mount Wilson a favorite vacation spot. Professor T.S.C. Lowe opened the **Mount Lowe Railroad** in 1893 to bring delighted tourists 3,000 feet up the steep incline to the mock-Alpine hamlet near Echo Mountain's peak. Fire destroyed the railway, but the famous **Mount Wilson Observatory** (free; 626/793.3100) still stands near the peak of the mountain. The observatory grounds and an astronomical photo exhibition are open Saturday and Sunday.

The San Gabriels are popular for hiking, bicycling, fishing, bird-watching, and, in winter, a variety of snow sports. The quiet trails are seldom crowded. There are great contrasts in vegetation and terrain; water makes all the difference (Crystal Lake is one of the most spectacular sights). One moment you may be walking in a fern dell, the next taking in an arid chaparral landscape. Wildflowers abound, including poppies, Indian paintbrush, lupines, and wild tiger lilies. Skunk cabbage grows near springs, and pine trees flourish at altitudes of more than 5,000 feet. Three levels of ranges add variety to hiking pleasure. The front slopes near **Altadena** are good for day hikes, with well-maintained trails leading through waterfalls and pools and near cliffs and ravines. In places such as **Bear Canyon,** the middle ranges take you to the last reserves of mountain lions and bighorn sheep in Southern California. At the top of the range, many of the slopes are stark—a rugged rock-climber's paradise. One of the most challenging of the higher areas is 10,064-foot Mount San Antonio, or **Old Baldy,** the county's highest peak. Much is virgin territory, so the thrill of trailblazing is still available. Visitors are advised to stop at the **Red Box Ranger Station** for trail and road information.

Restaurants/Clubs: Red | Hotels: Purple | Shops: Orange | Outdoors/Parks: Green | Sights/Culture: Blue

To phone ahead, dial 0 for the operator and ask for Red Box Ranger Station no. 2.

2 EATON CANYON COUNTY PARK AND NATURE CENTER

You can see native California plants at this 184-acre park just east of central Pasadena. The small museum contains displays of the area's ecology and gives leaflets for self-guided tours through the canyon. The **Naturalist's Room** houses live animals and natural history objects.♦ Free. Museum and park: daily. Naturalist's Room: Sa. Docent-led nature walks: Sa, 9AM. 1750 N Altadena Dr (between New York Dr and Canyon Close Rd). 626/821.3246

3 ART CENTER COLLEGE OF DESIGN

Established in 1930, the art center has an international reputation as a school of industrial design, photography, graphics, illustration, film, and fine arts. The Miesian steel-frame bridge that spans a ravine and now is an integral feature of the college was designed by Craig Ellwood and opened in 1976. The hilly 175-acre campus is an idyllic setting for artworks. Changing exhibitions of work by students and established artists and designers are held in the center's gallery. ♦ Campus and gallery: Tu, W, F-Su, noon-5PM; Th, noon-9PM. 1700 Lida St (between Pegfair La and Figueroa St). 626/396.2200

4 THE ROSE BOWL

Since 1902, the Midwest has met the West here in the most famous college football match of all, and **UCLA** plays its home games here. Recent highlights among the special events held here include the **1993 Super Bowl, 1994 World Cup** soccer finals, and the **1999 Women's Soccer Finals.** ♦ 1001 Rose Bowl Dr (just north of N Arroyo Blvd). 626/577.3100

Los Angeles' Wins in the Rose Bowl:

1923	USC over Penn State	14-2
1932	USC over Tulane	21-12
1933	USC over Pittsburgh	35-0
1939	USC over Duke	7-3
1940	USC over Tennessee	14-0
1944	USC over Washington	25-0
1945	USC over Tennessee	25-0
1953	USC over Wisconsin	7-0
1963	USC over Wisconsin	42-37
1966	UCLA over Michigan	14-12
1968	USC over Indiana	14-3
1970	USC over Michigan	10-3
1973	USC over Ohio State	42-17
1975	USC over Ohio State	18-17
1976	UCLA over Ohio State	23-10

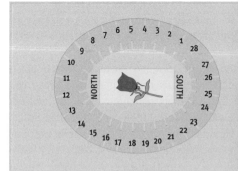

1977	USC over Michigan	14-6
1979	USC over Michigan	17-10
1980	USC over Ohio State	17-16
1983	UCLA over Michigan	24-14
1984	UCLA over Illinois	45-9
1985	USC over Ohio State	20-17
1986	UCLA over Iowa	45-28
1990	USC over Michigan	17-10

At the Rose Bowl:

ROSE BOWL FLEA MARKET

This bargain-picker's paradise offers everything from junk to antiques. ♦ Admission. Second Sunday of every month. 323/560.7469

4 KIDSPACE MUSEUM

Designed for children ages 2 to 12, the museum moved into a spiffy new, $13.5 million complex in 2004. Designed by LA architect **Michael Maltzan,** the 18,000-square-foot facility features galleries and a theater in which to showcase the interactive exhibits. ♦ 480 N Arroyo Blvd (at Seco St, next door to the Rose Bowl). Call for hours, which vary by season. 626/449.9144

5 JAMES IPEKJIAN

Cabinetmaker James Ipekjian sells handcrafted reproductions of **Greene and Greene** furniture. Call ahead for an appointment to visit the showroom. ♦ 768 N Fair Oaks Ave (between E Orange Grove Blvd and Painter St). 626/792.5025

6 PROSPECT BOULEVARD

The stone entrance gates at Orange Grove and Prospect Boulevards were designed by **Charles** and **Henry Greene** in the 1910s. Along this boulevard lined with camphor trees is the Greenes' 1906 **Bentz House** at No. 657. At No. 781 is **Alfred** and **Arthur Heineman's Hindry House,** half hidden behind shrubbery. A narrow street entered from the southwest side of the boulevard is Prospect Crescent, which leads to **Frank Lloyd**

Wright's 1923 **Millard House** at No. 645. (The studio house near the pond was designed by Wright's son Lloyd in 1926.) The house is set in a ravine, and there's a better view from below on Rosemont Avenue. All are private residences. ♦ Between N Orange Grove Blvd and Seco St

7 GAMBLE HOUSE

This recently restored 1908 house designed by **Charles** and **Henry Greene** is a masterpiece of craftsmanship and planning, from the polished teak and original furnishings to the cross-ventilation that provides natural air conditioning. The architects and designers have appointed it beautifully with tables, chairs, and Tiffany glassworks. The best known of the Craftsman-style bungalows was commissioned by Cincinnati's Gamble family (of Proctor & Gamble), who, like other affluent sun-starved Easterners, wintered here at the turn of the century. The USC School of Architecture now maintains it for visiting scholars. Docents lead public tours, pointing out the Japanese-influenced deep overhanging roofs and crafted woodwork. Next door, at 2 Westmoreland Place, is the **Cole House,** also designed by the Greenes; this 1906 house is now part of the Neighborhood Church. ♦ Admission. Tours: Th-Su, noon-3PM. 4 Westmoreland Pl (just north of Arroyo Terr). 626/793.3334. www.gamblehouse.org

7 ARROYO TERRACE

West of Westmoreland Place is the loop of Arroyo Terrace, with its colony of bungalows designed by **Charles** and **Henry Greene.** All are worth noting, although some are in better condition than others. They are: **Charles Sumner Greene House** (1906) at no. 368; **White Sisters House** (1903) at no. 370, home of Charles Greene's sisters-in-law; **Van Rossen–Neill House** (1903, 1906) at no. 400, which has a wall of burnt clinker brick and Arroyo boulders; **Hawkes House** (1906) at no. 408, which resembles a Swiss chalet; **Willet House** (1905) at no. 424, a remodeled bungalow; and, at no. 440, the **Ranney House** (1907). Also notable is the Greenes' **Duncan-Irwin House** (1900, 1906), which is close by at 240 North Grand Avenue. All are private residences. ♦ Between Westmoreland Pl and Live Oaks Ave

8 PASADENA MUSEUM OF HISTORY

Designed by **Robert Farquhar** in 1905, this neoclassical residence was formerly the home of the Finnish consul. The main floor retains its original furnishings, including antiques and

paintings, while the basement houses a display of memorabilia, paintings, and photographs chronicling Pasadena's history. The adjacent library is open to researchers as well as the general public. The beautifully landscaped grounds (four acres total) encompass a wandering stream with several pools, as well as the **Sauna House,** a replica of a 16th-century Finnish farmhouse with a display of Finnish folk art. This museum is also known as the **Fenyes Mansion.** ♦ Admission. Th-Su, 1-4PM. 470 W Walnut St (at N Orange Grove Blvd). 626/577.1660

9 NORTON SIMON MUSEUM

One of America's greatest collections of European, East Indian, and Southeast Asian art is housed in this 1969 **Ladd and Kelsey** building. Norton Simon installed his holdings at these spacious galleries after the failure of the Pasadena Museum of Modern Art (a good idea later reborn as **MOCA**). Notable pieces include Old Master paintings and drawings by Rubens, Rembrandt, Raphael, Botticelli, and Zurbarán; Goya etchings; Impressionist paintings and sculpture, including works by Cézanne, Toulouse-Lautrec, Renoir, and van Gogh; a large Degas selection, including an exquisite series of small bronze dancers; and works by Picasso, Matisse, and the German Expressionists. So rich is the permanent collection that outstanding exhibitions can be generated in-house without recourse to outside loans. The museum shop has one of the finest selections of art books in the city. The museum was renovated in 2000 under the direction of noted architect **Frank Gehry,** who reconfigured the galleries and added a seven-acre sculpture garden. ♦ Admission. W-Th, noon-6PM, F, Sa-M, noon-9PM. 411 W Colorado Blvd (between N Pasadena Ave and N Orange Grove Blvd). 626/449.6840. www.nortonsimon.org

10 COLORADO STREET BRIDGE

Pasadena's 1913 *Pont du Gard* has graceful concrete arches that span the Arroyo Seco. A local and national landmark, the bridge was closed in 1987 for a $27.4 million restoration and reopened in 1994. Dubbed "Suicide Bridge" because of the number of people (approximately 100) who have jumped to their deaths 160 feet below, it features a new spiked suicide-prevention fence and replicas of the original ornamental balustrade and lampposts. ♦ W Colorado Blvd (between Arroyo Blvd and N San Rafael Ave)

11 PASADENA CITY COLLEGE

The two-year accredited college is part of the **Pasadena Area Community District.** ♦ 1570

Restaurants/Clubs: Red | Hotels: Purple | Shops: Orange | Outdoors/Parks: Green | Sights/Culture: Blue

E Colorado Blvd (between S Bonnie and S Hill Aves). 626/585.7123

12 ACAPULCO

★$ The crab enchilada is famous at this casual spot, which offers imaginative interpretations of Mexican favorites. ♦ Mexican ♦ Daily, lunch and dinner. 2936 E Colorado Blvd (at El Nido Ave). 626/795.4248

13 TOURNAMENT HOUSE AND WRIGLEY GARDENS

This Italian Renaissance–style house, once owned by chewing-gum magnate William Wrigley Jr., is surrounded by a rolling lawn and well-kept gardens. An example of the grand mansions found on the boulevard in the first decades of the century, it is now the headquarters of the Tournament of Roses Association. ♦ Garden: daily. Tours: Tu, 2PM Feb-Aug. 391 S Orange Grove Blvd (between Lockehaven and Arbor Sts). 626/449.4100

14 CALIFORNIA INSTITUTE OF TECHNOLOGY

Albert Einstein once taught at this institute, which is world-famous for physics, engineering, and astronomy. The faculty and alumni have won 26 Nobel prizes, and the school has spawned a plethora of high-tech firms in the area. It is a far cry from Throop University, its forerunner, founded in 1891 to "foster higher appreciation of the value and dignity of intelligent manual labor." Architect **Bertram Goodhue** laid out the plan of the institute in 1930, which was inspired by a medieval scholastic cloister. Other buildings of that era were designed by **Gordon Kaufman,** notably the Spanish Renaissance **Atheneum Faculty Club** at 551 South Hill Avenue. ♦ Campus tours: M-F, 2PM Jan-June, Sept-Nov. Architectural tours: 11AM the fourth Th of every month (reservations required). 1201 E California Blvd (between S Hill and S Wilson Aves). 626/395.6327

Within the California Institute of Technology:

BECKMAN & RAMO AUDITORIUM

This auditorium hosts lectures, concerts, films, plays, and dance performances. ♦ 332 S Michigan Ave (just south of E Del Mar Blvd). Schedule and tickets 626/395.4562

15 THE RAYMOND

★★★$$$ Carefully prepared and refreshingly homespun food is served in this charming turn-of-the-century California bungalow, once home to the Raymond Hotel caretakers. The menu changes weekly but usually includes

veal, chicken, and beef entrées; steamed vegetables; and delicious, old-fashioned desserts. Colorfully landscaped patios offer quiet, bucolic dining. ♦ American ♦ Tu-Su, lunch and dinner. Reservations recommended. 1250 S Fair Oaks Ave (at Columbia St), South Pasadena. 626/441.3136

16 RITZ-CARLTON HUNTINGTON HOTEL & SPA

$$$$ This 392-room tile-roofed resort hotel from Pasadena's golden age offers six bungalows in a turn-of-the-century country club/estate setting and is home to the state's first Olympic-size pool. The two-story **Clara Vista Cottage,** designed as an executive retreat, features two bedrooms with private baths, full-size desks, and two-line phones, a living room, private study, kitchen, and wet bar. All the rooms are wonderful, with signature Ritz-Carlton appointments and top-notch service, be it room service, housekeeping, concierge assistance, or any personal need. William Hetrich designed the original gardens. A gracious covered picture bridge was later recreated on the 23-acre site at the base of the San Gabriel Mountains. Highlights include the full-service **Amadeus Spa,** a world-class facility offering the gamut of salubrious treatments, wet rooms, eucalyptus steam and shower, a private rest area, complimentary soft drinks, and a full fitness room (626/578.3404; email: amadeus@pacbell.net; www.amadeusspa. com). Believe us, this is one super spa. There are also luncheon garden tours led by a gardener, a traditional clublike grill that offers nightly entertainment, and old-fashioned tea dancing on Sunday afternoon. ♦ 1401 S Oak Knoll Ave (at Wentworth Ave). 626/568.3900, 800/241.3333; fax 626/792.6613. www.ritzcarlton.com

17 BRISTOL FARMS

You'll find the freshest produce and fish, a dazzling array of wines and groceries, and exemplary service at this four-star market. ♦ Daily, until 9PM. 606 Fair Oaks Ave (at Grevelia St), South Pasadena. 626/441.5450. Also at 837 Silver Spur Rd (between Crenshaw and Hawthorne Blvds), Rolling Hills Estates. 310/541.9157

18 BUSTER'S ICE CREAM & COFFEE STOP

★$ From blended yogurts to frosted mocha drinks, this place whips up a variety of delicious beverages to enjoy with the mellow live music that's featured five nights a week. Just off the railroad tracks, it's worth a visit, even with the occasional rattling as a locomotive rumbles by. ♦ Coffeehouse ♦ Daily; Tu-Su until 11PM. 1006 Mission St (between Fairview and Meridian Aves), South Pasadena. 626/441.0744

19 RESTAURANT SHIRO

★★★$$ Chef Hideo Yamashiro left **Cafe Jacoulet** to open this storefront restaurant, a great boon to the neighborhood. The freshness of the fish and the delicacy of the sauces have won acclaim. Standouts include seafood salad, ravioli stuffed with shrimp and salmon mousse, and sizzling catfish. ◆ French/Japanese ◆ W-F, lunch and dinner; Sa, Su, dinner. Reservations required. 1505 Mission St (at Mound Ave), South Pasadena. 626/799.4774. www.shirorestaurant.com

20 MILTIMORE HOUSE

Irving Gill designed this purified Mission Revival house in 1911. It is a private residence. ◆ 1301 Chelten Way (between Edgewood Dr and Monterey Rd), South Pasadena

21 PASADENA PUBLIC LIBRARY

The Renaissance-style building at the north end of the **Civic Center** axis was designed by **Hunt and Chambers** in 1927. ◆ Daily. 285 E Walnut St (between N Euclid and Garfield Aves). 626/744.4052

22 ARMORY CENTER FOR THE ARTS

Contemporary art shows are held at the center, which also has workshops offering kids hands-on experience of the arts. ◆ Free. Daily. 145 N Raymond Ave (between E Holly and E Walnut Sts). 626/792.5101

23 PLAZA LAS FUENTES

The $200 million, six-acre development by Maguire Thomas Partners, comprising a hotel, offices, retail, and restaurants to the east of **City Hall,** was designed by **Moore, Ruble, and Yudell** in 1989. In a break with the concrete boxes that have proliferated in recent years, the architects integrated buildings and gardens, drawing on the Beaux Arts spirit of the **Civic Center** as well as the Hispanic tradition. Pedestrian spaces are enlivened by fountains, with low buildings and plantings to soften the impact. Lawrence Halprin was the landscape architect. ◆ Bounded by N Los Robles and N Euclid Aves, and E Colorado Blvd and E Walnut St

Within Plaza Las Fuentes:

THE WESTIN PASADENA

$$$ The 350 rooms and suites at this luxury hotel offer low weekend rates. Within the hotel is **The Oaks on the Plaza** restaurant, which serves California specialties in a grand space. The bar offers tapas from 4 to 7PM and light

dining until midnight. ◆ 626/792.2727; fax 626/795.7669

24 PASADENA CITY HALL

John Bakewell Jr. and **Arthur Brown Jr.** designed this handsome domed Baroque structure at the junction of two broad avenues in 1925. (The same firm designed San Francisco's City Hall.) Equally impressive are the formal courtyard garden and fountain. ◆ 100 N Garfield Ave (between E Union and Ramona Sts). 626/744.4000

25 PASADENA MUSEUM OF CALIFORNIA ART

The newest addition to Pasadena's cultural scene was made possible by a $3 million gift from art collectors Bob and Arlene Oltman and local residents. The 30,000-square-foot, three-story museum features a dramatic entrance enhanced by fluctuating natural lighting from an overhead oculus. The second floor provides 8,000 square feet of gallery space and a bookstore. The Oltmans actually live in a 5,000-square-foot residence on the third level, while a rooftop terrace offers accessibility to the public. All exhibits are dedicated to in-state artists, architects, and designers from 1850 to the present. ◆ W-Su ◆ Admission. 490 East Union St (at N Los Robles Ave, just east of Pacific Asia Museum). 626/568.3665

26 PATAKAN

★$ Because of its obscure location on a one-way street, many customers stumble onto this Thai restaurant by accident. Winning entrées include *kang ka-lee* (a yellow curry with chicken, coconut milk, and vegetables) and any of the three ways they prepare pompano fish. ♦ Thai ♦ M-F, lunch and dinner; Sa, dinner. Reservations recommended. 43 E Union St (between N Raymond and N Fair Oaks Aves). 626/449.4418

26 YUJEAN KANG'S

★$$ Dine on a variety of gourmet Chinese dishes such as tea-smoked duck in black bean sauce and catfish with kumquats and passionfruit sauce—served sparingly but elegantly, much like the setting. ♦ Chinese ♦ Daily, lunch and dinner. Reservations recommended. 67 N Raymond Ave (between E Union and E Holly Sts). 626/585.0855. Also in West Hollywood at 8826 Melrose Ave (between La Cienega and Robertson Blvds). 310/288.0806

26 DOMENICO'S

★$$ A family-run establishment for more than 30 years, this pizzeria offers pies with fresh toppings. ♦ Pizza ♦ Tu-Su, until 10PM. 82 N Fair Oaks Ave (between Union and Holly Sts). 626/449.1948

26 XIOMARA

★★$$ Chef/owner Xiomara Ardolina bestows her culinary talents on this establishment, creating original dishes with a Cuban flair. Popular choices include ahi tuna, lamb malanga, Chilean sea bass on corn *guizo* (stew), and seared pork hash. ♦ California/French ♦ M-F, lunch and dinner; Sa, dinner. Reservations recommended. 69 N Raymond Ave (between E Union and E Holly Sts). 626/796.2520

27 MI PIACE

★★$ This restaurant is always busy, and with good reason. The excellent and well-priced Italian fare is served in a cheerful, bright, high-ceilinged interior. ♦ Italian ♦ Daily, lunch and dinner. Reservations recommended for four or more. 25 E Colorado Blvd (between N Raymond and N Fair Oaks Aves). 626/795.3131

Pasadena issues more than 400 film permits a year and has hosted shoots for such recent movies as *Hocus Pocus, Love Affair,* and *Significant Others.* Gamble House in Pasadena posed as Christopher Lloyd's *Back to the Future* digs, and *Beverly Hills Cop I* and *II, War of the Roses,* and *Witches of Eastwick* all filmed in houses on the campus of the California Institute of Technology. Even the popular 1960s TV sitcom *The Beverly Hillbillies* was shot in a house on Pasadena's Oakland Avenue because 20th Century-Fox couldn't find a house in Beverly Hills that it thought looked enough like Beverly Hills.

27 AKBAR

★★$ This funky little spot dishes out great tandoori fare to eat in or take out. Best bets are coco lamb done in coconut sauce flavored with fennel, *bhartha* (roasted eggplant sautéed with tomatoes and peas), and tandoori-grilled Chilean sea bass marinated in herbs. And for dessert, *kesari kheer* (rice pudding infused with saffron, nuts, and raisins) and mango cheesecake are sure winners. There's a surprisingly good wine list with personal selections from chef Avinash Kapoor. ♦ Indian ♦ Daily, lunch and dinner. 44 N Fair Oaks Ave (at Union St). 626/577.9916; fax 626/577.9919. Also in Marina Del Rey at 3115 Washington Blvd (one block west of Lincoln). 310/574.0666; fax 310/821.6686 ♿

28 PACIFIC ASIA MUSEUM

Grace Nicholson commissioned the firm of **Mayberry, Marston, and Van Pelt** in 1924 to design a traditional Northern Chinese building to house her extensive collection of Far Eastern art. The building, an imaginative amalgam of rare beauty and serenity, features changing exhibitions on the arts of the Far East and Pacific Basin. ♦ Admission. W-Su. 46 N Los Robles Ave (between E Colorado Blvd and E Union St). 626/449.2742

28 WARNER BUILDING

Don't miss the sensational Art Deco frieze of seashells on this 1927 building. ♦ 481 E Colorado Blvd (between N Oakland and N Los Robles Aves)

29 THE ICE HOUSE

You just might catch tomorrow's top talent at this friendly night spot, as this is the place where Lily Tomlin, Robin Williams, and Steve Martin got their starts. Blues musicians perform live at a small club. ♦ Cover. Shows: Tu-Su. Club: Th-Sa, until 2AM. 24 N Mentor Ave (between E Colorado Blvd and E Union St). 626/577.1894

30 OLD PASADENA

Who would expect to see the kind of action usually reserved for Melrose Avenue or Westwood Village in this bastion of old money? Though more tempered than their Westside counterparts, the streets of Old Pasadena bustle around small-scale vintage buildings, with several cinema complexes and interesting gift and antiques stores sharing the spotlight. Both sides of **Colorado Boulevard** between Arroyo Parkway and Pasadena Avenue are lined with small boutiques and eateries. Along **Holly Street,** shops sell antiques and memorabilia.

30 TANNER MARKET

This quaint, rehabilitated retail complex features more than 25 boutiques and restaurants that anchor the west end of Old Pasadena. ◆ W Colorado Blvd and S Pasadena Ave

Within Tanner Market:

OLD TOWN BAKERY

Many Southland restaurants and coffeehouses come to this bakery to purchase mouthwatering sweets such as peanut-butter-cup cheesecake, three-layer chocolate-raspberry cake, and double-crusted Snickerdoodle. ◆ Daily, until 11PM. 166 W Colorado Blvd. 626/792.2993

CIAO YIE

30 CIAO YIE

★$$ Though the blending of Occidental and Oriental spices and flavors isn't novel in this town, you'll find some refreshing tastes in kung pao chicken pizza, Shanghai ravioli, and mu shu duck calzone. ◆ International ◆ Daily, lunch and dinner. Reservations recommended. 54 W Colorado Blvd (between S Fair Oaks and S De Lacey Aves). 626/578.7501

30 Z GALLERIE

An affordable designer collection of gifts and home accessories is sold here, along with a wide selection of poster art. ◆ Daily, until 10PM. 42 W Colorado Blvd (between S Fair Oaks and S De Lacey Aves). 626/578.1538. Also at 230 Pine Ave (between E Maple Way and E Third St), Long Beach. 562/491.0766

31 SPENCER'S

★★$$$ If you have a craving for escargots, veal sweetbreads, goat cheese–stuffed swordfish, and cherries jubilee, this is the spot. The menu's Old World quirky and the L-shaped room is inviting. There's a fun patio with a wine bar, too. ◆ Continental ◆ M-Sa, lunch and dinner. Reservations suggested. 70 S Raymond Ave (at Green St). 626/441.3136 ⑤

31 DISTANT LANDS

Run by Adrian Kalvinskas, this traveler's bookstore offers maps, videos, and more than 8,000 book titles. ◆ Daily; F, Sa, until 9PM. 54 S Raymond Ave (between E Green St and E Colorado Blvd). 626/449.3220

32 PASEO COLORADO

This three-block-long indoor/outdoor shopping/condominium complex has everything under one urban roof, such as a **Macy's** department store, a multi-screen movie theater, a gourmet market, a health club, sidewalk cafés, and restaurants. ◆ East Colorado Blvd (between S Los Robles and S Marengo Aves). 626/795.8891. www.paseocolorado.com

33 PASADENA PLAYHOUSE

Founded in 1917, this theater flourished for more than 50 years, nurturing the careers of Gene Hackman, Kim Stanley, William Holden, and other leading actors. After closing in 1969 and staying dark for nearly 20 years, the 1925 building was elaborately restored and reopened in 1986 with Shaw's *Arms and the Man* in the proscenium-arch auditorium. There is also an Equity-waiver performance space. Both are flourishing under artistic director Sheldon Epps. Behind-the-scenes tours are led by theater alumni. ◆ 39 S El Molino Ave (at E Green St). Tickets 626/792.8672

34 BISTRO 45

★★$$ Ensconced in a 1939 Art Deco building, this unpretentious and elegant California-style French bistro is light and airy by day and romantic by night. Food served with artistry fits the bistro mold: pan-roasted sweetbreads, roasted lamb, and a hearty cassoulet with fresh sausage, duck, rabbit, and white beans. ◆ California/French ◆ Tu-F, lunch and dinner; Sa, Su, dinner.

Restaurants/Clubs: Red | Hotels: Purple | Shops: Orange | Outdoors/Parks: Green | Sights/Culture: Blue

Reservations recommended. 45 S Mentor Ave (between E Green St and E Colorado Blvd). 626/795.2478

35 PASADENA POST OFFICE

Oscar Wenderoth designed this Italian Renaissance building in 1913. ♦ 1022 E Colorado Blvd (at S Catalina Ave)

36 AUX DELICES

Old Town residents get an early start with a variety of croissants and pastries at this French-style bakery and café. ♦ Daily, until 10PM. 16 W Colorado Blvd (between S Fair Oaks and S De Lacey Aves). 626/796.1630

36 PENNY LANE

Shop here for new, used, and cutout CDs, tapes, and LPs. ♦ Daily, until 11PM. 12 W Colorado Blvd (between S Fair Oaks and S De Lacey Aves). 626/564.0161

37 HOTEL GREEN APARTMENTS

This is one of the two remaining examples of Pasadena's grand hotel era (the other is the **Ritz-Carlton Huntington Hotel**). Architect **Frederick Roehrig**'s Moorish and Spanish Colonial design is an immense extension to the older Hotel Green structure, originally known as the Webster Hotel, built in 1890 for promoter E.C. Webster and patent medicine manufacturer Colonel G.G. Green. In the 1920s, Roehrig more than tripled the hotel's size with elaborate bridged and arched additions, including the domed and turreted **Castle Green Apartments** (built across the street in 1897), and these apartments, which have been renovated and modernized as a senior citizens' home. ♦ 50 E Green St (between S Raymond and S Fair Oaks Aves)

38 PASADENA CIVIC AUDITORIUM

Built in 1932, this hall is the attractive home of the **Pasadena Symphony Orchestra,** music and dance events, and Broadway musicals. Don't miss a concert that showcases the mighty 1920s Moeller, the largest theater organ west of the Mississippi. The Italian

A 450-foot-long, 90-foot-high medieval castle was erected in Pasadena in 1922 for Douglas Fairbanks's version of *Robin Hood;* it was the largest single structure ever built as a movie set.

On 30 December 1940, a six-mile stretch of the Arroyo Seco Parkway, known today as the Pasadena Freeway, was opened as the first commuter freeway of Los Angeles. It was followed by the Hollywood Freeway, completed in 1947, linking LA with the San Fernando Valley.

Renaissance building is the centerpiece of a convention center built of concrete in a disagreeably brutal style in 1974. ♦ 300 E Green St (between S Euclid and S Marengo Aves). 626/449.7360

39 MIYAKO

★$$ The house specialty is sukiyaki, a mixture of meat and vegetables cooked in a seasoned sauce, prepared at your table by a kimono-clad waitress. Traditional Japanese décor enhances the meal. ♦ Japanese ♦ M-F, lunch and dinner; Sa, Su, dinner. Reservations recommended. 139 S Los Robles Ave (between Cordova and E Green Sts). 626/795.7005

40 HILTON PASADENA

$$ This 13-story, 291-room hotel is conveniently located within walking distance of Old Pasadena, the convention center, and the business district. **Trevos,** an Italian restaurant located inside the hotel, serves a nice Sunday brunch. ♦ 168 S Los Robles Ave (between Cordova and El Dorado Sts). 626/577.1000, 800/445.8667; fax 626/584.3148. www.hilton.com

41 CELESTINO OF PASADENA

★★★$$$ This neighborhood trattoria (formerly **Il Pastaio**), created by Celestino Drago and his three brothers, Giacomino, Calogero, and Tanino, specializes in antipasto, carpaccio, fresh and dried pasta, and risotto. Signature dishes include pumpkin lasagna, chestnut soup with sautéed duck liver, and roasted rabbit in sweet-and-sour sauce. All pastas and desserts, like the amazing hot chocolate ravioli with chocolate sorbet, are made in-house. The dining room is warmly decorated with antique pine furnishings, forest green walls, and touches of green-and-black marble. A charming patio provides alfresco dining. ♦ Italian ♦ M-F, lunch and dinner; Sa, dinner. 141 S Lake Ave (between Cordova and E Green Sts). 626/795.4006 ઇ

42 LAKE AVENUE

One of Pasadena's main shopping streets, it has numerous specialty shops clustered around **Macy's.** Three arcades are notable: **The Commons** (quality food stores); **The Colonnade** and **Burlington Arcade** (elegant imports); and **Haskett Court** (flowers, toys, and curios from "merrie England"). The Shops on Lake Avenue, a 333,766-square-foot high-end shopping center, opened in the spring of 2003, bringing 27 more shops and restaurants to the area. ♦ Corner of Lake Ave and Del Mar Blvd. ♦ Eclectic ♦ 110 S Lake

Ave (between Cordova and E Green Sts). 626/795.8950 &

42 CROCODILE CAFE

★★$ A junior version of the **Parkway Grill,** this café serves eclectic, trendy cuisine— including barbecued chicken, pizza, and spicy chicken salad—in a noisy, popular room. ◆ California ◆ Daily, lunch and dinner. 140 S Lake Ave (between Cordova and E Green Sts). 626/449.9900

43 FOLK TREE

Folk art, fine art, and books, mostly from Latin America, are sold here. Don't miss the seasonal theme exhibitions. Down the street is the **Folk Tree Collection** (217 S Fair Oaks Ave; 626/795.8733), specializing in ethnic-inspired beads, clothing, and textiles and rustic crafts and furniture. ◆ Daily. 199 S Fair Oaks Ave (at Valley St). 626/793.4828

44 PARKWAY GRILL

★★$$$ This is the place to chow down on some outstanding contemporary California cuisine in the aggressively creative tradition of Spago: gumbo, applewood-smoked chicken with chutney, oysters with corncakes, pasta, and, of course, the ubiquitous pizza served hot from the wood-burning oven. The obligatory bustling open kitchen is the centerpiece of the warm and attractive high-beamed brick room. ◆ California ◆ M-F, Su, lunch and dinner; Sa, dinner. Reservations recommended. 510 S Arroyo Pkwy (between E California Blvd and E Bellevue Dr). 626/795.1001

44 ARROYO CHOP HOUSE

★★★$$$ Bob and Gregg Smith opened this swank steak house next door to their popular **Parkway Grill,** much to the delight of Pasadena carnivores. In addition to some of the finest prime steaks and marbled cuts around, they also serve a great veal chop and rotisserie chicken; choice nonmeat options include fresh fish, corn on the cob, and divine sautéed wild mushrooms. Cigar smokers can puff away on the special smoking patio. ◆ Steak House ◆ Daily, dinner. Reservations required. Valet parking available. 536 S

Arroyo Pkwy (between E California Blvd and E Bellevue Dr). 626/577.7463

45 BURGER CONTINENTAL

★$ Gourmet hamburgers in native or exotic dress are offered at the self-serve counter or in the sit-down restaurant. Middle Eastern specialties are one of the surprises on this menu, and belly dancers perform on weekends. The rear patio is shaded by trees during the day and lit with Christmas bulbs in the evening. ◆ American/Middle Eastern ◆ Daily, breakfast, lunch, and dinner. 535 S Lake Ave (between E California and E Del Mar Blvds). 626/792.6634

46 PIE 'N' BURGER

★★$ Stop here for possibly the juiciest burgers in town—as good as the ones grilled in your own backyard. Remember to ask the waitress for a generous supply of napkins for the juices and dressing that drip with every bite. Top your meal off with a slice of old-fashioned peach-apple pie. ◆ American ◆ Daily, breakfast, lunch, and dinner. 913 E California Blvd (between S Catalina and S Lake Aves). 626/795.1123. Also at 9537 Las Tunas Dr (at Primrose Ave), Temple City. 626/287.5797

47 ROSE TREE COTTAGE

★$ Book a day early for an authentic English tea complete with fresh scones, Devonshire cream, and strawberry jam. It's a pretty place set in a British gift shop. ◆ English ◆ Daily, until 5:30PM. 824 E California Blvd (between S Lake and S Hudson Aves). 626/793.3337. e-mail: rosetree@aol.com

---

At the **California Institute of Technology** in Pasadena, **Charles Richter** invented the **Richter scale** for measuring the magnitude of earthquakes.

The **Pasadena City Council** outlawed tortilla tossing at the annual **Doo Dah** parade after spectactors pelted the marchers.

Restaurants/Clubs: Red | Hotels: Purple | Shops: Orange | Outdoors/Parks: Green | Sights/Culture: Blue

SAN GABRIEL VALLEY

The other Valley . . .

The first settlement of the Los Angeles region was made here in the San Gabriel Valley around 1771, when 14 soldiers, four mule drivers, and two priests chose a spot near the banks of the San Gabriel River and Rio Hondo to found the **Mission San Gabriel Archangel.** By the time California became part of the Union, the valley was a well-known stopping place on the route to Los Angeles. Several towns popped up in the San Gabriel region, as "ranchos" were broken up into small farm tracts. One of the first was **El Monte,** which started as a trading post and became the region's hog-ranching center. The site of **Alhambra** is part of the former **Rancho San Pascual,** which was acquired by J. D. Shorb

and Benjamin D. Wilson. Shorb and Wilson laid out a subdivision in 1874 and named it after Washington Irving's novel *The Alhambra*. Irving's "stern, melancholy country" reminded them of the landscape around the tract.

The next big spurt of development in this eastern valley came in 1903, when **Arcadia** and **San Marino** were founded by two of the wealthiest men of the times. E.J. "Lucky" Baldwin named his subdivision Arcadia after the district in Greece whose poetic name meant "a place of rural simplicity," while Henry E. Huntington named his palatial estate after the Republic of San Marino and created a small, independent city of luxurious houses.

In the 1920s and 1930s, the San Gabriel Valley was a near paradise, dense with orange, lemon, and walnut groves interspersed with such exotic attractions as lion, ostrich, and reptile farms. Over the past two decades, the Anglo population has sharply declined as Latinos and Asians have flocked to the area. And the small communities of the valley, nearly all independent cities, have sprawled one into another, creating a large suburban region of small stucco houses extending some 30 miles.

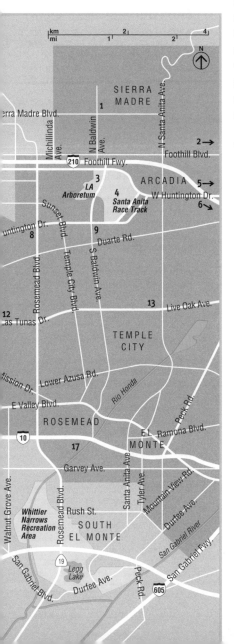

1 RESTAURANT LOZANO

★$$ The folksy setting provides a backdrop for black bean soup, stuffed peppers, AHA-approved burgers, and other flavorful, healthy dishes. ♦ Southwestern ♦ M-F, lunch; M-Sa, dinner. Reservations recommended. 44 N Baldwin Ave (between E Sierra Madre Blvd and E Montecito Ave), Sierra Madre. 626/355.5945

2 AZTEC HOTEL

This hotel, with its wonderfully eccentric, freshly restored stucco façade, was built in 1925 on a design by **Robert Stacy-Judd**, an enthusiastic advocate of the pre-Columbian Revival style. ♦ 311 W Foothill Blvd (between N Magnolia and Melrose Aves), Monrovia. 626/358.3231

3 LA ARBORETUM

There's no need to go to Africa or Brazil to visit a jungle—a trip to the arboretum and the lake where Humphrey Bogart heroically pulled the *African Queen* through the slimy muck, leeches and all, is certainly more economical. Located on a 127-acre portion of the former **Rancho Santa Anita**, the arboretum houses plant specimens from all over the world, arranged by continent of origin. The lake in the middle of the property is spring fed, a result of natural waters seeping up along the Raymond Fault, which runs across the property. The Gabrieleno Indians used this as a water source for hundreds of years before

197

E.J. "Lucky" Baldwin, a high-living and often outrageous silver-mining magnate, bought the ranch in 1875. The Baldwin property was not only a working ranch but one of the earliest botanical collections in the Southland. Witness several exceedingly tall *Washingtonia robusta* palm trees—at 121 feet they might set a world record. Peacocks and guinea fowl roam among the lush plantings, delightful with their vivid promenades and startling with their raucous cries. Demonstration gardens show California domestic horticulture at its best. A snack bar offers refreshments; a shop sells books and gifts. ♦ Admission. Daily. 301 N Baldwin Ave (across from the Santa Anita racetrack), Arcadia. 626/821.3222

Within the LA Arboretum:

Lucky Baldwin Queen Anne Guest Cottage

E.J. "Lucky" Baldwin created this Queen Anne–style building in 1881 as a lavish guesthouse for visitors. The red-and-white gingerbread cottage, with its delicately scrolled woodwork, is a favorite location for film and television crews. Close by, and in the same style, are stables, a doghouse, and an 1890 railroad station.

Hugh Reid Adobe

A reconstruction of Hugh Reid's original 1839 structure is built of more than 15,000 handmade adobe blocks. Reid owned the 13,319-acre **Rancho Santa Anita** between 1841 and 1847.

4 Santa Anita Park

Thoroughbred horses race against the backdrop of the San Gabriel Mountains on one of the most beautiful racetracks in the country. The park features a lushly landscaped infield, a children's playground, and numerous eating places that run the gamut from hot dogs to haute cuisine. Weekdays, the public is invited to watch morning workouts (a continental breakfast is served at **Clocker's Corner**); on Saturday and Sunday, a free tram tour of the grounds is offered. The action in the saddling enclosure and walking ring may be viewed just before post time. In addition to the regular season, the Oak Tree Racing Association sponsors thoroughbred racing from October through mid-November. ♦ Admission. Season: 26 Dec to late Apr. Post time: 1PM. Morning workouts: 7:30-9:30AM. Tram tours: Sa, Su,

8AM. 285 W Huntington Dr (between N Santa Anita and S Baldwin Aves), Arcadia. 626/574.7223. www.santaanita.com

Within Santa Anita Park:

FrontRunner Restaurant

★★$$$ One of the most elegant eateries of any sports site, this stylish luncheon spot is located in the Club House, where 400 feet of floor-to-ceiling sliding glass walls provide a 180-degree view of the finish line and the San Gabriel Mountains. Designed by Ray Gal, the décor is straight out of colonial Asia, with bamboo, rattan, ceiling fans, and mahogany and hand-carved wooden fixtures. For your betting convenience there's a nine-inch Sony TV and a pari-mutuel machine on every tabletop—which detract from the elegance, but gamblers like it. The menu is an eclectic assortment of everything from macadamia-crusted sea bass and grilled Sonoma lamb chops to pizzas, sandwiches, and hamburgers. And for dessert, the flourless chocolate cake and espresso anglaise, caramelized banana Napoleon with rum sauce, and raspberry cheesecake are well worth the caloric splurge. Access to the Club House is by an admission fee that's also applicable for seats at the track. ♦ Open during racing season only (Dec-Apr), 11AM-4PM. 626/574.1035

5 La Parisienne

★★$$ A venerable yet unpretentious restaurant, this place offers highly professional service and traditional French cooking. The portions are generous and the pastries win raves. ♦ French ♦ M-F, lunch; daily, dinner. 1101 E Huntington Dr (at S Mountain Ave), Monrovia. 626/357.3359

5 Monrovia Historical Museum

Built in the early 1920s and once the offices and changing rooms for the municipal pool, this Spanish Colonial Revival structure was saved from demolition to safeguard Monrovia memorabilia. Though the collections may not have mass appeal, the museum will interest those who enjoy discovering long-lost treasures in an attic. Among the highlights are items chronicling the life of city founder

FIT FOR STARDOM

In a city where your figure can be your fortune, Angelenos are quite possibly the most physically active people in the world. Spawned in the late 1970s and early 1980s by exercise gurus Richard Simmons and Jane Fonda, the fitness frenzy has touched an entire population of stars, wannabes, and just plain folk. Legions of joggers, power walkers, bicyclers, hikers, skaters, rollerbladers, bodybuilders, and surfers fill city streets, beaches, and gyms large and small. To most, exercise is considered tantamount to a religious experience.

Actually, fitness folk were doing their thing long before the advent of home exercise videotapes and posh health clubs. Back in the early 1930s, bodybuilders (remember Charles Atlas and the 97-pound weakling?) were pumping iron and doing calisthenics on what came to be known as **Muscle Beach,** just south of the Santa Monica Pier. Many Muscle Beach regulars went on to fitness fame and fortune, among them gymnasts Steve Hug and Cathy Rigby, Vic and Armand Tanny, Jack LaLanne, and Harold Zinkin (who developed the Universal weight machine).

Though a few diehards still lift barbells on the beach, modern-day muscle-seekers have turned to other venues where they can tone up in air-conditioned comfort—and maybe spot a celebrity or two. Herewith, some of our favorite fitness haunts.

Crunch

This super-hip "no attitude" workout emporium attracts a low-key celebrity crowd and ordinary folks who go to use the state-of-the-art equipment and/or participate in the quirky workouts. We're talking classes called "We'll Tumble 4 You," "Afro/Brazilian/Tango/Salsa," "EveryBodydance/Aerobagogo," and, well, you get the picture. It's zany, it's fun, and it's effective.

Steam baths, saunas, and massages are available, but all the frills are dedicated to the industrial-looking gym. Yearly memberships vary across the board from $900 to $1,200, although specials are offered regularly. Daily passes are $24. ♦ M-F, 5AM-midnight; Sa, Su, 7AM-10PM. 8000 Sunset Blvd (second level) (between Crescent Hgts and Laurel). 323/654.4550; fax 323/654.3935

Gold's Gym

This bodacious bodybuilding facility attracts celebrities and starlets from nearby Paramount Studios, aspiring actors, and ordinary folk. Even superstars feel at home here. Rows and rows of weight machines, nearly all occupied, line this serious muscle factory. There are lockers and showers, as well as a helpful staff. Cost is $15 a day, $567 a year (subject to change). Although there are dozens of Gold's branches throughout the Southland, this is the coolest spot to pump and flex. ♦ M-F, 5AM-11PM; Sa, Su, 7AM-9PM. 1016 Cole Ave (between Romaine St and Santa Monica Blvd). 323/462.7012

Joe's Gym

(formerly **The Gym**) Mariel Hemingway, Sharon Stone, Jamie Lee Curtis, and Jane March are alumni from the former location of this workout haven. Although in new digs, the drill's the same: savvy toning tactics combined with state-of-the-art matrix exercise equipment. The gym also features plasma TVs on all cardio equipment and four big-screen plasmas. There are no formal classes, but a knowledgeable staff teaches you proper techniques on the machines. Also available is computerized nutritional analysis and a staff chiropractor to work out the kinks. The cost is $15 for a day pass or $700 a year for unlimited use of the facility, and an additional $40 to $100 an hour for a personal trainer. ♦ M-F, 5AM-9PM; Sa, 6AM-6PM; Su, 8AM-2PM. 11601 Wilshire Blvd (in the World Savings Bldg at the corner of Wilshire Blvd and Federal Hwy). 310/966.1999

LA Private Trainers Lifestyle Centers

A host of hard-bodied celebrities stay in shape at this hip, holistic health center. Robin Del Pesco, owner/president/CEO and a personal trainer, caters his centers to the aesthetic self-improvement (nutrition, behavior modification, and lifestyle) and overall physical conditioning of baby boomers. Of course, all ages can join, but these clubs focus on *restoring* health. It costs $38 for a team workout, or $60 for a one-on-one with a personal trainer (which you must hire in order to gain access to the facility). ♦ M-F, 6AM-9PM; Sa, Su, 6AM-noon. 16542 Ventura Blvd (at Havehurst). 818/501.5142

If you don't have time to go to the gym, get fit while you sightsee with Cheryl Anker Agata, a running tour guide who takes tourists and locals on jogging tours of the city designed to keep visitors fit while they explore the area. The 40-something running enthusiast launched her company, **Off 'N Running Tours,** in July 1994 and runs with each group, happily tailoring trips to fit any request. One of her most popular routes is up to **Holmby Hills,** past the **Playboy Mansion,** past Aaron and Candy Spelling's massive estate and Humphrey Bogart's old home, down around the **Beverly Hills Hotel** and bungalows, over to **Beverly Drive** past the homes of Kate Jackson and Leslie Nielson, on to **Rodeo Drive** for a look at Carl Reiner's place. Other popular runs include **Universal Studios,** Santa Monica, the **South Bay beaches,** and **downtown LA.** Refreshments are provided during the tour and you get a "Running Keeps Me off the Street" T-shirt when you arrive at the finish line. Although the physically fit Cheryl can easily run 12 miles or more at a time, she leaves the distance up to her clients, most of whom, she says, prefer a 5- or 6-mile jaunt. The cost of a run is $35. For more information or to book a running tour, contact Cheryl at 310/246.1418 or at offnrun@westworld.com

William Monroe, and relics from the San Marino estate of General George Patton. ♦ Free. W-Th, Su, 1-4PM. 742 E Lemon Ave (between S Mountain and S Shamrock Aves), Monrovia. 626/357.9537

6 RAGING WATERS

Ⓟ Families flock to this 44-acre water park extravaganza, where waves, water slides, and a sandy beach offer welcome relief from scorching days. Revive yourself with **Thunder Rapids,** a five-person rafting adventure that culminates in a six-story drop; **High Extreme II,** a thrilling two-person raft ride; and **El Niño, the Ride,** which is guaranteed to get you soaked. ♦ Admission. Hours vary, so call ahead. 111 Raging Waters Dr (north of Via Verde), San Dimas. 909/802.2200. www.ragingwaters.com

7 HUNTINGTON LIBRARY, ART COLLECTIONS, AND BOTANICAL GARDENS

Ⓟ This 207-acre estate, formerly the home of pioneer railroad tycoon and philanthropist Henry E. Huntington (1850-1927), is one of the greatest attractions in Southern California. Designed by **Myron Hunt** and **Elmer Grey** in 1910, it now houses an art collection that emphasizes English and French painting of the 18th century. Among the works displayed are Gainsborough's *Blue Boy,* Lawrence's *Pinkie,* Reynolds's *Sarah Siddons as the Tragic Muse,* and Romney's *Lady Hamilton.* The gallery also exhibits an impressive collection of English and French porcelains, tapestries, graphics, drawings, and furniture. Acquisitions include a full-length Van Dyck portrait, *Mrs. Kirke,* and a late Turner canvas, *The Grand Canal, Venice.* The library, designed by Myron Hunt and H. C. Chambers in 1920, houses extensive holdings of English and American first editions, manuscripts, maps, letters, and incunabula. Displayed are a number of the most famous objects in the collection, including a Gutenberg Bible, the Ellesmere manuscript of Chaucer's *Canterbury Tales,* the double-elephant folio edition of Audubon's *Birds of America,* and an unsurpassed collection of the early editions of Shakespeare's works. In the west wing of the library is the **Arabella Huntington Memorial Collection** of French porcelain, furniture, sculpture, and Renaissance paintings.

With the 1984 opening of the **Virginia Steele Scott Gallery of American Art,** designed by Warner and Gray, the estate added another dimension to its collections. Works range in date from the 1730s to the 1930s, and include paintings by Mary Cassatt (*Breakfast in Bed*), Gilbert Stuart, Winslow Homer, John Singleton Copley, Edward Hopper, and Robert Henri. American artifacts and furniture,

including pieces by Gustav Stickley, are matched with paintings from the appropriate period. A permanent exhibition features furniture and decorative arts designed by Charles and Henry Greene. The beautiful and lush gardens were designed and developed by William Hertrich beginning in 1904. In addition to expansive lawns and formal planting arrangements that incorporate 17th-century Italian sculpture, they contain extensive rose and camellia gardens, a **Shakespearean Garden** of plants mentioned by the Bard, and a number of annual beds. The **Japanese Garden** is entered through a gate overlooking a half-moon-shaped bridge spanning a koi pond. It features an authentically furnished 18th-century-style house, specimens of bonsai, and a **Zen Rock Garden.** The astonishing 12-acre **Desert Garden** has one of the largest plantings of unique cactus and succulent varieties in the world. ♦ Admission. Galleries and gardens: Tu-Su. English tea (served in the Tea Room, behind the mansion): Tu-F, 1-3:30PM; Sa, Su, noon-3:30PM. 1151 Oxford Rd (between Euston and Orlando Rds), San Marino. Second entrance on Orlando Rd (between Oxford and Avondale Rds). General information 626/405.2100, tearoom reservations 626/584.9337, directions 626/405.2274. www.huntington.org

8 CLEARMAN'S NORTHWOODS INN

★$$ Kitschy log cabin architecture says it all— the Yukon in the heart of San Gabriel. The floors are covered with sawdust and peanut shells, which waitresses in frilly cocktail dresses encourage customers to toss freely. Good-size entrées are accompanied by delicious cheese breads and two salads. If you can't decide, try the hearty sampler—a steak, scallop, and chicken combination. ♦ American ♦ Daily, lunch and dinner. 7247 Rosemead Blvd (between E Fairview Ave and Huntington Dr), San Gabriel. 626/286.8284. Also at 14305 Firestone Blvd (between Phoebe and Valley View Aves), La Mirada. 714/994.4590

9 CHEZ SATEAU

★★★$$$ This oasis in the culinary desert is conveniently close to **Santa Anita Park** and the **LA Arboretum.** Japanese chef Ryo Sato combines his own traditions with inventive French cooking, delighting diners with such unusual dishes as grapefruit consommé and oyster-veal mousse. Nice service makes up for the plain décor. Sumptuous picnics to go can be purchased here and next door at **Chez Sateau Pâtisserie.** ♦ French ♦ Tu-F, lunch and dinner; Sa, dinner; Su, champagne brunch and dinner. 850 S Baldwin Ave (between Fairview Ave and Huntington Dr), Arcadia. 626/446.8806

10 JULIENNE

★$ Homemade bread, delicious salads, roast chicken, and daily specials are served at this charming café. ♦ French ♦ M-Sa, breakfast and lunch; dinner served only in summer, Th-F. 2649 Mission St (between El Molino and Los Robles Aves), San Marino. 626/441.2299

11 EL MOLINO VIEJO

Erected in 1816, the first water-powered gristmill in Southern California is maintained by the California Historical Society. ♦ Admission. Tu-Su, 1-4PM. 1120 Old Mill Rd (between Mill La and S Oak Knoll Ave), San Marino. 626/449.5450

12 TOKYO LOBBY

★$$ Decorated with folk art, this Japanese restaurant features generous entrées that appeal to Americans. ♦ Japanese ♦ M-F, lunch and dinner; Sa, Su, dinner. Reservations recommended for large parties. 927 E Las Tunas Dr (between Earle St and N Charlotte Ave), San Gabriel. 626/287.9972

13 ALEX DI PEPPE'S

★$$ Good pizza, good lasagna, and good value keep the regulars *molto contenti*. ♦ Italian ♦ M-Su, dinner. Reservations recommended on Friday and Saturday. 140 Las Tunas Dr (between S Santa Anita and El Monte Aves), Arcadia. 626/445.0544

14 MIDDLE EAST

★$ Bargain is the key word in this tiny shack of a restaurant, whether you're indulging in an aromatic stew, kabobs (which you must call ahead to order), or stuffed lamb with yogurt. All the traditional starters and desserts are available, as well as beer and wine. ♦ Lebanese ♦ Daily, breakfast, lunch, and dinner. 910 E Main St (between S Valencia St and S Granada Ave), Alhambra. 626/576.1048

15 SAN GABRIEL CIVIC AUDITORIUM

Designed especially for John Steven Groarty's *Mission Play*, Arthur Benton's authentic Mission-style playhouse was modeled after the **Mission San Antonio de Padua** in Monterey County. Heraldic shields of the Spanish provinces, donated by Spanish king Alfonso XIII on the auditorium's opening in 1927, adorn the immense interior. The fine theater organ is used for concerts and to accompany silent movies. ♦ Box office: M-F, 10AM-5PM. 320 S Mission Dr (between S

Santa Anita St and W Broadway), San Gabriel. 626/308.2865

15 MUSEUM OF THE SAN GABRIEL HISTORICAL ASSOCIATION

Visitors can obtain a walking-tour brochure from the headquarters of this society dedicated to the preservation of local history. At press time, a major historical site next door, the Victorian **Hayes House** (circa 1887), was undergoing restoration supervised by the museum. ♦ Free. W, Sa, Su, 1-4PM. 546 W Broadway (between S Santa Anita St and S Mission Dr), San Gabriel. 626/308.3223

15 MISSION SAN GABRIEL ARCHANGEL

Founded in 1771 by Fathers Pedro Cambon and Angel Somera, the present mission church consists of the renovated remains of the one built by Indian workers from 1791 to 1805. Constructed of stone, mortar, and brick, its capped buttresses and narrow windows were influenced by the style of the Cathedral of Cordova in Spain. The church originally had a vaulted roof, but it was damaged in the earthquake of 1803. In 1812, the church tower on the façade was toppled by another earthquake. When the church was completely restored in 1828, a bell tower was constructed on the north wall of the altar end. The bell-tower wall, with its three rows of arched openings, creates the characteristic image of the mission. ♦ 537 W Mission Dr (between Junípero Serra Dr and S Santa Anita St), San Gabriel. 626/282.5191

16 BABITA MEXICUISINE

★★$ The specialties of this local treasure include Yucatecan seafood dishes such as *pescado picado* (seared fresh catch of the day with bell pepper, tomato, jalapeño, and white wine), chicken tostadas topped with black bean paste, *cochinita pibil* (pork baked in banana leaves), and *carne asada* (skirt steak with salsa Mexicana). Try the bread pudding; you'll love it. ♦ Mexican ♦ Tu-F, lunch; Tu-Su, dinner. 1823 S San Gabriel Blvd (at E Norwood Pl), San Gabriel. 626/288.7265

17 EDWARD'S STEAK HOUSE

★$$ You can count on nicely grilled steaks and chops, a surprise or two (perhaps lamb shanks), and at least one fresh fish entrée. The sawdust-on-the-floor informality makes this place a good choice when you're with the kids. ♦ American ♦ M-F, lunch and dinner; Sa, Su, dinner. 9600 Flair Dr (at Fletcher Ave), El Monte. 626/442.2400

Restaurants/Clubs: Red | Hotels: Purple | Shops: Orange | Outdoors/Parks: Green | Sights/Culture: Blue

SOUTH AND EAST CENTRAL

Watt's up with this . . .

Edged by mountains and water and scored by railroad tracks, freeways, and rivers, South and East Central are the true Los Angeles basin. The flat geography, which offers no obstacles to the construction of factories and roads, is a main attraction to industry, which provides the economic base of the area. Development has largely depended on the Southern Pacific Railroad and the Pacific Electric Inter-Urban Railroad,

transportation giants that bought up huge tracts of land as they built their lines, and later subdivided their holdings into a series of communities for workers and their families.

The wide-open expanses, right-angled streets, and unimpeded vistas seemed familiar to newcomers from the Midwest and the South, who headed this way in response to the boosterism and land fever of the 1880s and 1920s. Many of these communities have remained unincorporated; like the jigsaw patterns of the other parts of Los Angeles County, the boundaries between city and county hop, skip, and jump around each other.

Culver City was formerly home to three major motion picture studios: Metro-

Goldwyn-Mayer, Selznick International Studios, and Hal Roach Studios. At one time, this small town produced half the films made in the United States.

From Boyle Heights to Whittier Hills, East LA has the largest concentration of Latinos in the United States, while Monterey Park is the preferred destination for Chinese immigrants and rivals Chinatown for authentic cuisine. South Central—from Baldwin Hills to the plains area that includes Watts, Willowbrook, and Compton—is home to the country's largest concentration of African-American residents, as well as a burgeoning Latino population. This area, hit hard by the 1992 riots, ranges from affluent hillside homes on the west to inner-city neighborhoods that have neatly trimmed older houses as well as run-down, dilapidated streets. A number of commercial strips were ravaged by arson and looting during the riots, especially the businesses between the 405 and 710 Freeways, but today it's becoming business as usual in this part of town. Although the ethnic mix makes the area more vital and interesting, it also can be a source of tension and crime; some of the historic sites are worth seeing, but we highly recommend visiting only during daylight hours.

1 LINCOLN PARK

More than 300 varieties of trees—a number of them rare and enormous—grace this 46-acre park. Some date back to the 1870s, when the park was created. ♦ Daily; M-F, until 9PM. 3501 Valley Blvd (between N Soto and N Main Sts). 213/847.1726

Within Lincoln Park:

PLAZA DE LA RAZA

Fronting the park's small lake is a complex with a theater, a classroom, and office space serving as a cultural and educational center. It is the main forum for activities of interest to LA's Spanish-speaking community. Activities include musical performances, dance, drama, and seasonal festivals based on themes related to Mexican holidays and family life. ♦ Nominal admission. 323/223.2475

2 LOS ANGELES COUNTY USC MEDICAL CENTER

The highly visible 20-story Moderne structure, completed in 1934, covers 89 acres and is one of the largest general acute-care hospitals in the country. The University of Southern California Health Sciences Campus, located seven miles northeast of the main campus, serves USC's Schools of Medicine and Pharmacy, the University Hospital, the Doheny Eye Institute, and the Kenneth Norris Jr. Comprehensive Cancer Center. The hospital is a training ground for students from the USC School of Medicine. ♦ Medical Center: 1975 Zonal Ave (between San Pablo and Biggy Sts). 323/342.2000; hospital: 1200 N State St (between Marengo St and Zonal Ave). 323/226.2622

3 CALIFORNIA STATE UNIVERSITY AT LOS ANGELES

A branch of the large California State University system. ♦ 5151 State University Dr (between San Bernardino Fwy and N Eastern Ave). 323/343.3000

4 OCEAN STAR SEAFOOD

★★$$ The chefs create no-frills authentic Cantonese seafood, including steamed live shrimp and scallops, baked lobster, and fish prepared in several distinctive ways. Duck soup with citrus peel and beef hot pot are likewise recommended. On Atlantic Boulevard, a much larger branch of this restaurant serves a variety of seafood delicacies in a palatial dining room with private banquet rooms. ♦ Chinese ♦ Daily, lunch and dinner. Reservations recommended for 10 or more. 145 N Atlantic Blvd (between W Garvey and W Emerson Aves), Monterey Park. 626/308.2128

5 COCARY

★$ This frantic and fun Mongolian restaurant lets you select (from refrigerated cases down one wall) such delicacies as tiger prawns, baby clams, and fish dumplings to grill or simmer in a pot at your table. Bring a crowd of friends and a big appetite. ◆ Mongolian ◆ Daily, lunch and dinner. 112 N Garfield Ave (at W Garvey Ave), Monterey Park. 626/573.0691

6 DIAMOND BAKERY

A wide selection of pastries and cakes offered at this place is complemented by a variety of *bao*—puffy steamed or fried rice-flour rolls filled with beef or chicken. ◆ Daily. 744-46 W Garvey Ave (at S Atlantic Blvd), Monterey Park. 626/289.5171

6 LITTLE SHEEP

★★$$ The extraordinary preparations of shrimp, crab, and sole put most Western seafood restaurants to shame. This place is crowded at lunchtime. ◆ Mongolian ◆ Daily, lunch and dinner. 120 S Atlantic Blvd (between W Newmark and W Garvey Aves), Monterey Park. 626/282.1089

7 YI-MEI DELI

This small, crowded deli and bakery features a wide selection of Chinese fast foods and sweets, including a popular soybean soup served with *yu jow gwui*, a tasty deep-fried bread. ◆ Daily. 736 S Atlantic Blvd (between El Mercado Ave and El Portal Pl), Monterey Park. 626/284.9306. Also at 18414 Colima Rd (at Batson Ave), Rowland Heights. 626/854.9246

8 HOLLENBECK PARK

This 21-acre park was donated to the city in 1892. A lovely stand of jacaranda sits amidst stately old trees and provides a pleasant setting for recreational programs sponsored by the clubhouse. ◆ M-F, until 10PM; Sa, Su, noon-4PM. 415 S St. Louis St (at E Fourth St). 323/261.0113

9 EL MERCADO

Experience the flavor of Mexico without leaving LA County at this south-of-the-border-style complex of bustling food markets, shops, and restaurants. The main floor houses stalls filled with all the ingredients necessary for Mexican cooking. The walls this level are lined with a *tortillaria*, a bakery, snack bars with food to go, and delicatessens. The mezzanine has a series of cafeteria-style restaurants. Mariachis perform here from noon until midnight and happily accept special requests for a small donation. Shops in the basement sell everything from furniture to Mexican crafts and utilitarian domestic goods. ◆ Shops: Daily. Restaurants: Daily until midnight. 3425

E First St (between N Indiana and N Lorena Sts). 323/268.3451

10 EAST LOS ANGELES COLLEGE

This two-year community college offers a variety of undergraduate courses and occupational programs. It was one of the first colleges to offer free, noncredit courses to anyone in the community. ◆ 1301 Avenida Cesar Chavez (between Collegian and Bleakwood Aves), Monterey Park. 323/265.8650

11 WHITTIER NARROWS NATURE CENTER

An enormous variety of birds, plants, and animals find sanctuary in this 419-acre nature center, located along the **San Gabriel River.** The small museum has exhibitions that describe the aquatic environment. Take a great hike along the nature trails. ◆ Free. Daily. 1000 N Durfee Ave (off Pomona and San Gabriel River Fwys). 626/575.5523

12 DO-NUT HOLE

This 1958 structure is one of the city's great pop monuments. Drive through the two giant doughnuts and pick up one (or a bag) for the road, any hour of the day or night. ◆ Daily, until midnight. 15300 Amar Rd (at Elliott Ave), La Puente. 626/968.2912

13 WORKMAN & TEMPLE FAMILY HOMESTEAD MUSEUM

Relive the colorful history of Los Angeles, from the first American settlers of the 1840s (when California was still under Mexican rule) through the boom years of the 1870s and 1920s. Each of these formative decades is dramatically evoked by historic buildings on a six-acre site restored by the City of Industry as an educational showpiece. The major attraction is a 26-room **Spanish Revival house,** built in the 1920s with the profits from an oil strike and furnished in period style, complete with a windup Victrola and a bearskin rug in the hall. The original mid-19th-century adobe, an English-style manor house, a lacy gazebo, and a private cemetery are also featured. ◆ Free. Tours available on the hour between 1 and 4PM. 15415 E Don Julian Rd (between Hacienda Blvd and Turnbull Canyon Rd), City of Industry. 626/968.8492

14 WILLIAM GRANT STILL ARTS CENTER

Named for the famous late African-American composer and longtime resident of LA, the center offers exhibitions, festivals, and workshops. ◆ Free. Daily, noon-5PM. 2520

Restaurants/Clubs: Red | Hotels: Purple | Shops: Orange | Outdoors/Parks: Green | Sights/Culture: Blue

West View St (just north of W Adams Blvd).
323/734.1164

15 CLARK MEMORIAL LIBRARY

English literature and music of the 17th and
18th centuries are well represented in this
research library, bequeathed to UCLA in 1934
by William Andrews Clark Jr. in memory of his
father, Senator William A. Clark. The Italian
Renaissance building is decorated with
murals and ceiling paintings by Allyn Cox, and
furnished with period antiques. Formal
gardens cover the underground vaults. Tours
can be arranged by appointment only. ♦
Open to researchers M-F. 2520 Cimarron St
(at W Adams Blvd). 323/731.8529

16 HAROLD & BELLE'S

★★$$ Generous helpings of fabulous gumbo,
jambalaya, hot sausage, shrimp creole, and
barbecued ribs draw enthusiastic crowds to
these pleasant surroundings. ♦ Cajun/Creole
♦ Daily, lunch and dinner. Reservations
recommended. 2920 W Jefferson Blvd
(between 9th and 10th Aves).
323/735.9023

17 CULVER STUDIOS

King Kong roared, Atlanta burned, and "Boy
Wonder" Orson Welles directed *Citizen Kane*
on this historic piece of land. Its Southern
plantation–style offices were built by pioneer
producer Thomas Ince, later housed RKO,
and were the trademark of David O.
Selznick's company long before he built Tara
on the land cleared by torching the surviving
sets of Cecil B. De Mille's *King of Kings.* All of
this history has gone with the wind, leaving
only the façade and a cluster of vintage
rental stages. ♦ Closed to the public. 9336
Washington Blvd (between Ince Blvd and Van
Buren Pl), Culver City. No general public
phone number

18 BALDWIN HILLS VILLAGE

Here is a rare model of planned housing that
became a tight-knit community. Completed
on the eve of America's entry into World War
II, this 80-acre complex of one- and two-story,
studio to three-bedroom dwellings was
considered a progressive urban experiment.
Though many units had private walled
gardens, the complex was well integrated,
with its generous landscape of spacious lawns
and giant sycamores and oaks. It was
renamed **Village Green** in the mid-1970s

when the units were converted into
condominiums, all of which are private
residences. ♦ 5300 Rodeo Rd (between S
Sycamore Ave and Hauser Blvd)

19 SONY PICTURES STUDIOS

How the mighty have fallen! Once an
empire with five lots, theaters and studios
around the world, and "more stars than
there are in heaven," Metro-Goldwyn-Mayer
(MGM) has surrendered its last piece of turf
to the producer of TV's *Dallas* and *Falcon
Crest* and now occupies a bland Beverly
Hills office building. Meanwhile, Columbia
Pictures, born on Gower Street's "Poverty
Row" the same year as MGM, relocated
here from Burbank—a poor-wretch-makes-
good story worthy of the movies. You can
see the exteriors of the two major buildings
on the lot: the 1916 **Triangle Company
office,** with its classical colonnades, that
MGM took over in 1924; and the
monumental Moderne **Thalberg Building** of
1939, named for MGM's legendary head of
production. It is also the lot where later
productions such as *Jeopardy!* and *Men in
Black* were filmed. ♦ Although closed to the
public, two-hour walking tours are offered
by appointment for a fee (323/520.TOUR).
10202 Washington Blvd (between Madison
and Overland Aves), Culver City.
310/280.8000

20 ALLIED MODEL TRAINS

One of the country's largest stores for model-
train buffs is set in a miniature replica of
Union Station. ♦ M-Sa 10AM–6PM. 4411
Sepulveda Blvd (between Braddock Dr and
Barman Ave), Culver City. 310/313.9353

21 KENNETH HAHN STATE RECREATIONAL AREA

Once an oil reservoir, this grassy 315-acre
park (named after the longtime LA County
supervisor) represents a sound, public-
oriented, adaptive reuse solution for an
otherwise bleak landscape of unimproved oil
wells nodding away like mechanical storks. A
forest was planted with 140 trees and shrubs
from around the world, representing every
nation that competed in the 1984 Summer
Olympics. The park has hiking trails and two
lakes for fishing. ♦ 4100 S La Cienega Blvd
(between Stocker and Aladdin Sts).
323/291.0199

22 MUSEUM IN BLACK

This collection includes more than 1,000
pieces of traditional African art and African-
American memorabilia. There is a shop with
items for sale. ♦ Free. Tu-Sa. 4331 Degnan
Blvd (between W 43rd Pl and W 43rd St).
323/292.9528

23 DWAH BOOKSHOP

One of the few stores of its kind specializing in African-American, Islamic, and children's literature. ♦ M-Sa. 4801 Crenshaw Blvd (between W 48th St and Brynhurst Ave). 323/299.0335

24 FARMER JOHN'S PIG MURALS

Little pigs romp and play in a life-size trompe l'oeil farm landscape that blends in with the building it's painted on. Live trees are indistinguishable from painted ones, and pigs peer into windows both real and painted. The murals were painted in 1957 by film studio artist Leslie A. Grimes. When Grimes fell to his death from a scaffold in 1968, the Arco Sign Company assumed responsibility for maintaining and extending the murals. ♦ 3049 E Vernon Ave (between Downey Rd and S Soto St), Vernon

25 THE CITADEL

This Assyrian fortress, only nine miles from downtown LA, offers 38 pseudo-discount outlets such as **Geoffrey Beene, Benetton, Old Navy, Joan & David, Perry Ellis, Eddie Bauer, Corning Revere, DKNY,** and **Nike.** Don't expect big bargains, though: 10–20% is more realistic. There's a stylish food court to fuel you for your shopping spree. Designed by **Morgan, Walls & Clements** in 1929 as an impressive façade for the Samson Tire and Rubber Factory and later remodeled and redeveloped by the Trammell Crow Company into its current incarnation, the 130,000-square-foot cut-rate emporium is the closest of its kind to the city. ♦ Daily. 100-150 Citadel Dr (between Tubeway Ave and Atlantic Blvd), City of Commerce. 323/888.1724

26 WINNIE AND SUTCH COMPANY BUILDING

These structures, designed by **William E. Myer** in 1939, represent the best examples of Streamline Moderne architecture in LA since the Pan Pacific Auditorium was torched by vandals in 1989. The grounds, landscaped with flowers and shrubs, were designed to draw attention away from the building's industrial purpose. ♦ 5610 S Soto St (between E Slauson Ave and E 54th St), Huntington Park

27 PIO PICO STATE HISTORIC PARK/CASA DE PIO PICO

Don Pio Pico, former governor of California, built this hacienda on his 9,000-acre **El Ranchito** in 1850. The U-shaped house, which has recently been renovated, is a 13-room, two-story adobe mansion with two- to three-foot-thick walls. Covered porches link the side wings to the central portion of the house; a well is located in the courtyard. Guided tours of the house are offered. ♦ Free. W-Su. 6003 Pioneer Blvd (at Whittier Blvd), Whittier. 562/695.1217

28 CHINA PAVILION

Once a restaurant, this place is now a nightclub featuring live performances of Chinese pop and rock 'n' roll bands. Disco dancing nightly. ♦ Cover. Daily, until 2AM. 2140 Hacienda Blvd (between La Monde St and Halliburton Rd). No phone

29 WESTFIELD SHOPPINGTOWN FOX HILLS

Macy's, Robinsons-May, and **JC Penney** anchor this shopping mall, with 137 other stores on three floors selling everything from fresh-roasted nuts to bolts of fabric and clothing for all ages. The electronic game center is a popular spot with youngsters. ♦ Daily; M-F until 9PM. Sepulveda Blvd and Slauson Ave, Culver City. 310/390.7833

30 HARRIET'S CHEESECAKES UNLIMITED

Choose from 50 flavors of cheesecake. If the exquisite French vanilla is too tame for you, try the chocolate amaretto, apple 'n' spice, or coffee flavors. ♦ Tu-Sa. 1515 Centinela Ave (between N Cedar and Beach Sts), Inglewood. 310/419.2259

31 MAIN POST OFFICE

LA's main mail distribution center is the nation's largest single-level post office, the size of 10 football fields. It processes five and a half million pieces of mail per day. ♦ Window service: M-Sa. 7001 S Central Ave (between E Florence and E Gage Aves). General information 323/585.1723, 323/585.1705, or 800/275.8777

32 CENTINELA ADOBE

Built in 1834 for Ignacio Machado, this well-preserved house is made of adobe with a wood-shingle roof, and furnished with 19th-century antiques. Some of the original planting is maintained. Within the site are a research library and the office once used by Daniel Freeman, whose 22,000 acres became the city of Inglewood. ♦ Free. W, Su, 2-4PM. 7634 Midfield Ave (between W 82nd and W 76th Sts), Inglewood. General information 310/649.6272. Tours 310/677.1154

Restaurants/Clubs: Red | Hotels: Purple | Shops: Orange | Outdoors/Parks: Green | Sights/Culture: Blue

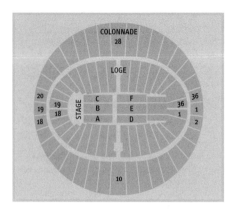

33 GREAT WESTERN FORUM

Until the Staples Center came on the scene, the Forum ruled as the main sports venue for the city. At press time the facility was in a state of flux after being purchased by an African-American religious group that plans to stage conferences, concerts, and events. ♦ 3900 Manchester Blvd (at S Prairie Ave), Inglewood. 310/673.1300

34 ACADEMY THEATRE

This 1939 Streamline Moderne landmark, designed by **S. Charles Lee,** is notable for its spiral-finned tower. The building is now used as a church. ♦ 3100 Manchester Blvd (at Crenshaw Blvd), Inglewood

35 HOLLYWOOD PARK

Thoroughbred racing occurs April through July and mid-November through December on a track landscaped with lagoons and tropical trees. A computer-operated screen offers patrons a view of the back stretch, as well as stop-action replays of photo finishes and racing statistics. Refreshments are available at the elegant **Turf Club Terrace, International Food Fair, Paddock Club,** and **Hollywood Bar.** The children's play area, designated **North Park,** now features a carousel. ♦ Admission. Call for post times. 1050 S Prairie Ave (between Century Blvd and W 90th St), Inglewood. 310/419.1500

36 WATTS TRAIN STATION

Restored as a railroad museum and office for the Department of Water and Power, the 1904 depot is meant as a symbol of the Community Redevelopment Agency's efforts to revitalize Watts. The **Metro Rail** Red Line from Long Beach to downtown LA stops close

by—much as the Big Red Cable Cars used to. ♦ E 103rd St and Grandee Ave

37 WATTS TOWERS

Paris has the Eiffel Tower, Barcelona has the Sagrada Familia cathedral, and LA has the Watts Towers. One of the world's greatest works of folk art, they were designed by Sam Rodia, an unlettered plasterer who created these masterpieces between 1921 and 1954 from salvaged steel rods, dismantled pipe structures, bed frames, and cement. He worked alone, building without a conscious plan (though he may have been inspired by childhood memories of similar structures used in an annual fiesta held near Naples) and scaling the heights of his work using a window-washer's belt and bucket. "How could I have been helped?" asked Rodia. "I couldn't tell anyone what to do. . . . Most of the time I didn't know myself." Rodia's glistening fretwork grew slowly over the years until the central tower topped out at 99.5 feet tall. Glass bottle fragments, ceramic tiles, china plates, and more than 25,000 seashells embellish his creation, encrusting the surface so thickly that they seem to be the primary building material, forming skin that has the calcified delicacy of coral.

When the towers were completed, Rodia deeded his property to a neighbor and left LA forever. He died in 1965 in Martinez, California, unwilling to the end to talk about his life's work. The spires were disfigured by vandals and threatened with demolition, but citizens rallied and saved them. The three towers have been completely renovated thanks to the Cultural Affairs Department of Los Angeles, and officially declared a National Historic Landmark. Public access to the interior is limited to weekends from noon to 4PM. Cultural events and exhibits are held here, such as the Day of the Drum, an ethnic foods and music festival celebrated in late September. Be aware of the high crime rate in the area. ♦ 1765 E 107th St (east of Graham Ave). 213/847.4646 or 213/485.1795. www.trywatts.com

Within the Watts Tower:

WATTS TOWERS ART CENTER

This community art center hosts exhibitions, art classes, and music, dance, and poetry readings. ♦ Tu-Sa. 213/847.4646

> The Lakers basketball team moved to Los Angeles from Minneapolis in 1960.

38 ALL AMERICAN HOME CENTER

This family-owned home-improvement store comprises 21 departments on four acres, with another six acres for parking. It claims to be the best-stocked store in the US and, more important, it motivates its staff through profit sharing. So, if you want to build your dream house . . . ◆ Daily. 7201 E Firestone Blvd (between Old River School Rd and Garfield Ave), Downey. 562/927.8666

39 HERITAGE PARK

The restored 1880s ranch and history museum is located in six acres of gardens. Close by is the 1919 **Clarke Estate,** one of the best-preserved works by landmark architect **Irving Gill.** ◆ Free. Heritage Park Dr (south of Telegraph Rd), Santa Fe Springs. 562/946.6476

40 EL POLLO INKA

★$ Marinated spit-roasted chicken is the signature dish, but just as delicious is the lamb stew served with rice and beans. ◆ Peruvian ◆ Daily, lunch and dinner. 15400-D Hawthorne Blvd (at W 154th St), Lawndale. 310/676.6665

41 PACIFIC SUPERMARKET

Foods of the Pacific Rim line the shelves in mind-numbing variety. ◆ Daily. 1620 W Redondo Beach Blvd (at La Salle Ave), Gardena. 310/323.7696

42 KAMPACHI

$$ While many sushi bars offer tempura and other batter-dipped dishes, this Japanese eatery concentrates solely on raw, fresh seafood. ◆ Japanese ◆ M-F, lunch and dinner; Sa, Su, dinner. Reservations recommended. 1425 W Artesia Blvd (between Normandie and Western Aves), Gardena. 310/515.1391

43 GOODYEAR BLIMP

One of the best-known, best-loved corporate symbols in the US is 192 feet long, 59 feet high, 50 feet in diameter, and 202,700 cubic feet in volume. Deflated, the dirigible weighs 12,000 pounds; filled with helium, its weight drops to 150 pounds. Its cruising speed is 35mph; its top speed, 53mph. The normal cruising altitude of 1,000 to 1,500 feet gives the blimp and its logo maximum recognition from the ground. In addition to advertising, the blimp acts as a camera platform for TV coverage of sports and public events, and assists the American Cetacean Society with the annual count of the California gray whales during their winter migration. Officially named the *Columbia,* the blimp travels six months out of the year, but you're most likely to see it on the ground in the early morning or at twilight from the intersection of the Harbor and San Diego Freeways. ◆ 19200 S Main St (between San Diego Fwy and E 192nd St), Carson. 323/770.0456

44 DOMINGUEZ RANCH ADOBE

A relic of the Spanish settlement of California, the adobe sits on property owned by Juan José Dominguez, a soldier who accompanied Father Serra on the original expedition from Mexico to found the California missions. In 1782, Dominguez was rewarded for his service with a land grant covering the harbor area south of the **Pueblo de Los Angeles,** more than 75,000 acres. His nephew built an adobe in 1826, and its interior has been restored as a historical museum, displaying many of the original furnishings. The adobe is now part of the **Dominguez Memorial Seminary,** operated by the Claretian Order. ◆ Free. Tu, W, 1-4PM; second and third Sunday of every month, 1-4PM. Groups of more than 15 must make advance reservations. 18127 S Alameda St (between Laurel Park Rd and Gardena Fwy). 323/636.6030

45 LA MIRADA THEATER FOR THE PERFORMING ARTS

This big, breezy theater features Tony award–winning performers, Off-Broadway productions, musicals, symphonies, and fabulous children's shows. ◆ 14900 La Mirada Blvd (between Ocaso and Rosecrans Aves), La Mirada. Box office 562/944.9801

Restaurants/Clubs: Red | Hotels: Purple | Shops: Orange | Outdoors/Parks: Green | Sights/Culture: Blue

By the bay, by the beautiful bay, but it's really an ocean . . .
   A cluster of colorful beachside communities snuggles against California's jagged coastline between Venice and Naples. Distinctively different, each offers an idyllic setting for swimming, sailing, surfing, and fishing. The South Bay area's sandy expanses are

broken up by **Marina del Rey,** the rocky outcrop of the **Palos Verdes peninsula,** and the industrial enclave around **Los Angeles Harbor, San Pedro,** and **Long Beach.** Further inland is **Los Angeles International Airport (LAX),** the third-busiest airport in the world. Note: The area code of most phone numbers in Long Beach, Lakewood, Whittier, Downey, Pico Rivera, and Norwalk is 562.

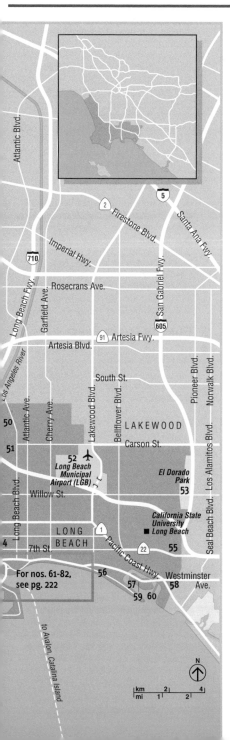

MARINA DEL REY

Pulsating with the young, the tan, the blond, and the restless, this waterfront community was laid out in the 1960s on marshy land between Venice Beach and LAX (see map at left). It's the world's largest artificial yacht harbor, with moorings for 10,000 private pleasure craft. The adjoining open space of **Playa Vista,** bought by Howard Hughes for aircraft testing in the 1940s, is currently being redeveloped as a planned community by a talented group of designers working for Maguire Thomas Partners. www.visitthemarina.com

1 DOROTHY GOLDEEN GALLERY

Contemporary painting, sculpture, and works on paper by emerging and mature artists, including Nam June Paik, Ed Paschke, and Robert Arneson, is exhibited here. ♦ Tu-Sa. 4223 Glencoe Ave (between Maxella and Beach Aves), Suite B-127. 310/577.8515

2 VILLA MARINA MARKETPLACE

A 1989 complex and a more-than-20-year-old center are oddly combined in this shopping area, which spans both sides of the street. Merchants include Gelson's gourmet supermarket, Petals & Wax (which carries cute candles and gifts), Electronics Boutique, Gap, and Tower Records, plus 12 movie screens and a southern restaurant. ♦ 13450 Maxella Ave (between Glencoe Ave and Lincoln Blvd). 310/827.0253

Within the Villa Marina Marketplace:

SOUPLANTATION

★★$ A healthful version of the all-you-can-eat smorgasbord, this salad-and-soup bar offers a wide array of fresh vegetables, fruits, and breads. Unlike most shopping center restaurants, it's airy and light. ♦ American ♦ Daily, lunch and dinner. 310/305.7669

2 AUNT KIZZY'S BACK PORCH

★★$ Catfish, fried chicken, short ribs, and smothered pork chops, just like in the old South, are served in a cabin-style restaurant. ♦ Southern ♦ Daily, lunch and dinner. 4325 Glencoe Ave (between Mindanao Way and Maxella Ave). 310/578.1005

3 MARINA INTERNATIONAL HOTEL AND BUNGALOWS

$$$ The main attractions at this waterfront property are the 25 adorable Europe-style bungalows and the commanding views of the marina from any of 135 rooms. A free airport shuttle is available to hotel guests. The **Crystal Fountain** restaurant serves seafood and continental dishes. ♦ 4200 Admiralty Way (at Palawan Way). 310/301.2000, 800/862.7462 in CA, 800/882.4000 in US; fax 310/301.8867 ♿

4 RITZ-CARLTON MARINA DEL REY

$$$$ This luxurious dockside property on the marina's north end is ideally situated for taking in the bustling waterfront. The 306 opulent guest rooms boast Italian marble bathrooms—complete with terry robes, hair dryers, and toiletries—an armoire, minibar, multiple phones, and a safe. Guests on the exceptional 46-room **Club Floor** are treated to complimentary breakfast, light meals and drinks, and other special services. As one would expect from a Ritz, amenities include just about anything your heart desires . . . just ask. The hotel's dinner restaurant, **Jer-ne** (formerly the Dining Room), offers fine French fare prepared by chef Troy Thompson, who makes a mean duck à l'orange (among other things). The **Terrace** serves all three meals daily; the more casual **Pool Café** is for light snacks, and cocktails can be enjoyed at the **Library Bar.** A pool, fitness center, and bicycle rentals can help work it all off. ♦ 4375 Admiralty Way (at Via Regatta). 800/241.3333, 310/823.1700; fax 310/823.8421. www.ritzcarlton.com

4 MARINA CITY TOWERS

Designed by **Anthony Lumsden** for DMJM in 1971, the towers' rounded shapes resemble enormous horseshoe magnets tugging at each other. ♦ 4333 Admiralty Way (between Via Regatta and Palawan Way)

5 CAFE DEL REY

★★★$$$ Just too trendy for words, with all the typical Westside accoutrements (sleek interiors and beautiful people), coupled with a magnificent view of the marina and great food, this restaurant is the area's best. Japanese chef Katsuo "Naga" Nagasawa brings his Italian and French training to the kitchen with creations such as grilled blackened swordfish with grilled banana, seared ahi tuna with mushroom potato ragout, red bell pepper linguine with smoked salmon, and wild mushroom ravioli. ♦ California ♦ Daily, lunch and dinner. Reservations recommended. 4451 Admiralty Way (between Bali Way and Via Regatta). 310/823.6395

6 THE CHEESECAKE FACTORY

$$ Specialty drinks are the name of the game at this branch of the popular restaurant chain. Sip a Flying Gorilla or Strawberry Creamsicle while looking out over the boat slips. Then enjoy a meal of really big portions of whatever you order—so much you'll need a doggie bag. And, if you really want to kiss your diet good-bye, order a slice of one of the 35 varieties of cheesecake. ♦ American ♦ Daily, lunch and dinner. 4142 Via Marina (between Panay and Admiralty Ways). 310/306.3344. There are half a dozen or so Cheesecake Factory restaurants throughout the Southland; two other very popular ones can be found at 364 N Beverly Dr (one block south of Little Santa Monica), Beverly Hills. 310/278.7270; 11647 San Vicente Blvd (between Barrington & Darlington Aves), Brentwood. 310/826.7111 (this one's popular with a young "uptown crowd")

7 MARINA DEL REY HOTEL

$$$ An ideal base for sailors, this nautical-style, 157-room luxury hotel is surrounded by water on three sides. The **Crystal Seahorse** restaurant overlooks the marina's main channel. Additional facilities include a pool, lounge, bike and skate rentals, and complimentary use of **LA Fitness Center.** ♦ 13534 Bali Way (southwest of Admiralty Way). 310/301.1000, 800/862.7462 in CA, 800/882.4000 in the US; fax 310/301.8167

8 BURTON CHACE PARK

This park is perfect for yacht-watching, fishing, kite-flying, or moon-gazing from the watchtower. Picnic facilities (with restrooms) attract families. ♦ Mindanao Way (southwest of Admiralty Way)

9 FISHERMAN'S VILLAGE

Sunday afternoon jazz concerts enliven this tourist attraction of quaint restaurants (with marginal food) and shops. A great spot for yacht-watching along the marina channel, it also offers harbor cruises. ♦ 13755 Fiji Way (southeast of Admiralty Way). 310/823.5411

10 SOUTHERN CALIFORNIA INSTITUTE OF ARCHITECTURE (SCI-ARC)

This creative design laboratory was established by Raymond Kappe in 1972 and is currently headed by Michael Rotondi, one of the first graduates and formerly a principal with Morphosis (he now heads his own firm, Roto). Four hundred students from 50 countries study with a talented and aggressive faculty in a nondescript two-story commercial and warehouse space. Exhibitions and lectures by the world's leading architects are open to the public free of charge. ♦ 5454 Beethoven St (at W Jefferson Blvd). 310/574.1123

11 INN AT PLAYA DEL REY

$$ In a terrific location—a few blocks from the beach and just a five-minute drive from LAX—this luxurious bed-and-breakfast is a real find. Each of the 22 guest rooms is decorated in charming Cape Cod style; all feature private baths, phones (with voice mail), cable TV, computer hookups, and views of the Channel; some also boast canopied beds, sunken Jacuzzi tubs, fireplaces, and decks or porches. Rates include full breakfast, afternoon tea, and wine and hors d'oeuvres in the evening. Guests may use the inn's bicycles to ride on a nearby path that overlooks the ocean, and there's also a bird sanctuary just outside the breakfast room. ♦ 435 Culver Blvd (at Pershing Dr). 310/574.1920. www.innatplayadelrey.com &

12 LOYOLA MARYMOUNT UNIVERSITY

Founded in 1865, this successor to St. Vincent's (the first college in Los Angeles) is now a coed private Catholic university. ♦ Loyola Blvd and W 80th St. 310/338.2700

13 LOYOLA THEATER

A luxurious former preview theater for Twentieth Century-Fox has been gutted and turned into offices. The 1946 swan's-neck façade survives. ♦ N Sepulveda Blvd and W Manchester Ave

14 AIRPORT MARINA HOTEL

$ Close to LAX but not on hotel row, this 770-room hostelry sits across from a city park with a 15-hole golf course, and next door to a bowling alley. Free shuttles to the airport and to Marina del Rey and Culver City shopping malls are available. ♦ 8601 Lincoln Blvd (at W Manchester Ave). 310/670.8111, 800/225.8126; fax 310/337.1883 &

15 SHERATON GATEWAY LOS ANGELES AIRPORT HOTEL

$$$ A $15 million renovation made this 807-room airport hotel much more appealing to both business travelers and tourists. The property boasts a fitness room, concierge, two club floors, a restaurant, and the only sushi bar in the airport area. A nice touch is the shuttle service to nearby beaches and Manhattan Beach shops. Room service is available around the clock. ♦ 6101 W Century Blvd (between Airport Blvd and Vicksburg Ave). 310/642.1111, 800/325.3535; fax 310/410.1267. www.sheraton.com &

15 WYNDHAM HOTEL AT LOS ANGELES AIRPORT

$$$ This prime business-traveler-oriented hotel has 591 soundproof rooms with lots of amenities, including special bath and body packages, coffeemaker, and shower massagers. Besides the gamut of business tools, there's a health spa, pool, steak house, café, and sports bar. Commuters have free 24-hour shuttle service to LAX. ♦ 6225 W Century Blvd (at Vicksburg Ave). 310/670.9000, 800/233.1234; fax 310/670.8110. www.wyndham.com &

16 LOS ANGELES AIRPORT HILTON & TOWERS

$$$ This deluxe property is embellished by an attractive porte-cochere that leads into its grand lobby. Each of its 1,236 rooms and suites features a California contemporary décor with original artwork, colorful bedspreads, and tapestries. If you book a Tower Level suite, it comes with concierge services and complimentary continental breakfast and hors d'oeuvres. Other facilities include four restaurants, a sports bar, a sundeck, four Jacuzzis, a heated outdoor pool, a fitness center, a conference center, and shuttle service to and from LAX. ♦ 5711 W Century Blvd (between Bellanca Ave and Airport Blvd). 310/410.4000, 800/445.8667; fax 310/410.6250. www.hilton.com &

16 LA AIRPORT MARRIOTT HOTEL

$$ Another caravansary for families and business travelers, this 1,000-room hotel offers a health club, a children's game room, a beauty salon, three restaurants, a 24-hour airport shuttle, and concierge service. ♦ 5855 W Century Blvd (at Airport Blvd). 310/641.5700, 800/228.9290; fax 310/337.5358. www.marriott.com &

16 RENAISSANCE LOS ANGELES HOTEL

$$$ There are 499 rooms and 16 function rooms, which tells you this hotel caters primarily to the business traveler, though it does offer somewhat of an intimate style and personal attention. The décor is upscale, with polished brass and mahogany appointments, marble floors, and a $10 million art collection. The rooms and suites feature marble baths, large soundproofed windows, fax machines, phones with voice mail, and coffeemakers. There are two restaurants (a steak house and a brasserie), an espresso bar, a lobby lounge, a small fitness center,

pool, and Jacuzzi; secretarial services are available. ◆ 9620 Airport Blvd (between W 98th and W 96th Sts). 310/337.2800, 800/647.6437 in CA, 800/228.9898 in the US; fax 310/216.6681. www.renaissancehotels.com ♿

17 QUALITY HOTEL LAX

$$ This 277-room hotel features an outdoor pool, exercise room, two restaurants, room service, a ballroom, conference rooms, and a complimentary 24-hour airport shuttle. ◆ 5249 W Century Blvd (between S La Cienega and Aviation Blvds). 310/645.2200, 800/228.5151; fax 310/641.8214. www.choicehotels.com ♿

18 LOS ANGELES INTERNATIONAL AIRPORT (LAX)

A general flying field in the early 1920s, LAX was first known as the Municipal Airport of Los Angeles. The postwar building boom and westward migration prompted city planners to greatly expand the airport between 1959 and 1962, with William Pereira Associates supervising the master plan. The airport was again expanded for the 1984 Olympic Games, and the five-level **Tom Bradley International Terminal** was added. In 1996, the terminal's mezzanine was redesigned to include a central waterfall, grand staircase, and gourmet food concessions. At the same time, Walt Disney Imagineering created the nearby **Theme Building,** which houses Encounter, an intergalactic restaurant complete with laser lights and "levitating" bar stools. Close to a million flights and upwards of 65 million passengers pass through any of the four east-west runways of the 3,500-acre site annually. The LA regional airport system includes Ontario International Airport to the east, Bob Hope Airport to the north, and Long Beach Municipal Airport and John Wayne Airport (Orange County) to the south. For detailed information on airlines, airport transportation, and parking, see "Airports" in the Orientation chapter on page 6.

In 1929, the Graf Zeppelin LZ 127 completed the first trans-Pacific flight from Japan to Los Angeles. It landed at the site of Los Angeles International Airport, then called Mines Field.

According to Ripley's Believe It or Not, the Skinny House (708 Gladys Ave) is the narrowest residence in the country. Nelson Rummond built it in 1932 on a bet that he couldn't construct a habitable structure on the tiny 10-by-50-foot lot. Rummond used unemployed workmen to erect the three-story, 860-square-foot Tudor-style home.

19 FOUR POINTS SHERATON

$$ Everything a business traveler could want and more can be found at this 573-room airport hotel. Accommodations are big, comfortable, and contain all the necessary creature comforts, from hair dryers to coffeemakers as well as free newspapers, cable TV, ironing board, and the like. Special executive-floor rooms come with all that plus data port hookups, complimentary water on arrival, and full American breakfasts. There are a couple of decent restaurants: **Palm Grill** ($$), where you can have breakfast, lunch, or dinner, a cup of Starbucks, a glass of Naked Juices, a slice of fantastic cheesecake, or a special anti–jet lag Body Clock meal (open 6AM-11PM); and **T.H. Brewsters,** a brew pub featuring an actual beer sommelier (no joke), light bar food, televised sporting events, and pop music (open 1PM-2AM). There's also 24-hour room service. Conveniently, the business and fitness centers are also open around the clock. And for your recreational needs, there's an Olympic-size pool, a huge sundeck, and a billiards/game room. Free shuttle service to and from LAX is also part of the deal. ◆ 9750 Airport Blvd (at 98th St). 310/645.4600, 800-LAXHOTEL (direct), 800/325-3535; fax 310/649.7047. www.fourpointslax.com

EL SEGUNDO AND MANHATTAN, HERMOSA, AND REDONDO BEACHES

A jumble of pastel cottages, posh condos, and huge beachfront homes that were once summer getaways are now year-round residences in a series of permanent communities. **El Segundo** has the least-developed waterfront and is hemmed in by the airport and a huge oil refinery. With its extravagant houses, pricey apartment complexes, and upscale restaurants, **Manhattan Beach** is a magnet for an affluent society of both married couples and swinging singles. South of Manhattan Beach is **Hermosa Beach,** the prototypical beach town with its concentration of surfers, volleyballers, and sun worshipers. And farther south is **Redondo Beach,** a mixture of the well-heeled new and the slightly seedy old, with a wonderful pier and marina complex offering boutiques, shops, and eateries galore.

20 HOUSTON'S

★★$ One of the most popular places in the beach area, this casual, friendly restaurant serves old-fashioned American food with some newfangled twists. The menu ranges from simple (but juicy) hamburgers and ribs to creative dishes like tortilla soup, grilled chicken salad, eggless Caesar salad, and spinach-and-artichoke dip. The dining room is handsomely decked out, with dark maple and cherry wood accents, a stone floor, and a long, marble-topped bar. ◆ American ◆ Daily, lunch and dinner. 1550-A Rosecrans Ave (between Apollo and S Nash Sts), El Segundo. 310/643.7211. Also at 10250 Santa Monica Blvd (at Century Park West), Century City. 310/557.1285; 5921 Owensmouth Ave (at Oxnard), Woodland Hills. 818/348.1095; 320 S. Arroyo Pkwy (at Del Mar Ave), Pasadena. 626/577.6001 ◈

21 BARNABEY'S

$$$ This 125-room Victorian fantasy hotel is adorably quaint, with its canopied four-poster beds, leaded glass, deep carpets, marble statuary, old books, and antiques, all enhanced by top-quality service. There's a pool and a pretty garden. The intimate Auberge restaurant serves traditional American cuisine, while Rosie's Pub offers nightly entertainment and dancing on weekends. ◆ 3501 Sepulveda Blvd (at N Valley Dr), Manhattan Beach. 310/545.8466, 800/552.5285; fax 310/545.8621; email: barnabeys@ix.netcom.com. www.barnabeys.com

At press time, Barnabey's was closed for a major renovation and scheduled to reopen sometime in 2004.

22 THE MURAD SPA

Scented by aromatic oils, this soothing day spa provides a salubrious sanctuary for those seeking the ultimate in pampering. Noted dermatologist Howard Murad also showcases his fabulous rejuvenating creams, bath and body treatments, and hair-care products, all of which are on sale here. ◆ Daily. 2141 Rosecrans Ave (at Park Way), Manhattan Beach. 310/726.0470

22 MANHATTAN BEACH MARRIOTT

$$$ This 385-room hotel offers comfortable but not exceptional accommodations designed for the in-and-out business traveler, for whom there's a special "Room that Works" equipped with a big work desk, ergonomic chairs, data ports, and other aids of the trade. Amenities include a nine-hole golf course, shuttle service to the airport (complimentary) and to the beach, concierge service, a full-service health club, and a pool. There's also Bleachers Sports Bar, the Terrace Restaurant (which is open for breakfast, lunch, and dinner), a lobby bar, and a Pizza Hut. ◆ 1400 Parkview Ave (east of Village Dr), Manhattan Beach. 310/546.7511, 800/228.9290; fax 310/546.7520. www.mariotthotels.com ◈

22 REED'S

★★★$$$ The subtle décor aptly showcases the inventive culinary style of the noted chef/owners, Joe Miller and Brandon Reed, who whip up sea bass with tequila sauce, white fish in Chardonney sauce, chicken ravioli, and other tempting dishes. ◆ California/Pacific Rim ◆ M, lunch; Tu-F, lunch and dinner; Su, brunch and dinner. Reservations required. 2640 Sepulveda Blvd (at 27th St), Manhattan Beach. 310/546.3299 ◈

23 CAFE PIERRE

★★$$ Franco-California cuisine visits the beach cities in this rustic and comfortable setting. The escargot du chef, Louisiana crab cakes, and Chilean sea bass are especially good. ◆ California/French Bistro ◆ M-F, lunch and dinner; Sa, Su, dinner. 317 Manhattan Beach Blvd (between N Morningside Dr and Valley Dr and N Highland Ave), Manhattan Beach. 310/545.5252. www.cafepierre.com

24 FONZ

★★★$$ Have a great steak in a comfortable, home-style setting where ocean breezes waft from across the street and a friendly wait staff makes you feel like you're visiting friends. The Angus beef is boffo, and so are the starters like braised Portobello mushrooms, seared ahi, and crab cakes. From the sea there's grilled albacore; sea bass with sautéed Asian veggies, papaya, and ginger sauce; and salmon done divinely. Carnivores can sink their teeth into tender New York steak, filet mignon, flank steak, or Fonz's meatloaf. There's a great wine list and lots of yummy dessert choices. ◆ Steak House/Seafood ◆ Daily, dinner; Sa, Su, brunch in summer. Reservations recommended. 1017 Manhattan Ave (between 10th Pl and 11th St), Manhattan Beach. 310/376.1536 ◈

25 HERMOSA BEACH PIER STRAND

Thanks to a restoration in 1997, this area near the fishing pier was converted into a charming, palm tree–lined walkway with benches, cafés, and restaurants. Pedestrians can stroll straight down to the ocean or out onto the pier. Some new spots include **Lapperts** (29 Pier Ave; 310/318.3953), the Hawaiian ice-cream vendor that scoops out the best sundaes this side of the islands; **Shirt Tales** (34 Pier Ave; 310/379.1073), a tiny but well-stocked T-shirt shop; and **Treasure Chest** (50 Pier Ave; 310/372.5644), a cool vintage outlet with far-out LA styles. Farther out on the pier is a tackle shop (310/372.2124) that rents equipment and sells bait. ◆ Pier: daily, 24 hours. Pier Ave (between Hermosa Ave and Hermosa Beach Pier), Hermosa Beach

Restaurants/Clubs: Red | Hotels: Purple | Shops: Orange | Outdoors/Parks: Green | Sights/Culture: Blue

Along the Hermosa Beach Pier Strand:

Il Boccaccio

★★$$ Pungent scents of garlic and aged Italian cheeses permeate this Old World trattoria, where good food is complemented by rich wood, white linens, and attentive service. The menu offers pastas, pizzas, great polenta, seafood, and more. ♦ Italian ♦ Daily, dinner. 39 Pier Ave. 310/376.0211

Down Town Bakery

Yummy desserts, pastries, muffins, coffees, teas, and juices can be taken to go or enjoyed on the adjacent patio (where a big basket filled with books keeps the kids entertained). ♦ Daily, 6AM-midnight. 37 Pier Ave. 310/374.0026

The Lighthouse

This is one of the best and oldest jazz clubs in Los Angeles. The fine music and top-flight performers have kept its doors open since the 1950s. Enjoy a weekend brunch enhanced by live jazz. ♦ Cover. Daily. 30 Pier Ave. 310/372.6911

Hennessey's Tavern

★★$ Big with the beach crowd, who throng here from dawn through midnight, this place is known for its unpretentious yet eclectic offerings: Irish nachos, quesadillas, Southern fried chicken, Caesar salad, burgers, sandwiches, and drinks. Rooftop dining overlooks the ocean. The lower-level bar is a happening watering spot, with its TV and friendly barkeeps. ♦ American/Irish/Mexican ♦ Daily, breakfast, lunch, and dinner. 8 Pier Ave. 310/372.5759

25 Comedy & Magic Club

Some of comedy's finest—Jay Leno, Rodney Dangerfield, Robin Williams, Garry Shandling—occasionally hit the stage here to try out new material. But even the lesser-known comedians and magicians at this Art Deco spot will keep you giggling. ♦ Cover. Hours vary; call ahead for show times. Reservations required. 1018 Hermosa Ave (between 10th St and Pier Ave), Hermosa Beach. 310/372.1193

25 The Lounge at the Beach

At press time, this adjunct to the Comedy & Magic Club was closed for a major renovation

A telephone "surf line" gives more than wave information. It includes a bacteria count for the water at LA's surfing hot spots.

In 1908, Long Beach became the first California city to organize a lifeguard service.

that will convert it into a jazz club. Plans are to open nightly Tuesday through Sunday. Call ahead. ♦ 1018 Hermosa Ave, Hermosa Beach (next door to the Comedy & Magic Club). 310/372.1193. www.comedyandmagicclub.com

26 Poulet du Jour

★$ Homemade specialties include barbecued lamb, hummus, baba ghanouj, and tabbouleh. ♦ Middle Eastern ♦ M-Sa, lunch and dinner. Reservations recommended F-Sa. 233 Pacific Coast Hwy (between Second and Third Sts), Hermosa Beach. 310/376.6620

27 Redondo Sportfishing Pier

The tackle shop at this privately owned pier rents and sells equipment and bait. There's a snack bar, too. ♦ Pier: daily. Tackle shop: daily. Portofino Way (west of N Harbor Dr), Redondo Beach. 310/372.2111

THE PORTOFINO
HOTEL and YACHT CLUB

A Noble House Hotel

27 Portofino Hotel and Yacht Club

$$$ Each of the 163 recently remodeled rooms in this midsize oceanfront hotel has a balcony and a view overlooking picturesque King Harbor. Amenities include a health club and the Breakwater Steak, Jazz and Seafood Restaurant. ♦ 260 Portofino Way (west of N Harbor Dr), Redondo Beach. 310/379.8481, 800/468.4292 in CA, 800/338.2993 in the US; fax 310/372.7329

27 Splash

★★$$ At this chic dining spot overlooking the Pacific and the Marina, Moroccan-born chef Malik Mekibes creates miracles with his sophisticated fusion cuisine. Start with an exotic appetizer like dim sum filled with truffles and foie gras and move along to the Chilean sea bass steamed in a banana leaf with date purée, saffron-scented apple, and quince compote, or the horseradish-encrusted salmon served on Thai rice with a heady vodka orange sauce. The glass-walled dining room is a dramatic leitmotif of purple, gold, and teal under a metal grid ceiling with a floor-to-ceiling aquarium, whimsical food art, and great ocean views. ♦ Eclectic California/Mediterranean ♦ Daily, breakfast, lunch, and dinner. Reservations recommended. Valet parking available. 350 N Harbor Dr (at Beryl St), Hermosa Beach. 310/798.5348 &

27 REDONDO SPORT FISHING

Choices from this charter service include a 45-minute harbor cruise, local offshore fishing, and deep-sea cruises to Catalina and Santa Barbara Islands. An exciting seasonal whale-watch allows you to observe the migration of the California gray whale from breathtakingly close range. ◆ Reservations required 24 hours in advance. 233 N Harbor Dr (south of Portofino Way), Redondo Beach. 310/372.3566

28 REDONDO BEACH PIER

This 70,000-square-foot landmark houses a cluster of small, touristy shops (offering T-shirts, bathing suits, postcards, and the like) and several casual and fast-food restaurants. Hundreds of people stroll through it each day. ◆ Coral Way (west of S Catalina Ave), Redondo Beach

28 MONSTAD BEACH PIER

In addition to a tackle shop that rents and sells equipment and bait, this privately owned 200-foot-long pier has **Tony's Fish Market Restaurant,** a casual spot where you can eat what others catch. ◆ Admission. Pier: daily, 24 hours. Tony's Fish Market Restaurant: daily, lunch and dinner. 310/376.6223. Redondo Coffee Shop Bait and Tackle: daily, breakfast, lunch, and dinner. Coral Way (west of S Catalina Ave), Redondo Beach. 310/318.1044

28 FISHERMAN'S WHARF

Everything from souvenir shops to places selling fresh fish (to buy or eat) lines the narrow path leading to the end of this pier. It's a popular place on summer nights, when many restaurants stay open late. ◆ Coral Way (west of S Catalina Ave), Redondo Beach

29 PALOS VERDES INN

$$$ This 110-room hotel is only three blocks from the beach. The guest rooms are attractively and simply decorated in shades of blue, sandy yellow, and beige; some feature four-poster beds and a Southwestern motif. There's also a restaurant (which offers room service from 8AM to 11PM), an enclosed outdoor pool and spa, complimentary bike rentals, and passes to a nearby fitness center. ◆ 1700 S Pacific Coast Hwy (at Palos Verdes Blvd), Redondo Beach. 310/316.4211, 800/421.9241 in the US; fax 310/316.4863

Adjacent to the Palos Verdes Inn:

CHEZ MELANGE

★★$$ True to its name, this cute eatery serves an international variety of victuals, from Japanese to Cajun. There's also a sushi bar, a wine counter, and a vodka/caviar/oyster bar. Chef Robert Bell whips up such standouts as warm lamb salad with mixed greens and fruit tarts. The wine-tasting dinners are celebrated citywide. ◆ International ◆ Daily, breakfast, lunch, and dinner. Reservations recommended. 310/540.1222

PALOS VERDES PENINSULA

In 1913, New York banker Frank Vanderlip bought most of this hilly peninsula and planned to turn it into a millionaires' colony. Slightly less ambitious developments began in the 1920s, leading to the creation of a series of exclusive residential enclaves and modest commercial centers, all in very conservative taste. Ranch houses alternate with Spanish haciendas, horse trails, and lovely hiking paths amid forests of eucalyptus trees. The hills are a succession of 13 marine uplift terraces created by Palos Verdes' slow rise from the ocean floor. www.palosverdes.com

30 PARADISE RESTAURANT

★$ Designer Scott Johnson created the exterior façade of this fun spot, which has a glass interior adorned with hanging lanterns and cozy colorful booths. The menu features a potpourri of exotic drinks and house specialties such as the baby greens salad with blue cheese and candied walnut herb vinaigrette, Szechuan chicken salad, pizza, grilled chicken and artichoke Sonora fettuccini, and paradise pot roast, with desserts like Key lime pie, flourless chocolate cake, and yin yang white-and-black cake. ◆ International ◆ M-F, lunch and dinner; Sa, dinner. Reservations recommended, especially on F-Sa. 889 190th St (at S Vermont Ave, at the junction of the Harbor and San Diego Fwys). 310/324.4800. www.paradiserestaurant.com

31 ALPINE VILLAGE

Quaff a stein of beer and down huge portions of German-Swiss food while listening to the band in the beer garden at this replica of an Alpine village. There's a restaurant and 24 shops offering an array of goods. ◆ Shops: daily. Restaurant: daily, lunch and dinner. Dancing: daily until midnight. 833 W Torrance Blvd (between Hamilton and S Vermont Aves). 310/327.4384

32 DEL AMO FASHION CENTER

With more than 350 stores in 2.6 million square feet of space, this is one of the largest retail centers of its kind. Department stores include **Sears, JC Penney, Robinsons-May, Macy's,**

Restaurants/Clubs: Red | Hotels: Purple | Shops: Orange | Outdoors/Parks: Green | Sights/Culture: Blue

and **Montgomery Ward.** Aside from these anchors, there are several independent fashion stores, more than 55 restaurants, and dramatic interior spaces. ♦ Daily. Bounded by Madrona Ave and Hawthorne Blvd, and Sepulveda Blvd and Fashion Way, Torrance. 310/542.8525 www.delamo.fashioncenter.com

33 CHEF SHAFER'S DEPOT

★★$$ With whitewashed brick walls, dark wood, classic tile work, and Moderne-style sconces, this popular eatery was carved out of a 1912 Red Car electric railway station. The food is offbeat and adventurous, ranging from Thai dyed chicken (a chicken breast covered in a blend of sweet spices on a bed of pasta) to Mexican hominy stew with lamb. ♦ California Eclectic ♦ M, Sa, Su, dinner; Tu-F, lunch and dinner. Reservations recommended. 1250 Cabrillo Ave (at Torrance Blvd), Torrance. 310/787.7501

34 MALAGA COVE PLAZA

In their 1922 plan for Palos Verdes, Charles H. Cheney and the Olmsted brothers envisioned four area community centers. This was the only one built. Designed by **Webber, Staunton & Spaulding** in 1924, it is a Spanish Revival design of two-story shops in an arcade. The plaza has a picturesque brick bridge over Via Chico and a fountain inspired by the Fountain of Neptune in Bologna, Italy. ♦ 200 Palos Verdes Dr W (at Via Corta), Palos Verdes Estates

34 LA RIVE GAUCHE

★★$$$ Classic French cuisine (try the veal chop with wild mushrooms) is served in this rustic but chic French-country setting. ♦ French ♦ M, dinner; Tu-Su, lunch and dinner. Reservations recommended. 320 Tejon Pl (just west of Via Corta), Palos Verdes Estates. 310/378.0267

35 RESTAURANT CHRISTINE

★★$$ Chef/owner Christine Brown has beefed up this cheerful bistro (formerly Fino) with Tucson hues of red, green, and orange, and offers an eclectic mix of Mediterranean, Pacific Rim, and California fare. Signature dishes include grilled Portobello mushrooms with scalloped potatoes, Louisiana crayfish and avocado salad, and fresh fish from around the world (like Costa Rican red silk snapper and African Lake Victoria perch). ♦ International ♦ M, W-F, lunch and dinner; Sa, Su, dinner. Reservations recommended. 24530 Hawthorne Blvd (between Newton and W 244th St), Torrance. 310/373.1952

36 LOMITA RAILROAD MUSEUM

Housed in a replica of the 19th-century Greenwood Station in Wakefield, Massachusetts, this museum displays memorabilia from the steam era of railroading.

An impeccably restored 1902 steam locomotive and a 1910 wooden caboose flank the station. Both are open to the public. The annex across the street offers picnic benches, a fountain, and a 1913 boxcar. ♦ Admission. W-Su. W 250th St and Woodward Ave, Lomita. 310/326.6255

37 SOUTH COAST BOTANIC GARDENS

Until 1956 this site was a diatomaceous earth mine. When mining activity ceased, the trash dumping began—3.5 million tons were poured in. Starting in 1960, though, the Los Angeles Department of Arboreta and Botanic Gardens initiated a landscaping program, and today the beautiful 87-acre gardens are a model experiment in land reclamation, containing mature specimens from all continents except Antarctica. There are also horticultural and botanical displays, a gift shop, gardening demonstrations every Sunday at 2PM, and a picnic area. ♦ Admission. Daily. 26300 Crenshaw Blvd (between Rolling Hills Rd and Palos Verdes Dr N), Rolling Hills Estates. 310/544.6815

38 GENERAL PHINEAS BANNING RESIDENCE MUSEUM

In 1864, Phineas Banning, father of the Los Angeles Harbor, built this Greek Revival clapboard home out of lumber from the Mendocino Coast and colored glass from Europe. Tours through the mansion include family and public rooms decorated in period furnishings. The **kitchen demonstration tour** focuses (naturally) on the restored kitchen, and food is cooked using Katherine Banning's recipes (call for schedule). The museum is located in 20-acre **Banning Park,** which has picnic facilities and a playground. Access to the house is by tour only. ♦ Donation requested. Tours: Tu-Su. 401 E M St (between Eubank and Broad Aves). 310/548.7777. www.banning.org

38 DRUM BARRACKS CIVIL WAR MUSEUM

This is the last remaining building of **Camp Drum,** a 7,000-soldier Union Army outpost that closed in 1871. Although California sympathized with the Confederacy during the Civil War, this large Union military presence kept the state in the blue ranks. The barracks have been refurbished as a museum of Civil War memorabilia. ♦ Admission. Tours: Tu-Sa. 1052 Banning Blvd (between E Opp and E L Sts). 310/548.7509

39 WAYFARER'S CHAPEL

Architect **Lloyd Wright**'s most-visited building occupies a prominent hillside location overlooking the ocean. The 1946 chapel is the national monument to Emmanuel

Swedenborg, a Swedish theologian and mystic. A redwood frame that blends nicely with the surrounding redwood grove supports the glass structure. ♦ Daily. Services: Su. 5755 Palos Verdes Dr S (between Narcissa Dr and Barkentine Rd), Rancho Palos Verdes. 310/377.1650

LOS ANGELES HARBOR

In 1876, the first railroad arrived in Los Angeles, but the city still lacked access to the sea. Despite its shallow, unprotected harbor, San Pedro (pronounced by locals as San Pee-dro) outmaneuvered Santa Monica for federal funding and became the main port of entry for the emerging metropolis. Work began in 1899 on a new breakwater and port expansion. In 1909, LA annexed San Pedro and Wilmington, creating the shoestring strip (at places only a half-mile wide) from downtown to the harbor, which provided for a seaport and transportation route within city limits. Today's harbor is the busiest import and export trade port in the nation, a hub of industry (notably oil refineries and aircraft plants), and the foremost port of call in Southern California for passenger vessels.

At the center of the harbor lies **Terminal Island,** linked to San Pedro by the Vincent Thomas Bridge and to Long Beach by the Gerald Desmond Bridge. The streets of downtown San Pedro retain much of the flavor of their colorful past as a seafarer's port town. The region's commercial fishing fleet employs many mariners of Portuguese, Greek, Serbian, and Croatian descent, resulting in an area rich in ethnically diverse shops and restaurants.

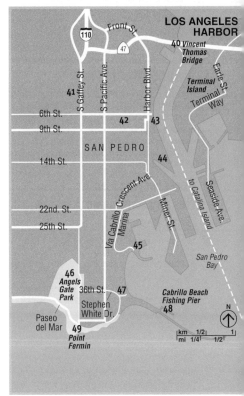

40 TERMINALS

On the west side of the main channel are passenger liner terminals and container terminals piled high with steel freight containers. The terminal for the *Catalina Express* and the Catalina helicopter (see page 227) lies just north of this point.

40 VINCENT THOMAS BRIDGE

Spanning the main channel between San Pedro and Terminal Island, this 6,500-foot-long turquoise suspension bridge clears the water by 185 feet so military planes can fly under it.

41 HOLIDAY INN

$$ This 60-room, European-style hotel boasts Victorian décor that is quite grand. The **Club 111** restaurant serves continental cuisine. ♦ 111 S Gaffey St (between Second and First Sts). 310/514.1414, 800/248.3188. www.holidayinnsanpedro.com

42 PAPADAKIS TAVERNA

★$$ If the mood is right, the waiters will dance in this lively, popular restaurant. ♦ Greek ♦ Daily, dinner. Reservations required. 301 W Sixth St (at S Centre St). 310/548.1186

43 LOS ANGELES MARITIME MUSEUM

A nautical history collection is appropriately housed in an old ferry building, refurbished by Pulliam & Matthews. Much of the old ferry gear remains, giving visitors a sense of imminent departure. Museum collections include ship models, the most impressive of which is a 16-foot scale model of the *Titanic*, fashioned from cardboard and matchsticks by a 14-year-old boy. The Naval Deck is replete with Navy memorabilia, including the bridge of the *Los Angeles*. ♦ Free. Tu-Su. Sampson Way (just south of E Sixth St). 310/548.7618

44 PORTS O' CALL VILLAGE

Nineteenth-century New England, a Mediterranean fishing village, and early California live again in this shopping and eating complex. It's beginning to show some wear and tear, but the complex is still worth a visit. The **Village Boat House** offers daily cruises of the harbor area, where visitors can see the inner harbor, yacht harbor, freighter operations,

---

Restaurants/Clubs: Red | Hotels: Purple | Shops: Orange | Outdoors/Parks: Green | Sights/Culture: Blue

scrapping yards, and the Coast Guard base. ♦ Tour hours vary with the season; call for hours and information. Nagoya Way (between Timms and Sampson Ways). 310/831.0287

45 MADEO RISTORANTE

★★$$$ A larger, more glamorous version of the Westside original, this ristorante serves great pasta, veal, and Florentine steak. ♦ Italian ♦ M-F, lunch and dinner; Sa, Su, dinner. Reservations recommended. 295 Whaler's Walk (east of Via Cabrillo Marina). 310/521.5333

46 FORT MCARTHUR RESERVATION AND ANGELS GATE PARK

The US Air Force still occupies part of this reservation (the fort dates back to 1888), but nearly 65 acres have been turned into a park and museum. The 20-acre park surrounding the **Korean Bell of Friendship** (a replica of a bronze bell made in AD 771, presented to the US by Korea during the 1976 Bicentennial celebration) offers picnic sites and a spectacular view of the Pacific and Point Fermin. A **military museum** preserves the workings (minus the guns) of the battery used as the biggest West Coast defense fortification during World War II, and also offers guided tours of the Port of Los Angeles control tower, by reservation. ♦ Free. Park: daily. Museum: Tu, Th, Sa, Su, noon-5PM. 3601 S Gaffey St (between Paseo del Mar and 30th St). 310/548.2631; email: curator_ftmac@juno.com. www.ftmac.org

47 CABRILLO MARINE AQUARIUM

A multimillion-dollar renovation of this aquarium saw the addition of an **Exploration Center** tailored to children. The youngsters can observe nature, work on experiments, and even dress like scientists. An aquatic nursery provides a nurturing area for young sea animals: grunion, garibaldi, and white sea bass. Children will also love the imaginative displays of marine life in this museum, designed by **Frank Gehry** in 1981. To emphasize the spirit of fun, Gehry created a village-like cluster of small buildings housing an aquarium, classrooms, and a theater in a dramatically enclosed, child-friendly playground with chain-link fencing. Visitors also can handle tide-pool creatures in a

Los Angeles County's top five industries are:
1. Business and professional services
2. Tourism
3. Health services
4. International trade
5. Motion picture and television

"touch tank." For information on whale-watching tours (offered from late December through early April), call 562/832.4444. ♦ Free; parking fee. Tu-Su. 3720 Stephen White Dr (at Oliver Vickery Circle Way). 310/548.7562. www.cabrilloaq.org

Next to the Cabrillo Marine Museum:

POINT FERMIN MARINE LIFE REFUGE

Brochures for a self-guided exploration of this tide-pool community are available at the museum.

48 CABRILLO BEACH FISHING PIER

A shop on the 1,500-foot-long publicly owned fishing pier sells equipment and live bait, but equipment rentals are not available. No license or fee is required to cast your fishing line. ♦ East of Oliver Vickery Circle Way

49 POINT FERMIN PARK

The 37 landscaped acres of this park along the palisades overlook the Pacific Ocean and Los Angeles Harbor. The lookout point has coin-operated telescopes, and the **whale-watching station** offers information on the California gray whales' annual winter migration to the Gulf of California. The Victorian Eastlake-style **lighthouse,** constructed in 1874 from bricks and lumber brought around Cape Horn by sailing ship, is not open to the public. The lighthouse used oil lamps approximating 2,100 candlepower until 1925, when electric power was installed. ♦ Free. Daily. Paseo del Mar and S Gaffey St. 310/548.7756

LONG BEACH

East of the harbor is California's fifth-largest city, Long Beach, which was founded in 1880 along five and a half miles of coastline. From the sandy strand south of the city, you can see the tropical camouflage of palm-clad islands created to conceal almost 600 still-producing offshore oil wells—each faux island covers 10 acres of soundproofed wells. The **Long Beach Harbor**, which opened in 1911, is a major port for electric machinery and Alaskan crude oil, and a significant West Coast port of entry.

Devastated by the 1933 earthquake, Long Beach has been rediscovering its unique combination of rustic seaside charm and urban sophistication in recent years. A complete urban renewal has brought trendy restaurants, nightspots, and shops. Long Beach hasn't completely lost touch with its past, either: Several historic landmarks and districts still remain outside the city center. In 1997, the $650 million Queensway Bay Project began development of 300 pristine acres along the downtown waterfront. Attractions include **Rainbow Harbor** and a bi-level public esplanade with rows of palm trees, plenty of restaurants, shops, and entertainment venues, and the new **Long Beach Aquarium of the Pacific.** A free Runabout shuttle service takes passengers to the city's points of interest, and in the downtown area, guides (easy to spot in their khaki pants, blue shirts, and caps) offer free advice about local attractions. The LA Rapid Transit District's Blue Line light rail runs from Long Beach's Transit Mall (W First St and Pacific Ave) to downtown LA daily from 5:30AM to 8PM; for more information, call 213/620.RAIL.

50 RANCHO LOS CERRITOS

The romance of the old rancho days is recalled in this renovated 1844 Monterey-style adobe. Don Juan Temple built the two-story residence on part of the 1790 Nieto land grant. Although later expanded, the house remains furnished as it was between 1866 and 1881, when the Bixby family used it as headquarters for their ranching empire. In addition to the children's room, the foreman's bedroom, and a blacksmith's shop, a wing features memorabilia of rancho life and a research library on California history. Some of the original walks and trees planted in the mid–19th century remain in the restored five-acre garden. ◆ Free. W-Su; Tours: Sa-Su. 4600 Virginia Rd (north of E San Antonio Dr). 562/424.9423

51 BIXBY HOUSE

One of the few remaining examples of English architect **Ernest Coxhead**'s residential work, this 1895 house was built for a member of the Bixby family. The wood-shingle Victorian has Craftsman design elements. It's a private residence. ◆ 11 La Linda Dr (between E Bixby Rd and Long Beach Blvd)

52 LONG BEACH MUNICIPAL AIRPORT

This airport is served by American Airlines and America West Airlines. Private bus companies provide transportation to Long Beach, and to destinations within Los Angeles and Orange Counties. ◆ 4100 Donald Douglas Dr (off Lakewood Blvd, between E Springs and Carson Sts). 562/570.2640

53 EL DORADO PARK

This 800-acre recreational facility is divided into two sections. **El Dorado East Regional Park** is an unstructured activity area containing meadows and several lakes (the largest rents paddleboats) where fishing is permitted, plus more than four miles of bicycle and roller-skating paths and an archery range. **El Dorado West City Park** offers an 18-hole golf course, night-lit tennis

courts, roller-skate rentals, six baseball diamonds, a children's playground, a band shell, and a branch of the Long Beach Public Library. The **El Dorado Nature Center,** located in the east section, is an 80-acre bird sanctuary. ◆ Vehicle admission fee. Parks: daily. Nature Center: Tu-Su. 7550 E Spring St (between San Gabriel River Fwy and Studebaker Rd). Parks information 562/429.6310, Nature Center information 562/421.9431

54 DRAKE PARK

Almost every architectural style known is found in this Long Beach historic district. ◆ Daisy Ave and Loma Vista Dr

55 RANCHO LOS ALAMITOS

Another part of the original 1790 Nieto land grant, this rancho's adobe house has been enlarged several times since it was built in 1806. The interior is very much as it was when the Bixby family occupied it during the 1920s and 1930s. The grounds contain cow and horse barns, a blacksmith's shop, and a lush five-acre garden planted with native California cacti and succulents, herbs, and exquisite Chinese and Japanese wisteria. Visitors to the buildings must join docent-led tours. ◆ Free. W-Su. 6400 Bixby Hill Rd (just east of Palos Verdes Ave). 562/431.3541

56 LEGENDS

★$ This rowdy sports bar and restaurant, founded in 1979 by rugby great John Morris and Rams all-pro Dennis Harrah, is filled with memorabilia, eight projection screens, and two news tickers. ◆ American ◆ Daily. 5236 E Second St (at Corona Ave). 562/433.5743

56 CAFFÈ GAZELLE

★$$ This pretty restaurant is famous for its hefty portions of pasta at reasonable prices. Be sure to try the creamy pine-nut soup. ◆ Italian ◆ Daily, dinner. No reservations. 191 Laverne Ave (at E Second St). 562/438.2881

56 Bono's

★★★$$$ The famous Bono daughter did it again with this hip and trendy California-style eatery just a stone's throw from Christy's. The décor is pure funk, with a glass-enclosed dining area, open ceiling with deep purple hues, and plenty of space between tables. As you might expect, the celebrity kid attracts her share of young tinsel-towners along with the usual complement of know-where-to-go stargazers. The food's good, too, and appeals to every appetite, with entrées ranging from BBQ shrimp to grilled ahi to New York steaks. ◆ California ◆ Daily, lunch and dinner.

Restaurants/Clubs: **Red** | Hotels: **Purple** | Shops: **Orange** | Outdoors/Parks: **Green** | Sights/Culture: **Blue**

Reservations suggested. 4901 E Second St (two blocks from Corona Ave). 562/434.9501

57 NAPLES

At the same time Abbot Kinney was creating his version of Venice in LA County, another American romantic, Arthur Parson, was dredging Alamitos Bay to create his own picture-perfect pastiche of Italy, building cottages on curving streets and along canals spanned by quaint footbridges. By the end of the 1920s, the community now known as Naples was complete. Today this residential neighborhood of Long Beach seems more American than Italian. The perimeter of the island is bordered by walkways that overlook the bay and a small beach. In the center, **Colonnade Park** is encircled by the Rivo Alto Canal. Although accessible by car, the island's true charm is seen only by the pedestrian.

57 THE GONDOLA GETAWAY

Take a one-hour cruise on an authentic Venetian gondola—with costumed gondolier—threading through the canals of Naples. Reserve months in advance for December (Christmas lights) and February (Valentine's Day), and one month ahead in summer. ◆ 5437 E Ocean Blvd (between 55th and 54th Pls). 562/433.9595

58 ANDIAMO

★★$$ Now that's Italian! This eatery, in the Marketplace Shopping Center, serves very good pastas, pizzas, and classic dishes. ◆ Italian ◆ Daily, lunch and dinner. Reservations recommended. 6509 Pacific Coast Hwy (just south of Westminster Ave). 562/493.5529

59 RUSSELL'S

★$ This tiny, busy coffee shop is part of a chain started in Long Beach in 1930; it offers the tastiest burgers and shakes anywhere, and good pie, too. ◆ American ◆ Daily, breakfast, lunch, and dinner. 5656 E Second St (between Ravenna and Campo Drs). 562/434.0226

59 MORRY'S OF NAPLES

Wine tastings are offered three nights a week at this long-established wine and liquor store. ◆ Daily. Tastings: W-F. 5764 E Second St (between Campo Walk and Ravenna Dr). 562/433.0405

60 ALAMITOS BAY LANDING

On this finger of land surrounded by Long Beach Marina boat slips, several chain restaurants, including the **Crab Pot** (562/430.0272), **Buster's Beach House Restaurant and Long Board Bar** (562/598.9431), **Khoury's** (562/598.6800), and **Joe's Crab Shack** (562/594.6551), serve standard steak and fresh seafood fare. ◆ 182 Marina Dr (south of E Second St). 562/799.3870

60 STAR PARTY CRUISES

Live reggae bands play on weekend cruises, and a Sunday champagne brunch features blues and jazz musicians aboard a 100-passenger boat. ◆ 140 Marina Dr (south of E Second St). 562/431.6833

61 MUSEUM OF LATIN AMERICAN ART (MoLAA)

Add a little salsa to your art appreciation at this thriving museum. Founded by Dr. Robert

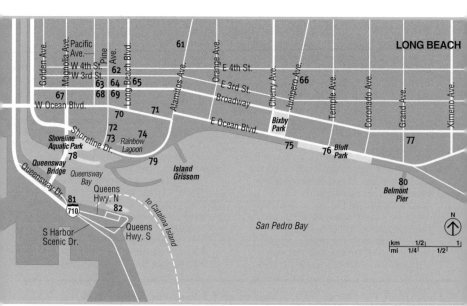

Gumbiner in November 1996, MoLAA is the only museum in the western US catering to contemporary Latin American Art. Located in the **East Village Arts District**, in the former Balboa Amusement Producing Company building (where silent films were once shot), MoLAA houses both a permanent collection and traveling exhibitions. A high vaulted ceiling and wooden floors, left over from a time when the building was a Hippodrome for skaters, provides a fitting showcase for the exhibits. There's the perfunctory museum gift shop, as well as a welcoming restaurant that's open from 11AM to 3PM called **Viva** that dishes out Latin American fare. ◆ Tu-Su. Admission except on F. 628 Alamitos Ave (at 7th St). 562/437.1680; fax 562/437.7043

62 RECREATION IN LONG BEACH MURAL

This 1936 Federal Arts Project mosaic by Henry Nord was originally in the now-demolished Municipal Auditorium. Currently installed on the Long Beach Plaza mall parking structure, it's slated to be moved to the new CityPlace open-air shopping center on the site of the Long Beach Plaza. ◆ E Third St (between Long Beach Blvd and Pine Ave)

63 M BARD GRILLE

This spare, high-tech café, coffeehouse, and art gallery is decorated with colorful tablecloths and carpets. Live jazz and blues music, performance art shows, and poetry readings can be enjoyed over dinner or a glass of wine or beer. ◆ California/American ◆ Daily. 213A Pine Ave (between W Broadway and W Third St). 562/435.2525

64 BLUE CAFE

How hip can you get? Blues bands, billiards, and a delightful café combine to make this an entertaining experience. ◆ Cover. Daily. 210 Promenade (between E Broadway and E Maple Way). 562/983.7111

65 ACRES OF BOOKS

Ray Bradbury acclaims this vast used-books emporium as a treasure. Nearly one million books line the miles of shelves in a 1922 Art Deco-style building. ◆ Tu-Sa. 240 Long Beach Blvd (between E Maple Way and E Third St). 562/437.6980

66 CARROLL PARK

The large houses here were built in the 1910s, and the bungalows in the 1920s. ◆ Bounded by Wisconsin and Junipero Aves, and E Third and E Fourth Sts

67 VISITORS' CENTER

Tourist and convention information is available here. ◆ M-F. 1 World Trade Center (at W Ocean Blvd), third floor. 562/436.3645

67 LONG BEACH HILTON

$$$ This 397-room mid-rise hotel in the World Trade Center offers a health club, an outdoor pool and Jacuzzi, 14 banquet rooms, a lobby bar, and the **City Grill** restaurant. Free LAX and Long Beach Municipal Airport shuttles are available. ◆ 2 World Trade Center (at W Ocean Blvd). 562/983.3400, 800/HILTONS; fax 562/983.1200

68 KING'S PINE AVENUE FISH HOUSE

★★$$ A classic grill ambience prevails in this corner restaurant, with rich wood textures and comfortable booths. The menu includes a variety of well-prepared fish dishes in unique sauces like Hawaiian swordfish  with papaya salsa and N'Awlins shrimp. A seasonal highlight is the Maryland soft-shell-crab piccata—blackened, deep fried. Also on the premises is the **King Crab Lounge,** an authentic New Orleans–style bar/oyster house, right down to the funky neon signs and Southern paraphernalia on the walls, offering six brands of microbrewery beers to accompany the seafood. ◆ Seafood/American ◆ M-F, lunch and dinner; Sa, Su, brunch, lunch, and dinner. Reservations recommended. 100 W Broadway (at N Pine Ave). 562/432.7463

68 L'OPERA

★★★$$$ This handsome, cosmopolitan restaurant is located in a turn-of-the-20th-century bank building with heavy green marble pillars, original high recessed ceilings, and modern touches of lighting that give it some contemporary verve. The menu, too, mixes the old and the new, with wonderful Roman fare that is both classic and modern. The vegetarian lasagna and ravioli are excellent. ◆ Italian ◆ M-F, lunch and dinner; Sa, Su, dinner. Reservations recommended. 101 N Pine Ave (at W First St). 562/491.0066

69 MUM'S

★$$ One of Long Beach's few hip dining spots, this modern urban restaurant and bar is brisk with professionals at lunchtime and lively

---

Restaurants/Clubs: Red | Hotels: Purple | Shops: Orange | Outdoors/Parks: Green | Sights/Culture: Blue

on Thursdays and weekends, when musicians (usually jazz) play on the patio or rooftop. Specialties include chestnut veal ravioli, mesquite-grilled fresh fish, and trendy pizza. ♦ Italian ♦ Daily, lunch and dinner. Reservations required. 144 N Pine Ave (at E Broadway). 562/437.7700

69 COHIBA CLUB

Taking its name from a legendary brand of Cuban cigar, this smoky nightclub features live bands as well as DJs. ♦ Cover. F-Sa. 110 E Broadway (between Tribune Ct and N Pine Ave). 562/437.7700

70 THE SKY ROOM RESTAURANT

★★★$$$ A 360-degree panoramic view of the downtown Long Beach skyline and the Pacific Ocean, combined with the historic Art Deco décor, superior service, and award-winning cuisine, makes this the perfect spot for special occasions. The menu satisfies all tastes with fresh fish, steaks, venison, lamb, and chicken entrées. Don't skip desserts here or you'll regret it. ♦ American ♦ Reservations suggested. M-Sa, dinner. 40 S Locust (at Ocean Blvd). 562/983.2703; e-mail: skyroom@earthlink.net. www.theskyroom.com

71 555 EAST

★★★$$$ Looking for traditional food and an old-fashioned dining experience? The dark but inviting interior with generous leather-upholstered banquettes can make you forget about "nouveau anything" restaurants. Dilled jumbo prawns or a pan-fried crab cake appetizer can be followed by juicy cuts of New York, porterhouse, and filet mignon, and a fine list of side dishes. ♦ American ♦ M-F, lunch and dinner; Sa, Su, dinner. Reservations recommended. 555 E Ocean Blvd (between Atlantic and N Linden Aves). 562/437.0626

72 LONG BEACH CONVENTION AND ENTERTAINMENT CENTER

The center is home to the acclaimed Long Beach Symphony Orchestra and International City Theater. The sports arena, which has recently become the home ice for the West Coast Hockey League team the Ice Dogs, also

The Beach Boys attended Hawthorne High, where Brian Wilson flunked a music class when he turned in the song that later became "Surfin' Safari."

The Academy Theatre (3100 Manchester Blvd, Inglewood) was built in 1939. Its distinctive pencil-like tower, crowned with a sunburst, rises 125 feet into the air.

hosts rodeos, rock concerts, and other events. ♦ S Pine Ave (between E Shoreline Dr and W Seaside Way). Ticket information 562/436.3661; Ice Dogs 562/436.3661

73 HYATT REGENCY

$$$ This luxurious 502-room atrium hotel near the convention center offers 19 suites with scenic harbor views, two restaurants, an outdoor pool, a spa, and business and banquet facilities. ♦ 200 S Pine Ave (between E Shoreline Dr and E Seaside Way). 562/491.1234, 800/233.1234; fax 562/432.1972. www.hyatt.com

74 PLANET OCEAN

Life-size gray whales and dolphins are depicted on the walls of the Long Beach Arena in this 122,000-square-foot mural—the largest in the world, created by internationally acclaimed environmental marine artist Wyland. ♦ Rainbow Lagoon Park, E Shoreline Dr (between S Linden and S Pine Aves)

75 LONG BEACH MUSEUM OF ART

Located in a 1912 Craftsman-style house, this museum sponsors changing exhibitions that emphasize contemporary Southern California art. The permanent collection includes works by the Laguna Canyon School of the 1920s and 1930s as well as WPA-sponsored pieces. The carriage house has a bookstore, gift shop, café, and gallery. ♦ Admission (free the first of each month). W-Su. 2300 E Ocean Blvd (between 20th and 19th Pls). 562/439.2119

76 BLUFF PARK

This historic district contains diversified houses fronting Ocean Boulevard. ♦ Temple Ave and E Ocean Blvd

77 CHRISTY'S RISTORANTE

★★$$$ This uptown neighborhood trattoria, owned by Christy Bono, daughter of Sonny and Cher, is spread out in four dining areas offering good, sturdy Northern and Southern Italian fare. The specialty bistecca Gorgonzola is an interesting presentation of stuffed prime filet. There are plenty of pastas and lots of salads and an extensive wine list to complement it all. ♦ Italian ♦ M-F, lunch and dinner; Sa, Su, dinner. Reservations a must. 3937 East Broadway at Termino Ave (between Mira Mar and Belmont). 562/433.7133

78 LONG BEACH AQUARIUM OF THE PACIFIC

LONG BEACH
AQUARIUM
OF THE PACIFIC®

This technologically advanced marine wonderland is recommended for kids of all ages. The $117 million facility offers up-close encounters with sharks, thousands of marine creatures representing 550 species, and myriad colorful fish. Waves crash overhead as visitors walk through the underwater tunnel of the seals' and sea lions' habitat. Throughout the complex, spectacular lighting and sound effects, touch tanks, hands-on wet labs, and multimedia activities make this a virtual walk through the Pacific. ♦ Admission. Daily. 100 Aquarium Way (south of W Shoreline Dr). 562/590.3100

79 SHORELINE VILLAGE

Part of the downtown marina, this is another ersatz historical waterfront shopping village with a few quaint tourist shops and popular restaurants (including two fish houses). A smaller reproduction of the 1906 Charles Looff **carousel** has replaced the original. For boat tours of Long Beach and Los Angeles Harbors and dinner cruises, call **Spirit Cruises** (562/495.5884) or **Shoreline Village Cruises** (562/495.5884). ♦ Daily. 407 E Shoreline Dr (between E Ocean Blvd and Queens Way). 562/590.8427

Within Shoreline Village:

ISLAND SUNFISH GRILL

★★$ Seafood lovers will delight in the fresh assortment of grilled, fried, and healthy choices at this casual indoor/outdoor waterfront bar and grill overlooking the Rainbow Harbor downtown marina. ♦ Daily, lunch and dinner. 432A Shoreline Village Dr. 562/285.2286. www.islandsunfish.com

80 BELMONT PIER

A bait shop (with tackle rentals) and a snack bar are located on this 1,300-foot municipal pier. ♦ Bait shop: daily. 39th Pl and Allin St. 562/434.6781

81 WEST COAST LONG BEACH HOTEL

$$ This five-story, 200-room waterfront hotel boasts a swimming pool and courts for tennis, volleyball, and basketball. The menu at the hotel's **Marina Pub & Cafe** includes everything from burgers and salads to pasta and seafood. ♦ 700 Queensway Dr (between Queens Hwy N and S Harbor Scenic Dr). 562/435.7676, 800/255.3050; fax 562/437.0866

82 QUEEN MARY

This majestic 81,237-ton passenger liner is berthed permanently in Long Beach Harbor. Launched in 1934, the vessel epitomized Art Deco luxury when she and her crew of 1,200 cruised the North Atlantic. In 1964 she was retired from service; in 1967 she was purchased by the City of Long Beach, and converted into a tourist attraction and luxury hotel with 365 cabins and three restaurants. If you're into nautical legend and lore, you'll find a treasure trove of maritime memorabilia. A variety of guided tours and exhibits help you explore everything from ghosts and myths to the behemoth ship's colorful history. By all means spend the night on board in one the staterooms, each of which provides the feel of yesterday with its wood paneling, Art Deco appointments, and portholes. Some suggest the presence of ghosts, so it could get a little eerie, but you'll get a good idea of what it must have been like to sail on this majestic Queen in her heyday. ♦ Queens Hwy N (between Windsor Way and S Harbor Scenic Dr). 562/435.3511, 800/437.2934, for stateroom reservations 562/432.6964. www.queenmary.com

Adjacent to the *Queen Mary*:

POVODNAYA LODKA B-427

Code-named "Scorpion," this 3,000-ton Soviet-built submarine was commissioned in 1973—during the height of the Cold War—by the Soviet government and went on to ply the seas for 21 years before being decommissioned. Formerly berthed in Sydney, Australia, the sub will be on view to the public here until 2009. ♦ Admission. Information 562/435.3511

CARNIVAL CRUISE LINES LONG BEACH TERMINAL

Carnival Cruises welcomes its Fun Ships *Ecstasy* and *Pride* passengers in style at this technologically advanced 30,000-square-foot terminal situated next to the *Queen Mary*. Designed by BEA of Coral Gables, Florida, the $40 million facility features a 300-foot-long, 35-foot-high passenger gangway, a 1,450-vehicle parking garage, and convenient drop-off and pick-up areas. The best part is the Carnival check-in lounge aboard the *Queen Mary*, where passengers can relax or tour the ocean liner prior to embarkation. ♦ For additional information, call Carnival Cruise Lines at 800/CARNIVAL, or the *Queen Mary* at 562/432.6964. www.queenmary.com; www.carnival.com

---

Restaurants/Clubs: **Red** | Hotels: **Purple** | Shops: **Orange** | Outdoors/Parks: **Green** | Sights/Culture: **Blue**

CATALINA ISLAND

Twenty-six miles across the sea, Santa Catalina is waiting for ye . . .

A cheerful little island that bustles in spring and summer and snoozes in winter, Catalina sits just 26 miles across the sea from the mainland. As you arrive by air or sea, the awesome misty green peaks of a mountain range that rises from the ocean floor to form this and the other Channel Islands seem to greet you with a smile. Next, your eyes will focus on the gleaming buildings climbing the hillside above the Mediterranean-style port of **Avalon** and its legendary casino. Finally you'll come into the thriving harbor, alive with pleasure boats and the occasional cruise ship. The picturesque, winding streets of the island are lined with red-tiled houses, boutiques, dive shops, quaint stores, and galleries. Alas, hotel rooms here are in short supply and are pricey during summer; many visitors simply take the ferry over for the day (it takes about an hour).

Catalina Island's resident population of 3,750 is far outnumbered by the influx of up to 12,000 visitors a day, and the town of Avalon, established in 1913, is straining at the seams. Fortunately, most of the island (21 miles long by 8 miles wide) has been preserved in its unspoiled natural state, and traffic is generally limited to golf carts and the buses that transport visitors along the back roads. (You can see even more of the island if you hike.) A 15-year plan to add houses, small hotels, and civic amenities—without sacrificing the small-town charm—is currently underway.

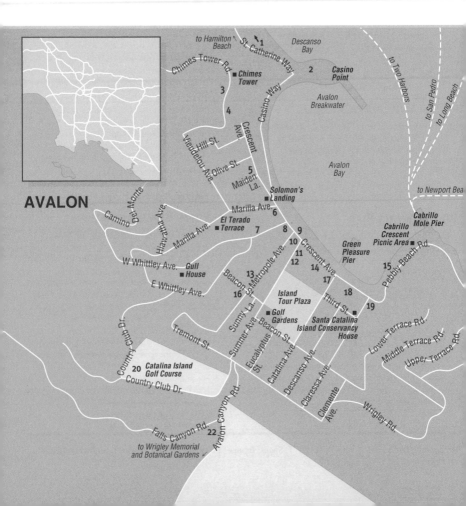

Most of the island has been privately owned since the native Indians were resettled on the mainland in 1811. Avalon was named in 1888 by the sister of an early developer, George Shatto, after the island of Avalon in Tennyson's *Idylls of the King,* the refuge of blessed souls in Celtic mythology. In 1919, William Wrigley Jr., the chewing-gum scion, purchased the Santa Catalina Island Company, built a casino in Avalon and a mansion for himself, and established a spring-training camp for his baseball team, the Chicago Cubs. Avalon became a popular tourist spot during the 1930s, but most of the interior of the island and much of the coastline remained undeveloped. A nonprofit conservancy acquired the title to about 86 percent of the island in 1975 and now administers this unique open space in conjunction with the County of Los Angeles.

The native wildlife in Catalina's underdeveloped interior is extraordinary. It is home to more than 100 species of birds and 400 species of native plant life (including eight types found only on this island, such as the Catalina ironweed, wild tomato, and *dudleya hassei,* which translates to "live forever"). Herds of wild bison (left by a movie crew several decades ago), boars, and goats roam free over the back region of the island.

For more visitor information, call 310/510.1520 or check out the web site at www. catalina.com.

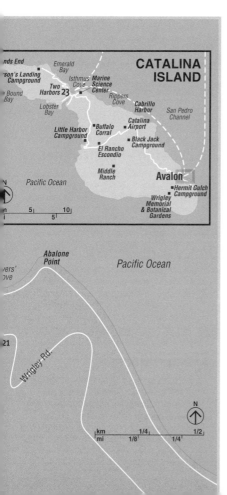

Getting to Catalina Island

By Boat

Your best bet is Catalina Express (310/519.1212, 800/622.2419, 800/315.3967; www.catalinaexpress.com), which operates three modern high-speed catamarans—the 300-passenger *Starship Express,* the 388-passenger *JetCar Express,* and the triple-deck, 360-passenger *Cat Express*—that make the trip to Avalon in less than an hour. Both sail round-trip from Long Beach, San Pedro, and Dana Point to Avalon daily year-round. For added comfort, pay a small extra fee for Commodore Lounge privileges, with which you get priority boarding, a free drink, a snack, and cushier seats. The company also operates four older vessels: a 56-passenger boat that takes campers to Two Harbors and three 150-passenger boats that arrive in Catalina in an hour from Long Beach or San Pedro and 90 minutes from Dana Point. The company also offers special hotel packages. The *Catalina Flyer* zips from Balboa Pavilion Newport in 75 minutes flat. 800/830.7744.

Rest rooms for the disabled can be found on the pier. Since most hotels and restaurants on the island were built before the California law mandating disabled access was put into effect, they are not necessarily wheelchair accessible. It's a good idea to ask when booking your room or making a restaurant reservation. For general visitor information, call 310/510.1520. www.catalinainfo.com

By Helicopter

The fastest, most convenient access to Catalina is by helicopter, though charter flights from Long Beach are available. The ride takes about 14 minutes in fair weather. **Island Express** (310/510.2525) flies from San Pedro and from beside the *Queen Mary* in Long Beach.

Getting Around Catalina Island

BY RENTAL CAR

Cars are not allowed in the interior. If you have a friend with a car on the island, you may obtain a temporary card key from the **Santa Catalina Island Conservancy** (310/510.1421) to drive outside of Avalon.

HIKING

Permits are required to hike into the interior and may be obtained at the Santa Catalina Island Conservancy (310/510.1421) in Avalon or at the **Catalina Cove and Camp Agency** (PO Box 5044, Two Harbors, Catalina; 310/510.0303) at the Isthmus.

TOURS

There are many sightseeing tours on Catalina Island, from glass-bottom boat excursions to scenic drives and fly-fishing boat trips. **Discovery Tours** (310/510.2000, 800/322.3434) offers semi-submersible boat excursions that provide passengers with awesome underwater views of sea life through large windows on the sides of the vessel. The boat departs twice daily from the Green Pleasure Pier in Avalon. Other tour operators include **Catalina Adventure Tours** (310/510.2888), **Catalina Safari Bus** (310/510.2800), and **Island Navigation** (310/510.0409).

FYI

Beach Realty (PO Box 2100, Avalon, CA 90704; 310/510.0039) can arrange cottage rentals. Note that most hotels require a two-day or even a one-week minimum stay during the summer.

The **Chamber of Commerce information office** on the Green Pleasure Pier in Avalon is open daily. To receive brochures describing the trails at Black Jack or Little Harbor or to make camping arrangements, call 310/510.0688 Monday through Friday. Information is also available at www.catalina.com and www.campingcatalinaisland.com.

Arrangements for camping at Little Fisherman's Cove (Two Harbors) must be made through **Catalina Cove and Camp Agency** (PO Box 5044, Two Harbors, CA 90704; 310/510.0303). All camping is by permit only and advance reservations are required. For additional information, call 310/510.3577 or check www.scico.com.

1 DESCANSO BEACH CLUB

Family cookouts are a popular event here— barbecue your own steaks or hamburgers, with salad and trimmings provided by the club. Descanso Beach Ocean Sports (310/510.1226), a private company on the premises, rents kayaks for exploring the ocean, guided or not. The beach is a short walk from the town of Avalon. The club is available for private parties. ♦ Call ahead for hours. Reservations required. St. Catherine Way (northwest of Casino Way). 310/510.2780. www.scico.com

2 CASINO

The island's signature building, a circular Spanish Moderne structure designed by **Webber & Spaulding** in 1928, is situated on a rocky promontory at the north end of Avalon Bay. It houses a beautiful 1,000-seat movie theater with fanciful underwater murals and an organ that is sometimes played during silent films. (Each theater seat has a hat rack on the back.) The grand ballroom hosts big-band concerts and other special events; there's also a small museum/art gallery. Tours of the structure and evening showings of movies are offered daily. ♦ 1 Casino Way (at St. Catherine Way). Movie schedule 310/510.0179, private parties 310/510.0550

3 ZANE GREY PUEBLO HOTEL

$$ Tahitian teak beams in an open-beam ceiling, a hewn-plank door, a log mantel, and walls of mortar mixed with goat's milk are combined with blessed isolation and an extraordinary view of the ocean and the hills in this former home of the foremost writer of the American West. The pueblo was originally built for Zane Grey in 1929 as a haven for his literary labors and fishing desires. There are 17 rooms, and amenities include free taxi pickup, an outdoor pool, and, although there is no restaurant, complimentary tea and coffee all day. The rates decrease in winter. ♦ 199 Chimes Tower Rd (east of Vieudelou Ave). 310/510.0966, 800/3-PUEBLO

4 WOLFE HOUSE

In 1928, **Rudolph Schindler** created this icon of Modernism, comprising a stack of balconied floors that exploit the steep site and its panoramic views. It's a private residence. ♦ 124 Chimes Tower Rd (east of Vieudelou Ave)

THE BEST

Dusty Fleming

Owner, Dusty Fleming beauty salon

Taking a drive up the **Pacific Coast Highway** for lunch in Malibu at **Geoffrey's** on the beach: the ride, beautiful and relaxing; the food, wonderful.

Getting a **shiatsu massage** at the **New Otani Hotel** in downtown LA. It's the perfect way to end a hard day of work. Not to mention, they give the best massages I've ever had.

Treating myself to dinner at **The Ivy–LA Desserts.** It has the best food in all of Los Angeles—and probably the country for that matter.

Katsu 3rd has some of the freshest seafood in the city. Be it sushi or grilled tuna, Chef Katsu will prepare food with expertise.

For a quiet afternoon, sitting up on **Sunset Plaza,** sipping on a cappuccino at one of the many restaurants, is always a plus. It's a great place to do some people-watching too!

For clothes shopping, **Maxfield** in West Hollywood has an incredible selection of top designer brands.

5 SEAPORT VILLAGE INN

$$$ Just steps from the beach, this pretty 30-room hotel features a spa, studio suites with views, and off-season packages. Additional amenities include color TV with cable, private baths, fully furnished kitchens, and wet bars (but no restaurant). ♦ 119 Maiden La (west of Crescent Ave). 310/510.0344, 800/2CATALINA. www.catalinacatalina.com

6 HOTEL VILLA PORTOFINO

$$$ Smack on the water's edge, this 34-room European-style hotel has two-bedroom units ideal for families, a large inviting sun deck, and the ambitious **Ristorante Villa Portofino,** next door, offering fine Italian cuisine. A complimentary breakfast is included in the rate, and there's a coffeemaker and refrigerator in each room. A special honeymooner's package is available. ♦ 111 Crescent Ave (between Whittley and Marilla Aves). 310/510.0555, 800/346.2326. www.villaportofino.com

7 HOTEL CATALINA

$$ The allure and style of yesterday prevails in this renovated 32-room Victorian hotel, only half a block from the beach. A nice touch is the complimentary movies shown every afternoon. The only other amenity is a Jacuzzi. There's no restaurant on premises, but plenty are within walking distance. ♦ 129 Whittley Ave (west of Crescent Ave). 310/510.0027, 800/540.0184; fax 310/510.1495. www.hotelcatalina.com

8 CHANNEL HOUSE

$ The food's just passable, but the setting is spectacular. Go for lunch and order a salad or sandwich on the terrace, where you can gaze out over the bustling harbor. ♦ American ♦ Daily, lunch and dinner June-Oct; F-Su, Mar-June. 205 Crescent Ave (between Metropole and Whittley Aves). 310/510.1617

9 ARMSTRONG'S SEAFOOD RESTAURANT

★★$$ Specialties include mesquite-grilled swordfish, fresh lobster, and abalone. Check the chalkboard for the day's specials. ♦ Seafood ♦ Daily, lunch and dinner. Reservations recommended for large parties. 300 Crescent Ave (at Metropole Ave). 310/510.0113

9 BUSY BEE

★★$ Chinese chicken salad with ginger dressing, hamburgers, and sandwiches are offered in this pleasant café. ♦ American ♦ Daily, breakfast, lunch, and dinner June-Oct; F-Su, lunch and dinner Mar-June. 306 Crescent Ave (between Sumner and Metropole Aves). 310/510.1983

10 LLOYDS OF AVALON

$ Saltwater taffy is an island institution, and watching the candy being made here is a popular activity. There's also a standard menu of grilled and fried items (hamburgers, fish and chips, etc.), as well as tacos, enchiladas, and tuna sandwiches. ♦ American ♦ M-W, F, Sa, lunch and dinner. 315 Crescent Ave (between Sumner and Metropole Aves). 310/510.1579

Restaurants/Clubs: **Red** | Hotels: **Purple** | Shops: Orange | Outdoors/Parks: **Green** | Sights/Culture: Blue

Los Angeles is a city, a county, and a region. The city is 467 square miles; the county covers 4,083 square miles; and the five-county region (including Los Angeles, Riverside, Ventura, Orange, and San Bernardino Counties) is 34,149 square miles. Los Angeles County has 88 incorporated cities, of which the city of Los Angeles is the largest.

10 CHI-CHI CLUB

Live jazz and bluegrass tunes keep this club hopping. ♦ Cover charge on weekends during the summer. Call ahead for hours and programs. 107 Sumner Ave (just south of Crescent Ave). 310/510.2828

11 SNUG HARBOR INN

$$ Originally built in the late 1880s, the former Hotel Monterey was completely renovated and reopened in the fall of 1997 as this charming six-room inn. Each deluxe guest room features a private bath, bay views, terry-cloth slippers, goose-down comforters, custom-made rugs, a fireplace, and nightly milk and cookies to enjoy by the fire. They also throw in a free continental breakfast and an evening wine-and-cheese reception. ♦ 108 Sumner Ave (at Crescent Ave). 310/510.8400; fax 310/510.8418. www.snugharbor-inn.com

12 GLENMORE PLAZA HOTEL

$$$ This charming Victorian hostelry, built at the turn of the 20th century, offers 45 rooms with whirlpool tubs that include a continental breakfast, afternoon wine and cheese, and shuttle to the boat area. There's no restaurant. ♦ 120 Sumner Ave (between Beacon St and Crescent Ave). 310/510.0017, 800/422.8254; fax 310/510.2833. www.catalina.com/glenmore.html

13 CASA MARIQUITA

$$ A quick jog from the beach, this precious hotel offers 22 cheerful guest rooms with king-size beds. Amenities include complimentary continental breakfast, shuttle service from the boat dock, cable TV, refrigerators, and a friendly staff. ♦ 229 Metropole Ave (between Beacon St and Crescent Ave). 800/545.1192, 310/510.1192. www.catalina.com/casamarq.html

14 AVALON BAY COMPANY

This little shop has the island's largest selection of women's clothing, shoes, and accessories. ♦ Daily. 407 Crescent Ave (between Catalina and Sumner Aves). 310/510.0178. www.avalonbaycompany.com

15 WET SPOT KAYAK RENTALS

Novice and experienced kayakers can explore the island's secluded coves and reefs on half-and full-day journeys (with guides on request). ♦ 120 Pebbly Beach Rd (northeast of Crescent Ave). 310/510.2229

16 HOTEL ST. LAUREN

$$$ Victorian décor and harbor views are two of the attractions of this charming 42-room hotel, located a block from the water. Amenities include king-size beds, whirlpool tubs, oceanfront views, and continental breakfast. ♦ 231 Beacon St (at Metropole Ave). 310/510.2999, 800/645.2478; fax 310/510.1365. www.stlauren.com

17 HOTEL VISTA DEL MAR

$$$ Located smack on the beach overlooking Avalon Bay, each of this hotel's 15 rooms has a fireplace, refrigerator, wet bar, ocean view, balcony, and a Jacuzzi tub, and comes with a free continental breakfast. There's no restaurant on site, but there is room service. ♦ 417 Crescent Ave (at Catalina Ave). 310/510.1452; fax 310/510.2917. www.hotel-vistadelmar.com

Below Hotel Vista del Mar:

BUOYS & GULLS

Shop for designer sportswear like Polo, Nautica, Reyn Spooner, and others, plus Speedo, Levi's, and more at this bi-level boutique. ♦ Daily. 310/510.0416. www.buoysandgulls.com

18 PAVILION LODGE

$$ A large central courtyard, free cable TV, and group rates can all be enjoyed at this 73-room lodge, which is one of the island's more popular hotels. No restaurant, however. ♦ 513 Crescent Ave (between Claressa and Catalina Aves). 310/510.2500, 800/322.3434. www.scico.com

19 CAFE PREGO

★$$ Old World warmth and charm are offered here, along with sautéed calamari, linguine with clams, and veal piccata. ♦ Italian ♦ Daily, dinner. 603 Crescent Ave (just east of Claressa Ave). 310/510.1218

20 CATALINA CANYON RESORT & SPA

$$ Nestled in the tranquil foothills above Avalon Bay, this Mediterranean-style resort offers 83 comfortable rooms with standard amenities: TVs, phones, king- or queen-size beds, and private baths. There's a full-service European spa, heated pool, restaurant, and courtesy shuttle. ♦ 888 Country Club Dr (between Tremont St and E Whittley Ave).

SONGS IN THE KEY OF LA LIFE

Los Angeles has been celebrated in many different types of music over the years. Artists in rock 'n' roll, country, and the blues have all taken the opportunity to serenade the city. The following are just a few of the results:

Song Title	Artist	Song Title	Artist
All I Wanna Do	Sheryl Crow	I Love LA	Randy Newman
Blue Jay Way	Beatles	It Never Rains in Southern California	Albert Hammond
Born in East LA	Cheech & Chong	La Bamba	Richie Valens
California Dreamin'	Mamas and the Papas	LA Freeway	Jerry Jeff Walker
California Girls	Beach Boys	LA's My Lady	Frank Sinatra
California Here I Come	Paul Martin	LA Woman	Doors
Celluloid Heroes	Kinks	Ladies of the Canyon	Joni Mitchell
Coldwater Canyon	Dory Previn	Life in the Fast Lane	Eagles
Coming into Los Angeles	Arlo Guthrie	Little Old Lady from Pasadena	Beach Boys
Creeque Alley	Mamas and the Papas		
Dead Man's Curve	Jan & Dean	Los Angeles	X
Do You Know the Way to San Jose?	Dionne Warwick	MacArthur Park	Richard Harris
		Mickey Mouse March	Mouseketeers
Free Fallin'	Tom Petty	Midnight Train to Georgia	Gladys Knight & the Pips
Heart of Gold	Neil Young	Route 66	Asleep at the Wheel
Hey Hey LA	Beverly Craveiro	Surfin' USA	Beach Boys
Hollywood Dream	Thunderclap Newman	That's Entertainment	Judy Garland
Hollywood Nights	Bob Seger	Trouble Every Day	Mothers of Invention
Hollywood Swinging	Kool & the Gang	Under the Bridge	Red Hot Chili Peppers
Hooray for Hollywood	Doris Day	Ventura Highway	America

310/510.0325, 888/478.7829; fax 310/510.0900

21 INN ON MOUNT ADA

$$$$ The Wrigley Mansion has been converted into a luxurious bed-and-breakfast with just six guest rooms, all featuring ocean or harbor views. Guests enjoy all meals, wine, and hors d'oeuvres, a gas-powered golf cart, and a free shuttle to and from the hotel. ♦ 398 Wrigley Rd (east of Clemente Ave). 310/510.2030

22 THE SAND TRAP

$This local favorite serves authentic Mexican fare. If you can stomach it, go for the menudo. © Mexican © Daily, breakfast and lunch; dinner during summer months only. Avalon Canyon Rd (south of Falls Canyon Rd). 310/510.1349

23 TWO HARBORS

Ⓟ Camping sites are available on this pretty stretch of beach reached by boat or Safari Bus (310/510.2800) from Avalon, 23 miles away. There's a general store, a snack bar, and a dive shop. ♦ Camping 310/510.2800. www.scico.com

At Two Harbors:

BANNING HOUSE LODGE

$$ This converted classic, perched on a hillside overlooking the Isthmus of Catalina and its harbor, provides a peaceful retreat from reality with only 11 rooms and no televisions. There's a dining room, solarium, and spectacular view of both sides of the island. Be sure to book well ahead. ♦ 310/510.2800, 888/510.7979; fax 310/510.0244. www.scico.com

---

Restaurants/Clubs: Red | Hotels: Purple | Shops: Orange | Outdoors/Parks: Green | Sights/Culture: Blue

ORANGE COUNTY NORTH/ DISNEYLAND

M-I-C-K-E-Y M-O-U-S-E . . .
Orange County, a sprawling, predominantly affluent metropolitan area, is now home to more than two and a half million people, but its development wasn't without some major growing pains. During the late 1980s, the county suffered a severe setback when mismanagement of county funds led to bankruptcy. The county is now safely back on its economic feet. The real financial history of the area started just four decades ago, beginning with the 1955 opening of **Disneyland** in **Anaheim** and followed in the 1970s

by the development of **Irvine Ranch.** Orange County is a maze of separate communities that can be divided into two areas: the less-prosperous north, with its ethnic and blue-collar enclaves and huge entertainment parks centered on Anaheim, and the affluent south, with its luxurious houses, hotels and restaurants, and burgeoning cultural scene.

During the Spanish and Mexican periods, in the middle of the 19th century, ranchos were turned into Yankee farms and orchards. In 1857, a group of 50 Germans established an agriculture cooperative they later named Anaheim—a combination of the name of the **Santa Ana River** and the German word for home, *heim.* Originally part of Los Angeles County, the area's autonomy was mandated by the California legislature in 1889. For the first 50 years of the 20th century, Orange County seemed a land of milk and honey, where

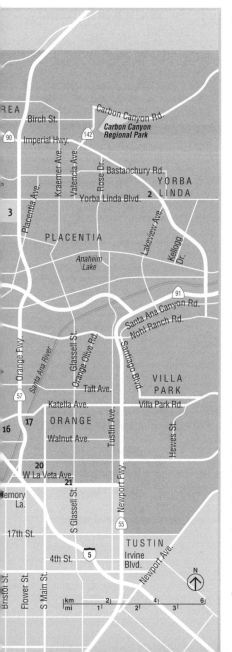

well-tended groves of Valencia orange trees perfumed the air with the fragrance of their blossoms. In the 1950s, land values began to skyrocket in response to a postwar generation eager for a suburban lifestyle. Soon, residential and commercial developments replaced the groves. Very soon the trees will be just a memory, immortalized in street and condominium names.

A $174 million program, completed in 2001, transformed the area southwest of **Interstate 5** between **Orangewood Avenue** and **Ball Road** into a more visually pleasing, pedestrian-friendly destination.

A $1.4 billion expansion of the **Disneyland Resort** culminated in 2001 with the opening of **Downtown Disney,** an eclectic assortment of adult-oriented shops, restaurants, and entertainment options; **Disney's Grand Californian Hotel;** and **Disney's California Adventure** theme park, which some critics say offers more commerce than theme.

More money in the area of $180 million went into remodeling the **Anaheim Convention Center** in 2003. The new design features $13 million worth of glass in a wave pattern that hugs the building. The Center is now the largest of its kind on the West Coast. The bottom line is that 50 years and a total $5 billion investment later, Anaheim, California's tenth-largest city, has been totally reinvented into a major tourist mecca. There really is more to the city—which, by the way, is not part of Los Angeles—than Disneyland.

Getting Around Orange County

Public transportation here is erratic at best. An unusual way to reach the **Disneyland Resort** is by a brief (about 35 minutes) and delightful ride on the **Amtrak** local to Fullerton from Union Station (for schedules and information, call 800/872.7245). From the Fullerton train station, walk about one and a half blocks to Commonwealth Avenue and Harbor Boulevard. From there you can board **Orange County Transit Authority** (OCTA) bus no. 435 to get to the Disneyland Hotel, Disney's Paradise Pier Hotel, and Disney's Grand Californian Hotel. OCTA has service throughout the county, but allow a lot of time; on many routes the buses run only once an hour. Call 714/636.7433 for more information.

The **Southern California Rapid Transit District** has service from its main terminal at East Sixth and South Los Angeles Streets in LA to major locations in Orange County. **Greyhound** (800/231.2222) serves Anaheim and Santa Ana from LA, and also covers Newport Beach and Laguna Beach en route to San Diego. From the Westside, a convenient way to get to Orange County is the regularly scheduled **Airport Coach Service** (800/772.5299) from LAX. The coaches service the major hotels, Disneyland, and John Wayne Airport.

For local transportation, there's **Anaheim Yellow Cab** (714/535.2211), **Orange County Shuttle Service** (714/978.8855), and **West Coast TaxiCab** (714/547.8000). For even easier area navigating, **ART** (Anaheim Resort Transit) shuttles visitors to Disneyland, Disney's California Adventure, Downtown Disney, the Anaheim Convention Center, and throughout the 1,100-acre Anaheim Resort District. Tickets are available at hotels, ART kiosks, and visitor's centers. www.atnetwork.org. For extensive travel away from the major tourist sites, a car is the only practical option. For more information about transportation, special events, sightseeing services, or accommodations, the **Anaheim/Orange County Visitor and Convention Bureau** (714/765.8888) has an office at the **Anaheim Convention Center** (800 W Katella Ave, between S Harbor Blvd and S West St).

1 CHILDREN'S MUSEUM AT LA HABRA

Railroad cars, hands-on displays (including a theater gallery with costumes and props), and a hands-off beehive are housed in a restored 1923 Union Pacific depot. ♦ Admission. M-Sa. 301 S Euclid St (between W Olive and W First Aves), La Habra. 310/905.9793

2 RICHARD NIXON LIBRARY & BIRTHPLACE

Admirers and detractors of the late thirty-seventh president should be equally rewarded by a visit to the Spanish-style museum designed by **Langdon & Wilson** in 1990 and built around Nixon's boyhood home. A treasure for political junkies, the museum has a Watergate exhibit, but one of the most popular items is the gun that Elvis Presley presented to Nixon in the Oval Office. The Nixon burial site rests here amid 1,300 rosebushes in a White House–style garden. ♦ Admission. Daily. 18001 Yorba Linda Blvd (at Eureka Ave), Yorba Linda. 714/993.5075, 714/993.3393, 800/872.8865. www.nixonfoundation.org

3 CALIFORNIA STATE UNIVERSITY AT FULLERTON

This 226-acre campus has 20 buildings and enrolls 25,000 students. It is a branch of the **California State University** system. ♦ 800 N State College Blvd (at Nutwood Ave), Fullerton. 714/773.2011

4 MUCKENTHALER CULTURAL CENTER

Located in a lovely 1923 Spanish Baroque house given to the city of Fullerton by the Muckenthaler family in 1965, the center is used for art exhibitions, classes, and receptions. ♦ Donation suggested. Daily. 1201 W Malvern Ave (at Buena Vista Dr), Fullerton. 714/738.6595

5 MOVIELAND WAX MUSEUM

More than 300 lifelike replicas of Hollywood and music stars are displayed in 150 sets from classic movies. Madonna, Arnold Schwarzenegger, Mel Gibson, Michael Jackson, Tom Selleck, and Gloria Estefan have joined the Marx Brothers, Bette Davis, the Keystone Kops, and Shirley Temple. Bring your camera for a close-up of your favorites, quake in the **Chamber of Horrors**, and shop for Hollywood memorabilia in the gift store. ♦ Admission. Daily. 7711 Beach Blvd (between La Palma Ave and Artesia Fwy), Buena Park. 714/522.1154. www.movielandwaxmuseum.com

6 MEDIEVAL TIMES

If you haven't overdosed on good cheer at the theme parks, end your day in a mock 11th-century castle that offers a tournament with knights on horseback, as costumed serfs and wenches serve your dinner—which you eat with your hands. ♦ Visits: M-F. Dinner shows: daily; call for times. 7662 Beach Blvd (between La Palma Ave and Artesia Fwy), Buena Park. 714/521.4740, 800/899.6600

7 KNOTT'S BERRY FARM

The nation's first theme park had its start in 1934 when Cordelia Knott began selling homemade chicken dinners to supplement income from the family's berry farm. Mrs. Knott's chicken kitchen survived the Depression and spawned a 150-acre entertainment facility that emphasizes the wholesome aspects of an idealized and simpler America. The six theme areas comprise 165 rides and attractions, live shows, restaurants, and stores. For thrill-seekers, there's a 30-story **Supreme Scream,** the tallest ride of its kind in the world, and **Ghost Rider,** the longest, fastest roller coaster known to man. Height and age restrictions apply on some rides. An admission ticket provides access to everything except Pan for Gold and the arcades. ◆ Admission. Daily, until 11PM June-Aug; daily, Sa until 10PM, Sept-May. 8039 Beach Blvd (at La Palma Ave), Buena Park. General information 714/827.1776, recorded information 714/220.5200. www.knotts.com

Within Knott's Berry Farm:

Joe Cool's GR8 SK8 (Great Skate)

A Peanuts' fan haven, with a Camp Snoopy Theater featuring Charlie Brown's Hoe-Down and Joe Cool's thrill ride, where riders do a 40-foot slide from the end of a giant skateboard.

Ghost Town

A replica of an 1880s Old West boomtown, complete with cowboys, cancan dancers, and gold panning, it includes several authentic buildings culled from real ghost towns. Old-time melodramas are presented in the **Birdcage Theatre.** The **Butterfield Stagecoach** tours the countryside, making riders bless the day that shock absorbers were invented. On the **Log Ride,** your log boat floats through sawmill and logging camps before splashing 42 feet in its final descent—plan on getting wet. A new multimedia laser extravaganza, **Edison International Electric Nights,** lights up the sky nightly. The swift **Ghost Rider** wooden roller coaster arrived in 1999.

The Boardwalk

This celebration of the California beach scene features the HammerHead, the Boomerang, Supreme Scream, and Perilous Plunge—exciting rides not for the fainthearted. The Good Time Theatre presents live shows daily.

Camp Snoopy

High in the Sierra Mountains, Snoopy and his Peanuts friends welcome youngsters to rides, shows, an 1896 merry-go-round, and performing animals. The new **Woodstock's Airmail** is a kid's-size version of Supreme Scream (see above).

Fiesta Village

A tribute to California's Latino heritage, with piñatas, mariachis, a *mercado* (market), and

a turn-of-the-century hand-carved merry-go-round within a lushly landscaped and tiled plaza. The 2,700-foot-long **Jaguar!** roller coaster thrills riders with swerves, circles, and 60-foot surges. One of the most popular rides is **Montezooma's Revenge,** a roller coaster with cars that spin through a 360-degree loop at 55mph and then shoot backward.

Wild Water Wilderness

Turn-of-the-century California is featured here, with **Bigfoot Rapids,** a white-water river raft trip. Within Wild Water Wilderness:

Thunder Falls

This mystical place has trees native to the Northwest Pacific coast, Native American artifacts and paintings, and a lake with four towering waterfalls. Its centerpiece is **Mystery Lodge,** one of the park's most technologically advanced projects. Inside this full-scale replica of a traditional tribal house, a storyteller sets the stage for a multisensory experience with special visual effects.

Knott's California MarketPlace

Just outside the park is a separate dining and shopping village where you can sample the chicken dinners and boysenberry pies that launched the farm; enjoy **Knott's Family Restaurant** (714/220.5067), the **Cable Car Kitchen** (714/220.5100), or a salad, burger, or barbecue.

Indian Trails

One of America's only live Native American interpretative centers educates and entertains visitors.

8 Hansen House

Built in 1857, this white clapboard house with a narrow front porch was designed in the Greek Revival style. Also known as the Mother Colony House, it was the first house in Anaheim, built by George Hansen, founder of the Mother Colony, a group of Germans who left San Francisco to grow grapes in Southern California. Inside the restored structure is an interesting exhibition on Anaheim's history. ◆ Free. Tours usually held W mornings; call for an appointment. 414 N West St (between W Lincoln Ave and W Sycamore St), Anaheim. Library 714/254.1850

9 Angelo's

$ This classic drive-in, with pert carhops on roller skates and occasional rallies of vintage wheels, has a terrific neon sign. ◆ American ◆ Daily; Sa until 12:30AM. 511 S State College

---

Restaurants/Clubs: Red | Hotels: Purple | Shops: Orange | Outdoors/Parks: Green | Sights/Culture: Blue

Blvd (between Chelsea Dr and E Santa Ana St), Anaheim. 714/533.1401

10 HOBBY CITY

This six-acre cluster of old-fashioned collectors' shops has 23 buildings, including a log cabin shop that carries Native American memorabilia. ◆ Daily. 1238 S Beach Blvd (between Starr St and W Ball Rd), Anaheim. 714/527.2323

11 LOS ALAMITOS RACE COURSE

One of LA's top tracks features quarter-horse racing and harness racing; call ahead for racing dates. ◆ Admission. Post time: 7PM. 4961 Katella Ave (between Walker St and Portal Dr), Los Alamitos. 714/995.1234

12 DISNEYLAND HOTEL

$$$ Three towers surround the Peter Pan–inspired Never Land swimming pool, complete with a pirate ship and 110-foot water slide. The 990 rooms and 62 suites are decorated in classic Disney. All have views of either the Never Land Pool or Disneyland, and some have balconies. There are also three other pools, a tropical beach, a shopping mall, and 11 restaurants and lounges. ◆ 1150 W Magic Way (between Disneyland Dr and Walnut St), Anaheim. 714/956.6425; fax 714/956.6582. www.disneyland.com

12 DISNEY'S PARADISE PIER HOTEL

$$$ The hotel offers many guest rooms with views directly into the Paradise Pier section of Disney's California Adventure. It represents the ultimate beachfront amusement zone, featuring the unique boardwalks that used to line the California coast. Its premier location also features an exclusive private entry gate for hotel guests to access the new park. Facilities include a pool with intimate poolside cabanas, two restaurants, and a coffee bar, fitness center, and retail shop. ◆ 1717 S Disneyland Drive (between Magic Way and Katella Ave), Anaheim. 714/956.6425. www.disneyland.com

12 DISNEY'S CALIFORNIA ADVENTURE PARK

Located next to the original Disneyland Park, Disney's California Adventure offers three themelands: Hollywood Pictures Backlot, Golden State, and Paradise Pier.◆ 714/781.2154. www.disneyland.com

Within Disney's California Adventure Park:

HOLLYWOOD PICTURES BACKLOT

This themeland celebrates the magic of the movie business and the glamour, culture, fame, and celebrity atmosphere that surrounds it. Guests enter through the majestic studio gates and discover a place where reality blends seamlessly into illusion. Among the attractions featured are the **Hyperion Theater,** a 2,000-seat venue for a variety of stage productions; **Jim Henson's Muppet Vision 3-D;** and **Disney Animation,** where guests view pencil test scenes from animation features that are still in production.

GOLDEN STATE

Golden State has six districts and is highlighted by the enormous bear-shaped mountain called **Grizzly Peak,** part of the **Grizzly River Run** white-water rafting ride that twirls guests 360 degrees as they drop down two waterfalls. The eight-acre mini-wilderness pays tribute to California's spectacular wilderness areas, featuring redwood trees, authentic Gold Country artifacts, and nature trails. The **Condor Flats** district celebrates California's aviation heritage in the design of the high desert airfields. **Soarin' Over California** suspends guests in their flying theater seats as they lift off, float, and soar in a thrilling flight over California's most spectacular scenic wonders. Celebrating the state's rich agricultural heritage is the **Bountiful Bounty Farm** district, where guests can walk through areas growing with citrus, walnuts, avocados, and artichokes or sit in the Bug's Life Theater and watch It's Tough to Be a Bug!, a stunning and comical 3-D presentation. In partnership with Robert Mondavi Wines, the new theme park also has its taste of Napa Valley. The **Pacific Wharf** district of the Golden State is inspired by Monterey's Cannery Row and gives guests a firsthand look at sourdough bread baking at the Boudin Bakery and fresh tortilla making at the Mission Tortilla Factory. In **The Bay Area,** guests can experience Golden Dreams, a filmed theatrical celebration of California's cultural diversity. It's hosted by actress Whoopi Goldberg, who pays tribute to the people whose courage and creative spirit have made and continue to make California a dynamic and trend-setting state.

PARADISE PIER

The ultimate beachfront amusement zone, decked out in spectacular lighting and elegant graphics associated with the heyday of the great amusement park piers. One of the main attractions is **California Screamin',** a steel coaster disguised as a white wooden coaster, but with a Disney twist: Guests are looped upside-down around a Mickey Mouse silhouette! Another major attraction is the unique Ferris wheel, featuring a revolving sunburst. On this **Sun Wheel,** the carriages are on tracks that slide to the center of the wheel, adding an exciting gravity element to an already spectacular visual experience.

GRAND CALIFORNIA HOTEL

$$$ This 751-room luxury hotel provides uptown accommodations for the more discerning Disney visitor. Still typically thematic with turn-of-the-20th-century designs created by Peter Dominick of the Urban Design Group of Denver, the décor attempts to capture California's ruggedly beautiful coastline while evoking memories of the Arroyo craftsmen. The hotel provides 24-hour room service; a health spa (Eureka Springs) with workout equipment, steam, sauna, and massage rooms; two pools (one with a water slide); and lots of dining options. 714/635.2300

Within the Grand Hotel California:

THE NAPA ROSE RESTAURANT

★★$$$$ This uncharacteristically fine dining spot stars chef Andrew Sutton (formerly of Napa Valley's deluxe Auberge du Soleil), who creates magical menus served in a typically Disney-esque room where waiters wear vests with little roses embroidered on them and colors clash under a 20-foot-high vaulted ceiling. Floor-to-ceiling windows provide a view of California Adventure's Grizzly Peak. Adding to the mood is a display kitchen, lounge, and a vast wine cellar. Sutton's menu includes good seared rock scallops in a lemon lobster sauce, a creative Portobello mushroom cappuccino with a thyme froth, prime rib of pork, and a mean mustard-crusted rack of lamb. Best desserts are the Meyer lemon mousse brûlée served with a blood orange sorbet and the goat cheese flan with fresh fruit. ◆ California ◆ Daily, dinner; Su, brunch. Reservations suggested. 714/300.7170, 714/781.3436, or dial *86 on any resort pay phone. Valet parking available

13 THE DISNEYLAND RESORT

A $1.4 billion expansion, completed in 2001, transformed the world-famous amusement park into one mega-theme-resort with the addition of **Downtown Disney, Disney's California Adventure,** and two new hotels (see above). **Disneyland Park, The Happiest Place on Earth** is Walt Disney's original theme park, with eight themelands that showcase classic Disney characters, favorite attractions, and lots of live entertainment. Every day on **Main Street USA** (see below) brings the Parade of the Stars starring Mickey Mouse, Donald Duck, Snow White, and more than 40 other Disney characters. The parade presents vivid interpretations of scenes from *Beauty and the Beast, The Lion King, The Little Mermaid, Tarzan,* and *Fantasia 2000,* among others. Showcased on Friday, Saturday, and Sunday evenings is

FANTASMIC!, a unique extravaganza of music, live performers, and sensational special effects, starring Mickey Mouse and his imagination, conjuring up fanciful images from a variety of Disney classics.

Included in the admission price is access to all rides and shows. Some rides have height and age minimums. Guided tours are available. ◆ Admission. For hours and show schedules, call 714/781.4565. S Harbor Blvd (between W Katella Ave and Santa Ana Fwy), Anaheim. 714/999.4000. www.disneyland.com

Within Disneyland Park:

MAIN STREET USA

This idealized turn-of-the-20th-century town is close to the entrance to the park. Small shops, with wooden floors that resound under your feet and glass display cases at precisely the right height for children's noses, sell a variety of nostalgic merchandise. The **Walt Disney Story** featuring "Great Moments with Mr. Lincoln" brings the sixteenth president to life through the magic of audio-animatronics.

ADVENTURELAND

The **Indiana Jones Adventure** takes you deep into the jungles to the Temple of the Forbidden Eye. Watch out for snakes, insects, rats, fire, poison darts, and the deadly rolling rock. The **Jungle Cruise** takes you in a flat-bottomed boat down simulated Nile, Congo, and Amazon Rivers, with lots of audio-animatronic magic.

NEW ORLEANS SQUARE

On the **Rivers of America,** filigreed balconies overlook winding streets ablaze with flowers and lined with quaint shops. Take a ride with the **Pirates of the Caribbean** on flat-bottomed boats that explore a haunted grotto hung with Spanish moss, and glide into a seaport for pillage and plunder. Ghosts inhabit the **Haunted Mansion,** which uses holography-like imagery to bring many of the 999 residents to wonderfully disembodied life.

CRITTER COUNTRY

Adventures of Winnie the Pooh takes toddlers on a gentle ride through the Hundred-Acre Wood to see Pooh as he dreams of Heffalumps and honey. We said it was for kids. **Davy Crockett's Explorer Canoes** let you paddle along the Rivers of America. Another attraction is **Splash Mountain,** a spectacular log flume adventure.

FRONTIERLAND

This area has battles, a blazing fort, and, through the swinging doors of a western

---

Restaurants/Clubs: Red | Hotels: Purple | Shops: Orange | Outdoors/Parks: Green | Sights/Culture: Blue

saloon, the **Golden Horseshoe Jamboree,** complete with cancan dancers. The Rivers of America run along the shore and are plied by an amazing assortment of vessels such as the **Mark Twain Riverboat** and the sailing ship *Columbia*. **Big Thunder Mountain Railroad** is a roller-coaster ride through a deserted mine enhanced by special effects (an earthquake, a swarm of bats, and so on).

FANTASYLAND

Enter this magical land through the **Sleeping Beauty Castle.** Over the drawbridge and through the stone halls is the world of familiar storybook characters. The **Casey Jr. Circus Train** chugs past Cinderella's castle, Pinocchio's village, and the home of the Three Little Pigs. The whirling teacups of the **Mad Tea Party** will leave your head spinning. Boats glide through **It's a Small World,** filled with scenes of animated children from many lands all singing the same tune in their native tongues. The most popular ride in Fantasyland is the **Matterhorn,** a 14-story replica of the Swiss mountain built for white-knuckle fun. **Videopolis** is a popular nightspot featuring live musical revues.

MICKEY'S TOONTOWN

Cute is the operative word for this attraction, which features houses that belong to Mickey and Minnie and a whole toon-inspired town. The big draw, though, is the **Roger Rabbit Car Toon Spin,** the longest black-light ride in Disneyland history.

TOMORROWLAND

Sporting a fresh new futuristic look, complete with giant gardens of edible plants, this land of sci-fi now features an exciting 3-D experience, **Honey, I Shrunk the Audience.** The whimsical show combines 3-D techniques with zany antics by Rick Moranis, reprising his role in the similarly titled Disney films. Also new are **Innoventions,** an interactive technology pavilion; **Rocket Rods,** a high-speed rocket journey into the future; and the 64-foot-high **Astro Orbitor,** where self-piloted spaceships soar and plunge through an animated system of planets and constellations. The perils of outer space will thrill you on **Space Mountain,** a spectacular high-speed journey to the stars in which showers of meteors illuminate portions of the ride. To fill that black hole in your stomach, the food court at **Redd Rockett's Pizza Port** offers everything from salads to pasta and pizza.

In 1923, Walt and Roy Disney established the Disney Brothers Studio in Silverlake.

14 ANAHEIM CONVENTION CENTER

Across the street from Disneyland Park, this huge convention center—the most successful on the West Coast—is used for events ranging from concerts to conventions. ♦ 800 W Katella Ave (between S Harbor Blvd and S West St), Anaheim. 714/765.8888; e-mail:mail@anaheimoc.org. www.anaheimoc.org

14 DOWNTOWN DISNEY

Just when you think you've had enough Disney already, enter **Downtown Disney,** a new public pedestrian esplanade that connects the two theme parks—Disney's California Adventure and Disneyland—together with the Disneyland Resort hotels.The complex of commerce hosts a plethora of entertainment and dining venues such as a 21-screen megaplex theater with 3,000 stadium-like seats; a branch of Hollywood's **House of Blues;** a Rainforest Café; a New Orleans branch of **Ralph Brennan's Jazz Kitchen,** offering spicy food and hot jazz; branches of the popular La Brea Bakery, Wetzel's Pretzels, and Häagen-Dazs ice cream shops, and more. 714.781.DINE. www.disneyland.com

Within Downtown Disney:

CATAL RESTAURANT AND UVA BAR

★★$$ Yet another Patina Group/Joachim Splichal venture, this one a dual-concept restaurant offering two different dining experiences. Uva, a part of Catal, is a casual indoor/outdoor affair with a large menu of tapas and 40 wines by the glass. Catal, on the upper level, features Mediterranean cuisine. ♦ Spanish/Mediterranean ♦ Tu-Sa, lunch and dinner. Reservations suggested. 714/774.4442

14 JW'S STEAKHOUSE

★★★$$$ A carnivore's delight of New York steaks, porterhouses, and filet mignons served in a romantic, library-like dining room in the Anaheim Marriott. Specialties might include rack of lamb with garlic sauce, veal medallions with mushrooms, and Grand Marnier soufflé. ♦ International ♦ M-Sa, dinner. Reservations recommended. 700 Convention Way (between S Harbor Blvd and S West St), Anaheim. 714/750.8000

14 WEST COAST ANAHEIM HOTEL

$$ Formerly the Inn at the Park, this 480-room, 14-story hotel is next to the convention center and just down the street from the Disneyland Resort. The décor is contemporary, highlighted by pastel colors. Guest rooms have balconies overlooking either an

expansive stretch of park or Disneyland's Matterhorn and the nightly fireworks display. There's a coffee shop, a restaurant serving American food, and a swimming pool with a sundeck. ♦ 1855 S Harbor Blvd (between Convention Way and W Katella Ave), Anaheim. 714/750.1811, 800/421.6662; fax 714/971.3626 ♿

15 HANSA HOUSE

★$ Families especially like this Scandinavian all-you-can-eat smorgasbord. The groaning boards feature some unusual dishes (like corn fritters and a herring plate) as well as a wide range of entrées and unusually good salads. ♦ Scandinavian/American ♦ Daily, breakfast, lunch, and dinner. 1840 S Harbor Blvd (between W Orangewood and W Katella Aves), Anaheim. 714/750.2411

15 DOLL CITY USA

Claiming to be the largest of its kind, this 7,700-square-foot specialty store has thousands of dolls, buggies, and related books. ♦ M-Sa. 2080 S Harbor Blvd (at W Orangewood Ave), Anaheim. 714/750.3585, 800/954.3655

16 EDISON INTERNATIONAL FIELD OF ANAHEIM

Past improvements made this home of the Anaheim Angels more spectator-friendly by reducing seating capacity from 70,000 to 45,000. The stadium is a dedicated baseball-only sports venue. ♦ 2000 Gene Autry Way (between E Orangewood and E Katella Aves), Anaheim. Stadium 714/254.3000, Angels information 714/634.2000. www.angelsbaseball.com

17 ARROWHEAD POND OF ANAHEIM

The National Hockey League's Mighty Ducks push the puck around at this 17,250-seat facility across the freeway from Anaheim Stadium. ♦ 2965 E Katella Ave (between Struck Ave and Orange Frwy), Anaheim. 714/704.2500. www.arrowheadpond.com

18 HYATT REGENCY ORANGE COUNTY

$$$ The flamingos, pools, and 60-foot palms in the glass atrium of this 17-story, 400-room hotel provide a resort-like ambience. There's tennis, a spa, three restaurants, and stylish décor. ♦ 100 Plaza Alicante (at Harbor Blvd and Chapman Ave), Garden Grove. 714/750.1234, 800/972.2929; fax 714/740.0460. www.hyatt.com

19 CRYSTAL CATHEDRAL

Hailed as the most spectacular place of worship on earth, this architectural marvel is just a few blocks from Disneyland Park but light years away. Made of 10,000 panes of tempered silver glass covering a translucent, weblike frame of white steel trusses set in the shape of a four-pointed star, this cathedral of the Garden Grove Community Church was designed by **Johnson & Burgee** and dedicated in 1980. Seating 2,736, it's a shimmering extravaganza, 415 feet long, 207 feet wide, and 128 feet high. The 236-foot Crean Tower, built in 1990 of highly polished stainless-steel prisms, has a 52-bell carillon. Architect Richard Neutra designed the church's previous center in 1961. The International Style steel-and-glass church was first used for drive-in services (passengers in 1,400 cars could congregate without ever leaving their autos). Today it hosts Sunday evening services complete with a cast of live animals, flying angels, and dynamic special effects, as well as weddings, meetings, and the annual "Glory of Christmas" and "Glory of Easter" pageants. Neutra's son Dion designed the adjacent 15-story Tower of Hope for the expanding church administration in 1967. Yet another architectural wonder opened in 2003: a cylindrical $20 million Hospitality Center. The **Richard Meier**-designed geometric gem houses a café, bookstore, auditorium, and exhibition rooms. ♦ Tours: M-Sa, 9AM-3:30PM every half-hour. Services: Su, 8:30AM (Chapel), 9:30AM, 11AM, 12:30PM (Spanish), 6:30PM. 12141 Lewis St (between Dawn and Chapman Aves), Garden Grove. 714/971.4000. www.crystalcathedral.org

20 LA BRASSERIE RESTAURANT

★$$ This intimate and relaxed bistro specializes in home-style soups, well-prepared fish, and veal. The library dining room is appealing. ♦ French ♦ M-F, lunch and dinner; Sa, dinner. 202 S Main St (between W Palmyra and W Almond Aves), Orange. 714/978.6161

21 YEN CHING

★★$$ Wonderful food is served in a cool, modern setting; the unusually friendly service makes this place a consistent favorite. Specialties include Mandarin and Szechuan-style crispy duck, pot stickers, and whole fish with garlic sauce. ♦ Chinese ♦ Daily, lunch and dinner. 574 S Glassell St (between Garden Grove Frwy and W La Veta Ave), Orange. 714/997.3300

Restaurants/Clubs: Red | Hotels: Purple | Shops: Orange | Outdoors/Parks: Green | Sights/Culture: Blue

ORANGE COUNTY SOUTH

Back from bankruptcy big time . . .

This gilded area has picked itself up and dusted itself off to become one of the priciest, ritziest sections of Southern California. Home prices have skyrocketed. There's so much money in the till that even teenagers own BMWs.

There is little of tourist interest in the interior hills of Orange County South, where edu-

cation and high-tech industry are the mainstays. The **California Gold Coast,** on the other hand, is an earthly paradise devoted to boating, golf, and tennis, with a temperate climate, sandy beaches, rocky promontories, green canyons, and rolling hills. The beaches along this stretch of coast boast distinctive personalities: **Huntington Beach** is a surfer's paradise, **Newport Beach** and **Balboa** are havens for the yachting crowd, **Corona del Mar** is a quiet beachside community, **Laguna Beach** is an artists' colony, **Dana Point** boasts a large marina, and **San Juan Capistrano** and **San Clemente** are gracious residential areas.

For everything you want to know about Newport Beach, go to www.newport beach-cvb.com or call 800/94 COAST.

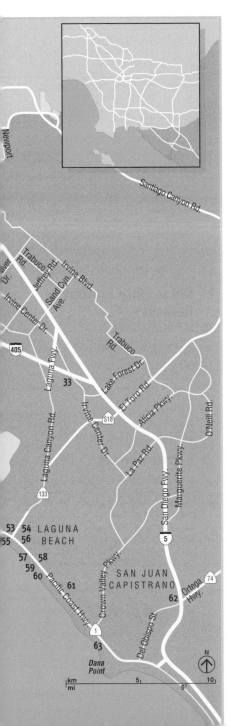

1 WESTFIELD SHOPPINGTOWN MAIN PLACE

The Jerde Partnership remodeled this 1958 indoor mall in 1987 in **Jon Jerde**'s trademark style, with colorful tiles, neon, and whimsical signs. The cramped, two-story, skylit center, anchored by **Nordstrom, Bullock's,** and **Robinsons-May** department stores, includes six movie screens and 190 specialty shops. ◆ Daily. 2800 N Main St (between Santa Ana and Garden Grove Fwys), Santa Ana. 714/547.7800, 714/547.7000

2 THE HACIENDA

★★★$ This side-street restaurant, with a shaded flagstone courtyard and authentic Mexican artifacts, is such a popular wedding spot that the owners sell wedding dresses in the back. Try the best margarita in the county, blue-corn chicken enchiladas, and a chile relleno made strictly with chilies grown in New Mexico's Sandia Valley. Everything comes with homemade *sopapillas* (sweet bread). ◆ Southwestern ◆ M-F, lunch; Th, dinner; Su, brunch. Call ahead on Sunday, as it is often closed for weddings. Reservations recommended for large parties. 1725 N College Ave (between W 17th and W 19th Sts), Santa Ana. 714/558.1304

3 SEAFOOD PARADISE II

★★$$ Three dozen varieties of dim sum for connoisseurs are served daily for lunch. The regular Cantonese menu includes such treats as drunken chicken, roast duck, shredded jellyfish, and five-flavor beef. ◆ Chinese ◆ Daily, lunch and dinner; dim sum served daily, 10AM-3PM. 8602 Westminster Ave (between Shirley and Newland Sts), Westminster. 714/893.6066

4 NGOC SUONG

★$ Aficionados of Euro/Vietnamese cuisine think this restaurant serves some of the best in Little Saigon. The menu's unique and delicious, with offerings such as a sliced banana flower salad with clams, shredded green papaya salad with steamed string beans, and shrimp and shredded pork, and for dessert, the Euro-influenced crème brûlée. ♦ Asian Euro Fusion ♦ W-M, 10AM-3PM and 5PM-11PM. 10112 Westminster Ave (at Brookhurst St), Westminster. 714/539.8811

5 PAGOLAC

★$ Another great place to grab a bite while browsing through Little Saigon, this one offers seven-course meals of beef—delicate tender morsels that melt in your mouth, charbroiled or rolled in rice paper and served with lettuce, mint, and cilantro. ♦ Vietnamese ♦ Daily, 11AM-9:30PM. 14580 Brookhurst St (between Bolsa and Hazard Aves), Westminster. 714/531.4740

6 ZOV'S BISTRO & BAKERY

★★$$ It's located in a drab commercial center, but this little restaurant has the feel of a European bistro. Chef/owner Zov Karamardian's menu offers delicious Armenian pizza, fresh fish (try the salmon), rack of lamb, and mouthwatering desserts. The servers are sometimes curt, but meeter-and-greeter Gary Karamardian is always there with warmth and a handshake. ♦ Eastern Mediterranean ♦ M-Sa, breakfast and lunch; Tu-Sa, lunch and dinner. 17440 17th St (between Enderle Center Dr and Yorba St), Tustin. 714/838.8855

7 SEAL BEACH INN

$$ *Country Inns Magazine* added this charming inn to their 1997 list of the "Top 12 Country Inns in America." Each of the 23 rooms is furnished with antiques, pre–Civil War beds with Ralph Lauren spreads, and French Mediterranean appointments. Fourteen rooms have fully equipped kitchens, and the **Wisteria bedroom** boasts a 200-year-old Persian mural. A miniature Victorian garden and a quaint brick courtyard with a centuries-old fountain add to the charm of this hideaway, where notable privacy-seeking guests have included Bo Derek, Lesley Ann Warren, and Sandy Koufax. A lavish complimentary breakfast, prepared daily by the house chef, includes freshly baked muffins, quiche, waffles, homemade granola, and fresh fruit. The beach, restaurants, and fishing pier are a short two blocks away. ♦ 212 Fifth St (at Central Ave), Seal Beach. 562/493.2416, 800.HIDEAWAY; fax 562/799.0483. www.sealbeachinn.com

8 PHO 79

★$ This Vietnamese eatery, situated in the heart of Little Saigon, is not suited to all tastes, but it's about as authentic as it gets with its noodles, soups, barbecue shrimp, and adventuresome meals in a bowl. ♦ Vietnamese ♦ Daily, lunch and dinner. No credit cards accepted, or reservations. 9200 Bolsa Ave (between Bushard and Magnolia Sts), Westminster. 714/893.1883 &

9 BANH MI CHE CALL

★★$$ Customers line up here for freshly baked puffs which are prepared at the counter at this Little Saigon bakery, which also sells killer *banh mi* (hoagie-style sandwiches) and *che*, flan-like desserts with sticky rice, tapioca, or mung beans and coconut milk. It's not for every sweet tooth, but it's good. ♦ Bakery ♦ Daily, 7AM-9PM. 9848 Bolsa Ave (at ABC Market Mall, between Newland and Bushard Sts). 714/897.3927

10 GEN KAI

★$$ The décor consists of simple wooden tables, a long sushi bar, and a lone tatami platform, but don't be deterred: This is a favorite eating place for local Japanese chefs, and the rustic dishes taste wonderful. Highlights include marinated squid, asparagus and sausage, stewed fish with vegetables, and hot-pepper eggplant with onion. ♦ Japanese ♦ M-F, lunch and dinner; Sa, Su, dinner. Reservations recommended. 16650 Harbor Blvd (between Warner and Edinger Aves), Fountain Valley. 714/775.3818

11 BOLSA CHICA ECOLOGICAL RESERVE

🅟 This wildlife sanctuary is the largest salt marsh preserve in the Los Angeles/Orange County metropolitan area. Its 300 acres provides an oasis for shorebirds and millions of transiting birds that migrate between the Arctic and South America along the Pacific Flyway. There are guides handy to take you on hikes and tours. ♦ Free. Daily. Pacific Coast Hwy (between Golden West St and Warner Ave). 714/846.1114. www.coastalconservancy.ca.gov

12 GUSTAF ANDERS

★★★$$$ Spacious elegance and wonderful food are found here. The standouts are the gravlax with wild rice pancakes topped with smoked salmon, caviar, and crème fraîche; filet of beef with Stilton cheese; Chilean sea bass with seaweed and shrimp salad; and crusty home-baked breads. There's a fabulous smorgasbord spread out in the Back Pocket in the rear of the restaurant, where you can feast on everything from gravlax pizza to Swedish meatballs and grilled chicken. The pastries here are to die for. ♦ Scandinavian ♦ M-Sa, lunch and dinner; Su, dinner. Reservations recommended, especially on Friday and Saturday. 3851 Bear St (at Sunflower Ave), Santa Ana. 714/668.1737. www.gustaf-anders.com

13 ANTONELLO

★★$$ This splashy spot is where OC's powerful politicos, social leaders, and businesspeople congregate. Owner Antonio Cagnolo is your typical friendly Italian host who will happily suggest menu options such as a divine veal chop with porcini mushrooms and truffles or outstanding pasta. There's also an exceptional wine list. ♦ Italian ♦ M-F, lunch and dinner; Sa, dinner. 1611 Sunflower Ave (between Bristol St and Plaza Dr), Santa Ana. 714/751.7153

14 ORANGE COUNTY PERFORMING ARTS CENTER

From the **Kirov Ballet** and the **American Ballet Theatre** to *Cats,* this performing arts center has rivaled LA's Music Center since it opened in 1986. The auditorium is named for developer Henry T. Segerstrom, who spearheaded the effort to make it a center for the arts. Concerts and opera are also regularly featured. ♦ M-Sa. 600 Town Center Dr (at Ave of the Arts), Costa Mesa. 714/556.2787. www.ocpac.org

15 SOUTH COAST PLAZA

This upscale shopper's heaven has more than 270 stores on the main landscaped plaza and the adjoining Crystal, Carousel, and Jewel Courts, including department stores such as **Nordstrom, Saks Fifth Avenue, Sears, Macy's, and Robinsons-May.** In between is a selection of designer boutiques to rival those in Beverly Hills: Gucci, Cartier, Chanel, Tiffany, Emporio Armani, Fendi, Escada, Hermès, Liz Claiborne, La Perla, Laundry by Shelli Segal, Book Soup, Brookstone, Jaeger, Louis Vuitton, and Godiva Chocolatier, to name a few. You can also pamper yourself with spa treatments at Aida Grey, Aveda, Georgette Klinger, or José Eber. To fuel shoppers there are dozens of eateries, including **Pinot Provence, Morton's of Chicago, Royal Kyber,** and **Darya.** Shuttle service is available from area hotels for about $8 round-trip. This ranks as the busiest retail center in Southern California, with more than 18 million visitors a year (as many as any theme park). ♦ Daily. 3333 Bristol St (at San Diego Fwy), Costa Mesa. 800/782.8888, 714/435.2000. 714/435.2034. www.southcoastplaza.com

16 WESTIN SOUTH COAST PLAZA HOTEL

$$$$ The weekend specials are a good value at this 17-story, 390-room hotel, which features tennis and volleyball courts, a pool, 24-hour room service, and the **Garden Court Cafe.** ♦ 686 Anton Blvd (at Bristol St), Costa Mesa. 714/540.2500, 800/228.3000; fax 714/662.6695; email: south@westin.com. www.westin.com

17 SOUTH COAST REPERTORY THEATRE

The Mainstage and Second Stage present a diversified program of live comedy and drama from September through June. ♦ Box office: daily. 655 Town Center Dr (between Ave of the Arts and Bristol St), Costa Mesa. 714/957.4033. www.scr.org

18 PLAZA TOWER

The curved façade and stainless-steel panels of this 1991 **Cesar Pelli** office building gleam in the light and capture the color of the sunset. The sophisticated structure has a formal front, a double grid of round-edged horizontal and vertical ribs, and double loggias and setbacks at the 17th and 21st floors. ♦ 600 Anton Blvd (at Ave of the Arts), Costa Mesa

19 CALIFORNIA SCENARIO

Artworks are scattered throughout **South Coast Plaza,** but the real treasure (worth the drive from LA) is Isamu Noguchi's 1.6-acre sculpture garden. Framed by reflective glass towers and the blank white walls of parking structures, this oasis is often overlooked by visitors. Noguchi created a contemporary version of a traditional Japanese garden in which natural rocks, sandstone structures and paving, trees, cacti, and running water symbolize different aspects of the state of California. ♦ Free. Daily. 611 Anton Blvd (between Ave of the Arts and Park Center Dr), Costa Mesa

20 MANDARIN GOURMET

★$$ The showcase of Michael Chiang, who also owns **Chinatown** in Irvine, this restaurant serves fine Mandarin and Szechuan dishes in a contemporary setting. Aromatic shrimp is a standout, but the menu is full of interesting discoveries. ♦ Chinese ♦ Daily, lunch and dinner. Reservations recommended. 1500 Adams Ave (at Harbor Blvd), Costa Mesa. 714/540.1937

21 JOHN WAYNE/ORANGE COUNTY AIRPORT

Ten commercial and two commuter carriers serve this busy alternative to LAX, providing direct flights to 19 domestic destinations. As the population of Orange County exploded (from 200,000 in 1950 to well over 2.4 million today), the airport's capacity became strained. Fortunately, major expansion was completed in 1990. **Leason Pomeroy Associates** and **Gensler & Associates** designed an award-winning new terminal, taking inspiration from

---

Restaurants/Clubs: Red | **Hotels: Purple** | **Shops: Orange** | **Outdoors/Parks: Green** | **Sights/Culture: Blue**

the shape of an airplane fuselage. The rounded, bronze-tinted roofs of its three long, sleek, parallel vaults run perpendicular to the San Diego Freeway. For ground transportation to **LAX,** call 949/252.5171. ♦ 3151 Airway Ave (at Paularino Ave), Costa Mesa. 714/252.5200. www.ocair.com

22 CHANTECLAIR

★★$$$ The French farmhouse décor offers a romantic setting for fillet Wellington, veal Oscar, grilled swordfish, and like entrées. ♦ Continental ♦ M-F, lunch and dinner; Sa, dinner. 18912 MacArthur Blvd (just north of Campus Dr), Irvine. 949/752.8001

22 BISTANGO

★★$$ This modern restaurant with a granite bar, rough slate floor, chic Italian furniture, and nearly a hundred contemporary gallery artworks (they're for sale) is a power-lunch meeting place by day and a jazz hot spot at night. Menu choices include inventive pastas, designer pizzas, and grilled meat and seafood. There's also a super four-course tasting menu. There's music nightly. ♦ International ♦ M-F, lunch and dinner; daily, dinner. Reservations recommended. Atrium Building, 19100 Von Karman Ave (between Campus and Dupont Drs), Irvine. 949/752.5222. www.bistango.com

22 PREGO

★★$$ Modeled on a Tuscan villa, this happy, crowded place serves innovative pizzas, rabbit, duck, and free-range chicken from the rotisserie, and such special treats as ravioli filled with ricotta, chard, and sage. ♦ Italian ♦ M-F, lunch and dinner; Sa, Su, dinner. Reservations recommended. 18420 Von Karman Ave (at Michelson Dr), Irvine. 949/553.1333

23 PARK PLACE

Developed by Fluor Corporation, this complex of futuristic glass-clad structures along the San Diego Freeway has become an Orange County landmark. It's best viewed from the road. It was designed by **Welton Becket & Associates** and completed in 1976. ♦ 3333 Michelson Dr (between Harvard Ave and Jamboree Blvd), Irvine

24 SUTTON PLACE HOTEL

$$$$ This striking ziggurat-shaped property has a Newport Beach address, but it's located well inland, across from the airport. It has 435 rooms, a swimming pool, fitness center, sauna, Jacuzzi, and two tennis courts, **Accents Dining Room** (contemporary French cuisine), and a lounge. ♦ 4500 MacArthur Blvd (at Birch St), Newport Beach. 949/476.2001, 800/810.6888; fax 949/476.0153; email: info@npb.suttonplace.com. www.suttonplace.com

25 PASCAL

★★$$$ Superb seafood is served here, with a hint of Provence in the bold colors and seasonings. Mussels steamed with saffron, bass with thyme, and chicken with olives are among the signature dishes. ♦ French ♦ M-F, lunch and dinner; Sa, dinner. Reservations recommended. 1000 N Bristol St (at Jamboree Rd), Newport Beach. 949/752.0107

26 HUNTINGTON PIER

🅟 The first surfing contests were held at Huntington Beach, and today it remains a destination for surfers from around the world. This pier is the best place to watch the year-round action. ♦ Pacific Coast Hwy and Main St, Huntington Beach

27 HILTON WATERFRONT BEACH RESORT

$$$ This 12-story hotel, just across the road from a four-mile stretch of sandy beach, has 290 ocean-view rooms decorated in light woods and soothing florals. The casually elegant property also offers an outdoor pool, a fitness center, meeting facilities, a nightclub, a restaurant, and four tennis courts. ♦ 21100 Pacific Coast Hwy (between Huntington and Second Sts), Huntington Beach. 714/960.7873, 800/822.7873; fax 714/960.3791. www.waterfrontbeachresort.hilton.com

27 HYATT REGENCY HUNTINGTON BEACH RESORT & SPA

$$$ Luxury personified best describes this four-story, 517-room resort with its sweeping views of the Pacific Ocean and tasteful Andalusian décor. Three restaurants, two lounges, a mega shopping plaza, a pool, tennis courts, a fitness center, and a 20,000-square-foot Pacific Waters Spa provide the guest diversions. Each room and suite is stocked with robes, a coffeemaker, a refrigerator, data ports and high-speed Internet access, an oversized desk, down comforters, and a private balcony or patio. There's even shuttle service to Disneyland and environs. ♦ 21500 Pacific Coast Hwy (at Beach Blvd), 714/698.1234; 800/233.1234. www.hyatthuntingtonbeach.com

28 CRAB COOKER

★$$ This popular, crowded fish restaurant doesn't accept reservations—not even, as one story has it, from the late President Richard Nixon, who wanted to circumvent the line. The Manhattan clam chower is a big seller, but the specialty is any mesquite-broiled seafood, and if you like lobster, well, it's the best. The adjacent fish market opens at 10AM. ♦ Seafood ♦ M-Sa, lunch and dinner; Su, dinner. 2200 Newport Blvd (at 22nd St), Costa Mesa. 949/673.0100

29 KITAYAMA

★★★$$ This *kaiseki* restaurant (serving multicourse sushi, sashimi, noodle, and tempura meals in tatami rooms with kimono-clad waitresses) is so authentic you might want to bring a Japanese friend along to translate the menu—or you could always have a seat at the more accessible and likewise excellent sushi bar. The fixed-price *omakase kaiseki* (chef's choice) is your best bet if you don't want to spend time figuring out the menu. Other good choices are the beef shabu shabu that you cook at the table, buckwheat soba, and sukiyaki. Finish with red-bean ice cream, then take a walk through the pretty bonsai garden. ♦ Japanese ♦ M-F, lunch and dinner; Sa, dinner. Reservations recommended. 101 Bayview Pl (at Bristol St), Newport Beach. 949/725.0777

30 GOLDEN TRUFFLE

★★$$ Chef/owner Alan Greeley continues to please the crowd that gathers nightly at this convivial neighborhood eatery. Much of the clientele are regulars who have eaten here for more than two decades. They bring wines by the bottle (corkage is charged) or order from his extensive list, and spend hours savoring such dishes as crispy roast duck with raspberry peppercorn sauce, baked artichoke ravioli, or Jamaican fried chicken with Caribbean mashed potatoes and gravy. On the other hand, many simply sit back and let the chef "surprise" them with his off-the-menu prix-fixe dinner. There's even a spa menu for waist watchers. ♦ French Continental ♦ Tu-Sa, lunch and dinner. Reservations recommended. 1767 Newport Blvd (at W 18th St), Costa Mesa. 949/645.9858

30 THE YARD HOUSE RESTAURANT

★★★$$$$ This massive 10,000-square-foot eating emporium with its exhibition kitchen and signature Oval Bar serves lobster tails like no other in clarified butter and blanched garlic, finishing with lemongrass beurre blanc and tomato oil. Executive chef Carlito Jocson does a kick-ass job with grilled New Zealand chops, too, wrapping the tender meat around an herb crust and lathering on sweet balsamic syrup. Other great choices include a spinach salad with grilled Portobello mushrooms and gouda cheese, and pan-roasted Chilean sea bass with bok choy and a miso glaze. To wash it down, there's the world's largest selection of draft beers (about 180) and a super wine list, served by the glass or bottle. And then there are desserts: warm chocolate soufflé cake with vanilla-bean ice cream, macadamia nut

cheesecake with warm caramel sauce, warm lemon soufflé cake with raspberry sauce, and more. ♦ American Fusion ♦ Daily, dinner; Sa, Su, lunch. Reservations suggested. Valet parking. 1875 Newport Blvd (at Harbor Blvd), Costa Mesa, 949/642.0090. Also at 401 Shoreline Dr (in Shoreline Village), Long Beach. 562/628.0455; 71 Fortune Dr (at Irvine Spectrum), Irvine. 949/585.9477. www.yardhouse.com

30 Goat Hill Tavern

Beer lovers, lift your mugs. This place rocks with more than 150 different brewskis on tap. The 35-year-old saloon is manned by good-natured barkeeps and sports a popular billiards table and lots of action all hours of the day and night. ♦ Daily. 1830 Newport Blvd (across from the Yard House Restaurant, near Harbor). 949/548.8428

31 UPPER NEWPORT BAY

Surrounded by the bluffs of Newport Bay, this remarkable and idyllic 741-acre spot is a preserve for ducks, geese, and other avian users of the Pacific Flyway. Paths along the far reaches of the estuary are wonderful for quiet early-morning walks. ♦ Backbay Dr, Newport Beach. 949/640.6746

32 UNIVERSITY OF CALIFORNIA AT IRVINE

UC Irvine was founded in 1965 on a thousand acres donated by the Irvine Company. Twenty-five buildings house five major schools and a number of interdisciplinary and graduate departments. Full-time enrollment is about 17,000. The campus was laid out as an arboretum; more than 11,000 trees from all over the world form a green grove in the center of the tan hills of the **Irvine Ranch.** A self-guided tree-tour brochure is available at the Administration Building. Rare exceptions to the prevailing architectural mediocrity of UC campuses are the **Information Computer Sciences and Engineering Research Facility**—a splendid complex of buildings by **Frank Gehry** located on the southeast edge of the inner ring—and works by **Morphosis** and other cutting-edge architects. The free **School of the Arts Gallery** sponsors exhibitions of 20th-century art and is open Tuesday through Sunday. Theatrical performances are held in the **Fine Arts Village Theatre,** the **Concert Hall,** and **Crawford Hall.** ♦ Campus Dr (between Culver and University Drs). 949/824.5011

33 WILD RIVERS

A water park with 40 rides and attractions is set on a lush tropical site formerly occupied

---

Restaurants/Clubs: Red | Hotels: Purple | Shops: Orange | Outdoors/Parks: Green | Sights/Culture: Blue

by Lion Country Safari. You can shoot the rapids on an inner tube, be fired over water on the **Wipeout,** or simply lie back and work on your tan. Paddling pools keep the smallest children happy. Refreshments are available, as are group picnic sites by advance reservation. ◆ Admission. Daily, June-Oct; some weekends off-season. 8770 Irvine Center Dr (between Lake Forest Dr and San Diego Fwy), Irvine. 949/768.9453

34 Bistro 201

★★$$$ David Wilhelm's contemporary restaurant is modeled after sophisticated New York bistros. This time Wilhelm applies his exotic flair to traditional fare, with dishes such as roast rack of lamb on garlicky lima beans. The bar is zinc-topped and angular, the banquettes covered in raw silk, and the atmosphere cosmopolitan. Jazz musicians play Wednesday through Saturday. ◆ International ◆ M-F, lunch and dinner; Sa, Su, dinner. Reservations recommended. 3333 W Coast Hwy (just east of Newport Blvd), Newport Beach. 949/631.1551

35 Balboa Bay Club & Resort

$$$$ Catering to a prototypical country-club clientele who inhabit the multimillion-dollar manses of the surrounding area, this 132-room beauty is the only full-service waterfront hotel in Newport. Designed by Barry Design Associates of Los Angeles, the décor harbors an understated elegance orchestrated by soft classical columns, cream and gold stone floors, natural rattan furnishings, and tropical touches. Accommodations are spacious and attractively furnished with colorful drapes over plantation shutters, dark woods pitted with apricot, and rust-colored fabrics. Rooms are equipped with coffeemakers and the usual but upscale amenities you'd expect. The makeup mirrors are about the best we've encountered. Bay-front rooms are choice, with views of multimillion-dollar boats and pricey town houses and homes across the narrow arm of Newport Bay on Lido Island. There's a large, inviting pool, a well-equipped, compact fitness room, and optional fee activities, such as use of the spiffy spa (an utter pamper emporium offering head-to-toe services) and the gym (a large, bustling body-buffing facility) at the **Balboa Bay Racquet Club**. There are also nearby boat rentals and golf. The culinary highlight is chef Josef Lageder's creative California cuisine served in the **First Cabin** (★★★$$$) dining room. Room service is available whenever and well worth it. In the evening, Duke's Place dishes out drinks and entertainment. Complimentary transportation to and from Orange County Airport provides a pleasant extra. ◆ 1221 W Coast Hwy (between Dover Dr and Tustin Ave). 888/445.7153, 949/645.5000. www.balboabayclub.com

35 Duffy Electric Boat Co.

If you want to fit right in with Newport's chic set, rent an electric boat and spend an afternoon barhopping or just drive it to a bayside restaurant for lunch or dinner. The in mode of transportation for the locals who lunch, dine, or drink, these comfortable, smooth-running boats remind one of sailing around the canals of Venice, except you do the steering. You can rent one by the hour or day. ◆ Located just steps from the Balboa Bay Club at 2002 W Coast Hwy, Newport Beach. 949/645.6812. www.duffyboats.com

36 Newport Dunes

This upscale aquatic RV park on a 15-acre lagoon is not only for campers; visitors may rent all sorts of sports equipment, from paddleboats to sailboats, kayaks, windsurfers, boogie boards, roller skates, and bicycles. There are also meeting facilities, a launching ramp, and dressing rooms. ◆ 1131 Backbay Dr (just west of Jamboree Rd), Newport Beach. General information 949/729.3863, resort watersports 949/729.3863, 949/729.1155

37 Hyatt Newporter

$$$ Located on **Upper Newport Bay,** this 26-acre resort has 405 rooms and four three-bedroom villas with private pools. The sporting options here include a nine-hole golf course, tennis, and swimming, and a spa with Jacuzzis for post-workout fun. **Duke's,** an English pub filled with John Wayne memorabilia (he used to frequent the resort, and started the tennis club), offers live entertainment Wednesday through Saturday. Summer concerts are held Friday evenings in an outdoor amphitheater. ◆ 1107 Jamboree Rd (just east of Backbay Dr), Newport Beach. 949/729.1234, 800/233.1234; fax 949/644.1552; email: info@hyattnewporter.com. www.hyattnewporter.com

38 Orange County Museum of Art

Changing exhibitions of contemporary art and a permanent collection of 20th-century art emphasizing works by California artists are presented in this internationally famous museum. The **Sculpture Garden Cafe** offers light meals and snacks; the gift shop sells catalogs and books. ◆ Admission. Tu-Su. 850 San Clemente Dr (between Santa Cruz and Santa Barbara Drs), Newport Beach. 949/759.1122

39 Four Seasons Hotel

$$$$ Staying at any Four Seasons hotel is about as good as it gets, and naturally this flagship of the prestigious hotel chain is no exception. One of the few hotels that can cater to business travelers and vacationers

with equal élan, this 20-story urban oasis offers 285 outstanding rooms and sensational service and amenities. The décor is refined, the art of typical exceptional Four Seasons quality, and the gardens and views spectacular. Facilities include a pool where every lounge chair is wired with data ports for folks who need their daily Internet fix, and eight private cabanas for those who just want to plotz in a chaise. There's also a well-equipped fitness center, spa, free bicycles, exercise classes, tennis courts, a business center, and restaurants. ◆ 690 Newport Center Dr (at Santa Cruz Dr), Newport Beach. 949/759.0808, 800/332.3442; fax 949/759.0568. www.fourseasons.com

Within the Four Seasons Hotel:

PAVILION

★★$$$$ Crab fritters, lobster ragout, lamb with turnip pancakes, and other specialties are enhanced by the sophisticated décor at this elegant dining room. ◆ California ◆ M-F, breakfast, lunch, and dinner; Sa, dinner; Su, brunch and dinner. Reservations recommended. 949/760.4920

THE GRILL AT PELICAN HILL

★★★$$$ This charming Mission-style restaurant, with its beamed white ceiling, whitewash exterior, and hand-painted tiles, overlooks the eighteenth hole of Pelican Hill Golf course. The food's great too. ◆ American. ◆ Daily, lunch and dinner Sa, Su, brunch. Reservations required for dinner. 949/717.6000

40 THE RITZ

★★★$$$$ Don't confuse it with the Ritz-Carlton hotel down the coast (see page 212), even though Hans Prager's luxury restaurant draws the same well-heeled crowd. Its bouillabaisse has been acclaimed as the best west of the Mississippi, and the carousel appetizer (with fresh foie gras, sweet smoked trout, and gravlax), the liver with crispy onion sticks, and the classic osso buco have also won devoted fans. This place is kind of dressy, so don your best duds. ◆ Continental ◆ M-F, lunch and dinner; Sa, dinner. Reservations recommended. 880 Newport Center Dr (between Farallon and Santa Barbara Drs), Newport Beach. 949/720.1800. www.theritz.com

41 FASHION ISLAND

This spiffy 1960s mall serves as both a marketplace and gathering spot, with more than 200 shops, restaurants, and movie theaters under one roof. Anchored by Neiman Marcus, Robinsons-May, Macy's Women's Store, and Bloomingdales, the center houses 40-plus eateries including the ever popular Hard Rock Café (with a 50-foot guitar), Cheesecake Factory, Wolfgang Puck Cafe, two food courts, and a farmers' market. The Jerde Partnership's Mediterranean-themed design, completed in 1990, is so popular that families come just to stroll through the plazas and catch views of the Pacific. Located in the 75-acre Newport Center complex, the mall is 20 minutes south of Anaheim. Shuttle service is available from area hotels. ◆ Daily. Newport Center Dr (north of E Coast Hwy), Newport Beach. 949/721.2000. www.shopfashionisland.com

Within Fashion Island:

TUTTO MARE

★$$ This stylish trattoria specializes in seafood and pasta. ◆ Italian ◆ M-F, lunch and dinner; Sa, Su, dinner. Reservations recommended. 545 Newport Center Dr. 949/640.6333

ROY'S OF NEWPORT BEACH

★★★$$-$$$ Anyone who has ever sampled Roy Yamaguchi's food knows it's downright sensational, and this West Coast branch of his Hawaii-based chain is no exception. The appetizers are so good some people make an entire meal out of them, ordering straight down the list of dim sums. But every one of his exquisitely presented Pacific Rim items, from seared ahi tuna to fresh fish dishes, tastes terrific. ◆ Pacific Rim/Asian/California ◆ M-Sa, dinner. Reservations recommended. 453 Newport Center Dr. 949/640.ROYS. www.roys-restaurants.com

EL TORITO GRILL

★$ From the zingy salsa to the creative tortilla fillings, everything is freshly made and served with flair in this casual hot spot. ◆ Southwestern ◆ Daily, lunch and dinner. 951 Newport Center Dr. 949/640.2875. Also at 633 Anton Blvd (between Avenue of the Arts and Park Center Dr), Costa Mesa. 949/640.2875

42 HO SUM BISTRO

★$ Set in a stark white room, this little bistro enchants your taste buds with delicious chicken, dim sum, noodles, and assorted snacks. ◆ California/Chinese ◆ Daily, lunch and dinner. 3112 Newport Blvd (at 32nd St), Newport Beach. 949/675.0896

42 THE CANNERY

★★$$ This chimerical landmark restaurant, festooned with jellyfish lights, provides an animated, fun setting with excellent service and good food. There's seating outside on a balcony overlooking the bay and in an informal upstairs bar, lounge, and dining area with hardwood floors under an exposed-beam ceiling. The place, which actually was a real cannery circa 1921, called Western Canners, bustles day and night. The fresh fish dishes, like the halibut, Chilean sea bass, or king salmon, are excellent. Go early and join the crowd for drinks. ♦ Seafood ♦ Daily, lunch and dinner. 3010 Lafayette Ave (near 32nd St), Newport Beach. 949/566.0060. www.cannerynewport.com

43 BAYSIDE

★★★$$$ There's a pleasant uptown style to this restaurant by the bay on Balboa Island. The food is quite good, but the service can be spotty. You can dine inside or out on a pretty porch. As at so many seaside eateries, the fish is the best choice here. ♦ Seafood ♦ Daily, dinner. Reservations required. 900 Bayside Dr (between Balboa and Harbor Islands), Newport Beach. 949/721.1222. www.BaysideRestaurant.com

44 21 OCEANFRONT RESTAURANT

★★$$$ At this clublike restaurant, chef Luiz Tzorin prepares an especially fine abalone and a popular fresh Colorado rack of lamb. ♦ Continental ♦ Daily, dinner. Reservations recommended. 2100 W Ocean Front (at McFadden Pl), Newport Beach. 949/673.2100

44 DORYMAN'S OCEANFRONT INN

$$$ This 10-room bed-and-breakfast inn offers ocean views and Victorian décor in a converted 1891 commercial building—the first in the city. ♦ 2102 W Ocean Front (between McFadden and 21st Pls), Newport Beach. 949/675.7300

45 LOVELL BEACH HOUSE

One of the great monuments of modern architecture, this 1926 beach house was designed by **Rudolph Schindler** for the same progressive doctor who was to commission a house by Richard Neutra in Los Feliz a few years later. It is a fine example of Schindler's early Constructivist style, combining grace, lightness, and strength in a design far ahead of its time. It's a private residence. ♦ 1242 W Ocean Front (at 13th St), Newport Beach

46 NEWPORT HARBOR

There are 10 yacht clubs and 10,000 boats in this aquatic playground. The bay surrounds Lido Isle, Linda Isle, Harbor Island, Bay Isle, and Balboa Island. Boat slips or moorings can be rented through the county sheriff's **Harbor Division** (949/723.1002). **Hornblower Yachts** (800/950.1920) offers brunch and dinner/dancing cruises. ♦ Lower Newport Bay, Newport Beach

Within Newport Harbor:

BALBOA ISLAND

Balboa is actually three islands (in descending size, the Big Island, the Little Island, and Collins Island) connected by bridges. A favorite island pastime is an evening stroll among the luxury houses.

47 BALBOA FERRY

Three tiny ferries take you between the Balboa Peninsula and Balboa Island. ♦ Daily, 24 hours. Palm St (just north of E Bay Ave), Newport Beach

48 BALBOA PAVILION

Built as a Victorian bathhouse and electric Red Car terminal in 1906, this was a trendy destination for fashionably dressed bathers from the greater LA area. It is now the most visible point on the bay, outlined by twinkling lights at night, with a harbor-view bar and restaurant. It is the Newport Terminal for **Catalina Island tours, whale-watching expeditions,** and cruises aboard the *Pavilion Queen*, which last 45 to 90 minutes and take you around Newport Harbor. ♦ 400 Main St (just north of E Bay Ave), Newport Beach. General information 949/673.5245, sport fishing and skiff rentals 949/673.1423

49 RUBY'S

★$ The lovingly re-created Streamline diner helped launch a trend—and a growing chain, now in more than 30 locations—toward white Formica, red vinyl, and quilted stainless steel. Cuddle up in a booth to feast on omelets, mountains of fries, big salads, hot dogs, hamburgers (and really good veggie burgers), and milk shakes. There are also great views of the Pacific Ocean that's just across the street. ♦ American ♦ Daily, breakfast, lunch, and dinner. Balboa Pier, Newport Beach. 949/673.7829

50 SHERMAN LIBRARY AND GARDENS

This jewel of a botanical garden and library specializes in the horticulture of the Pacific Southwest. The well-maintained grounds are vibrant with unusual flowers and hanging baskets. The tea garden serves pastries and coffee, while a gift shop sells horticultural items. ♦ Admission. Gardens: daily. Library: Tu, Th, 9AM-4:30PM. 2647 E Coast Hwy (between Fernleaf and Dahlia Aves), Newport Beach. 949/673.2261

51 CARMELO'S

★★$$ The well-rounded menu, friendly service, and live music draw crowds to this unpretentious trattoria. Entrées to try include pasta Sorrentina (with fresh porcini mushrooms and zucchini flowers), pumpkin-flavored gnocchi, and Dover sole Milanese. ♦ Italian ♦ Daily, dinner (music and dancing until 1AM). Reservations recommended. 3520 E Coast Hwy (between Orchid and Narcissus Aves), Newport Beach. 949/675.1922

52 FIVE CROWNS

★★$$$$ Fine food, professional service, and a charming ambience account for the popularity of this improved version of England's oldest inn (Ye Old Bell at Hurley, opened in 1135). Herb-roasted free-range chicken, roast duckling with apple-prune compote, and prime rib are dependable choices. ♦ Continental ♦ M-Sa, dinner; Su, brunch and dinner. Reservations recommended. 3801 E Coast Hwy (at Poppy Ave), Corona del Mar. 949/760.0331

53 HORTENSE MILLER GARDEN

Docents lead two-hour tours through this spectacular two-acre private garden, overgrown with native flora and exotic plants. More than 1,200 species are represented. Reservations are required two weeks in advance. ♦ Admission. Tours: W, Sa, and occasionally Tu. 22511 Allview Terr (north of High Dr), Laguna Beach. 949/497.0716

54 FESTIVAL OF ARTS/PAGEANT OF THE MASTERS

Showbiz and technical wizardry are combined to simulate great works of art, such as *The Last Supper,* using live models. Artists apply innovative makeup to the models, who must remain motionless for up to a minute and a half during the performance. For seven or eight (it changes slightly) weeks each year, some 600 volunteers and a small staff of trained professionals draw oohs and aahs from thousands of wide-eyed spectators. Book well ahead for the July and August performances. ♦ Admission. 650 Laguna Canyon Rd (north of Forest Ave), Laguna Beach. 949/494.1145, 800/487.3378. www.foapom.org

55 LAGUNA BEACH

So beautiful it can take your breath away. So peaceful it could melt Rambo. Add to that a Mediterranean climate combined with a three-mile beach and an artsy atmosphere and you have the reason why even Angelenos flock here for summer weekends or rent seaside cottages for weeks or months at a time. To maintain its pristine environment, the city strictly prohibits neon signs, T-shirt vendors, and buildings higher than three stories. The town bustles year-round with locals and visitors browsing through boutiques (this is where to find nifty bikinis), shopping for art or antiques, eating at sidewalk cafés, and playing beach volleyball 'til they literally drop on the soft sand beach. Laguna Beach is where John Steinbeck lived while penning *Tortilla Flat,* and Bette Davis made this her home during the 1940s. For adventurers, explorers, or just plain sybarites, Laguna's South Coast Wilderness—a 17,000-acre greenbelt—offers an opportunity to commune with nature. You can snorkel, dive, go mountain biking, hiking, horseback riding, or camping, or take guided tours. Nature lovers can catch glimpses of rare monkey flowers and bush lupine, while explorers will discover hidden caves and coves. It's easy to spend days trekking through this eco-friendly area that includes **Aliso and Wood Canyons Wilderness Park,** 28373 Alicia Parkway (949/923.2200); **Crystal Cove State Park,** 8471 Pacific Coast Highway (949/494/3539); **Laguna Coast Wilderness Park,** 20102 Laguna Canyon Road (949/923.2235), and **Laguna Beach Open Space and Marine Sanctuaries,** Mouton Meadows Park at Del Mar and Balboa Aves (949/497.0716). Beyond recreation and tourist services, the community also supports a thriving cottage industry of boutiques, art galleries, artisan shops, and antiques dealers. For visitor information, call 800/877.1115 or see www.lagunabeachinfo.org. Although the town's filled with great dining spots, should you just want to eat in or take a picnic, call **Restaurants on the Run** (949/951.2500, fax 949/951.7700; www.ontherun.com) and they'll deliver food from any restaurant in the area, 11AM-2PM and 5:30-9PM daily.

55 LAGUNA MUSEUM OF ART

A permanent collection and changing exhibitions of work by California artists are displayed here. ♦ Admission. Tu-Su. 307 Cliff Dr (at N Coast Hwy), Laguna Beach. 949/494.6531, 800/487.3378. www.lagunaartmuseum.org

55 LAS BRISAS—SEAFOODS OF MEXICO

★★★$$$ This landmark 1938 restaurant, perched on a seaside cliff, fills up with locals, tourists, and folks who drive several hours for the great margaritas and spectacular view of Laguna Beach and the Pacific Ocean. The food is good, too, especially the fresh seafood and Mexican specialties. ♦ Mexican ♦ Daily, dinner; M-Sa, breakfast and lunch; Su,

Restaurants/Clubs: Red | Hotels: Purple | Shops: Orange | Outdoors/Parks: Green | Sights/Culture: Blue

brunch. Reservations recommended. 361 Cliff Dr (between N Coast Hwy and Jasmine St), Laguna Beach. 949/497.5434. www.leonardneilproductions.com &

56 CAFE ZINC MARKET

★★★$ A quiet sidewalk patio fronts this gourmet food market and vegetarian restaurant, where patrons line up to wrap their hands around a tall, hot mug of the county's best cappuccino. Enjoy bread from **La Brea Bakery,** along with homemade granola, plate-size gourmet pizzettes, sandwiches, and salads. ◆ Vegetarian ◆ M, breakfast; daily, breakfast and lunch. Market: Daily. 350 Ocean Ave (between Beach St and Forest Ave), Laguna Beach. 949/494.6302

56 VERTICAL WINE BAR

★★$$$ The thing to do at this hip spot is sit back and enjoy some wine with your lunch or dinner. Just order a bottle from among the 800 labels and enjoy while mulling over the menu. Begin with the mesclun salad with goat cheese and pesto vinaigrette or white bean soup with mussels, and continue on with grilled scallops topped with hazelnuts or the tender peppered New York steak with brie mashed potatoes. For dessert, savor the chocolate saverin tart. ◆ Bistro ◆ Daily, lunch and dinner. 234 Forest Ave (between S Coast Hwy and Beach St), Laguna Beach. 949/494.0990. www.verticalwinebar.com

56 FIVE FEET

★★★$$$$ East meets West in this modern, arty restaurant, where chef/owner Michael Kang surprises and delights with such dishes as *kung pao* calamari (in a caramelized sauce of soy, Thai red chilies, peanuts, and scallions), a whole catfish with a variety of sauces, pot stickers, and even a yummy veal chop. Expect to wait for your table, as this is one popular spot. ◆ Chinese/European/California ◆ Daily, dinner. Reservations recommended. 328 Glenneyre St (between Mermaid St and Forest Ave), Laguna Beach. 949/497.4955. Also at Fashion Island, Newport Center Dr (north of E Coast Hwy), Newport Beach. 949/497.4955

57 VACATION VILLAGE

$$ This beachfront resort is a relative bargain, particularly in late September and October, when the rates drop but the weather is ideal. Accommodations include apartments with kitchenettes, studios, and 130 rooms (50 with ocean views). Among the amenities are two pools, a whirlpool and sauna, and a kids'

game room. The delightful **Beach House Restaurant** (949/494.9707), on site but under separate ownership, serves California cuisine. ◆ 647 S Coast Hwy (between Cleo St and Sleepy Hollow La), Laguna Beach. 949/494.8566, 800/843.6895; fax 949/494.1386. www.vacationvillage.com

57 EILER'S INN

$$ Warm European hospitality is dished out at this charming bed-and-breakfast by the sea. There are 11 rooms and one suite with a kitchen and fireplace. The morning repast is a gourmet treat worth leaping out of bed for. ◆ 741 S Coast Hwy (between St. Ann's Dr and Cleo St), Laguna Beach. 949/494.3004; fax 949/497.2215

58 THE CARRIAGE HOUSE

$$ This charming New Orleans–style bed-and-breakfast (yet another in the area) has six suites with private entrances, and five with kitchens. There's a pretty garden, a friendly dining room, and it's just a three-minute walk from the beach. ◆ 1322 Catalina St (between Mountain Rd and Cress St), Laguna Beach. 949/494.8945. www.carriagehouse.com

59 LA CASA DE LA CAMINO

$$ This charming Mediterranean-style bed-and-breakfast, built in 1927, features 39 units and eight mini-suites with whirlpool tubs, all adorably decorated with antiques and pretty pieces and most with ocean views. Although refurbished, the décor retains some wonderful holdovers from the 1920s and 1950s. A 2,500-square-foot rooftop deck offers panoramic views of the Pacific, and complimentary continental breakfast is served daily in a lovely courtyard. On cool nights, the lobby lounge offers a cozy retreat where guests can relax beside a wood-burning fireplace. ◆ 1289 S Coast Hwy (between Cress and Brooks Sts), Laguna Beach. 949/497.2446, 888/FOR.LCDC; fax 949/494.5581; email: casacamino@aol.com. www.casacamino.com

60 SURF & SAND HOTEL

$$$$ One of the few Southern California hotels right on the ocean, this local standard with Mediterranean décor has 160 rooms with sea-view balconies overlooking the Pacific. There's a fun, three-meal-a-day restaurant called **Splashes** (★★$$$) that serves a mix of Mediterranean/California cuisine with an ocean view (714/497.4477) and meeting facilities and an outdoor pool. The **AquaTerra Spa** provides a cozy sea-front sanctuary for myriad salubrious treatments. 949/376.2SPA ◆ 1555 S Coast Hwy (between Bluebird Canyon Dr and Calliope St), Laguna Beach. 949/497.4477, 800/524.8621; fax 949/494.2897. www.surfandsandresort.com

61 DIZZ'S AS IS

★$$ Kind of funky, with a typical Laguna Beach bohemian crowd that dresses to please themselves, this eclectic, Art Deco joint is designed for serious eating. The food's great, the menu changes daily, and the plates don't match. Cioppino and filet mignon are standouts. ♦ International ♦ Tu-Su, dinner. 2794 S Coast Hwy (between Nyes Pl and Highland Rd), Laguna Beach. 949/494.5250

61 MONTAGE RESORT & SPA LAGUNA BEACH

$$$$ What can we say? This is the most impressive beachfront hotel in Southern California. The rooms are magnificent. The ambience exudes warmth, while the spa outdoes itself. A deep regard for nature permeates the 30-acre facility with individually crafted designs through pottery and ceramic tiles, woodwork, and outstanding metalwork, all done by local artisans. Once known as Treasure Island, named for the Robert Louis Stevenson novel that was shot there in 1934, the grounds are indeed a treasure. Each of the 262 spacious (the smallest is 500 square feet) ocean-view rooms and suites is dynamite. Designed by Wilson & Associates of Dallas, Texas, each is done in dark woods and light fabrics. High beds are covered in feather tops and down. Televisions feature flat screens with DVD players and state-of-the-art sound systems. Bathrooms are big with lots of marble, shaving mirrors in the showers, and lavish tubs adorned with three candles to enhance the soaking experience. There are 51 spectacular suites and 37 equally extravagant bungalows. In-room amenities include the usual Internet accessories, iron and ironing board, and all the comforts of a luxury resort. And, ah, the spa, with cushy outdoor lounges set by a large Jacuzzi and cold-plunge pool, is so inviting, once you're inside you'll want to spend the day. Treatments are top-of-the-line, with hand-picked therapists to work on you head to foot. No expense was spared doing the fitness center, either. Fully equipped, it's one of the best around, with ocean views, a private lap pool, plenty of bottled water, and a TV at each piece of machinery. However, it would be a shame to spend too much time in the room, since the outdoors is what this resort is all about, with a long stretch of sandy beach providing opportunity for a variety of water sports. There are three large, very inviting pools on premises. Room service, available around the clock, is always efficient and well done. There are three restaurants, **The Loft** (★★$$), a casual bistro offering three meals daily; the **Mosaic Bar and Grille** (★★$$), situated bluff style, for California beach fare, open for breakfast and lunch on Sunday and dinner Friday and Saturday; and **Studio** (★★★★$$$$), the pièce de résistance, created by super-chef James Boyce, a personal pick to head the restaurant of Alan Fuerstman, the hotel's founder and CEO. Studio occupies a charming bluff-side bungalow that provides 280-degree views of the Pacific Ocean through huge open-air windows. The décor incorporates the resort's light and airy theme with a 20-foot-high raised ceiling of rustic, stained wood beams, two custom-built Paul Wyatt wine vaults perched in the entryway, and early California art gracing the walls. To really get a sense of Boyce's talents, order from his seasonally changing tasting menu, which he will happily tailor to any dietary needs or taste. ♦ French ♦ Reservations a must. Sa, Su, lunch; T-Su, dinner. For reservations, call 949/715.6420. 30801 S Coast Hwy (between Nyes Place and Wesley St). 866/271.6953. www.montagelagunabeach.com

62 MISSION SAN JUAN CAPISTRANO

Founded in 1776 by Father Junípero Serra, this simple adobe is one of the oldest churches in California. In 1796, Indian laborers under the charge of a Mexican stonemason began a grand stone church that was completed in 1806, only to be destroyed by earthquake six years later. The monumental structure was not rebuilt, and services resumed in an older adobe church. In the 1890s, the Landmarks Club saved this church from destruction, and in the 1920s it underwent major restoration. The famous swallows that return to Capistrano each 19 March, St. Joseph's Day, are cliff swallows that build their gourdlike nests in the broken arches of the ruins of the stone church. ♦ Admission. Daily. Camino Capistrano and Ortega Hwy, San Juan Capistrano. 949/248.2049

62 SARDUCCI'S CAPISTRANO DEPOT RESTAURANT

★★$$ Soak in the beauty of Old San Juan while enjoying Italian/American cuisine in this quaint eatery situated in an 1894 train depot. Stone walls and brick archways lead to an indoor dining room warmed, in winter, by several fireplaces. In summer, dine outside in the charming courtyard, where graceful fountains provide the sensory background. The food is surprisingly good, with Sarducci's signature papaya-mango halibut, shrimp and rainbow tortellini, and lamb Wellington leading the list of favorites. Desserts rule here, with an amazing hazelnut mousse and

Restaurants/Clubs: **Red** | Hotels: **Purple** | Shops: **Orange** | Outdoors/Parks: **Green** | Sights/Culture: **Blue**

Florentine cookie tower, or a four-layer chocolate cake that serves three. ◆ Italian/American ◆ Daily, lunch and dinner. 926701 Verdugo St (just west of Camino Capistrano), San Juan Capistrano. 949/488.7600

62 San Juan Capistrano Library

The harmonious but slightly tongue-in-cheek use of anachronism is a hallmark of celebrity Postmodern architect **Michael Graves,** who designed this 1983 library. The buildings are arranged around an arcaded courtyard, a lovely fountain, and gazebos for reading and resting, and the polychrome interior echoes the nearby Spanish mission. ◆ M-Th, Sa. 31495 El Camino Real (between El Horno St and Don Juan Ave), San Juan Capistrano. 949/493.1752

63 Ritz-Carlton Laguna Niguel

$$$$ Knock-down gorgeous, with views to match, this crème de la crème of super-luxury beachfront resort hotels unites East Coast style and West Coast atmosphere on its perch atop a dramatic bluff overlooking the Pacific Ocean. Excellent service coupled with superb amenities—fantastic fitness center and spa, two swimming pools, four tennis courts, direct access (by foot or shuttle) to a two-mile-long beach below, and sailing accommodations at nearby **Dana Point**—enhance a stay here. Dining is an event at any of its four restaurants: **The Dining Room, Club Grill & Bar, The Wine Room,** or the **Terrace Restaurant.** There's also a lobby lounge where you can enjoy a light breakfast, lunch, or dinner, dessert, or drinks. The library, with its floor-to-ceiling bookshelves, is the perfect place to sip high tea while looking out at spectacular ocean views. The **Wine Room** sets the stage for special wine tastings and cigar-smoking events. Suites are spectacular at this resort (one even has its own Steinway), especially on the Club Floor, accessible by a special elevator key and available at an extra charge, which gets you such privileges as complimentary breakfast, gourmet snacks, drinks, hors d'oeuvres, and more. © Ritz Carlton Dr and Pacific Coast Hwy, Dana Point. 949/240.2000, 800/241.3333; fax 949/240.1061. www.ritzcarlton.com ᕤ

Within the Ritz-Carlton Laguna Niguel:

The Dining Room

★★★$$$$ Every meal here comes up a winner, from the simple (grilled fresh fish or

tender veal chop) to the exotic (pheasant mousse with blueberry vinegar sauce, sweetbreads in Port and caper sauce, and saddle of rabbit with basil cream sauce). Add an outstanding wine list and sublime service in an ultra-handsome décor, and the overindulgence seems well worth the splurge. ◆ Mediterranean ◆ Tu-Sa, dinner. Reservations recommended. 949/240.2000

The Wine Room

★★★$$$ Extravagantly furnished with rich, dark mahogany wine cabinets cradling $200,000 worth of wine, the room is available for romantic dinners for two or groups of 12. Fine china and Riedel crystal serve as backdrops for the personalized menus created by chef de cuisine Yvon Goetz and executive chef Christian Rassinoux. Monthly wine seminars are also hosted here. ◆ Reservations required. 949/240.5008

The Club Grill & Bar

★★★$$$ A casual-chic supper club where you can enjoy live jazz and blues music while savoring an all-American menu of hearty meats and seafood. 949/240.5008

63 St. Regis Monarch Beach Resort & Spa

$$$$ Perched just across Pacific Highway and up the road about a half mile, this 400-room Tuscan-style gem looks like it stepped out of a Renaissance painting with its tall palms, gracious fountains and courtyards, mosaic tiles, European stone, marble floors, oversized crystal chandeliers, and sweeping stairways. Walls are adorned with a one-of-a-kind art collection featuring original Picassos and Chagalls that sit among four Dale Chihuly glass pieces. When it opened in 2001, the hotel fast became a getaway for the Hollywood crowd, attracting Sarah Michelle Gellar, Selma Bair, and other tinsel-town types—many who went to sample the lavish **Gaucin Spa** and famed **Aqua Restaurant**. The mood is genial and relaxed. And sometimes so is the service. Rooms are amazing, especially suites. All sport balconies or terraces and come equipped with high-tech tools like plasma televisions, digital sound, high-speed Internet access, and other techno gadgets. Attention to detail prevails, with gorgeous Filido Italian bed linens, goose-down comforters, Lissedell Irish terry towels, and Lady Primrose bath products. Even the hair dryers are top-of-the-line. Outdoor play areas include three pools, two Jacuzzis, tennis, jogging trails, nearby golf, and access to a 6.1-acre stretch of beach. The spa and fitness center are lavish affairs, offering head-to-toe treatments and every workout option known to fitness buffs. There are plenty of

---

The first Jewish religious services took place in predominantly Catholic LA in 1854, and the first Protestant church was built 10 years later.

THE BEST

Mark Morrison

West Coast Editor, *In Style*

Breakfast at the never-closed **Original Pantry** downtown.

The Deco floors and ceilings of **Union Station.**

Running, walking, or riding a bike around **Lake Hollywood,** a pine-fringed reservoir built in the 1920s, set in the hills below the **Hollywood sign.**

Anything by Joachim Splichal at **Patina, Pinot Bistro,** or **Cafe Pinot.** The downtown café is set in a park alongside the landmark Art Deco **LA Library,** where you have that rare feeling—for LA—that you're in a pulsating urban center.

Cruising **Mulholland** for the changing landscape, scenic lookouts, and some of the best city and valley views (lots of photo ops).

Strolling the **Venice canals** and feeding the ducks.

Hiking to the top of **Runyon Canyon** in Hollywood, past the ruins of the old Huntington Hartford estate to a bluff overlooking the entire LA basin.

The **Third Street Promenade** in Santa Monica for shopping, strolling, and street performers.

A picnic dinner at the open-air **Hollywood Bowl** (home to the LA Philharmonic) during the summer.

The carousel, homemade potato chips, and Jody Maroni sausages at the **Santa Monica Pier.**

Margaritas and nachos at **Marix Tex-Mex** in Santa Monica Canyon.

The **Getty Villa** with its elegant gardens, palatial architecture, and alfresco dining.

The two-headed snake at the **LA Zoo.**

The pony rides and kid-sized railroad at **Griffith Park.**

Having a drink atop the revolving restaurant at the **Bonaventure Hotel**—the elevator ride alone is worth the trip, and the panoramic LA view can't be beat.

The **La Brea Tar Pits** and the **George C. Page Museum,** an abundant archaeological dig right in the heart of the city.

The **Gumbo Pot** at **Farmers' Market** for fast-food Cajun cooking at a measly price.

Universal CityWalk, a two-block, theme-park–style shopping strip that's more fun during the week (and in the winter), when it's less crowded.

House of Blues, a hot-blooded (if somewhat touristy) bayou-style music club on Sunset Strip, owned by former Blues Brother Dan Aykroyd.

Indian artifacts at the **Southwest Museum.**

Dinnertime at **Typhoon** at the neighborly Santa Monica Airport, where you can have a cocktail, munch on Pan-Asian delights, and watch small planes take off and land as the sun sets.

---

dining choices, from **Motif** (★★$$$), specializing in small-plate cuisine with an international flair; the **Pool Bar & Grill** ($$) for casual light American fare; and the star, Aqua (see below), the award-winning showcase for chef Bruno Chemel's extraordinary talents. ♦ 1 Monarch Beach Resort Dr (just up from Pacific Coast Hwy; turn left at Starbucks and Ritz Carlton Dr), Dana Point. 800/772.1543, 949/234.3200. www.stregismb.com

Within the St. Regis Monarch Beach Resort & Spa:

AQUA

★★★★$$$$ This is one dynamite restaurant, both esthetically and gastronomically.

Floor-to-ceiling windows dressed with burgundy drapes, large columns, and comfortable banquettes set the mood for chef Bruno Chemel's cuisine. The wait staff are helpful and efficient; the wine steward is one of the most knowledgeable in the business. The food speaks for itself. We really recommend the chef's tasting menu just so you don't miss a scrumptious morsel. A recent impeccably prepared and served tasting menu began with an appetite-tempting ahi tuna sashimi for an *amuse-bouche* and continued to please the palate with a tomato-miso soup, salmon cake, miso-glazed Chilean sea bass, grilled Angus prime New York steak, and Tahitian vanilla-bean crème brûlée. ♦ Contemporary Seafood. ♦ Daily, dinner. Reservations required. 949/234.3200

Restaurants/Clubs: Red | Hotels: Purple | Shops: Orange | Outdoors/Parks: Green | Sights/Culture: Blue

GAY LOS ANGELES

The movie and entertainment capital of the world, Los Angeles is a megalopolis of 3.6 million people (9.4 million in LA County as a whole), where a riot of orientations, lifestyles, and cultures make for a festive, colorful mosaic. What the gay English writer (and longtime Angeleno) Christopher Isherwood once fondly observed—that this is "perhaps the ugliest city in the world"—is no longer the case. A full-on cosmopolitan city of its own design, LA has plenty of beauty (and beauties) if you know where to look. Whatever your pleasure, from simple to sophisticated to sinful, the City of Angels can deliver.

Antsy for an electric night on the town? Looking for chic boutiques, world-famous restaurants, homey coffeehouses, and trendy nightclubs packed with bronzed, buffed revelers? Then head over to **West Hollywood** (commonly called "WeHo"), the epicenter of Los Angeles homo-heaven and the home of the recently revitalized **Sunset Strip,** all sandwiched between glitzy **Hollywood** and palm-tree-lined **Beverly Hills.** Prefer the rough-and-tumble biker crowd? Then vroom over to the **East Hollywood** neighborhood of **Silverlake,** home to the burgeoning homocore music scene (see "LA's Lesbigay Music Scene" on page 265) and stomping ground of "daddies" and "bears," leather and denim. Something a bit more suburban? Wander through the beautiful **Hollywood Hills** to the **San Fernando Valley,** with its cabarets, country-western clubs, cozy neighborhood haunts, and of course the infamous **Queen Mary,** a cabaret catering to drag divas and their admirers. For a seaside adventure, head for one of Los Angeles's nearby beach communities and find a charming and casual setting for everything from a romantic meander along the shore to dancing till dawn—just throw on a tank top and spend a golden afternoon or cool evening in **Santa Monica, Venice, Long Beach,** or the popular **Laguna Beach.**

It has been noted, with some reason, that in Southern California, image and style are everything—the right car, the right pecs, the right coffee beans, etc. But there's more to the gay world here than the very visible sculpted-bod boys. If that's not your scene, there are also large gay communities in Silverlake, Santa Monica, and the San Fernando Valley.

The gay dollar speaks loud and proud in LA, too. While there's a multitude of unique homo-owned and/or-operated establishments, most mainstream shops, restaurants, and clubs are respectful of the community and its influence. Many predominantly straight venues, such as the **House of Blues,** the **Hollywood Palladium,** and even Anaheim's family-oriented **Disneyland,** often open their doors to gay and lesbian events, and most locals won't bat an eye should you decide to take your same-sex squeeze for a hand-in-hand stroll through Santa Monica or along sandy **Malibu Beach.**

With economic clout comes a measure of political power. In West Hollywood, at least half the city council members at any given time are gay, and the mayor (who serves a one-year term) often is as well. The local unified school system of Greater LA offers same-sex domestic partner benefits, and many consider the current (Republican!) mayor of Los Angeles, Richard Riordan, to be one of the country's best on homo civil rights and AIDS issues. The relationship hasn't been without strains, though. Despite an official liaison to the gay and lesbian community, the LA Police Department has aroused indignation with its harassment of bar and bathhouse patrons, especially in Silverlake.

A great part of this city's magic lies, of course, in the fact that here literally anything can happen. Like Harrison Ford being discovered while working construction, it could happen to you. But even if it doesn't, and you go home no more famous than before, don't worry; you'll have enough memories of this singular city and its dynamic queer community to last a lifetime.

Area code 310 unless otherwise noted.

Symbols

♂ predominantly/exclusively gay-male-oriented

♀ predominantly/exclusively lesbian-oriented

♂♀ predominantly/exclusively gay-oriented, with a male and female clientele

1 QUEEN MARY

For more than 25 years, female impersonators have been strutting their stuff for a diverse crowd of gays, lesbians, and straights at this kitschy Valley nightclub that's light pink outside, very 1970s inside. You can always find a seat in the expansive lounge to watch recreations of all the gay icons take the stage from Liza to Barbra to Bette to Madonna. Had enough? A quaint back bar provides a cozy place to mingle. ♦ Cover. Back bar: Daily, 1PM-2AM. Shows: W-Th, 9:30PM; F-Sa, 9PM. 12449 Ventura Blvd (between Rhodes and Whitsett Aves). 818/506.5619 ♿

2 OASIS

♂♀ Life is a cabaret, old chum, at this cozy Valley piano bar and show lounge that attracts a friendly, sophisticated crowd of guys and some gals in their late thirties and up. Every seat in the house offers a close-up of the nightly shows, and darts and pool provide distraction between sets. The décor has been described as "weird Egyptian hi-tech with chintz." ♦ M-F, Su, 3PM-2AM; Sa, 2PM-2AM. 11916 Ventura Blvd (between Carpenter Ave and Laurel Canyon Blvd). 818/980.4811 ♿

2 APACHE TERRITORY

♂ It may be small, but most weekends this video bar is *the* place to be for cruisy, cute, young Valley Boys, who rock the tiny dance floor to the latest dance tunes under disco balls. Wallflowers can shoot pool or play pinball or just ogle the buff underwear-clad barkeeps; an adjacent patio offers a break from the noise inside. ♦ Cover, Tu, Sa. Daily, 3PM-2AM. 11608 Ventura Blvd (at Blue Canyon Dr). 818/506.0404 ♿

2 OIL CAN HARRY'S

♂♀ A friendly mix of urban cowpersons calls this Valley country-western bar home, where classic and new country tunes and videos keep the Stetson- and Wrangler-clad crowd boot scootin' on the huge central dance floor, which is sandwiched between two bars. A side stage hosts live bands on occasion. ♦ Cover. Tu, Th, 7:30PM-2AM; F, Sa, 9PM-2AM. 11502 Ventura Blvd (at Berry Dr). 818/760.9749

3 THE GETTY CENTER

In late 1998, millionaire J. Paul Getty's extensive collections of Roman and Greek antiquities, European paintings, and French decorative arts were reopened to the public in their new home, a six-building, 110-acre campus designed by **Richard Meier** in nearby Brentwood (so sprawling, in fact, that a special tram has been built to take visitors from the parking lot uphill to the galleries).

Restaurants/Clubs: Red | Hotels: Purple | Shops: Orange | Outdoors/Parks: Green | Sights/Culture: Blue

Outside, the lovely gardens offer mazes, streams, waterfalls, and terraces; inside the overwhelming array of art includes drawings by the homosexual genius Michelangelo. A bookstore on the premises completes the intellectual nourishment, and two cafés and a restaurant take care of the physical. ♦ Free; fee for parking. Tu-Su. 1200 Getty Center Dr (off N Sepulveda Blvd, between Moraga Dr and I-405). 440.7300 ♿

4 Renaissance Beverly Hills

♂♀ $$ A snazzy boutique hotel perched on a hilltop, it offers 140 quaint rooms decked out in soothing shades of salmon and cream, each with its own private balcony with a panoramic view. Other amenities include a swimming pool; the **Tiara** restaurant, serving California cuisine; 24-hour room service; and valet parking. ♦ 1224 Beverwil Dr (at W Pico Blvd). 277.2800, 800/421.3212; fax 203.9537

5 Jewel's Catch One

♂♀ Still going strong after more than a quarter-century, this large westside dance spot is popular with a mixed gay and lesbian, mostly African-American crowd who groove on the cutting-edge urban dance music. Chicago-style house heats up **Catch One** upstairs, while Top 40 and hip-hop keep the two lower-level dance areas in **Jewel's Room** busy. Friday nights are especially popular with the boys, while Saturday is unofficially girls' night. ♦ Cover. Jewel's Room: Daily, 5PM-2AM. Catch One: W-F, 9PM-3AM; Sa, Su, 9PM-5AM. 4067 W Pico Blvd (at S Norton Ave). 213/734.8849 ♿

6 Geffen Contemporary at MOCA

Renamed after gay mogul David Geffen coughed up $5 million in 1996, the facility (an ex-warehouse renovated by **Frank Gehry** in 1983 and formerly known as **MOCA at the Temporary Contemporary**) counts Jasper Johns and Pop daddy Andy Warhol among the homo members of its distinguished modern art stable (a list studded with stars such as Robert Rauschenberg, Jackson

Pollock, Mark Rothko, Claes Oldenburg, and Diane Arbus). Gehry skillfully preserved the raw character of the 55,000-square-foot interior, adding a steel-and-chainlink canopy over the street to create an outdoor lobby. There's low-cost parking and easy access from the **DASH** shuttle—as well as, of course, a shop on the premises. ♦ Admission (also covers the MOCA on S Grand Ave); free Th, 5PM-8PM. Tu, W, F-Su, 11AM-6PM; Th, 11AM-8PM. Gallery tours: Tu, W, F-Su, noon, 1PM, 2PM; Th, noon, 1PM, 2PM, 6PM. 152 N Central Ave (just north of E First St). 213/626.6222, 213/621.2766

6 Museum of Contemporary Art (MOCA)

Works by such homosexual heavyweights as Jasper Johns, David Hockney, and Félix González-Torres are included among the permanent pieces in this huge museum, the first major US building designed by **Arata Isozaki**, Japan's leading architect. Built in 1986, a sequence of luminous galleries with exposed vaults opens off a sunken courtyard; Isozaki has even incorporated his fascination with Marilyn Monroe in the sensuous curve of the parapet overlooking the courtyard. It's here you'll find a well-stocked shop and the elegant **MOCA Café,** along with a bar, free hors d'oeuvres, and, in summer, live entertainment. Below the galleries is a 162-seat auditorium used for film, video, and performing arts. Artists, critics, and curators give informative tours of current exhibitions. Parking is available at First and Grand Avenues (Lot 16) and at the nearby **Music Center;** the **DASH** shuttle will also get you there. ♦ Admission; free Th, 5-8PM. Tu, W, F-Su, 10AM-6PM; Th, 11AM-8PM. 250 S Grand Ave (between W Fifth and W First Sts). 213/621.2766, 213/626.6222

7 Akbar

★★$ This location was once a watering hole-in-the-wall for the down and out, but now offers one of the hippest bars for trendy Hollywood gays and lesbians. The early evening starts with eclectic songs from the jukebox and then segues into nightly DJs spinning next to the front door, entertaining a closely packed crowd of the young and retro. The bartenders are among the most talented of any in town, able to fix any fun concoction you can think of, and then some. The décor is '40s Hollywood style, with pictures of Ratpackers from way back mingling with other memorabilia. ♦ Daily, 6PM-2AM. 4356 Sunset Blvd (at Fountain). 323/665.6810

8 Highways

Founded in 1989 by writer Linda Frye Burnham and gay performance artist Tim Miller, this is Southern California's center for cutting-edge

---

It started in Los Angeles:

1967—*The Advocate*, the US's oldest continuing national gay and lesbian periodical.

1969—The Metropolitan Community Church, the nation's largest gay and lesbian Christian denomination.

1972—Beth Chayim Chadashim, America's first gay synagogue.

1988—Lambda Delta Lambda, UCLA, the country's first lesbian sorority.

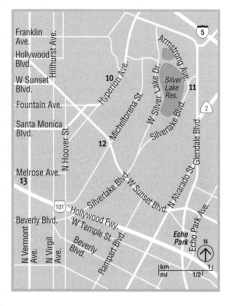

one-room shack, so dim that its few shards of décor barely register. The joint's busiest on weekends, when curious WeHo boys mix with the regulars in a scene that can get raunchy, with plenty of groping (and sometimes more) going on in the rear; even the bathrooms, set up just right for voyeurs, offer no escape. You have been warned. ♦ Cover. M-Th, 4PM-2AM; F, 4PM-4AM; Sa, 2PM-4AM; Su, 2PM-2AM. 1941 Hyperion Ave (between De Longpre and Lyric Aves). 323/660.2649 ⚇

11 LE BARCITO

♂ Locally known simply as "Le Bar," this neighborhood Silverlake haunt is popular with Latino men who come for the fiery salsa and disco and to take in an occasional live show or a game of pool. Hunky strippers also make the place worth a visit. The crowd who hangs out here can also be found on occasion at the nearby and similar **Silver Lake Lounge** (2906 Sunset Blvd, at Silverlake Blvd, 323/953.0471). ♦ Daily, from 8PM. 2375 Glendale Blvd (between Deane St and Silverlake Blvd). 323/660.7595

12 MILLIE'S

★★$ Tiny and trendy, the main attraction at this no-frills Silverlake diner is certainly not the standard burgers, sandwiches, and omelets, or the tacky vinyl tablecloths. It's the entertaining crowd—especially the waiters and waitresses, mostly struggling musicians with more piercings than Pinhead. Famous and not-yet-famous rockers are also among the patrons; don't be surprised to see some of them on MTV one day. ♦ Diner ♦ Daily, breakfast and lunch. 3524 W Sunset Blvd (between Golden Gate and Maltman Aves). 213/664.0404 ⚇

13 FAULTLINE

♂ Located in a seedy area where Silverlake and Hollywood meet, this denim-and-leather joint has a large indoor bar, a huge outdoor patio with a stage, and a shop hawking everything from T-shirts to leather whips and masks. As in most Silverlake bars, inside it's dim and black, and posters of hunky NFL players and leathermen pass for décor. The masculine, often cigar-smoking crowd is fairly tame, but can get carried away at once-a-month events such as a night for bears or a watersports soirée. Faultline is an orgy of hard rock and homocore that draws a bevy of pierced and tattooed grungemeisters, and Sunday's beer bust is popular with local leather dudes. ♦ Cover. Tu-F, 4PM-2AM; Sa, Su, 2PM-2AM. 4216 Melrose Ave (between N Vermont and N New Hampshire Aves). 213/660.0889. www.faultlinebar.com ⚇

talent, highlighting works from LA's diverse creative worlds—including the gay and lesbian HIV/AIDS communities. Featured here are prominent and emerging artists, with some 200 programs by solo performers, small theater ensembles, and dance companies, including appearances by gay artists such as Sir Ian McKellen, Marga Gomez, and Michael Kearns. In addition, the performance space sponsors a variety of annual festivals, such as "Ecce Lesbo/Ecce Homo," featuring eclectic works by performers from across the nation. ♦ 1651 18th St (between Olympic Blvd and Colorado Ave), Santa Monica. 453.1755; ticket information 660.8587

9 ROOSTERFISH

♂ ★★ After 10PM, the crew at this laid-back Venice bar is an interesting hodgepodge of handsome beach boys, low-attitude WeHo types, and young collegiates. The front provides an airy space to lounge and play pinball or darts, while the back area is more cruisy and houses a CD jukebox playing everything from R.E.M. to Cher; a small back patio offers a bit of fresh air and weekend barbecues. Friday nights are most popular here, when the crowd is wall-to-wall and looking for Mr. Right (or Mr. Right Now). ♦ Daily, 11AM-2AM. 1302 Abbot Kinney Blvd (at Santa Clara Ave). 392.2123 ⚇

10 CUFFS

♂ A mostly older and fairly fierce bunch of pierced fetishists and bewhiskered leather daddies give character to what's basically a

Restaurants/Clubs: Red | **Hotels: Purple** | **Shops: Orange** | **Outdoors/Parks: Green** | **Sights/Culture: Blue**

257

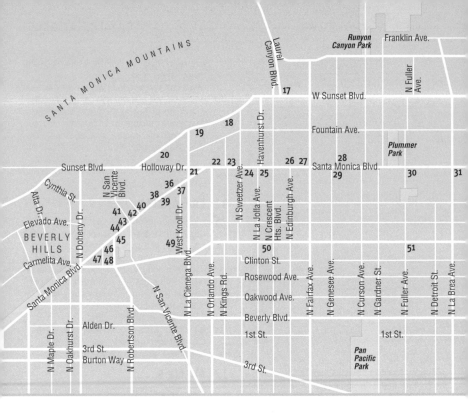

14 L.A. GAY AND LESBIAN COMMUNITY SERVICES CENTER

♂ Besides an abundance of health, legal, and youth-oriented services, this pillar of the community (since 1971) offers plenty of activities of interest to visitors, including lectures, exhibitions, parties, and movies. You also can catch meetings of groups such as Bears L.A., the Coalition of Older Lesbians, and even the Gay & Lesbian Postal Employees Network. *And* the center's got its own line of merchandise. ◆ M-Sa, 9AM-9PM. 1625 N Hudson Ave (between Selma Ave and Hollywood Blvd). 213/993.7400; fax 213/993.7699. www.gay-lesbian-center.org

15 HOLLYWOOD SPA

♂ This huge bathhouse offers a gym, sauna, steam room, Jacuzzi, café, and a live DJ—plus three floors of lads in white towels looking for a quick, uncomplicated date. Whatever your taste, you'll find him here—from fey boys to rock-hard gym types to hairy bears and beyond. Evenings and weekends, not surprisingly, are busiest, and gym cards get admission discounts on Wednesdays. ◆ Admission. Daily, 24 hours. 1650 Ivar Ave (between Selma Ave and Hollywood Blvd). 213/463.5169

16 MING'S DYNASTY

♂ Under new ownership, the former **Mugi** still draws a fun mix of East Asian and Caucasian gays and lesbians, who mix easily in the simple, modern space; there is, however, no dance floor. ◆ Daily, 5PM-2AM. 5221 Hollywood Blvd (between N Kingsley Dr and N Harvard Blvd). 213/462.2039 &

17 NUMBERS

♂ ★★$ Once upon a time, the image of the place was one of randy old men and twinkies for hire, but in its new location, this bar and restaurant actually serves creditable French and continental fare, specializing in steaks and seafood. Mirrored walls and a 1970s décor make for an unintentional retro appeal, while black leather booths provide a comfortable perch for checking out the scene while you eat your dinner. At the bar, it can be assumed that one is looking for a date for an hour or two, though it is becoming a stopping point for the hip and handsome to have a drink and take in the "atmosphere." Valet parking is available. ◆ French/Continental ◆ Restaurant: Daily, lunch and dinner. Bar: Daily, 11AM-2AM. 8741 Santa Monica Blvd (just west of the Ramada). 652.7700 &

18 THE ARGYLE

$$$$ Known for its shameless pampering of guests, this 16-story Art Deco landmark hotel began life in the 1920s as the **St. James Club;** before and since its renovation in the 1980s, it has hosted Bette Davis, River Phoenix, Mariah Carey, Sharon Stone, and

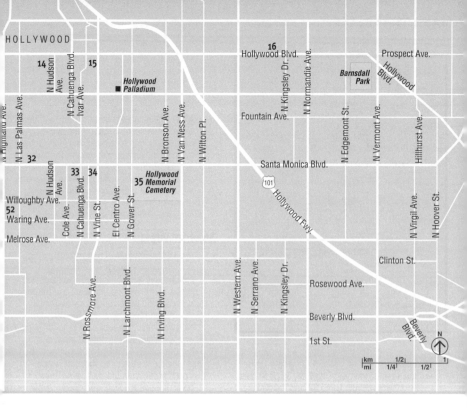

other celebrities. There are 20 charming, well-appointed rooms and 44 apartmentlike suites with great city views, along with a health spa and a fine continental restaurant, **Fenix at the Argyle**. Next to the hotel, a cute little neighborhood park is perfect for hanging and chilling out. ♦ 8358 Sunset Blvd (between N Sweetzer Ave and Olive Dr), West Hollywood. 323/654.7100, 800/225.2637; fax 323/654.9287 &

19 MONDRIAN

$$$ Hip, happening, and homo-friendly, this 12-story hotel has been under the ownership of Ian Schrager since 1995. He painted it white, made it all-suite, and brought in frequent accomplice Phillippe Starck to freshen up the place with his sleek trademark look. Not surprisingly, once again they've cranked out yet another hot flophouse—and nightspot. Expect the same scene you'd find at their other properties (like the **Delano** in South Beach): party boys and girls mingling with artists, rockers, and the occasional celebrity (especially at the heated rooftop pool and adjoining star-power watering hole, the **Skybar**). The 245 units all have minibars, stereo systems, and full kitchens. Other amenities include the **Coco Pazzo** Italian restaurant, a lobby bar, lounge, newsstand, 24-hour gym, room service, concierge, and valet parking. ♦ 8440 Sunset Blvd (between Olive Dr and N La Cienega Blvd),

West Hollywood. 213/650.8999, 800/525.8029; fax 213/650.5215

19 HOUSE OF BLUES

♂ $$ This usually straight venue electrifies with once-a-month all-male bashes that draw LA's prettiest hotties. Popular dance and Top-40 tunes keep the floor sweaty and packed while buff go-go dudes shake it up on the main stage. Aside from the hot crowd, the big club space is a sight to behold, and the back patio provides a breathtaking view of the city. Partly owned by actor Dan Aykroyd and the band Aerosmith, the two-level club/restaurant recreates the ambience of a Southern Delta home, with juke-joint décor and folk art by Delta-based black artists; the corrugated gray metal exterior was salvaged from a shack in Louisiana. Call to check for special events. ♦ Cover. Su, 9PM-2AM. 8430 Sunset Blvd (between Olive Dr and N La Cienega Blvd), West Hollywood. 213/650.0247 &

20 CHIN CHIN

★★★$ Dim sum, pot stickers, noodles, and roast meats are the thing at this hip, gay- and lesbian-friendly Chinese restaurant in the heart of Sunset Boulevard's trendy **Sunset Plaza.** Bright and airy, though a heavy hangout for the young and newly inducted Industry kids, it offers a welcome escape from the WeHo scene and is the perfect oasis for a romantic

---

Restaurants/Clubs: Red | Hotels: Purple | Shops: Orange | Outdoors/Parks: Green | Sights/Culture: Blue

Monica Boulevard is always packed. This is especially true on Friday and Saturday nights, when all the party *muchachos* and *muchachas* pile in for drinks or a spicy late dinner of fajitas and blue-corn tortillas before hitting the clubs. A tiny side patio offers respite from the throngs squeezed in near the back of the house, waiting their turn for a table. The fare's above average, the atmosphere electric, the humongo margaritas near-legendary, and the crowd is classic WeHo: drop-dead gorgeous. ♦ Tex-Mex ♦ Daily, lunch and dinner. 1108 N Flores St (between Santa Monica Blvd and Fountain Ave), West Hollywood. 213/656.8800 &

24 EAT WELL

♂ ★★★$ One of WeHo's hottest eating spots is a hip, homey little diner with a cool coffeehouse-ish atmosphere and great—yet cheap—eats. Burgers, omelets, and the rest of the simple but extensive menu draw a young, good-looking, and surprisingly low-attitude bunch of people. A 15- to 20-minute wait is practically guaranteed on weekends, but the sociable, cruisy types waiting with you help pass the time. The staff is also incredibly easy on the eyes. ♦ American ♦ Daily, breakfast, lunch, and dinner. 8252 Santa Monica Blvd (between N La Jolla and N Harper Aves), West Hollywood. 213/656.1383 &

25 GOLD COAST

♂ This neighborhood spot attracts mostly men in their late thirties and older. Managed by Melissa Etheridge's uncle Carl, it's laid-back yet cruisy, with dance tunes spun by a DJ but no dance floor. Others may prefer the notoriously active parking lot out back, where some hang out in the alley, others sit in their cars, and still others circle and circle around the block. Busy, busy, busy . . . ♦ M-F, 11AM-2AM; Sa, Su, 10AM-2AM. 8228 Santa Monica Blvd (between Havenhurst Dr and N La Jolla Ave), West Hollywood. 213/656.4879 &

26 FRENCH QUARTER MARKET

★★$ For a campy experience, visit this expansive New Orleans–themed restaurant, considered the epicenter of gay and lesbian LA since the mid-1970s. An indoor terrace, fountains filled with live fish, patio tables with green-and-white canopies, and ubiquitous hanging plants lend a quirky charm. The reasonably priced, eclectic menu (from pancakes to baked orange roughy) makes the place popular with a varied crowd, from the WeHo gym boys to Silverlake bikedykes to straights. On weekend afternoons there's always a 15- to 20-minute wait for patio tables, but since the crowd is always friendly and the scene is always cruisy, no one minds a bit. ♦ Eclectic ♦ Daily, breakfast, lunch, and

late-night BYOB dinner; expect a brief wait for a seat on the front patio. ♦ Chinese ♦ Daily, lunch and dinner. Sunset Plaza, 8618 Sunset Blvd (between Alta Loma Rd and Palm Ave), West Hollywood. 652.1818 &Also at various locations throughout the area

21 HOLLOWAY MOTEL

$ This gay-run affair in the thick of it all is styled like a little villa with 20 clean, no-frills rooms. Suites with small kitchens are also available. Don't be surprised if a (presumably off-duty) porn star is staying just down the hall. There's no restaurant. ♦ 8465 Santa Monica Blvd (between Hacienda Pl and N La Cienega Blvd), West Hollywood. 213/654.2454; fax 213/848.7161 &

22 HUGO'S

★★★$$ Tinseltown movers and shakers used to cut multimillion-dollar deals on their cell phones at this hip and charming WeHo eatery, which is still way popular but way less pretentious than in those days. Today it draws a young queer clientele with a homey but lively (and, on weekends, often noisy) atmosphere. The menu's a blend of Cal and Ital—pumpkin pancakes for breakfast, a juicy burger for lunch, and chicken piccata for dinner—all served in generous portions. The best tables in the house are along the front wall, where windows overlook the boulevard. ♦ California/Italian ♦ M, breakfast and lunch; Tu-Su, breakfast, lunch, and dinner. 8401 Santa Monica Blvd (between N Kings Rd and Olive Dr), West Hollywood. 213/654.3993 &

23 MARIX TEX MEX

★$$ Undoubtedly WeHo's most popular cantina, this loud and lively spot off Santa

dinner. 7985 Santa Monica Blvd (between N Hayworth and N Laurel Aves), West Hollywood. 213/654.0898 &

27 Figs

★★★$$ A nice mix of gay men and women—young and older, pretty and sophisticated—come to this private home turned charming restaurant for a romantic dinner or a low-key night out. Jazz, soft lighting, and a warm yellow interior help set the mood, and the menu's a down-home blend of comfort food including pasta, chicken, meat loaf, and vegetarian dishes; the Sunday brunch is quite popular. ♦ American ♦ M-Sa, dinner; Su, brunch and dinner. 7929 Santa Monica Blvd (between N Fairfax and N Hayworth Aves), West Hollywood. 213/654.0780 &

28 The Pleasure Chest

Whatever your pleasure—tame to tawdry, mild to wild—this clean and bright sex supermarket has it all. Domination buffs will be drawn to the first floor, home to a vast array of whips, chains, handcuffs, and bondage and leather gear, while the upstairs holds an extensive selection of gay, lesbian, bi, and straight porn vids, just across from a huge stock of sex toys. Safe-sex supplies abound (including virtually every shape, size, flavor, and color of condom), and the staff's knowledgeable and reasonably friendly, too. ♦ M-Th, Su, 10AM-12:30AM; F, Sa, 10AM-1AM. 7733 Santa Monica Blvd (at N Genesee Ave), West Hollywood. 213/650.1022

29 Spike

♂ Dark and cavelike, this leather-and-Levi's joint entertains a rugged but not intimidating crowd with the usual pinball, pool table, and porn flicks; there's a back patio as well. Its popularity peaks on weekends after other clubs close, even though they stop serving liquor at some point during the night. Sunday's beer bust is fun and popular. ♦ Cover W-Sa. M-Th, Su, noon-2AM; F, Sa, 24 hours. 7746 Santa Monica Blvd (between N Spaulding and N Genesee Aves), West Hollywood. 213/656.9343 &

29 TomKat Theatre

♂ For those into adult movie houses, here's a seedy specimen that should do the trick. It screens the latest gay porn releases on its wide screen and is open practically around-the-clock. Don't be surprised to see some of the patrons "acting out." ♦ Admission. Daily, 10AM-2:30AM. 7734 Santa Monica Blvd (between N Spaulding and N Genesee Aves), West Hollywood. 323/650.9551 &

30 Yukon Mining Company

★$ More popular for its scene than for its greasy diner vittles, this gay landmark is packed with club kids and drag divas every weekend after the clubs let out and the Ecstasy wears off. The Gold Rush–themed dining room is dark, rustic, and especially easy on bloodshot eyes. There's also a side patio where smokers can light up. The rest of the week finds the all-night dining room frequented by locals who stop by for a quick omelet in the morning or fried chicken for dinner. ♦ Diner ♦ Daily, 24 hours. 7328 Santa Monica Blvd (between N Poinsettia Pl and N Fuller Ave), West Hollywood. 323/851.8833 &

31 Celebration Theatre

♂♀ A 64-seat venue catering to gay and lesbian theatergoers, this house specializes in comic productions on the order of *Naked Boys Singing*. High drama it isn't, but fun it is—and you can also catch more serious-minded dramaturgy here, too, such as the Lesbian Playwrights Festival. ♦ 7051B Santa Monica Blvd (between N Sycamore and N La Brea Aves). 213/957.1884, tickets 289.2999

32 Circus Disco

♂ Located in a rather seedy part of Hollywood and modeled after a big-top arena, this huge and usually straight dance club heads south on Tuesday and Friday nights, turning into a hot spot for gay Latinos and their admirers. A *calientito* mix of disco, hi-energy, hip-hop, and house keeps the *machos* and salsa queens grooving on four separate dance floors. ♦ Cover after 10PM. Tu, F, 9PM-2AM. 6655 Santa Monica Blvd (between Seward St and N Las Palmas Ave). 213/462.1291

33 Gold's Gym Hollywood

Sure, Fabio, Jodie Foster, and members of the group Kiss have been spotted working out at this huge two-level gym, but with all the bodybuilders, models, and aspiring actors of all sexual persuasions pumping iron here, you might not even notice the celebs. White walls and floor-to-ceiling windows make this an airy place to work on your abs, delts, pecs, and glutes among a buff and beautiful "A-list" crowd. ♦ M-F, 5AM-midnight; Sa, Su, 7AM-9PM. 1016 Cole Ave (between Romaine St and Santa Monica Blvd). 213/462.7012 &

34 The Zone

♂ Lots of hot-looking, seemingly unapproachable WeHomos end up at this private sex club at one time or another, especially from early Friday evening until the

---

Restaurants/Clubs: Red | Hotels: Purple | Shops: Orange | Outdoors/Parks: Green | Sights/Culture: Blue

THE BEST

Lisa Phillips

Police Officer/Liaison to the Gay and Lesbian Community for the Los Angeles Police Department

Drive through the hills of **Silverlake** and take in the wonderfully different architecture of the houses, many of which overlook the **Silver Lake Reservoir.** Lots of gay-owned homes, which is evident by the many rainbow flags hanging in the doorways. You will want to move here.

Go to the **"dog park"** (the animal!!) and mingle with the almost exclusively gay pet owners! Very, very fun and a great place to meet people and mix with the locals. The park is located right next to the Silver Lake Reservoir. Very pretty area!!!

small hours of Sunday night, when the joint is packed with shirtless jarheads, pretty boys, and average Joes cruising the dim maze of halls. There are tiny rooms with door locks and glory holes, a video room, and a back room with a sling in near-total darkness. The dress code (such as it is) is heavy on T-shirts, Levi's, or leather, and a loud industrial rock soundtrack makes conversation all but impossible—but so what? ♦ Cover. Daily, 8PM-dawn.1037 N Sycamore. 213/464. 8881 &

35 HOLLYWOOD MEMORIAL CEMETERY

A galaxy of top stars has found final refuge from its fans in this 65-acre oasis. Tinseltown biggies who were in the closet, out of it, or somewhere in between while aboveground include **Tyrone Power** and **Rudolph Valentino** (in wall crypt no. 1205); sadly, the lady in black who used to bring flowers on the anniversary of the latter's death comes no more. Also here are gravesites of the likes of **Douglas Fairbanks** (whose memorial is the most elaborate) and **Cecil B. DeMille** (who helped establish Paramount Studios, located just over the garden wall). ♦ Daily. 6000 Santa Monica Blvd (between N Van Ness Ave and N Gower St). 213/469.1181

36 RAMADA WEST HOLLYWOOD

$$ Designer Peter Shire's colorful metal flowers greet guests at this white-stucco Deco hotel right in the heart of WeHo. Its bright interior is also adorned with Warholesque portraits of Cher, Elvis, Janis Joplin, and other such famous mugs. The 135 rooms and 40 suites offer everything you'd expect from this worldwide chain; the back patio, though, is much more interesting, with lounge chairs, shaded tables, and a small, sparkling pool usually filled with studly sun worshipers.

There's also a large health club across the street, 24-hour room service, a **Starbuck's** (which has become the major gathering spot for the buff and beautiful), and a Mexican eatery called **Baja Buds** on the premises; for lesbians, the popular club **The Palms** (see page 263) is directly across the street. ♦ 8585 Santa Monica Blvd (between West Knoll and Westmount Drs), West Hollywood. 652.6400, 800/228.2828; fax 652.2135

Within the Ramada West Hollywood:

PIZZERIA UNO/CHICAGO BAR & GRILL

★★$ It ain't just pizza at this huge outlet of the national chain, but also pasta, chicken, steak, and full bar service; hotel guests can even be served poolside or in their rooms. The polished dark wood interior and laid-back ambience attract a goodly crowd heavy with gay thirtysomethings and families staying at the **Ramada.** A front patio overlooking Santa Monica Boulevard offers a distracting view straight into the gym across the street. ♦ Pizza ♦ Daily, breakfast, lunch, and dinner. 652.9263 &

36 RAYMOND DRAGON

♂ This small boutique, owned by the eponymous and couture-conscious former Colt model, sells form-fitting—and pricey—duds both casual and dressy. Mostly in Lycra, they bulge in all the right places on many a WeHo muscle man. A few of the nonsartorial goods are bulgy too, like the clony "Billy" doll. ♦ M-F, 11AM-8PM; Sa, 11AM-7PM; Su, noon-7PM. 8587 Santa Monica Blvd (between West Knoll and Westmount Drs), West Hollywood. 659.5044 &

36 SUMMERFIELD SUITES HOTEL

$$ Tucked away in a residential neighborhood, these 103 upscale gay- and lesbian-friendly suites make a quiet, wonderful getaway just steps from bustling Santa Monica Boulevard. Amenities include a workout room and a rooftop swimming pool and Jacuzzi, but there's no restaurant on the premises. ♦ 1000 Westmount Dr (at West Knoll Dr), West Hollywood. 657.7400, 800/253.7997; fax 854.6744

37 BENVENUTO

★★★$$ The perfect place to impress dates or cohorts, the former recording studio of Jim Morrison and the Doors is now a charming two-level trattoria with an upstairs lounge serving up a killer view of the Hollywood Hills. Dive into the wonderful traditional Italian concoctions, including individual gourmet pizzas, moist Roman-style gnocchi, and a *favoloso* tiramisù. The upstairs lounge with plush booths and light jazz is perfect for pre-

Visit a Los Angeles-Area Museum Today

2-FOR-1 ADMISSION

Museum of the American West
4700 Western Heritage Way
(323) 667-2000

ART+ MUSEUMS LOS ANGELES

MEMBER FOR A DAY

The Museum of Contemporary Art
250 South Grand Avenue
(213) 626-6222

ART+ MUSEUM LOS ANG

MEMBER FOR A DAY

The Museum of Television & Radio
465 North Beverly Hills Drive, Beverly Hills
(310) 786-1000

ART+ MUSEUM LOS AN

2-FOR-1 ADMISSION

Japanese American National Museum
369 East First Street
(213) 625-0414

ART+ MUSEUM LOS ANG

2-FOR-1 ADMISSION

Pacific Asia Museum
46 North Los Robles Avenue, Pasadena
(626) 449-2742

ART+ MUSEUMS LOS ANGE

MEMBER FOR A DAY

Museum of Latin American Art
628 Alamitos Avenue, Long Beach
(562) 437-1689

ART+ MUSEUMS LOS ANGEL

2-FOR-1 ADMISSION

Museum of Tolerance
9786 West Pico Boulevard at Roxbury Drive
(310) 553-8403

ART+ MUSEUMS LOS ANGEL

2-FOR-1 ADMISSION

Long Beach Museum of Art
2300 East Ocean Boulevard, Long Beach
(562) 439-2119

ART+ MUSEUMS LOS ANGEL

Visit a Los Angeles-Area Museum Today

MUSEUMS LOS ANGELES

| 2-FOR-1 ADMISSION | Good through Aug 31, 2005 | **Museum of the American West**
Tue-Sun 10-5, Thu 10-8
2-for-1 admission |

| MEMBER FOR A DAY | Good through Aug 31, 2005 | **The Museum of Contemporary Art**
Mon 11-5, Thu 11-8, Fri 11-5, Sat-Sun 11-6
Free general admission for one family and
10% discount at The MOCA Store.
Excludes admission to specially ticketed exhibits
and education events. Not valid with other offers. |

| MEMBER FOR A DAY | Good through Aug 31, 2005 | **The Museum of Television & Radio**
Wed-Sun 12-5 |

| 2-FOR-1 ADMISSION | Good through Aug 31, 2005 | **Japanese American National Museum**
Tue-Sun 10-5, Thu 10-8
2-for-1 admission |

| 2-FOR-1 ADMISSION | Good through Aug 31, 2005 | **Pacific Asia Museum**
Wed-Sun 10-5, Fri 10-8
2-for-1 admission |

| MEMBER FOR A DAY | Good through Aug 31, 2005 | **Museum of Latin American Art**
Tue-Fri 11:30-7, Sat 11-7, Sun 11-6
Free admission for two and 10% discount
at the museum store. |

| 2-FOR-1 ADMISSION | Good through Aug 31, 2005 | **Museum of Tolerance**
Mon-Thu 11:30-6:30, last entrance at 4,
Fri 11:30-5, last entrance at 3, Sun 11-7:30,
last entrance at 5.
2-for-1 admission |

| 2-FOR-1 ADMISSION | Good through Aug 31, 2005 | **Long Beach Museum of Art**
Tue-Sun 11-5, Thu 11-8
2-for-1 admission |

dinner drinks; post-dinner, the place turns into a popular rendezvous spot where LA's movers and shakers (Madonna, for one) linger over frothy cappuccinos and divine desserts. ♦ Italian ♦ Daily, lunch and dinner. 8512 Santa Monica Blvd (between N La Cienega Blvd and West Knoll Dr), West Hollywood. 659.8635 ♿

37 ALTA CIENEGA MOTEL

$ Once a popular stay for up-and-coming rock stars on the order of Jim Morrison, Deborah Harry, and the Pretenders' Chrissie Hynde, this unassuming motel offers 21 bargain rooms in the heart of WeHo. There is no restaurant, swimming pool, or other luxuries to speak of, but the basic rooms are clean and comfortable. Light sleepers take note: The loud traffic noise may bug you. ♦ No credit cards accepted. 1005 N La Cienega Blvd (at Santa Monica Blvd), West Hollywood. 652.5797 ♿

38 STONEWALL GOURMET COFFEE COMPANY

♂
♀ ★★$ Named in honor of the historic 1969 Stonewall uprising that jump-started the gay rights movement, West Hollywood's newest coffeehouse is located in the heart of WeHo, offering specialty coffees, teas, and gourmet desserts in a relatively quiet, well-lit atmosphere. Occasionally, live jazz bands perform on the front patio (which is also a great spot to people-watch and cruise passersby). ♦ Coffeehouse ♦ Daily, 6AM-midnight. 8717 Santa Monica Blvd (between Westbourne Dr and Hancock Ave), West Hollywood. 659.8009, 888.STONWAL ♿

39 24-HOUR FITNESS SPORT

♂
♀ Previously called the **Sports Connection** (and, by some, the "Sports Erection," considering the friskiness of the men's steam room, sauna, showers, and Jacuzzi), this health club recently underwent a head-to-toe shape-up, with all-new top-of-the-line equipment. Four floors offer two aerobics rooms, large areas for cardio and weight training, and a sundeck and lap pool outdoors. Despite attempts to attract more straight men and women and keep the wet-area shenanigans under control, the beat goes on. ♦ M-F, 6AM-11PM; Sa, Su, 8AM-8PM. 8612 Santa Monica Blvd (between West Knoll and Westbourne Drs), West Hollywood. 652.7440

39 THE PALMS

On weekends, long lines of the butch and the beautiful await entry to this way popular lesbian bar. Inside, it's a tad dark, but mirrors, a verdant wall mural, and *Baywatch*-quality barmaids help liven things up. When the DJ isn't spinning the latest dance tunes or a live band isn't doing its thing, a CD jukebox keeps the house hopping with rock and Top 40—the large dance floor and billiards tables are always in use. Wednesday dollar drink nights and Sunday beer blasts are major events. Men are admitted, but might get a stare or two. ♦ Cover. M-F, 1PM-2AM; Sa, Su, noon-2AM. 8572 Santa Monica Blvd (between West Knoll and Westbourne Drs), West Hollywood. 652.6188 ♿

39 THE ATHLETIC CLUB

♂ Two decades and several names later, this huge gym is still one of LA fagdom's most popular. You may find yourself next to a porn star or *Playgirl* model at the indoor or outdoor workout areas, by the pool or hot tub on the outside patio, or on the rooftop sundeck—not to mention in the very popular sauna and steam room. As pretty as the crowd is, though, the attitude level is low. Meet the locals while downing a power drink at the small café beside the main workout area. ♦ M-F, 5:30AM-11PM; Sa, Su, 7AM-9PM. 8560 Santa Monica Blvd (between West Knoll and Westbourne Drs), West Hollywood. 659.6630

40 TANGO GRILL

★★$ If you could take your eyes off the foxy gym bunnies that frequent this Argentine-style bistro, you might notice that the service is quick and friendly and the no-nonsense skinless chicken and steak dishes reasonably priced. A high ceiling, a brick and blond-wood interior, and pop and dance tunes give this hip eatery a festive, airy atmosphere; it's the perfect place to bring a date. Smokers can enjoy their dinner on the sidewalk patio, which is most advantageous for people-watching. Inside or out, the place is always packed, but the wait for a table is rarely longer than 15 minutes. Reservations recommended. ♦ Argentine ♦ Daily, lunch and dinner. 8807 Santa Monica Blvd (between Palm Ave and Larrabee St), West Hollywood. 659.3663 ♿

41 SAN VICENTE INN/RESORT

♂ $ Within stumbling distance of the hottest nightlife, Rocky Farren and Terry Snyman run one of LA's best-kept secrets: WeHo's only gay guest house. Arranged around a sparkling pool and Jacuzzi, 30 spacious, immaculate rooms and three garden cottages offer cable TV with VCR and private phone with answering machine; half have private baths. The pastel yellow and white exterior recalls Miami's South Beach, and the cruisy crowd sunbathing in the altogether might make you think you've found your way to heaven. There's also an in-house library, but no restaurant on the premises. ♦

Restaurants/Clubs: Red | Hotels: Purple | Shops: Orange | Outdoors/Parks: Green | Sights/Culture: Blue

THE BEST

Dennis Hensley

Jounalist/Author, *Misadventures in the (213)*

Will Geer Theatricum Botanicum—It feels like you're totally away from LA, under the stars in the pitch-black. There's a sense of the place being family-owned and -operated. You can just show up, it's not a fussy credit card-type experience, and at $10 to $15, tickets for plays are really reasonable.

Groove Thing—I take dance classes at the **Dance Center** in North Hollywood (a throwback to my old days as a dancer on a cruise ship). A great way to get out of bed and start your weekend shakin' your groove.

All Star Theater Café at the Knickerbocker Hotel—A speakeasy-type place with tons of history. Open really late and supposedly haunted by Rudolph Valentino. If the ghosts don't show, the owner, Max, has lots of stories about models.

Battle for the Tiara at the Wilshire Ebell Theatre—An AIDS benefit that's a beauty pageant in drag. That says it all, don't you think?

Oil Can Harry's—Whether you're shit-kicking with the cowboys on Friday night or shaking your groove thang on retro disco Saturday, it's a good time with a fun, friendly crowd.

Outfest—Great gay films and tons of lobby crush material . . .

845 N San Vicente Blvd (between Santa Monica Blvd and Cynthia St), West Hollywood. 854.6915; fax 289.5929 &

42 DON'T PANIC!

♂
♀ Take your pick of sassy T-shirts and sweats (how about "Sometimes You Feel Like a Slut, Sometimes You Don't"?) at the flagship location of a three-branch nationwide mini-chain that started out in a tiny WeHo apartment. Other offerings include rainbow flags and stickers, disco and dance music CDs, and *Absolutely Fabulous* mugs and shirts. ♦ M-Th, Su, 10AM-11PM; F, Sa, 10AM-midnight. 802 N San Vicente Blvd (at Santa Monica Blvd), West Hollywood. 652.9689

42 MICKEY'S

♂ Similar in style to the Valley's **Apache Territory**, this roomy video/dance bar appeases its youthful crowd with pinball, sugary-sweet dance tunes, sweaty go-go boys, and studly (usually shirtless) barkeeps. A side lounge provides an overview of the crowd, and the sidewalk patio is good for cruising fellow bar patrons and passersby alike. It tends to attract the same "new clone"/twinkie crowd as the nearby **Rage** of the WeHo clubs it's also the most popular with Hispanics, Asians, and blacks. Check local gay papers for theme parties and 18-and-over nights. The **Sidewalk** patio has become a haven for smokers. ♦ Daily, noon-2AM. 8857 Santa Monica Blvd (between Larrabee St and N San Vicente Blvd), West Hollywood. 657.1176 &

42 A DIFFERENT LIGHT

♂
♀ Everyone has a grand old time browsing through aisles and aisles of gay and lesbian books, magazines, and CDs at this bookshop. There's also a jolly miscellany of items ranging from calendars and magnets to address books. The cruisy back of the store, meanwhile, is more suited to connoisseurs of "adult-oriented" periodicals. Check the signs in the window for open readings, book signings, and concerts, and don't forget to pick up a free copy of the local gay and lesbian magazines on your way out. ♦ Daily, 10AM-midnight. 8853 Santa Monica Blvd (between Larrabee St and N San Vicente Blvd), West Hollywood. 854.6601, 800/343.4002

42 REVOLVER

♂ A WeHo staple since 1981, this laid-back two-room video bar is all about campy film clips and the latest dance-pop videos on screens big and small. The music is always fun, but unfortunately there's no dance floor. There are, however, fun theme nights dedicated to show tunes, comedy, and sports. It's cruisier in front, while the back bar offers a spot to sit and relax amid colorful Pop art on the faux-finished walls. Be forewarned: Given the crowd, the scent of the latest trendy cologne is always in the air. ♦ Cover, F-Sa after 9:30PM, holidays, and special events. M-F, 4PM-2AM; Sa, Su, 2PM-2AM. 8851 Santa Monica Blvd (at Larrabee St), West Hollywood. 550.8851 &

43 RAGE

♂ This still-trendy video/dance bar's famous blue neon logo lit up Santa Monica Boulevard through the '80s, packing a hot mix of locals and tourists—mostly of the tanned-and-toned twinkie variety—into a drab black-lit interior virtually every night. Now, with its reported $2 million renovation, it's more packed than ever. The large dance floor literally throbs; an overhead lounge offers seating and an observation deck, but here, too, conversation usually loses out to blaring amps. Pinup-quality studs in tank tops always man the huge bars, and Monday "Alternative Music Nights" draw a rugged early-twenties to mid-thirties grunge crowd. There's also a weekly talent show and occasional drag events. ♦ Cover. Daily,

LA's Lesbigay Music Scene

The closets of the mainstream music scene are, like other sectors of the entertainment industry, plenty crowded. There are, however, more and more music makers coming out every year. Consider "homocore," the latest trend, hot on the heels of Seattle grunge. Best described as brash hard rock with an out-and-proud gay and lesbian edge, homocore is thriving in tiny queer and queer-friendly clubs throughout LA, especially in **Silverlake.** Locally, its most visible pioneers are Glue, led by drag diva Sean D'Lear, and Extra Fancy, started and fronted by sole gay member Brian Grillo, whose songs address everything from outing to his role as an HIV-positive activist. Extra Fancy's "Sinnerman" was the first explicit homoerotic music video ever to play on MTV, and the band has been splashed across the pages of The *Advocate* and *Out* and has also been featured in the likes of *Rolling Stone* and *Details*.

With a style of music similar to that of Extra Fancy, Slojack has amassed a cult following of alterna-queers who identify with the band's socio-political musings on the AIDS crisis and the gay rights movement. Meanwhile, smoking sets by lesbian quartet Girl Jesus always includes their signature rocker, "No Way Out," which expresses the pain of oppression. The Johnny Depp Clones, a seven-member glam rock band, features porn star Chris Green on vocals and guitar, with drag divas/adult film directors Chi Chi LaRue and Karen Dior (aka Geoff Gann) on backing vocals.

Not everything is frantic, though: For music fans who like their sound mellow, there's folk rocker Melissa Ferrick and pop rock band Sally & Michelle (featuring lovers Sally Mangione and Michelle Landers). Unthinkable a few years ago, the current queer music scene in LA has something for just about every taste.

2PM-2AM. 8911 Santa Monica Blvd (between N San Vicente Blvd and Hilldale Ave), West Hollywood. 652.7055 &

44 Cafe d'Etoile

★★$ Soft lighting, mellow music, and cozy booths make for an intimate, casual setting popular with a sophisticated thirty- to forty-something public that appreciates the solid, well-executed pasta, chicken, and seafood. The bar stretching along one wall is nearly always packed, and Sunday brunch is a big draw. ♦ American/International ♦ M-Sa, lunch and dinner; Su, brunch and dinner. 8941½ Santa Monica Blvd (between Hilldale Ave and N Robertson Blvd), West Hollywood. 278.1011 &

45 The Abbey

★$ By far WeHo's hottest alternative to the club scene, this huge coffeehouse is also casual and cruisy. Most of the movement takes place on the outdoor patio, where java junkies gather for conversation or to take in a game of chess or backgammon over great coffee and desserts (including killer lemon squares) amid plants and cement sculptures. Light fare, including salads and sandwiches (try the chicken on focaccia) and a full bar are also available. The back is relatively quiet, housing billiards, Internet terminals, and two couches. When a folksinger isn't warbling, the music ranges from peppy pop and alterna tunes to ambient grooves. ♦ Coffeehouse ♦ M-Th, 7AM-2AM; F, Sa, 7AM-3AM; Su, 8AM-2AM. 692 N Robertson

Blvd (between Melrose Ave and Santa Monica Blvd), West Hollywood. 289.8410 &

45 The Firehouse

♂ ♀ With flaming torches at the entrance and both the inside and out painted fire-engine red, it's hard to miss one of WeHo's trendiest clubs, red-hot since opening in late 1996. The exposed brick dance floor is one of the area's biggest, and there are front and back patios for further mingling. Wednesday nights are dedicated to women, but everyone is welcome; ditto for the popular tea dance on Sundays. The house specialty, appropriately called "The Fireball" (Absolut Citron with fruit juices and Chambord), is about as hot as this club's humpy crowd. ♦ Cover. M-F, 5PM-2AM; Sa, Su, 3PM-2AM. 696 N Robertson Blvd (between Melrose Ave and Santa Monica Blvd), West Hollywood. 289.1353 &

45 Mother Lode

♂ This popular imbibing den with its rustic wood interior may sit right in the heart of WeHo on Santa Monica Boulevard, but it has a friendly, neighborhoody feel. Dance, pop, and alt-rock tunes cater to the jeans and T-shirt crowd in its two bars, packed to the rafters on weekends and especially during Sunday afternoon beer busts, when it's too jammed to take advantage of the arcade games or pool table (not that you'll care, with everything else there is to do . . .). ♦ Daily, noon-2AM. 8944 Santa Monica Blvd (between N San Vicente and N Robertson Blvds), West Hollywood. 659.9700 &

Restaurants/Clubs: Red | Hotels: Purple | Shops: Orange | Outdoors/Parks: Green | Sights/Culture: Blue

45 DRAKE'S

♂ Brightly lit, cheery, and friendly, this adult novelty shop takes the awkwardness out of shopping for the latest gay and bi erotic videos, lube, or condoms. The store also sells T-shirts sporting gay-positive slogans, posters, postcards, magnets, stickers, and nifty doohickeys, so it's worth the trip just for a browse. ♦ Daily, 10AM-2:30AM. 8932 Santa Monica Blvd (between N San Vicente and N Robertson Blvds), West Hollywood. 289.8932. Also at 7566 Melrose Ave (between N Sierra Bonita and N Curson Aves). 213/651.5600 ♿

46 BOSSA NOVA

★★$ Just across the street from the **Abbey** (page 265), this hip eatery's jam-packed covered patio gives some refuge from the hustle and bustle of "the scene," allowing you to watch the boys go by at a peaceful distance. Its vivid canary-yellow interior mixes well with the colorful crowd and spicy fare, which combines sandwiches, pastas, and grilled meats with Brazilian touches like croquetes de camarão (shrimp and cheese, breaded and deep-fried). Don't be surprised to find yourself sitting next to your favorite porn star or even one of the Red Hot Chili Peppers. ♦ Brazilian/International ♦ Daily, lunch and dinner. 685 N Robertson Blvd (between Melrose Ave and Santa Monica Blvd), West Hollywood. 657.5070 ♿

47 INTERNATIONAL MALE/ IM SPORT

♂ What gay man hasn't leafed through IM's titillating mail-order catalogs, more for the beefcake than the outfits? This airy, split-level WeHo shop sells all the duds in those pages, from sexy bikinis and snug T-shirts to dressier fare and funky accessories (such as designer belts, bracelets, and watches). These clothes look fabulous on gym queens and hipsters alike, but no matter what your waistline, the cruising—er, browsing—is great here. ♦ M-Sa, 10AM-9PM; Su, 11AM-8PM. 8465 Holloway Drive (at Santa Monica Blvd), West Hollywood. 275.0285 ♿

48 AXIS/LOVE LOUNGE

♂
♀ Same ownership, but separate clubs with separate entrances, these nightspots attract a young, pretty crowd. **Axis** is in the front, with a pool table in the front bar, followed by a huge dance floor, beyond which is a small bar. All three spaces are slick and painted black, with plenty of video monitors all around. At the plush **Love Lounge** at the rear of the building is a rococo bar with red velvet curtains and a small stage usually staffed by go-go boys. Here patrons groove to pop and club music on the huge main dance floor, where most of the action takes place: three stages with muscular dancers, large video monitors, and plenty of cruising space. Theme events, often celebrating the release of gay-oriented films or albums (Madonna once put in a surprise appearance at one of these), are held nightly in both clubs. The popular lez party **Hot Box** (394.6451) takes over Axis on Friday and Love Lounge on Saturday. The hotly attended homo party **Cherry** takes over Love Lounge on Friday nights. ♦ Separate cover for each. Tu-Su, 9PM-2AM. Axis: 652 N La Peer Dr (between Melrose Ave and Santa Monica Blvd). Love Lounge: 657 N Robertson Blvd, West Hollywood. 659.0472

48 COBALT CANTINA

♂ ★★★$$ Sister restaurant to the **Cobalt** in Silverlake, this Spanish adobe–style restaurant is fast becoming the see-and-be-seen locale for WeHo's hip and well-heeled. The atmosphere provides everything from muscleboys to fashion queens to dads-'n'-sons, and the menu is equally diverse. A combination of Tex-Mex, Italian, and down-home entrées, all with a decidedly Spanish flair, are served in ample portions. Prices are reasonable for this part of town and many nights feature specials (second Margarita for 25 cents on Tuesdays). The **Blue Bar** in the back is an art-filled and boy-packed place to wait for your table and sip on one of the notorious Blue Margaritas—as tasty as the view. ♦ Tex-Mex ♦ M-Th, Su, lunch and dinner to 11PM; Sa, Su, lunch and dinner to midnight. 616 N Robertson Blvd (at Melrose Ave). 659.8691. Also at 4326 Sunset Blvd (at Fountain). 323/953.9991 ♿

49 LE PARC

$$$ Gay- and lesbian-friendly and popular with the celebrity elite (including popster George Michael), this exquisite 154-suite hotel is nestled in a quiet WeHo neighborhood just steps from the many homo hot spots lining Santa Monica Boulevard. Pampered guests enjoy a pool, on-site gym, rooftop tennis courts, and the **Cafe Le Parc**, serving fine cuisine française. ♦ 733 West Knoll Dr (between Melrose Ave and Sherwood Dr), West Hollywood. 855.8888, 800/424.4443; fax 659.7812

50 FRED SEGAL

A favorite of hip "industry" types (like queer REM front man Michael Stipe, supermodel Rachel Hunter, and crooner Rod Stewart), this block-wide gay-popular complex of stores hawks everything from pricy designer duds by Prada, Gucci, and Armani to funky, relatively inexpensive T-shirts, accessories, and gadgets in a fun, youthful atmosphere. Bargains can be found, and the late-September sale fills every parking spot for six blocks around. The

GONE TO LAGUNA

When gay and lesbian Angelenos want a break, many opt for a getaway to the beautiful resort and arts community of **Laguna Beach,** a 60-mile cruise south on the scenic Pacific Coast Highway. In the tradition of other arts colonies turned gay, the arrival here in 1903 of painter Norman St. Claire started this hamlet of rocky cliffs and eucalyptus trees on the road to becoming a vibrant, upscale town of 25,000, a haven for artsy types, Hollywood celebs, and a large but fairly discreet homo population of both sexes. Yes, it's in Bob Dornan/John Birch Society territory, but there are enough progressive types around that Laguna Beach actually had a gay mayor, Bob Gentry, as far back as the early 1980s.

Laguna's hottest spot—and a favorite with the WeHo set—is the **Boom Boom Room,** a four-bar nightclub inside the **Coast Inn** ($; 1401 S Pacific Coast Hwy, at Mountain Rd; 949/494.7588, 800/653.2697; fax 949/494.1735). For more than three decades, this beachside complex has also been feeding the boys in its **Coast Inn Cafe** (★★$) and putting them up in 24 rooms with sundecks, fireplaces, a heated pool, and ocean views. (By the way, if taking a moonlit stroll along the beach below the inn, keep your wits about you: Gay bashings are a rare but occasional problem here.) Up the road a ways, the gay-and-lesbian-welcoming **Casa Laguna Inn** ($$; 2510 S Pacific Coast Hwy, between Solana Way and Upland Rd; 949/494.2996, 800/233.0449; fax 949/494.5009) offers 21 charming rooms, plus a pool, lovely grounds, and great views.

About halfway between Laguna Beach and WeHo, the **Ozz Supper Club** (★★★$; 6231 Manchester Blvd, at Western Ave, Buena Park; 714/522.1542), popular with a youngish gay male crowd (and with some lesbians and straights), serves hearty steak, seafood, and pasta dishes, while the adjacent unnamed nightclub is a good place to dance, cruise, and play. The more mellow set will want to hit **Main Street** (1460 S Pacific Coast Hwy,

between Calliope St and Mountain Rd; 714/494.0056), a very nice piano bar with nightly entertainment.

Other restaurant options include the homo-friendly **Royal Thai** (★★★$$; 1750 S Pacific Coast Hwy, at Pearl St; 714/494.8424), with delicious spicy fare. Hungry literature buffs could check out the excellent Mexi-Cal cuisine at **Tortilla Flats** (★★$; 1740 S Pacific Coast Hwy, between Pearl and Agate Sts; 714/494.6588), though its connection with the novel of that name is tenuous (Steinbeck was living in Laguna Beach when he wrote it). For something sweet, head over to Laguna's gay-owned and homo-popular coffeehouse **Cafe Zinc** (★$; 350 Ocean Ave, between Beach St and Forest Ave; 949/494.6302).

Shopping here is fun, too, with many galleries and boutiques, including **Gaymart** (168 Mountain Rd, at S Pacific Coast Hwy; 949/497.9108); **Jewelry by Poncé** (1417 S Pacific Coast Hwy, between Calliope St and Mountain Rd; 800/969.7464), specializing in commitment rings; and the local lesbigay bookstore **Different Drummer Books** (1294 S Pacific Coast Hwy, at Cress St; 949/497.6699). The main attraction, however, is naturally the **beach.** There's a gay section below the **Coast Inn,** but the queerest male stretch of sand in town is farther south, at **West Street Beach.**

Gay and lesbian Laguna Beach is covered by the biweekly *Orange County Blade,* available free at homo-popular venues. More information is available from the **Laguna Beach Chamber of Commerce** (357 Glenneyre Ave, Laguna Beach, CA 92652; 949/494.1018) or the **Gay and Lesbian Community Center of Orange County** (12832 Garden Grove Blvd, Suite A, Laguna Beach, CA 92843, 949/534.0961, 949/534.3261; www.centeroc.org). For accommodations information, contact **California Riviera 800** (714/376.0305, 800/621.0500).

patio and coffee shop offer copacetic settings for watching celebs while sipping frosty mochaccinos. ♦ M-Sa; Su, noon-6PM. 8100 Melrose Ave (at N Crescent Heights Blvd). 213/651.4129 &

51 CONDOMANIA

It's latex-o-rama: colored condoms, lollipop condoms, scented condoms, glow-in-the-dark condoms, kitty condoms (don't ask), and every other variety you could possibly imagine. Inventive safe sex is the message, and browsing through this funky outlet is almost as much fun as the main event. ♦ Daily; F, Sa until 10PM. 7306 Melrose Ave (at N Poinsettia Pl). 323/933.7865 &

52 PROBE

♂ This huge warehouselike space in Hollywood, a gay fixture since 1978, caters heavily to the "A-list" and circuit-party crowd. On Saturday it's boys, boys, and more boys, from well-known porn stars lounging at the bar to chiseled, sweaty, shirtless sides of beef jamming the dance floor to the hi-energy beat. Such infamous once-a-month bashes as the **Underwear Party** and the **Black Ball** last practically the entire weekend; the cover for such events can get steep, but many say it's often worth it. ♦ Cover. Sa, 10PM to early Su afternoon. 836 N Highland Ave (between Waring and Willoughby Aves). 323/461.8301 &

Restaurants/Clubs: Red | Hotels: Purple | Shops: Orange | Outdoors/Parks: Green | Sights/Culture: Blue

DESERT AREAS

Macho Macho Man . . .

The Southern California Desert, or "high desert," attracts the macho crowd who ride their dirt bikes and dune buggies or dive into daredevil hijinks on the tall sand mounds of **Lancaster** at the mouth of **Antelope Valley.** Other adventurers go for the bungee jumping and hot-air ballooning offered in **Perris Valley** near **Riverside.** Many visitors simply wander through the many natural splendors of the unusually varied terrain. **Palm Springs,** a popular weekend getaway destination sometimes referred to as the city of "the newlywed and the nearly dead," flourishes during spring break with crowds of sun-worshiping collegians, and year round as a haven for golfers, tennis players, and senior citizens who want a warm, dry climate.

Around the mid-1990s the gay community began flocking to the Springs, buying up teardowns and lavishly remodeling them into weekend and winter getaways. Vacationing gays who don't own property can take advantage of the more than 30 gay-friendly inns in areas such as Warm Sands, San Lorenzo Road, and along Palm Canyon Drive. An additional three are for lesbians. The hub of the gay social scene, known as the **Castro district,** houses a variety of bars, coffeehouses, shops, and a live theater. The Palm Springs Visitors Association offers a dedicated toll-free number to assist members of the gay community (888/866.2744) as well as a *Gay Visitor's Guide* available by calling 800/347.7746 or online at www.palm-springs.org/08.

If you're into golf, you've got more than 100 impeccably landscaped courses to choose from throughout the lower desert. Seekers of spiritual self-discovery or splendid isolation, however, can feel free—or lost—among the prickly yuccas of **Joshua Tree National Monument,** a natural wonder less than three hours from LA.

ANTELOPE VALLEY

This arid region north of LA County is no longer the peaceful place it once was. A major building boom dotted the once sparsely populated and undeveloped area with lots of new homes, and urban blight followed, bringing with it drugs, crimes, and gangs. The air is still smog-free, but it just isn't the great escape it once was.

1 EDWARDS AIR FORCE BASE

See the space shuttle land on the dry surface of Rogers Lake. There's also the **Air Force Flight Center Museum** where you can see exhibits on aircraft hardware, rocket engines, ancient lake-bed formations, early homesteading, the very first military uses of Edwards, and the story of Glen Edwards. Daily tours of Edwards Air Force Base are offered except on federal holidays and during shuttle operation. ♦ Free. You must call ahead for sponsorship (661/277.8050). There is also an open-house and air show held each October. Rosamond Blvd (east of Sierra Hwy). 661/277.3510. www.edwards.af.mil/index-static.html

2 WILLOW SPRINGS INTERNATIONAL RACEWAY

This "fastest road in the west" is one of the best tracks in the country for watching top car and motorcycle racing year-round, with weekend races that last all day. Light refreshments are available. There's also a new **Racer School** that is open from 7AM to 5PM when there are WSMC weekend events. ♦ Admission. Call ahead for hours. Rosamond Blvd (between 60th St W and 90th St W). 661/256.1234; fax 661/256.1583; email: racewillow@aol.com. www.race-wsmc.com

3 ANTELOPE VALLEY CALIFORNIA POPPY RESERVE

Two thousand acres have been set aside for the preservation of the golden poppy, the California state flower. During springtime, the reserve is carpeted with a solid covering of flowers. ♦ Daily, Mar-May. Lancaster Rd (between 120th St W and 160th St W)

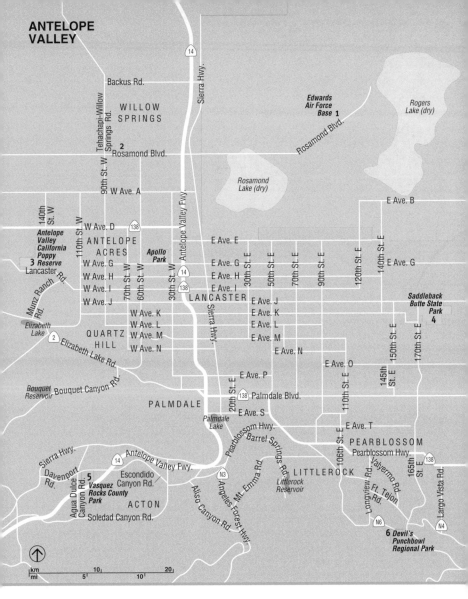

ANTELOPE VALLEY

Backus Rd.

WILLOW
SPRINGS

Tehachapi-Willow Springs Rd.

90th St. W.

2
Rosamond Blvd.

W Ave. A

14
Sierra Hwy.

Edwards
Air Force
Base **1**

Rosamond Blvd.

Rogers
Lake (dry)

Rosamond
Lake (dry)

E Ave. B

140th St. W.
110th St. W.

W Ave. D

138

E Ave. E

**Antelope
Valley
California
Poppy
3 Reserve**
Lancaster

ANTELOPE
ACRES

Munz Ranch Rd.

70th St. W.
60th St. W.
30th St. W.

**Apollo
Park**

Antelope Valley Fwy.

W Ave. G
W Ave. H
W Ave. I
W Ave. J

14
138

E Ave. G
E Ave. H
E Ave. I

LANCASTER

E Ave. J

30th St. E
50th St. E
70th St. E
90th St. E

120th St. E
140th St. E

E Ave. G

**Saddleback
Butte State
Park
4**

Elizabeth
Lake

2

QUARTZ
HILL

Elizabeth Lake Rd.

W Ave. K
W Ave. L
W Ave. M
W Ave. N

Sierra Hwy.

E Ave. K
E Ave. L
E Ave. M

E Ave. N

E Ave. O

150th St. E
170th St. E

110th St. E
145th St. E

**Bouquet
Reservoir** Bouquet Canyon Rd.

PALMDALE

20th St. E

E Ave. P

138 Palmdale Blvd.

E Ave. S

Palmdale
Lake

Pearblossom Hwy.
Barrel Springs Rd.

E Ave. T

105th St. E

PEARBLOSSOM
Pearblossom Hwy.

165th St. E

138

Sierra Hwy.

Davenport
Rd.

14

Antelope Valley Fwy.

Agua Dulce Canyon Rd.

**5
Vasquez
Rocks County
Park**

Escondido
Canyon Rd.

N3

ACTON

Soledad Canyon Rd.

Aliso Canyon Rd.

Angeles Forest Hwy.

Mt. Emma Rd.

LITTLEROCK

Littlerock
Reservoir

Valyermo Rd.

Longview Rd.
Ft. Tejon Rd.

N6

Largo Vista Rd.

N4

**6 Devil's
Punchbowl
Regional Park**

km   10   20
mi   5   10

---

4 SADDLEBACK BUTTE STATE PARK

🅟 Native chaparral can be seen on a sandstone bluff here. There is also a magnificent stand of Joshua trees, bizarrely shaped plants that are, improbably, members of the lily family. ♦ Admission. Daily, 24 hours. 170th St E and E Ave J. 661/942.0662

5 VASQUEZ ROCKS COUNTY PARK

🅟 The surrealistic tumble of lacy sandstone rocks, some several hundred feet high, is great for climbing. The area is named for Tiburcio Vasquez, a 19th-century bandit who used it as one of his numerous hideouts. ♦ Escondido Canyon Rd (between Antelope Valley Fwy and Agua Dulce Canyon Rd)

6 DEVIL'S PUNCHBOWL REGIONAL PARK

🅟 Located in the high desert area near Pearblossom, the rocky landscape of this 1,310-acre county park is rich in native plants and includes a number of hiking trails. The park also has a lovely stream (the size of which varies greatly with the season) ringed with willows and other water-loving plants. The **Punchbowl** is a natural depression in a slope of tumbled boulders. ♦ 2800 Devil's Punchbowl Rd (southeast of Tumbleweed Rd). 661/944.2743

Restaurants/Clubs: Red | Hotels: Purple | Shops: Orange | Outdoors/Parks: Green | Sights/Culture: Blue

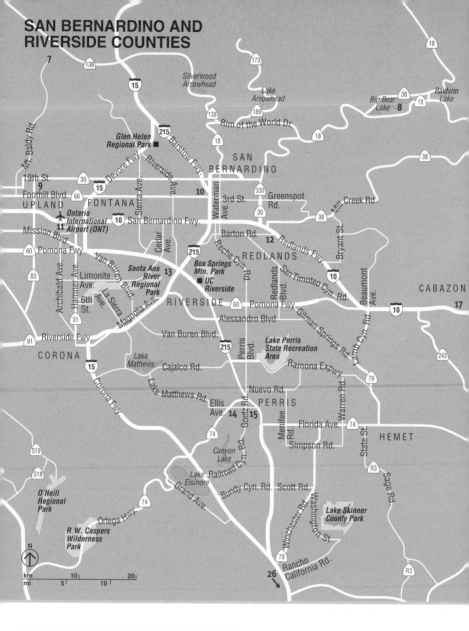

SAN BERNARDINO AND RIVERSIDE COUNTIES

Silverwood
Arrowhead

Lake
Arrowhead

Big Bear
Lake 8

Baldwin
Lake

Glen Helen
Regional Park

Rim of the World Dr.

SAN
BERNARDINO

CABAZON

19th St.

Foothill Blvd.

UPLAND   FONTANA

Ontario
International
Airport (ONT)

Mission Blvd.

Pomona Fwy.

Santa Ana
River
Regional
Park

Box Springs
Mtn. Park

UC
Riverside

REDLANDS

3rd St.

Greenspot
Rd.

Barton Rd.

Mill Creek Rd.

San Bernardino Fwy.

Limonite
Ave.

6th
St.

Riverside Fwy.

CORONA

Lake
Mathews

Cajalco Rd.

Lake Matthews Rd.

RIVERSIDE

Pomona Fwy.

Alessandro Blvd.

Van Buren Blvd.

Lake Perris
State Recreation
Area

Ramona Expwy.

Ellis
Ave. 14   15

PERRIS

Nuevo Rd.

Florida Ave.

Simpson Rd.

HEMET

Canyon
Lake

Lake
Elsinore

Railroad Cyn. Rd.

Bundy Cyn. Rd.   Scott Rd.

Lake Skinner
County Park

O'Neill
Regional
Park

Ortega Hwy.

R. W. Caspers
Wilderness
Park

N

km   10   20
mi   5   10

Rancho
California Rd.

26

Just an hour from desert, beach, or mountains, San Bernardino is ideally located for beaching, biking, hiking, or just soaking in the view of often snowcapped mountains. While its relatively affordable land has attracted some of the ugliest developments in the state—and while it does often have the worst smog in the country—there are a number of things well worth seeing and doing here.

7 MOUNT BALDY

Ski this mountain in winter or hike it in summer. By lift or on foot, it's more than 10,000 feet to the top and worth it for the view. ♦ Mt. Baldy Rd (north of Mountain Ave). 909/982.2829, 818/335.1251

8 BIG BEAR LAKE

At 9,000 feet and surrounded by forests, this lake has a tranquillity sadly lacking in Lake Arrowhead to the west. You can stay at **Gold Mountain Manor** (909/585.6997; www/bigbear.com/goldmtn), a historic 1938 log mansion where Clark Gable and Carole Lombard honeymooned, replete with wood-burning fireplaces and antiques; at the

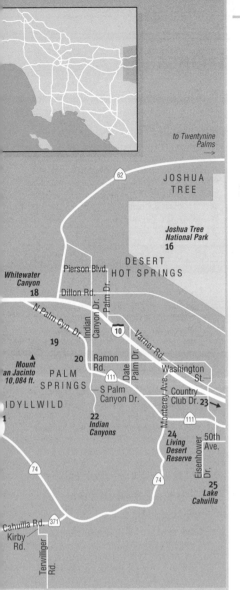

9 SYCAMORE INN

★$$ Built on the site of a historic stagecoach stop, this restaurant continues an old tradition of warm hospitality and service. Prime rib steaks, chops, and 20 wines by the glass plus a huge stone fireplace and wing-back chairs warm the atmosphere. ♦ American ♦ M-F, lunch and dinner; Sa, Su, dinner. 8318 Foothill Blvd (between Carnelian St and Red Hill Country Club Dr), Rancho Cucamonga. 909/982.1104

10 SAN BERNARDINO

There's a **City Hall** (300 N D St) designed by **Cesar Pelli,** and to the west on the old Route 66, a marvelous folly: the **Wigwam Village Highway Hotel** (2728 W Foothill Blvd; 909/875.0241). www.sanbernardino.org

Within San Bernardino:

BOBBY RAY'S TEXAS BBQ

★$ Ribs, chicken, and links are slowly cooked in a smoky oven and served with a zesty sauce. ♦ American ♦ W-Sa, lunch and dinner. 1657 W Baseline St (at Medical Center Dr). 909/885.9177

11 ONTARIO INTERNATIONAL AIRPORT

This features lots of glass, bright surfaces, and $1.6 million art exhibits. It is also a very attractive alternative to LAX, offering 12 major passenger carriers. Designed by the architectural firm of **Daniel, Mann, Johnson & Mendenhall**, the passenger-friendly twin terminals offer a choice of 14 restaurants and 21 retail shops. The airport is about 35 miles east of LA and 20 miles west of San Bernardino, northwest of Riverside, between the Pomona and San Bernardino Freeways. Long-term and short-term parking are available, as is parking in several privately operated lots outside the airport. Public transportation to the surrounding areas is limited, although local hotels operate free shuttles to and from the airport. Information kiosks on local hotel pickups, car rentals, and shuttle services, including **Inland Express** (909/626.6599) and **SuperShuttle** (800/258.3826, 714/517.6600), can be found in the baggage-claim areas. ♦ Archibald Avenue, just off exit I-10 of the San Bernardino Fwy, Ontario. 909/937.2700. www.lawa.org

12 REDLANDS

An architectural gem created during the early citrus-farming period, this city is notable for the Tuscan-style loggia of the **Santa Fe Railroad Station** (Orange St, between

historic **Knickerbocker Mansion** (909/866.8221; www.knickerbockermansion.com), a restored 1920 log mansion and carriage house; or at any of a number of unique mountain hideaways. There are great places to eat, like **Le Bistro** for hearty French fare (909/866.6666), **Mozart's Bistro** (909/866.9497) for good international cuisine, and **Cowboy Express Steak House** (909/866.1486) for big, juicy cuts of beef cooked just right. ♦ Rtes 18 and 38. Information 800-4-Big-Bear; fax 909/866.5671; email: bblra@bigbearinfo.com. www.bigbearinfo.com

Restaurants/Clubs: Red | Hotels: Purple | Shops: Orange | Outdoors/Parks: Green | Sights/Culture: Blue

PLACE YOUR BETS ON THE SPRINGS

Much to the consternation of many, gambling came to Palm Springs in the late 1990s. Although full-scale gaming is prohibited in California, a federal law and a Supreme Court ruling allow Native American tribes to offer on their reservations any type of gaming. While high-stakes Las Vegas–like action is still pending approval, inveterate gamblers can now try their luck at a number of casinos that operate 24 hours a day year-round. In addition to the usual card games, the following casinos offer video blackjack and poker, bingo, and off-track betting: **Spa Casino** (inside the historic Spa Resort Casino in downtown Palm Springs; 800/258.2WIN) is operated by the Agua Caliente band of Cahuilla Indians; **Fantasy Springs Casino** (located north of Interstate 10 near Indio; 800/827.2WIN) is operated by the Cabazon band of Mission Indians and includes a Las Vegas–style show; **Casino Morongo** (west of Palm Springs off Interstate 10; 800/252.4499) is run by the Morongo band of Mission Indians; **Spotlight 29 Casino** (located on Interstate 10 east of Fantasy Springs; 619/775.5566) is owned by the Twenty-Nine Palms band of Mission Indians.

Redlands Blvd and Redlands Fwy); the picturebook 1890 **Morey Mansion** (190 Terracina Blvd, 909/793.7970), a bed-and-breakfast inn that may be toured on Sundays; and the grand Victorian mansions along **Olive Street.**

Within Redlands:

KIMBERLY CREST HOUSE AND GARDENS

The flamboyant 1897 château features Tiffany glass, formal gardens, lily ponds, and citrus groves recalling the city's heyday. ♦ Admission. Tours: Th-Su, 1-4PM every half hour. 1325 Prospect Dr (off Highland Ave, between Cajon St and Ramona Dr). 909/792.2111

13 MISSION INN

$$$ The centerpiece of Riverside's historic downtown, this 232-room (including 32 suites) architectural treasure began life in 1876 as a 13-room adobe house, and was opened as a hotel by town father Frank Miller in 1902. The design incorporates an eclectic ensemble of Mission Revival, Victorian, and Beaux Arts architectural styles inspired by Miller, who had a penchant for travel and collecting. Over the years the hotel has hosted a celebrated guest registry, from aviation pioneers Amelia Earhart and Charles Lindbergh to industry barons Andrew Carnegie and Henry Ford. But the inn rapidly declined after Miller's death in 1935, and was dangerously close to demolition until rescued by the Riverside Redevelopment Agency. Further protection was guaranteed when the inn entered the National Register of Historic Places in 1977. ELS/Elbasani & Logan led the painstaking renovation process, which involved extensive seismic upgrading and interior restoration. Several unique architectural elements, including domed ceilings, wrought-iron balconies, tile floors, and leaded-glass windows, characterize the guest rooms. One of the two wedding chapels (the Nixons were married here) features a 17th-century altar.

The inn has an Olympic-size swimming pool (heated year-round), a Jacuzzi, health club, and three restaurants. The charming **Duane's Prime Steak Restaurant,** also known for its seafood dishes, is a Spanish-tiled room with outdoor patio dining; **The Mission Inn Restaurant** features vaulted ceilings, colorful tiles, ornate wall sconces, and marble accents; and the **Spanish Patio** offers alfresco dining amid lush plants and a graceful fountain. ♦ 3649 Mission Inn Ave (between Orange and Main Sts), Riverside. 951/784.0300, 800/843.7755; fax 951/784.5525. www.missioninn.com

13 RIVERSIDE MUNICIPAL MUSEUM

This Renaissance-Revival building contains several exhibits on local and natural history, including a variety of flora and fauna, birds, and a gallery devoted to the city's citrus industry. ♦ Free. Tu-Su. 3720 Orange St (between University and Mission Inn Aves), Riverside. 951/782.5273

13 RIVERSIDE ART MUSEUM

The gallery spaces in this 1929 **Julia Morgan**–designed structure showcase a full range of artwork, from historical exhibits to works of contemporary Southern California artists. Located within the museum's courtyard is **A Moveable Feast,** a charming café serving light fare for lunch. There's also a gift shop. ♦ Admission. Tu-Sa. 3425 Mission Inn Ave (between Lime and Lemon Sts), Riverside. 951/684.7111

13 CALIFORNIA MUSEUM OF PHOTOGRAPHY

Stanley Saitowitz remodeled a downtown Kress store in 1990 to house this photography collection, which rivals those of Eastman House and the Smithsonian. Director Jonathan Green presents a lively program of exhibitions and events. Researchers may use the study center. ♦ Admission; free on Wednesday. W-Su. 3824 Main St (between Ninth St and University Ave), Riverside. Recording 951/784.3686, office 951/787.4787

PERRIS

In 1882, real estate and railway development helped establish the town of Perris, named after Fred T. Perris, the chief engineer of the California Southern Railroad line, which stretched from San Diego to Riverside. The city prospered with the wool trade, but fortunes declined in the 1890s when the water system failed to keep up with demand and many residents fled westward toward Riverside.

14 ORANGE EMPIRE RAILWAY MUSEUM

This museum displays more than 150 rail vehicles, including steam, diesel, and electric locomotives and streetcars. You can ride several of these on the property. For special events the museum allows locomotives to make trips into town, where there's a fine surviving train station. ♦ Free, except for some special events. Daily. 2201 S A St (between Mapes Rd and Ellis Ave). Recording 909/657.2605, office 909/943.3020

15 PERRIS VALLEY AIRPORT

You won't find any commercial airlines landing on the runways here, just gliders, hot-air balloons, ultralight planes, and parachuters. ♦ 2091 Goetz Rd (between Mapes Rd and Ellis Ave). 909/657.3904

PALM SPRINGS

A smartly casual resort at the base of Mount San Jacinto, the **Palm Springs Desert Resorts** has become the generic name for a group of resort and residential areas spread out around the Coachella Valley: Desert Hot Springs, Cathedral City, Rancho Mirage, Palm Desert, Indian Wells, La Quinta, and Indio. At the beginning of the 1980s, Palm Springs was a prime tourist destination, boasting more than 7,000 hotel rooms. As the decade ended, though, American companies began tightening their belts, reducing the business and convention travel that had fueled the area's economy. As a result, some hotels folded, real estate values plummeted, and residents started moving away. Palm Springs was definitely on the skids.

But the region has rebounded, thanks to some aggressive promotion on the part of the Palm Springs

Desert Resorts Convention and Visitors Authority, not to mention a few boosts from its late mayor and congressman, Sonny Bono. Many also credit the gay population, which turned deteriorating houses into palatial estates and added a *je ne sais quoi* aura to the area. It still rules as the golf capital of the world, with more than 100 golf courses spread throughout the 150-square-mile valley. And the sublime climate remains the primary draw, with light-as-a-feather air quality, low humidity and rainfall (an average of 5.39 inches annually), and an average daytime temperature of 88°F (though it can easily reach a broiling 120°F in summer or a freezing 20°F on winter nights). Gay couples and singles account for a major portion of the winter and weekend population. College kids take over Palm Springs at spring break. The numerous hot springs attract a health-conscious crowd that goes to "take the waters."

Many celebrities keep second homes in Palm Springs. Throughout the city are some remarkable modern desert houses designed by **Richard Neutra** and **John Lautner**. For information on hotels, restaurants, and other attractions in the greater Palm Springs area, call 800/34.RELAX or 760/770.9000, or try the Palm Springs web site at www.palmspringsusa.com.

16 JOSHUA TREE NATIONAL PARK

A natural wonder just two and a half hours from LA, this park is 874 square miles of beautiful mountain and desert flora, the highlight of which is the unusual Joshua tree, a member of the lily family whose crooked limbs can grow to 50 feet long, producing clusters of greenish-white flowers. Mormon settlers, who thought it resembled the prophet Joshua showing them the way, named the tree and the park. **Keys View** has the best sampling of Joshua trees. More than 80 percent of the park is designated wilderness area, and it is a haven for rock climbers. Over thousands of years, the elements have formed the granite monoliths of the **Wonderland of Rocks** in Hidden Valley into bizarre shapes that challenge the skills of climbers. A trail from the Oasis Visitors Center leads to the **Oasis of Mara,** one of the world's most popular climbing sites. The park has plenty to offer those who enjoy remote desert hiking; experienced hikers should stop at a visitors' center for a map and to learn the rules and regulations before beginning their trek, and should carry at least a gallon of water per person per day. More than 500 campsites are available; all are filled on a first-come, first-served basis, except for Black Rock (for reservations, call MISTIX at 800/365.2267, ext 5674). ♦ Oasis (main) Visitors Center: Utah Tr (south of Rte 62), Twentynine Palms. 760/367.7511. Cottonwood Visitors Center: Cottonwood Spring Rd (north of I-10). Black Rock Visitors Center: Quail Springs Rd (south of Rte 62), Joshua Tree

---

Restaurants/Clubs: Red | Hotels: Purple | Shops: Orange | Outdoors/Parks: Green | Sights/Culture: Blue

Aw, Go Take a Hike (or Climb a Rock)

Hiker alert: There are plenty of great options to explore, either on your own or with a guide. The **Palm Springs Desert Museum** (619/321.5778) offers biweekly mountain hikes led by a naturalist. **Designer Nature Tours & Outings** (619/251.1717) do personalized hikes and health walks. And, yes, there is rock climbing in the desert offered by **Uprising Outdoor Adventure** (619/320.6630) and at Joshua National Park (619/367.5500), where only the truly experienced need apply.

17 Desert Hills Premium Outlets

Clever developers have found a way to attract discount shoppers to the remotest corners of Southern California. More than 120 factory outlet stores here offer designer men's and women's apparel, footwear, home furnishings, toys, and leather goods. If the kids get bored, treat them to nearby **Dinosaur Gardens** (see below). ♦ Daily. 48400 Seminole Dr (at Millard Pass), Cabazon. 909/849.6641

17 Dinosaur Gardens

Claude Bell designed and built the 150-foot-long brontosaurus and matching Tyrannosaurus rex that occupy a garden in the San Gorgonio Pass, 18 miles northwest of Palm Springs. ♦ Nominal admission; children under 10 free. Hours vary, call ahead. 5800 Seminole Dr (at Main St), Cabazon. 909/849.8309

18 Whitewater Canyon

The canyon offers interesting scenery and a trout farm. Tackle and bait are available to rent, and those who get lucky can cook their catch on grills in the picnic area. ♦ Whitewater Canyon Rd (north of Whitewater Cutoff), Whitewater

19 Palm Springs Aerial Tramway

A spectacular tram ride—the largest vertical cable rise in the US—climbs to an altitude of 8,516 feet on Mount San Jacinto for a fantastic view of the surrounding area. In October 2000, spiffy, roomier 80-passenger Rotair tramcars from Switzerland finally replaced the original cars, which were installed in 1963. At the top is a bar, restaurant, shops, and 54 miles of hiking trails. The cars run every 30 minutes. There's camping (by permit only) at **Mount San Jacinto State Park and Wilderness;** reservations required. ♦ Daily. Tramway Rd (west of N Palm Canyon Dr). Recording 760/325.1391, office 760/325.1449, camping information and reservations 909/659.2607. www.pstramway.com

20 Palm Springs Desert Museum

This 100,000-square-foot cultural center houses the **Steve Chase Art Wing and Education Center,** where more than 120 of the interior designer's large-scale contemporary works are on display. Also here are changing exhibitions of contemporary and historical art, including a fine collection of more than 1,300 American Indian artifacts. ♦ Admission. Tu-Su. 101 Museum Dr (at W Tahquitz Canyon Way). 760/325.7186; fax 760/327.5069. www.psmuseum.org

20 Viceroy Palm Springs

$$$ Looking for a special spot to get away from it all? This stylish, upscale celebrity hideaway is just the ticket. Book a Grove bungalow and entrench yourself amid pristine white walls. Enjoy a blazing fireplace (in winter), flat-screen TV viewing, a private patio with a Jacuzzi, a big comfortable bed with Frette linens and down comforters, and plush terry robes to wear during your stay. For additional comfort, reserve one of the spiffy bungalows that come with kitchens equipped with a coffeemaker and refrigerator, a large living room, and high-tech equipment for Internet access and phone service. Stay fit in the well-equipped gym. Take a steam bath and enjoy a massage or facial at the jaunty, well-run spa. Then swim night and day in one of two inviting pools, relax in the outdoor whirlpool baths, or take the short stroll into town. At night join locals and other hotel guests at the bustling bar, then enjoy a fantastic dinner in the attractive indoor/outdoor restaurant.

Within Viceroy Palm Springs:

Citron

★★★$$$ Revelers from nearby and out of town swarm into this stylish restaurant nightly. A chic combination of black and white with splashes of vibrant yellow swathes the walls and furnishings. Gaiety prevails, with a noise level to match. Still, the mood can prove intimate if you sit off to the side. The food is truly special. Any fish dish (oven-roasted cod; Rhode Island black bass) on the menu will delight, as will starters such as heirloom tomatoes with slice watermelon, topped with baby greens and blue cheese. Crunchy crab cakes are served in a salad with fava bean purée, bacon, and peppercorns. Pea soup is served chilled with crème fraiche, and the veal tenderloin melts in your mouth. The chocolate soufflé and panna cottas are truly distinctive. Citron ranks as a major celebrity hangout, so keep your eyes peeled, but please act judiciously. ♦ California/French ♦ Daily, breakfast, lunch, and dinner. Reservations for dinner are essential. 415 S Belardo Rd (at Ramon Rd). 800/237.3687. www.viceroypalmsprings.com

20 THE FALLS

★★★$$$ If you like your steaks large and your drinks big and potent, this is the place. Every selection (porterhouse, rib-eye, or New York) is served to order. The beef is some of the tenderest and best you can get. The clientele is high energy, and the wait staff fast on their feet and eager to please. There are all sorts of sides to go with your meat, and plenty of dessert choices. On a warm night, opt to sit out on the balcony so you can view all the action on the busy promenade below. ♦ Steak House ♦ Daily, dinner. Reservations suggested. 155 Palm Canyon Dr (between Arenas and Tahquitz Canyon). 714/416.8656. www.thefallsprimesteakhouse.com

21 IDYLLWILD

A community nestled in mile-high mountains, Idyllwild has tall pines, a tumbled rock formation for climbing, and trails for hiking in summer and cross-country skiing in winter. Drive-in campgrounds for overnight stays are located within Idyllwild and **Stone Creek Park.** ♦ Rte 243 (north of Rte 74). Reservations 800/444.7275 (ask for C6161 for Idyllwild camp; C6162 for Stone Creek camp)

22 INDIAN CANYONS

Andreas, Murray, and Palm Canyons offer large and unusual rock formations, good hiking trails, and a stand of majestic Washingtonian palms believed to be almost 2,000 years old. ♦ S Palm Canyon Dr (south of Canyon Heights Dr)

23 SALTON SEA

Not quite the pristine spot it once was, this 38-mile-long inland sea, which lies 235 feet below sea level, has been plagued with dead fish washing up on its shores. However, there's still a **National Wildlife Refuge,** located at the southern end, and a **Visitors Center** that offers wildlife exhibitions and tourist information. ♦ Rte 111 (southeast of Mecca). West Shores Chamber of Commerce 760/394.4112

24 LIVING DESERT RESERVE

This 1,200-acre endangered species habitat houses the rare cheetah—the fastest land animal on earth—and presents "Wildlife Wonders," a show featuring exotic creatures such as the South African serval and the fennec fox, as well as birds of prey like the red-tailed hawk and the barn owl. **African Savanna** houses the tallest giraffes and the largest ostriches in a virtual two-acre setting that is also inhabited by lions, baboons, rhinoceros, and Nile crocodiles. There are also nature trails, a botanical garden, a visitor center, the **Meerkat Cafe,** and a gift shop/bookshop. Group tours are available. ♦ Admission. Daily, Sept to mid-June. 47900 Portola Ave (between Mariposa and W Vintage Drs), Palm Desert. 760/346.5694; fax 760/568.9685. www.livingdesert.org

25 LAKE CAHUILLA

Twenty-five miles southeast of Palm Springs, this lake is great for fishing, swimming, boating, and picnicking. ♦ Daily. Keller Pit Rd (just southwest of Ave 58), La Quinta. 760/564.4712

26 ANZA BORREGO DESERT

This 470,000-acre state park is a well-maintained desert preserve with unusual varieties of flora and fauna. The striking geological formations resemble a miniature Grand Canyon. ♦ Free. Visitors Center: Rte S22 (between Rtes S3 and 79). 760/767.4205, park information 760/767.5311

There are about 30,000 swimming pools in Palm Springs alone, both in hotels and private homes.

At last count, in 1997, there were more than 30 major movie studios in Los Angeles.

Restaurants/Clubs: Red | Hotels: Purple | Shops: Orange | Outdoors/Parks: Green | Sights/Culture: Blue

BEACHES: NORTHERN TOURS

By the sea, by the sea, by the beautiful sea . . .

PACIFIC COAST HIGHWAY TOUR

Area: A drive up and down the Pacific Coast Highway past some of the loveliest beaches in Los Angeles County

Mileage: 53 miles round-trip from the intersection of the Santa Monica Freeway (I-10) and Route 1

Take the **Santa Monica Freeway** to its end at **Santa Monica,** where it will merge with **Route 1.** Continue north on this road for the tour. Although much of the beachfront is free and open to the public, you will see private homes, many of which are elaborate residences belonging to the rich and famous. You may have to pay for parking in the adjoining lots. Getting across the Pacific Coast Highway on foot or turning your car around is dangerous; extreme caution is advised.

The first major public beach is **(1) Will Rogers Beach State Park,** named for the famous cowboy humorist. This beach stretches for several miles along the Pacific Coast Highway and is well provided with parking, facilities, and volleyball areas. Surfers congregate in the area opposite **Sunset Boulevard.**

You may want to detour up Sunset Boulevard to visit the **(2) Self-Realization Fellowship Lake Shrine** or **(3) Will Rogers State Historic Park.** See page 111.

At the corner of Coastline Drive is the **(4) Getty Villa;** for more information, see page 110.

At Topanga Canyon Boulevard, a right turn will take you to the semirural community of **(5) Topanga,** to

Topanga State Park (see page 149), or on a drive to the **(6) San Fernando Valley** through a winding and scenic canyon. For more information, see the "San Fernando Valley" chapter on page 154.

The seaside community of **(7) Malibu** is as famous for its residents as for its scenery. The area on the right side of the Pacific Coast Highway is subject to landslides; note retaining walls holding back the earth. Much of the beach is walled off by "cottages" owned by celebrity types, but there are about 10 public-access paths, with parking, posted on the highway. You also can walk down from the pier.

The **(8) Malibu Pier,** located about 10 miles along this route, was closed for years for much-needed repairs, but should be open to the public again by the time you read this.

Just east of **(9) Malibu Point** is **Surfrider State Beach,** a favorite with surfers. About 12 miles out, you may take a detour right onto Malibu Canyon Road/Las Virgenes Road, which traverses the **Santa Monica Mountains** to the San Fernando Valley, following the edge of a colorful and rugged canyon. **(10) Malibu Creek State Park** is located beside this road. **(11) Pepperdine University** is just west of Malibu Canyon Road on the Pacific Coast Highway.

(12) Paradise Cove is just east of **Point Dume,** approximately 16 miles along this route. It is a sheltered beach with white sand, tumbled sandstone cliffs, and fishing and boat-launching facilities. Admission is charged.

(13) Zuma Beach, on the west side of Point Dume, is a broad, flat beach offering volleyball, picnic facilities, easy parking, miles of smooth sand, and good body- and board-surfing.

Beautiful and secluded **(14) Leo Carrillo State Beach** is located in a wide cove that is slightly sheltered by rocks at either end. The northern portion of the beach is very popular with surfers. Swimmers should go to the center of the cove to avoid underwater rocks.

Across the Pacific Coast Highway, approximately 26 miles from the start of this tour, is **(15) Point Mugu State Park.** For more information on this park and other sites mentioned above, see the "Malibu/The Canyons" chapter on page 144.

To return, retrace your route on the Pacific Coast Highway to the Santa Monica Freeway.

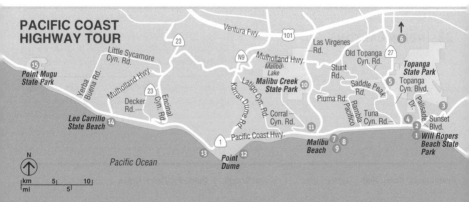

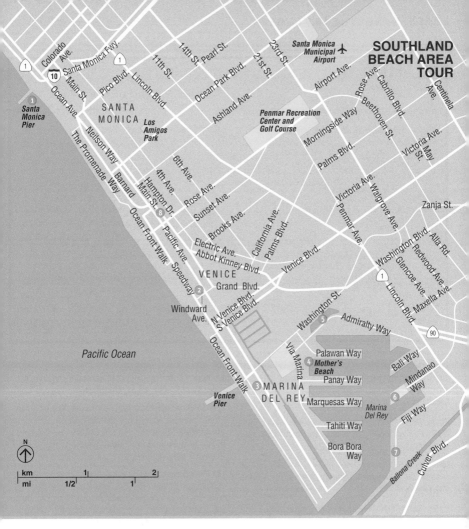

SOUTHLAND BEACH AREA TOUR

Area: Santa Monica, Venice, and Marina del Rey, the most popular and colorful of the Southland beach areas.

Mileage: Four miles round-trip from the Santa Monica Pier

Santa Monica/Marina del Rey is a compact area best seen on foot or by bicycle. (The use of a car is preferable only to get from neighborhood to neighborhood.) The bike path begins at the **Santa Monica Pier** and parallels the beach south to **Torrance,** a distance of some 18 miles. A short ride through the marina to **Playa del Rey** is highly recommended. The best walking and skating sites are on **The Promenade** and **Ocean Front Walk,** between the Santa Monica Pier and **Venice Pier,** and along **Main Street.**

To get into the proper playful mood for the tour, you might want to begin with a carousel ride at the **(1) Santa Monica Pier** at the end of Colorado Avenue in Santa Monica. Take Ocean Avenue south to the intersection with Pico Boulevard, where the road forks, then follow the right-hand fork that parallels the ocean; this is **Barnard Way.** Stay on Barnard around to the left until it hits **Neilson Way.** Turn right at Neilson and continue. The street becomes Pacific Avenue in the next block as you enter **Venice.**

Continue down Pacific past the corner of **(2) Windward Avenue,** whose beachfront is now a frenetic mixture of skaters, cyclists, joggers, entertainers, and assorted eccentrics. At Washington Street, a short stroll takes you to the **Venice Pier** for views, fishing, people-watching, and snacks. Continue down Pacific. You are now entering **(3) Marina del Rey,** about three miles from the Santa Monica Pier. The marina section of Pacific takes you past frayed relics of old Venice: canals, bridges, and a few disguised oil wells.

At the end of Pacific, where it abuts **Via Marina,** a small promenade area and jetty look out over the Marina del Rey entrance channel. This is a fine place to stop and

277

THE BEST

Felice Richter

Marketing Liaison, Museum of Tolerance

For jazz aficionados, **St. Mark's** in Venice is a happening spot.

I can quote the menu from **Remi** by heart. My friends all know that if the dinner reservations are up to me, we'll be dining at Remi and after dinner strolling along the **Promenade** in Santa Monica, where you'll find an assortment of shops, each with its own eclectic taste (and always something that you *must* have!).

I am fortunate that most of my driving around Los Angeles takes me through some of the most beautiful canyons in the West. From the **Hollywood Hills,** where you can visit **Lake Hollywood,** to the funky architecture of the houses of **Beverly Glen,** a drive through these canyons shows a side of Los Angeles that most visitors don't know about or get to see.

About one hour north of Los Angeles on I-5, you can find hiking trails up to **Mt. Pinos** that are easy on the novice hiker. The upper levels are closed during the winter months, but that only means February here! And if you are interested in snow, the town of **Frazier Park** is quaint and accommodating—and surprisingly warm considering you're in the snow!

For a bit of Los Angeles history, the **Central Library** houses four levels of books, interactive computers, storytelling hours, and more. After you've exhausted yourself learning, you can step out the front entrance to the **Cafe Pinot** for delicious food and wine in the outdoor sculpture garden, designed by artist Jud Fine.

One of the newest museums in Los Angeles, the **Museum of Tolerance,** addresses today's issues of racism, prejudice, and anti-Semitism. It's definitely a one-of-a-kind experience that must not be missed!

The bar at the **Westwood Marquis** in Westwood is one of my favorite romantic spots, with its dark lush interior. (And you never know who you might run into there!)

---

watch the sailboats glide by. Via Marina curves around the entrance channel and enters a densely built area of apartments and condominiums until it reaches **Admiralty Way.**

At the corner of Admiralty Way and Via Marina is **(4) Mother's Beach,** with a children's swimming area and picnic facilities.

Turn right onto Admiralty. After about half a mile you will pass the **(5) Bird Sanctuary** on the left and the **Marina City Towers** on the right.

Follow Admiralty to **Mindanao Way** and turn right. Continue to the end of the street, where you will find the entrance to **(6) Burton Chace Park.** The well-maintained park has picnic areas, barbecues, soft grassy knolls, rest rooms, and a tower you can climb to watch the boats in the marina.

Return to Admiralty and turn right to the next peninsula, **Fiji Way.** Go right again to **(7) Fisherman's Village,** a place for shopping, eating, and strolling.

Follow Fiji back to Admiralty and veer left. At the corner of Admiralty and Via Marina, turn right. Go to **Washington Street** and turn left. Continue a few blocks to Pacific and turn right. At **Rose Avenue,** turn right, go one block to Main Street, and turn left.

(8) Main Street, beginning near Marine Street and continuing almost to Pico Boulevard, is a delightful small shopping and dining area. Many of the restaurants along this street have rear patios that face the Pacific Ocean. Park in the city lots west of Main Street. To return to downtown LA on the **Santa Monica Freeway,** follow Main Street to Pico, turn right, and at **Lincoln Boulevard,** turn left. The freeway intersects Lincoln in two blocks.

BEACHES: SOUTHERN TOUR

Area: The Gold Coast beaches of Orange County from Newport Beach to Laguna Beach, and the planned community of Irvine; an alternate route leads to Mission San Juan Capistrano

Mileage: 150 miles round-trip from the downtown LA Civic Center

Take the **Santa Ana Freeway (I-5)** south from the Civic Center; an alternate route is the **San Diego Freeway**

(I-405). At 34 miles, take the **Newport Freeway (Route 55)** south. At the end of the freeway it becomes Newport Boulevard, a four- to six-lane street. Continue through Costa Mesa into **(1) Newport Beach.** For more information, see the "Orange County South" chapter on page 240.

At 44 miles, get into the left lane and go over the bridge onto the **(2) Newport Peninsula.**

You'll notice the yacht anchorage in the **Lido Channel** on your left as you pass over the bridge. Continue on Newport Boulevard, which curves to the left as it follows the peninsula. Opposite the **(3) Newport Pier,** Newport Boulevard becomes **Balboa Boulevard.**

At Palm Street, turn into the parking lot for a visit to the **(4) Balboa Pier** to enjoy the ocean view. You can also rent roller skates here.

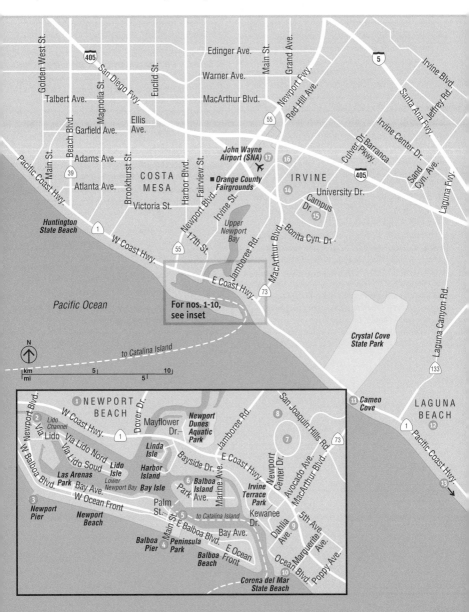

Walk across Balboa Boulevard into the **Fun Zone** for some snacks and a visit to the **(5) Balboa Pavilion** (see page 248).

To get to the ferry to **(6) Balboa Island** (see page 248), follow the signs from the parking lot to the crossing. The three-minute cruise across the Main Channel can be made aboard the *Admiral, Commodore,* or *Captain.* When you disembark at Agate Avenue, continue straight for one block to **Park Avenue.** Go left on Marine, through the center of the business district, and over **Back Bay Channel** on a little bridge. Continue straight a short distance to Bayside Drive, veer left, and continue up the hill to the Coast Highway. Go right, past the **(7) Fashion Island shopping center** (see page 247).

For a detour, turn left at Newport Center Drive and visit the **(8) Orange County Museum of Art** (see page 246).

Continue straight on the Coast Highway, past the **(9) Sherman Gardens,** and turn right on Marguerite Avenue. Go through the beautifully manicured residential streets to Ocean Boulevard. Turn left and park near the knoll that tops **(10) Corona del Mar State Beach.** This beautiful seaside area is rocky on the south and sandy on the north, and boasts a superb view. There is excellent swimming in the northern waters, which are protected by the east jetty of the Newport Harbor entrance.

Follow Ocean to Poppy Avenue and turn left, back to the Coast Highway. Turn right onto **Coast Highway** and continue south. The stretch between Poppy and Laguna Beach has rolling hills coming down to meet the undeveloped beach, giving a glimpse of what the coast was like prior to the 20th century. **(11) Cameo Cove,** just north of Laguna Beach, is a breathtaking scene, with a rock promontory and emerald-green water.

At approximately 55 miles, you enter **(12) Laguna Beach,** an area known for its beautiful scenery and painters devoted to capturing that scenery on canvas. Go left at Forest Avenue. Find a parking spot and stroll down pleasant shop-lined streets, or cross the Coast Highway to follow the Pacific Ocean along the boardwalk. For more information, see the "Orange County South" chapter on page 240.

To return to LA from this point, go north a short distance on the Coast Highway to Broadway. Go right to Laguna Canyon Road (Route 133), and then to the San Diego Freeway (I-405).

At this point, hardy souls with unflagging energy may wish to continue south to **(13) Mission San Juan Capistrano** (see page 251), where the famous cliff swallows return annually to this Spanish adobe church. Follow the Coast Highway down to **Del Obispo Street,** which is just past Dana Point. Go left to **Ortega Highway (Route 74),** then left to the mission at the intersection of Ortega Highway and Camino Capistrano. To return to LA from San Juan Capistrano, take the San Diego Freeway (I-5) north from its intersection with Ortega Highway.

To continue back up to **(14) Irvine** from Laguna Beach, return north on the Coast Highway to MacArthur Boulevard (Route 73). Turn right.

Lovers of trees, education, and/or architecture may wish to detour to the **(15) University of California at Irvine.** From MacArthur, go right on University Drive to Campus Drive. Go right on Campus to Bridge Road. Go right on Bridge to North Circle View Drive, then turn left. The **Administration Building** and **Visitor Center** are located on the right-hand side of North Circle View Drive (see page 245).

Meanwhile, the future may be taking shape in the **(16) Irvine Industrial Park,** located on both sides of MacArthur Boulevard. The simple, monolithic shapes of these structures contain businesses whose products vary from computer software to advanced technological hardware.

(17) John Wayne Airport, located on the left side of MacArthur Boulevard, is a busy commercial and small-craft airport. The terminal, designed by Leason Pomeroy Associates and Gensler & Associates in 1990, takes its shape from an airplane fuselage: three sleek vaults with rounded metal roofs (see page 243).

To return to LA, go to the **San Diego Freeway (I-405)** off MacArthur Boulevard and head north.

MOUNTAIN TOURS

COASTAL MOUNTAINS TOUR

Area: Some of the most scenic but easily driven coastal routes showing rugged mountains and beautiful ocean views

Mileage: Minimum of 47 miles round-trip from Ocean Avenue and Route 1 in Santa Monica; maximum of 100 miles round-trip with alternate routes from Ocean Avenue and Route 1

Begin at **Route 1** where the Santa Monica Freeway (I-10) ends near the **Santa Monica Pier.** Follow Route 1 north for five and a half miles to **Topanga Canyon Boulevard;** turn right. The highway winds past a sycamore-shaded creek. The 10,000-acre **Topanga State Park**—which by the time you read this may have become part of a massive conservation effort to preserve the entire sweep of land from Pacific Coast Highway, relocate business and homes, and turn it into an even larger state park (see Topanga Canyon, page 149)—features 18 miles of bicycle trails and 32 miles of hiking trails. Camping is permitted through special reservations; call 818/880.0350.

About two miles north of Topanga State Park is the main part of the rustic community of **(1) Topanga.** The narrowness of this winding road sometimes slows traffic, particularly on the weekends.

At 15.2 miles, the road descends to a panoramic view of the **San Fernando Valley,** the **Simi Hills,** and the **Santa Susana Mountains.** This is a good place to stop and appreciate the huge expanse of the valley.

At 16.9 miles, turn left on **(2) Mulholland Drive.** A great deal of housing construction is going on in this once rural area.

At this point, those who wish to make only a short trip can continue straight on Topanga Canyon Boulevard to the **Ventura Freeway (Highway 101),** which takes you back to LA.

For those who wish to continue this tour, at 17.5 miles make a left near the Woodland Plaza Shopping Center onto **Mulholland Highway.** The road widens to four lanes near Daguerre Avenue but narrows back to two soon afterward.

At about 19 miles, the intersection of **Old Topanga Canyon Road** and Mulholland Highway is confusing, but continue driving straight ahead and soon a sign will appear confirming that you are indeed on **(3) Mulholland Highway.** Steep rock, jagged hills, and abrupt terrain become an interesting backdrop for the road at around 23.7 miles. Breathtakingly beautiful scenery and rock formations begin with all the drama of an old western movie begin at around 25.5 miles.

At 27 miles is a stoplight intersection for **Las Virgenes Road.** Turn left. The two-lane highway passes rugged, wide-open vistas of classic western scenery and horseback-riding trails. Coming up soon on the right is 7,000-acre **Malibu Creek State Park,** with more than 15 miles of hiking and equestrian trails; for information, call 818/880.0350.

At 28.7 miles is **(4) Tapia Park,** a wilderness park near Malibu Creek with great hiking paths. This is an ideal place for picnicking and relaxing.

Just south of Tapia Park the highway's name changes to **Malibu Canyon Road.** At about 30 miles, a series of gorges and steep valley formations begins. Many turnouts provide opportunities to stop and examine the intricate stratification of rock layers, all tilted upward.

At 32.5 miles, several palm trees announce the **(5) Hughes Research Laboratories,** where the first practical laser was built. The lab is at the peak of a hill, and just at the other side is a spectacular ocean view.

The road to **(6) Pepperdine University** soon appears. The intersection of the Pacific Coast Highway and Malibu Canyon Road is at 33.4 miles. Turn left to return to Santa Monica.

Alternate routes: At the intersection of Las Virgenes and Mulholland Highway, continue straight on Mulholland and go west past **(7) Malibu Lake.**

At the intersection of **Kanan Dume Road (Route N9)** and Mulholland Highway, a detour can be made through the rugged scenery of Latigo Canyon by going south (left) for a short while on N9 and then turning left on **(8) Latigo Canyon Road.**

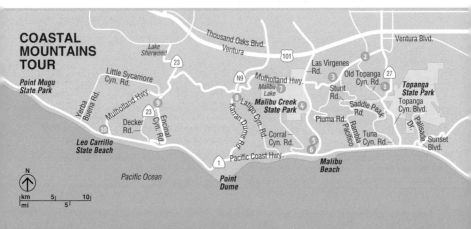

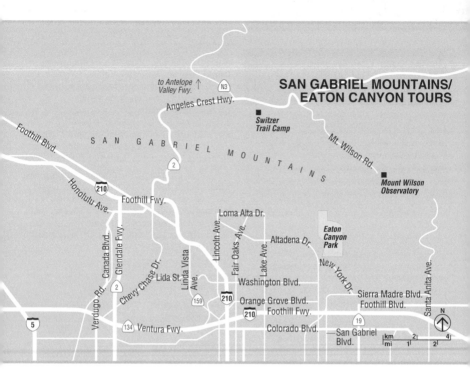

SAN GABRIEL MOUNTAINS/
EATON CANYON TOURS

Mulholland Highway (Route 23) loses its state highway designation to **(9) Decker Road.** You can follow Decker south to the ocean from the intersection, or continue west on Mulholland, skirting the Ventura County line until Mulholland takes you onto the **(10) Pacific Coast Highway** at **Leo Carrillo State Beach.**

Follow the Pacific Coast Highway back south to Santa Monica. For information, call the **National Park Service** (818/597.9192) or the **Santa Monica Mountains National Recreation Area** (818/597.9192).

section of **Route 2** and the **Angeles Forest Highway (Route N3),** turn right off Route 2 at the **Switzer Trail Camp.** (For information, call the **Clear Creek Station** at 818/797.9959.) The foot trail then crosses the **Arroyo Seco,** whose waters abruptly drop off into a 50-foot fall. Follow the trail uphill to a fork. Take the left branch of the fork into the gorge beneath the falls. To return, retrace your steps. Drive back to the intersection of Route 2 and the Angeles Forest Highway (Route N3). Go right for 30 minutes to the intersection with the **Antelope Valley Freeway (Route 14).** Go west to the **Golden State Freeway (I-5),** a distance of 20 miles.

SAN GABRIEL MOUNTAINS/ EATON CANYON TOURS

Area: A vigorous driving and hiking expedition that traverses the San Gabriels from La Cañada–Flintridge to the Antelope Valley, with a hiking stop at the Arroyo Seco Cascades

Mileage: 60 miles by car from the intersection of Interstate 210 and Route 2 to the intersection of Route 14 and Interstate 5, and a four-mile hike

From the **Foothill Freeway (I-210),** take the **Angeles Crest Highway (Route 2)** north into the mountains for 10.5 miles. At approximately a half-mile past the inter-

Area: Hikes within Eaton Canyon, ranging from a short hike to Eaton Falls to a 16-mile jaunt to Mount Wilson; for information, call 818/398.5420 and see the map above

Mileage: 30 miles by car round-trip from the Foothill Freeway (I-210), and a half-mile to 16-mile hike

The starting point may be reached by car or bus.

Bus: Take **No. 79** north on Olive Street in downtown LA to the intersection of Huntington Drive and San Gabriel Boulevard, then transfer to **No. 264.** Get off at **New York** and **Altadena Drives** and walk one block north on Altadena to the gate of **Eaton Canyon Park.**

Car: From the **Foothill Freeway (I-210),** turn on Altadena Drive to No. 1750, which is the entrance to **Eaton Canyon Park.**

Go through the gates to the **Robert M. McCurdy Nature Center,** a quarter-mile down the path. The center has brochures for the self-guided **Arroyo Nature Trail,** as well as information on the other trails in the park and canyon. Among the possibilities are a half-mile hike to **Eaton Falls;** a three-mile climb to the **Henninger Flat Campground and Ranger Station;** a three-mile excursion to the natural stone pools in **Upper Eaton Canyon;** and a 16-mile overnighter to **Mount Wilson.**

The **San Gabriel Mountains** tower above the city to the north. A century ago, naturalist John Muir described them as among the "most rigidly inaccessible" mountains he had ever trod. Today, these guardians are laced with trails and roads. The visitor who tours by car will see spectacular vistas from **Angeles Crest Highway (Route 2)** and **Angeles Forest Highway (Route N3),** but the serenity and majesty of the range is revealed only to those who explore it on foot. Information and maps are available from the **Angeles National Forest San Gabriel Canyon** entrance station (Route 39; 818/969.1012) or from the **National Park Service** (30401 Agoura Rd, No. 100, Agoura Hills, CA 91301; 818/597.9192). Hikers are no longer required to have entry permits but are strongly urged to advise friends of their itinerary in case of an accident. All visitors should bring water and take special precautions during the fire season (from June through December).

Don't touch the shiny clusters of trilobed serrated leaves; they are poison oak. And the rattlesnakes that live in this wilderness strike only to protect themselves, so if you leave them alone, they will leave you alone.

ARCHITECTURE TOURS

Los Angeles boasts a vast architectural heritage which, while do-able on your own, is easiest explored through guided tours offered by a plethora of knowledgeable companies. The following itineraries provide roadmaps for a self-guided wide-ranging

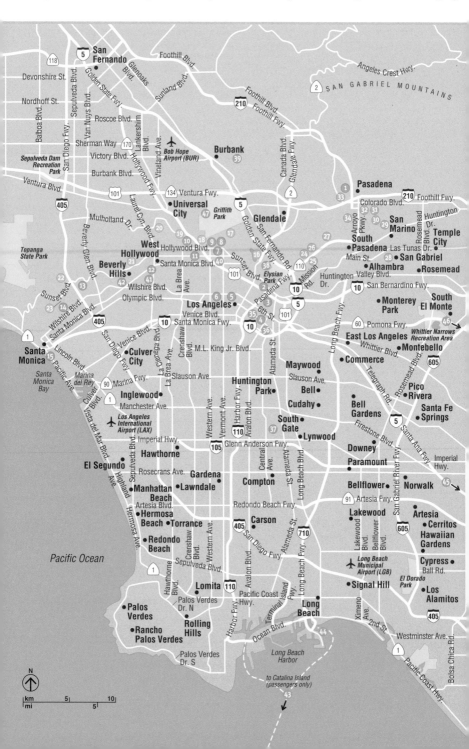

pilgrimage to some of LA's most distinctive landmarks. The tours are color-coded. Occasionally you'll drive by a featured site that's in a color different from that of the tour you're following. Relax. Enjoy. As you'll soon find out, LA has many surprising charms. If you'd prefer to let someone else do the navigating, contact **architours** (323/294.5821, fax 323/294.5825; info@architours.com; www.architours.com). The company offers a series of day and overnight tours that includes "Rediscovering the Southland," plus downtown walking tours, art and architecture tours, and others designed for individuals or groups.

Our **ACCESS guided tour** will delight those who prefer a modicum of walking—in typical LA fashion, you hardly have to leave your car to make this 46-mile excursion. Plan on driving about five hours. And please bear in mind that the private residences should be viewed only from the street.

THE MOSTLY ORANGE TOUR

For this tour follow the orange numbers on the map. Set out from **Pasadena,** an area rich in fine turn-of-the-20th-century domestic architecture. Slightly north of the interchange of the Foothill (I-210) and Ventura (Route 134) Freeways, or north from the Orange Grove Avenue exit of the Pasadena Freeway (Route 110), is the **(1) Gamble House** (4 Westmoreland Pl; open Thursday through Sunday; admission charge), a large vacation bungalow designed in 1908 by Pasadena Craftsman architects **Charles and Henry Greene.** Other houses by the Greenes can be seen all along **(1) Arroyo Terrace,** to the west of the Gamble House.

Take Orange Grove Boulevard south to the **Pasadena Freeway.** Head south on the freeway, stay to the right, and connect with the **Hollywood Freeway (Hwy 101)** going north. Exit at Echo Park–Glendale Boulevard and turn right at the end of the exit onto Bellevue Avenue. Turn left (north) on Edgeware Road East and left again on Carroll Avenue. The 1300 block of Carroll is the **(2) Carroll Avenue Historic District.**

Take Edgeware south to Temple Street, turn left (east), continue into downtown, and turn right on Broadway. At Third Street on the left is the **(3) Bradbury Building,** which you must see from the inside in order to appreciate its interior court. Saturday tours of the lobby are conducted by the LA Conservancy (admission charge); for more information, call 213/623.2489. To continue the tour, take a right on Third, drive through the tunnel, turn right on Flower Street, and stay left at the fork. The construction on the right is the architectural wonder **(3) Walt Disney Concert Hall** designed by **Frank Gehry.** Take a right on First Street and a right on Grand Avenue. On your left at 250 Grand Avenue is the **(3) Museum of Contemporary Art (MOCA),** by internationally renowned Japanese architect **Arata Isozaki.** Continue to Fifth Street, and on your left is the **(3) Gas Company Tower** (555 W Fifth St), designed in 1991 by **Skidmore, Owings & Merrill/R. Keating, Designer.** On your right at the southwest corner is the 1926 Beaux Arts landmark **(3) Central Library** by **Bertram Goodhue** and **Carleton Winslow Sr.** Turn left on Sixth Street and left on Olive Street. On your right is **(3)**

Pershing Square, renovated at a cost of $14 million by Ricardo Legorreta and Hanna Olin. On your left is the restored Italianate Beaux Arts **(3) Regal Biltmore Hotel,** designed by **Schultze & Weaver** in 1923.

Turn left onto Fifth Street and on your right is the tallest building in LA, the 73-story **(3) First Interstate World Center** (633 W Fifth St), designed in 1990 by **Pei Cobb Freed & Partners Associates/Harold Fredenburg.** Next door are **Lawrence Halprin**'s 1990 **Bunker Hill Steps.** Continue west and on your right you will see the cylindrical towers of the **(3) Westin Bonaventure Hotel** (404 S Figueroa St), designed by **John Portman** in 1976. Turn left (south) on Flower Street, right (west) on Eighth Street, and right on Figueroa. Ahead on your left you'll find the **(4) Sanwa Bank Plaza,** designed in 1991 by **AC Martin Partners.** Turn left (west) on Wilshire to see some Modernist commercial buildings. Visible at a distance is the tan terra-cotta and green-copper-trimmed tower of the **(5) I. Magnin Wilshire** building (3050 Wilshire Blvd), which was designed by **John and Donald Parkinson** in 1929. Farther west is the **(6) Wiltern Center** (3790 Wilshire Blvd), a zigzag Modernist complex of turquoise terra-cotta designed in 1931 by **Morgan, Walls & Clements.**

Turn right (north) on Western Avenue and then right (east) at Hollywood Boulevard. Enter **Barnsdall Park** on the right, before the intersection with Vermont Avenue. Here is **Frank Lloyd Wright**'s first Los Angeles project, the **(7) Hollyhock House,** which was completed in 1920. Tours are offered Tuesday through Sunday (nominal admission charge); for more information, call 213/662.7272. Return to Hollywood going right (east) and turn left at Vermont Avenue. Turn right (east) on Franklin Avenue. Between Myra Avenue and St. George Street is the **Shakespeare Bridge,** a handsome open spandrel with long Gothic arches. Turn back in a westbound direction on Franklin and turn right at Vermont Avenue. Cross Los Feliz Boulevard, and where Vermont forks, go to the left on Glendower Avenue. In a spectacular setting in the hills at 2607 Glendower Avenue is **Frank Lloyd Wright**'s stunning concrete **(8) Ennis-Brown House,** designed in 1924.

Return to Vermont and at Franklin Avenue, turn right (west). On the right is the dramatic **(9) Sowden House** (5121 Franklin Ave) by **Lloyd Wright,** Frank Lloyd Wright's son. Continue on Franklin. Three blocks past

THE BEST

Ron Salisbury

Owner, El Cholo and Sonora Cafe

Taking my seven-year-old early to a **Dodgers game** to watch batting practice.

Dining at **Valentino,** with their incredible Italian food and wine list.

Sitting at the community tables at sawdust-floored **Phillipe's** eating roast beef sandwiches and drinking $15 glasses of wine.

Picnicking before a **USC football game,** then going to the **Clipper Gate** in the second half (when the *real* game starts).

Highland, turn left (south) on Orange Drive and come up the back way to **Meyer & Holler**'s extravagant **(10) Mann's Chinese Theatre** (designed in 1927), at 6925 Hollywood Boulevard.

Turn right (south) onto Highland and left (east) onto Sunset Boulevard. At 6671 Sunset Boulevard is the **(11) Crossroads of the World,** a group of international theme shops designed by **Robert Derrah** in 1936 as a tourist attraction. Turn right (south) on Cahuenga Boulevard and right again (west) on Santa Monica Boulevard. Continue on to San Vicente Boulevard and turn left (south). The large blue-and-green glass structure at the corner of San Vicente and Melrose Avenue is the **(12) Pacific Design Center,** designed in 1975 by **Cesar Pelli** for Gruen Associates.

Backtrack on San Vicente to Sunset and turn left (west). Continue on Sunset past the University of California, Los Angeles (UCLA), and turn left at Veteran Avenue. At the first street, Cashmere, turn right, then right again on Greenfield Avenue. **Rudolph Schindler**'s **(13) Tischler House** (designed in 1949) is at 175 Greenfield Avenue. Take Greenfield to the end of the block and turn left (west) on Sunset. At Bundy Drive turn left (south) and at Montana Avenue turn right. Turn left on 22nd Street. At Washington Avenue and 22nd is **Frank Gehry**'s dramatic **(14) Gehry House,** a 1977-78 remodeling of an older house, using corrugated steel, wood, and glass. Go east on Washington Avenue to 26th Street and turn right. At Broadway turn right and at Ocean Avenue turn left.

To conclude the tour, drive past the white cubistic **(15) Horatio West Court Apartments** (140 Hollister Avenue) designed in 1919 by **Irving Gill,** one of California's leading Modernist architects. To get back to the Santa Monica Freeway, take Neilson Way north to Pico Boulevard and turn right. At Lincoln Boulevard turn left and you will see signs for the Santa Monica Freeway, which heads toward downtown.

THE MOSTLY GREEN TOUR

LA living has been established in style by trend-setting architects. The second tour is a sampling of the finest houses designed by modern architects (with the addition of a few excellent Revival-style homes) from Silverlake west through Hollywood to Santa Monica. For this tour, follow the green numbers on the map (on page 284).

The tour is approximately 37 miles long and takes at least three hours. The following sites are all private residences and should be viewed only from the street. Begin in **Silverlake.** The Silverlake area cannot be entered directly from Sunset. To get there, turn south on Reno Street from Sunset Boulevard, then onto Silverlake Boulevard. Follow Silverlake to the right around the reservoir. At 2300 Silverlake Boulevard is the **(16) Neutra House,** an International Style structure designed in 1933 and rebuilt in 1963 by Viennese immigrant **Richard Neutra.** Down the street are other houses by the architect: **nos. 2250, 2242, 2240, 2238, 2226, 2218, 2210,** and **2200.**

Continue north on Silverlake and turn left at its end onto Glendale Boulevard. At the fork, go left on Rowena Avenue, and at Los Feliz Boulevard turn left. Two blocks farther, at Commonwealth Avenue, turn right (north). Turn left at the third block on Dundee Drive. At the end of the street is Neutra's **(17) Lovell House** (No. 4616), designed in 1929. Return to Los Feliz and turn right (west). At Vermont Avenue turn right and veer to the left to Glendower Avenue. Winding up the hill you will reach **Frank Lloyd Wright**'s spectacular 1924 **(8) Ennis-Brown House** at 2607 Glendower Avenue.

Return to Vermont and turn right at Hollywood Boulevard. On the left is **Barnsdall Park.** See **Frank Lloyd Wright**'s first Los Angeles project, the **(7) Hollyhock House,** designed in 1917-20. Tours are held Tuesday through Sunday (admission charge); for more information, call 213/485.4581.

Return to Hollywood and turn left. At Normandie Avenue turn right (north), and at Franklin Avenue turn left (west). **Lloyd Wright**'s dramatic 1926 **(9) Sowden House** is at 5121 Franklin Avenue. Continue on Franklin and turn right (north) on Western Avenue. Take Western to its end where it veers right, connecting with Los Feliz. Get in the left lane in preparation to turn left at the first street, Ferndell Drive. Turn left again on Black Oak Drive. Turn left on Live Oak Drive East and right on Verde Oak Drive. Veer to the left on Valley Oak Drive to see **Lloyd Wright**'s copper-trimmed **(18) Samuels-Navarro House** (no. 5609), built in 1922-24.

Retrace back to Los Feliz, and at Western turn left (south). At Franklin, turn right and continue past the jog to the left at Highland Avenue. Three blocks past Highland, turn right on Sycamore Avenue and drive up to **(19) Yamashiro's Restaurant** at 1999 North

Sycamore Avenue, designed as an authentic Chinese palace by **Franklin Small** in 1913.

Return to Franklin, turn right (west), then left on Sierra Bonita and right on Hollywood, which turns into Laurel Canyon Boulevard. Follow it up to Mulholland Drive and turn right (east). At Torreyson Place turn right again. From here you can see the **(20) Malin House,** also known as the **Chemosphere House,** a residence designed by **John Lautner** in 1960.

Return to Mulholland and turn left (south) on Laurel Canyon. When you reach Sunset, turn right (west). At the intersection of Cory Avenue and Sunset, take the small street to the right on Sunset Boulevard, going straight onto Doheny Road. In **Greystone Park,** the English Tudor **(21) Greystone Mansion** (501 Doheny Rd; open daily; no admission charge) was designed by **Gordon Kaufman** in 1923 for oil millionaire Edward Doheny, and today is owned by the city of Beverly Hills. For more information, call 310/550.4654.

Return to Loma Vista and head south. At Mountain Drive, veer left and turn right (west) at Sunset Boulevard. Continue on Sunset and pass the **University of California, Los Angeles (UCLA).** Turn left on Veteran Avenue and then right at Cashmere Street. Turn right on Greenfield Avenue and see Viennese immigrant architect **Rudolph Schindler**'s ingenious **(13) Tischler House** (175 Greenfield Ave), designed in 1949. Continue north on the street to return to Sunset and turn left (west). Just west of Bundy Drive turn right onto Kenter, and at the second block on the right (Skyeway Road), turn right to see **Frank Lloyd Wright**'s redwood-and-stucco 1939 **(22) Sturgis House** at no. 449.

Return to Sunset and turn right (west). One block past Mandeville Canyon, turn right at Riviera Ranch Road. Here and on Old Oak Road are architect **Cliff May**'s original ranch houses, a style popularized throughout America during the 1940s and 1950s. Return to Sunset and turn left (east). Turn right at Rockingham Avenue. Across 26th Street, Rockingham becomes La Mesa Drive. From 26th to 19th Streets, La Mesa is draped by huge Moreton Bay fig trees, and in the 2100 to 1900 block of La Mesa are a number of **(23) Spanish Colonial Revival homes** by **John Byers** from the 1920s to 1930s. They are **nos. 2153, 2101, 2034,** and **1923.**

At the end of the road is San Vicente Boulevard. Take it to the left one block and turn right on 20th Street, jogging left at Montana Avenue. Turn left on Washington Avenue. At 1002 22nd Street, you will see the dramatic **(14) Gehry House,** a Dutch Colonial structure remodeled in 1977-78 by architect **Frank Gehry** using corrugated metal, wood, and glass. The tour concluded, you can return to the Santa Monica Freeway by heading west on Washington. At 20th, turn left to connect with the freeway.

THE MOSTLY BLUE TOUR

The next tour views a number of Spanish Colonial, Mexican, and Mission Revival buildings. It also concentrates on the Craftsman movement from the turn of the century. For this tour, follow the blue numbers on the map (on page 284).

The Pasadena area abounds in fine architecture of many styles, but the English-based Arts and Crafts movement found one of its strongest American outlets here. This tour is approximately 19 miles long and takes at least four hours. Private residences should be viewed only from the street. Begin at a location adjacent to the Pasadena Freeway (Route 110). On the west side of the freeway at the Avenue 43 exit is the **(24) Lummis House** (built between 1898 and 1910) at 200 East Avenue 43. The boulder home was built by **Charles F. Lummis,** enthusiast of the Spanish, Mexican, and Indian heritage of Southern California (tours are held on Saturday and Sunday; admission charge). Across the freeway, **(25) Heritage Square** is a bright cluster of Victorian mansions in various stages of renovation.

Now take Avenue 43 left (west) to Figueroa Street and turn left. At Marmion Way, turn right. On the corner of Marmion and Museum Drive is the **Southwest Museum,** which was designed in 1912 by **Sumner Hunt** and Silas Burns and houses an impressive collection of Southwest Indian art. A monument to the Mission style, it is embellished with architectural references to the Alhambra in Spain. Return to Figueroa and turn left. At 4603 Figueroa Street is the **(26) Casa de Adobe,** a 1917 reconstruction of a Mexican adobe house by **Theodore Eisen.** Continue on Figueroa going northeast to Arroyo Glen Street and turn right. At 6211 Arroyo Glen is the **(27) San Encino Abbey** (built between 1909 and 1925), a private residence designed by **Clyde Brown** in a combination of Spanish Mission and European Gothic styles.

Return to Figueroa and turn right, continuing northeast. At York Boulevard, turn right (east). The turn-of-the-19th-century **(27) Judson Studios** (200 S Avenue 66) are famous for their Craftsman glass and mosaic work. Return to York and turn right. Continue on as the road becomes Pasadena Avenue and then Monterey Road. At Huntington Drive, jog left and turn right (south) on San Marino, and at a fork in the road, go to the right onto Santa Anita Street. At the corner of Santa Anita and Mission Drive is the **(28) Mission Playhouse** (320 S Mission Dr), designed in 1927 by **Arthur Benton** to appear similar to the Mission San Antonio in Monterey County. Go east one block to visit the **(28) Mission San Gabriel Archangel** at 537 West Mission Drive, the fourth mission established by Father Junípero Serra. The mission was built between 1791 and 1805 and is open daily; there's an admission charge.

Now head north on Serra Drive and turn left on San Marino Avenue. Turn left on **(29) Lombardy Road** and notice the Spanish Revival homes, all private residences, in the 1700 to 2000 blocks, especially **no. 1750** by architect **Roland E. Coate; no. 1779** by George **Washington Smith,** at the corner of Allen Avenue; **665 Allen Avenue,** another Smith house; and two **Wallace Neff** houses at **nos. 1861** and **2035 Lombardy.** Turn right (north) on Hill Avenue and go one block to California Boulevard. Across California is the campus of the **(30) California Institute of Technology.** The oldest buildings, from the 1930s, were designed by **Gordon Kaufman** in the Spanish Renaissance and Spanish Baroque styles. Note especially the **(30) Atheneum Club** facing Hill Avenue and the adjacent dorms seen as you turn left (west) onto California Boulevard. Continue on California to El Molino Avenue and turn right (north).

At 37 South El Molino Avenue is the Spanish Colonial **(31) Pasadena Playhouse,** designed in 1924-25 by architect **Elmer Grey.** Turn left at the corner of Colorado Boulevard heading west and at Fair Oaks Avenue turn left again. One block away is Green Street. Turn left and then right at Raymond Avenue. You will be in front of the large turretted Spanish Colonial **(32) Hotel Green & Castle Green Apartments,** designed in 1890-99 by architect **Frederick Roehrig.** Head north on Raymond and at Colorado Boulevard turn left (west). Turn right on Orange Grove Boulevard. Just past Walnut Street, you will see a small street flanking Orange Grove Boulevard on the left. This is Westmoreland Place. At no. 4 is the **(1) Gamble House,** built in 1908 by famous Pasadena Craftsman architects **Charles and Henry Greene** (open Thursday through Sunday; admission charge; call 818/793.3334 in advance for tours). To the west of the house is **(1) Arroyo Terrace,** which has a number of houses designed by the Greenes. All are private residences. Pay particular attention to **nos. 368, 370, 400, 408, 424,** and **440,** which were built between 1902 and 1913.

Return to Orange Grove Boulevard and turn right. At Holly Street, one block away, turn right on Linda Vista Avenue. Turn left and then go one block to **(33) El Circulo Drive,** then turn left. At **95 El Circulo** and **825 Las Palmas Road** are two rural Spanish Revival homes designed by amateur architect **Edward Fowler** in 1927. Backtrack to Linda Vista Avenue. Turn right (north) on Holly Street and then right (east). At Orange Grove Boulevard turn right (south). Turn right at California Boulevard and note the **(34) E. J. Cheesewright House** at 686 West California Boulevard, a 1910 Craftsman house that looks like an English snuggery with its thatch roof. At Arroyo Boulevard turn left (south). See the **(34) Batchelder House** (626 S Arroyo Blvd), built in 1909 by **Ernest Batchelder,** Pasadena craftsman and renowned tilemaker. Conclude this tour with the finest example of a Spanish Monterey-style house, the home at **(34) 850 South Arroyo Boulevard,** designed by **Donald McMurray** in 1927.

To return to the Pasadena or Ventura Freeways, turn left at Grand Avenue and right on Bellefontaine Street to get to Orange Grove. From Orange Grove you can connect with the Pasadena Freeway (Route 110) by turning right and heading south, and with the Ventura Freeway (Route 134) by turning left.

THE MOSTLY PURPLE TOUR

The next tour is a sampling of some of LA's next fantastic architecture, from the serious to the whimsical. For this tour, follow the purple numbers on the map (on page 284).

A bit of fantasy abounds on almost every street of LA, so along the way you might note additional structures that have adopted the styles of other areas and other cultures, or buildings that are straightforwardly indulgent and delight in commercialism, futurism, and personal eccentricities. This route leads you around the city in an extremely broad sweep from downtown to Watts, and north to Glendale, ending in Beverly Hills.

The tour is approximately 52 miles long and takes at least four hours. Please keep in mind that the private residences should be viewed only from the street. In downtown LA the shimmering futuristic apparition at 404 S Figueroa Street is the **(3) Westin Bonaventure Hotel** by architect **John Portman.** Take Flower Street south to Olympic Boulevard and turn left. At Hill Street turn right to see the former **(35) Mayan Theater,** now the Mayan Nightclub, at 1038 South Hill Street. The pre-Columbian façade was designed by **Morgan, Walls & Clements** in 1927. Continue on Hill to Pico Boulevard and turn left (east). At the end of Pico you will come to Central Avenue and the shiplike **(36) Coca-Cola Building** (1334 S Central Ave), designed in 1935-37 by **Robert Derrah** with enormous Coke bottles at the entrance to the plant. Turn right onto Central and follow the signs on the right to enter the Santa Monica Freeway (I-10) going west (to Santa Monica). After a short distance, connect with the Harbor Freeway (I-110) south (toward San Pedro).

Turn off at the Manchester Avenue exit and go left (east). Manchester turns into Firestone Boulevard. At Elm Street turn right (Elm turns into Wilmington Avenue), and at the intersection of 107th Street, turn right again. At 1765 E 107th Street you will see the unique, monumental **(37) Watts Towers,** a personal vision fashioned of broken tile, glass, and debris between 1921 and 1954 by Italian immigrant tile-layer **Sam Rodia.** The three-tower structure was completely renovated in 2001.

Retrace your way back to the **Harbor Freeway (I-110).** Go north on the freeway (toward Pasadena) and connect with the Hollywood Freeway (Highway 101). Take the Hollywood Freeway west and get off after a short distance at the Echo Park exit. Proceed north on Echo Park Avenue to Baxter Street and turn right. At Avon Street turn left (driving the streets around here is like riding a roller coaster). You will want to park and walk on the right (east) side of Avon, to Avon Park Terrace. There you will see what looks like an authentic Indian pueblo, the **(38) Atwater Bungalows** at 1431-33 Avon Park Terrace, built in 1931 by **Robert Stacy-Judd.**

Return to your car and at Baxter turn right. At Alvarado Street turn left and at Glendale turn right. Proceed north to Rowena Avenue and turn left. Glendale continues at the right; take it to San Fernando Road and turn left. At Grandview Avenue turn right and take it to its end.

At the intersection of Mountain Street and Grandview you will enter the **(39) Brand Library,** formerly the Brand House (built in 1902), an exotic East Indian and Moorish mansion that is now a public library. Return to Grandview and at San Fernando turn left. At Los Feliz Road turn right. Turn left at Vermont Avenue and right onto Sunset Boulevard, and you will pass the Indian **(40) Self-Realization Temple** at 4860 Sunset Boulevard and the **(11) Crossroads of the World** at 6671 Sunset Boulevard. The latter, a 1935 tourist attraction, presents a ship sailing into a courtyard of shops representing various European countries. At Highland Avenue turn right and at Hollywood Boulevard

turn left. At 6925 Hollywood Boulevard you will see **(10) Mann's Chinese Theatre** (formerly **Grauman's**), an extravagant and exotic Chinese design dating from 1927.

Continue west on Hollywood and at La Brea turn left. At Santa Monica Boulevard turn right and at San Vicente Boulevard turn left (south). On the right, just north of Beverly Boulevard, is the **(41) Tail-o'-the-Pup** hot dog stand, at 329 North San Vicente Boulevard. On the corner of the Beverly Center (San Vicente and Beverly Blvds) is the **Hard Rock Café,** with a 1959 Cadillac and a palm tree on its roof. There is also a large digital billboard displaying the diminishing number of the world's rain-forest acreage and the alarming rise in the global population.

Turn right on La Cienega Boulevard, right again on Wilshire Boulevard, and continue west into Beverly Hills. Right after the intersection of Wilshire and Santa Monica, turn right on Carmelita Avenue. At the corner of Walden Drive and Carmelita is the **(42) Spadena House** (516 Walden Dr), a 1921 Hansel-and-Gretel cottage that was originally a combined movie set and production office. From Wilshire going west, you can connect with the San Diego Freeway (I-405) to the Santa Monica Freeway (I-10).

This tour by no means covers all the fantasy architecture in Southern California. Interested viewers should also make a point to see the **(43) Avalon Casino, (44) Queen Mary, (45) Crystal Cathedral, (45) Disneyland, (46) Drive-thru Donut,** and **(47) Hollywood Sign.**

HISTORY

1771 Founding of **Mission San Gabriel.**

1781 On 4 September, Los Angeles is officially incorporated as a city. A plan for its initial settlement and layout is unveiled by Felipe de Neve, California's first governor. The population is 44 people, primarily a mix of Spanish, Mexican, Indian, and black farmers.

1818 **Avila Adobe** is built by Don Francisco Avila, mayor of the pueblo, as his town house. It later serves as the headquarters for Commodore Robert Stockton during the Mexican-American War.

1822 **La Iglesia de Nuestra Señora La Reina de Los Angeles** (Church of Our Lady of the Queen of the Angels), the city's first Catholic church, is dedicated.

1825 California becomes a territory of Mexico.

1826 The **Biscailuz Building** is constructed to house the headquarters of the United Methodist Church. It is named after Eugene Biscailuz, a Los Angeles County sheriff who helped protect the area.

1842 Gold is discovered in California near the **San Fernando Mission,** six years before the discovery at Sutters Mill.

1848 The Treaty of Guadalupe Hidalgo is signed, ending the Mexican-American War. California officially becomes part of the United States.

1850 California becomes a state.

1853 Don Matteo Keeler plants the state's first orange trees. Within a decade, Southern California becomes the top orange producer in the United States.

1869 Pio Pico, California's last Mexican governor, builds the **Pico House.**

1872 In an attempt to promote train travel to the area, the Southern Pacific Railroad hires Charles Nordhoff to write the first guidebook to Southern California. The book, *California: For Health, Pleasure, and Residence,* is a tremendous success, bringing hundreds of visitors to the state.

Biddy Mason, a former slave who became one of the richest women in the city, organizes the **First African Methodist Church** in her home.

1876 The first transcontinental railroad—the **Southern Pacific**—arrives in Los Angeles, followed shortly by the **Santa Fe Railroad** in 1885.

1880 The **University of Southern California** is founded. It has 12 teachers and 53 students.

1881 The *Los Angeles Times* publishes its first issue. (It also features home delivery—by horse-drawn carriage.)

1884 The *Los Angeles Times* begins a carrier pigeon service to and from **Catalina Island.** The birds bring information between the summer vacation colony and the mainland. The service lasts until 1887.

1892 Edward Doheny discovers oil in what is now downtown Los Angeles.

Palisades Park, encompassing more than 26 acres overlooking the Pacific Ocean, is dedicated.

1893 The **Bradbury Building** is erected. It's now the city's oldest commercial building.

1896 Welsh newspaperman Griffith J. Griffith donates 4,400 acres to the city. It becomes **Griffith Park,** one of the nation's largest urban parks.

1900 Los Angeles's population increases tenfold in 20 years (from 10,000 in 1880 to 100,000 in 1900).

1902 The **Electric Theatre,** the world's first movie house, opens on Main Street.

1904 The first Buddhist temple in the United States opens in Los Angeles.

1906 The first **Rose Bowl** football game is played.

1907 **Hollywood** becomes an incorporated city.

1909 The **Santa Monica Pier** is erected.

1910 The **Beverly Hills Hotel** is built, luring movie industry people to Beverly Hills from Hollywood.

Hollywood is annexed to the City of Los Angeles.

1911 The Nestor Company rents the old **Blondeau Tavern and Barn** at Sunset Boulevard and Gower Street and begins making movies.

1912 The first gas station in the country opens at the corner of Grand Avenue and Washington Boulevard.

1913 **Cecil B. DeMille** makes the industry's first full-length film, *The Squaw Man,* in a barn near Selma Avenue and Vine Street. (Declared a state monument, the barn has been moved and now houses the **Hollywood Studio Museum.**)

William Mulholland, head of the Los Angeles Water Department, spearheads efforts to install an aqueduct that brings water to Los Angeles and to the San Fernando Valley from some 233 miles away in the Owens Valley.

The nation's first public defender, Walton J. Wood, begins his practice on 13 June.

1914 Carl Laemmle opens **Universal Studios Hollywood,** operating on the concept that filmmaking itself is an attraction.

The first air-conditioned railroad cars begin service between Los Angeles and Chicago aboard the Atchison, Topeka, and Santa Fe Railroad's *California Limited.*

1915 D.W. Griffith produces *The Birth of a Nation.* It paves the way for the great movie palaces that were soon to take over Los Angeles and the rest of the country. Eventually, the film drew controversy over its favorable portrayal of the Ku Klux Klan.

1916 The Watts district sends the first black man, **Frederick Roberts,** to the California State Assembly.

1917 **Mary Pickford** is the first movie star to sign a million-dollar contract with a studio.

1919 William Wrigley Jr. purchases **Santa Catalina Island.**

1920 Douglas Fairbanks builds the **Pickfair mansion** in Beverly Hills for his young bride, Mary Pickford.

1923 The nation's first chinchilla farm opens in Los Angeles.

A 50-foot-high sign reading **"Hollywoodland"** is built to advertise a real estate development. In 1949, the Hollywood Chamber of Commerce buys the sign, removes the "land," and a civic symbol is born.

1927 **Grauman's Chinese Theatre** (now Mann's) opens. Norma Talmadge makes cement imprints of her hands and feet in the sidewalk out front, and a tradition is born.

On New Year's Eve, the **Beverly Wilshire Hotel** celebrates its grand opening.

The **Academy of Motion Picture Arts & Sciences** is officially incorporated. During the celebratory dinner at the Biltmore Hotel's Crystal Ballroom, plans for the first award ceremonies are laid, and the first sketch of the trophy is scrawled on a linen napkin by Cedric Gibbons.

1928 Los Angeles's first airport, **Mines Field,** opens on the current site of LAX. It's a single dirt strip.

1929 The airship *Graf Zeppelin* completes the first trans-Pacific flight, from Japan to Los Angeles.

1930 The **Polo Lounge** is added to the **Beverly Hills Hotel,** creating a hub for Hollywood deals and the social elite.

1931 The **California Edison Building,** the first all-electric structure, opens for business.

1932 The **Summer Olympics** take place in Los Angeles. Automatic timing and the photo-finish camera are introduced during the games.

1935 The **Griffith Observatory** is built, the legacy of a trust fund left by Griffith J. Griffith.

1939 **Union Station** is built in downtown Los Angeles. The historic landmark is one of the finer examples of California Mission-style architecture.

1940 The six-mile stretch of the new **Arroyo Seco Parkway** (later known as the Pasadena Freeway) opens for traffic. It's the first freeway in Los Angeles.

1942 New Year's Day brings an unprecedented one inch of snowfall in Los Angeles.

1945 The **Mattel company** is founded in Hawthorne. Boosted by skyrocketing sales of Barbie, it becomes the world's largest toy manufacturer.

1947 The **Hollywood Freeway** opens, linking Los Angeles with the San Fernando Valley.

KTLA, the first TV station west of the Mississippi, begins broadcasting.

The **Rams,** a professional football team, come to Los Angeles from Cleveland, Ohio.

Howard Hughes designs and builds the largest wooden plane in the world, the *Spruce Goose,* and takes it out on a taxi run in the **Long Beach Harbor.** At the last minute, Hughes takes off and flies for about a mile, surprising even the flight crew.

1949 The **Pantages Theatre** in Hollywood begins hosting the Academy Awards ceremony. It will do so until 1960.

1955 **Disneyland** opens in Anaheim.

1956 The **Capitol Records Tower,** the nation's first circular office building, opens. The architectural concept is the brainchild of Capitol recording stars Nat King Cole and Johnnie Mercer.

1957 Walter O'Malley, owner of the **Brooklyn Dodgers,** moves the team west to Los Angeles.

The next year, the team plays its first games at the **Coliseum**—a doubleheader, defeating the New York Yankees and the San Francisco Giants.

1960 **John F. Kennedy** is named the Democratic presidential candidate at the party's national convention, held in Los Angeles.

The **Lakers** basketball team comes to Los Angeles from Minneapolis.

1961 Hollywood's **Walk of Fame,** which honors the leading names in entertainment, is started by the Hollywood Chamber of Commerce.

1962 **Dodger Stadium** is built on land purchased by team owner Walter O'Malley.

1964 Beatlemania comes to Los Angeles as the Fab Four perform in what will be remembered as a legendary concert at the **Hollywood Bowl.**

1966 The new **Los Angeles Zoo** opens with 1,000 animals. It will become one of the world's major collections of rare and endangered species.

1967 The *Queen Mary* docks permanently at Long Beach.

1973 Thomas Bradley, LA's first African-American mayor, is elected.

1980 According to the US census, the population of the Los Angeles/Orange County area is 10 million. Since 1880, the region has changed from a small, rural town to a world-class metropolis.

1984 The **Summer Olympic Games** are held again in LA. It is the first Games to make a profit for the Olympic Committee.

1986 The **Museum of Contemporary Art (MOCA),** designed by Arata Isozaki, is unveiled as a showplace for contemporary California artists.

1988 The **Gene Autry Western Heritage Museum,** an institution dedicated to western movie stars and the country's rodeo heritage, opens.

1990 The 62-story **First Interstate Tower,** designed by I. M. Pei, opens. As the tallest building west of Chicago, it changes the formerly low-rise skyline.

LA begins construction on its first subway system. The **Metro Rail**'s **Blue Line** opens, connecting downtown Los Angeles with Long Beach.

1991 **Malibu** becomes a separate city.

1993 The newly expanded **Los Angeles Convention Center** reopens. It's now the largest meeting facility on the West Coast.

1994 The **World Cup soccer finals** take place at the Rose Bowl.

1995 The trial of **O.J. Simpson** for the murder of ex-wife Nicole Brown Simpson and Ronald Goldman focuses the world's attention on Los Angeles for most of the year. In the end, Simpson is acquitted in a jury decision that ignites controversy throughout the country.

1997 The **Getty Center,** a 110-acre expansion of the J. Paul Getty Museum, opens in Bel Air.

1999 The **Staples Center,** lavish home of four pro sports franchises, opens its doors with a concert by Bruce Springsteen.

The **Democratic National Convention** takes LA by storm, costing the city more than they bargained for.

The **Hollywood and Highland Development Project,** a $567 million revitalization of the area between Highland Boulvard east along Hollywood Boulevard, heralds the opening of a massive retail/entertainment complex that includes the **Kodak Theater,** the new home for the annual Academy Awards spectacular.

The Archdiocese of Los Angeles **Cathedral of Our Lady of Angels** opens between Grand Avenue and Hill Street in downtown LA. The $163-million house of worship, which acts as the mother church for the Archdiocese of LA, was designed by Spanish architect José Rafael Moneo and features a 20,000- square-foot plaza, with Mission-style colonnades.

2002 The **Kodak Theater,** touted as the central landmark at the heart of TrizecHahn's **Hollywood & Highland** entertainment complex, opens. The theater seats 3,500 audience members and will be the future home of the Academy Awards ceremonies, movie premieres, entertainment events, and other major celebrations.

The Frank Gehry–designed **Walt Disney Concert Hall** finally reaches completion. Located in downtown LA, the 2,290-seat home of the LA Philharmonic and Los Angeles Master Chorale features an outdoor park, restaurant, café, bookstore, and gift shop.

2003 California Governor Gray Davis is recalled in an unprecedented election that puts Hollywood's Terminator Arnold Schwarzenegger in the state's driver seat. Stay tuned, folks.

INDEX

E

H

Q

R

X

Y

Z

RESTAURANTS

Only restaurants with star ratings are listed below. All restaurants are listed alphabetically in the main (preceding) index. Always call in advance to ensure a restaurant has not closed, changed its hours, or booked its tables for a private party. The restaurant price ratings are based on the average cost of an entrée for one person, excluding tax and tip.

★ Good
★★ Very Good
★★★ Excellent
★★★★ An Extraordinary Experience

$ The Price Is Right (less than $35)
$$ Reasonable ($35–$50)
$$$ Expensive ($50–$80)
$$$$ Big Bucks ($80 and up)

★★★★

★ ★ ★

★★

$$

$

CREDITS

Writer and Researcher
for the Eleventh Edition

Patti Covello Pietschmann

The writer wishes to thank the
following for all their help and
efforts in the care and making of
this guide: Carol Martinez and the
Los Angeles Convention &
Visitors Bureau, Holly Barnhill,
Eliot Setulac and Universal
Studios, Richard Pietschmann,
George Yu, Marty Leshner,
Victoria King Public Relations,
Long Beach CVB, Newport CVB,
and Daniel Guerrero of the West
Hollywood CVB.

Gay Los Angeles Writers

David Appell
Paul Balido
David Ciminelli

Editorial Director

Edwin Tan

Senior Production Editor
Penelope Haynes

Jacket Design
Chin-Yee Lai

Design Director
Leah Carlson-Stanisic

Design Supervisor
Nicola Ferguson

Map Designer
Patricia Keelin

Associate Director of Production
Dianne Pinkowitz

Look for these other Access Guides at your local bookstore.

ACCESS Boston
ACCESS California Wine Country
ACCESS Chicago
ACCESS Florence & Venice
ACCESS London
ACCESS Montreal & Quebec City
ACCESS New Orleans
ACCESS New York City
ACCESS Philadelphia
ACCESS Rome
ACCESS San Francisco
ACCESS Seattle
ACCESS Washington, DC

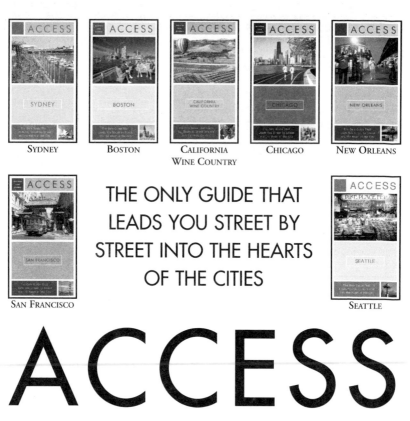